Collectables
PRICE GUIDE 2005

Collectables
PRICE GUIDE 2005

Judith Miller
with Mark Hill

A DORLING KINDERSLEY BOOK

LONDON, NEW YORK,
MELBOURNE, MUNICH AND DELHI

A joint production from DORLING KINDERSLEY
and THE PRICE GUIDE COMPANY

THE PRICE GUIDE COMPANY LIMITED

Publisher Judith Miller

Collectables Specialist Mark Hill

Publishing Manager Julie Brooke

European Consultants Martina Franke,
Nicolas Tricaud de Montonnière

Managing Editor Carolyn Madden

Assistant Editors Sara Sturgess, Claire Smith

Digital Image Co-ordinator Ellen Spalek

Editorial Assistants Jessica Bishop,
Dan Dunlavey, Sandra Lange

Design and DTP Tim Scrivens, TJ Graphics

Additional Design Jason Hopper, District 6

Photographers Graham Rae, Bruce Boyajian,
John McKenzie, Byron Slater, Steve Tanner,
Heike Löwenstein, Andy Johnson, Adam Gault

Indexer Hilary Bird

Workflow Consultant Bob Bousfield

Business Advisor Nick Croydon

DORLING KINDERSLEY LIMITED

Category Publisher Jackie Douglas

Managing Art Editor Heather McCarry

Managing Editor Julie Oughton

Designer Martin Dieguez

DTP Designer Mike Grigoletti

Production Sarah Dodd

Production Manager Sarah Coltman

While every care has been taken in the compilation of this guide, neither the authors
nor the publishers accept any liability for any financial or other loss incurred by
reliance placed on the information contained in *Collectables Price Guide 2005*

First published in 2004 by
Dorling Kindersley Limited
80 Strand, London WC2R 0RL

A Penguin Company

The Price Guide Company (UK) Ltd
Studio 21, Waterside
44–48 Wharf Road
London N1 7UX
info@thepriceguidecompany.com

2 4 6 8 10 9 7 5 3 1

This edition published 2005 for Index Books Ltd

A CIP catalogue record for this book is available from the British Library.

1 4053 0597 5

Printed and bound in Singapore by Star Standard PTE Ltd.

Discover more at
www.dk.com

CONTENTS

INTRODUCTION

W elcome to the third edition of my Collectables Price Guide, published in association with Dorling Kindersley. Over the thirty years that I have been collecting and writing about collectables, I have found this market to be one of the most exciting and innovative areas around. Constantly expanding to take in new areas as well as developments in more established subjects, it's not surprising that it has become one of the most popular hobbies in the world.

By publishing our price guides annually and by covering a completely new selection of collectables in each edition, we are able to reflect this innovation and growth by covering as a huge range of subjects – presented this year across more than 65 subject headings. As well as more traditional collecting areas, such as pot lids and posters, we cover a number of newer areas such as men's clothing, character collectables, early computers and contemporary glass. Each image is specially commissioned in full-colour and you can learn more about many items from the numerous footnotes and 'Closer Look' features, as well as discovering other useful resources through 'Find out more'. With this much change every year, I'm sure you'll agree with me that our Collectables Price Guides build up over the years to become an invaluable reference library for experienced and new collectors alike.

Judith Miller.

LIST OF CONSULTANTS

Advertising

David Huxtable
Huxtins, London

Automobilia

G.G. Weiner
C.A.R.S, Brighton

Bottles & Potlids

Alan Blakeman
BBR, South Yorkshire

Ceramics

Judith Miller
The Price Guide Company (UK) Ltd

Coins & Scripophily

Yasha Beresiner
Intercol, London

Costume

Kate Peters
Beyond Retro, London

Costume Jewellery

Steven Miners
Cristobal, London

Glass

Jeanette Hayhurst
Jeanette Hayhurst Fine Glass
London

Mark Hill
The Price Guide Company (UK) Ltd

Dr Graham Cooley
graham.cooley@metalysis.com

Militaria

Roy Butler
Wallis & Wallis
Lewes, East Sussex

Posters

Patrick Bogue
Onslows, Dorset

Nicholas D. Lowry
Swann Galleries, New York

Royal Memorabilia

John Pym
Hope and Glory, London

Toys

Glenn Butler
Wallis & Wallis
Lewes, East Sussex

New Collectables

Harry Cowdy & Pauline Solven
Cowdy Gallery, Gloucestershire

We are also very grateful to our friends and experts who gave us so much help - Leo Harrison of Biblion, Peter Layton of London Glass Blowing, John Mackie of Lyon & Turnbull, Alvise Schiavon & Veronika Leibetseder of Vetro & Arte Gallery in Venice, Simon Smith of Vectis Auctions Ltd and Beth & Beverley Adams, Keith Baker, Jean Scott, Roxanne Stuart.

HOW TO USE THIS BOOK

HOW TO USE THIS BOOK

Subcategory Heading
Indicates the subcategory of the main category heading and describes the general contents of the page.

A Closer Look at...
Here, we highlight particularly interesting items or show identifying features, pointing out rare or desirable qualities.

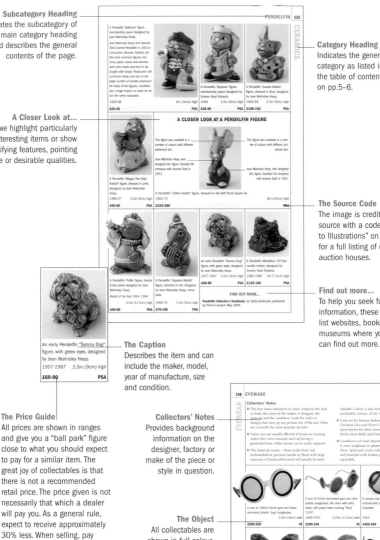

Category Heading
Indicates the general category as listed in the table of contents on pp.5–6.

The Source Code
The image is credited to its source with a code. See the "Key to Illustrations" on pp.576–580 for a full listing of dealers and auction houses.

Find out more...
To help you seek further information, these boxes list websites, books, and museums where you can find out more.

The Caption
Describes the item and can include the maker, model, year of manufacture, size and condition.

The Price Guide
All prices are shown in ranges and give you a "ball park" figure close to what you should expect to pay for a similar item. The great joy of collectables is that there is not a recommended retail price. The price given is not necessarily that which a dealer will pay you. As a general rule, expect to receive approximately 30% less. When selling, pay attention to the dealer or auction house specialist to understand why this may be, and consider that they have to run a business as well as make a living. When buying, listen again. Condition, market forces and location of the place of sale will all affect a price.

Collectors' Notes
Provides background information on the designer, factory or make of the piece or style in question.

The Object
All collectables are shown in full colour, which is a vital aid to identification and valuation.

COLLECTORS' NOTES

■ Coca-Cola was developed by Dr John Styth Pemberton of Atlanta in 1886. It was initially marketed as a refreshing 'pick-me-up' and sold by pharmacists. Frank Robinson, Pemberton's bookkeeper, devised the name 'Coca-Cola' and his distinctive script remained in the logo.

■ From 1888-91 Pemberton sold the company to Asa Griggs Candler for around $2,300. Candler was a shrewd businessman who began to expand the company. The first magazine advertisement appeared in 1902 and advertising expanded soon after to many formats and media, in different countries and languages.

■ During the 1920s and 1930s, the Great Depression caused a lull in sales, but Coca-Cola was cleverly marketed as being able to give a lift when 'at pause', as well as a tonic to be enjoyed in a group such as a family. This latter theme has continued and since then Coca-Cola has always celebrated enjoyment, togetherness and tradition in its advertisements.

■ Any genuine advertising items produced before 1910 are very rare. Visual impact, rare characters, popular artists and the changing face of the brand and how it represents itself are some of the indicators of value. Condition is also important, with worn or damaged goods being less valuable, unless extremely scarce or early. Since the 1970s, 'heritage' products featuring advertisements from previous decades have been produced. Collectors should familiarise themselves with the look and feel of these in order to recognise them.

A 1930s Coca-Cola lithographed tin advertising sign, with thermometer.

16.5in (42cm) high

£200-250   ATA

A Coca-Cola embossed tin advertising door push.

The shape of a Coca Cola bottle can help to date a piece, as well as the style of the design of the piece itself. Before 1916, bottles were straight-sided and not contoured as the bottle in this example.

c1931   12.25in (31cm) long

£300-400   SOTT

A very rare Coca-Cola calendar for 1946 showing the 'Sprite Boy', in near mint condition.

The perky 'Sprite Boy', developed by legendary Coke artist Haddon Sundblom, is rarer than most advertising characters as he was only used between 1942 and 1958.

1946   21in (53cm) high

£550-650   SOTT

A 1950s German Coca-Cola printed and laminated card advertising sign.

13in (33cm) high

£250-350   ATA

A 1950s American Coca-Cola gold-plated illuminated electric advertising wall clock, by Synchron.

11.75in (30cm) high

£120-180   PA

A very rare Coca-Cola printed tin-over-cardboard advertising plaque.

This piece is placed firmly in the 'Roaring Twenties' by the style of the dress and the short, boyish hair of the 'flapper'. This, together with her direct invitation to drink and a clear display of the legendary Coca-Cola logo, make this a desirable piece.

c1927

£800-1,200

11in (28cm) wide

SOTT

A Coca-Cola lithographed tin advertising tray, with holiday theme.

c1955   13.25in (33.5cm) long

£40-60   **DH**

A Coca-Cola advertising tin tip tray, with artwork by Hamilton King.

Born in Lewiston, Maine, Hamilton King is ranked amongst the most famous designers for Coca-Cola along with Norman Rockwell and Haddon Sundblom. He died in 1952 and is known for his series of ladies with elegant and fashionable hats or hair for Coca-Cola amongst other designs.

c1919   6in (15cm) long

£350-450   **SOTT**

A 1950s Coca-Cola 'Picnic Basket' advertising card bottle topper.

8.25in (21cm) wide

£60-80   **SOTT**

A pack of Coca-Cola advertising 'Service Woman' playing cards.

c1943   3.5in (9cm) high

£50-60   **SOTT**

A pack of Coca-Cola advertising playing cards.

c1951   3.5in (9cm) high

£40-60   **SOTT**

Two 1950s Coca-Cola Thanksgiving advertising carton stuffers.

7.5in (19cm) high

£15-20 set   **SOTT**

A Coca-Cola 'Toy Town' advertising cut-out.

c1927   15in (38cm) wide

£70-100   **SOTT**

A 1940s Coca-Cola 'Gold Bottle' advertising match book.

1.5in (4cm) wide

£7-10   **SOTT**

A Coca-Cola paper advertising bottle protector.

c1948   6.75in (17cm) wide

£3-4   **SOTT**

A Budgie No. 228 Karrier Bantam Bottle Lorry advertising Coca-Cola.
1959-64   *5.25in (13.5cm) wide*

£80-120   SOTT

A late 1950s Matchbox No. 37 Karrier Bantam Coca-Cola advertising lorry, with 'even' load, boxed.

£60-80   SOTT

A 1950s Coca-Cola 'Rock 'n' Roll' promotional charm bracelet, with box.

Charm bracelets were popular in the 1950s, most notably for Elvis Presley.

£40-60   SOTT

A 1950s/60s Coca-Cola 15-year service pin, set with three stones.
                                        0.75in (2cm) wide

£60-80   SOTT

A 1950s Coca-Cola bottle novelty lighter.

These lighters were also available in the form of cans.
                                        2.5in (6.5cm) high

£15-20   SOTT

A 1950s Coca-Cola advertising plastic music box cooler.
                                        2.75in (7cm) wide

£40-50   SOTT

An American 'Vendo 80' Coca-Cola coin-operated vending machine, restored.

Large pieces like this are considered decorative and almost 'architectural' pieces. They have become popular with those who like to live in modern loft or warehouse conversions.

c1955   *58in (147cm) high*

£800-1,200   ATK

A Pepsi Evervess sparkling water advertising tin tip tray.
                                        6in (15cm) wide

£30-40   SOTT

A 1950s Coca-Cola advertising celluloid pencil, with bottle-shaped clip.
                                        8.5in (21.5cm) long

£20-25   SOTT

A 1950s Pepsi-Cola advertising miniature toy truck, with applied paper label.
                                        2in (5cm) wide

£25-35   SOTT

FIND OUT MORE...

'Petretti's Coca-Cola Collectibles Price Guide', *by Allan Petretti, published by Krause Publications, 11th edition, July 2001.*

'Petretti's Soda Pop Collectibles Price Guide', *by Allan Petretti, published by Krause Publications' 3rd edition, March 2003.*

COLLECTORS' NOTES

■ Tins were usually sold containing biscuits, sweets or tobacco. The designs and shapes became progressively more complex and, by the 1890s, could be found in the form of anything from musical instruments and houses to vehicles and luggage. Once empty they could be used as decorative storage objects or toys for children. This wide range of shapes also means that many tins have a crossover appeal.

■ The fierce competition between biscuit-producing companies such as collectors' favourite Huntley & Palmers, Crawfords and Jacobs, also contributed to the complexity of the tins as each company tried to out-do each other.

■ Tins remained popular through the turn of the 20th century and survived the privations of WWI. The need for metal during WWII and the development of

cheaper alternatives led to the demise of tin as the standard material for containers.

■ Collectors often focus on one company and Huntley & Palmers are the most desirable. Novelty shapes, particularly those with moving parts, are also sought-after as well as examples featuring artwork by famous artists such as Alphonse Mucha.

■ Condition has a dramatic effect on value and mint or near mint examples will always fetch a premium. Be sure to examine tins, inside and out, for any signs of rust, dents or scratches to the artwork.

■ Tins should not be immersed in water as this can cause rust and damage the artwork. They should be stored out of direct sunlight as this can lead to fading.

A Crawford 'House of Knowledge' lithographed tin money box.

c1939   *7.75in (20cm) wide*

£80-120   **DH**

A Crawford's 'Stage Coach' lithographed biscuit tin.

c1928   *8in (20cm) high*

£550-650   **DH**

A Barringer, Wallis & Manners lithographed biscuit tin, in the form of a coffee pot, decorated with Dickensian scenes.

c1910   *12.25in (31cm) high*

£150-200   **DH**

A late 1950s Gay Dunn lithographed biscuit tin, in the form of a suitcase.

8.5in (21.5cm) wide

£20-30   **DH**

A Huntley and Palmers novelty biscuit tin, modelled as a long narrow suitcase.

8in (20cm) long

£50-70   **F**

A Huntley & Palmers 'The Cricket Match' lithographed biscuit tin.

c1935   *7.25in (18.5cm) high*

£15-25   **DH**

A Huntley & Palmers 'Artist' lithographed palette-shaped biscuit tin.

c1900   *10in (25.5cm) high*

£180-220   **DH**

A rare Jacob's 'Gypsy Caravan' lithographed biscuit tin.

c1935   *6.5in (16.5cm) wide*

£300-400   **DH**

A rare Felix Cream Toffee lithographed tin, by R.K. Confectionery Co. Hull, marked "By Kind Permission of Pathé Freres Cinema".

This tin would appeal to collectors of cartoon character Felix as well, making it doubly collectable.

A French Biscuits Olibet 'Globe Terrestre' lithographed biscuit tin.

c1905   10in (25.5cm) high

£200-250   DH

c1930   6in (15cm) high

£650-750   DH

A Cremorna Park lithographed tin, by A.S. Wilkins Ltd.

c1960   3.75in (9.5cm) diam

£10-15   DH

A 1950s Kelller's 'Portable Radio' lithographed sweet tin.

7.5in (19cm) wide

£25-35   DH

A Mackintosh's Toffee de Luxe 'Santa's House' lithographed sweet tin, with pull-out sledge.

c1925   3.5in (9cm) high

£200-250   DH

A 1940s Dean's Peacock 'Reservoir Ends' lithographed condom tin.

2.25in (5.5cm) wide

£25-35   DH

A Mackintosh's Toffee deluxe 'Toffee Shop' lithographed sweet tin, with pull-out canopy.

This and the other Mackintosh sweet tin on this page are part of a set of four tins, together with a zoo and an ark, and each features a pull-out section. The Toffee Shop is the rarest and most valuable, and Santa's House the most common.

1925   3.5in (9cm) high

£300-400   DH

A Lightning Soap lithographed tin advertising peg game, by Ed. Cook & Co. Ltd.

1910   3.25in (8.5cm) wide

£50-70   DH

A Nugget Black Boot Polish lithographed tin money box.

c1920   3.75in (9.5cm) high

£55-65   DH

FIND OUT MORE...

'Biscuit Tins 1868-1939: The Art of Decorative Packaging', by M.J. Franklin, published by New Cavendish Books, USA, 2002.

'Decorative Printed Tins: The Golden Age of Printed Tin Packaging', by David Griffith, published by Studio Vista, 1996.

Museum of Reading, Balgrave Street, Reading, RG1 1QH, www.readingmuseum.org.uk - this museum houses a display of over 300 tins made by local biscuit maker Huntley & Palmer.

A blue and white tea pot, based on the Huntley & Palmer 'Indian' biscuit tin, with reg. design mark.

The manufacturers of this teapot were successfully sued by Huntley & Palmers for breach of copyright as the design was so similar.

1898   *6in (15cm) high*

£350-450   **DH**

A Batty & Co. Patent Mustard Co. ceramic pot.

c1900   *4.5in (11.5cm) high*

£35-45   **DH**

A 1950s Horlicks advertising mug, by Alfred Meakin.

         3.75in (9.5cm) high

£12-18   **DH**

A Capstan Cigarettes & Tobacco ceramic match striker, made in Stoke-on-Trent.

c1905   *3in (7.5cm) diam*

£100-150   **DH**

A 1950s ESSO advertising pocket penknife.

         2.5in (6.5cm) high

£25-35   **DH**

A Player's Navy Cut Tobacco lithographed tin advertising tray.

c1910   *12.5in (31.5cm) wide*

£100-150   **DH**

A Triumph bras advertising plaster mannequin, with original hand-colouring.

c1930   *29.5in (75cm) high*

£450-550   **ATK**

A 1920s News of the World lithographed tin promotional tray.

The News of the World presented these trays to couples that celebrated their 50th wedding anniversary.

         12.25in (31cm) wide

£25-35   **DH**

A 'London Mail, "Smart as Paint", Every Monday' enamel advertising sign, some chips, losses and rusting to edges.

         28in (71cm) high

£450-550   **ON**

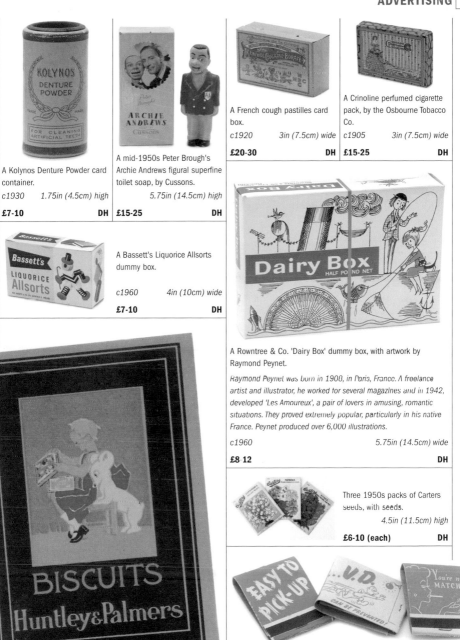

A Kolynos Denture Powder card container.

c1930   *1.75in (4.5cm) high*

£7-10   **DH**

A mid-1950s Peter Brough's Archie Andrews figural superfine toilet soap, by Cussons.

5.75in (14.5cm) high

£15-25   **DH**

A French cough pastilles card box.

c1920   *3in (7.5cm) wide*

£20-30   **DH**

A Crinoline perfumed cigarette pack, by the Osbourne Tobacco Co.

c1905   *3in (7.5cm) wide*

£15-25   **DH**

A Bassett's Liquorice Allsorts dummy box.

c1960   *4in (10cm) wide*

£7-10   **DH**

A Rowntree & Co. 'Dairy Box' dummy box, with artwork by Raymond Peynet.

Raymond Peynet was born in 1908, in Paris, France. A freelance artist and illustrator, he worked for several magazines and in 1942, developed 'Les Amoureux', a pair of lovers in amusing, romantic situations. They proved extremely popular, particularly in his native France. Peynet produced over 6,000 illustrations.

c1960   *5.75in (14.5cm) wide*

£8-12   **DH**

Three 1950s packs of Carters seeds, with seeds.

4.5in (11.5cm) high

£6-10 (each)   **DH**

A Huntley & Palmers Biscuits Saint's day calendar, for Reading and Lourdes.

1932   *3.5in (9cm) high*

£30-40   **DH**

Three WWII V.D. match books, by the Universal Match Corp. St Louis.

In an effort to curb the incidence of venereal disease in the army, these educational match books were given to soldiers, informing them of the dangers of fraternising with the local women.

2in (5cm) high

£4-6 (each)   **DH**

COLLECTORS' NOTES

■ The variety of animation art available can seem bewildering and, as the type also dictates the value and desirability, it is important to understand the differences.

■ The most desirable form is a hand-painted original production cel that appears in the final feature. Collectors look for scenes with main characters, particularly from key scenes. Be aware that some original cels are never screened and these are not as desirable.

■ Due to the huge interest in collecting animation art, animation studios are now releasing limited editions in a number of formats.

■ The most sought-after are hand-painted cels. These may be reproductions of original cels or new images; they are unlikely to have been painted by the original artists although they may have signed the piece. Edition runs tend to be quite small and can sell out quickly.

■ Machine-produced serigraphs or sericels are more affordable and easier to obtain as they are produced in greater numbers.

■ Today, very little animation is produced completely by hand, meaning original production cels do not exist for modern films and series such as "Ice Age", "Monsters, Inc." and "The Simpsons". Scenes are drawn by hand and scanned into a computer where they are coloured and converted straight to film.

A Walt Disney original production cel from "Mother Goose goes to Hollywood", featuring three men in a wooden tub.

The 'Mother Goose goes to Hollywood' story featured various nursery rhymes. The voices for the men were provided by Charles Laughton, Spencer Tracy and Freddie Bartholomew, with Kathryn Hepburn as Mother Goose.

1938   11in (28cm) wide

£650-750   **AAC**

An MGM original production cel from "Deputy Droopy", featuring Slim Jim.

1955   12in (30.5cm) wide

£750-850   **AAG**

A 20th Century Fox hand-painted cel from "Futurama", together with the original production drawing, featuring Leela and Fry.

30.5in (77.5cm) wide

£250-350   **AAG**

A limited edition 20th Century Fox giclee 'The Herd' from "Ice Age", from an edition of 750, featuring Sid, Manny, Diego and Scrat.

A giclee is a high resolution digital scan printed with archival quality inks.

2002   20.5in (52cm) wide

£300-400   **AAG**

A 20th Century Fox 'Simpsons on Sunday' original production cel from "The Simpsons", featuring the family in their Sunday best.

16.5in (42cm) wide

£450-550 AAG

A 20th Century Fox key set-up from "The Simpsons", featuring the family running to the couch in an M.C. Escher-style image.

This scene is used in the opening sequence of the episodes 'The PTA Disbands' and 'Homer the Great'.

c1995 16.5in (42cm) wide

£1,500-2,000 AAG

A 20th Century Fox 'Water Pistols at Dawn' original production cel, from "The Simpsons" episode 'Lady Bouvier's Lover', featuring Jackie, Mr Burns and Bart.

1994 16.5in (42cm) wide

£350-450 AAG

A limited edition 20th Century Fox 'Happy Hour' serilitho cel, from "The Simpsons" and an edition of 2,000, taken from original artwork and reference material archived at the studio.

38in (96.5cm) wide

£280-320 AAG

A limited edition Warner Bros hand-painted cel, from an edition of 50, featuring Sylvester, Tweety Pie and Spike, signed by Warner Bros. animator Virgil Ross.

A limited edition Warner Bros hand-painted cel 'Bacall to Arms', from an edition of 250, taken from original 1946 cartoon of the same name and featuring "Bogey Gocart", "Laurie Becool" and "Wolf".

17in (43cm) high

£800-900 AAG

15.25in (38.5cm) wide

£800-900 AAG

A Warner Bros original production cel from Road Runner, featuring "Flying Coyote".

11.5in (29cm) wide

£650-750   **AAG**

An original hand-painted cel, featuring Astérix, Obélix and Dogmatix.

22.5in (57cm) wide

£8,000-11,000   **AAG**

A Klasky Csupo original production cel from "Duckman", featuring Eric Duckman.

16.5in (42cm) wide

£400-500   **AAG**

A Paramount original production cel from the open sequence of "Grease", featuring Danny Zukko.

1978   *9.75in (25cm) wide*

£320-380   **AAG**

A Fantasy Films original production cel from "The Lord of the Rings", featuring Frodo Baggins and two other hobbits.

1978   *11in (28cm) wide*

£250-350   **AAG**

A Warner Bros. original production cel from the animated sequence of Oliver Stone's "Natural Born Killers".

11.75in (30cm) wide

£700-800   **AAG**

An original production cel from "Peanuts", featuring Woodstock and Snoopy, from the Bill Melendez studio.

10in (25.5cm) wide

£600-700   **AAG**

A Don Bluth Productions original production cel from "The Pebble and the Penguin", featuring Hubie and Rocko.

1995   *17in (43cm) wide*

£300-400   **AAG**

A Universal Studios original production cel from "Who Framed Roger Rabbit", featuring Jessica Rabbit.

1988   *15.5in (39.5cm) w*

£1,200-1,800   **AAG**

A DePatie-Freleng original production cel of the "Pink Panther", from the opening credits of the feature film.

The Pink Panther was created by Friz Freleng for the title sequence of Blake Edward's 1964 comedy farce "The Pink Panther". The character proved so popular that a series of cartoons soon appeared.

10in (25.5cm) wide

£800-1,200   **AAG**

A Klasky Csupo original production cel from "Rugrats", featuring Didi and Tommy Pickles.

12.25in (31cm) wide

£350-450   AAG

An Aardman Animations limited edition "Wallace and Gromitt" giclee 'A Grand Day Out', signed by director Nick Park, Peter Sallis (the voice of Wallace) and producer Peter Lord.

23.5in (60cm) wide

£700-800   AAG

An original pen and ink drawing, featuring 'The Cat In The Hat' signed by Dr Seuss, 'The Pink Panther' signed by Friz Freleng and 'Linus Van Pelt' from "Peanuts" signed by Charles M. Schultz.

5.5in (14cm) wide

£3,000-4,000   AAG

A set of four Apple Films animation art cels from The Beatles 'Yellow Submarine', featuring three back-views of the Beatles and Ringo driving a car.

1968   Each 25in (63cm) wide

£2,200-2,800   CO

An Apple Films limited edition reproduction hand-painted cel 'Love, Love, Love' from "Yellow Submarine", from an edition of 175, featuring the Beatles, Jeremy Hilary Boob and the Blue Meeney, signed by George Martin.

20.25in (51.5cm) wide

£1,200-1,800   AAG

An Apple Films original production sketch from "Yellow Submarine".

1968   12in (30.5cm) wide

£500-600   AAG

An MGM original production cel from "Pink Floyd The Wall".

1982   16.25in (41.5cm) wide

£700-800   AAG

An MGM original production cel from "Pink Floyd The Wall".

15in (38cm) wide

£700-800   AAG

An MGM original production cel from "Pink Floyd The Wall", together with the original production sketch.

1982 Image 14in (35.5cm) wide

£1,200-1,800   AAG

An MGM original production cel from "Pink Floyd The Wall", featuring the Warlord.

1982   15.5in (40cm) w.

£750-850   AAG

A Virgin Films key set-up from "The Great Rock N Roll Swindle", featuring members of the Sex Pistols.

A key set-up is a combination on an original production cel and a background.

1980   14.25in (36cm) high

£750-850   AAG

COLLECTORS' NOTES

- Autograph collecting has been popular for as long as there have been 'famous' people, however the value depends on more than just the fame of the signer.

- Signed personal property such as credit cards or cheques feature at the high end of the market as they are obviously extremely rare.

- Hand-written letters are among the most sought-after examples as they provide a glimpse into the author's life with particularly interesting, controversial or historically important content fetching a premium. Typed correspondence and documents are also desirable, though to a slightly lesser degree.

- When it comes to signed photographs, the bigger the better. An image taken from an actor's most famous

film or scene, or a performer in a typical pose, are the most popular. They will be worth more than the same autograph on an image from a less popular film or period of work.

- Signatures in ink are better than pencil as pencil can fade over time and is usually not as crisp. Look for group signatures on a single image or piece of paper, as they are more desirable than a collection of individually signed examples.

- Always purchase from a reputable seller, as fakes are common. If in doubt ask for the item's provenance and compare the example to an authentic signature.

- Good condition is also vital, as tears, rips and stains will lower the value.

A signed Dirk Bogarde 'The High Bright Sun' video insert.

10in (25.5cm) wide

£70-90　　　　　　　　　　　　　　**LCA**

A signed Michael Caine publicity photograph.

10in (25.5cm) high

£30-50　　　　　　**LCA**

A signed Robert De Niro publicity photograph.

10in (25.5cm) high

£65-75　　　　　　**LCA**

A Bette Davis American Express credit card, mounted with a signed credit card slip and a signed postcard and engagement contract.

Card 3.25 (8.5cm) wide

£5,000-6,000　　　　　　　　　　　　　　　　　　　　**LCA**

A signed Leonardo DiCaprio 'Titanic' publicity photograph.

10in (25.5cm) high

£40-50　　　**LCA**

A signed John Gielguid publicity postcard.

6in (15cm) high

£10-20　　　　　　　　　**LCA**

A signed Alec Guiness publicity photograph.

10in (25.5cm) high

£35-45　　　**LCA**

A signed Tippi Hedren 'The Birds' publicity photograph.

10in (25.5cm) high

£35-45   **LCA**

A signed Charlton Heston publicity photograph.

10in (25.5cm) high

£25-35   **LCA**

A signed Harvey Keitel publicity photograph.

10in (25.5cm) high

£30-40   **LCA**

A signed Ian McKellan publicity postcard.

6in (15cm) high

£10-15   **LCA**

A signed Eric Morcombe and Ernie Wise publicity photograph.

11.5in (29cm) high

£150-200   **LCA**

A pair of Stan Laurel and Oliver Hardy autographs, mounted with a publicity photograph.

13.5in (39.5cm) high

£650-750   **LCA**

A signed Al Pacino publicity photograph.

10in (25.5cm) high

£75-85   **LCA**

A signed Arnold Schwarzenegger 'Predator' publicity photograph.

10in (25.5cm) high

£35-45   **LCA**

A signed Sylvester Stallone publicity photograph.

10in (25.5cm) high

£55-65   **LCA**

A signed Eric Clapton publicity photograph.

£50-60　　　　　**GAZE**

A signed Barry Gibb "Now Voyager" promotional single.

£25-35　　　　　　　　　　　　**GAZE**

A signed Janet Jackson publicity photograph.

£12-18　　　　　**GAZE**

A signed Mick Jagger photograph, with certificate of authenticity.

£50-70　　　　　**GAZE**

A signed Madonna publicity photograph, with certificate of authenticity.

£45-55　　　　　**GAZE**

A signed Kylie Minogue publicity photograph, mounted with a 'Je Ne Sais Pas Pourquoi' single, with certificate of authenticity.

£50-70　　　　　　　　　　　　**GAZE**

A rare signed Prince publicity photograph, mounted with the quote "So tonight I'm gonna party like it's 1999...".

£80-120　　　　　**GAZE**

A signed Justin Timberlake photograph.

10in (25.5cm) high

£55-65　　　　　**LCA**

A signed Barbara Streisand cheque, mounted with a publicity photograph.

10in (25.5cm) high

£700-1,000　　　　　**LCA**

A signed Tony Blair publicity postcard.

6in (15cm) high

£25-35   LCA

A signed John Major publicity postcard.

6in (15cm) high

£10-15   LCA

A Winston Churchill signature, mounted with a publicity photograph.

Photo 9.5in (12.5cm) high

£1,200-1,600   LCA

A signed Isambard Kingdom Brunel cheque, mounted with photograph.

15.5in (39.5cm) high

£450-550   LCA

A Diana, Princess of Wales handwritten letter, mounted with a publicity photograph.

Letter 7in (18cm) high

£2,500-3,000   LCA

A signed Elizabeth R Christmas card.

15in (38cm) wide

£250-300   LCA

A signed David Hockney postcard.

10in (25.5cm) high

£65-75   LCA

A signed Chris Bonnington publicity postcard.

6in (15cm) high

£10-15   LCA

COLLECTORS' NOTES

■ Car badges, for placing on the front grille or another part of the car, typically show membership of an organisation such as a motorist's club or owner's club. They are often made from cast brass or white metal and colourfully enamelled.

■ The most sought-after will often be those from the golden age of motoring from the early 1900s to the 1930s and those for the owner's clubs of the most famous marques or from notable clubs, such as the B.A.R.C.

■ Badges for the Automobile Association and Royal Automobile Club have undergone stylistic changes over nearly a century and form a popular and diverse collecting area, with many different examples to be found.

■ Look for badges in the best condition possible with attractive artwork and fine quality workmanship and materials. Bear in mind that some local club badges may only have been produced in limited numbers for a small society membership, so can be rare.

A limited edition R.A.C. Silver Jubilee commemorative car badge.
1977   *4.5in (11.5cm) high*

£150-200   **CARS**

A 1930s/40s National Motorists Association member's badge.

Clubs like the N.M.A. were eventually superseded by the A.A. and R.A.C. although the name is still used by North American and Australian clubs, amongst others. The superb perspective, form and artwork with motto make this a popular badge.

5.5in (14cm) high

£100-150   **CARS**

A limited edition R.A.C. 1897-1997 Centenary commemorative car badge.
1997   4.75in (12cm) high

£100-150   **CARS**

A limited edition R.A.C. Golden Jubilee commemorative car badge, boxed.
2002   3.5in (9cm) high

£80-100   **CARS**

A 1950s/60s British Motor Racing & Sports Car Club car badge.
4.5in (11.5cm) high

£70-80   **CARS**

A British Motor Racing Marshals Club car badge.
4.5in (11.5cm) high

£120-180   **CARS**

A British Automobile Racing Club car badge, 1980s-2003.

The British Automobile Racing Club was founded in 1912 as The Cyclecar Club and still organises races at venues across Britain.

3.75in (9.5cm) high

£50-70   **CARS**

A CLOSER LOOK AT A CAR BADGE

The reverse bears an inscription relating to John Cobb and is dated 1947.

The piece is gilded – a rare feature relating to the fame of the owner.

John Cobb took the land speed record in Utah in 1947 at 394.19 mph, but exceeding 400mph one way, and this was presented to him by the BARC.

This car badge has been mounted as a presentation piece.

A special presentation British Automobile Racing Club Brooklands car badge.
A similar, standard un-engraved badge would usually fetch around £400-600.

4in (10cm) high

£5,000-6,000 CARS

A 1980s Brooklands Society plastic grill badge.

4.5in (11.5cm) high

£70-90 CARS

A 1960s Brighton & Hove Motor Club enamel club badge.

3.5in (9cm) high

£50-80 CARS

An Institute of Advanced Motoring car badge.

5in (12.5cm) high

£12-15 CARS

A limited edition Morgan 4/4 1951-1991 Morgan Sports Car Club badge.

3.25in (8.5cm) wide

£70-100 CARS

A 'Morgan's Finest Hour' Le Mans commemorative car badge, 23-24 June 1962.

3.75in (9.5cm) wide

£30-40 CARS

A Bugatti Owner's Club enamelled and chromed motor vehicle badge.

3.75in (9.5cm) high

£70-90 F

A post-WWII Aston Martin Owner's Club car badge.

5.75in (14.5cm) wide

£70-90 CARS

A Ferrari Owners Club grill badge.

3.25in (8.5cm) high

£70-90 CARS

A CLOSER LOOK AT A CAR MASCOT

The larger versions were usually fitted to saloons, whilst the smaller versions were fitted to open cars, although they could be customised.

Early Bentley mascots have two wings extending from the sides of the 'B', later examples have wings extending from the back of the 'B'.

The majority were made by Joseph Fray of Birmingham for Bentley.

Smaller examples, roughly half the size of this example, are usually worth around half the value.

A Bentley 'B' car mascot, with large outstretched wings.

c1920

£400-500

3.5in (9cm) high

CARS

A Bentley 'B' single wing car mascot.

In 1931, Charles Robinson Sykes, famous for his 'Spirit of Ecstasy' design for the Rolls Royce 'Silver Ghost', was commissioned to redesign Bentley's mascot. He changed the side wings to a single wing extending from the back of the 'B'. The design was not produced for long before Bentley reverted to double wings, but still extending from the back, not the sides. As such, single-wing Bentley mascots are rare and sought-after.

1931   2.5in (6.5cm) high

£550-650   **CARS**

A 1930s large Bentley 'B' car mascot, with upswept wings.

Bentley car mascots with two wings extending from the back of the 'B' usually date from the 1930s and 1940s and are more common than those with one wing. The 'B' can be found leaning forward or backwards and the shape can vary widely.

5.25in (13.5cm) wide

£500-600   **CARS**

A Rolls Royce Silver Cloud 'Spirit of Ecstasy' car mascot.

The famed 'Spirit of Ecstasy' mascot was designed by Charles Sykes in 1911 and was reputedly firstly based on a secret lover of his initial patron John Walter Edward-Scott-Montagu, later the second Earl Montagu.

5.25in (13.5cm) high

£350-400   **CARS**

A pre-WWI Morgan flying 'M' winged mascot, on car radiator cap.

As they were not supplied by the factory, these are 'accessory' rather 'manufacturer' mascots.

3.25in (8.5cm) wide

£100-150   **CARS**

A 'Schneider Trophy' car mascot, in the form of the Rolls Royce-powered Supermarine S6B seaplane designed by R.J. Mitchell, stamped "Rolls Royce".

1931

£650-750   **CARS**

A Morgans Three-Wheeler Club key fob.

1in (2.5cm) high

£8-10 CARS

A Morgan Sports Car Club 4/4 winged logo key fob.

1.5in (4cm) high

£6-8 CARS

A Morgan commemorative three- and four-wheeler key fob.

1in (2.5cm) high

£8-10 CARS

A modern Morgan 4/4 winged logo key fob.

1.5in (4cm) high

£5-6 CARS

A large Ferrari enamel commemorative key fob.

1.75in (4.5cm) high

£40-50 CARS

A Ferrari Owners Club chrome and enamel key fob.

1.5in (4cm) high

£12-15 CARS

A Mini Cooper key fob.

1.25in (3cm) high

£10-12 CARS

A Riley Elf key fob.

1.25in (3cm) high

£20-25 CARS

A Mini E.R.A. ringed logo key fob.

This fob was made for a 1989-91 'Mini-ERA Turbo' special edition car, of which only 500 were made. The ERA (English Racing Automobiles) logo relates to Brooklands race track and dates back to the 1930s.

c1989 *1.5in (4cm) wide*

£25-30 CARS

A Brooklands Society Re-Union pin badge.
1988

£12-15　　　　　　　　　　　　CARS

A 1980s Brooklands Museum pressed tin pin badge.

£5-8　　　　　　　　　　　　CARS

A Brooklands Racing Club annual entry members and guests boxed badges.
1920

£250-300　　　　　　　　　　　　CARS

A British Racing Drivers' Club coloured enamel lapel pin.

£35-45　　　　　　　　　　　　CARS

A Riley Motor Club enamel membership badge.
2.5in (6.5cm) wide

£30-35　　　　　　　　　　　　CARS

A 1960s Brighton & Hove M.C. Christmas invitation, showing the club bar interior.

£10-12　　　　　　　　　　　　CARS

A Brighton & Hove Motor Club Christmas menu, dated 1955.

£12-15　　　　　　　　　　　　CARS

An unusual bound model book, titled 'The Camelliard-Fullagar Balanced Marine Internal Combustion Oil Engine', by White and Pike Ltd, Birmingham.
10.25in (26cm) high

£35-45　　　　　　　　　　　　F

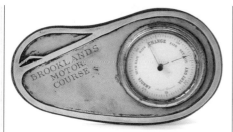

A barometer with decorative case, in the form of Brooklands racing circuit.

c1930

£250-300   **CARS**

An American 1930s green-gold Cadillac logo pocket watch, by Hamilton, with original box.

£180-220   **ML**

A Mini Special grill badge.

3.5in (9cm) wide

£8-10   **CARS**

A 1980s Mini Special boot lid badge.

6.25in (16cm) wide

£15-20   **CARS**

A Riley boot lid badge, for a Riley Elf.

3.25in (8.5cm) wide

£15-20   **CARS**

A Morgan plastic centre steering wheel boss logo.

2in (5cm) diam

£5-8   **CARS**

A Desmo brass motor vehicle horn.

c1915   *14.5in (37cm) long*

£25-35   **F**

A Sadlers racing car ceramic teapot and cover, glazed in yellow with silvered highlights, moulded marks.

8.75in (22cm) wide

£80-120   **L&T**

A Ferrari racing poster, with facsimile drivers' signatures.

1995

£12-15   **CARS**

FIND OUT MORE...

'Car Badges of The World', *by Timothy Robin Nicholson, published by American Heritage Press, 1970.*

'Motor Car Mascots & Badges', *by Peter Card, published by Hyperion Books, 1989.*

The National Motor Museum, John Montagu Building, Beaulieu, Hampshire www.beaulieu.co.uk

COLLECTORS' NOTES

- Paper money first appeared in China in the 7th century and was initially issued by merchants in place of large and bulky consignments of copper coins.

- Sweden was the first European country to follow suit in the 1660s and the Bank of England issued its first notes in 1695.

- Examples from collapsed currencies, while worthless in themselves, are popular with collectors, as well as siege notes, and invasion and occupation notes issued during both World Wars.

- Security features such as watermarks, holograms and guilloche flourishes add interest.

- Condition is crucial and, unlike coins, paper money is more easily damaged. 'Uncirculated' or 'mint state' items are usually the most desirable.

Three English George VI one shilling postal orders, two inscribed with payees' names, all three stamped by issuing office, dated 1943, 1950 and 1953.

5.25in (13.5cm) wide

£7-10   **INT**

A Bank of England ten shilling note, of the last series printed without the Queen's head, brown design featuring Britannia on white ground, watermark, not dated.

This format, using the signature of Leslie K. O'Brien, Governor of the Bank of England (1955-62), was only used for this one year.

c1955   *5.5in (14cm) long*

£20-25   **INT**

One of five consecutively numbered British Armed Forces second series one pound notes, issued by the Army Council, blue, red and purple design on white ground, printed by Thomas de la Rue & Co, London.

1948   *5.25in (13.5cm) wide*

£2-3 (set)   **INT**

A 1923 German thousand million mark note, overprinted on a thousand mark note from 1922.

During this period of German history inflation peaked at 300 million percent. As printed currency became worthless, higher denominations were stamped onto the faces of existing notes to increase their value.

1923   *7in (18cm) wide*

£4-6   **INT**

A 500 peso specimen bank note, issued by El Banco Americano de Guatemala, printed with harbour scene with two female figures, ships and local produce on obverse, four holes punched in base.

6.75in (17cm) wide

£220-280   **INT**

A CLOSER LOOK AT A COMMEMORATIVE BANK NOTE

The contrast between the colours in this metameric window changes under certain lighting conditions.

Text is printed in both vertical and horizontal axis and in varying sizes, making the note more difficult to reproduce.

The transparent panel is a model security feature only possible in polymer substrate bank notes. It is also used on Australian currency.

The colourful design, created by Nicolae Saftoiu, depicts the path of the 1999 solar eclipse through Romania.

Nearly all paper currency produced today has a unique serial number to make it easier to trace in the event of fraud.

A Romanian 2,000 lei polymer note, issued to commemorate the 1999 total solar eclipse, featuring solar system motif and plan of the path of the eclipse as visible from Romania on reverse, presented in plastic folder, number 001A0662676.

The 2,000 lei denomination was chosen to mark the impending turn of the new millennium.

1999   5.75in (14.5cm) wide

£6-8   **INT**

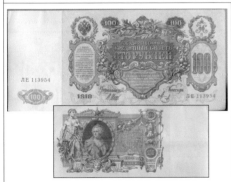

A Russian 100 rouble note, with very fine portrait of Catherine the Great framed by elaborate decoration of fruits and leaves, watermark of portrait on side panel.

Following the Russian revolution, many of these notes, including 500 rouble denomination notes bearing portraits of Alexander the Great, were brought to the UK by fleeing Russian citizens. The condition of the notes is a crucial factor in determining their value.

1910   10.25in (26cm) wide

£10-15   **INT**

A Thai 60 baht note, issued to commemorate the King of Thailand 60th birthday, depicting the throned King in state dress on obverse, and in audience with Thai women on reverse.

This was the first Thai banknote to include a colour-changing security feature.

1987   6.25in (16cm) long

£8-12   **INT**

FIND OUT MORE...

International Bank Note Society (IBNS) *General Secretary, PO Box 1642, Racine, WI 53404 USA*

COLLECTORS' NOTES

- George Baxter (1804-1867) was the son of a publisher and printer. Following in the family business, he patented an oil colour printing process in 1835, initially for the production of colour frontispieces in books. His invention was to make reasonably priced colour prints available to the general public for the first time.

- The process began with a black outline from a steel 'key plate', producing a monochrome image. Then up to 20 differently coloured blocks were applied, each adding another layer of coloured ink. The colour blocks had to be applied carefully to ensure there was no overlapping, and only two colours could be added each day as they had to dry properly.

- The prints ranged in subject from news and current events, personalities and royalty, to landscapes, flora and fauna. As well as decorative prints, the images were used as book illustrations, box labels and in music books.

- Although his prints were popular, Baxter was bankrupt within 30 years of inventing his process and it was replaced with the cheaper chromolithographic process.

- Prints were sold either with or without a stamped mount and examples with an original mount will generally be more desirable. Prints of famous personalities and Royalty, such as Queen Victoria, were very popular at the time and are common today. Fakes and reproductions are known, so examine the quality of the printing carefully.

An 'Australia' Baxter print, featuring diggers at the gold-field, in their hut, surrounded by dogs, fire arms, and other accessories of a settler's life.

This image also appeared on the cover of the sheet music book "News from Home Quadrille", published by Jullien & Co in 1853, and is worth slightly more in this version.

1853   6in (15cm) wide

£30-80   **NBS**

A '"Copper your honour?"' Baxter print, on stamped mount.

1853   6.25in (16cm) high

£40-60   **NBS**

An 'England's Queen', or 'Her Most Gracious Majesty the Queen' Baxter print.

Hundreds of thousands of copies of this print were sold. It was also used on needle boxes and reversed on a rare pot lid.

1848   6in (15cm) high

£30-50   **NBS**

An unmounted 'Figures and Landscapes Set' Baxter print, with ten oval landscapes and figures on one card.

The individual scenes can be found on small needle boxes.

1859   5in (12.5cm) wide

£80-120   **NBS**

A 'First Impressions' Baxter print.

1850   4in (10cm) high

£40-60   **NBS**

A 'Gem No. 3' Baxter print, from the 'Gems of the Great Exhibition' series, featuring a scene from the Russian department.

1852   9.75in (25cm) wide

£40-60   **NBS**

A 'Grand Entrance to the Great Exhibition' Baxter print, showing Queen Victoria opening the exhibition on 1st May 1851.

1851   4in (10cm) wide

£50-70   **NBS**

A 'Greek Dance' and 'The Harem Set' Baxter print, printed in two strips, on stamped mount.

This print was often cut into five prints and used on needle boxes.

1850   *5in (12.5cm) wide*

£50-80   **NBS**

A 'Houses of Parliament' Baxter print, showing the newly built houses from the river Thames.

1851   *4in (10cm) wide*

£40-60   **NBS**

A 'Jenny Lind, Madelle' Baxter print.

This portrait of the famous Swedish songstress known as the 'Swedish Nightingale' (1820-87) appeared on two sheet music books: "Jullien's Album for 1851" and "Deutsche Lieder Valse".

1850   *6in (15cm) high*

£60-80   **NBS**

A 'Hindoo and Mohamedan Buildings' Baxter print.

It is believed that Baxter first used oil colour printing during the production of this print. Only the later versions are printed with oil ink, which is indicated in the wording on the mounts.

1834   *8in (20cm) high*

£15-25   **NBS**

A 'His Royal Highness Prince Albert' Baxter print.

This was one of the first prints that produced a profit for Baxter.

1848   *6in (15cm) high*

£30-50   **NBS**

A 'Lake Lucerne, Switzerland' Baxter print, possibly after J. M. W. Turner.

1857   *15in (38cm) wide*

£100-150   **NBS**

An unmounted 'Southdown Sheep' Baxter print, with an extensive view of the Sussex Weald in the background.

1836   *5in (12.5cm) high*

£30-40   **NBS**

A rare 'Review of the British Fleet, &.,c., Portsmouth' large Baxter print.

1854

10in (25.5cm) wide

£100-200   **NBS**

A 'Vélocipède' pedal-driven bicycle, unmarked although probably by Pierre Michaux of Paris, solid iron frame and rims, wooden wheels, excellent working condition.

Michaux, once erroneously credited with inventing the bicycle, did develop the first bicycle pedal and cranks in the early 1860s. He went on to manufacture bicycles, known as 'Michaulina' but nicknamed 'bone shakers'.

c1870

£3,000-4,000 **ATK**

A Doulton Lambeth stoneware cycling jug, with three white vignettes, inscribed "Military", "Road" and "Path".

c1900   9in (23cm) high

£280-320 **TEN**

A 'penny farthing' bicycle, with sprung leather saddle, finished in green and white livery.

So named as the wheels were proportioned like a larger penny is to a smaller farthing, it was realised that the larger the drive wheel, the further one could travel with one rotation.

c1880s   57in (145cm) high

£2,000-3,000 **LC**

A Crown Devon musical cycling jug, playing 'Daisy Bell'.

8in (20.5cm) high

£220-280 **TEN**

A CLOSER LOOK AT A TRICYCLE

The seated rider braces himself with this handle.

It is steered by turning this handle which moves the small wheels.

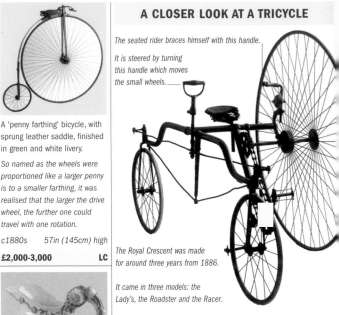

The Royal Crescent was made for around three years from 1886.

It came in three models: the Lady's, the Roadster and the Racer.

A Daniel Rudge's patent 'Royal Crescent' tricycle, with handle steering mechanism.

c1886   large wheel 48in (122cm) diam

£8,000-9,000 **LC**

A cabinet card by A. Huber, Vienna, featuring rider with high-wheel bicycle, dated on reverse, with some soiling on the reverse.

1892

£150-200 **AAC**

Two 'Aha' bicycle lamps, including headlamp, rear-lamp and dynamo, black-coloured metal, in original, unused condition.

c1925

£100-150 **ATK**

A large scrapbook relating to cycling, containing prints and cuttings.

12.5in (32cm) high

£100-150 **TEN**

FIND OUT MORE...

The British Cycling Museum, The Old Station, Camelford, Cornwall.

The National Cycle Collection, The Automobile Palace, Temple Street, Llandrindod Wells. www.cyclemuseum.org.uk.

COLLECTORS' NOTES

■ Bonds, share or stock certificates are issued to investors as proof of capital invested in a company, government or other public body, or an individual.

■ The first shares in the modern sense were maritime shares and were traded in the Italian port of Amalfi from around AD1000, although certificates were not issued.

■ The first certificates were issued in the late 17th century in England, France, Holland and Italy. However the majority of collectable certificates available today are from the 19th and first half of the 20th centuries.

■ As this field is so wide, collectors often specialize in one area such as a particular country or period of issue, printing or casting errors, or unusual serial numbers. Shares for automobile, railroad and mining companies are also particularly sought-after.

■ Manuscript signatures, especially of famous people, can also have a profound effect on value.

■ As with all other paper-based collectables, condition is crucial in terms of market value.

A certificate for three 500 rupee shares in the private Bank of Bengal, featuring a fine vignette representing the Empire, dated 24th September 1909, complete with the seal of the bank, fine script security device and various manuscript signatures and endorsements.

13.75in (35cm) wide

£15-25   **INT**

A General Motors Corporation common stock certificate.

12in (30.5cm) long

£6-8   **INT**

A Chinese government 5% interest gold loan bond certificate, the first ever issue by the new Republic of China, issued in 1912, £100 denomination, green border and background design.

18in (46cm) long

£30-40   **INT**

A Russian 5% interest bond certificate, 'Loan of the City of Nikolaef', complete with detachable coupons redeemable for 10 shillings, dated 1912, printed in Russian and English.

15.5in (39cm) long

£10-20   **INT**

A certificate for 100 francs stock in the Société des Cafés de l'Indochine, complete with all 24 redeemable coupons, very attractive red and brown Oriental designs on a green ground, dated 25th August 1926, certificate number 011756.

This certificate is unusual in that it was issued in Saigon rather than the seat of the Colonial government in Vietnam.

14in (36cm) long

£10-20   **INT**

An interest bond certificate issued by Bank Zerubabel, Central Institution of the Palestine Cooperative Movement.

Bank Zerubabel continued operations after the creation of the state of Israel in 1948 - however, pre-1948 bond certificates are worth 4-5 times as much as later examples.

1945   *14in (36cm) wide*

£40-50   **INT**

A "cancelled" certificate for 5% guaranteed preferred shares, in the Waterford, Dungarvan & Lismore Railway Co.

1897   *10.5in (27cm) w*

£8-12   **INT**

A Turkish Ottoman Empire 1/4 livres certificate, printed on one side only with the 'tughra' seal of the Sultan.

1912   *8in (20cm) wide*

£15-20   **INT**

FIND OUT MORE...

'Scripophily: Collecting Bonds and Share Certificates', *by Keith Hollender, published by Book Sales, 1985.*

www.scripophily.org, the International Bond and Share Society.

COLLECTORS' NOTES

- First editions books are popular as they represent the most original version of the book and the one closest to the author's intent. Later examples can also be sought-after, but only if they contain important additional information.

- Copies signed by the author will add to the value and, as authors become celebrities in their own right, book signings are becoming more common. Inscriptions by other people, unless they are famous themselves, generally decrease the value of a book.

- Classic works by writers such as Agatha Christie and Ian Fleming are always popular, but contemporary writers like Margaret Atwood, Vikram Seth, Nick Hornby, Irvine Welsh and Donna Tartt are all sought-after. Look out for authors who have won literary prizes as this adds to the desirability of their current and earlier books. Titles that have been made into films will also be worth more.

- The condition of a book has a huge impact on the value, and mint copies will always command a premium. The presence of a dust jacket is also important, particularly for post-1950 books.

Monica Ali, "Brick Lane", first edition, published by Doubleday, signed by the author.
2003

£50-70　　　　　　　　　　　　　　　**BIB**

Jack Arnott, "The Long Firm", first edition, published by Hoddard and Staunton General.
1999

£15-25　　　　　**BIB**

Margaret Atwood, "The Blind Assassin", first edition, published by Bloomsbury, signed by the author.
2000

£15-25　　　　　**BIB**

Margaret Atwood, "Oryx & Crake", first edition, published by Bloomsbury.
2003

£10-20　　　　　**BIB**

Iain M. Banks, "Feersum Endjinn", first edition, published by Orbit.
1994

£10-15　　　　　**BIB**

Iain M. Banks, "Inversions", first edition, published by Orbit.
1998

£25-35　　　　　**BIB**

Clive Barker, "Abarat", uncorrected proof of first US edition, published by Harper Collins.

2002

£55-65　　　　　**BIB**

Julian Barnes, "Something to Declare", first edition, published by Picador.
2002

£7-10　　　　　**BIB**

Stephen Baxter, "Titan", first edition, published by Voyager.

1997

£15-20 BIB

William Boyd, "Armadillo", first UK edition, published by Hamish Hamilton.

1998

£18-22 BIB

Greg Bear, "Eon", first UK edition, published by Gollancz.

1986

£40-50 BIB

A.S. Byatt, "Babel Tower", first edition, published by Chatto and Windus.

1996

£18-22 BIB

Peter Carey, "The Unusual Life of Tristan Smith", first edition, published by Faber and Faber.

1994

£25-35 BIB

J.M.Coetzee, "Disgrace", first edition, published by Secker and Warburg, signed and dated "25/10/99" by the author.

The date is significant and adds to the value, as it was the day Coetzee was awarded the Booker prize for this book.

1995

£300-400 BIB

Tracy Chevalier, "Falling Angels", first edition, published by Harper Collins, signed by the author.

2001

£15-25 BIB

Paul Coelho, "The Devil and Miss Prym", first English-language edition, published by Harper Collins.

2000

£15-25 BIB

Douglas Coupland, "Microserfs", first edition, published by Harper Collins.

1995

£7-10 BIB

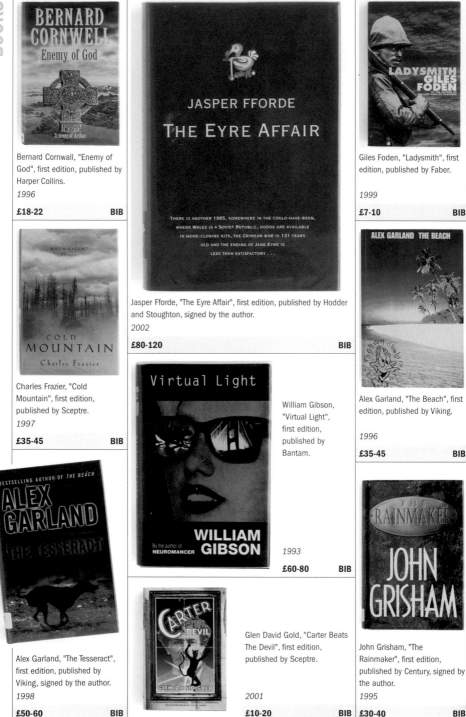

Bernard Cornwall, "Enemy of God", first edition, published by Harper Collins.
1996
£18-22 BIB

Jasper Fforde, "The Eyre Affair", first edition, published by Hodder and Stoughton, signed by the author.
2002
£80-120 BIB

Giles Foden, "Ladysmith", first edition, published by Faber.
1999
£7-10 BIB

Charles Frazier, "Cold Mountain", first edition, published by Sceptre.
1997
£35-45 BIB

William Gibson, "Virtual Light", first edition, published by Bantam.
1993
£60-80 BIB

Alex Garland, "The Beach", first edition, published by Viking.
1996
£35-45 BIB

Alex Garland, "The Tesseract", first edition, published by Viking, signed by the author.
1998
£50-60 BIB

Glen David Gold, "Carter Beats The Devil", first edition, published by Sceptre.
2001
£10-20 BIB

John Grisham, "The Rainmaker", first edition, published by Century, signed by the author.
1995
£30-40 BIB

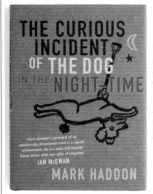

Mark Haddon, "The Curious Incident of the Dog in the Night-Time", first edition, published by Jonathan Cape, with adult version dust jacket.

Mark Haddon, "The Curious Incident of the Dog in the Night-Time", first edition, published by David Fickling Books, with children's version dust jacket.
2003

£15-25   BIB

Joanne Harris, "Five Quarters of the Orange", first edition, published by Doubleday, signed by the author.
2001

£20-30   BIB

Like J.K. Rowling's Harry Potter series and Philip Pullman's 'His Dark Materials' trilogy, this children's book is a popular adults' read, so the publishers re-issued it with an 'adult' cover. This was released in smaller numbers, making it more desirable to collectors.

2003

£36-45   BIB

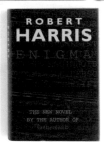

Robert Harris, "Enigma", first edition, published by Hutchinson, signed by the author.
1995

£20-30   BIB

James Hawes, "Rancid Aluminium", first edition, published by Jonathan Cape.
1997

£12-18   BIB

Peter Høeg, "Miss Smilla's Feeling For Snow", first UK edition, published by Harvill.
1993

£100-150   BIB

Nick Hornby, "High Fidelity", first edition, published by Victor Gollancz, signed, some underlining.
1995

£15-25   BIB

Kazuo Ishiguro, "The Remains of the Day", first edition, published by Faber.
1989

£100-140   BIB

Helen Fielding, "The Edge of Reason", first edition, published by Picador, signed by the author.
1999

£50-70   BIB

Jonathan Lethem, "Motherless Brooklyn", first edition, published by Faber.

1999

£12-18 BIB

Michael Marshall, "The Straw Men", first edition, published by Harper Collins, signed by the author.

2002

£10-15 BIB

Frank McCourt, "'Tis", first edition, published by Flamingo.

1999

£10-20 BIB

David Mitchell, "Number 9 Dream", first edition, published by Sceptre.

2001

£10-15 BIB

Kim Newman, "Bad Dreams", first edition, published by Simon and Schuster.

1990

£7-10 BIB

Jeff Noon, "Pollen", first edition, published by Ringpull.

1995

£10-15 BIB

Terry Pratchett, "Carpe Jugulum", first edition, published by Doubleday, signed by the author.

1988

£25-35 BIB

Terry Pratchett, "The Wee Free Men", first edition, published by Doubleday, signed by the author.

2003

£50-70 BIB

Robert Rankin, "Snuff Fiction", first edition, published by Doubleday.

1999

£10-15 BIB

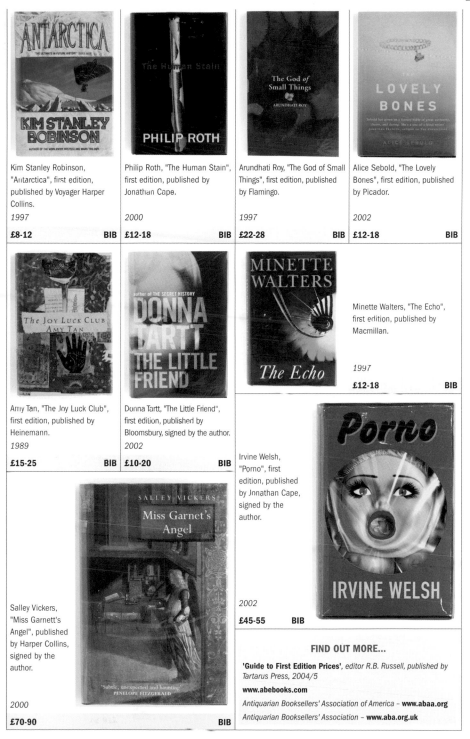

Kim Stanley Robinson, "Antarctica", first edition, published by Voyager Harper Collins.

1997

£8-12 BIB

Philip Roth, "The Human Stain", first edition, published by Jonathan Cape.

2000

£12-18 BIB

Arundhati Roy, "The God of Small Things", first edition, published by Flamingo.

1997

£22-28 BIB

Alice Sebold, "The Lovely Bones", first edition, published by Picador.

2002

£12-18 BIB

Amy Tan, "The Joy Luck Club", first edition, published by Heinemann.

1989

£15-25 BIB

Donna Tartt, "The Little Friend", first edition, published by Bloomsbury, signed by the author.

2002

£10-20 BIB

Minette Walters, "The Echo", first edition, published by Macmillan.

1997

£12-18 BIB

Irvine Welsh, "Porno", first edition, published by Jonathan Cape, signed by the author.

2002

£45-55 BIB

Salley Vickers, "Miss Garnett's Angel", published by Harper Collins, signed by the author.

2000

£70-90 BIB

FIND OUT MORE...

'Guide to First Edition Prices', *editor R.B. Russell, published by Tartarus Press, 2004/5*

www.abebooks.com

Antiquarian Booksellers' Association of America – **www.abaa.org**

Antiquarian Booksellers' Association – **www.aba.org.uk**

Rev. W. Awdry, "Duck and the Diesel Engine - Railway Series, No. 13", first edition, published by Edmund Ward, London.

1958

£40-50   BIB

Rev. W. Awdry, "The Little Old Engine - Railway Series, No. 14", first edition, published by Edmund Ward, London.

1959

£60-80   BIB

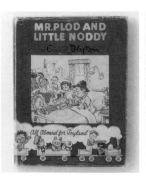

Enid Blyton, "Mr Plod and Little Noddy", first edition, published by Sampson Low, Marston & Co., London.

1961

£25-35   BIB

Rev. W. Awdry, "The Twin Engines - Railway Series, No. 15", first edition, published by Edmund Ward, London.

1960

£70-90   BIB

Enid Blyton, "New Big Noddy Book", first edition, published by Sampson Low, Marston & Co., London.

1950s

£60-80   BIB

Enid Blyton, "A Rubbalong Tale, A Werner Laurie Show Book", first edition, published by Werner Laurie, with original hard paper picture boards.

1951

£350-400   BIB

Enid Blyton, "Noddy's Own Nursery Rhymes", first edition, published by Sampson Low, Marston & Co., London.

1958

£70-100   BIB

Enid Blyton, "Tales of Toyland", first edition, published by George Newnes Ltd, London, contains owner's inscription.

1944

£80-120   BIB

Enid Blyton, "Tales About Toys", published by Brockhampton Press, Leicester.

c1950

£15-20   BIB

Enid Blyton, "Well Done Noddy", first edition, published by Sampson Low, Marston & Co., London.
1952
£40-50   BIB

Laurent de Brunhoff, "Babar's Visit To Bird Island", first edition, published by Methuen, London, with cloth spine.
1952
£100-140   BIB

Laurent de Brunhoff, "Babar's Fair", first edition, published by Methuen, London.
1969
£20-24   BIB

Laurent de Brunhoff, "The Story of Babar, the Little Elephant", first edition, published by Methuen, London.
1934
£100-150   BIB

Kate Greenaway, "Language of Flowers", published by George Routledge and Sons, illustrations by Kate Greenaway, written inscription dated Sept. 20th 1888.
£80-120   BIB

Andrew Lang, "The Brown Fairy", first edition, published by Longmans, Green & Co., London.
1904
£250-300   BIB

A A. Milne, "The House At Pooh Corner", first edition, published by Methuen, London, illustrated by E.H. Shepard.
1928
£700-1,000   BIB

A.A. Milne, "Now We Are Six", first edition with illustration by E.H. Shepard, published by Methuen, London.
1927
£650-750   BIB

A.A. Milne, "Toad of Toad Hall", first edition, published by Methuen, London.
1929
£120-180   BIB

A.A. Milne, "Winnie-the-Pooh", first edition, with illustrations by E.H. Shepard, published by Methuen, London.
1926
£100-150   BIB

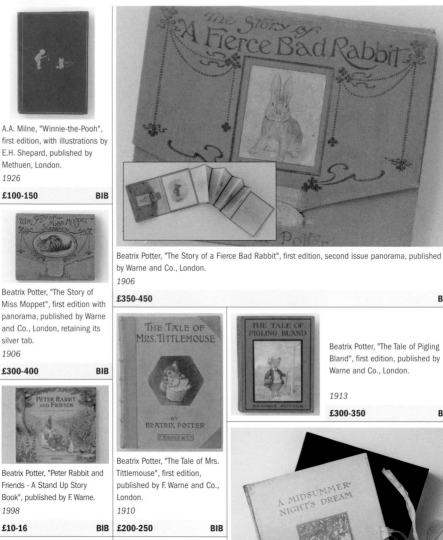

Beatrix Potter, "The Story of a Fierce Bad Rabbit", first edition, second issue panorama, published by Warne and Co., London.
1906
£350-450   BIB

Beatrix Potter, "The Story of Miss Moppet", first edition with panorama, published by Warne and Co., London, retaining its silver tab.
1906
£300-400   BIB

Beatrix Potter, "The Tale of Mrs. Tittlemouse", first edition, published by F. Warne and Co., London.
1910
£200-250   BIB

Beatrix Potter, "The Tale of Pigling Bland", first edition, published by Warne and Co., London.
1913
£300-350   BIB

Beatrix Potter, "Peter Rabbit and Friends - A Stand Up Story Book", published by F. Warne.
1998
£10-16   BIB

Maurice Sendak, "In the Night Kitchen", first edition, published by Harper & Row.
1970
£20-30   BIB

"Dean's Surprise Model Series No. 1 - Surprise Model Picture Book", published by Dean & Son, London, very scarce.
c1895
£120-180   BIB

William Shakespeare, "A Midsummer-Night's Dream", published by Heinemann, from a limited edition of 1,000, illustrated by Arthur Rackham with 40 mounted plates, signed and numbered by Rackham, inscription on front inside cover, with dust slip cover.
1908
£2,000-2,500   BIB

COLLECTORS' NOTES

■ Known today for its teddy bears, Dean's Rag Book Co. originally made children's cloth story books, illustrated with brightly coloured pictures, at its London factory. The company was founded by Henry Samuel Dean in 1903 and made bears from 1917 onwards.

■ For collectors, the most interesting period runs from 1903 until the 1930s, when the company employed popular artists of the day to design the illustrations. These included F.M. Barton, Stanley Berkeley and John Hasall.

■ As well as English, the books were also produced in French, German, Dutch and, rarest of all, Russian.

■ The materials used, and the fact that these books were handled by children, means that condition affects value greatly except in the scarcest examples. Look for examples in good, clean condition with no tears or stains.

Gladys Hall and Eugenie Richards, "The Nursery Rhyme Book", Book No. 161, and "Look Here!", Book No. 158, both colour-printed illustrated picture books.

1916   *Largest 11.25in (28.5cm) high*

£80-120   **BONC**

"Just Off", a colour-printed illustrated picture book.

1905   *9in (23cm) wide*

£40-50   **BONC**

Yoshio Markino, "Old English Nursery Rhymes", Book No. 188, colour-printed illustrated storybook.

1916   *8in (20cm) wide*

£25-35   **BONC**

A. Herouard, "The Playtime Book", Book No. 254, colour-printed illustrated picture book.

1927   *11in (28cm) high*

£35-45   **BONC**

John Hassell, 'Ding! Din! Don!', Book No. 9, French language colour-printed illustrated storybook, cover slightly dirty.

1903   *11.5in (29cm) high*

£35-45   **BONC**

John Hassall, "Entre Dans la Danse", colour-printed illustrated storybook.

1913   *10.75in (27.5cm) high*

£80-120   **BONC**

G.H. Dodd, "Le Cirque Pig & Cie", Book No. 81, French language with colour-printed illustrations.

1910   *8.75in (22.5cm) high*

£25-35   **BONC**

Stanley Berkeley and Eugenie Richards, "Les Memoires De Toby Par Lui Même", Book No. 47, French language, colour-printed illustrated storybook.

1905   *11.5in (29cm) high*

£50-60   **BONC**

E. Travis, "Le Train Siffle!", Book No. 150, French language, colour-printed illustrated train book.

1916   *11.5in (29.5cm) wide*

£70-80   **BONC**

John Hassall, "Mironton, Mirontaine!", French language colour-printed illustrated storybook.

1913   *11.5in (29cm) high*

£80-120   **BONC**

F. M. Barton, "Puff! Puff!", Book No. 20, French language with colour-printed illustrations.

1903   *8.75in (22.5cm) wide*

£25-45   **BONC**

Left: Chas K. Cook, "Eisenbahnen", Book No. 61, German language colour-printed illustrated train book.

1910   *8.5in (21.5cm) high*

£35-45   **BONC**

Right: Chas K. Cook, "Eins-Zwei-Drei", Book No. 48, German language colour-printed illustrated number book.

1905   *8.25in (21cm) high*

£30-40   **BONC**

A Flip the Frog factory production rag toy sheet, colour printed on orange velvet.

1930   *39.25in (100cm) long*

£100-200   **BONC**

A Flip the Frog factory production rag toy sheet, colour printed on yellow velvet and a part Flip sheet.

1930   *39.25in (100cm) long*

£180-220   **BONC**

An Oswald the Lucky Rabbit factory production rag toy sheet, on printed velvet, with various sized heads.

1933   *29in (74cm) long*

£100-150   **BONC**

Six Dean's shop display cards, comprising "Lost Dismal Desmond", "Tatters the Hospital Pup", "Patient Pat Son of Tatters", "Lazybones", "Wabbly Wally" and "Gallopin' Gus the Lucky Gee Gee".

c1930   *11.75in (30cm) wide*

£180-200   **BONC**

Six Dean's shop display cards, comprising "Oswald the Lucky Rabbit", "Bosco and Honey", "Dean's Dancing Dolls" and "Hetty the Help Yourself Girl", together with "Lazybones", and "Ma-Coney".

c1930

£180-220   **BONC**

FIND OUT MORE...

'Dean's Rag Book Co. - The First 100 Years', *by Neil Miller.*

Enid Blyton, "Enid Blyton's Famous Five Go Adventuring Again" annual.

1978

£10-15　　　　　　　　　**BIB**

Mary Tourtel, "Rupert In More Adventures" annual, published by the Daily Express.

1944

£70-90　　　　　　　　　**BIB**

Mary Tourtel, "More Adventures of Rupert" annual, published by the Daily Express.

1947

£120-180　　　　　　　　**BIB**

Mary Tourtel, "The Monster Rupert" annual, published by the Daily Express.

1948

£30-40　　　　　　　　　**BIB**

Mary Tourtel, "More Adventures of Rupert" annual, published by the Daily Express.

1949

£40-60　　　　　　　　　**BIB**

Mary Tourtel, "More Rupert Adventures" annual, published by the Daily Express.

1952

£80-120　　　　　　　　**BIB**

Mary Tourtel, "Rupert" annual, published by the Daily Express.

1949

£100-150　　　　　　　　　　　　　　　　　**BIB**

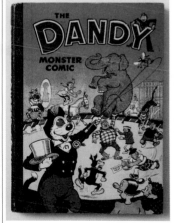

"The Dandy Monster Comic" annual, published by D.C. Thomson, front boards featuring Korky the Cat as ringmaster at a circus.

These annuals are hard to find in such clean condition, making it more desirable.

1951

£100-150　　　　　　　　**BIB**

Mary Tourtel, "Rupert" annual, published by the Daily Express.

1958

£30-50　　　　　　　　　**BIB**

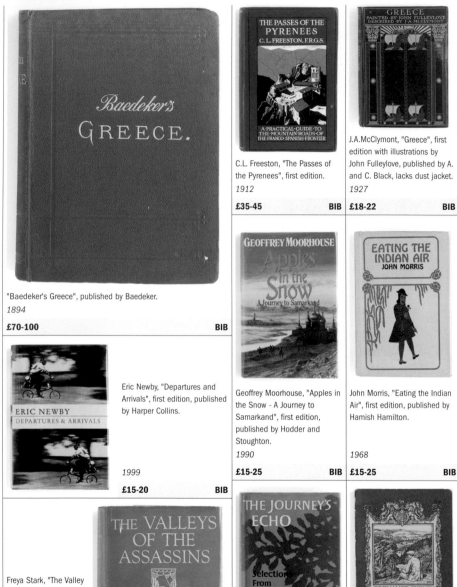

"Baedeker's Greece", published by Baedeker.
1894
£70-100   BIB

Eric Newby, "Departures and Arrivals", first edition, published by Harper Collins.
1999
£15-20   BIB

Freya Stark, "The Valley of the Assassins", first edition, published by John Murray.
1934
£250-350   BIB

C.L. Freeston, "The Passes of the Pyrenees", first edition.
1912
£35-45   BIB

Geoffrey Moorhouse, "Apples in the Snow - A Journey to Samarkand", first edition, published by Hodder and Stoughton.
1990
£15-25   BIB

Freya Stark, "The Journey's Echo", first edition, published by John Murray.
1963
£30-50   BIB

J.A.McClymont, "Greece", first edition with illustrations by John Fulleylove, published by A. and C. Black, lacks dust jacket.
1927
£18-22   BIB

John Morris, "Eating the Indian Air", first edition, published by Hamish Hamilton.
1968
£15-25   BIB

An Ordnance Survey map of Clacton-on-Sea and Harwich.
£10-15   BIB

J. Coutts, "Everyday Gardening", reprint, published by Ward, Lock and Co.

£7-10   BIB

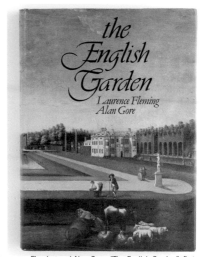

F. Hadfield Farthing, "Saturday In My Garden", third edition revised by A. Cecil Bartlett, published by McDonald & Co.
1947

£10-15   BIB

L.J.F. Brimble, "Flowers in Britain", published by Macmillan.
1980

£15-25   BIB

A.G.L. Hellyer, "Garden Plants in Colour", first edition, published by W.H. and L. Collingridge Ltd.
1958

£7-10   BIB

Denis Wood, "Practical Garden Design", first edition, published by J.M. Dent and Sons.
1976

£10-15   BIB

Laurence Fleming and Alan Gore, "The English Garden", first edition, second impression, published by Michael Joseph Ltd.
1980

£15-25   BIB

Edward Step, "Wild Flowers Month by Month", first edition, published by Frederick Warne and Co., two volumes.
1905

£15-20   BIB

Richardson Wright, "The Practical Book of Outdoor Flowers", first edition, published by J.B. Lippincott.
1924

£15-25   BIB

Frank S. Smythe, "The Valley of Flowers", published by Hodder and Stoughton.
1947

£10-15   BIB

COLLECTORS' NOTES

■ Before glass bottles became the norm, household liquids were usually stored in tan- or cream-coloured stoneware vessels with black lettering, sometimes made by well-known potteries such as Doulton & Co. Blue or green glass bottles, older etched glass versions, and those decorated with pictures are particularly sought-after.

■ Glass was increasingly used for storing drinks from the end of the 18thC. Following the invention of a method for carbonating water in the late 18thC, a torpedo-shaped bottle was introduced that prevented bubbles escaping.

■ Patented medicines became popular in the early 19thC, and were often attractively packaged, making the bottles appealing to today's collector. Warner's Safe Cure is a popular example and a collecting area in its own right. Standard bottles can be easily picked up.

■ Glass and earthenware ink bottles, especially those in unusual shapes such as cottages, birdcages and figures, are also popular with enthusiasts. Ink Bottles made after 1840 are especially common, as more were produced to meet the rising demand caused by improving literacy and the Penny Post.

■ Good condition is essential and a crack or chip in the wrong place can make an otherwise valuable bottle almost worthless; a missing stopper can also decrease value. Be wary of the large number of fake coloured bottles on the market and look out for photocopied 'original' labels by carefully examining tears and dirt.

A rare and early Daffys Elixir bottle, dark olive green glass, rectangular cross section, bevelled corners, base cross hinged and pontilled, short neck with crude applied rolled lip, embossed "True Daffys/Elixir" to front and rear, one small patch of iridescence, very good condition.

This early version is identifiable by the lack of lettering on the smaller side panels.

c1830-40   4.5in (11.5cm) high

£2,500-3,000   **BBR**

An unusual Savory & Moore wooden boxed bottle, clear glass with paper label "The Cordial Stomach Mixture/Savory & Moore/Chemists To The Queen", complete in boxwood case with screw-off top.

1880-1900   4.5in (11.5cm) h

£80-100   **BBR**

A Hooper & Company bottle, dark olive green glass, rectangular shape with rounded shoulders and bevelled corners embossed "Hooper & Compy/55/Grosvenor St/And At/7 Pall Mall East/London Laboratory/Mitcham/Surrey".

1870-80   7.5in (19cm) high

£180-220   **BBR**

A Warners Safe Cure bottle, olive green glass, embossed "Warners/Safe Cure London", with pictorial safe trade mark, good condition.

1890-1910   7.25in (18.5cm) h

£45-55   **BBR**

A Warners Nervine bottle, olive green glass, weakly embossed "Warners Safe Nervine/London", with the safe pictorial trade mark, misshapen shoulders, top embossing weak, very good condition.

1900-10   7.5in (9cm) high

£30-40   **BBR**

A rare Warners Safe Compound bottle, golden amber glass, embossed "Warners/Safe/Compound", with pictorial safe trade mark, a few tiny dings.

1910-20   5.5in (14cm) high

£80-100   **BBR**

A Warners Safe Cure bottle, fine deep amber glass, embossed "Warners/Safe/Cure/London", with safe trade mark, very good condition.

1890-1900   7.5in (19cm) high

£25-35   **BBR**

A scarce hair restorer bottle, cobalt blue glass, rectangular shape, embossed "The Maison Benbow/Specialists For The Hair/St Leonards-On-Sea", very good condition.

1910-20   6in (15cm) high

£22-28   **BBR**

A rare large late 19th/early 20thC Crescent green glass poison bottle, embossed "Not To Be Taken" to centre panel with diagonal ribs and dots, "RD NO 461701" to base, together with a small cobalt blue glass example, very good condition.

Poison bottles had to be easily discernable from other bottles and are typically blue or green with ribbed or quilted exteriors and embossed "Not To Be Taken" or "Poison". Clear glass examples are rare and shaped bottles such as skulls are sought-after.

Large 6.75in (17cm) high

£50-60   **BBR**

Small 3.5in (9cm) high

£20-30   **BBR**

A CLOSER LOOK AT A WINE BOTTLE

The Nailsea factory is best known today for it tableware produced from 'end of shift' dark bottle glass leftovers. The name became a general term for similar glass made at numerous factories.

The first glass wine bottles date from the 17thC. Early designs tended to be globe or onion-shaped, by the early 18thC the mallet shape was introduced, followed by the cylinder.

This type of glass is often referred to as black glass, when it is actually dark green or brown.

This is possibly the first recorded example of a Nailsea-style bottle with a seal incorporating both a date and pictorial image.

A dated Nailsea-style sealed wine bottle, globular body with longish neck and applied collar, dark olive green with white enamelled flecks of varying size, pictorial seal reads "1830/ AC", with a horse pictured.

1830   9.5in (24cm) high

£4,000-5,000   **BBR**

A Hyde cobalt blue glass cylinder ink bottle, with pouring lip, embossed "Hyde/London", very good condition.

1900-1910 6in (15.5cm) high

£12-18   **BBR**

An early Hamilton cobalt blue glass bottle, very heavily embossed with large coat of arms, minor neck mark, otherwise extremely good condition.

8.75in (22cm) long

£1,500-2,000   **BBR**

An early Schweppes dark olive green glass Hamilton bottle, with applied rolled lip "J Schweppe & Co./Genuine Superior/Aerated Waters/ 79 Margaret Street", minor wear.

7.5in (19cm) long

£1,200-1,800   **BBR**

A sealed dark olive green glass wine bottle, applied collar lip and base pontil, seal with the initials "A S", small hairline crack to base.

1870-80   11in (28cm) high

£180-220   **BBR**

An 1880s sealed dark olive green glass wine bottle, applied heavy double collar lip, seal with wild boar and coronet, deep kick-up pontil base.

11.25in (28.5cm) high

£250-300   **BBR**

A Prices Patent Candle bottle, cobalt blue glass wedge-shaped bottle embossed to front "Prices/ Patent/ Candle/ Company/ Limited", with diamond registration mark, good condition.

£80-100   7.5in (19cm) high

£80-100   **BBR**

An unusual small 1880s Weston Super Mare Sykes Macvay patent aqua glass bottle, embossed "Ross & Co./Weston Super Mare" to front, "Sykes Macvay & Co./Patent 1877/Castleford", complete with lead and rubber insert to neck, minor star body crack.

6in (15cm) high

£150-200 **BBR**

A teakettle dark amethyst coloured glass ink bottle, fluted sloping octagonal shape with upturned spout, good condition.

c1840-50 *2in (5cm) high*

£250-350 **BBR**

A very rare 1870s-80s amethyst glass target ball, criss-cross embossing, central band embossed "W W Greener St Marys Works Birmm & Haymarket London".

3in (7.5cm) high

£400-500 **BBR**

A Hardens Star fire grenade, cobalt blue glass, vertically ribbed, embossed star to front, central band embossed "Harden Star Hand Grenade Fire Extinguisher", complete sealed with contents and paper label around neck, good condition.

1880-1900 *6.5in (16.5cm) h*

£120-180 **BBR**

A Hardens Star fire grenade, cobalt blue glass, vertically ribbed embossed star to front, weakly embossed around central band, sealed with contents, good condition.

1880-1900 *6.5in (16.5cm) h*

£60-80 **BBR**

A Napoleon mid-brown saltglaze ink bottle, probably London, formed as a naturalistically modelled Napoleon's head, impressed to rear "Findleys/Napolion", slight flake to hat front.

This is a previously unrecorded figural Napoleon ink bottle. Napoleon died in 1821 and it is possible this could have commemorated his death, which would make it significantly early.

c1830 *2.25in (5.5cm) h*

£1,200-1,500 **BBR**

A Mr Punch saltglaze figural ink bottle, formed as a seated Mr Punch, mid-brown saltglaze with touches of dark brown highlights, rear with raised diamond registration mark and particularly well impressed "Gardners Ink Works/Lower White Cross St London", very good condition.

c1840-50 *5in (12.5cm) high*

£500-600 **BBR**

A Bellowing Man light and mid-brown saltglaze ink bottle, formed as a bellowing man's head, quill hole to forehead with elaborate side embossing, minor bottom edge flake.

c1840-50 *3in (7.5cm) wide*

£200-250 **BBR**

A Manchester Railway slab seal porter, grey-green glaze, applied seal reads "Midland/B.B." (Midland Hotel Buffet Bar) very crude, very good condition.

The hotel still stands beside Victoria Station in Manchester.

1860-70 *7in (18cm) high*

£220-280 **BBR**

A Sheffield slab seal flask, grey-green glaze, seal reads "Old No. 12", good condition.

Old No. 12 is the name of a public house in Sheffield.

c1850-60   8in (20cm) high

£80-120   **BBR**

An S.H. Ward & Co. Ltd ginger beer bottle, standard two-tone bottle with "Home Brewed Ginger Beer/S.H. Ward & Co. Ltd Renton Street/Sheffield".

This is the rarest of all the Wards variations.

1890-1910   7.5in (19cm) h

£35-45   **BBR**

A Firths Darlington ginger beer bottle, standard two-tone Blue transfer "Firths Darlington/Brewed Ginger Beer", locomotive pictorial trade mark Gray Portobello pottery mark, good condition.

1890-1910   7in (18cm) high

£30-40   **BBR**

An Arliss Robinson & Co. ginger beer bottle, standard blue top "Arliss Robinson & Co./Home Brewed/Ginger Beer/Sutton Surrey", Bourne Denby pottery mark, slight hairline.

1890-1910   6.75in (17cm) h

£22-28   **BBR**

A scarce Comrie & Co. ginger beer bottle, transfer "Special/Old Scotch Ginger Beer Comrie & Co./Helensburgh", large pictorial of man holding aloft a bottle of ginger beer, Port Dundas Glasgow pottery mark.

1890-1910   8in (20cm) high

£60-80   **BBR**

A rare late Victorian Tyrconnell whisky jug, off-white glaze, black transfer "Tyrconnell Whisky" depicting Donegal Castle's building ruins, rear handle broken off, Grosvenor Glasgow pottery mark.

9in (23cm) high

£35-45   **BBR**

A Cruiskeen Lawn two-tone whisky jug, handle to rear, black transfer "Cruiskeen Lawn/Mitchells Old/Irish Whisky/Belfast", with cautionary lines to rear, Midland Pottery Melling pottery mark, good condition.

c1900   7.25in (18.5cm) high

£35-45   **BBR**

A Watsons two-tone whisky jug, pouring lip to neck, transfer showing highlander, "Watsons/Dundee/Whisky", Port Dundas pottery mark.

1880-90   8.5in (21.5cm) h

£35-45   **BBR**

An unusual Ivanhoe whisky jug, top off-white glaze, base tan, black transfer "Ivanhoe/Old Scotch Whisky", Port Dundas Glasgow pottery mark.

1900-10   8in (20cm) high

£100-150   **BBR**

FIND OUT MORE...

'Antique Glass Bottles - Their History and Evolution (1500-1850), Willy van den Bossche, Antique Collectors Club, 20001.

'Stoneware Bottles: Bellarmines to Ginger Beers', Derek Askey, published by BBR Publishing, 1998.

www.antiquebottles.com

CANES

COLLECTORS' NOTES

■ Canes first became popular during the 16th century. Their fashionable high point was from the 19th century until WWI and most canes found today date from this period. A gentleman may have had a number of canes for day and evening use. The materials and quality of workmanship indicated a person's status and continue to be important factors for collectors today.

■ Examine the different parts including the handle or rounded pommel, the shaft and the ferrule on the end, as all should be original and not replacements. Missing ferrules are rarely a problem unless it was an intrinsic, decorated part of the cane. Hardwood is used for the shaft, usually Malacca which does not warp or bend.

■ Examples with fine carving, materials such as ivory, gold or inset precious stones are desirable as are 'folk art' canes, which are usually charmingly or naively carved. 'Gadget' canes with hidden or added uses are much sought after, and the more complex, the more valuable a piece usually is.

An erotic walking stick, the ivory handle carved with a reclining naked woman, Malacca shaft with an ivory collar engraved with flowers.
c1850

£1,600-1,800   SEG

A 19thC riding crop, with carved ivory handle of a monkey's head with a long brimmed stylized riding hat, with gilded engraved collar.

£350-450   SEG

A CLOSER LOOK AT A CANE

A walking stick with a carved ivory handle, in the form of a reclining mastiff guard dog, with a Malacca shaft, with a gold, engraved collar.
c1870

£650-750   SEG

An early 19thC ivory mounted cane, with an ivory skull handled grip, shaft made out of a snake's vertebral column.

The skull has long been identified as a 'momento mori' (remember death). It famously appears in Holbein's 1533 painting 'The Ambassadors'.

£2,000-2,500   SEG

This is a pilgrimage cane used by pilgrims walking to religious towns, they are often called 'bourdons'.

The pommel is carved with a skull and the faces of Christ and Mary, reflecting its religious use and acting as a 'memento mori'.

The carving is extremely fine and realistic, and the good condition and early date makes this exceptionally rare and desirable.

A 19thC 'Seditious' cane, with turned ivory pommel.

Whilst appearing to be an ordinary cane, its shape casts a shadow of a man's profile. These were often used by organisations such as the Freemasons to identify each other. Canes of this type were also used to discreetly demonstrate political allegiances to certain factions or parties.

£1,500-2,000   SEG

An historic walking stick, the figural ivory pommel carved with the head of French King Francis I, with a Malacca shaft, decorated silver collar and brass ferrule.
c1850

£2,000-2,500   SEG

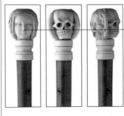

Traces of colour can be found on the face of Mary, who was once painted possibly with her traditional colours of blue, red and white.

A 17th/18thC carved ivory pilgrimage cane, with a Malacca shaft and an ivory pommel mounted on a turned ivory collar, the large brass ferrule with an iron spike for gripping the ground.

£5,000-6,000   SEG

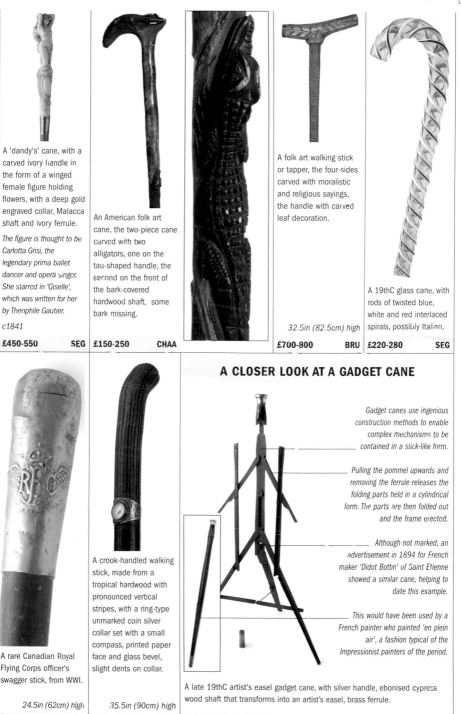

A 'dandy's' cane, with a carved ivory handle in the form of a winged female figure holding flowers, with a deep gold engraved collar, Malacca shaft and ivory ferrule.

The figure is thought to be Carlotta Grisi, the legendary prima ballet dancer and opera singer. She starred in 'Giselle', which was written for her by Theophile Gautier.

c1841

£450-550   SEG

An American folk art cane, the two-piece cane carved with two alligators, one on the tau-shaped handle, the second on the front of the bark-covered hardwood shaft, some bark missing.

£150-250   CHAA

A folk art walking stick or tapper, the four-sides carved with moralistic and religious sayings, the handle with carved leaf decoration.

32.5in (82.5cm) high

£700-800   BRU

A 19thC glass cane, with rods of twisted blue, white and red interlaced spirals, possibly Italian.

£220-280   SEG

A rare Canadian Royal Flying Corps officer's swagger stick, from WWI.

24.5in (62cm) high

£80-120   TAM

A crook-handled walking stick, made from a tropical hardwood with pronounced vertical stripes, with a ring-type unmarked coin silver collar set with a small compass, printed paper face and glass bevel, slight dents on collar.

35.5in (90cm) high

£70-100   CHAA

A CLOSER LOOK AT A GADGET CANE

Gadget canes use ingenious construction methods to enable complex mechanisms to be contained in a stick-like form.

Pulling the pommel upwards and removing the ferrule releases the folding parts held in a cylindrical form. The parts are then folded out and the frame erected.

Although not marked, an advertisement in 1894 for French maker 'Didot Bottin' of Saint Etienne showed a similar cane, helping to date this example.

This would have been used by a French painter who painted 'en plein air', a fashion typical of the Impressionist painters of the period.

A late 19thC artist's easel gadget cane, with silver handle, ebonised cypress wood shaft that transforms into an artist's easel, brass ferrule.

£5,000-6,000   SEG

COLLECTORS' NOTES

■ Lorna Bailey was born in 1978 and studied at Stoke-on-Trent College. Stoke was the successor to the notable Burslem School of Art where Susie Cooper, Clarice Cliff and Charlotte Rhead studied.

■ In the 1990s, her father acquired many of the assets of Wood & Sons upon its liquidation and began to produce traditional hand decorated pieces such as toby jugs. Lorna soon began to create pieces for the shop and demand grew so rapidly that by 1998, she had two decorators solely producing her designs. Her designs are now collected widely with an ever-expanding, loyal base of collectors,

■ Her designs are very like Clarice Cliff's early designs, in terms of form, their exuberance and bright colours. However, considering her range, she is clearly not exclusively governed by this inspiration. Look out for her unique prototype pieces, as well as those produced in strictly limited numbers.

A limited edition Lorna Bailey large bird beak water jug.

The form of this vase is similar to Myott's 'bowtie' jugs of the 1930s, showing Bailey's fascination with 1930s ceramics.

12in (30.5cm) high

£80-120 **PSA**

A Lorna Bailey rocket sugar shaker.

6.5in (16.5cm) high

£30-40 **PSA**

A limited edition Lorna Bailey comet conical sugar sifter, with two 'star' shaped handles.

5.75in (14.5cm) high

£60-80 **PSA**

A limited edition Lorna Bailey triangular tea pot.

7.75in (19.5cm) high

£50-70 **PSA**

A Lorna Bailey large Sputnik jar and cover.

8in (20cm) high

£60-80 **PSA**

A Lorna Bailey Metropolis milk jug.

3.5in (9cm) high

£25-35 **PSA**

A Lorna Bailey large prototype vase, highly decorated with bands of brightly coloured, stylized floral and geometric designs.

23in (58cm) high

£350-450 **PSA**

A Lorna Bailey small butterfly vase.

3.75in (9.5cm) high

£30-40 **PSA**

A Lorna Bailey for Carltonware
Art Deco charger.
13.25in (33.5cm) diam

£120-180   **PSA**

A limited edition Lorna Bailey Art Deco lady embossed charger.

*As well as having a striking design incorporating a 'flapper' girl of
the 1920s and a bright choice of period colours, this piece features
embossing, adding to its decorative appeal.*

13.5in (34.5cm) diam

£220-280   **PSA**

A prototype Lorna Bailey
Christmas charger.
13.5in (34.5cm) diam

£180-220   **PSA**

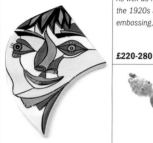

A limited edition Lorna Bailey
abstract face wall plaque, from
an edition of 50.
13.5in (34.5cm) high

£50-70   **PSA**

A limited edition Lorna Bailey
figure of a showgirl, hand
signed and numbered "47"
from an edition of 100.
8.25in (20cm) high

£60-80   **PSA**

A prototype Lorna Bailey
dancing showgirl figure, in a
yellow and green outfit.
7.5in (19cm) high

£150-200   **PSA**

A limited edition Lorna Bailey
lady as a sunbather figure, from
an edition of 100.
7in (18cm) long

£80-120   **PSA**

A limited edition Lorna Bailey
large grotesque bird, from an
edition of 75.

11.5in (29cm) high

£200-250   **PSA**

A limited edition Lorna Bailey
large ginger cat, playing with a
mouse, from an edition of 75.
11.5in (29cm) high

£150-200   **PSA**

COLLECTORS' NOTES

- John Beswick founded a pottery at Loughton, Stoke-on-Trent, in 1894. Animal figures were added to production in the 1930s and it is this line for which Beswick is renowned.

- Many collectors focus on a type of animal or bird, and aim to own one in every available colour. Cattle are popular and have risen in desirability and value recently, some fetch over £2,000.

- Certain colours are rarer or more desirable than others, and thus often more valuable. Also look for minor variations in form, such as tails that hang free, or differently positioned legs as this indicates a different version and can also affect value.

- Models made for short periods of time can also be more desirable and valuable, especially if from the mid-20th century. Condition is important, with protruding horns, thin legs and tails being easily broken, so examine a piece carefully.

- Interest in Beswick animals has risen over the past two years and so have the values, partly as the factory closed in late 2002. Many prices are now exceeding their 'book' values, so collectors should pay close attention to annual price guides, auctions and specialist dealers. Rarer models and those in mint condition are the most likely to appreciate in value.

A Beswick 'Jay' gloss figure, MN2417, modelled by Graham Tongue.

1972-82   *5in (12.5cm) high*

£120-180   **PSA**

A Beswick 'Songthrush' gloss figure, MN2308, modelled by Albert Hallam.

The matte version of this model produced 1983-89 is usually worth around 60% of the value of the gloss version.

1970-89 5.75in (14.5cm) high

£100-150   **PSA**

A Beswick 'Large Barn Owl' gloss figure, MN1046a, modelled by Arthur Gredington.

This is the first version with 'split' tail feathers. Produced from 1946, the date of retirement of this version is not known. The second version with a single row of tail feathers is worth around 50% less.

7.25in (18.5cm) high

£50-70   **PSA**

A Beswick 'Kingfisher' gloss figure, MN2371, modelled by Albert Hallam.

1971-91   5in (12.5cm) high

£70-100   **PSA**

A Beswick pottery cock pheasant, modelled by Arthur Gredington, impressed number "1225".

The version without flowers on the base is usually worth around 20% less than the version with flowers.

1951-67   9.75in (25cm) long

£100-150   **CHEF**

A Beswick 'Golden Eagle' matte figure, MN2062, modelled by Graham Tongue.

Look out for the slightly more desirable gloss finish version, produced from 1966-74.

1970-72   9.5in (24cm) high

£50-80   **PSA**

A Beswick 'Parakeet' gloss figure, MN930, modelled by Arthur Gredington.

1941-75   6in (15cm) high

£70-100   **PSA**

A Beswick 'Friesian Cow Champion Claybury Leegwater' gloss figure, MN1362a, modelled by Arthur Gredington.

The matte version, produced only between 1985 and 1989 is usually more desirable.

1954-97   *4.5in (12cm) high*

£150-200   **PSA**

A Beswick 'Ayrshire Bull Whitehill Mandate' gloss figure, MN1454b, modelled by Colin Melbourne.

1957-90   *5.25in (13.5cm) high*

£300-400   **PSA**

A Beswick 'Dairy Shorthorn Bull Champion Gwersylt Lord Oxford 74th' figure, MN1504, modelled by Colin Melbourne.

This is a desirable model, only produced in this colourway.

1957-90   *5.25in (13.5cm) high*

£800-1,000   **PSA**

A Beswick 'Charolais Bull' gloss figure, MN2463a, modelled by Alan Maslankowski in 1973.

1979-97   *5in (12.5cm) high*

£200-300   **PSA**

A Beswick 'Large Hereford Calf' gloss figure, MN854, modelled by Arthur Gredington.

This example is in an unusual light sandy brown colour. The gloss, roan colourway is the most sought after.

1940-57   *4.25in (12cm) high*

£120-180   **PSA**

A Beswick 'Hereford Calf' figure, MN901b, second version with closed mouth.

Look out for the roan colourway of this model, especially if its mouth is open, indicating the first version of the model.

c1940-1957   *3.75in (9.5cm) high*

£80-120   **PSA**

A Beswick 'Friesian Calf' gloss figure, MN1249c, modelled by Arthur Gredington in 1952.

c1950-97   *2.75in (7cm) high*

£150-200   **PSA**

A Beswick 'Large Racehorse' grey gloss figure, MN1564, modelled by Arthur Gredington.

As with many other horses, 'rocking horse grey' is the most desirable and valuable colour.

1959-82   *11.25in (28.5cm) high*

£120-180   **PSA**

A CLOSER LOOK AT A BESWICK HORSE

This piece was modelled by Arthur Gredington, known for his horses and prolific designs for Beswick.

This is one of the rarest colourways for this model – other rare colours include blue, palomino and iron grey.

It is not known how long this colour was produced for, but it is likely to have been a very short period.

Look out for the black gloss commemorative horse produced in an edition of 135 in 1990 to celebrate 50 years of production of this model.

A rare Beswick 'Shire Mare' piebald gloss figure, MN818, light crazing.

8.5in (21.5cm) high

£1,000-1,500   **PSA**

A Beswick 'Shire Mare' rocking horse grey gloss figure, MN818, modelled by Arthur Gredington.

c1940-62

£600-700   **PSA**

A Beswick 'Welsh Mountain Pony Coed Coch Madog' grey gloss figure, MN1643, first version, modelled by Arthur Gredington, introduced in 1961 and retirement date unknown.

6.25in (16cm) high

£150-200   **PSA**

A Beswick 'Arab Xayal' rocking horse grey figure, MN1265, modelled by Arthur Gredington.

This colourway is the most desirable for this model, which is available in a number of different colours.

1953-62   6.25in (16cm) high

£400-500   **PSA**

A Beswick piebald 'Pinto Pony' gloss figure, MN1373, first version modelled by Arthur Gredington, introduced 1972, retirement date unknown.

6.5in (16.5cm) high

£150-200   **PSA**

A Beswick large 'Thoroughbred Stallion' chestnut gloss figure, MN1772, modelled by Arthur Gredington.

One leg of this horse has been restored, lowering his value.

1961-69   8in (20.5cm) high

£250-350   **PSA**

Two Beswick pottery foals, MN836, stretching with splayed forelegs and MN915, reclining, modelled by Arthur Gredington.

c1941-1980   tallest 4.75in (12cm) h

£20-30   **CHEF**

A Beswick pottery 'English Setter' grey gloss figure, probably MN1220, modelled by Arthur Gredington.

1951-73   *8in (20cm) high*

£60-80   **CHEF**

A Beswick 'Solomon of Wendover' golden yellow gloss figure, MN1548, modelled by Arthur Gredington.

1958-94   *5.5in (14.5cm) high*

£30-40   **CHEF**

A Beswick 'Corgi' golden brown gloss figure, probably MN1299B, modelled by Arthur Gredington.

1953-94   *5.5in (14cm) high*

£30-50   **CHEF**

A Beswick 'Lioness' golden gloss figure, facing left, MN1507, modelled by Colin Melbourne.

This colourway is more desirable and valuable than the black one.

1957-67   *4.75in (12cm) high*

£40-60   **CHEF**

A rare Beswick 'Chi Chi The Panda' figure, MN2613, first version with bamboo shoot.

This version of the model, where the bear is eating a bamboo shoot, was produced for The London Natural History Museum for around two years only.

1978-c1980   *3.75in (9.5cm) high*

£120-180   **PSA**

A Beswick 'Atlantic Salmon' figure, MN1233, modelled by Arthur Gredington.

1952-70   *6.5in (16.5cm) high*

£200-300   **CHEF**

A Beswick 'Loch Ness Monster' gloss full whisky flask for Benegals Whisky, MN2051, modelled by Albert Hallam.

These flasks are also available in eagle, otter and badger forms. They must be in mint condition, unopened and full to command maximum values.

1965-86   *3in (7.5cm) high*

£20-30   **PSA**

A Beswick 'Seal' gloss figure, MN1534, modelled by Arthur Gredington.

1958-66   *5.75in (14.5cm) high*

£60-80   **PSA**

COLLECTORS' NOTES

■ Arthur Gredington started a new chapter in the history of John Beswick's pottery when he designed the Jemima Puddle-Duck figurine in 1947. The initial range, consisting of ten characters, was a great success and today over 100 versions of more than 40 different figures are known to exist.

■ Beswick was acquired by Royal Doulton in 1969. Over the following six years, the Beatrix Potter line underwent a number of changes, which although designed to standardize the range, in the short term created the myriad variations that continue to fascinate the collecting community today.

■ The different types of backstamps that were used attract great interest – the original gold "Beswick England" stamps are generally more sought-after and command higher prices than the later brown stamps which were used after 1972.

■ Other changes included the phasing out of lead-based paints and fine details and fragile protrusions on the models. Earlier examples that pre-date these changes are much harder to find today.

■ Look for characters that were discontinued at an early date or were produced in smaller quantities.

■ Production of Beatrix Potter figures continues today under Border Fine Art and it will be interesting to see how this will affect the price of original Beswick pieces.

A Beswick Beatrix Potter's 'Anna Maria' figure, BP3, brown backstamp.

1973-83   *3in (7.5cm) high*

£100-150   **CHEF**

A Beswick Beatrix Potter's 'Appley Dapply' figure, BP3, version two, brown backstamp.

1975-89   3.25in (8.5cm) high

£80-120   **CHEF**

A Beswick Beatrix Potter's 'Cecily Parsley' figure, BP3, first version with head down, brown backstamp.

1973-85   *4in (10cm) high*

£30-50   **CHEF**

A Beswick Beatrix Potter's 'Flopsy, Mopsy and Cottontail' figure, BP3, brown backstamp.

1973-89   *2.5in (6.5cm) high*

£35-45   **CHEF**

A Beswick Beatrix Potter's 'Ginger' figure, BP3b, brown backstamp.

1976-82   3.75in (9.5cm) high

£180-220   **CHEF**

A Beswick Beatrix Potter's 'Fierce Bad Rabbit' figure, BP3b, first version with feet out, brown backstamp.

A later version of this figure with less protruding feet and a lighter coat is worth at least half the value of this earlier version.

1977-80   4.75in (12cm) high

£100-150   **CHEF**

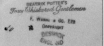

A Beswick Beatrix Potter's 'Foxy Whiskered Gentleman' figure, BP2a, gloss finish, gold oval backstamp.

1955-72   4.75in (12cm) high

£80-120   **CHEF**

A Beswick Beatrix Potter's 'Goody Tiptoes' figure, BP3, with brown backstamp.

1973-89   3.5in (9cm) high

£25-35   CHEF

A Beswick Beatrix Potter's 'Jemima Puddleduck' figure, BP2, first version, first variation, gold backstamp.

1955-72   4.75in (12cm) high

£60-70   CHEF

A Beswick Beatrix Potter's 'Johnny Town Mouse' figure, BP2, gold oval backstamp.

1955-72   3.5in (9cm) high

£50-60   CHEF

A Beswick Beatrix Potter's 'Lady Mouse' figure, BP3, brown backstamp.

1973-1989   4in (10cm) high

£40-50   CHEF

A Beswick Beatrix Potter's 'Mrs Flopsy Bunny' figure, BP3, light blue dress, brown backstamp.

1974   4in (10cm) high

£50-60   CHEF

A Beswick Beatrix Potter's 'Little Black Rabbit', BP3, brown backstamp.

1977 89   4.5in (11.5cm) high

£30-50   CHEF

A Beswick Beatrix Potter's 'Little Pig Robinson' figure, BP3, first variation with striped outfit.

The later variation with a checked outfit is less sought-after.

1973-74   4in (10cm) high

£50-70   CHEF

A Beswick Beatrix Potter's 'Mr. Jeremy Fisher' figure, BP2, first version with spotted legs, gold oval backstamp.

1955-1972   3in (7.5cm) high

£100-150   CHEF

A Beswick Beatrix Potter's 'Mr Alderman Ptolemy' figure, BP3b, brown backstamp.

This brown back stamp was used between 1974 and 1985, it was used on 63 Potter figures as well as 16 variations.

1974-85   3.5in (9cm) high

£30-40   CHEF

A Beswick Beatrix Potter's 'Mrs Tittlemouse' figure, BP1, style one, gold backstamp.

1948-54   3.5in (9cm) high

£120-180   CHEF

A Beswick Beatrix Potter's 'Mrs Rabbit' figure, BP3, second version with umbrella moulded to dress, brown backstamp.

An earlier version of this figure with the umbrella sticking out is worth approximately four times as much.

1975-89   4.25in (11cm) high

£100-150   CHEF

A Beswick Beatrix Potter's 'Old Mr Brown' figure, BP3, brown owl and red squirrel, brown backstamp.

1975-89   3.5in (8.5cm) h

£30-50   CHEF

A Beswick Beatrix Potter's 'Peter Rabbit' figure, BP2a, first version, first variation, gold oval backstamp.

1955-72   4.5in (11.5cm) high

£60-70   CHEF

A Beswick Beatrix Potter's 'Pigling Bland' figure, BP3, first variation with purple jacket, brown backstamp.

Later versions of this figure have a pale lilac jacket which is less desirable and worth less than a third of this version.

1973-74   4.25in (11cm) high

£180-220   CHEF

A Beswick Beatrix Potter's 'Pickles' figure, BP3, brown backstamp.

1973-82   4.5in (11.5cm) high

£120-180   CHEF

A Beswick Beatrix Potter's 'Poorly Peter Rabbit' figure, BP3, brown back stamp.

1976-89   3.75in (9.5cm) high

£40-60   CHEF

A Beswick Beatrix Potter's 'Sally Henny Penny' figure, BP3, brown backstamp.

1974-89   4in (10cm) high

£30-50   CHEF

A Beswick Beatrix Potter's 'Pickles' figure, BP2, gold oval backstamp.

Although this figure is identical to later figures, such as the one centre left, this earlier figure is worth considerably more as it was only produced with this backstamp for one year.

1971-72   4.5in (11.5cm) high

£250-300   GORL

A Beswick Beatrix Potter's 'Simpkin' figure, BP3b, brown backstamp.

1975-83   *4in (10cm) high*

£150-200   **CHEF**

A Beswick Beatrix Potter's 'Tailor of Gloucester' figure, BP2, copyright F. Warne & Co Ltd, gold mark.

1955-72   3.5in (9cm) high

£60-90   **CHEF**

A Beswick Beatrix Potter's 'Sir Isaac Newton' figure, BP3, brown backstamp.

1973-84   *3.75in (9.5cm) high*

£180-220   **CHEF**

A Beswick Beatrix Potter's 'Timmie Willie from Johnny Town Mouse' figure, BP3, brown backstamp.

1973-89   2.5in (6.5cm) high

£100-150   **CHEF**

A Beswick Beatrix Potter's 'Squirrel Nutkin' figure, BP3, first version, second variation, brown backstamp.

1980-89   3.75in (9.5cm) high

£40-50   **CHEF**

A Beswick Beatrix Potter's 'Timmy Tiptoes' figure, BP2, first variation with brown-grey squirrel in red jacket, gold backstamp.

1955-72   3.25in (8.5cm) high

£60-90   **CHEF**

A Beswick Beatrix Potter's 'Tom Kitten' figure, BP3, first version, second variation with light colour base and suit, with brown backstamp.

1980-89   3.5in (9cm) high

£35-45   **CHEF**

A Beswick Beatrix Potter's 'Tommy Brock' figure, BP3, first version, first variation with spade handle out and small eye patches, brown backstamp.

1973-74   3.5in (9cm) high

£100-150   **CHEF**

A Beswick Beatrix Potter's 'The Old Woman Who Lived In A Shoe' figure, BP3, brown backstamp.

1973-89   *3.745in (9.5cm) long*

£40-60   **CHEF**

FIND OUT MORE...

'Beswick Quarterly', *Laura Rock-Smith, 10 Holmes Court, Sayville, N.Y. 11782-2408, U.S.A.*

'The Charlton Standard Catalogue of Beswick Animals', *by Diana Callow, The Charlton Press, Toronto, Ontario, 1996.*

'Royal Doulton Beswick Storybook Figurines', *by Jean Dale, (6th edition), published by Charlton International Inc, U.S.A., 2000.*

COLLECTORS' NOTES

■ Bing & Grøndahl was founded in Copenhagen, Denmark in 1853 by Frederick Grøndahl (1819-56) and brothers Jacob and Meyer Bing. The majority of their pieces are coloured under the glaze in white, pale blue or grey. They are marked with a 'three tower' mark based on the city of Copenhagen's coat of arms, over the 'B&G' initials. Seconds are indicated with a horizontal scratch through the towers.

■ Pieces can be dated to a period by the style and colour of the printed mark. The 'B&G' initials were blue from 1853-1947 and once again from 1970-83 and black, grey or green at other times. From around 1970, the towers became highly stylized, and much less detailed, being simply tall rectangles with triangular apexes. However, there are many variations so it is best to consult a reference work to date a piece more precisely.

■ Figures were introduced c1895 and proved immensely popular, with their fine modelling and delicacy of colour. In 1987, Bing & Grøndahl merged with their rival Royal Copenhagen factory and pieces were then marked with the Royal Copenhagen marks. The numbering system for models changed too. They were numbered from 400 upwards and had a prefix of 1020 for animals and 1021 for people.

■ Look for size, complexity, date, designer and the appeal of the model, as larger, earlier or more complex models will often fetch the higher values, as will those that are no longer in production. Models produced over a long period may be less desirable. Examine a model carefully for variations in terms of form (such as a differently tilted head), pattern and colour. Damage such as cracks and chips will reduce value.

A Bing & Grøndahl porcelain model of a cocker spaniel, No. 2072, by Laurits Jensen.

6in (15cm) long

£150-200　　　　**LOB**

A Bing & Grøndahl porcelain model of a cocker spaniel, No. 2172, by Svend Jespersen.

4.25in (11cm) long

£75-85　　　　**LOB**

A Bing & Grøndahl porcelain model of a terrier, No. 2072, by Laurits Jensen.

4.25in (11cm) long

£50-70　　　　**LOB**

A Bing & Grøndahl porcelain model of a wirehaired terrier, No. 2967, designed by Ingeborg Plockross Irminger.

6.75in (17cm) long

£150-200　　　　**LOB**

A Bing & Grøndahl 'Pessimist' porcelain model of a titmouse, No. 1635.

This bird was designed by Dahl-Jensen and has remained popular.

c1904

5in (13cm) long

£70-80　　　　**LOB**

A Bing & Grøndahl porcelain model of a sealyham puppy, No. 2027, by Dahl-Jensen.

Jens Peter Dahl-Jensen (1874-1960) was a Danish sculptor who trained at the Copenhagen Academy. He joined Bing & Grøndahl as a designer in 1897, and worked there for 20 years. He is known for his small figurines, especially dogs. In 1925 he set up his own factory.

4in (10cm) long

£80-120　　　　**LOB**

A Bing & Grøndahl porcelain model of beagle lying, No. 2565.

6.5in (16.5cm) long

£70-100　　　　**LOB**

A Bing & Grøndahl 'Optimist' porcelain model of a titmouse, No. 1633, designed by Dahl-Jensen.

5in (13cm) long

£70-80 LOB

A Bing & Grøndahl porcelain model of a parrot, No. 2019, original design by Dahl-Jensen.

c1985 *5.5in (14cm) high*

£60-80 LOB

A Bing and Grøndahl Copenhagen seagull.

10.75in (27.5cm) wide

£70-80 CHEF

A Bing & Grøndahl porcelain model of a seated guinea pig, no. 2489.

3.25in (8cm) long

£70-100 LOB

A Bing & Grøndahl porcelain model of a deer, No. 1929, designed by Niels Nielsen.

This figure is available in stoneware.

6.75in (17cm) high

£80-120 LOB

A Bing & Grøndahl porcelain model of a seal, designed by Knud Moller.

7.5in (19cm) high

£80-120 LOB

A Bing & Grøndahl porcelain model of a walking bear, No. 2213.

c1950 *4in (10cm) long*

£100-150 LOB

A CLOSER LOOK AT A BING & GRØNDAHL ANIMAL

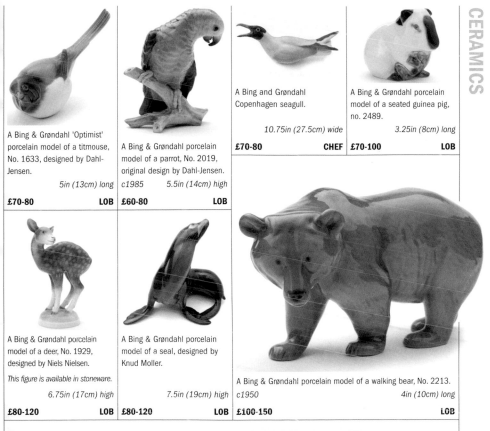

This figure is comparatively large. There are also other variations of the polar bear, making it a popular subject to collect.

As it does not have a 400 series number, this example is vintage and was made around 1962.

It was modelled by noted modeller Knud Kyhn (1880-1969) who studied animals in Germany, Lapland and Greenland, and is well-known for his animal work.

The colour and well-modelled form of the bear work well with Bing & Grøndahl's colour scheme and style.

A Bing & Grøndahl large porcelain model of a polar bear, marked 1857.

c1962 *14.5in (37cm) long*

£400-500 LOB

A Bing & Grøndahl 'Who is Calling?' porcelain model, No. 2251, designed by Michaela Ahlman.

6in (15cm) high

£70-90   **LOB**

A Bing & Grøndahl 'Kaj' porcelain model, No. 1617, designed by Ingeborg Plockross Irminger.

8in (20cm) high

£70-100   **LOB**

A Bing & Grøndahl 'Flute Player' porcelain model, No. 1897, designed by Ingeborg Plockross Irminger.

11.5in (29cm) high

£100-170   **LOB**

A Bing & Grøndahl 'Paddling About' porcelain model, No. 1757, designed by Ingeborg Plockross Irminger.

8in (20cm) high

£80-120   **LOB**

A Bing & Grøndahl 'Love Refused' porcelain model, No. 1614, designed by Ingeborg Plockross Irminger.

6.75in (17cm) high

£120-180   **LOB**

A Bing & Grøndahl 'Youthful Boldness' porcelain model, No. 2162, designed by Claire Weiss.

8in (20cm) high

£80-120   **LOB**

A Bing & Grøndahl 'Else' porcelain model, No. 1574.

This model is found in either a blue or white dress and is one of Bing & Grøndahl's (later Royal Copenhagen's) most familiar figurines. It was designed around 1900 by the sculptor Ingeborg Plockross Irminger, who is well known for her designs of children and animals. Irminger had trained at the Royal Academy in Copenhagen between 1893 and 1899. She began work at the Bing & Grøndahl factory in 1898, while also working independently as a sculptor in marble and bronze.

6.75in (17cm) high

£80-120   **LOB**

A Bing & Grøndahl 'Children Reading' porcelain model, No. 1567, designed by Ingeborg Plockross Irminger.

c1900   *4in (10cm) high*

£100-150   **LOB**

A Bing & Grøndahl 'Fish Market' porcelain model, No. 2233, designed by Alex Locher.

8in (20cm) high

£250-300   **LOB**

A Bing & Grøndahl 'Girl with Calves' porcelain model, No. 2270, by Alex Locher.

8in (20cm) high

£220-280   **LOB**

FIND OUT MORE...

'Bing & Grøndahl Figurines', *by Nick & Caroline Pope, published by Schiffer Books, 2003.*

COLLECTORS' NOTES

- Briglin pottery founders Brigitte Goldschmidt (later Appleby) and Eileen Lewenstein originally worked together at Donald Mills' London pottery from 1945. After a bad contract forced Mills' business to close, Eileen and Brigitte opened their own pottery in fashionable Crawford St, London in 1948.

- They aimed to make pots that were decorative, functional, but affordable. Their designs and style were unlike most available at the time and became highly successful, being stocked by leading retailers Heal's and Peter Jones. They bear some similarities to Scandinavian pottery of the period. Both founders helped build the Craft Potters Association.

- Lewenstein left the pottery in 1959, but production continued and grew. During the 1970s, many of the pieces were decorated with sgraffito patterns, or patterns where the colour and roughness of the clay body contrasts against the glossy colour of the glaze. Patterns tended to be natural in inspiration, using flower or leaf forms.

- The pottery closed in 1990 and its works are just beginning to be more widely appreciated. Pieces are often clearly stamped 'BRIGLIN', sometimes 'AB', not for Brigitte Appleby, but for a decorator Anthony Barson.

A 1970s Briglin Pottery beige and brown glazed vase, with sycamore leaf design, the leaves with scored decoration and showing the colour of the clay.
9.5in (24cm) high

£25-35   **GC**

A 1970s Briglin Pottery light blue and cream glazed vase, with maple leaf design.
9.5in (24.5cm) high

£25-35   **GC**

A Briglin Pottery small vase, with all-over glaze with green floral pattern and stamped "BRIGLIN".
5.5in (14cm) high

£20-30   **GROB**

A 1970s Briglin Pottery lamp base, with catkin-shaped pattern in natural clay and creamy white glaze.
10in (25.5cm) high

£40-50   **GROB**

A Briglin Pottery small cup, with chrysanthemum pattern in natural rough clay.
3in (8cm) high

£7-10   **GROB**

A Briglin Pottery large mug, with lost wax swirling pattern in natural rough clay.
4.5in (11.5cm) high

£15-20   **GROB**

A Briglin Pottery footed coffee cup, glazed all-over with blue bamboo pattern.
4.5in (11.5cm) high

£15-20   **GROB**

A Briglin Pottery small goblet, with fern-shaped pattern in natural rough clay.
4.5in (11.5cm) high

£10-15   **GROB**

An unusual Briglin Pottery green-glazed lidded soup bowl, with a highly tactile, matte finish.
5.5in (14cm) diam

£20-30   **GROB**

FIND OUT MORE...

'**Briglin Pottery 1948-1990 The Story of a Studio Pottery in the West End of London**', *by Anthea Arnold, published by Briglin Books, 2002.*

COLLECTORS' NOTES

- The Bunnykins series began as a range of nurseryware and was based on the illustrations of Augustinian nun Sister Barbara Vernon, the daughter of Royal Doulton manager Cuthbert Bailey. Early pieces bearing her facsimile signature, produced before 1952, are highly sought-after today.

- The tableware range was launched in 1934 and was originally fashioned from earthenware or white china. The range proved popular and figures were added in 1939, modelled by Royal Doulton's Art Director Charles Nokes. However, production was soon disrupted by WWII and only six characters were initially available.

- The original set of six, which bear little resemblance to Sister Barbara Vernon's drawings, are now extremely rare and can fetch up to £1,000-2,000 each.

- Albert Hallam joined Royal Doulton when the company obtained the Beswick factory in 1969. As he worked on their Beatrix Potter range he was given the task of expanding the line and designed another nine figures.

- Since the early 1970s, Bunnykins figures have carried identifying 'DB' numbers. So far over 250 have been allocated and many collectors aim to find one of each – no mean feat since figures are frequently retired and replaced by newcomers.

- Bunnykins is popular all over the world and there are collector's clubs as far afield as Australia and the US. An 'Australian Bunnykins' was specially designed to celebrate the country's bicentenary in 1988.

A Royal Doulton 'Drummer' Bunnykins figure, DB26A, from the Oompah Band Series, version 1.

This figure was released to celebrate the Golden Jubilee of Doulton. A standard version exists and it is worth approximately the same amount. The third version, released in an edition of 250, can be worth around four times as much.

1984   3.5in (9cm) high

£45-55   **PSA**

A Royal Doulton 'Brownie' Bunnykins figure, DB61.

Examples with unpainted belts have also been found.

1987-93   4in (10cm) high

£70-100   **PSA**

A Royal Doulton 'William' Bunnykins figure, DB69, boxed.

This figure is based on the 'Tally Ho!' figure released in 1973. A second variation, also called 'Tally Ho!, was released in 1988 and is worth about 30% more.

1988-93   4in (10cm) high

£50-60   **PSA**

A Royal Doulton 'Paperboy' Bunnykins figure, DB77, boxed.

1989-93   4.5in (11.5cm) high

£70-90   **PSA**

A Royal Doulton 'Fisherman' Bunnykins figure, DB84.

1990-93 4.25in (12.5cm) high

£55-65   **PSA**

A Royal Doulton 'Cook' Bunnykins figure, DB85.

1990-94   4.25in (11cm) high

£50-60   **PSA**

A Royal Doulton 'Aussie Surfer' Bunnykins figure, DB133.

1994-97   4in (10cm) high

£45-55   **PSA**

A limited edition Royal Doulton 'Out For A Duck' Bunnykins figure, DB160, from the Cricketers Series and an edition of 1,250.

1995　　　　4in (10cm) high

£100-150　　　　**PSA**

A limited edition Royal Doulton 'Clarinet' Bunnykins figure, DB184, from the Jazz Band Collection and an edition of 2,500, boxed with certificate.

1999-2000　4.5in (11.5cm) high

£45-55　　　　**PSA**

A limited edition Royal Doulton 'Double Bass' Bunnykins figure, DB184, from the Jazz Band Collection and an edition of 2,500, boxed with certificate.

1999-2000　4.5in (11.5cm) high

£45-55　　　　**PSA**

A limited edition Royal Doulton 'Saxophone Player' Bunnykins figure, DB184, from the Jazz Band Collection and an edition of 2,500, boxed with certificate.

1999-2000　4.5in (11.5cm) high

£45-55　　　　**PSA**

A limited edition Royal Doulton 'Drummer' Bunnykins figure, DB250, from the Jazz Band Collection and an edition of 2,500, boxed with certificate.

2002　4.5in (11.5cm) high

£50-70　　　　**PSA**

A limited edition Royal Doulton 'Boy Skater' Bunnykins figure, DB187, from a limited edition of 2,500, boxed.

A standard version of this figure was released in 1995 and is of the same value.

1998　　　　4in (10cm) high

£30-40　　　　**PSA**

A limited edition Royal Doulton 'Santa's Helper' Bunnykins figure, DB192, from a limited edition of 2,500, boxed.

This figure is based on 'Christmas Surprise', released between 1994-2000, and worth approximately the same amount.

1999　　　　3.5in (9cm) high

£25-35　　　　**PSA**

A limited edition Royal Doulton 'Trumpeter' Bunnykins figure, DB210, from the Jazz Band Collection and an edition of 2,500, boxed with certificate.

2000　　　4.5in (11.5cm) high

£45-55　　　　**PSA**

A limited edition Royal Doulton 'Easter Surprise' Bunnykins figure, DB225, from a limited edition of 2,500, boxed.

This figure is based on 'Easter Greetings' released between 1995-99 and of approximately the same value.

2000　　　　3.5in (9cm) high

£25-35　　　　**PSA**

FIND OUT MORE...

'Royal Doulton Bunnykins, A Charlton Standard Catalogue', *by Jean Dale & Louise Irvine, published by Charlton Press, 2002.*

COLLECTORS' NOTES

■ Carlton Ware is a trade name used from the mid-1890's by Wiltshaw & Robinson Ltd of the Carlton Works, Stoke. They became Carlton Ware Ltd. in 1958.

■ In the 1920s and 1930s the company produced a range of richly decorated pieces, many in the Art Deco style, with Oriental or Persian designs and a lustrous finish. The 1930s saw the introduction of mass-produced floral and fruiting designs. These are

not usually as valuable as the lustre pieces, but look out for unusual shapes and rare colour variations.

■ To attract fashionable postwar buyers, forms in the 1950s became more streamlined and patterns more modern. The 1960s saw many cylindrical forms, echoing the output of other factories.

■ Condition is important. Look out for wear to enamelling and gilding on the lustre ranges.

A Carlton Ware 'Fish & Seaweed' pattern circular bowl, printed marks.

8in (20cm) diam

£120-180　　　　**L&T**

A Carlton Ware 'Devil's Copse' pattern circular bowl, with printed and painted marks.

This pattern is exactly the same as the background of the pattern known as 'Mephistopheles', although it does not contain the figure of the Devil himself.

7in (17.5cm) diam

£120-180　　　　**L&T**

A Carlton Ware 'Hollyhocks' pattern ovoid jug, printed and painted marks, No. 3973.

'Hollyhocks' is known on a green, black or orange background.

7.5in (19cm) high

£120-180　　　　**L&T**

A Carlton Ware 'Hollyhocks' pattern ovoid jug, printed and painted marks.

10.75in (18cm) high

£50-80　　　　**L&T**

A Carlton Ware 'Bluebells' pattern large jug, printed and painted marks, No. 3862.

14.2in (35.5cm) high

£350-450　　　　**L&T**

A CLOSER LOOK AT A CARLTON WARE VASE

The stepped rim and inverted conical form is very Art Deco, and is partly inspired by period architecture.

The 'Bell' pattern can also be found on cream, pale blue, green and dark red glazes.

The two dimensional 'flat design' with the diagona stripe, and Oriental inspiration shows some of the important artistic influences of the Art Deco style.

'Bell' is one of the most important stylized flower patterns in Carlton Ware and is based on harebell flowers.

A Carlton Ware 'Bell' pattern conical shaped vase, printed and painted marks.

8.25in (20.5cm) high

£600-700　　　　**L&T**

A Carlton Ware 'New Mikado' pattern vase, on a pale pink ground, printed marks.

'New Mikado' was made in many colours from the 1920s up until the 1960s, and always features an evergreen tree and a Chinese style house.

6in (15.5cm) high

£150-250   **WW**

A Carlton Ware 'Armand' lustre vase, of tapering cylindrical form with canted angles, printed and painted in gilt and colours with exotic moths on a pale blue ground, printed and painted marks 2134/136.

7.75in (19.5cm) high

£120-180   **L&T**

A Carlton Ware 'New Mikado' pattern Bleu Royale tall vase.

11in (28cm) high

£150-250   **PSA**

A 1930s Carlton Ware 'Blackberry' pattern biscuit barrel.

This barrel is more valuable than most pieces from the floral and fruiting range produced by Carlton Ware during the 1930s as its shape is extremely unusual and typical of the Art Deco style. Most pieces are shaped more like stylized leaves or flowers.

5.5in (14cm) high

£200-250   **BAD**

Two Carlton Ware 'Spangle Tree' and 'New Anemone' Aztec dishes, pattern No. 4626, printed and painted marks.

12.5in (32cm) wide

£150-250   **WW**

An unusual 1930s Carlton Ware 'Cherry' pattern jam pot and base.

4.5in (11.5cm) diam

£70-90   **BAD**

A Carlton Ware 'Hollyhocks' pattern two-handled dish, with an orange lustre glaze, very minor wear to gilding.

12.5in (32cm) long

£180-220   **PSA**

A Carlton Ware Art Deco-style bowl, in a blue and pink floral pattern on a cream ground with satin glaze.

9.5in (24cm) diam

£80-120   **PSA**

A Carlton Ware crinolined lady napkin holder.

3.75in (9.5cm) high

£60-80   **BAD**

A Carlton Ware 'Walking Ware' egg-cup, with feet in pink shoes, standing, printed mark "Carlton Ware England Lustre Pottery 1978".

2.25in (5.5cm) high

£20-25 **CHS**

A Carlton Ware 'Walking Ware' teacup, with feet in green shoes, walking.

4.25in (11cm) high

£30-35 **CHS**

A Carlton Ware 'Walking Ware' teacup, with feet in brown shoes standing, printed mark "Carlton Ware England Lustre Pottery 1980".

The 'Walking Ware' series was designed by Roger Michell and Danka Napiorkowska of the Lustre Pottery in the 1970s. The first series comprised of feet standing still, but designs became more adventurous with the addition of 'Running', 'Jumping' and 'Big Feet' series. Despite being popular the company was in financial trouble and the series was not produced for long. Pieces usually bear the Lustre Pottery and Carlton Ware marks as can be seen from the thumbnail illustration of the mark on this piece.

4.25in (11cm) high

£20-30 **CHS**

A Carlton Ware 'Walking Ware' egg-cup, with feet in yellow shoes, walking, printed mark "Carlton Ware England Lustre Pottery 1976".

3in (7.5cm) high

£25-35 **CHS**

A Carlton Ware 'Walking Ware' sugar bowl, with feet in blue shoes, crossed, printed marks.

c1973 *6.5in (16.5cm) high*

£30-40 **CHS**

A scarce Carlton Ware 'French Maid' 'Walking Ware' tea cup.

5in (13cm) high

£70-100 **BAD**

A 1970s Carlton Ware coffee pot, sugar bowl and two mugs.

coffee pot 13in (33cm) high

£60-70 **DTC**

A Carlton Ware egg-cup, the base and handle formed as a tuba-playing man, printed mark "CW England".

2.5in (6.5cm) high

£25-30 **CHS**

A set of three Carlton Ware circular psychedelic dishes.

largest 8.5in (21cm) diam

£50-70 **MTS**

COLLECTORS' NOTES

- The Celtic Pottery was founded around 1965 by William and Margaret Fisher in the tiny fishing village of Mousehole (pronounced 'maowsel'), near Penzance. They became known for their abstract designs known as 'Folk', often based on animals.

- With a mottled yellow background with black detailing, angular animals such as cockerels and unicorns are hand-painted on thickly built vessels such as cups, mugs, vases and dishes. Look for yellow paper labels indicating the piece was designed and made by William Fisher.

- When the couple split up, Margaret moved the pottery and its designs to Newlyn. The company was amalgamated with the Gwavas Pottery whose 'Medallion' range was taken into the newly expanded Celtic Pottery fold. The label changed, and included a 'stickman' and the town's name. During the late 1970s the pottery was renamed 'Sunset Pottery', but closed within a few years.

A Newlyn dish, with a design of a stylized bird.

8.75in (22cm) long

£30-40   **B&H**

A Newlyn dish, with a design of a stylized bird.

6.5in (16.5cm) long

£30-40   **B&H**

A Newlyn dish, with a painted design of a fishing boat, blue border.

5in (12.5cm) diam

£30-50   **B&H**

A Newlyn vase, of bulbous form decorated with stylized flying birds.

6.75in (17cm) high

£15-25   **B&H**

A Newlyn vase, with a stylized bird design.

6in (15cm) high

£20-40   **B&H**

A pair of small Newlyn vases.

3.5in (9cm) high

£25-35   **B&H**

A Newlyn cylindrical mug, decorated with stylized birds.

5in (12.5cm) high

£20-40   **B&H**

Two Celtic Pottery cats.

£50-70   **CHEF**

A pair of stylized Newlyn pottery cat figures, in Celtic design.

The cats are amongst the best-known of Celtic Pottery's animal designs and are typical of the colourway and designs developed.

7.75in (19.5cm) high

£120-180   **B&H**

A 1930s Royal Winton 'Sunshine' teacup and saucer.

6in (15cm) diam

£50-70   **BAD**

A 1950s Royal Winton 'Summertime' pattern geometrically shaped dish.

9.5in (24cm) wide

£100-150   **BAD**

A 1950s Royal Winton 'English Rose' pattern cup and saucer.

4.5in (11.5cm) diam

£60-80   **AD**

A 1950s Royal Winton 'Cheadle' pattern butter dish.

Objects as covered in design as possible, even on the handle, are amongst the most sought after by collectors, especially in the more popular, bright colourways.

6.25in (16cm) wide

£180-220   **BAD**

A 1930s Royal Winton 'Welbeck' pattern scalloped edge fruit bowl.

9in (23cm) wide

£70-90   **BAD**

A 1950s Royal Winton 'Julia' pattern ring or candy dish.

6in (15cm) wide

£80-120   **BAD**

A 1930s Royal Winton 'Welbeck' pattern milk jug.

3.25in (8cm) high

£70-90   **BAD**

A Grimwades Royal Winton chintz toast rack, printed in typical bright colours.

6in (15cm) wide

£35-45   **GORL**

A 1930s Royal Winton hand-painted 'Anemone' pattern sugar sifter.

This sifter is unusual as the design is hand-painted, rather than being applied by coloured transfer.

6.25in (16cm) high

£70-100   **BAD**

A 1930s Lancasters Ltd 'Pansy' pattern sugar bowl, with chrome-plated lid.

Although it looks as though the lid has been replaced, it has not. Chrome parts are commonly found on chintzware.

3.75in (9.5cm) high

£55-65   **BAD**

COLLECTORS' NOTES

- Clarice Cliff was born in 1899 in Tunstall, Stoke-on-Trent, in the heart of the Potteries. In 1912 she joined Linguard Webster & Co. as an apprentice enameller and, after further study, went to A.J. Wilkinson Ltd of Burslem in 1916.

- Cliff's colourful designs were influenced by the art of the period, and by flowers and botany. Collectors tend to prefer the patterns that typify her work. The shape and pattern of the vessel is also important – pieces that display the pattern well, such as chargers, plates, Lotus shape jugs and vases, are all popular.

- The pottery was impressed with Cliff's skill and in 1927 gave her a studio of her own in the recently acquired Newport Pottery. She was given the opportunity to experiment and produced a range of bright and colourful geometric designs – different from anything previously produced. The range was named 'Bizarre' and launched in 1928. The line proved so successful that the entire pottery was soon devoted to its production.

- Condition affects the value; any damage or wear will reduce the value on all but the rarest pieces.

- Due to the popularity of Cliff's work, fakes are on the market. Beware of poor quality painting, smudged designs, washed-out colours and uneven glazes.

A Clarice Cliff Fantasque 'Alton' pattern bowl, with a landscape pattern against green borders.

1933-34   *8in (20cm) diam*

£180-220   **GORL**

A Clarice Cliff Bizarre 'Aurea' pattern planter, of twin-handled oval shape, shape No.450, black printed mark.

1935-7   *13in (33cm) wide*

£250-350   **CHEF**

A Clarice Cliff 'Blue Chintz' pattern octagonal plate, on chromium-plated stand, printed mark, introduced in 1932/3.

The Chintz pattern was also produced in an orange and a scarce green colourway.

c1932   *8.75in (22cm) diam*

£120-180   **L&T**

A Clarice Cliff Fantasque Bizarre 'Blue Chintz' pattern Athens jug, the bellied octagonal shape painted with stylised blue green and pink flowers and foliage, printed marks and moulded shape No.42.

1932   *6in (15cm) high*

£200-250   **CHEF**

A Clarice Cliff Bizarre 'Blue Chintz' pattern biscuit barrel, with chrome lid, mounts and swing handle, the ovoid shape supported on three blue edged buttress legs and painted with pink flowers and circular leaves, printed marks.

1932   *6in (15cm) high*

£300-400   **CHEF**

A Clarice Cliff Bizarre 'Blue Chintz' pattern vase, the barrel shape painted with pink flowers and blue leaves between the flared rim and foot, printed marks and moulded shape No.264.

c1932   *8in (20cm) high*

£220-280   **CHEF**

A Clarice Cliff Fantasque 'Broth' pattern vase, the ovoid girth painted with brown bubbles above horizontal rib moulding emphasized in orange, blue and purple, printed marks and impressed shape No.362.

1929-30   *8in (20.5cm) high*

£350-450   **CHEF**

A Clarice Cliff 'Canterbury Bells' pattern sugar bowl.

1932-33   *3.5in (9cm) diam*

£400-500   **SCG**

A Clarice Cliff 'Crocus' pattern preserve jar and cover, of drum form, painted in colours, the cover with drum finial, on sledge feet, two chips to inner rim, printed Bizarre marks.

Produced in a number of colourways over 35 years, Purple Crocus is the rarest.

c1930   *4in (10cm) high*

£220-280   **HAMG**

A 1930s/40s Clarice Cliff Bizarre 'Crocus' pattern flower rock, with painted flowers at the base of the pierced shape, and printed marks.

4in (10cm) high

£100-150   **CHEF**

A Clarice Cliff Honeyglaze 'Crocus' pattern sandwich plate, the canted rectangular shape painted with the flowers either side of a brown roundel within a green-lined yellow rim, printed marks and moulded shape No.449.

1928-63   *12in (30cm) wide*

£150-200   **CHEF**

A Clarice Cliff Bizarre 'Forest Glen' pattern bowl, the interior repainted coral red, the horizontally ribbed exterior painted with a cottage in a glen, printed marks and shape No.633.

Produced in a different colourway as 'Newlyn'.

1936-37   *9.5in (24cm) diam*

£350-450   **CHEF**

A Clarice Cliff Bizarre 'Delecia Pansies' pattern single-handled Lotus jug, printed mark.

The 'Delecia' effect was created by mixing turpentine with colour to produce hazy washes of colour, with various flowers painted into the design.

1933-34   *12in (30cm) high*

£1,000-1,500   **WW**

A Clarice Cliff 'Gayday' pattern cylindrical beaker, of tapered outline, printed marks.

1930-34   *3.75in (9.5cm) high*

£80-120   **L&T**

A Clarice Cliff Bizarre 'Gayday' pattern beehive honey pot and cover, the black-winged orange bee finial above the rope moulded sides painted with bright floral border, printed marks.

1930-34   *3.75in (9.5cm) high*

£300-400   **CHEF**

A Clarice Cliff 'Gayday' pattern single-handled jug, of ovoid form, shape No.634, printed marks.

1930-34   *7.25in (18.5cm) high*

£350-450   **L&T**

A large Clarice Cliff 'Latona Tree' pattern bowl, painted and glazed ceramic.

The Latona range, introduced in 1929, featured a milky-white glaze which formed the base for a number of simple but striking designs.

1929-31   16.25in (40.5cm) diam

£1,200-1,800   **FRE**

A Clarice Cliff 'Lily' pattern ovoid biscuit barrel and cover, with wicker handle, printed marks and retailer's marks.

c1929   5.5in (14cm) high

£280-320   **L&T**

A Clarice Cliff Bizarre Honeyglaze 'Limberlost' pattern plate, painted with two white flowerheads in the foreground and distant trees within target rim bands of greens, coral and brown, printed marks and impressed "6/37".

c1932   9.75in (25cm) diam

£350-450   **CHEF**

A Clarice Cliff Bizarre 'Lydiat' pattern plate, painted to one side with flower-heads and black leaves on a streaky autumnal ground, printed marks and impressed "35".

This is a rare colourway variation of the 'Jonquil' pattern.

c1933   9in (23cm) diam

£150-200   **CHEF**

A Clarice Cliff Bizarre 'Marguerite' pattern beehive honey pot and cover, the latter moulded and blue painted with three pink-centred flowerheads about the bud knop, the base of the rope moulded sides with blue band, printed marks.

c1932   4in (10cm) high

£200-250   **CHEF**

A Clarice Cliff 'May Blossom' pattern Bonjour shape preserve pot and cover, badly damaged.

1935-36   4in (10cm) high

£50-70   **BAR**

A Clarice Cliff Fantasque 'Melon' or 'Picasso Fruit' pattern jardinière, brightly painted with a band of stylised melons between chocolate brown lines and orange bands, the tapering cylindrical shape rounding to the three strap feet, with printed marks.

1930-32   8.5in (21.5cm) diam

£550-650   **CHEF**

A Clarice Cliff 'Nasturtium' pattern Le Bon Dieu bowl, of organic form, printed marks.

c1932   7in (18cm) diam

£150-200   **L&T**

A Clarice Cliff 'My Garden Surprise' pattern circular bowl, with applied foot, moulded with lines.

1934-39   6.5in (16.5cm) diam

£80-120   **L&T**

A Clarice Cliff 'Nasturtium' pattern cheese dish and cover, printed marks.

1932   *7.5in (19cm) wide*

£180-220   **L&T**

A pair of Clarice Cliff 'Nasturtium' pattern sugar sifters.

1932   *3in (7.5cm) high*

£180-220   **GORL**

A Clarice Cliff 'Nasturtium' pattern preserve jar and cover, of cylindrical form, printed marks.

1932   *3.5in (9cm) high*

£200-250   **L&T**

A Clarice Cliff Bizarre 'Sunshine' pattern Bonjour biscuit barrel and cover, each of the flat sides of the cylindrical shape painted with hollyhocks, the bamboo handle swinging on yellow-edged knops, printed marks.

c1930   *6in (15.5cm) high*

£200-250   **CHEF**

A Clarice Cliff Bizarre 'Rhodanthe' pattern wall plaque, painted with orange, grey, ochre and yellow flowers growing from greyish brown mounds, printed marks, introduced 1934.

1934   *10.25in (26cm) diam*

£250-350   **CHEF**

A Clarice Cliff galloping horse, the stylised pale mushroom-glazed animal racing with gilt details, blue printed marks.

6in (15cm) high

£180-220   **CHEF**

A Clarice Cliff 'Rhodanthe' pattern coffee pot and cover, the flared cylindrical sides painted with stylised orange, yellow and grey flowers growing from grey stems on grey mounds, the handle and spout triangular, printed marks.

1934   *7.5in (19cm) high*

£450-550   **CHEF**

A Clarice Cliff Bizarre 'Viscaria' pattern 'Bonjour' preserve pot and cover, painted with green and blue flowers on the cylindrical body, printed marks.

This is a version of the 'Rhodanthe' design.

1934   *4.25in (11cm) high*

£350-450   **CHEF**

A pair of Clarice Cliff 'Yuan' pattern vases, the cylindrical shapes tapering to spreading feet and horizontally ribbed below a celadon green glaze, printed marks.

1937   *10in (25.5cm) high*

£150-200   **CHEF**

COLLECTORS' NOTES

■ Susie Cooper was born in 1902. She began work as a paintress in 1922 at A.E. Gray & Co. Ltd, a noted ceramic decorating factory and pottery. She designed a number of floral patterns for Gray's, most marked with a new backstamp including her name. By 1929 she had gained a wealth of experience and left to set up the Susie Cooper Pottery, decorating white 'blanks' made elsewhere.

■ In 1931 she took residence at the now famous 'Crown Works', part of Woods & Sons in Burslem. Woods both supplied blank white wares to be decorated and, from around 1932, started to make Cooper's own shapes. It is this that distinguishes Cooper from her contemporary Clarice Cliff, who did not design her own shapes.

■ As with Clarice Cliff, Susie Cooper's Art Deco style work is the most sought after. Produced up until the 1930s, these wares are hand-painted with boldly coloured flowers or geometric shapes.

■ Many of her designs were inspired by nature, using floral or foliate motifs. Some pieces were hand-painted and others applied by lithographic transfer – examine the pattern closely to spot telltale hand-painted brushstrokes.

■ Look for Cooper's classic and very modern shapes, such as 'Kestrel' or 'Rex'. Typical patterns such as 'Dresden Spray' are likely to retain their popularity.

■ In 1950 Cooper acquired a factory and produced bone china, which tends to be less desirable and valuable than her earlier earthenware pieces. In 1966, the factory was acquired by Wedgwood and new bone china designs were produced, many reflecting the styles of the age. As with her other bone china pieces, these tend to be less valuable, but usually offer a more affordable entry point to her designs.

■ Cooper resigned as Director in 1972, and worked solely as a designer. The Crown Works were closed in late 1979 and Cooper worked as a freelance designer from 1986 until her death in 1995.

An early Susie Cooper hand-painted lidded butter/cheese dish, with Art Deco geometric pattern, unmarked.

c1930   6.75in (17cm) diam

£250-300   **BAD**

A Susie Cooper three handled 'studio ware' earthenware vase, of ovoid form, handpainted with leaves, printed marks.

Demonstrative of Cooper's desire to control both shape and pattern, and in line with studio pottery of the time, this range was made to celebrate hand-painting and hand-throwing pottery.

c1933   6.25in (16cm) high

£70-100   **L&T**

A Susie Cooper for Gray's Art Deco styled four-piece hand-painted 'Moons and Mountains' pattern part teaset, comprising a teapot, teacup, plate and cream jug, blue enamel worn.

c1930 Teapot 3in (7.5cm) high

£700-800   **GORL**

A Susie Cooper hand-painted dessert plate, with black spiral centre.

c1933

£50-70   **SCG**

A Susie Cooper Art Deco Kestrel shape teapot, with floral pattern.

7.25in (18.5cm) high

£60-70   **BAD**

A Susie Cooper Kestrel shape teapot, with hand-painted green leaf and circle design and pink lid.

7.5in (19cm) high

£80-120   **BAD**

A Susie Cooper green 'Dresden Spray' pattern Rex shape hot water jug.

7in (17.5cm) high

£80-120   **BAD**

A Susie Cooper green 'Dresden Spray' pattern Rex shape teapot.

c1960   9.75in (24.5cm) long

£70-100   **BAD**

CERAMICS

A 1950s Susie Cooper bone china 'Romance Pink' pattern Quail shape teapot.

This shape was introduced at the 1951 Festival of Britain. The traditional form appealed to a certain area of the market and draws attention to the elegance of the bone china material.

8in (20cm) long

£70-90　　　　　　**BAD**

A Susie Cooper for John Lewis blue 'Polka Dot' pattern Kestrel shape teapot.

c1930　　5.75in (14.5cm) high

£80-120　　　　　　**BAD**

A Susie Cooper 'Gardenia' pattern lidded butter dish, crack to lid.

1958　　　　7.25in (18.5cm) diam

£100-150　　　　　　**BAD**

A Susie Cooper 'Patricia Rose' pattern plate, with broad yellow border.

c1940　　8.25in (21cm) diam

£70-100　　　　　　**BAD**

A Susie Cooper trio set, with hand-painted floral pattern surrounded by a green border.

saucer 7in (17.5cm) diam

£70-100　　　　　　**BAD**

A Susie Cooper Kestrel shape small coffee can, with hand-painted green leaf and circle design to exterior and pink interior.

2.25in (6cm) high

£30-50　　　　　　**BAD**

A Susie Cooper Kestrel shape cup and saucer, the pink ground with leaf and dots decoration, with old repair to handle.

saucer 4.5in (11.5cm) diam

£8-12　　　　　　**BAD**

A 1970s Wedgwood Susie Cooper Design jade 'Flower Motif' pattern cup and saucer, printed marks.

Part of a set of Wildflower designs, each with different colourways.

saucer 5.5in (14cm) diam

£20-30　　　　　　**CHS**

A 1960s Wedgwood Susie Cooper Design 'Blue Anenome' pattern cup and saucer, printed marks.

saucer 6in (15cm) diam

£20-30　　　　　　**CHS**

A Wedgwood Susie Cooper Design 'Diablo' pattern side plate, cup and saucer, printed marks.

c1965　　plate 7in (18cm) diam

£30-50　　　　　　**CHS**

A Royal Winton Cottageware cheese dish and stand.

Of the 1930s Cottageware makers, Royal Winton is known for the quality of its decoration and mouldings. The watermill is a popular and desirable shape.

c1935 7.25in (18.5cm) wide

£150-250 JF

A Wade Heath cheese dish.

Wade Heath launched its Cottageware range in 1933 and continued manufacture until 1971.

c1935 6.75in (17.5cm) wide

£120-150 JF

A Cantonware 'Cheese Inn' two-piece cheese dish.

7.5in (19cm) long

£60-80 JF

A Beswick 'Cottage' circular cheese dish.

c1935

£80-120 JF

A Price Bros. three-storey coffee pot and cover.

c1945 10in (25.5cm) high

£60-80 JF

An English creamer, probably by Price Bros.

1930s 3in (8cm) high

£60-80 JF

An English creamer, probably by Price Bros.

1930s 3in (8cm) high

£60-80 JF

A Price Bros. Cottageware stovey jug.

c1945 2.5in (6.5cm) high

£50-60 JF

A Kensington Pottery double jam pot.

1930s 8in (20.5cm) wide

£80-100 JF

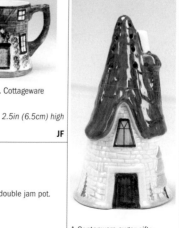

A Cantonware sugar sifter.

1930s

£60-90 JF

An Aynsley 'Japanese Bridge' pattern bone china trio set.
c1920   *7in (18cm) diam*

£30-50   **JL**

A CLOSER LOOK AT A CUP AND SAUCER

The saucer is divided into the 12 signs of the Zodiac and the cup has mystical motifs representing different facets of human life as well as rays with astrological planetary signs.

The registration number 442928 printed on the base dates the design to 1905, but the cup was produced for a number of years after this date.

The outside of the cup reads 'Would'st Learn Thy Future With The Tea, This Magic Cup Will Show It Thee' making the design functional as well as decorative.

The shallow cup is ideal for reading tea-leaves, indicating the drinkers future when read against the design.

An Aynsley 'The Nelros Cup of Fortune' fortune telling cup and saucer, with transfer-printed design.
c1930   *Saucer 5.75in (14.5cm) diam*

£50-60   **BEV**

c1935   *Plate 6in (15.5cm) wide*

£50-70   **JL**

A Carlton china trio set, with hand-painted flowers and gilt details to the rims and foot of the cup.

A 'Chapman' Longton Ltd cup and saucer, with Art Deco styled angular handle and hand-coloured transfer-printed design.
c1935

£15-25   **JL**

A 'Chapman' Longton coffee trio set, decorated with a hand-painted and transfer-printed Grecian or Neo-Classical garland design.
c1920   *7in (17.5cm) diam*

£20-40   **JL**

A 'Chapmans' Longton trio set, with a design of sprays of blue flowers
c1935   *Plate 5.75in (14.5cm) wide*

£30-40   **JL**

A Copeland Garrett cup and saucer, with transfer-printed design of grey flowers and shaped, gilt rim.
1833-47   *Saucer 6in (15cm) wide*

£40-60   **JL**

A Crown Derby blue and white transfer-printed cup and two saucers, with Oriental scene similar to the 'Willow' pattern.
c1935   *Plate 6.25in (16cm) diam*

£40-60   **JL**

A Crown Derby cup and saucer, with cobalt blue and gilt scrolling rococo-style design incorporating a phoenix.

c1935   *6.25in (16cm) d.*

£60-80   **JL**

A Davenport coffee cup and saucer, with cobalt blue, red and gilt chinoiserie design, slight chip on saucer.

1870-86   *Saucer 4.5in (11.5cm) diam*

£70-100   **JL**

A Duchess China cup and saucer, made by Edwards and Brown, the interior of the cup and saucer decorated with hand-painted flowers.

1910-33   *5.5in (14cm) diam*

£15-25   **JL**

A 'Ye Olde English Grosvenor China' Dulang trio set, with a fuchsia ground and hand-painted flower decoration.

Plate 7in (18cm) diam

£30-40   **JL**

A Habitat 'Scraffito' pattern cup and saucer, printed marks.

This range was named after the decorative technique 'sgraffito' where a design is created by scoring through a coloured layer to reveals the contrasting underlying colour.

Saucer 6.5in (16.5cm) diam

£10 15   **CHS**

A Habitat 'Bistro' pattern cup and saucer, printed marks.

Saucer 6in (15cm) diam

£7-10   **CHS**

A Minton cup and saucer, with hand-painted flower motif and gilt rim and handle.

1866   *Saucer 5.25in (13.5cm) diam*

£70-90   **JL**

A 1970s Noritake 'Progression' cup and saucer, printed marks.

Saucer 5.5in (14cm) diam

£7-9   **CHS**

A Paragon Star China Company bone china trio set, with a green floral wreath pattern, moulded trellis design in leaf shapes and a scalloped and gilt edge.

Plate 7.25in (18.5cm) diam

£25-35   **JL**

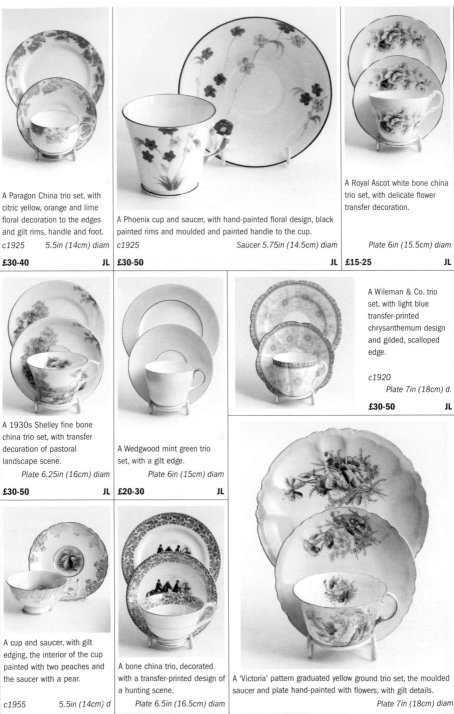

A Paragon China trio set, with citric yellow, orange and lime floral decoration to the edges and gilt rims, handle and foot.

c1925   *5.5in (14cm) diam*

£30-40   **JL**

A Phoenix cup and saucer, with hand-painted floral design, black painted rims and moulded and painted handle to the cup.

c1925   *Saucer 5.75in (14.5cm) diam*

£30-50   **JL**

A Royal Ascot white bone china trio set, with delicate flower transfer decoration.

Plate 6in (15.5cm) diam

£15-25   **JL**

A 1930s Shelley fine bone china trio set, with transfer decoration of pastoral landscape scene.

Plate 6.25in (16cm) diam

£30-50   **JL**

A Wedgwood mint green trio set, with a gilt edge.

Plate 6in (15cm) diam

£20-30   **JL**

A Wileman & Co. trio set, with light blue transfer-printed chrysanthemum design and gilded, scalloped edge.

c1920

Plate 7in (18cm) d.

£30-50   **JL**

A cup and saucer, with gilt edging, the interior of the cup painted with two peaches and the saucer with a pear.

c1955   *5.5in (14cm) d*

£25-35   **JL**

A bone china trio, decorated with a transfer-printed design of a hunting scene.

Plate 6.5in (16.5cm) diam

£25-35   **JL**

A 'Victoria' pattern graduated yellow ground trio set, the moulded saucer and plate hand-painted with flowers, with gilt details.

Plate 7in (18cm) diam

£60-80   **JL**

COLLECTORS' NOTES

■ Denby Pottery was started by William Bourne in 1806 in Denby, Derbyshire, after the discovery of a clay seam in the area.

■ It was originally called the Joseph Bourne Pottery after William's son, who ran the business. Production of quality salt-glazed pottery, in particular bottles, began in 1809.

■ By the end of the 19th century the pottery moved away from containers and expanded its kitchenware line, developing the luxurious, coloured glazes for which Denby became famous.

■ The 'Danesby Ware' range of the 1920s was a popular range of functional kitchenware, decorative items and giftware. More popular ranges appeared in the 1930s such as 'Electric Blue' with a glossy blue glaze and 'Orient ware' with a matte blue or brown glaze, both

of which are sought-after today. This decade also saw the introduction of kitchenware lines such as 'Cottage Blue', 'Manor Green' and 'Homestead Brown', which remained in vogue into the early 1980s.

■ In the 1950s the Pottery again changed direction. It concentrated on tableware and employed designers such as Glyn Colledge, Gill Pemberton and Kenneth Clark to create patterns like 'Greenwheat' (1956), 'Echo and Ode' (1950s), 'Studio' (1961) and 'Arabesque', known as 'Samarkand' in the US, (1964).

■ The pottery continued to move with the times and produced striking tableware, with styles becoming less formal in the 1980s to meet the demand for 'casual dining'. It remains a popular choice for good quality, stylish tableware today.

A Denby Pottery 'Dreamweaver' pattern mug, with printed marks.

1975-6   3.5in (9cm) high

£10-15   **CHS**

A Denby Pottery 'East Midlands' mug, with printed marks.

Originally commissioned by Cadbury's as a set of 13 'regional' mugs, including Scotland. It appears that the range was eventually produced without any connection to Cadbury's.

c1976   4in (10cm) high

£8-10   **CHS**

A Denby Pottery 'Green Wheat' pattern side plate, Albert College cup and saucer, printed marks.

1950s-1977 6.5in (16.5cm) diam

£15-20   **CHS**

A Denby Pottery 'Savoy' pattern side plate, cup and saucer, printed marks.

1982-87   Plate 6.5in (16.5cm) diam

£12-18   **CHS**

A late 1950s Denby Pottery 'Gourmet' pattern jug, designed by Kenneth Clark, with lid.

c1957   12.5in (31.75cm) high

£150-200   **GGRT**

A Denby Pottery 'South East' mug, with printed marks.

c1976   4in (10cm) high

£8-10   **CHS**

A 1950s Denby Pottery 'Spring' pattern side plate, cup and saucer.

6.75in (17cm) diam

£20-25   **CHS**

A mid-1970s Denby Pottery 'Verona' pattern side plate, cup and saucer, designed by Gill Pemberton, printed marks.

Plate 7in (18cm) diam

£22-28   **CHS**

A 1970s Denby Pottery 'Trees' pattern side plate, cup and saucer, designed by Diana Woodcock-Beckering, printed marks.

Plate 6.5in (16.5cm) diam

£18-22   **CHS**

FIND OUT MORE...

'Denby Pottery 1809-1997 Dynasties and Designers', *by Irene Gordon Hopwood, published by Richard Dennis Publications, 1997.*

'Denby Stonewares: a Collector's Guide', *by Graham and Alva Key, published by Ems and Ens Ltd, 1995.*

www.denbypottery.co.uk - *Official pottery website.*

COLLECTOR'S NOTES

■ Doulton was founded in 1815 at Vauxhall Walk in Lambeth, London by John Doulton, Martha Jones and John Watts. It became known as Doulton and Co. in 1853. It first produced utilitarian wares, such as pipes and bottles, in stoneware. From around 1871, students of the Lambeth School of Art began to create decorative wares, most notably George Tinworth and Hannah, Florence and Arthur Barlow.

■ Around 1877 78, the Pindar, Bourne and Co. factory at Burslem in Staffordshire was acquired and its name changed to Doulton and Company Ltd in 1882. It soon became known for fine porcelain. In 1901, the company gained the title 'royal' from Edward VII, and the first new 'Royal Doulton' marks appeared in 1902. Since 1955, it has been known as Doulton Fine China Ltd. The Lambeth factory closed in 1956.

■ Over the past decade there has been a slight decline in demand for all but the finest pieces of Doulton, particularly the stoneware, as the style has become somewhat unfashionable. Now may be a good time to buy as a revival would cause values to rise once again.

■ Look out for work signed by notable artists such as the Barlows – examine bases for their monograms and designs for their typical motifs.

A CLOSER LOOK AT A DOULTON LAMBETH VASE

These vases were decorated by Florence Barlow, part of the notable Barlow family who worked for Doulton.

Florence Barlow is especially noted for her birds and flowers, whilst her sister Hannah is known for her horses and other animals.

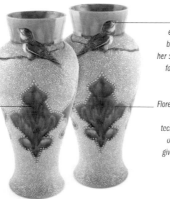

The bodies are decorated with 'tube lining' where white glaze is 'piped' onto the body like icing – this particular pattern is sometimes known as 'vermicelli'.

Florence Barlow often used the 'pâte-sur-pâte' technique, whereby layers of colour are built up to give texture and create a design in low relief.

An unusual pair of Doulton Lambeth vases, by Florence Barlow, incised in relief with sparrows to the neck, impressed marks.

Many artists at Lambeth practised the pâte-sur-pâte technique, used here on the bird's feathers, particularly between1878 and 1906.

11.25in (28.5cm) high

£800-1,200   **WW**

A Doulton Lambeth stoneware bottle vase, by George Tinworth, incised and applied with scrolling seaweed pattern in shades of blue and brown, impressed mark, incised monogram.

10.5in (27cm) high

£650-750   **WW**

A Doulton 'Moon' vase, with blue and gilt detailing in the 'Spray' pattern.

The form and pattern of this vase are both Eastern in origin, the 'Moon' name being taken from the Oriental circular doorways known as 'moon gates'.

c1885   9.5in (24cm) high

£70-100   **BAD**

A Royal Doulton 'Chang' vase, by Charles Noke and Harry Nixon, covered in a running and pitted flambé glaze, signatures.

7in (17.5cm) high

£1,000-1,500   **WW**

A Doulton Lambeth stoneware inkwell, in the form of an old lady, inscribed "Votes For Women".

3.5in (9cm) high

£350-420   **PSA**

A 20thC Doulton Lambeth ring tray, modelled as a large billed bird, impressed mark and numerals 11497 to base.

4.25in (11cm) high

£250-300   **BONS**

CERAMICS

A Doulton vase with blue and gilt detailing, stamped "2055".

c1900   7.25in (18.5cm) high

£100-150   **BAD**

A Royal Doulton two-handled hand-painted and gilt transfer vase on stem.

6.5in (16.5cm) high

£100-150   **BAD**

An unusual Royal Doulton ribbed art pottery vase, marked and impressed.

6.5in (16.5cm) high

£250-350   **PSA**

A large Royal Doulton water pitcher, painted with sailboats at sea in dark brown and amber on bottle-green ground, minimal crazing, two small nicks to rim, Royal Doulton ink stamp, and registry mark.

10.5in (26.5cm) high

£180-220   **DRA**

A Royal Doulton Art Deco style 'De Luxe' pattern tea set, each green piece divided by a black and silver arc to leave one third white, comprising: sandwich plate, sugar bowl, milk jug, six teacups, saucers and tea plates, impressed dates.

This tea set was featured in an advertisement for Lipton's Tea in 1933. It's the angular handles, the bright colours and the geometric pattern with simple lines that make this teaset typical of this stylistic movement.

c1933

£350-450 set   **CHEF**

A 1930s Royal Doulton hand-painted hexagonal planter, marked "D4365" on the base.

6in (15.5cm) widest

£60-70   **BAD**

A Royal Doulton "Votes For Women" and "Toil For Men" cruet set, boxed.

3.25in (8.5cm) high

£50-60   **PSA**

A Royal Doulton 'Shakespeare Jug', produced in a limited edition of 1000, this no.548 depicting Shakespeare characters, complete with certificate of authenticity.

A series of jugs or loving cups with heavily embossed scenes and decoration was designed by Harry Fenton between 1920 and 1938, and once again in 1952. Edition sizes vary between 350 and 1,000 and it is always good to look out for the original certificate bearing the matching limited edition number, which will help make a piece more desirable by 'completing' it.

c1933   10.75in (27cm) high

£400-600   **ROS**

A Royal Doulton stoneware figure of the Cheshire Cat.

'The Charlton Standard Catalogue of Royal Doulton Animals' attributes this model to Mark Marshall.

3.5in (9cm) wide

£350-450   **CHEF**

A Royal Doulton 'Sealyham Begging' figure, K3.

1931-77   2.5in (6.5cm) h

£35-45   **PSA**

A Royal Doulton 'Seated Bulldog' figure.

4.75in (12cm) high

£40-50   **PSA**

A rare Royal Doulton prototype 'Study of an Australian Blue Heeler Dog' figure, in matt finish.

5in (12.5cm) wide

£1,000-1,500   **PSA**

A Royal Doulton 'Dog Licking Plate' figure, HN1158.

5in (12.5cm) wide

£45-55   **PSA**

A mid-20thC Royal Doulton 'Lying St Bernard' figure, K19.

£30-40   **PSA**

A Royal Doulton 'Tabby Kitten' figure, HN2580, seated licking its paw.

1941-85   2.25in (5.5cm) h

£40-50   **CHEF**

A limited edition Royal Doulton 'The Walking Cat' figure, DA148, from an edition of 1,000, boxed with certificate.

5.5in (14cm) high

£15-25   **PSA**

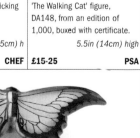

A Royal Doulton 'Butterfly On A Stump' figure, HN141.

2.75in (7cm) high

£180-220   **PSA**

A 1990s Royal Doulton 'Badger' paperweight.

4in (10cm) wide

£180-220   **PSA**

COLLECTORS' NOTES

■ Character jugs depict well-known fictional or real-life personalities and have their roots in the early English 'toby' jugs. Whereas toby jugs are modelled on a whole body, character jugs portray just the head, or head and shoulders.

■ The first 20th century character jug is generally thought to be Charles Noke's 1934 John Barleycorn design, although Royal Doulton did produce a Lord Nelson jug as early as the 1820s.

■ Royal Doulton manufacture character jugs in four sizes usually referred to as large, small, miniature and tiny. Over the years the exact dimensions have varied, although the largest jugs measure around 7.25in (18cm) high and the smallest only 1.25in (3cm).

■ In recent years Royal Doulton have undertaken a great many special commissions, some of which are only released in small quantities, which makes them instantly desirable to collectors.

■ Royal Doulton character jugs will usually carry a mark to help confirm their authenticity. Most jugs made before 1973 will also bear a registration number.

■ Collectors should make themselves familiar with the various colour variations that exist on some jugs, many due to shortages during WWII. Examples that were only made for a short period of time and therefore are in short supply are the most sought-after.

A Royal Doulton 'Paddy' small character jug, D5768, with green hat.

1937-60   *3.5in (9cm) high*

£45-55   **GORL**

A Royal Doulton 'John Peel' small character jug, D5731, with orange riding crop.

1937-60   *3.25in (8.5cm) high*

£35-45   **PSA**

A Royal Doulton 'John Peel' all white small character jug, D5731.

Apart from three models, all white jugs are factory rejects. White versions of recent or current production are scarce as the factory tries to stop their release.

1937-60   *3.25in (8.5cm) high*

£150-200   **PSA**

A Royal Doulton 'John Barleycorn' all white miniature character jug, D6041.

1939-60   *2in (5cm) high*

£60-80   **PSA**

A Royal Doulton 'Old Charley' all white tiny character jug, D6144.

1940-60   *1.25in (3cm) high*

£350-450   **PSA**

A Royal Doulton 'Drake' all white small character jug, D6174.

1941-60   *3.25in (8.5cm) high*

£80-120   **PSA**

A Royal Doulton 'Samuel Johnson' small character jug. D6296.

1950-60   *3.25in (8.5cm) high*

£70-90   **PSA**

A Royal Doulton 'Jarge' small character jug, D6295.

1950-60   *3.25in (8.5cm) high*

£80-120   **PSA**

A Royal Doulton 'Gulliver' small character jug, D6563, small glaze fault.

1962-67   *4in (10cm) high*

£120-180   **PSA**

A CLOSER LOOK AT A CHARACTER JUG

This jug is based on "Arry" which was released between 1947-60.

This jug has the addition of moulded buttons on the cap and collar.

Pearly Boy comes in four variations: three in brown, and this one with a blue coat.

All versions are rare, but the blue coat is the rarest.

A rare Royal Doulton blue 'Pearly Boy' small character jug.

3.25in (8.5cm) high

£1,200-1,500   **PSA**

A Royal Doulton 'Mine Host' large character jug, D6468.

1958-82

£45-55   **GORL**

A Royal Doulton 'Punch And Judy Man' small character jug, D6593.

1964-69   *4in (10cm) high*

£200-250   **PSA**

A Royal Doulton 'Captain Hook' small character jug, D6601, version 1.

1965-71   *4in (10cm) high*

£150-200   **PSA**

A Royal Doulton 'Ugly Duchess' small character jug, D6603.

The design of this jug is based on Sir John Tenniel's original illustrations for 'Alice In Wonderland'.

1965-73   *4in (10cm) high*

£150-200   **PSA**

A Royal Doulton 'Winston Churchill' large character jug, D6907.

This jug proved very popular and over 30,000 were sold.

1992   *7in (18cm) high*

£120-180   **PSA**

A limited edition Royal Doulton 'Charlie Chaplin' large character jug, D6949, from an edition of 5,000, with certificate.

1993   *7in (18cm) high*

£100-150   **PSA**

COLLECTORS' NOTES

■ Royal Doulton modeller Charles Noke conceived the idea of reviving the Staffordshire tradition of figurine modelling in the late 19th century. He invited sculptors to submit their design ideas and soon had enough for a collection.

■ Since the 1913 launch, most of the figures made in Doulton's Burslem factory have been given 'HN' numbers after Harry Nixon, then manager of the painting department. More than 4,000 of these numbers have been assigned to date.

■ One of Doulton's most prolific modellers was Leslie Harradine, a freelancer who submitted a vast number of designs to the factory throughout the 1920s, '30s and '40s. Always popular, many of Harradine's designs are still in production today. Other names to look for include Nada Pedley and Peggy Davies.

■ Doulton figures are usually impressed or stamped with the company's lion and crown mark on the base. Some also have date codes, and it is often possible to ascertain the rough age of a figure from the type of stamp used.

■ Older, discontinued figures, especially those with fine modelling and in good condition, attract the highest prices. Pre-war models are among the most desirable as they were produced in low numbers and seldom come onto the market today.

A Royal Doulton 'Captain Macheath' figure, HN464, designed by Leslie Harradine, from the Beggar's Opera Series, minor restoration.

1921-49   *7in (18cm) high*

£220-280   **PSA**

A Royal Doulton 'Polly Peacham' figure, HN549, designed by Leslie Harradine, style two from the Beggar's Opera Series, light restoration.

1922-49   *4.25in (11cm) high*

£150-200   **PSA**

A Royal Doulton 'Mendicant' figure, HN1365, designed by Leslie Harradine, hand damaged.

1929-69   *8in (20cm) high*

£50-70   **PSA**

A Royal Doulton 'Miss Muffet' figure, HN1936, designed by Leslie Harradine.

1940-67   *5.5in (14cm) high*

£70-100   **PSA**

A Royal Doulton 'The Ermine Coat' figure, HN1981, designed by Leslie Harradine.

1945-67   *7in (18cm) high*

£100-150   **PSA**

A Royal Doulton figure 'Diana', HN1986, designed by Leslie Harradine, style one.

Two earlier versions were released in 1935 and are both worth about twice the value for this later figure.

1946-75   *6in (15cm) high*

£60-80   **GORL**

A Royal Doulton 'Bluebeard' figure, HN2105, designed by Leslie Harradine.

1953-92   *11in (28cm) high*

£150-200   **PSA**

A Royal Doulton 'Christmas Morn' figure, HN1992, designed by Margaret Davies.

1947-96   *7in (18cm) high*

£60-80   **GORL**

A Royal Doulton 'Gentleman from Williamsburg' figure, HN2227, designed by Margaret Davies, from the Figures of Williamsburg Series.

1960-83   *6.25in (16cm) h*

£70-100   **GORL**

A limited edition Royal Doulton 'The Mask' figure, HN4141, designed by Leslie Harradine, from an edition of 1,500.

1999   *10in (25.5cm) high*

£150-200   **PSA**

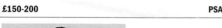

A limited edition Royal Doulton 'West Indian Dancer' figure, HN2384, designed by Margaret Davies, from the Dancers Of The World series and an edition of 750, boxed with certificate.

1981   *9in (23cm) high*

£280-320   **PSA**

A Royal Doulton 'Lady From Williamsburg' figure, HN2228, designed by Margaret Davies, from the Figures of Williamsburg series.

1960-83   *6in (15cm) high*

£70-100   **PSA**

A Royal Doulton 'Premiere' figure, HN2343, designed by Margaret Davies.

1969-79   *7.75in (19.5cm) high*

£80-120   **PSA**

A Royal Doulton 'Lorna' figure, HN2311, designed by Margaret Davies.

1965-85   *8.5in (21.5cm) high*

£50-70   **PSA**

A Royal Doulton 'Good King Wenceslas' miniature figure, HN3262, designed by Margaret Davies, style two.

1989-92   *4.25in (11cm) high*

£55-65   **PSA**

A Royal Doulton 'The Potter' figure, HN1493, designed by Charles Noke.

1932-92   *7in (18cm) high*

£170-200   **PSA**

A Royal Doulton 'Belle O The Ball' figure, HN1997, designed by R. Asplin.

1949-79   8.5in (21.5cm) wide

£170-200   **PSA**

A Royal Doulton 'Symphony' figure, HN2287, designed by D.B. Lovegrove.

1961-65   5.25in (13.5cm) h

£100-150   **GorL**

A Royal Doulton 'The Moor' figure, HN2082, designed by Charles Noke.

1952-   *17in (43cm) high*

£800-1,000   **PSA**

A Royal Doulton figure 'Mantilla', HN2712, designed by Eric J. Griffiths, from the Haute Ensemble Series.

1974-79   11.75in (29cm) high

£120-180   **L&T**

A Royal Doulton 'Harlequin' figure, HN2737, designed by Douglas V. Tootle.

1982-present 13in (33cm) high

£800-1,000   **PSA**

A Royal Doulton 'Columbine' figure, HN2738, designed by Douglas V. Tootle.

1982-present 13in (33cm) high

£700-900   **PSA**

A Royal Doulton 'Guy Fawkes' miniature figure, HN3271, originally designed by Charles Noke, style two.

1989-91   4in (10cm) high

£65-75   **PSA**

A Royal Doulton 'Samantha' figure, HN2954, designed by Pauline Parsons, style one from the Vanity Fair Ladies Series.

1982-84   7.25in (18.5cm) high

£55-65   **PSA**

A Royal Doulton 'Falstaff' miniature figure, HN3236, originally designed by C. Noke.

1989-90   4in (10cm) high

£35-45   **PSA**

A limited edition Royal Doulton 'Christopher Columbus' figure, HN3392, designed by Alan Maslankowski, from an edition of 1,492, boxed with certificate.

This limited edition, issued in 1992 celebrates the 500th anniversary of Columbus discovering America.

12in (30.5cm) high

£350-450   **PSA**

A limited edition Royal Doulton 'Countess Of Harrington' figure, HN3317, designed by Peter Gee, from the Reynolds Ladies Series and an edition of 5,000.

1992   9.25in (23.5cm) high

£150-200   **PSA**

A Royal Doulton 'Anniversary' figure, HN3625, designed by Valerie Annand.

1994-98   8.5in (21.5cm) high

£120-180   **PSA**

A limited edition Royal Doulton 'Eastern Grace' flambé figure, HN3683, designed by Pauline Parsons, from the Flambé Series and an edition of 2,500.

1995   12.5in (31.5cm) high

£150-200   **PSA**

A Royal Doulton 'Jessica' figure, HN3850, designed by Nada Pedley, style two, Figure of the Year.

Style one (1988-95) is worth slightly less.

1997   8in (20cm) high

£70-90   **PSA**

A Royal Doulton 'Off To School' figure, HN3768, designed by Nada Pedley.

1996-98   5.5in (14cm) high

£100-150   **PSA**

A Royal Doulton 'Wisdom' figure, HN4083, designed by Alan Maslankowski, from the Sentiments Series.

c2000   6in (15cm) high

£35-45   **PSA**

A Royal Doulton 'Bethany' figure, HN4326, designed by Valerie Annard.

c2000   8.5in (21.5cm) high

£40-60   **PSA**

COLLECTORS' NOTES

- Devised by Charles Noke in the mid-1890s, seriesware was a range of utilitarian ceramic pieces decorated with scenes by theme. Some sets, such as 'Rip van Winkle' comprise a few pieces whilst other, such as 'Dickens' comprises many hundreds of different pieces. Advertised as "made to adorn, yet serve some useful purpose", the public took to them immediately.

- The decoration is applied by transfer, which is then highlighted with a little hand-colouring. Many fashionable illustrators were used, such as Cecil Aldin, Kate Greenaway, the humourous Henry Bateman, and poster artist John Hassall. Seriesware was mass-produced for over 50 years until public taste moved on in the 1950s, and new shapes and pattern combinations are often found.

- Themes are taken from literature, folklore, plays and sports. Most collectors focus on a particular series, most notably the extremely varied 'Dickensware'. Sporting series, such as 'Golfing', are often highly valued, primarily as they will be of interest to collectors of sporting memorabilia as well as Doulton seriesware collectors.

- Look out for rare shapes from popular series, which will command a premium from collectors keen to add unusual objects to their collections. Cracks, chips and excessive wear will reduce value as will any damage to the decoration.

A Royal Doulton Dickensware water jug, with 'Old Peggoty' scene.

7in (18cm) high

£100-150   **PSA**

A Royal Doulton Dickensware water jug, with 'Mr Pickwick' scene.

7in (18cm) high

£120-180   **PSA**

A Royal Doulton Dickensware water jug, with 'Poor Joe' scene.

6.25in (16cm) high

£100-150   **PSA**

A Royal Doulton Dickensware two-handled vase, with 'Barnaby Rudge' scene.

6in (15cm) high

£150-200   **PSA**

A Royal Doulton Dickensware tankard, with 'Mr Micawber' scene.

4.75in (12cm) high

£80-120   **PSA**

A Royal Doulton Dickensware teapot, with 'Bill Sykes' scene and an undecorated lid.

6in (15cm) high

£25-35   **PSA**

A Royal Doulton Dickensware two-handled vase, with 'Sgt Buz Fuz' scene.

8.5in (22cm) high

£250-350   **PSA**

A rare Royal Doulton Dickensware match striker, with 'Fagin and the Artful Dodger' scene, slight hairline and nip.

£180-220   **PSA**

A Royal Doulton 'Bayeux Tapestry' series small water jug, light hairline crack.

5in (12.5cm) high

£15-25   PSA

A Royal Doulton 'Blue Sky' 'Coaching' series hot water jug, with pewter fitting.

6.25in (16cm) high

£180-220   PSA

A Royal Doulton 'Coaching' series plate.

£20-30   CHEF

A Royal Doulton 'Cock A Doodle Do' series beaker.

3.25in (8cm) high

£100-150   PSA

A Royal Doulton 'Dutch' series small water jug.

5in (13cm) high

£45-55   PSA

A Royal Doulton 'Gallant Fishers' series tall water jug.

8in (20cm) high

£70-100   PSA

A Royal Doulton 'Gaffers' series small teapot.

5.5in (14cm) high

£100-150   PSA

A Royal Doulton 'Golfing' series water jug, with the motto "Every Dog Has His Day And Every Man His Hour".

£400-500   PSA

A rare Royal Doulton 'Golfing' series match box holder, light restoration to top.

3.5in (9cm) high

£350-450   PSA

A Royal Doulton 'Historic England' series coffee pot, with 'Shakespeare and Stratford-upon-Avon' scene.

6.25in (16cm) high

£60-80   **PSA**

A Royal Doulton 'Hunting' series embossed water jug.

10.25in (26cm) high

£150-200   **PSA**

A rare Royal Doulton 'Motoring' series plate, crazed.

10.5in (27cm) diam

£550-650   **PSA**

A Royal Doulton 'Isaac Walton' series water jug.

5.5in (14cm) high

£50-60   **PSA**

A Royal Doulton 'The Old Wife' series vase, decorated in low relief with fish under the sea.

1938-55   *6.25in (16cm) high*

£50-70   **PSA**

A Royal Doulton 'Plough Horses' series tankard.

5.5in (14cm) high

£70-100   **PSA**

A Royal Doulton 'Robbie Burns' series water jug.

4.5in (11.5cm) high

£70-100   **PSA**

A limited edition Royal Doulton seriesware twin-handled vase, moulded in relief with 'The Three Musketeers' and other figures, titled 'The Great Romance of Louis XIII's reign', from an edition of 600.

10in (25cm) high

£500-600   **GORL**

A Royal Doulton 'Tutankhamen' series flask, with Titanian glaze, lacks lid.

£70-100   **PSA**

FIND OUT MORE...

'Royal Doulton Seriesware', *Vols 1-4, by Louise Irvine, published by Richard Dennis Publications, 1980-88.*

A Royal Doulton 'Stylish Snowman' figure, DS3.

1985-94   *5in (12.5cm) high*

£100-150   **PSA**

A Royal Doulton 'Cowboy Snowman' figure, DS6.

1986-92   *5in (12.5cm) high*

£120-180   **PSA**

A Royal Doulton 'Highland Snowman' figure, DS7.

1987-93   *5.25in (13.5cm) high*

£120-180   **PSA**

A Royal Doulton 'Snowman Money Bank' figure, DS19, boxed.

1990-94   *8.5in (21.5cm) high*

£120-180   **PSA**

A Royal Doulton 'Snowman Snowballing' figure, DS22, boxed.

1990 94   *5in (12.5cm) high*

£150-200   **PSA**

A Royal Doulton Snowman Gift Collection 'Balloons' pattern lidded box.

4in (10cm) diam

£40-50   **PSA**

A Royal Doulton 'Skier Snowman' figure, DS21.

1990-92   *5.5in (14cm) high*

£450-550   **PSA**

COLLECTORS' NOTES

■ Piero Fornasetti was born in Milan in 1913 and studied in Brera and Milan. His love of opulent surface designs set him apart from his Modernist peers who dismissed him. Nevertheless, he was popular with the public during the 1950s.

■ Fornasetti is well known for his interior decoration work and the striking furniture designs he produced with Gio Ponti. His work underwent a renaissance in the 1980s. By the 1990s a popular revival of interest developed and an exhibition of his work was held at the Victoria & Albert Museum, London.

■ Look for pieces that typify the style, with Classical motifs in a modern design. Condition is important, particularly as the gold surface is prone to wear and scratching, which reduces value. Fornasetti died in 1988. His son Barnaba continues to produces his designs, many with Rosenthal.

A Fornasetti plate.

8.5in (21.5cm) diam

£80-120 FM

A Fornasetti Italian artist plate, featuring Giorgio Barbarelli.

9.5in (24cm) diam

£100-140 FM

A Fornasetti Italian artist plate, featuring Tiziano Veneziano (Titian).

Fornasetti was heavily influenced by Renaissance painters such as Titian and Bellini.

9.5in (24cm) diam

£100-140 FM

A Fornasetti Italian artist plate, Antonello da Messina.

9.5in (24cm) diam

£100-140 FM

A Fornasetti opera plate, featuring Pollione from 'Norma' by Vincenzo Bellini (1801-1835).

10in (25.5cm) diam

£120-160 FM

A Fornasetti opera plate, featuring Carmen from 'Carmen' by George Bizet (1838-1875).

10in (25.5cm) diam

£120-160 FM

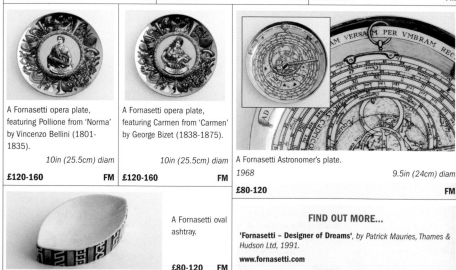

A Fornasetti Astronomer's plate.

1968

9.5in (24cm) diam

£80-120 FM

A Fornasetti oval ashtray.

£80-120 FM

FIND OUT MORE...

'Fornasetti – Designer of Dreams', by Patrick Mauries, *Thames & Hudson Ltd, 1991.*

www.fornasetti.com

A London crested china model of the Cenotaph.	A Willow crested china model of Florence Nightingale, bearing the crest of Epsom, missing hand.	An unmarked crested model of a candlestick as a lifebelt, the stem as a man's head, bearing the crest of Padstow.
6in (15cm) high	*6.25in (16cm) high*	*3.75in (9.5cm) diam*
£10-15 **GAZE**	**£20-30** **GAZE**	**£100-150** **GAZE**

A Carlton crested model of a kitchen range, inscribed "Keep the home fires burning until the boys come home", bearing the crest of the City of Sheffield.

This model is comparatively complex, requiring extra decoration and transfers as well as illustrating a popular theme related to WWI, which explains its higher value.

A crested model of a British soldier in a trench, inscribed "A Tommies Dugout".

3.5in (9cm) wide

3.25in (8.5cm) wide

£45-55 **GAZE**	**£70-100** **GAZE**

A Porcelle crested model of an ambulance, bearing the crest of Scarborough, some wear to gilt.

A Grafton crested model of the battleship Dreadnought, bearing the crest of Sawbridgeworth, one frontal gun broken.

5.5in (14cm) long

4.25in (11cm) long

£30-40 **GAZE**	**£40-50** **GAZE**

A Clifton crested model of a British tank, bearing the crest of West Hartlepool, some wear.

5in (12.5cm) long

A Porcelle crested model of a plane, bearing the crest of Inverness.

5in (12.5cm) long

£30-40 **GAZE**	**£45-55** **GAZE**

A Hornsea Pottery mug, decorated with pigs.

c1967   *3.5in (9cm) high*

£5-7   **DTC**

A Hornsea Pottery mug, decorated with owls.

c1967   *3.5in (9cm) high*

£5-7   **DTC**

A Hornsea Pottery mug, decorated with a three-coach train.

Typical of the late 1960s ranges in gloss and matte such as 'Heirloom', this mug is commonly found. Clappison's humour is evident in the design, with a bearded train driver, a worker in the second class carriage and a burglar complete with crowbar in the third class carriage!

c1967   *3.5in (9cm) high*

£5-7   **DTC**

A Hornsea Pottery bird ashtray.

6in (15cm) wide

£18-22   **CHS**

A pair of Hornsea Pottery salt and pepper shakers, shaped as fish.

3in (7.5cm) high

£25-35   **CHS**

A Hornsea Pottery lion salt shaker, printed marks.

3.25in (8.5cm) high

£15-20   **CHS**

An unusual Hornsea Pottery moulded earthenware vase, designed by Ronald Mitchell, model 723, cast in low relief with fish, printed marks, small chip to foot rim.

Royal College of Art graduate Ronald Mitchell was a friend of the Hornsea chief designer, John Clappison. This vase was part of the 'Pisces' range, sold only in 1961. See 'Austerity to Affluence: British Art and Design 1945-1962', Fine Art Society, p54.

1961   *6in (15.5cm) high*

£450-550   **WW**

A Hornsea Pottery sugar storage jar.

5in (12.5cm) high

£5-10   **CHS**

COLLECTORS' NOTES

■ Goebel's Hummel figurines were inspired by the charming drawings of children drawn by Sister Berta Hummel, who was born in 1909 in Bavaria, Germany. They were first released in 1935 and since then, over 500 different models have been made, offering great scope to collectors. Examine the base for an impressed mark showing a number as this helps to identify the model and also the name, particularly if there is no transfer showing the model name on the base.

■ Always examine the style of the factory mark stamped on the underside of the base as this helps to date a piece. It is primarily the older pieces from the 1930s and 1940s, followed by the 1950s-1960s, that are the most valuable, along with rare variations in colour and form. Larger pieces are also usually more valuable.

■ The first mark used was a 'crown' mark from 1934-50, with the name 'Goebel' in script. In 1950, a mark including a bee was introduced and over the following decades the bee became smaller and moved further inside the V mark. In c1960 it became a dot with two simple triangles as wings. In 1964, the entire motif was placed beside three lines of text reading '© by W. Goebel W. Germany' and from 1972, the motif sits in top of the word Goebel and the 'G' becomes larger and almost circular in form.

■ Condition is important as the material is fragile and chips, cracks or breaks extremely easily. Always examine protruding parts, heads and the rims of bases for damage or repairs, which devalue a piece. Take care when moving pieces around, especially when on display as if they are too close they can easily get damaged. Hummel figurines are still produced today.

A Hummel 'Little Gardener' figure, stylized bee mark, stamped "74".

This has the stylized bee mark used from 1960-72.

1960-72   4.25in (10.5cm)

£50-70   EAB

A Hummel 'Meditation' figure, with stylized bee mark, stamped "13".

c1962   4.5in (11.5cm)

£40-50   EAB

A Hummel 'Sister' figure, with full bee mark, restored fringe, stamped "98".

c1950   5.75in (14.5cm)

£70-100   EAB

A Hummel 'Forever Yours' special Club Edition figure, with special club edition mark, stamped "793".

Note the difference in form, and the graduated colour of the dress which indicates the later Club Edition.

c1996–97   4.25in (10.5cm)

£60-70   EAB

A Hummel 'Spring Cheer' figure, late bee mark, stamped "72".

Designed in 1934 by Reinhold Ungar, earlier versions than this example have yellow dresses and hold no flowers in the right hand.

c1972–79   5in (13cm)

£70-90   EAB

A Hummel 'Weary Wanderer' figurine, stamped "204".

Look out for the very rare variation with blue painted eyes which can fetch up to £1,000 if undamaged.

c1949   5.75in (14.5cm)

£100-150   GCA

A Hummel 'Kiss Me' figure, restoration to the doll's neck, three-line mark, stamped "311".

Look out for the early examples that use the 'full' bee mark and inspect pieces carefully for damage as the protruding parts are easy to damage. Later examples, which are less desirable, make the doll look less like a young girl.

c1964–72	6.25in (16cm)
£150-200	**EPO**

A Hummel 'Mother's Darling' figure, stylized bee mark, stamped "175".

Earlier examples with 'pre-bee' crown marks are the most sought after - one of the best ways to check is to look at the colour of the bags, which are light pink and yellow-green on older versions.

c1960–72	5.75in (14.5cm)
£100-150	**AGO**

A Hummel 'Signs of Spring' figure, perched bluebird, three-line mark, stamped "203/1".

c1960–72	5in (13cm)
£100-150	**AGO**

A Hummel 'Doll Mother' figure, full bee mark, stamped "67".

c1940–56	4.5in (12.5cm)
£100-170	**EAB**

A Hummel 'Favourite Pet' figure, stylized bee mark, stamped "361".

1964–72	4.25in (11cm)
£80-120	**EAB**

A Hummel 'Good Friends' figure, with full bee mark, stamped "182".

This example has the first of the many 'full' bee marks used from 1940-59.

c1948–59	4in (10cm)
£100-170	**EAB**

A Hummel 'Apple Tree Girl' figure, full bee mark, stamped "141".

c1940–59	
	6in (15cm)
£100-170	**AGO**

A Hummel 'Chick Girl' figure, incised crown and full bee mark, stamped "57".

c1934-50	3.75in (9.5cm)
£150-200	**AGO**

A Hummel 'Baker' figure, with original "Baker" label, stylized bee mark, stamped "128".

Although there have been a number of variations over the years, unlike many models, the baker does not vary much in value.

A Hummel 'Little Hiker' figure, with full bee mark, restored staff, stamped "16 2/0".

c1956   4.25in (11cm)

£40-60   **EAB**

A Hummel 'Soloist' figure, three-line mark, some restoration, stamped "135".

£60-80   **EAB**

c1970–79   5in (12.5cm)

£80-120   **EAB**

A Hummel 'Village Boy' figure, stylized bee mark, stamped "51".

This figurine was released in 1936 but withdrawn in the 1960s, to be then reintroduced around 20 years later. Early versions with crown marks and full bee marks are rare, as are those with blue jackets.

c1979   3.75in (9.5cm)

£50-70   **EAB**

A Hummel 'Little Drummer' figure, full bee mark, stamped "240".

c1960–63   4.25in (11cm)

£40-50   **EAB**

A Hummel 'Let's Sing' figure, no base, full bee mark, stamped "110".

c1938   3.75in (9.5cm)

£80-120   **IW**

A Hummel 'Garden Treasures' limited Club Edition figure, base marked "I must keep on digging" and stamped "727".

Designed by Helmut Fischer in 1996, this example was released in the US as a special edition in 1998-99 upon renewing a subscription to the M.I. Hummel Club.

c1998–99   3.75in (9.5cm)

£40-60   **EAB**

A Hummel 'Singing Lesson' figure, stylized bee mark, stamped "63".

c1958–72   3.75in (9.5cm)

£70-90   **AGO**

A Hummel 'Skier' figurine, with wooden poles and stylized bee mark, stamped "59".

Older examples have wooden poles, but check the style of the mark as they can easily be replaced.

c1960   *5in (13cm)*

£180-220   **GCA**

A Hummel 'She Loves Me, She Loves Me Not' figure, stylized bee mark, stamped "174".

c1958-72   *4.25in (11cm)*

£80-120   **EAB**

A Hummel 'Barnyard Hero' figure, three-line mark, stamped "195 2/0".

c1964-72   *4in (10cm)*

£70-100   **AGO**

A Hummel 'Joyful' ashtray, full bee mark for December 1984, slight chip on sole of right foot, stamped "33".

This piece was removed from production on 31st December 1984 and is unlikely to be made again. Look out for versions with orange dresses and blue shoes, and faïence painted examples as these are rare and much sought after.

4.5in (11.5cm)

£50-70   **EAB**

A Hummel 'Begging His Share' figure, with 'Goebel' mark with no bee and stamped "9" on the base.

1979-91   *5.5in (14cm)*

£70-100   **ROX**

A Hummel 'Strolling Along' figure, with Goebel mark with no bee and stamped "5".

1979-89   *5in (13cm)*

£70-100   **ROX**

A Hummel 'Apple Tree Boy' table lamp figure, with a small, stylized bee, stamped "230".

This piece was modelled by Arthur Moeller in 1953 and uses the standard 'Apple Tree Boy' figure as a base. Older pieces have a proportionately larger figure, although the whole piece is the same size. It was withdrawn from production in 1989.

c1954-89   *9.75in (25cm)*

£180-220   **AGO**

A Hummel 'Smart Little Sister' figure, three-line/stylized bee mark "No. 346".

c1964-72   *4.5in (11.5cm)*

£70-100   **EAB**

A Hummel 'Apple Tree Boy' figure, stamped "142 3/0'.

Larger versions than this have a bird perched on the branch.

c1958–72   *3in (10cm)*

£40-60   **EAB**

FIND OUT MORE...

'Luckey's Hummel Figurines & Plates Price Guide – 12th Edition', *by Carl F. Luckey and Dean A. Genth, published by Krause Publications, 2003.*

'No.1 Price Guide to Hummel Figurines, Plates and More', *by Robert L. Miller, published by Portfolio Press, 2003.*

COLLECTORS' NOTES

- The Midwinter Pottery was founded by William Robinson Midwinter in 1910 and was based in Burslem, Stoke-on-Trent. Initial production comprised Art Deco-styled tablewares and nurseryware.

- The company had a fairly small output until 1946 when Roy Midwinter, William's son, joined. He worked his way up through the company and began modernising the designs and the operating processes.

- Much of Roy's inspiration came from a trip to the US in 1952 where he saw work by designers such as Eva Meisel and Raymond Loewy.

- As a result of this trip, the Stylecraft range was launched at the 1953 Blackpool Fair, aimed at younger buyers in the export and domestic market. The job of designing the patterns for this range fell to designer Jessie Tait who had joined the company around the same time as Roy. Some of the first patterns included 'Primavera', 'Fiesta' and the popular 'Zambesi'. Designs could be hand-painted, lithographed or a combination of the two.

- Roy followed the success of Stylecraft with the Fashion range, first shown at the 1955 British Industries Fair, which featured even more modernised designs with abstract patterns and bright colours.

- Again, Tait was responsible for most of the designs, but a young Terence Conran and architect Hugh Casson also provided artwork.

- Shapes, patterns and colours that typify the period are most popular with collectors. Condition should also be considered, as damage will reduce the value.

A Midwinter Pottery 'Red Domino' pattern hand-painted milk jug, from the Stylecraft range, designed by Jessie Tait.

A blue variation of this pattern was also made and is harder to find.

c1953   2.25in (5.5cm) high

£12-18   **FFM**

A Midwinter Pottery 'Fiesta' pattern charger, from the Stylecraft range, designed by Jessie Tait.

c1954   13.75in (35cm) wide

£100-140   **GGRT**

A Midwinter Pottery 'Tonga' pattern tube-line decorated plate, designed by Jessie Tait.

c1954   12.25in (31cm) diam

£100-150   **GGRT**

A Midwinter Pottery 'Autumn' pattern small plate, designed by Jessie Tait.

c1955   6.75in (15.5cm) diam

£50-70   **GGRT**

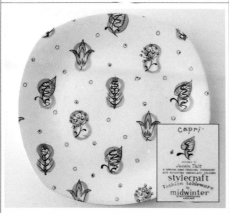

A Midwinter Pottery Fashion shape 'Capri' pattern plate, designed by Jessie Tait.

c1955   9.75in (24.5cm) diam

£70-90   **GGRT**

A Midwinter Pottery 'Fashion Check' pattern small plate, designed by Jessie Tait.

c1955   6.75in (15.5cm) diam

£70-90   **GGRT**

A Midwinter Pottery Fashion shape 'Pierrot' pattern small plate, designed by Jessie Tait.

c1955   6.75in (15.5cm) diam

£40-60   **GGRT**

A Midwinter Pottery 'Monaco' pattern plate, designed by Jessie Tait.

c1956   *8.75in (22.5cm) diam*

£20-40   **GGRT**

A Midwinter Pottery 'Savannah' pattern teapot, designed by Jessie Tait.

c1956   *5in (12.5cm) high*

£70-90   **BEV**

A Midwinter Pottery 'Stardust' pattern plate, designed by Jessie Tait.

These were made for the American market and had a speckled background, which was not very popular in England.

c1956   *9.75in (25cm) diam*

£80-120   **GGRT**

A Midwinter Pottery 'Savanna' pattern dish, designed by Jessie Tait.

c1956   *8.5in (21.5cm) diam*

£80-130   **GGRT**

A Midwinter Pottery 'Toadstool' pattern small plate, designed by Jessie Tait.

c1956   *6.75in (15.5cm) diam*

£80-120   **GGRT**

A Midwinter Pottery 'Savanna' pattern hors d'oeuvres dish, designed by Jessie Tait.

c1956   *6.25in (16cm) diam*

£20-40   **GGRT**

A Midwinter Pottery 'Zambezi' pattern hand-painted coffee set, designed by Jessie Tait, including six cups and saucers.

This pattern was extremely popular and was copied by other factories at the time.

c1956   *coffee pot 7.5in (19cm) high*

£600-700   **GGRT**

A Midwinter Pottery 'Zambezi' pattern hand-painted dish, designed by Jessie Tait.

c1956   *7.25in (18.5cm) diam*

£25-35   **GGRT**

A Midwinter Pottery 'Cuban Fantasy' hors d'oeuvres dish, designed by Jessie Tait.

c1957   *10.25in (26cm) wide*

£100-150   **GGRT**

A Midwinter Pottery 'Flowermist' pattern plate, designed by Jessie Tait.

c1958　　　　　　9.75in (25cm) diam

£70-90　　　　　　**GGRT**

A 1950s Midwinter Pottery 'Cherokee Variant' pattern mug, designed by Jessie Tait.

This pattern is based on 'Cherokee', designed by Jessie Tait in 1957.

4in (10.5cm) high

£60-80　　　　　　**GGRT**

A Midwinter Pottery 'Galaxy' pattern coffee pot, designed by Jessie Tait.

c1960　　　　7in (18cm) high

£120-180　　　　　**GGRT**

A rare 1950s Midwinter pottery 'Elephant' pattern nursery mug, designed by Jessie Tait.

Midwinter nurseryware is hard to find and is much sought-after.

3.5in (9cm) high

£280-320　　　　　**GGRT**

A Midwinter Pottery 'Quite Contrary' pattern vegetable tureen, designed by Jessie Tait.

c1959　　　9.5in (24cm) diam

£65-85　　　　　**GGRT**

A Midwinter Pottery 'Graphic' pattern trio set, designed by Jessie Tait.

c1964 plate 7in (17.5cm) diam

£15-25　　　　　**GGRT**

A Midwinter Fine shape 'Sienna' pattern transfer-printed plate, designed by Jessie Tait.

This was one of the most popular designs from the Fine range, which was launched in 1962.

c1962　　　　8in (20.5cm) diam

£3 5　　　　　**FFM**

A 1960s Midwinter Pottery 'Homespun' pattern plate, designed by Jessie Tait.

9.75in (25cm) diam

£60-80　　　　　**GGRT**

A Midwinter Pottery 'Elstree' pattern small plate, designed by Jessie Tait.

8in (20.5cm) wide

£55-65　　　　　**GGRT**

A Midwinter Pottery 'Nature Study' pattern plate, from the Stylecraft range, designed by Terence Conran.

Conran produced designs for Midwinter between 1955-7 as well as re-designing the factory's showrooms. All of his designs proved popular and are sought-after by collectors today.

c1955   *8.5in (22cm) d.*

£45-55   **GGRT**

A Midwinter Pottery 'Nature Study' plate, from the Stylecraft range, designed by Terence Conran.

c1955   *9.5in (24cm) diam*

£70-90   **GGRT**

A Midwinter pottery 'Saladware' pattern small plate, designed by Terence Conran.

1955   6.75in (15.5cm) diam

£35-45   **GGRT**

A Midwinter pottery 'Saladware' pattern Boomerang dish, designed by Terence Conran.

1955   8.25in (21cm) wide

£55-65   **GGRT**

A CLOSER LOOK AT A MIDWINTER VASE

This vase was intended to serve celery, but also doubled as a flower vase.

Unusual shapes such as this will fetch a premium. Plates are the most common pieces available and tend to be less popular with collectors.

The Salad Ware range was hand-painted making it more desirable than lithographed patterns.

This modern design was aimed at the post-war generation who wanted tableware that reflected their modern way of life and less formal dining arrangements.

A Midwinter Pottery 'Salad Ware' pattern hand-painted celery vase, designed by Terence Conran.

7in (18cm) high

£100-150   **BEV**

A Midwinter Pottery 'Saladware' pattern hand-painted dish, from the Stylecraft range, designed by Terence Conran.

c1955   8.5in (21.5cm) wide

£80-120   **GGRT**

A Midwinter Pottery 'Saladware' pattern hand-painted salt and pepper, from the Stylecraft range, designed by Terence Conran.

c1955   5.75in (14.5cm) high

£120-180   **GGRT**

A Midwinter Pottery 'Saladware' pattern hand-painted salad set, including one large bowl and six smaller bowls from the Stylecraft range, designed by Terence Conran.

c1955   large bowl 9in (23cm) w

£550-650   **GGRT**

A Midwinter Pottery 'Plant Life' pattern plate, designed by Terence Conran.

c1956   *11.75in (30cm) wide*

£100-140   **GGRT**

Three Midwinter Fashion shape 'Transport' pattern transfer-printed dishes or pin trays, designed by Terence Conran, with a bicycle, a train and a ship.

These dishes come from a series of black and white designs, all featuring forms of transport.

c1955   *3.25in (8.5cm) diam*

£20-30 each   **FFM**

A Midwinter Pottery 'Plant Life' pattern small plate, designed by Terence Conran.

c1956   *6.75in (15.5cm) diam*

£50-70   **GGRT**

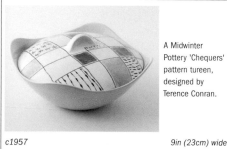

A Midwinter Pottery 'Chequers' pattern charger, designed by Terence Conran.

c1957   *12.25in (31cm) high*

£220-280   **GGRT**

A Midwinter Pottery 'Chequers' pattern cup and saucer, designed by Terence Conran.

c1957   *saucer 6.25in (16cm) diam*

£45-55   **GGRT**

A Midwinter Pottery 'Chequers' pattern tureen, designed by Terence Conran.

c1957   *9in (23cm) wide*

£100-170   **GGRT**

A Midwinter Pottery 'Melody' pattern plate, designed by Terence Conran.

9.75in (24.5cm) diam

£60-80   **GGRT**

A 1950s Midwinter Pottery 'Fishing Boat' pattern plate, designed by Charles Cobelle.

8.75in (22cm) diam

£60-80 GGRT

A 1950s Midwinter Pottery 'Fishing Boat' pattern plate, designed by Charles Cobelle.

9.5in (24cm) wide

£70-90 GGRT

A 1950s Midwinter Pottery 'Fishing Boat' pattern gravy boat, stand and ladle, designed by Charles Cobelle.

boat 9in (23cm) wide

£100-150 GGRT

A Midwinter Pottery 'Riviera' pattern plate, from the Stylecraft range, designed by Hugh Casson.

Casson's inspiration for this pattern came from a holiday in the South of France. Originally issued as part of the Stylecraft range and including a number of different scenes, the pattern was re-issued as 'Cannes' in the Fashion shape in 1960.

c1954

6.25in (16cm) diam

£25-35 GGRT

A Midwinter Pottery 'Cannes' pattern chop plate, designed by Hugh Casson.

These were made for the American market, and are larger in size than the standard domestic issue.

c1960 12.25in (31cm) wide

£100-170 GGRT

A Midwinter Pottery 'Cannes' pattern celery vase, designed by Hugh Casson.

c1960 6.75in (17cm) high

£280-320 GGRT

A Midwinter Pottery 'Cannes' pattern cup and saucer, designed by Hugh Casson.

c1960 saucer 6.25in (16cm) diam

£45-55 GGRT

A Midwinter Pottery 'Marguerite' pattern charger, by an unknown designer.

14in (35.5cm) wide

£65-85 GGRT

COLLECTORS' NOTES

■ William Moorcroft (1872-1945) joined the James MacIntyre & Company pottery at a time when it was actively trying to move away from utilitarian wares to increasingly popular art pottery. His designs, such as Florian ware, became successful and were one of the building blocks of the Art Nouveau style.

■ He used the 'tube lining' technique where the pattern is drawn onto the surface using liquid clay – like icing, before being coloured. Middle and Far Eastern styles influenced many of his patterns, while Classical forms influenced the shapes.

■ Built on the acclaim he had gained at MacIntyre's, he set up on his own with financial backing from Liberty & Co. in 1913. Success followed him. William died in 1945, and his son Walter took over. His exotic floral designs became very popular and a hallmark style for the company.

■ From the 1960s-80, the company did not prosper and in 1984 a controlling stake was sold to the Churchill Group. Production was streamlined, and some patterns were stopped. Sales did not meet the new owners' approval and the pottery was sold to collector Hugh Edwards and dealer Richard Dennis in 1986.

■ Dennis' wife Sally Tuffin injected new life into the pottery until her departure in 1996. She was replaced by Rachel Bishop, who continues to both be inspired by and develop the stylised, naturalistic style for which Moorcroft has become renowned.

■ William's comparatively more complex early floral and foliate designs, such as Florian ware, are desirable. Look for rare patterns including animals such as fish.

■ Collectors look for uncommon shapes, such as rounded cube biscuit barrels, and unusual colourways. Large pieces such as jardinières on stands, those made for Liberty are also sought after. Those incorporating metal parts, sometimes designed by Archibald Knox can fetch high prices.

■ Modern limited editions by Sally Tuffin and Rachel Bishop can also fetch high prices. This section is arranged alphabetically by pattern name.

A Moorcroft 'Anemones' pattern saltglazed shouldered ovoid vase, impressed mark, signed in blue.

9.5in (24cm) high

£750-850   **L&T**

A 1990s Moorcroft 'Anemones' pattern baluster vase, impressed marks, initialled in green.

The 'Anemones' range was redrawn by Walter Moorcroft in 1989 and was released in yellow, green and blue, the first two were withdrawn in 1991.

8.75in (22cm) high

£180-220   **L&T**

c1955   *5.75in (14cm) high*

£180-220   **GORL**

A Walter Moorcroft 'African Lily' bowl and cover, decorated in shades of red and yellow and green against a blue-green ground, impressed marks, restored chips to rim of bowl.

A Moorcroft 'Anna Lily' pattern bowl, designed by Nicola Slaney, of circular shape with tube lined decoration on a cream and cobalt blue ground, printed and painted marks.

c2001   *10.25in (26cm) diam*

£150-200   **CHEF**

A Moorcroft 'Black Tulip' pattern bowl, designed by Sally Tuffin, decorated against a blue-green ground, impressed and painted marks.

1991-2   *6.25in (16cm) high*

£180-220   **GORL**

A Moorcroft 'Buttercup' pattern baluster vase, designed by Sally Tuffin, impressed mark, initialled in green.

c1991   *10.5in (26cm) high*

£320-380   **L&T**

A mid-1990s Moorcroft 'Charles Rennie Mackintosh' pattern ovoid vase, designed by Rachel Bishop, decorated in shades of blue, red and green, impressed and painted marks.

7in (17.5cm) high

£180-220   **GORL**

A Moorcroft 'Claremont' pattern tapering vase, with flared rim, impressed marks, signed in blue.

The toadstool design was introduced in 1903 and received its Claremont title from Liberty. However not all pieces with mushroom decoration are from the 'Claremont' range. Later examples have bold and dark colours.

8.5in (21cm) high

£1,800-2,200   **L&T**

A Moorcroft 'Claremont' pattern circular plate, impressed mark, initialled in blue.

7.5in (18.8cm) diam

£250-350   **L&T**

A Moorcroft 'Blue Finches' pattern shouldered tapering vase, designed by Sally Tuffin, impressed mark, initialled in green.

1988   *10.25in (25.5cm) high*

£200-250   **L&T**

A Moorcroft 'Ochre Finches' pattern shouldered tapering vase, impressed marks, initialled in green.

1989-90   *10in (25cm) high*

£220-280   **L&T**

A 1930S Moorcroft 'Fish' pattern flambé baluster vase, restored rim, impressed marks, signed in blue.

7.25in (18cm) high

£700-800   **L&T**

A Moorcroft 'Flamminian' pattern circular twin-handled bowl, with printed Liberty & Co. mark, impressed signature mark.

The red and green pieces from the Flamminian range were produced for Liberty and are from 1906-13, while the blue examples were made at Cobridge in 1914.

1906-13   *7.5in (19cm) diam*

£250-300   **L&T**

A Moorcroft Florian ware flared vase, printed MacIntyre marks, initialled in green.

8.25in (20.5cm) high

£1,800-2,200   **L&T**

A Moorcroft Florian ware biscuit barrel and cover, with electro-plated mount, decorated with poppies and highlighted with gilt, printed "MacIntyre" mark.

5.25in (13cm) high

£800-1,200   **L&T**

A Moorcroft Florian ware circular bowl, with silver mounts, printed "Florian Ware" mark, initialled in green.

5.5in (14cm) high

£1,200-1,800   **L&T**

A Moorcroft Florian ware vase, of tapering cylindrical form, small restoration to rim, printed MacIntyre mark, signed in green.

6in (15cm) high

£750-850   **L&T**

A Moorcroft 'Hazeldene' pattern ovoid vase, small restoration to rim, printed Liberty & Co. mark, signed in green.

c1914   6.5in (16cm) high

£1,000-1,500   **L&T**

A late 1980s limited edition Moorcroft 'HMS Sirius Bicentenary' ovoid vase, designed by Sally Tuffin, from an edition of 150, decorated in shades of green, brown, cream and light blue, painted and impressed marks.

Made to commemorate the Australian Bicentenary of 1988.

14.5in (37cm) high

£300-400   **GORL**

A Moorcroft 'Hibiscus' pattern vase, of flattened spherical shape, the design against a green ground, probably 1960s.

4in (10cm) high

£120-180   **GORL**

A limited edition Moorcroft 'Jasmine Carousel' bottle vase, No. 1180, decorated overall in shades of brown and green against a green ground, impressed and painted marks.

1997   9in (22.5cm) high

£120-180   **GORL**

A late 1920s/early 1930s Moorcroft 'Leaf and Berry' pattern baluster vase, impressed marks, initialled in blue.

10in (25cm) high

£450-550   **L&T**

A Moorcroft 'Magnolia' pattern vase, of globe and shaft form, the design against a dark blue ground.

c1976   6in (15cm) high

£70-100   **GORL**

A Moorcroft 'Nasturtium' pattern ginger jar and cover, designed by Sally Tuffin, printed Collectors Club mark, initialled in green.

This jar was made exclusively for the Moorcroft Collectors Club.

1992   7.25in (18cm) high

£70-100   **L&T**

A late 1990s limited edition Moorcroft 'New Swallows' ovoid vase, designed by Rachel Bishop, from an edition of 500, with everted rim, decorated in shades of red, green, purple and blue against a pale green ground, painted and impressed marks.

10in (25.5cm) high

£650-750   **GORL**

A Moorcroft 'Oberon' pattern ovoid vase, designed by Rachel Bishop, with everted rim, decorated in shades of pinks, greens and yellows against a pink and blue ground, impressed marks and painted initials.

c1997   *10.75in (27cm) high*

£600-800   **GORL**

A Moorcroft 'Orchid' pattern bowl, painted against a deep blue ground, painted initials mark, cracked.

9in (23cm) diam

£120-180   **GORL**

A late 1990s Moorcroft 'Phoenix' pattern vase, designed by Rachel Bishop, with waisted neck and decorated in shades of blue, green and orange against a brown-green ground, impressed marks, signed.

11.5in (29cm) high

£550-650   **GORL**

A Moorcroft 'Peacock' pattern vase, designed by Sally Tuffin for Liberty, decorated in shades of turquoise, green and brown against a green ground, impressed and painted marks.

1988-90   *8in (20cm) high*

£200-300   **GORL**

A Moorcroft 'Pomegranate' pattern baluster vase, with flared rim, impressed marks, signed in green, restored rim.

1915-30   *9.5in (24cm) high*

£800-1,200   **L&T**

A Moorcroft 'Pomegranate' pattern miniature ovoid vase, impressed mark, initialled in green.

1915-30   *2.5in (6.5cm) high*

£150-250   **L&T**

A Moorcroft 'Pomegranate' pattern miniature ovoid vase, impressed marks.

1915-30   *2.5in (6.5cm) high*

£180-220   **L&T**

A Moorcroft 'Pomegranate' pattern circular bowl, with 'Tudric' beaten pewter foot, stamped mark "Tudric 01306".

1915-30   *7.5in (19cm) diam*

£400-500   **L&T**

A Moorcroft 'Poppies' pattern flambé shouldered tapering vase, restored rim, impressed mark, signed in blue.

8.5in (21cm) high

£550-650   **L&T**

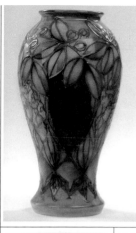

An early 1990s Moorcroft 'Rain Forest' baluster vase, designed by Sally Tuffin, decorated with various tropical flowers in shades of yellow, green and red against a green ground, impressed marks and painted initials.

12.25in (30.5cm) high

£500-700   **GORL**

A Moorcroft 'Robin' pattern baluster vase.

1991-92

£70-100   **L&T**

A late 1990s Moorcroft 'Rockpool' pattern squat vase, designed by Wendy Mason, from a numbered edition, decorated in various coloured shades against a blue-green ground, impressed marks and painted "Wendy Mason" signature.

6.5in (16cm) high

£250-350   **GORL**

A large Moorcroft 'Spring' pattern shouldered cylindrical vase, impressed marks, initialled in blue.

11.5in (28.5cm) high

£850-950   **L&T**

A 1930s Moorcroft 'Waving Corn' pattern ovoid vase, impressed signature mark and bearing initials.

6.5in (16cm) high

£350-450   **L&T**

A large 1920s Moorcroft 'Wisteria' pattern jardinière, of deep tapering cylindrical form, decorated with tube lined and painted decoration, restored chip to rim, initialled in green, impressed marks.

16.75in (42cm) diam

£1,000-1,500   **L&T**

A 1980s Moorcroft bottle vase, painted with a mauve plant and green leaves against a cream ground, impressed marks.

6in (15cm) high

£70-100   **GORL**

A 1930s Moorcroft orange lustre vase.

7.25in (18.5cm) high

£100-150   **CHEF**

A 1930s William Moorcroft teapot, of circular shape decorated in shades of yellow and red with freesias on a mottled green ground, impressed marks.

c1935   6in (15cm) high

£150-200   **CHEF**

FIND OUT MORE...

'Moorcroft, A Guide to Moorcroft Pottery 1897-1993', by Paul Atterbury, published by Richard Dennis & Hugh Edwards, 1998.

www.moorcroft.co.uk - official company website.

A Keith Murray for Wedgwood moonstone bulbous ribbed vase, with late Etruria "KM" mark.

c1940   7in (18cm) high

£300-400   **PSA**

A Keith Murray for Wedgwood moonstone small hooped bulbous vase, with "KM" mark.

c1935   6.75in (17cm) high

£180-220   **PSA**

A Keith Murray for Wedgwood moonstone vase, decorated with horizontal bands of two widths.

6.5in (16.5cm) h

£650-750   **BEV**

A Keith Murray for Wedgwood moonstone ridged vase.

Murray was born in 1892 and trained as an architect. He was approached by Wedgwood in 1932. His training is clear in his simple, stylish designs, which typify the Art Deco style. His first design was released in 1933 and his work was produced until the late 1960s.

6in (15cm) high

£250-350   **BEV**

A Keith Murray for Wedgwood moonstone stepped bowl.

8in (20cm) diam

£650-750   **BEV**

A Keith Murray for Wedgwood large white bowl, with a wide rim.

7.5in (19cm) high

£350-450   **BEV**

A Keith Murray for Wedgwood moonstone hooped cake stand, with signature mark.

c1933   9in (23cm) diam

£60-80   **PSA**

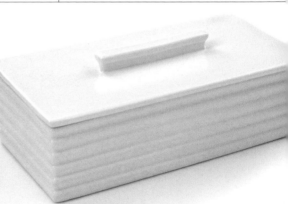

A Keith Murray for Wedgwood moonstone rectangular cigarette box and cover, with signature mark.

Around 1934, Wedgwood introduced a less expensive line of smaller objects, such as this cigarette box (model No. 3871) and an inkstand. They were formed from less expensive and faster to produce slipware. Condition is very important as lids are often chipped or missing.

c1932   7.5in (19cm) long

£220-280   **PSA**

A Keith Murray for Wedgwood dark green large tapered ribbed vase, with signature mark.

c1933   11.5in (29cm) high

£250-350   **PSA**

A Keith Murray for Wedgwood matte green vase, the sides decorated with horizontal lines.

11in (28cm) high

£750-950   **BAD**

A Keith Murray for Wedgwood matte green ribbed tapered vase, with "KM" mark.

c1935   7.5in (19cm) high

£120-180   **PSA**

A Keith Murray for Wedgwood matte green ribbed vase, with signature mark.

c1933   6in (15cm) high

£220-280   **PSA**

A Keith Murray for Wedgwood matte green bulbous ribbed vase, with signature mark.

c1933   9.5in (24cm) high

£250-350   **PSA**

A Keith Murray for Wedgwood matte green vase, with an ovoid body, decorated with horizontal lines.

6.75in (17cm) high

£300-400   **BEV**

A Keith Murray for Wedgwood dark green pedestal ribbed bowl.

10.25in (26cm) diam

£100-150   **PSA**

A Keith Murray for Wedgwood dark green scalloped fruit bowl, with signature mark.

c1933   8.75in (22.5cm) diam

£80-120   **PSA**

A Keith Murray for Wedgwood matte green beer mug, model number 3971.

c1935   8in (20cm) diam

£60-80   **BEV**

A Keith Murray for Wedgwood celadon and cream-glazed footed bowl, with "KM" mark.

c1935   11in (28cm) diam

£280-320   **PSA**

A Keith Murray for Wedgwood matte straw vase, with regular line decoration.

7.5in (19cm) high

£450-550   **BEV**

A Keith Murray for Wedgwood matte straw vase, with an ovoid body and ridged decoration, printed marks and facsimile signature.

9in (23cm) high

£550-650   **BEV**

A Keith Murray for Wedgwood straw water jug, with signature mark.

c1933   8in (20cm) high

£450-550   **PSA**

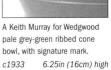

A Keith Murray for Wedgwood light blue ribbed tapered vase, with "KM" mark.

c1935   7.5in (19cm) high

£150-200   **PSA**

A Keith Murray for Wedgwood blue footed bowl, with hooped foot and rim and "KM" mark.

c1935   10in (25.5cm) diam

£280-320   **PSA**

A Keith Murray for Wedgwood grey vase, with a fluted body and a wide rim.

7.25in (18.5cm) high

£450-550   **BEV**

A Keith Murray for Wedgwood pale grey-green ribbed cone bowl, with signature mark.

c1933   6.25in (16cm) high

£450-550   **PSA**

A Keith Murray for Wedgwood black basalt bowl, with signature mark.

Black Basalt pieces are scarcer than other colours and tend to fetch higher prices. They are always signed with a red signature on the base. The technique for the black body was perfected by Josiah Wedgwood in the late 1760s.

c1935   9in (23cm) diam

£250-350   **PSA**

A rare Keith Murray for Wedgwood commemorative beer mug, the printed puce decoration by Victor Skellern, made to commemorate the opening of a new electrically fired tunnel oven at Barlaston and from the first firing Biscuit & Glost, Summer 1940.

4.75in (12cm) high

£250-350   **DN**

A set of four Keith Murray for Wedgwood moonstone egg cups, with ribbing to foot, two with minor chips.

£200-250   **PSA**

COLLECTORS' NOTES

- Popular during the 1920s and 1930s, wind-up musical mechanisms were fitted to a range of objects. Makers included Royal Winton (known primarily for their chintz pattern ceramics), Fielding's Crown Devon and Carlton Ware. Jugs and tankards were among the most popular forms, but cigarette boxes can also be found, as can decorative vases.

- Scenes are often pastoral in theme, ranging from fairs to scenes of people near cottages, or country personalities. Mechanisms should work for a piece to fetch the highest value. Some mechanisms are replaced and this also has a bearing on values. The condition of the piece itself is also important – wear or damage such as crazing or chips will reduce value.

- Also look for well-decorated or detailed scenes, and notable makers. Musical tunes will often echo the scene on the jug such as 'Daisy Daisy' with a 'Daisy Bell' cycling jug by Crown Devon. Detailed handles will also usually add to desirability, particularly if shaped or very decorative. Certain characters and themes are also popular and be aware that pieces that have a cross-market interest may fetch higher values.

A Royal Winton 'Underneath the Spreading Chestnut Tree' musical tankard, working order, some crazing.
6.25in (16cm) high
£70-100 PSA

A Royal Winton 'Annie Laurie' musical tankard, working order.
6.25in (16cm) high
£100-150 PSA

A Royal Winton 'The Floral Dance' musical tankard, working order, some crazing.
6.25in (16cm) high
£70-100 PSA

A Royal Winton 'Come to the Fair' musical tankard, working order, some crazing.
6in (15cm) high
£35-45 PSA

A Fielding's Crown Devon 'Daisy Bell' musical water jug, working order, some crazing.
8in (20cm) high
£150-200 PSA

A Royal Winton musical tankard, with the handle as a tinker looking over the rim.
8in (20cm) high
£80-120 PSA

A Fielding's Crown Devon 'Widdecombe Fair' musical water jug, working order, some crazing.
7.5in (19cm) high
£100-150 PSA

A Fielding's Crown Devon 'Roamin' in the Gloamin' musical water jug, working order, some crazing.
8in (20cm) high
£200-250 PSA

A Fielding's Crown Devon 'John Peel' musical tankard, working order, minor roughness to lip and some crazing.

4.75in (12cm) high

£60-80   **PSA**

A Crown Devon 'Auld Lang Syne' musical tankard, working order.

4.5in (11.5cm) high

£100-150   **PSA**

A Crown Devon 'Daisy Bell' musical tankard, working order.

6.25in (16cm) high

£70-100   **PSA**

A Carlton Ware 'John Peel' musical tankard, working order.

5.25in (13.5cm) high

£25-35   **PSA**

A musical tankard, with a 'John Peel' hunting scene, working order, some crazing.

5in (12.5cm) high

£35-45   **PSA**

A 'Come Landlord Fill the Flowing Bowl' musical tankard, working order, some crazing.

6in (15cm) high

£70-100   **PSA**

A Fielding's Crown Devon musical cigarette box, with a hunting scene, working order, minor chip to underside of lid and some crazing.

This box has much cross market appeal, being of interest to collectors of smoking memorabilia and musical ceramics, as well as sporting and hunting collectors. It also has a finely detailed and realistic scene with gilt highlights.

c1930   *2.75in (7cm) high*

£600-700   **PSA**

A Fielding's Crown Devon 'John Peel' musical footed fruit bowl, in working order, some crazing.

This example, although in a comparatively complex form, has been fitted with a new movement.

9in (23cm) high

£300-400   **PSA**

A Fielding's Crown Devon musical cigar box, working order, some crazing.

£70-100   **PSA**

A Pendelfin 'Bellman' figure, membership piece designed by Jean Walmsley Heap.

Jean Walmsley Heap and Jeannie Todd started Pendelfin in 1953 in Burnley, Lancashire. Rabbits are the most common figures, but mice, pixies, ducks and witches were also made and tend to be sought-after. Production still continues today and due to the large number of models produced, condition has a huge impact on value for all but the rarest examples.

1995-96

4in (10cm) high

£35-45 PSA

A Pendelfin 'Buttons' figure, membership piece designed by Doreen Noel Roberts.

1994 3.5in (9cm) high

£30-40 PSA

A Pendelfin 'Gussie Rabbit' figure, dressed in blue, designed by Jean Walmsley Heap.

1960-68 3.5in (9cm) high

£100-150 PSA

A Pendelfin 'Megan The Harp Rabbit' figure, dressed in pink, designed by Joan Walmsley Heap.

1960-67 3.5in (9cm) high

£50-80 PSA

A CLOSER LOOK AT A PENDELFIN FIGURE

The 'Father Rabbit' figure, issued in 1955, was one of the first designed and originally wore dungarees.

The figure was available in a number of colours with different patterned ties

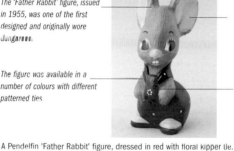

The earlier version of this figure was very top heavy and tended to fall over, damaging the ears, so it was redesigned.

This kipper tie-wearing example replaced the earlier design in 1970 and is worth about half the value of the earlier models.

A Pendelfin 'Father Rabbit' figure, dressed in red with floral kipper tie.

c1970 8in (20cm) high

PSA

A Pendelfin 'Puffer' figure, Family Circle piece designed by Jean Walmsley Heap.

Model of the Year 1994.

4.5in (11.5cm) high

£40-60 PSA

A Pendelfin 'Squeezy Rabbit' figure, dressed in red, designed by Jean Walmsley Heap, minor wear.

1960-70 3.5in (9cm) high

£70-100 PSA

An early Pendelfin 'Tammy Dog' figure, with green eyes, designed by Jean Walmsley Heap.

1957-87 3.5in (9cm) high

£60-80 PSA

A Pendelfin Metallion 'Elf Tree' candle holder, designed by Doreen Noel Roberts.

1980-85 3in (7.5cm) high

£120-180 PSA

FIND OUT MORE...

'Pendelfin Collector's Handbook', by Stella Ashbrook, published by Francis Joseph, May 2004.

COLLECTORS' NOTES

■ The Carter & Co. Pottery was started by Jesse Carter in Poole, Dorset in 1873 and produced mainly tiles and architectural products.

■ In 1921, the company formed a subsidiary with designers Harold Stabler and John Adams, called Carter, Stabler and Adams, with the intention of producing decorative wares.

■ John Adams' wife, Truda (later Carter), had a background in embroidery design and became a leading designer at the pottery. She produced a range of designs with Art Deco styled floral, foliate and geometric motifs using bright colours against a white ground. These hand-painted pieces proved extremely popular and the company gained two gold medals at the 1925 Paris Exhibition.

■ After WWII, Ruth Pavely became head of the painting department where traditional designs continued to be made. In an effort to recover from WWII, the pottery employed lamp designer Alfred Burgess Read, who, with senior thrower Guy Sydenham, created the 'Contemporary' range of hand-thrown and hand-painted free-form pieces.

■ Read resigned in 1957 and was replaced by Robert Jefferson in 1958, who designed the 'Delphis' range of studio ware. The 1960s public approved of the pieces' bright colours and individual styling and the 'Aegean' range was added in 1970. It is often difficult to tell which range a piece came from, but the 'Delphis' pieces generally have a finer texture than 'Aegean'.

■ Collectors should look for pieces that exemplify their period, examples by Truda Adams and Ruth Pavely are always popular. As 1930s wares are becoming increasingly rare, pieces from the 1950s and later are gaining more attention.

A small Poole Pottery hand-painted bowl, painted by Phyllis Ryal (1928-37), date code "21".

1925-34   *4.5in (11.5cm) diam*

£50-70   **BEV**

A 1930s small Poole Pottery hand-painted vase, the base indistinctly painted "/EN [G]" and inscribed "968".

4in (10cm) high

£70-100   **BAD**

A 1930s Poole Pottery hand-painted 'Comic Bird' pattern vase.

10.25in (26cm) high

£400-500   **ADE**

A Poole Pottery hand-painted 'Blue Bird' pattern vase.

1934-7   *5.5in (14cm) high*

£70-100   **BEV**

A Poole Pottery red earthenware dish, designed by Truda Carter and painted by Mary Brown, in unusual colours, impressed "Carter Stabler & Adams" mark, painter's mark and "662/BK".

12in (30.5cm) diam

£350-450   **DN**

A Poole Pottery oviform vase, designed by Truda Carter and painted by Marian Heath (De'Ath), impressed "Poole England", marked "596/KD?".

9.25in (23.5cm) high

£220-280   **DN**

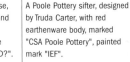

A Poole Pottery sifter, designed by Truda Carter, with red earthenware body, marked "CSA Poole Pottery", painted mark "IEF".

1924-34   *4.75in (12cm) high*

£70-100   **CHS**

A Poole Pottery 'Sugar for the Birds' plate, designed by Olive Bourne and painted by Betty Gooby, with the head of a young woman amid flowers and foliage, marked "Poole England" with a dolphin mark and painter's mark.

10in (25.5cm) diam

£220-280   **DN**

A Poole Pottery white earthenware tray, moulded and pierced in the centre with a bird in flight amid highly stylized flowers and foliage, impressed "Poole England".

12.25in (31cm) wide

£60-80   **DN**

A 1930s Poole Pottery Sylvanware vase.

£150-200   **ADE**

A pair of Poole Pottery 'Elephant' bookends, designed by Harold Brownsword, covered with a 'café-au-lait' glaze, Impressed "Carter Stabler and Adams" mark and hexagonal "trial" mark.

Similar bookends were shown in the exhibition of Industrial and Decorative Art, Monza, Italy, 1930.

6in (15.5cm) high

£400-500   **DN**

A pair of Poole Vases, the waisted cylindrical shapes painted in smoky grey and pink with alternating vertical vines of pink fruits, impressed marks and "E/PH".

c1950   *11in (28cm) high*

£300-500   **CHEF**

A Poole Pottery 'Contemporary' style vase.

1952-55   *10.5in (27cm) high*

£140-160   **ADE**

A Poole Pottery 'Contemporary' style vase.

1952-55   *7.75in (19.5cm) high*

£140-160   **ADE**

A Poole Pottery 'Spiral Leaf' pattern 'Contemporary' style vase, designed by Alfred B. Read.

1952-55   *9.75in (25cm) high*

£250-350   **ADE**

A Poole Pottery 'Contemporary' style vase, designed by Alfred B. Read.

1952-55   *10in (25.2cm) high*

£300-400   **ADE**

CERAMICS

A Poole Pottery 'Freeform' style bowl, decoration designed by Ruth Pavely.

1955-59   *7.25in (18.5cm) high*

£110-130   **ADE**

A Poole Pottery 'Freeform' style vase.

1955-59   *7.5in (18.5cm) high*

£220-250   **ADE**

A Poole Pottery 'Freeform' style vase.

1955-59   *12.25in (31cm) wide*

£250-325   **ADE**

A 1970s Poole Pottery 'Aegean' plate, chip to rim, reglued.

10.25in (26cm) diam

£15-20   **GAZE**

A 1970s Poole Pottery 'Aegean' plate.

8in (20.5cm) diam

£60-70   **ADE**

A 1970s Poole Pottery 'Aegean' plate.

10.5in (26.5cm) diam

£80-90   **ADE**

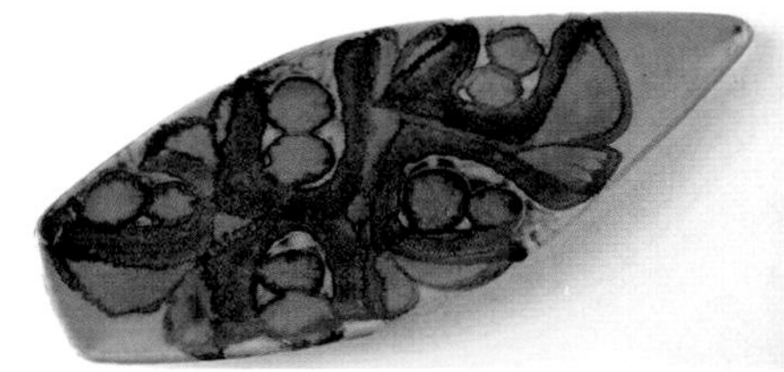

A 1960s Poole Pottery 'Delphis' spear-shaped dish, in yellow, greens and brown glazes.

10.25in (26cm) diam

£70-100   **GAZE**

A Poole Pottery stoneware charger, designed by Guy Sydenham, decorated in slip with a central boss of concentric circles surrounded by a similar band, impressed mark.

13.5in (34cm) high

£200-300   **DN**

A 1970s Poole Pottery charger, marked "Poole Pottery" and "54".

16in (40.5cm) diam

£180-220   L

A 1970s Poole Pottery vase, marked "Poole England" and "83" with a dolphin.

6.25in (16cm) high

£50-70   L

A 1970s Poole Pottery tall vase, impressed "Poole Pottery" and "93?".

12in (30.5cm) high

£80-120   L

A 1970s Poole Pottery vase, marked "Poole England" and "79" with a dolphin.

5.25in (13.5cm) high

£40-60   L

A 1970s Poole Pottery tall vase, with printed and painted marks.

15.75in (40cm) high

£250-300   CHS

A 1970s Poole Pottery 'Atlantis' hand-thrown vase, decorated by Beatrice Bolton.

7in (18cm) high

£350-450   ADE

A 1970s Poole Pottery dish, with printed marks, boxed.

6.5in (16.5cm) wide

£30-40   CHS

A 1970s Poole Pottery dish, with printed marks, boxed.

7in (18cm) wide

£18-25   CHS

A 1970s Poole Pottery 'Atlantis' hand-thrown vase, by Jennie Haigh.

8in (20.3cm) high

£250-300   **ADE**

A 1970s Poole Pottery 'Atlantis' vase, 'A20'5', by Catherine Connett, impressed mark.

8in (20.5cm) high

£180-220   **WW**

A Poole Pottery vase, by Guy Sydenham, impressed marks.

6.75in (17cm) high

£250-350   **WW**

A small Poole table lamp base, with glass shade.

11.75in (30cm) high

£18-22   **GAZE**

A Poole Pottery tankard.

4.5in (11.5cm) high

£35-45   **CHS**

A Poole Pottery square dish, with "medieval" scene, printed marks.

7in (18cm) wide

£18-22   **CHS**

A late 1970s Poole Pottery candlestick, from the Aubrey Beardsley collection, designed by Sue Pottinger.

5in (12.5cm) high

£20-25   **CHS**

A Poole Pottery teapot, cup and saucer, with coffee bean decoration, printed marks.

Teapot 5.5in (14cm) high

£45-55   **CHS**

Poole
England
436 Scene VI

A Poole Pottery display plate, printed mark "436 Scene VI".

6in (15cm) wide

£8-12   **CHS**

FIND OUT MORE...

'Poole Pottery', *by Leslie Hayward and Paul Atterbury, published by Richard Dennis Publishing, 1999.*

'Collecting Poole Pottery', *by Robert Prescott-Walker, published by Kevin Francis Publishing, 2001.*

www.poolepottery.co.uk - *official company website.*

COLLECTORS' NOTES

- Susan Williams-Ellis is the daughter of Sir Clough Williams-Ellis, creator of the famous Portmeirion village in North Wales. Susan took over the souvenir shop in the village in 1953. She designed patterns for ceramics, which were applied to blank bodies by the famous Gray's Pottery of Stoke-on-Trent.

- In 1960 she and her husband bought Gray's, and later acquired Kirkhams Pottery in 1961. This enabled her to create shapes as well as decorate them. Portmeirion is best known for the floral and foliate 'Botanic Garden' range of the 1970s onwards, however the 1960s ranges now have a growing base of collectors.

- Patterns were moulded, such as the innovative 'Totem' design, and transfer printed, with printed designs often showing Susan's background in textile design. Inspirations were numerous, including personal memories. Forms tend to be clean lined and cylindrical, reflecting 1960s ceramic design and allowing transfers to be applied and displayed easily and fully

- Pattern, colour and condition are the main indicators of value. Early patterns and those produced for short periods such as 'Moss Agate' are sought after and valuable. Some patterns are also more desirable than others, and different colourways can attract different prices. Condition is important, with wear and damage reducing value considerably.

A Portmeirion Pottery 'Talisman' pattern medium storage jar, designed by Susan Williams-Ellis, in yellow and orange.

c1962   *6in (15.5cm) high*

£50-70   **GGRT**

A Portmeirion Pottery 'Talisman' pattern large storage jar, designed by Susan Williams-Ellis, in blue and green.

c1962

8in (20cm) high

£80-120   **GGRT**

A Portmeirion Pottery 'Talisman' pattern medium storage jar, designed by Susan Williams-Ellis, in blue and plum.

c1962   *8in (20cm) high*

£60-90   **GGRT**

A Portmeirion Pottery 'Jupiter' pattern 'Serif' shape petrol blue coffee pot, designed by Susan Williams-Ellis, printed marks.

The petrol blue colourway is hard to find in good condition, as the colour faded when washed.

12.5in (32cm) high

£50-80   **CHS**

A Portmeirion Pottery 'Phoenix' pattern coffee pot.

Unlike most Portmeirion, this pattern was not designed by Williams-Ellis, but her assistant John Cuffley. A large pattern, it works best on coffee pots.

13in (33cm) high

£15-30   **CHS**

A Portmeirion 'Phoenix' pattern milk jug and sugar bowl.

4in (10cm) high

£6-10   **GAZE**

A Portmeirion 'Tivoli' pattern milk jug.

The Tivoli pattern was inspired by Copenhagen's Tivoli Gardens.

c1964   *5.75in (14.5cm) high*

£50-60   **ADE**

Two Portmeirion 'Velocipedes' range pieces.

jug 4in (10cm) high

£10-20   **GAZE**

A Grays pottery for Portmeirion 'Moss Agate' pattern jar, designed by Susan Williams-Ellis.

'Moss Agate' was an early design, dating back to the early 1960s. It is extremely desirable today as it was hard and expensive to produce. It was made in limited quantities. Made to resemble the stone moss agate, each gilt disc has a cameo-like shadow pattern, clearly seen here.

3.75in (9.5cm) high

£300-400   **GGRT**

A Portmeirion 'Dolphin' pattern tea storage jar, designed by Susan Williams-Ellis, printed marks.

3.5in (9cm) high

£30-50   **CHS**

A Portmeirion 'Dolphin' pattern tea storage jar, designed by Susan Williams-Ellis, printed marks.

4in (10cm) high

£30-40   **CHS**

A Portmeirion 'Dolphin' pattern sugar sifter, designed by Susan Williams-Ellis, printed marks.

5.25in (13.5cm) high

£80-100   **CHS**

A Portmeirion 'Dolphin' pattern tea storage jar, designed by Susan Williams-Ellis, printed marks.

Designed in 1958, this is one of the earliest patterns and was produced by Gray's. It is an increasingly sought-after pattern due to its early date.

6.5in (16.5cm) wide

£100-150   **CHS**

A Portmeirion 'Greek Key' pattern 'Cylinder' shape mug, designed by Susan Williams-Ellis, printed marks.

A black 'Greek Key' pattern on any colour base is an early design. After 1968, a gold pattern, usually on a black body, was introduced.

5in (12.5cm) high

£15-20   **CHS**

A Portmeirion 'Greek Key' pattern 'Cylinder' shape spice jar, handled, designed by Susan Williams-Ellis, printed marks.

3.75in (9.5cm) high

£12-18   **CH**

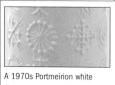

A 1970s Portmeirion white 'Totem' pattern sifter.

6.5in (16.5cm) high

£20-40   **CHS**

A Portmeirion casserole dish, marked "Portmeirion Pottery 1 Made in England".

10.25in (26cm) wide

£30-50   **CHS**

A Portmeirion 'Tiger Lily' pattern bowl, designed by Susan Williams-Ellis, with printed marks.

This pattern was designed in 1961 and based on Williams-Ellis' love for painted barge ware.

11in (28cm) diam

£100-150   **CHS**

COLLECTORS' NOTES

■ The Royal Copenhagen Porcelain Manufactory was founded by Franz Heinrich Müller in Copenhagen in 1775. It gained royal patronage in 1779 after running into such severe financial problems that the King of Denmark, Frederick V, had to step in to save the company. Pieces are marked with three wavy lines symbolising the seas isolating the country.

■ It was known primarily for its fine porcelain, often inspired by Meissen. But from 1885-1916, Danish architect and painter Arnold Krog revived the factory's fortunes with under-glaze designs based on the popular Art Nouveau style, as well as Japanese designs. Look closely at backstamps - a bar above or below a letter in the names 'Royal Copenhagen' or 'Denmark' will identify the year it was made.

■ During the 1950s and 1960s the factory produced a range of stoneware and porcelain 'art ware' designed by a series of notable designers, including Nils Thorsson and Axel Salto. These were often designed in 'modern' styles, which reflected both the fashions of the period and the Scandinavian ceramic tradition.

■ They were hand-painted with designs that showed the Scandinavian obsession with nature and the environment, a source of inspiration that was also reflected in period glass design. Pieces can often be dated to a period by noting the painter's number or initials and referring to a reference work. An 'X' implies that it was painted by the person whose initials also appear. Look for the work of notable designers and at larger pieces with hand-painted designs. Blue, often seen in the Marselis range, is a popular colour.

A 1970s Danish Royal Copenhagen 'Baca' vase, designed by Nils Thorsson.

4.75in (12cm) high

£35-45   **RWA**

A 1960s Danish Royal Copenhagen 'Baca' vase, by Nils Thorsson.

7.5in (19cm) high

£50-60   **RWA**

A 1970s Danish Royal Copenhagen 'Baca' vase, by Joanne Gerber.

9in (23cm) high

£80-120   **RWA**

A Danish Royal Copenhagen 'Tenera' vase, by Grete Helland-Hansen, with fruit design.

c1969-74   7.5in (19cm) high

£80-120   **RWA**

A 1970s Danish Royal Copenhagen 'Tenera' vase, by Bert Jessen.

7.5in (19cm) high

£80-120   **RWA**

A Danish Royal Copenhagen 'Baca' kiln-shaped vase, by Nils Thorsson, with Aluminia backstamp.

The Aluminia factory was purchased by Royal Copenhagen in 1882. The name continued to appear as a backstamp until 1969.

c1966   8in (20cm) high

£100-120   **RWA**

A 1960s Danish Royal Copenhagen stoneware vase, designed by Jørgen Morgensen, in Sung glaze, with abstract design.

9.5in (24cm) high

£150-180   **RWA**

A 1970s Danish Royal Copenhagen 'Tenera' cigarette box, by Marianne Johnson, with stylized design.	A 1970s Danish Royal Copenhagen vase, by Ellen Malmer, with abstract design.	A Danish Royal Copenhagen vase, by Ellen Malmer, with brown heart-shaped design.	A 1950s Royal Copenhagen fine porcelain vase, with geometric decoration, printed marks to underside.

4.25in (11cm) high — *6.5in (17cm) high* — *1969-74   3.25in (8cm) high* — *5.75in (14.5cm) high*

£40-60   **RWA** | **£80-120**   **RWA** | **£30-35**   **RWA** | **£80-100**   **MHT**

A Danish Royal Copenhagen 'Marselis' vase, by Nils Thorsson, with green glaze and Aluminia backstamp.

c1960   4.25in (11cm) h

£80-100   **RWA**

A Danish Royal Copenhagen 'Marselis' vase, designed by Nils Thorsson, in blue glaze, with diamond pattern.

This vase displays rich and deep Scandinavian blues. It has an excellent detailed pattern and an attractive and classic form based on Oriental shapes while still appearing 'modern' in a particularly Scandinavian style.

c1969

£120-140   **RWA**

A Danish Royal Copenhagen 'Marselis' vase, by Nils Thorsson, with blue glaze with Aluminia backstamp.	A Danish Royal Copenhagen 'Marselis' gourd-shaped vase, designed by Nils Thorsson, with blue striped glaze and Aluminia backstamp.

c1960   5.5in (14cm) high — *5in (13cm) high*

£80-120   **RWA** | **£100-120**   **RWA**

A Danish Royal Copenhagen tall porcelain vase, painted with a white cattleya orchid on a shaded grey ground, stamped "ROYAL COPENHAGEN/Denmark/XL9".

12.5in (30.5cm) high

£450-550   **DRA**

A CLOSER LOOK AT A ROYAL COPENHAGEN POT

This pot was designed by sculptor Bode Willumsen, (1895-1987) who worked for Royal Copenhagen between 1925 and 1930 and again from 1940-47.

The pot is decorated in the Sung glaze, Royal Copenhagen's most typical and common stoneware glaze. This is a relatively large example in good condition.

Due to the way the glaze changes when painted on and fired, the mottling and streaking on each piece differs, making each piece effectively unique.

The form is complex and is Oriental in inspiration. It also highlights the 'handmade' and 'studio' aspects of Royal Copenhagen stoneware.

A 1960s Danish Royal Copenhagen pot, designed by Bode Willumsen, in Sung glaze, with figural lid and relief design.

8in (20cm) high

£160-180   **RWA**

A 1960s Danish Royal Copenhagen 'Tenera' bowl, by Marianne Johnson.

4.25in (11cm) diam

£40-50   **RWA**

A unique Royal Copenhagen studio pottery bowl, the flared stoneware vessel covered with a black and streaked milky blue phosphatic glaze which pools on the underside near the turned foot-rim, with a painted wave mark and "Denmark" on base.

7.75in (19.5cm) diam

£150-200   **DN**

A 1970s Danish Royal Copenhagen hand-painted bowl, by Nils Thorsson, with underwater fish design.

6.75in (17cm) diam

£80-120   **RWA**

A 1960s Danish Royal Copenhagen 'Baca' dish, by Nils Thorsson, abstract design.

6.75in (17cm) wide

£40-50   **RWA**

A 1960s Danish Royal Copenhagen 'Tenera' trinket pot, by Kari Christensen.

4in (10cm) high

£30-50   **RWA**

A 1960s Danish Royal Copenhagen 'Baca' egg vase, by Nils Thorsson.

3in (7.5cm) high

£55-65   **RWA**

A pair of Royal Copenhagen porcelain mounted cufflinks, each of circular form inset with gilt squares and silver beaded decoration, with painted marks.

1.25in (3cm) diam

£60-80   **L&T**

A Royal Copenhagen stoneware model of a bear, glazed with Sung glaze, modelled by Knud Kyhn.

A Royal Copenhagen stoneware model of a bear, by Knud Kyhn.

4in (10cm) high

£30-40　　　　**LOB**

A Royal Copenhagen stoneware model of a bear, by Knud Kyhn.

4in (10cm) high

£30-40　　　　**LOB**

Knud Kyhn (1880-1969) is considered one of the most prolific and accomplished modellers in stoneware at Royal Copenhagen. He also worked for Bing and Grøndahl. His observations of animals in zoological gardens as well as natural environments, such as Greenland, can clearly be seen in his understanding of their poses and expressions.

7in (18cm) long

£100-150　　　　**LOB**

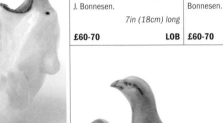

A Royal Copenhagen porcelain model of a polar bear, by Carl J. Bonnesen.

7in (18cm) long

£60-70　　　　**LOB**

A Royal Copenhagen porcelain model of a polar bear playing, number 321, by Carl J. Bonnesen.

5.5in (14cm) long

£60-70　　　　**LOB**

A Royal Copenhagen porcelain model of polar bear cubs playing, number 1107, by Knud Kyhn.

9.5in (24cm) high

£80-120　　　　**LOB**

A Royal Copenhagen porcelain model of a cock, number 1126, designed by Chr. Thomsen.

4.75in (12cm) long

£70-100　　**LOB**

A Royal Copenhagen porcelain model of a pheasant, number 862, designed by Jais Nielsen.

Jais Nielsen worked at Royal Copenhagen from 1920 until his death in 1961. He trained under Patrick Nordstrom and is known for his religious models. This complex and well-painted model is also a sought-after example of his work.

6.75in (17cm) high

£220-280　　　　**LOB**

A Royal Copenhagen porcelain model of a kingfisher, number 1769, designed by Peter Herold.

4.25in (11cm) high

£100-150 **LOB**

A Royal Copenhagen 'Penguins Pair' porcelain model, number 1190, designed by Anna Trap.

4in (10cm) high

£70-90 **LOB**

A Royal Copenhagen figure of a sparrow, number 1081.

3.25in (8cm) high

£18-22 **CLV**

A Royal Copenhagen porcelain model of a dachshund, number 1408, by Olaf Mathiensen.

c1969 *4.25in (11cm) long*

£70-100 **LOB**

A Royal Copenhagen porcelain model of a dachshund, number 1407, designed by Olaf Mathiensen.

4.25in (11cm) long

£70-100 **LOB**

A Royal Copenhagen 'Setter with Pheasant' porcelain model, number 1533, designed by Knud Moller.

c1968 *3.25in (8cm) long*

£70-100 **LOB**

A Royal Copenhagen stoneware model of a deer.

4in (10cm) high

£30-40 **LOB**

A 1990s Royal Copenhagen porcelain figure of a kid.

4in (10cm) high

£35-45 **CLV**

A Royal Copenhagen 'Mouse on Corn Cob' porcelain model, number 512, designed by Svend Jespersen.

5.5in (14cm) long

£50-70 **LOB**

A Royal Copenhagen porcelain dish with a lobster, number 3277.

6.25in (16cm) diam

£70-100 **LOB**

A Royal Copenhagen 'Vanity' porcelain model, number 2318, designed by Svend Jespersen.

5.5in (14cm) high

£70-100 LOB

A Royal Copenhagen 'Girl with Cat' porcelain model, number 4631, designed by John Calster.

6in (15cm) high

£100-170 LOB

A Royal Copenhagen porcelain model of children with a dog, number 707, designed by Chris Thomsen.

c1986 *6in (15cm) high*

£250-300 LOB

A 1990s Royal Copenhagen 'The Little Mermaid' porcelain model, number 4431, designed by Edvard Eriksen.

The original famous 'Little Mermaid' bronze sculpture found in Copenhagen's harbour was designed by Eriksen and was erected in August 1913. She was sponsored by brewer Carl Jacobsen, owner of the Carlsberg brewery.

8.75in (22cm) high

£350-450 LOB

A Royal Copenhagen porcelain figure of a girl with a goose, number 528.

7.25in (18.5cm) high

£45-55 CLV

A Royal Copenhagen 'Boy Cutting Stick' porcelain model, designed by Chris Thomsen.

c1969 *7.5in (19cm) high*

£100-150 LOB

A Royal Copenhagen porcelain model of a boy with a calf, No. 772.

c1975 *6.75in (17cm) high*

£150-200 LOB

A Royal Copenhagen 'Boy Naked on a Tray' porcelain model, number 1660.

8.75in (22cm) diam

£80-120 LOB

A Royal Copenhagen porcelain group, designed by Christian Thomsen, marked "Royal Copenhagen" and "1012 498".

5in (13cm) high

£120-180 DN

A Royal Copenhagen 'Mermaid in Water' porcelain figure, factory marks and numbered "1212".

7.75in (19.5cm) long

£120-180 DN

A Royal Crown Derby 'Owl' paperweight, with gold-coloured stopper.

Although not realistic, the form is derived from a terracotta model found in Corinth dating back to the 7thC BC.

1981-92

£150-200　　　　**PSA**

A Royal Crown Derby 'Pheasant' paperweight, with gold-coloured stopper.

1983-98

£50-70　　　　**PSA**

A Royal Crown Derby 'Snake' paperweight, with gold-coloured stopper.

1989-92

£150-200　　　　**PSA**

A Royal Crown Derby 'Dragon' paperweight, with gold-coloured stopper.

This paperweight was released in 1988 to commemorate the Chinese year of the Dragon. In 1890 Crown Derby was given the Royal Warrant by Queen Victoria.

1988-92

£200-250　　　　**PSA**

A Royal Crown Derby 'Chipmunk' paperweight, his chest decorated with maple/sycamore leaves and seeds, with gold-coloured stopper.

1986-97

£70-100　　　　**PSA**

A Royal Crown Derby 'Frog' paperweight, with gold-coloured stopper.

1983-97

£70-100　　　　**PSA**

A Royal Crown Derby 'Walrus' paperweight, decorated with an all-over pattern of marine motifs, including the Pole star, sea anemones, calm and rough seas and limpets, with gold-coloured stopper.

1987-91

£180-220　　　　**PSA**

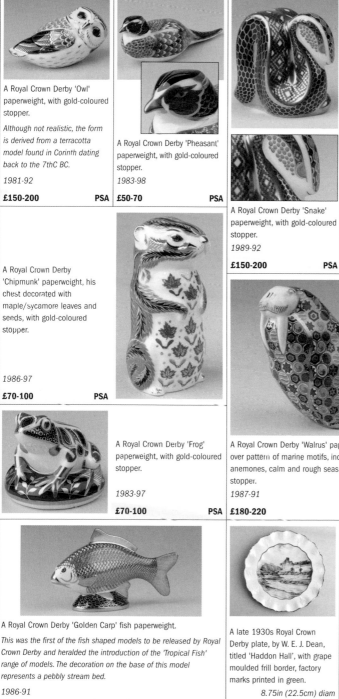

A Royal Crown Derby 'Golden Carp' fish paperweight.

This was the first of the fish shaped models to be released by Royal Crown Derby and heralded the introduction of the 'Tropical Fish' range of models. The decoration on the base of this model represents a pebbly stream bed.

1986-91

£120-180　　　　**PSA**

A late 1930s Royal Crown Derby plate, by W. E. J. Dean, titled 'Haddon Hall', with grape moulded frill border, factory marks printed in green.

8.75in (22.5cm) diam

£250-350　　　　**CHEF**

A Royal Crown Derby 'Posies' pattern vase, boxed.

7in (18cm) high

£20-40　　　　**PSA**

CERAMICS

COLLECTORS' NOTES

- Bjørn Wiinblad was born in 1918 in Copenhagen. He studied at Copenhagen's Technical High School and Royal Academy of Arts and worked at the Lars Syberg Studio in Taastrup. He had his first exhibition in 1945 and soon grew to prominence alongside noted Swedish designer Stig Lindberg.

- Wiinblad has worked in many different media, from poster design and book illustrations to ceramics and glass and has also designed theatrical sets. His style and designs are instantly recognisable and highly personal. They are popular world-wide, but particularly in his home country and the US.

- He worked at Nymølle from 1946-56 and then at Rosenthal from 1957 until the late 1970s when he took

ownership of Nymølle, which had run into problems and was facing closure. He continued at Nymølle until the 1990s when the factory finally closed.

- He also runs his own successful studio, and once had one in New York, where many of his most recognisable and collected designs are made in brightly decorated, glazed clay. Look out for large figures, figurative candlesticks and bowls, as these tend to be the most popular.

- His pieces are available at many different price levels, from under £20 for more commonly found transfer-printed mugs produced by Rosenthal or Nymølle to many hundreds of pounds for one of his hand-painted Studio figures.

A set of 12 Danish Nymølle ceramic 'Month' plaques, designed by Bjørn Wiinblad.

6in (15cm) diam

£50-70   **GAZE**

A Danish Nymølle transfer-printed red calendar plaque for 'July', designed by Bjørn Wiinblad.

A complete set of plaques tells the story of a courting couple and came in three colourways. They were also produced by Rosenthal.

1950s-90s   6in (15cm) diam

£5-7   **RWA**

A Danish Nymølle transfer gold calendar plaque for 'June', designed by Bjørn Wiinblad.

The gold colourway is more desirable and valuable than the red or white versions.

1950s-90s   6in (15cm) diam

£8-12   **RWA**

A pair of limited edition Danish Nymølle wall plaques, designed by Bjørn Wiinblad, in original box.

Although a standard pattern, these plaques were produced in an edition of 600 to celebrate the opening of the new Inspirations shop in Herning, Denmark and bear special wording to the back. It is unusual to find the box.

1978

£40-50   **RWA**

A Danish Nymølle 'Four Seasons' plate for 'Winter', designed by Bjørn Wiinblad.

These sets of four plates were made in four different sizes from 6in to 14in diam, each with a different design.

c1960s/90s   11in (28cm) wide

£35-45 each   **RWA**

A 1980s Danish Nymølle wall plate, designed by Bjørn Wiinblad, decorated with girl, with flower border.

12in (30cm) diam

£50-60   **RWA**

A Danish Nymølle transfer-printed candle wall sconce, designed by Bjørn Wiinblad.

10in (25.5cm) high

£60-75   **CHS**

A 1980s Danish Nymølle calendar mug for 'October', designed by Bjørn Wiinblad.

A complete set of calendar mugs tells the story of a courting couple.

3.5in (9cm) high

£15-20 RWA

A 1980s German Rosenthal 'Weihnachten' hand-painted porcelain postcard, in original box, designed by Bjørn Wiinblad.

These were produced to be bought, dedicated on the blank reverse and sent through the post in the box as gifts. They can be found in a number of different colourways and designs.

Box 8in (20.5cm) wide

£40-50 RWA

A German Rosenthal '1001 Nights' cylindrical vase, designed by Bjørn Wiinblad, with a vaguely erotic pattern, marked "Rosenthal Studio-Linie" to base.

£100-150 RWA

A 1970s German Rosenthal '1001 Nights' vase, designed by Bjørn Wiinblad.

7in (17cm) high

£120-140 RWA

A 1970s German Rosenthal '1001 Nights' vase, designed by Bjørn Wiinblad.

This pattern was one of Wiinblad's most popular for Rosenthal. This large vase was expensive at the time, costing 832 Krona in 1975, which roughly equates to around £80.

8.5in (22cm) high

£180-200 RWA

A Danish Wiinblad Studio hand-painted 'Hat Lady' figure, signed and dated on the base, designed by Bjørn Wiinblad.

Examples larger than this are very rare and valuable. The earlier the piece, the more colours it tends to include, later examples tend to be in blue only. This is a typical mark as found on the bases of Studio produced pieces. The 'L13' relates to the model number, the '70' to the year of production and the 'BW' monogram to the Bjørn Wiinblad studio.

1970

19.75in (50cm) high

£500-600 RWA

A Danish Wiinblad Studio 'Four Seasons' figure for 'Autumn', model No. M22, designed by Bjørn Wiinblad, signed and dated on the base.

These figures are top heavy and prone to damage, so examine carefully to ensure that they have not been broken and re-glued. They are still in production today, costing around £350, and can be found in blue or green, rarely in other colours. Examples from the 1970s are the most collectable.

1974   14in (35.5cm) h

£300-400 RWA

A Danish Wiinblad Studio lidded dish, model J115, designed by Bjørn Wiinblad, with unusual brown glaze, the lid formed as a hat, signed "BW" and dated.

1968

£180-220 RWA

A CLOSER LOOK AT A BJØRN WIINBLAD BOWL

This bowl is very large and impressive and the image is typical of his designs. The imperfect circular shape shows that it was hand-thrown.

As well as being produced unusually early in his career, it is a unique design.

The signature on the base includes a 'character' face, the personal signature used by Wiinblad to indicate his own handiwork.

Rather than being painted by his decorators, this piece was hand-painted by Wiinblad himself.

An early and unique Danish Bjørn Wiinblad large bowl, decorated with a lady and bird sitting amidst foliage and grass, dated. *1956*

18.5in (47cm) diam

£700-900   **RWA**

A Swedish Gustavsberg wall plaque, by Lisa Larson, with stylized bird design.

11in (28cm) wide

£220-280   **RWA**

A 1950s Swedish Gustavsberg Studio 'Karnavel' dish, by Stig Lindberg.

6.25in (16cm) wide

£80-120   **RWA**

A 1940s/50s Swedish Gustavsberg dish, designed by Stig Lindberg.

Founded in Sweden in 1825, Gustavsberg was the most important of the Scandinavian factories.

Designs were dominated by Wilhelm Kage and Stig Lindberg, his successor. Lindberg's designs are much sought after today for their clean shapes and brightly coloured, modern and abstract designs.

10in (25.5cm) wide

£250-300   **GGRT**

A Swedish Gustavsberg 'Sunflower' wall tile, by Lisa Larson.

From the Unik series of nine different design tiles produced between 1967-86.

9in (23cm) wide

£80-120   **RWA**

A Swedish Gustavsberg 'Sunflower' wall plaque, by Lisa Larson, in production 1967-72.

10.75in (27.5cm) high

£130-150   **RWA**

A 1950s/60s Swedish Gustavsberg 'Domino' conical-shaped vase, by Stig Lindberg, with brown glaze with herringbone design.

5.25in (13.5cm) high

£100-120   **RWA**

A 1950s Swedish Gustavsberg 'Endiv' vase, by Stig Lindberg, in grey-ish glaze.

7in (18cm) high

£120-140   **RWA**

COLLECTORS' NOTES

- Danish studio potter Arne Bang was born in 1901, the brother of internationally famous architect Jacob Bang. In 1926 he set up a studio with Carl Halier (1873-1948), who had been working as technical manager at Royal Copenhagen.

- Bang opened his own studio in 1932 and was extremely successful, winning many prizes for his designs. His work also had a great impact on Scandinavian ceramic design in the 1960s and 1970s. Bang's designs often combine Bauhaus elements with a Neoclassical feel. His glazes are rich in colour and texture when examined closely. The forms are simple, often featuring vertical ribbing or wide, deep incisions. Arne Bang died in 1983.

A 1930s/40s Danish Arne Bang beige stoneware vase, with ribbed, cog design.
2.25in (5.5cm) high
£40-60 RWA

A 1930s/40s Danish Arne Bang stoneware vase, with ribbed, cog design.
3.25in (8cm) high
£60-80 RWA

A rare 1920s Danish Arne Bang bowl, produced at Holmegaard Glassworks, with Aluminia backstamp.
7.5in (19cm) diam
£120-180 RWA

A 1930s/40s Danish Arne Bang green stoneware vase, with ribbed, cog design.
4.5in (11.5cm) high
£80-100 RWA

A Danish Arne Bang vase, of ribbed gourd form, with speckled blue and brown running glaze.
5in (13cm) high
£100-140 RWA

A 1930s/40s Danish Arne Bang studio bowl, in speckled blue glaze, with ribbed decoration.
7.5in (19cm) diam
£130-150 RWA

A 1930s/40s Danish Arne Bang studio vase, in beige matte glaze.
5.5in (14cm) high
£80-120 RWA

A 1930s Danish Arne Bang ice bucket, with wicker handle and brown and tan glaze, incised studio mark.
5.25in (13.5cm) high
£150-200 RWA

A 1930s/40s Danish Arne Bang jug, with lizard design cane handle mount, in a mottled blue glaze.
5.5in (14cm) high
£150-200 RWA

CERAMICS

A Finnish Arabia hand-decorated stoneware vase, with decorators and potters marks.

9.25in (23.5cm) high

£50-70   **GAZE**

A Finnish Arabia studio made vase.

10.25in (26cm) high

£40-60   **GAZE**

A pair of Finnish Arabia oil bottles, designed by Kaj Frank, with dark brown glaze.

5.5in (14cm) high

£35-45   **GAZE**

A set of six Swedish Ganiopta small storage jars, with rosewood tops.

3in (7.5cm) high

£22-28   **GAZE**

A 1970s large Finnish Arabia tile, with stylized flower design, signed on the front "RU/".

Arabia was founded in 1873 and grew to be the most prominent factory in Finland, with designs being led by Kaj Franck, who is also known for his Scandinavian glass designs for Nuutajarvi Nosjo.

18in (46cm) wide

£200-230   **RWA**

A Finnish Arabia hand-painted bowl, by Hikkla-Liisa Ahola, with blue and green glazes giving an almost iridescent appearance.

13.75in (25cm) diam

£150-170   **RWA**

A 1950s Danish Nymølle vase, by Gunnar Nylund.

10.75in (27.5cm)

£150-200   **ADE**

A Danish Nymølle vase, designed by Axel Brüel.

9in (23cm) high

£120-140   **RWA**

A 1950s Danish Palshus 'Torpedo' vase, by Per Linnermann-Schmidt, in blue haresfur glaze.

Scandinavian ceramics finished in blue glazes are popular and desirable, particularly if the glaze is richly and deeply coloured as with this example.

8.5in (22cm) high

£180-200   **RWA**

A 1950s Danish Palshus 'Torpedo' vase, by Per Linnermann-Schmidt, with olive haresfur glaze.

5in (12.5cm) high

£100-150   **RWA**

A 1950s Danish Palshus cylinder vase, designed by Per Linnermann-Schmidt, in caramel haresfur glaze.

9.25in (23.5cm) high

£200-230   **RWA**

A Swedish Rorstrand tall and narrow porcelain vase, by Carl-Harry Stalhane, covered in ochre, apricot and gunmetal microcrystalline glaze, incised "R" with "crowns/Sweden/CHS/SYT".

11.5in (29cm) high

£300-400   **DRA**

A Swedish Rorstrand vase, by Carl Harry Stalhane, with speckled black glaze.

6.25in (16cm) high

£160-180   **RWA**

A Swedish Rorstrand ovoid porcelain bowl, by Gunnar Nyland, with brown and black mottled matte glaze, incised "R" with "crowns/GN/Sweden/AXK".

6in (15cm) high

£120-180   **DRA**

A 1950s Danish Saxbo vase, designed by Edith Sonne Brunn, with brown mottled glaze.

Founded in 1930 and closed in 1968, Saxbo grew to be the most important and influential independent Danish pottery. Its look is characterised by Oriental style glazes and simple, clean lined shapes.

8.5in (21.5cm) high

£200-230   **RWA**

A Swedish Upsala Ekeby vase, with scraffito decoration.

9.75in (24.5cm) high

£50-70   **GAZE**

A Danish Saxbo bowl, unknown designer.

9in (23cm) diam

£100-120   **RWA**

A 1950s Swedish Upsala Ekeby dish, by Mari Simmulson.

7.75in (20cm) wide

£70-100   **ADE**

A Norwegian Stavangerflint bowl, with hand-painted decoration, printed and painted marks and two labels including retail sticker from Steen & Strøm A/S Oslo.

Founded in 1949 in Stavanger, Stavangerflint employed the design services of Kari Nyquist and Kaare Fjeldsaa during the 1950s and 60s. After a merger in 1968, it closed in 1979.

1957   *4.5in (11.5cm) high*

£40-60   **CHS**

A mid-20thC Shelley vase, the cone shape with recess above the foot streaked with horizontal bands of grey, orange and yellow, printed marks.

9.5in (24cm) high

£120-180   **CHEF**

A 1930s Shelley 'Melody' pattern chintz and yellow ribbed vase.

4.5in (11.5cm) high

£50-70   **BAD**

A 1930s Shelley 'Kingfisher' vase.

30-40   **BAD**

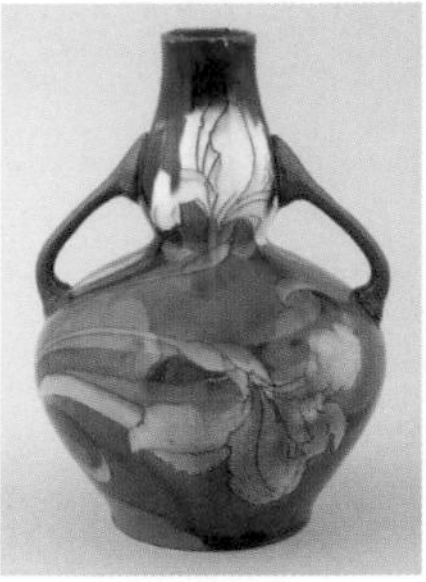

£30-40   **BAD**

A Shelley 'Intarsio' vase, of gourd form with twin handles, painted with sinuous plant forms in bright enamels, pattern 3573, neck repaired.

7.25in (18.5cm) high

£80-120   **GORL**

A 1930s Shelley double eggcup, with gilt rim.

This double-ended eggcup could hold either a hen's egg or a smaller duck's egg.

3.75in (9.5cm) high

£70-90   **BAD**

A 1930s Shelley Mabel Lucie Attwell 'To Fairy Town' mug, with motto reading "Fairies love motoring all about, two wouldn't keep still, so they fell out".

3in (7.5cm) high

£50-70   **BAD**

A Shelley late Foley Oriental-style octagonal jug.

c1910   *6in (15cm) high*

£150-200   **BAD**

A small shaped Shelley teapot, with floral motifs and blue detailing.

7.75in (19.5cm) long

£100-150   **BAD**

A 1930s Shelley trio set, painted marks "12072 F".

7in (17.5cm) wide

£100-150   **BAD**

A Shelley Art Deco trio set.

saucer 6.25in (16cm) diam

£80-120   **GCL**

A 1930s Shelley Art Deco tea set, each piece decorated with the 11755 pattern of an orange, comprising milk jug, sugar bowl, sandwich plate, four cups, five saucers and six tea plates.

£800-1,000 set   **CHEF**

A 1930s Shelley Art Deco tea set, the Vogue shapes printed in black and overpainted in orange with the 11792 pattern of interlocking rectangles within rim bands of the same colours, comprising milk jug, sugar bowl, two sandwich plates, 12 cups, saucers and tea plates.

£2,500-3,000 set   **CHEF**

A Shelley 'Boo Boo' nursery figure, designed by Mabel Lucie Attwell, modelled watering flowers, printed mark "LA29".

3in (7.5cm) high

£450-550   **WW**

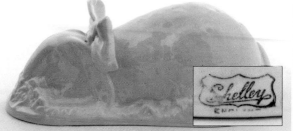

A Shelley white jelly mould, in the form of a crouching rabbit, printed mark in green.

10in (25.5cm) long

£220-280   **LFA**

A Shelley 'Diddums' figure, designed by Mabel Lucie Attwell, painted in colours, printed and painted marks "LA18".

Illustrator Mabel Lucie Attwell's designs for Shelley are much sought after - particularly the rare nursery figurines. 'Diddums' was one of her most popular and famous drawings. Fakes are known so check the marks and quality of the paintwork carefully.

6.25in (16cm) high

£1,800-2,200   **WW**

A Shelley 'Howm'I Doin' figure, designed by Mabel Lucie Attwell, LA16, painted in colours, printed marks.

6.75in (17cm) high

£1,600-2,000   **WW**

A Shelley 'Our Pets' figure, designed by Mabel Lucie Attwell, painted in colours, printed green mark.

8.25in (21cm) high

£1,700-2,000   **WW**

CERAMICS

COLLECTORS' NOTES

■ Studio pottery is characterised by hand-thrown and hand-decorated wares made in small 'personal' studios. It was produced from the 1930s, but primarily after WWII. Although pioneering and notable names such as Bernard Leach and Lucie Rie usually fetch very high sums, more affordable pieces can be found that are typical of their styles, particularly smaller examples. Also look at other, currently less sought-after names and try to buy pieces that represent their style the best.

■ The market is lively, constantly innovative and provides great scope for the collector. Those interested in collecting should also consider looking away from individual personalities towards some of the currently less notable but often prolific potteries such as Troika, Newlyn and Briglin, covered elsewhere in this book. Many of these, particularly Troika, have become more sought-after and collectable recently and their importance may continue to grow.

An Ian Auld square ashtray, with slightly nibbled corners.

3.5in (9cm) wide

£35-45   **GROB**

A Richard Batterham stoneware charger, pale celadon glaze, unmarked.

Batterham was born in 1936 and has become one of Britain's finest living studio potters. His forms and glazes are typically minimal.

15.75in (40cm) diam

£180-220   **WW**

An Aldermaston Pottery punch or large tea pot, by Alan Caiger-Smith, painted with brown scrolls.

The Aldermaston Pottery was founded in 1955 by Caiger-Smith and continues to produce today. It has employed many fine potters, with only a few working there at any one time. Caiger-Smith and his pottery are particularly known for their tinglazes.

10.25in (26cm) high

£350-450   **CHEF**

An Aldermaston Pottery oviform vase, by Alan Caiger-Smith, painted in manganese, olive green and muted red in broad brushstrokes with bands of linear decoration against white, painted pottery mark on base.

10.75in (27.5cm) high

£180-220   **DN**

A Winchcombe Pottery vase, by Michael Cardew.

Michael Cardew (1901-1983) was a noted, inspirational potter who studied under Bernard Leach. He set up the Winchcombe Pottery in 1926 but sold it in 1939 to set up a pottery at Wenford Bridge, Cornwall. He also travelled, most notably to Africa, where he founded a third pottery and taught.

c1930   *5.75in (14.5cm) high*

£300-350   **ADE**

A Michael Cardew 'Kingwood' slipware jug, the red pottery partially covered in white slip and having combed and banded decoration, impressed 'K' in circle seal mark.

8.75in (22.5cm) high

£120-180   **DN**

An unusual Chelsea Pottery flared circular bowl, decorated by Joyce Morgan, with a pair of cockerels with extending tail feathers, in autumnal colours, signed "JEM" and "Chelsea P England" on back.

1952-97   *12in (30.5cm) diam*

£100-150   **DN**

CERAMICS

A cruet set, made by Harry Davis at the Crowan Pottery, Cornwall, with iridescent cream and green glaze.

mustard 2.25in

1945-62 *(6cm) high*

£25-35 **GROB**

A Janet Leach wheel-shaped vase, in cream with a brown stripe.

c1970 *7.75in (20cm) high*

£350-400 **ADE**

A Janet Leach stoneware vase, simple temmoku cross brushstrokes over mottled ochre ground, impressed "JL" monogram and St Ives mark.

5.75in (14.5cm) high

£180-220 **WW**

A Janet Leach pitted stoneware vase, the everted rim covered in an olive green glaze, impressed "JL" with St Ives mark.

5.5in (14cm) high

£250-350 **WW**

A Janet Leach stoneware dish, square section, painted with temokku cross motif, impressed "JL" and St Ives mark.

6in (15cm) wide

£150-200 **WW**

A David Leach teapot, from Lowerdown Pottery.

c1960 *5.75in (14.5cm) high*

£200-250 **ADE**

A David Leach jug, with temmoku glazed rim and oatmeal body, "L" mark.

7.75in (19.5cm) high

£80-120 **CHEF**

A small David Leach ramekin dish, with green glazed interior and handle.

5in (12.5cm) long

£10-20 **GROB**

An ovoid jug, decorated by Katie Muir, painted with foliate panels in shades of green, painted monogram.

5in (12.5cm) high

£15-20 **L&T**

A William Staite Murray bowl, covered in a crackled pale blue glaze, impressed seal mark.

3.75in (9.5cm) diam

£100-150 **WW**

A CLOSER LOOK AT A STUDIO VASE

Coldstone was founded during the 1950s by Chris Harries who built his own kiln at Ascott-under Wychwood, Oxfordshire. His work typifies the studio pottery movement.

The faces resemble the drawings of Italian artist Modigliani, who was influenced by African tribal and Oceanic art.

This vase was thrown and decorated by Dieter Kunzemann, the chief thrower at Coldstone. It is a unique piece, probably having been made as a 'Christmas Special' between 1960-63.

The style departs from Coldstone's typical designs, which are characterised by crossed wheat-ear and matchstick like decoration. Kunzemann is known for developing his own individual style.

A 'Coldstone' pottery oviform vase, decorated with incisions to the beige clay and heightened with dark staining rubbed in to the incisions, impressed on base "Coldstone".

c1960

8in (20.5cm) high

£200-300 **DN**

A Katherine Pleydell-Bouverie stoneware bowl, impressed seal mark, incised "280".

Pleydell-Bouverie (1895-1985) studied under Bernard Leach. She became known for her work on ash glazes, which is much sought after.

5.75in (14.5cm) diam

£180-220 **WW**

A Katherine Pleydell-Bouverie vase, impressed seal mark.

3in (7.5cm) high

£120-180 **WW**

A Katherine Pleydell-Bouverie vase, impressed seal mark.

3.5in (9cm) high

£120-180 **WW**

A Bernard Rooke studio pottery vase, with leaves and birds.

7.5in (19cm) high

£30-40 **GAZE**

A Bernard Rooke Studio pottery vase.

£40-60 **GAZE**

A Bernard Rooke Studio pottery table lamp base.

£40-50 **GAZE**

A Bernard Rooke pottery wall pocket.

Born in 1938, Bernard Rooke produces pottery that is eminently saleable and simple to produce. Lamp bases have become a mainstay of his production.

8.25in (21cm) long

£20-30   **GAZE**

A pair of Bernard Rooke pottery tankards.

4in (10.5cm) high

£25-35   **GAZE**

A small terracotta planter, by Marianne de Trey, with applied glazed bosses.

2.75in (7cm) high

£15-25   **GROB**

A Robin Welch pottery bowl, with green mottled glazed interior.

Born in 1936, Welch worked part-time at the Leach Pottery from 1953-59, before opening his own pottery in London which ran from 1960-62. He then set up the Stadbroke Pottery in Eye, Suffolk. He has worked for leading companies including Midwinter and Wedgwood.

c1960   4.75in (12cm) diam

£35-45   **GROB**

A large studio pottery vase, with impressed decoration, signature to base.

13.75in (35cm) high

£15-20   **GAZE**

A studio pottery bottle vase.

10.5in (26.5cm) high

£15-20   **GAZE**

A St. Ives celadon vase, cracked.

9.5in (24cm) high

£40-60   **CHEF**

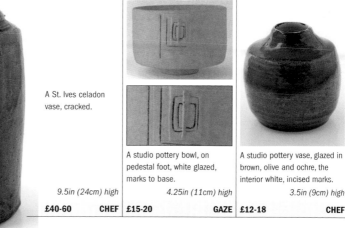

A studio pottery bowl, on pedestal foot, white glazed, marks to base.

4.25in (11cm) high

£15-20   **GAZE**

A studio pottery vase, glazed in brown, olive and ochre, the interior white, incised marks.

3.5in (9cm) high

£12-18   **CHEF**

COLLECTORS' NOTES

- The SylvaC factory, originally known as Shaw and Copestake, was started by William Shaw and William Copestake in 1894. The name SylvaC did not come into use until c1936 and was a combination of the names Sylvan Works, where the factory was based at the time, and Copestake. The company produced decorative and household ware.

- The animal and novelty figures, or 'fancies', that SylvaC is most closely associated with were introduced in the late 1920s and were initially sold at fairgrounds and as novelties.

- The company was liquidated in 1982 but production limped on under Longton Ceramics and later Crown Winsor until 1989. Portmerion Pottery purchased the factory and sold all the remaining stock, including display pieces, which are much sought-after today.

- Models are identified by their mould numbers and figures of the same design but different sizes will have different numbers. Dates connected to mould numbers are the date of the introduction of the shape – not the date of the model as models were used for many years.

- As well as rare shapes/moulds, size and colour are the most important factors determining value and the general rule is the larger the better. The most common colours are fawn and then green, with blue and pink the rarest.

- Condition also affects value; the matt glazes are easily chipped, so handle them with care.

A SylvaC 'Cat', stamped "1086".

This is the smallest of three sizes and is a common shape, however it is in a rare finish.

5in (12.5cm) high

£30-50   **MCOL**

A SylvaC 'Boxing Cat', stamped "184".

5in (12.5cm) high

£70-100   **MCOL**

A SylvaC green 'Long-necked Cat', stamped "3457".

1963-4   *13in (33cm) high*

£50-80   **MCOL**

A SylvaC 'Cat', with back paw to ear, stamped "3406".

5in (12cm) high

£50-70   **MCOL**

A SylvaC bronze glaze 'Cheetah', from the 'Modus 80' range, stamped "5212".

10.5in (26.5cm) long

£60-80   **MCOL**

A SylvaC 'Flat Cat', stamped "2722".

From a set of three different-sized figures.

c1960   *5in (12.5cm) high*

£70-100   **MCOL**

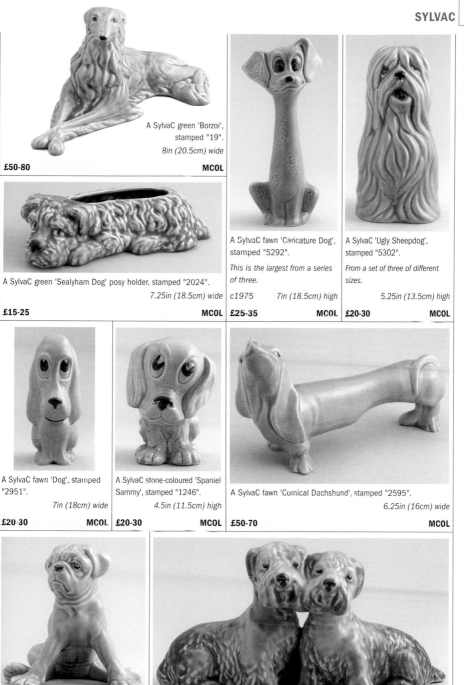

A SylvaC green 'Borzoi', stamped "19".
8in (20.5cm) wide
£50-80   MCOL

A SylvaC green 'Sealyham Dog' posy holder, stamped "2024".
7.25in (18.5cm) wide
£15-25   MCOL

A SylvaC fawn 'Caricature Dog', stamped "5292".
This is the largest from a series of three.
c1975   *7in (18.5cm) high*
£25-35   MCOL

A SylvaC 'Ugly Sheepdog', stamped "5302".
From a set of three of different sizes.
5.25in (13.5cm) high
£20-30   MCOL

A SylvaC fawn 'Dog', stamped "2951".
7in (18cm) wide
£20-30   MCOL

A SylvaC stone-coloured 'Spaniel Sammy', stamped "1246".
4.5in (11.5cm) high
£20-30   MCOL

A SylvaC fawn 'Comical Dachshund', stamped "2595".
6.25in (16cm) wide
£50-70   MCOL

A SylvaC stone-coloured 'Boxer Pup', stamped "2331".
5.5in (14cm) high
£70-100   MCOL

A rare SylvaC fawn 'Two Sealyhams Joined', stamped "166".
6.25in (16cm) high
£100-150   MCOL

A SylvaC green 'Koala Bear', stamped "1391".

6in (15.5cm) high

£60-90   **MCOL**

A SylvaC green 'Squirrel and Acorn', stamped "1146".

This is the largest in a set of five. This design was also available as a cottonwool holder.

£80-120   **MCOL**

A very rare SylvaC green 'Seated Pigeon', stamped "1376".

3.25in (8.5cm) high

£100-150   **MCOL**

A CLOSER LOOK AT SYLVAC FIGURE

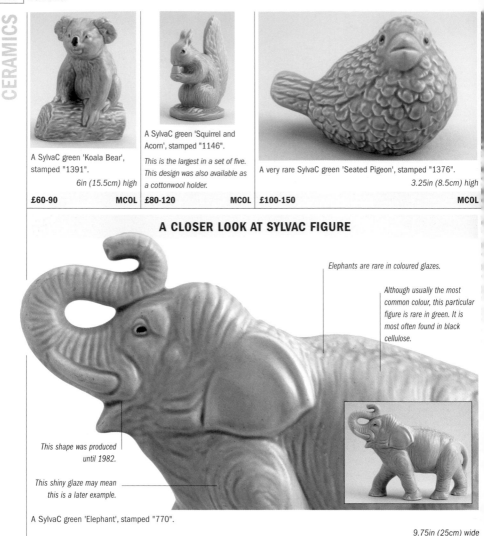

Elephants are rare in coloured glazes.

Although usually the most common colour, this particular figure is rare in green. It is most often found in black cellulose.

This shape was produced until 1982.

This shiny glaze may mean this is a later example.

A SylvaC green 'Elephant', stamped "770".

9.75in (25cm) wide

£40-60   **MCOL**

A SylvaC green 'Seated Horse', stamped and marked "SylvaC England".

£30-50   **MCOL**

A rare SylvaC blue 'Hippo', stamped "1425".

This piece is rare because of its shape and colour.

2in (5cm) high

£120-180   **MCOL**

A SylvaC fawn 'Seated Mule', stamped "183".

5.75in (14.5cm) high

£70-100   **MCOL**

A SylvaC 'Duck', stamped "1499".

5.25in (13.5cm) long

£50-70   **MCOL**

A SylvaC green 'Frog' money bank, stamped "5097".

5.75in (14.5cm) high

£20-40   **MCOL**

A rare SylvaC green 'Fish' money bank, stamped "5662".

7in (18cm) long

£60-80   **MCOL**

A SylvaC 'Elephant' money bank, stamped "5659".

6in (15cm) high

£40-60   **MCOL**

A SylvaC brown 'Chipmunk' money bank, stamped "5105".

6.25in (16cm) high

£20-30   **MCOL**

A SylvaC 'Owl' money bank, stamped "5106".

5in (12.5cm) high

£20-30   **MCOL**

A SylvaC beige 'Rabbit' money bank, stamped "5658".

6in (15cm) high

£40-60   **MCol**

A SylvaC 'Pig' money bank, stamped "5657".

6in (15cm) high

£40-60   **MCOL**

A SylvaC orange 'Bear' money bank, stamped "5104".

Money banks were produced with and without painted-in eyes. Those without painted-in eyes are less popular and less desirable.

6in (15cm) high

£30-50   **MCOL**

FIND OUT MORE...

'The SylvaC Story', *by Susan Jean Veerbeek, published by Pottery Publications, 2002.*

'Collecting SylvaC', *by Mick and Derry Collins, published by The SylvaC Collectors' Circle, 1998.*

A 1950s Adderley teapot, with transfer decoration of sprigs of hazel.

The streamlined handle of the lid and the simplified form is typically 1950s.

6.75in (17cm) long

£20-30　　　　　　　**JL**

A 1950s Crown Dorset teapot, with rose transfer.

10.25in (26cm) wide

£25-35　　　　　　　**JL**

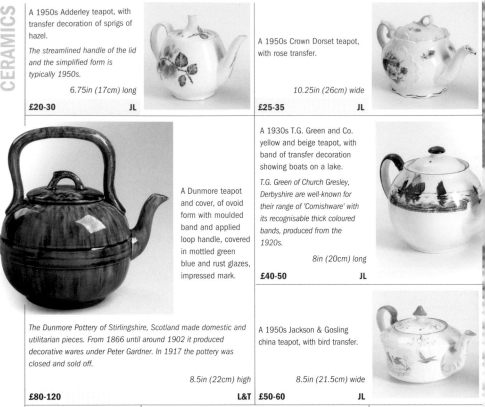

A Dunmore teapot and cover, of ovoid form with moulded band and applied loop handle, covered in mottled green blue and rust glazes, impressed mark.

A 1930s T.G. Green and Co. yellow and beige teapot, with band of transfer decoration showing boats on a lake.

T.G. Green of Church Gresley, Derbyshire are well-known for their range of 'Cornishware' with its recognisable thick coloured bands, produced from the 1920s.

8in (20cm) long

£40-50　　　　　　　**JL**

The Dunmore Pottery of Stirlingshire, Scotland made domestic and utilitarian pieces. From 1866 until around 1902 it produced decorative wares under Peter Gardner. In 1917 the pottery was closed and sold off.

8.5in (22cm) high

£80-120　　　　　　　**L&T**

A 1950s Jackson & Gosling china teapot, with bird transfer.

8.5in (21.5cm) wide

£50-60　　　　　　　**JL**

A Johnson Bros. coffee pot, decorated with a flock of Canada geese in flight, printed marks.

7in (18cm) high

£40-50　　　　　　　**CHS**

A Johnson Bros 'Mill Stream' blue and white transfer decorated earthenware teapot.

9in (23cm) long

£30-40　　　　　　　**JL**

A Minton 'Mirabeau' hand-painted bone china teapot, with floral and gilt detailing.

10.5in (27cm) high

£40-50　　　　　　　**JL**

A Royal Winton Grimwades beehive shaped teapot, with bee knop on lid.

Royal Winton, owned by the Grimwade brothers, is better known for its prolifically produced chintzware. Beehive objects such as these and honey pots are also popular.

c1935　　　　　　　6in (15cm) high

£220-280　　　　　　　**BAD**

A Royal Worcester cream fireproof teapot, with obtusely placed handle.

5.75in (14.5cm) high

£20-40　　　　　　　**P&I**

A 1950s Royal Worcester 'Fiesta' coffee pot, stamped "Shape 3 Size 6".

7in (18cm) high

£40-60 **BAD**

A 1980s Strangeways 'Teddy Boy' ceramic teapot.

7.5in (19.5cm) wide

£30-40 **MA**

A Wade Heath 'Donald Duck' hand-painted novelty teapot, his beak as a spout, in typical colours, printed mark, restored cover.

4in (10cm) high

£350-450 **WW**

A 1930s Wade Art Deco style hand-painted octagonal coffee pot, with jolly floral pattern and printed marks to base.

8in (20cm) high

£70-100 **JL**

A 1940s Wood and Sons 'Yuan' Oriental style pattern blue and white transfer printed teapot, the base with printed marks and Registered No. 656368 for 1916.

8.5in (22cm) long

£40-60 **JL**

An Enoch Wood's blue and white transfer printed teapot, with design of English scenery.

c1960 *9in (23cm) wide*

£40-60 **JL**

A novelty automobile teapot, in yellow-glazed earthenware, cover with drivers head handle, registration "OK T42".

Available in a range of colours, the silvered areas are prone to wear, particularly on the corners and the driver's helmet and handle, which reduces value considerably.

c1930 *9in (22.5cm) long*

£70-100 **GORL**

A 1950s Bavarian octagonal transfer printed souvenir teapot, from and with dedication for Canvey Island.

8.25in (21cm) wide

£20-30 **JL**

A Victorian chocolate brown teapot, with hand-painted marguerite decoration.

c1895 *8.25in (21cm) wide*

£40-50 **JL**

A 1950s West German zone teapot, with lotus bud-shaped handle to lid, flower transfers and gilt detailing.

10.25in (26cm) wide

£40-50 **JL**

CERAMICS

COLLECTORS' NOTES

■ Tiles have been used in decorative architectural designs for centuries, notably in Turkey and the Middle East. The collector has greater scope to choose from: look out for Grueby and Claycraft from the US, William de Morgan and Minton from the UK and Dutch Delft tiles.

■ Condition is important, with cracks and losses devaluing a piece, unless very old and rare. Many tiles are hand-painted, but from the mid-19th century onwards they tend to be transfer-printed. Beware of modern reproductions, which tend to be lighter and thinner. Look for tiles that are decorated in a style typical of the factory, designer or period.

■ De Porceleyne Fles literally means 'the porcelain jar', which relates to the jar-shaped mark used by this Dutch, Delft-based factory. Established c1635, it is said to be the longest lived and most famous of the 32 earthenware factories founded there.

■ Joost Thooft, an engineer, bought the company in 1876 and revolutionised materials and processes. To restore the fame of Delft, the name was added to the mark, along with Thooft's monogram. The company received Royal designation in 1919. Although better known for its blue and white wares, the company also produced Arts and Crafts and Art Nouveau stylized designs around the turn of the century.

A De Porceleyne Fles large horizontal tile, with peacock, minute flecks to walls, stamped bottle "TL, Delft" mark.

17in (42.5cm) wide

£450-550 DRA

A De Porceleyne Fles tall tile, with a peacock in polychrome on a brick wall, stamped bottle "TL, Delft" mark.

13in (32.5cm) high

£280-320 DRA

A pair of De Porceleyne Fles tall vertical tiles, with a pair of ibises at an oasis in front of pyramids, surrounded by green-glazed border tiles, mount hiding marks.

13.5in (34cm) high

£450-550 DRA

A De Porceleyne Fles vertical tile, with a goose landing in a marsh with fishing boat, stamped bottle "J, Delft" mark.

8.75in (22cm) high

£180-220 DRA

A De Porceleyne Fles horizontal tile, depicting a deer hunt in the snow, restoration to one edge and top back, stamped bottle "TL, Delft" mark.

17.25in (43cm) wide

£350-450 DRA

A De Porceleyne Fles tile, decorated in cuenca with a hare leaping below branches, two small nicks to upper right edge, stamped bottle with "TL" and "Delft" mark.

8.25in (20.5cm) wide

£350-450 DRA

A De Porceleyne Fles large tile, decorated in cuenca with a Viking ship with seahorse prow, a few small nicks to cuenca walls, framed.

8in (20cm) wide

£350-450 DRA

A De Porceleyne Fles horizontal tile, with Viking ship, stamped bottle "TL, Delft" mark.

8.75in (22cm) wide

£220-280 DRA

A De Porceleyne Fles horizontal tile, with a regatta of tall ships, small nicks to corners, stamped bottle "TL, Delft" mark.

8.25in (20.5cm) wide

£80-120 DRA

A CLOSER LOOK AT TILES

Six unusual Californian tiles, depicting a desert scene, unmarked.

28.5in (70cm) wide

£1,500-2,000 **DRA**

Groups of tiles that form a picture are more scarce than standard tiles, particularly if complete and undamaged.

At 60cm wide, the image is easier to display in modern houses than larger scenes, but makes much more of a visual impression than a single tile.

A Claycraft tile, decorated in cuenca with a bowl of flowers in brilliant polychrome on a black ground, several minute flecks to high points, stamped "CLAYCRAFT".

7.75in (19cm) square

£450-550 **DRA**

Although not by a notable factory, the colours and modern style of the image with its flat planes of colour are strongly in the Arts & Crafts tradition.

The decoration is tube-lined, where the design is hand-applied by trailing liquid clay onto the tiles though a pipe before adding the colours.

An Arts and Crafts twelve-tile panel, decorated with an autumnal landscape with trees, hills and water, restoration to chip on side of top right tile, reglued top left tile, unmarked.

24in (60cm) wide

£3,500-4,500 **DRA**

A Claycraft G3 tile panel, decorated in cuenca, brilliant polychrome matte and glossy glazes, tiles numbered, unmounted, small nicks to some edges, loose.

The 'cuenca' technique, like tube-lining, uses ridges to separate coloured glazes.

34.5in (86cm) high

£2,500-3,500 **DRA**

A rare Federal Seaboard Terra Cotta Co. architectural faïence tile, Perth Amboy, New Jersey, carved and moulded with a fox and grape vines, in polychrome matte and semi-matte glazes, several chips to edges and a few to surface, unmarked.

14in (35cm) wide

£1,200-1,800 **DRA**

A Franklin tile, decorated in cuenca with yellow daffodils on a cobalt ground, mounted in an Arts and Crafts frame, mark covered.

9in (23cm) wide

£220-280 **DRA**

A rare Georgia Tech Ceramics tile, of partly unglazed clay impressed with the college spire against green foliage and blue sky, above "GA TECH CERAMICS '40".

1940   4.75in (12cm) wide

£200-300 **DRA**

A Muresque horizontal panel, moulded with a medieval village scene with a woman with basket in front of thatched roof cottages, mounted in an Arts and Crafts frame, stamped "MURESQUE TILES OAKLAND".

12in (30cm) wide

£550-650 **DRA**

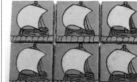

Six Mosaic tiles, decorated in cuerda seca with a sailboat in brown and beige on a blue ground, each stamped "MTC".

3in (75cm) wide

£550-650 **DRA**

COLLECTORS' NOTES

■ Toby jugs probably take their name from the old French word 'tope' meaning 'to drink or toast'. The first Toby jug was given the name 'Toby Fillpot', after the heavy-drinking subject of a popular ballad.

■ Royal Doulton are generally recognized as one of the largest manufacturers of Tobies, although a number of other companies have also made them, including Wood & Sons, Spode and Kevin Francis.

■ The standard Toby jug, sometimes called the 'ordinary Toby', depicts a seated figure in a tricorn hat holding a tankard and a pipe. Toby jugs also portray literary creations, folk characters and popular statesmen.

■ Value is determined by a combination of age, scarcity and quality. Jugs that have been withdrawn from production, especially those only made in small quantities, will be more expensive.

■ A number of companies, particularly brewers and distillers, have commissioned promotional Toby jugs. These are often released in limited editions and are very collectable.

■ Toby jugs are available in various sizes, ranging from large 9in (23cm) high examples to small sized jugs, measuring around 4in (10cm) high.

■ The range of small 'Doultonville Tobies', created by William Harper, is accompanied by a series of stories based on the characters.

A Royal Doulton 'The Best Is Not Too Good' Toby jug, D6107.

1939-60   4.25in (11cm) high

£100-150   **PSA**

A Royal Doulton 'Sir John Falstaff' small Toby jug, D6063.

1939-91   5.5in (14cm) high

£35-45   **PSA**

A Royal Doulton 'Old Charley' small Toby jug, D6069.

1939-60   5.5in (14cm) high

£120-180   **PSA**

A Royal Doulton 'Sherlock Holmes' large Toby jug, D6661.

1981-91   8.75in (22cm) high

£50-60   **PSA**

A Royal Doulton 'Cliff Cornell' large Toby jug, in blue jacket.

A variety of colour combinations exist for this Toby jug. This medium size was also produced with a brown jacket and a beige jacket.

c1956   9.5in (24cm) high

£180-220   **PSA**

A Royal Doulton 'Winston Churchill' medium Toby jug, D6172.

5.5in (14cm) high

£40-60   **PSA**

A limited edition Royal Doulton 'Charles Dickens' Toby jug, D6997, from an edition of 2,500.

1995   5.25in (13.5cm) high

£70-90   **PSA**

COLLECTORS' NOTES

■ The Toni Raymond Pottery was established by Raymond Smith in 1951, in a humble workshop in Babbacombe near Torquay, Devon. The name is derived from the first names of the husband and wife team. The earliest products were wall-mounted heads of pirates and Mexicans and small models of birds made from a clay-like material called 'barbola'.

■ In 1954, Smith's friend Geoff Hiscock joined as partner and the business began to flourish. A line of ceramic jewellery was added, which was sold at Selfridges and Fortnum & Mason in London. Soon tableware, commonly found today, was added to the range. By the late 1960s, the pottery employed over 80 people in three locations including the Babbacombe Pottery, which was bought in 1967.

■ With its bright, hand-painted designs on a white background showing Spanish and South American influences, it was quite unlike the designs being produced at the time and was immensely popular. The range was extended and also included decorative items such as door plaques, vases and lamps.

■ The pottery was sold by 1978 and founder Raymond Smith died in 1990. Since then, interest in his pottery has grown rapidly and continues to do so. Pieces can be identified by a printed or impressed backstamp, which often includes a flying mallard duck, the Toni Raymond or the Babbacombe Pottery name. Look for his most characteristic works and those in the best condition as damage reduces value considerably.

A hand-painted Toni Raymond Pottery 'Biscuits' storage jar.

Look for the 'Dried Potatoes' version of these storage jars, which, being an unusual ingredient, is very rare.

6.5in (16.5cm) high

£12-17   **MTS**

A rare hand-painted ceramic Toni Raymond Pottery 'Bouquet Garni' pot, with wooden lid.

4in (10cm) high

£20-26   **MTS**

A rare hand-painted Toni Raymond Pottery 'Tobacco' jar.

3.25in (8cm) high

£20-24   **MTS**

A rare hand-painted Toni Raymond Pottery 'Crispbread' jar, with wooden lid.

6in (15.5cm) wide

£32-38   **MTS**

A hand-painted Toni Raymond Pottery lidded 'Jam' pot.

3.75in (9.5cm) high

£10-14   **MTS**

A 1960s hand-painted Toni Raymond Pottery lidded pot scourer box.

3.5in (9cm) diam

£10-16   **MTS**

A hand-painted Toni Raymond Pottery 'Mops & Things' sink-side pot.

5in (13cm) high

£12-16   **MTS**

A hand-painted Toni Raymond lidded 'Cheese' dish.

5.5in (14cm) diam

£20-24   **MTS**

A hand-painted Toni Raymond Pottery cucumber dish.

5in (12.5cm) diam

£10-14   **MTS**

A hand-painted Toni Raymond Pottery 'Sugar' sifter.

5in (12.5cm) high

£6-11 MTS

A hand-painted Toni Raymond Pottery double egg cup.

2.5in (6.5cm) high

£10-14 MTS

A hand-painted Toni Raymond Pottery pepper pot.

4.25in (10.5cm) high

£3-4 MTS

An unusual hand-painted Toni Raymond Pottery 'Spoon Rest'.

8in (20cm) high

£18-22 MTS

A hand-painted Toni Raymond Pottery 'Milk Saver'.

This was placed in the bottom of a saucepan to stop the milk boiling over.

4.5in (11cm) diam

£7-9 MTS

A hand-painted Toni Raymond Pottery 'Mary's Room' door sign.

4in (10cm) high

£12-18 MTS

A hand-painted Toni Raymond Pottery 'Ivan's Room' door sign.

4in (10cm) high

£12-18 MTS

A hand-painted Toni Raymond Pottery cat mask string dispenser.

One of the pottery's most recognisable designs, these string holders also came in the form of a dog, fox and mole.

5.5in (14cm) wide

£18-22 MTS

A hand-painted Toni Raymond Pottery Mexican 'Sugar' sifter.

The design of this sifter clearly demonstrates the South American influences on style.

6.25in (16cm) high

£10-14 MTS

CERAMICS

COLLECTORS' NOTES

■ The Troika Pottery Company was founded at the Wells Pottery at Wheal Dream, St Ives on the 1st May 1963. The three founders were sculptor and painter Leslie Illsley, potter Benny Sirota and architect Jan Thompson, who left in 1965.

■ Illsley primarily worked on shapes, which were produced in moulds, while Sirota handled surface design and glazes. The first pieces were small domestic wares such as teapots, mugs and vases. Although many associate Troika with matte, textured pieces, most of these early pieces were glazed, giving a glossy or shiny finish.

■ Early decoration included circle designs which were usually austere and sober in terms of both form and colour. Scandinavian ceramics of the period were a strong influence. Leslie Illsley admired artist Paul Klee and sculptor Constantin Brancusi whose work strongly influenced designs, as did the work of local artists.

■ The 1960s saw much growth, spurred on by the tourist industry and a number of prestigious London stores stocked their wares, including Selfridges, Heal's, (where an exhibition was held in 1968) and Liberty . In 1970 the pottery expanded and moved to Newlyn, where new shapes and designs were introduced – by 1974 textured ware dominated the range.

■ Much Troika can be dated from the mark and the decorator's initials – consult a reference work to learn about each decorator. Dates given here show when the decorator worked. Marks including 'St Ives' generally date from 1963-70, and a trident-shaped mark was used until 1967. If a piece is not marked 'St Ives', then it is likely to have been made at Newlyn, although 'Newlyn' never appears in any mark.

■ Look for large or sculptural pieces and those dating from the first years of the pottery, especially if by the founders. Typical shapes, surface designs and attractive colours are also popular features. The pottery closed in 1983 due to less expensive foreign imports and more people holidaying abroad rather than in Cornwall.

A rare early Troika St Ives Pottery 'chimney' vase, with green/blue glazed ground, the geometric embossed panels to either side impressed with printers block lettering, indistinct monogram.

8in (20cm) high

£600-700   **B&H**

A rare late 1960s Troika St Ives Pottery 'chimney' vase, by Marilyn Pascoe, in blues and browns with plain high black glazed sides, the back and front with embossed geometric Aztec designs and impressed printers block lettering.

7.75in (19.5cm) high

£600-700   **B&H**

A Troika Pottery 'chimney' vase, with blue glazed sides and embossed Aztec designs to either side, monogrammed "B.E.".

8in (20cm) high

£280-320   **B&H**

A rare early Troika St Ives Pottery 'slab' vase, the embossed geometric decorated back and front with impressed printers block lettering.

6.75in (17cm) high

£600-700   **B&H**

A Troika Pottery 'slab' vase, with abstract designs in blue and beige, the base with the as yet unidentified monogram of "E.W.".

£250-350   **B&H**

£220-280

A late 1970s Troika Pottery 'slab' vase, by Annette Walters, in greys and browns with mottled blue glazed sides and textured embossed Aztec stylized designs to the back and front.

7in (18cm) high

B&H

CERAMICS

A Troika Pottery 'wheel' vase, probably by Jane Fitzgerald, cast in low painted relief, painted "Troika LF" monogram, small chips.

1977-83   *7.75in (20cm) high*

£400-500   **WW**

A Troika Pottery small 'wheel' vase, by Alison Brigden, with embossed stylized design depicting woman with a basket to one side and grid design to the other.

1976-83   *4.5in (11.5cm) high*

£120-180   **B&H**

A late 1970s Troika Pottery 'wheel' vase, modelled in relief with face design, with painted marks for Tina Doubleday.

7.75in (19.5cm) high

£450-550   **WW**

A Troika Pottery small 'wheel' vase, by Louise Jinks, in blues and browns with mottled blue ground and embossed geometric designs to both sides.

1976-81   *4.5in (11.5cm) high*

£150-200   **B&H**

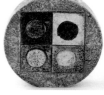

A Troika Pottery small 'wheel' vase, by Sue Bladen, with embossed domino and Aztec designs to either side.

1975   *4.75in (12cm) high*

£80-120   **B&H**

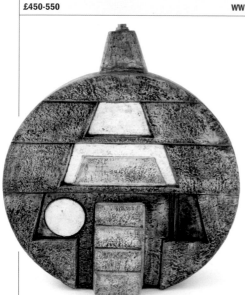

A Troika Pottery giant 'wheel' lamp base, with raised Aztec designs to one side and a fireplace to the opposing side, in blue greens and browns by Head Decorator Avril Bennett.

Wheel vases were available in four sizes, from the smallest 'No. 1' at 4.5in (11.5cm) in diameter to the 'Giant' at around 14in (35.5cm) in diameter. The 'Giant' size was also available as a lamp base, as with this example.

1973-79   *14.5in (37cm) high*

£1,000-1,500   **B&H**

A Troika Pottery 'wheel' vase, painted mark, chips.

2in (5cm) high

£250-300   **WW**

A Troika Pottery small 'wheel' vase, monogrammed "C.H." and probably by Honor Curtis.

1966-74   *4.75in (12cm) high*

£120-180   **B&H**

A late 1970s Troika Pottery 'wheel' lamp base, by Tina Doubleday, with textured green ground and embossed domino and arch designs to either side, in greens and browns.

10.25in (26cm) high

£280-320   **B&H**

A Troika Pottery 'cylinder' vase, restoration to rim.

5.5in (14cm) high

£70-100 GAZE

A 1960s Troika St Ives Pottery 'cylindrical' vase, with mottled brown glazes, marks to base.

6in (15cm) high

£100-150 GAZE

A Troika Pottery large 'cylinder' vase, by Honor Curtis, with mottled blue ground and painted double band of geometric disks.

1966-74   14.5in (37cm) h

£280-320 B&H

A late 1970s Troika Pottery large 'cylinder' vase, by Tina Doubleday, with textured green ground and geometric bands in high oranges and blues.

14.5in (37cm) high

£400-500 B&H

An early 1970s Troika Pottery medium 'cylinder' vase, by Linda Thomas, with painted disk design band.

7.5in (19cm) high

£120-180 B&H

A Troika Pottery small 'cylinder' vase, by Ann Jones, with brown textured ground and painted disk design band.

c1977   5.75in (14.5cm) high

£100-150 B&H

A Troika Pottery 'cylinder' vase, in blues, with a band of linked diamond decoration.

10in (25.5cm) high

£80-120 WW

An early Troika St Ives Pottery medium 'cylinder' vase with neck, by Stella Benjamin, with mottled brown ground and a painted disk design band.

1963-67   7.75in (20cm) h

£150-200 B&H

A Troika St Ives Pottery medium 'cylinder' vase with neck, by Stella Benjamin.

1963-67 7.75in (19.5cm) high

£220-280 B&H

CERAMICS

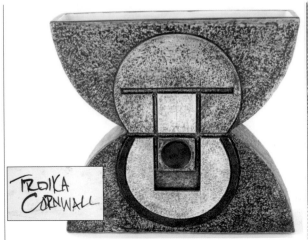

A 1970s Troika Pottery 'doublebased' vase, incised and painted with geometric devices, painted mark "Troika, Cornwall".

A late 1970s Troika Pottery 'anvil' vase, by Louise Jinks, with textured green ground and stylized embossed domino and mask designs to either side.

Anvil vases were designed and produced after 1965. Louise Jinks worked at Troika from 1976-81 and as Head Decorator from 1979-81. The form, pattern and glazes work extremely well together on this example.

8.5in (21.5cm) high

£550-650   **GORL** | £1,500-2,000   **B&H**

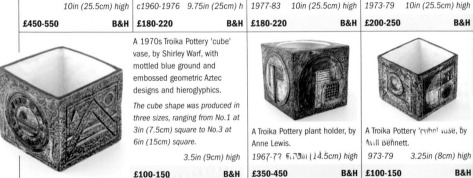

A rare early Troika St Ives Pottery 'urn' vase, with all-over white treacle glaze and bands of wax resist disks in matte black, trident mark to base.

10in (25.5cm) high

£450-550   **B&H**

A Troika Pottery 'urn' vase, by Penny Black, with mottled green ground and painted disk design band.

c1960-1976   9.75in (25cm) h

£180-220   **B&H**

A Troika Pottery 'urn' vase, by Jane Fitzgerald, with mottled green ground and painted band of geometric disks in high blues and browns.

1977-83   10in (25.5cm) high

£180-220   **B&H**

A Troika Pottery 'urn' vase, by Avril Bennett, with blue ground and brown painted disk design band.

1973-79   10in (25.5cm) high

£200-250   **B&H**

A 1970s Troika Pottery 'cube' vase, by Shirley Warf, with mottled blue ground and embossed geometric Aztec designs and hieroglyphics.

The cube shape was produced in three sizes, ranging from No.1 at 3in (7.5cm) square to No.3 at 6in (15cm) square.

3.5in (9cm) high

£100-150   **B&H**

A Troika Pottery plant holder, by Anne Lewis.

1967-73   5.75in (14.5cm) high

£350-450   **B&H**

A Troika Pottery 'cube' vase, by Avril Bennett.

973-79   3.25in (8cm) high

£100-150   **B&H**

A late 1970s Troika Pottery 'coffin' vase, by Tina Doubleday, with textured blue ground and embossed domino and brick kiln designs to either side.

A Troika Pottery 'coffin' vase, modelled in low relief, painted marks, chip to top rim, nicks to paintwork.

6.75in (17cm) high

£200-250   **WW**

A Troika Pottery 'coffin' vase, by Colin Carbis, embossed with stylized designs of a brick kiln and domino to either side.

c1977   6.75in (17cm) high

£200-250   **B&H**

A Troika 'coffin' vase, modelled in low relief, painted marks, nicks to paintwork.

6.75in (17cm) high

£200-250   **WW**

The 'coffin' vase was introduced in 1970 when the pottery moved to Newlyn, and was immensely popular during that decade. It is one of the most common shapes found by collectors today.

6.5in (16.5cm) high

£100-150   **B&H**

A Troika Pottery 'rectangle' vase, with unidentified monogram "E.W".

8.5in (21.5cm) high

£220-280   **B&H**

A rare early Troika St Ives Pottery lidded vessel, in blues and purples, with painted geometric designs, retailer's price "16/-" on base.

5.5in (14cm) high

£600-700   **B&H**

A Troika Pottery 'rectangle' vase, by Marilyn Pascoe, with embossed abstract helmet and arrow designs, blues and browns.

1970-74 8.75in (11.5cm) high

£250-350   **B&H**

A CLOSER LOOK AT A TROIKA WALL PLAQUE

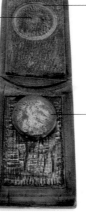

Wall plaques were one of the first products produced at Troika, while still in St Ives. This shape is similar to the later 'coffin' vases.

This piece is by Benny Sirota, co-founder of the pottery and bears his fingerprints at each end.

The combination of raised circles and geometric shapes is typical of Troika, as are the muted, almost Scandinavian inspired colours.

This is an early piece, dating from around a year after the pottery was founded in 1963.

A unique Troika Pottery wall plaque, by Benny Sirota, with raised circle and disk designs in blues and browns, on a textured ground.

c1964   15.5in (39.5cm) high

£3,200 1,200   **B&H**

A rare early Troika St Ives Pottery shallow dish, with mottled blue ground and stylized hieroglyphic designed centre panel, with impressed trident mark to the base.

1963-7   *11.75in (30cm) wide*

£1,500-2,000   **B&H**

An early Troika St Ives D-plate, of rounded square form, having embossed geometric flower head and leaf designs, in blues and greens, with impressed trident mark to base.

7.25in (18.5cm) diam

£350-450   **B&H**

A rare Troika St Ives Pottery floor tile, with blue painted Aztec sun design, marked on reverse.

Floor tiles were amongst the earliest objects produced and were discontinued not long after the pottery was founded.

5.75in (14.5cm) diam

£450-550   **B&H**

A Troika Newlyn Pottery pocket vase, by Louise Jinks, with embossed geometric stylized designs in greens and browns.

1976-81   *8in (20cm) high*

£700-800   **B&H**

A Troika St Ives Pottery double eggcup, with plain high white ground and blue painted geometric designs to base.

Double egg-cups were introduced in 1965 at the request of London retailer Heal's. Although expensive, costing a guinea each, a great many were made and sold.

c1965   *3.5in (9cm) high*

£100-150   **B&H**

A rare Troika St Ives Pottery teapot, of cylindrical form decorated with black-glazed shoulders, a painted disk design band in browns and blues, with original bent cane handle.

Teapots and coffee pots ceased to be produced just after 1967, having been made for around four years.

1963-67   *7in (18cm) diam*

£400-500   **B&H**

A Troika Pottery tin mine lamp base, by Alison Brigden, in the form of a stone building and chimney, in browns and greens.

1976-83   *8.5in (21.5cm) high*

£600-700   **B&H**

A CLOSER LOOK AT A TROIKA MASK

The piece is signed with an "SK" monogram, it was decorated by Simone Kilburn, who worked at Troika from 1976-77.

Masks are large and visually impressive display pieces and were introduced in the early 1970s and made until closure in 1983.

Masks are much rarer than other, more functional, objects as they did not sell well at the time and would have been expensive.

The design shows the influence of Paul Klee and Aztec designs and is in mint condition with no damage or wear.

A Troika Newlyn Pottery double-sided mask, by Simone Kilburn, one side with stylized Aztec design, the other depicting a Cycladic mask, blue and browns.

c1977   *10in (25.5cm) high*

£3,000-4,000   **B&H**

A CLOSER LOOK AT TWO WADE CATS

These figures are known as 'Blow-Ups' and are much larger than the standard 'Hatbox' figures. They are also rarer and more valuable.

They were produced later than the initial Hatbox' series, from 1961-65, and are slip-cast.

The colours are different to the 'Hatbox' figures, being beige and black with pink interiors to the ears.

Although similar, the design is different to the 'Hatbox' – Si's tail is integral to his body, rather than curling backwards and his facial expression is slightly different.

Two Wade Disney Series 'Si' and 'Am' Siamese cat figures, from "Lady & the Tramp". *1961-65*

smallest 5.5in (14cm) high

£180-220   **CHEF**

A Wade Disney Series 'Si' Siamese cat figure, from 'Lady & The Tramp'.

Despite its unpleasant face, this cat is worth 25% more than similar Siamese cats with pleasant or smiling faces from the same series.

1.75in (4.5cm) high

£20-30   **LG**

A Wade Disney series 'Am' Siamese cat figure, from 'Lady & The Tramp'.

1.75in (4.5cm) high

£15-25   **LG**

A set of four Wade 'Bengo and his Puppy Friends' TV Pets figures, including 'Chee Chee', 'Bengo', 'Fi Fi' and 'Pipi'.

These were based on the popular TV series of the time, based on characters devised by William Tlmym. They originally cost 3/11d each!

1959-65

largest 2.5in (6.5cm) high

£70-100   **PSA**

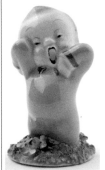

A Wade 'Nod' figure, first version with flowers to base.

These three figures were based on the children's poem 'Wynken, Blynken & Nod' by Eugene Field (1850-95). They were produced by Wade between 1948 and 1958. Watch out for Japanese copies, which are made from thinner and cheaper ceramic. They are virtually identical but are often marked "MADE IN JAPAN".

2.5in (6.5cm) high

£40-60   **PSA**

A Wade 'Blynken' figure, first version with flowers to base.

2.5in (6.5cm) high

£30-40   **PSA**

A Wade 'I've A Bare Behind' figure, first version with flowers at base.

2.75in (7cm) high

£15-20   **PSA**

CERAMICS

A Wade Fairytale 'I've a Bare Behind' figure, version two.

The first version of the figure had a floral base, which is removed on this second version. Presumably this cut costs and made the figures easier to mould and decorate. Version two was produced for a shorter period than the first version, making it rarer.

2.75in (7cm) high

£45-55   **PSA**

A Wade Fairytale 'Nod' figure, version two.

2.75in (7cm) high

£50-70   **PSA**

A limited edition Wade 'Brown Spaniel Dog' figure.

This model is from a limited edition of 1,000 produced to commemorate the Motorcycle Museum Wade Fair.

1994   3in (7.5cm) high

£30-40   **PSA**

A CLOSER LOOK AT WADE'S NATWEST PIGGY BANKS

Lady Hilary and Sir Nathaniel.are often considered the rarest pigs. Less were produced as they were only given to account holders with higher savings - £100 was a considerable sum for a child to save in the 1980s.

'Woody' was the first pig and early examples were made by Sunshine Ceramics, so do not bear the Wade backstamp.

Maxwell was reputedly named after disgraced tycoon Sir Robert Maxwell, who fell from grace after this pig had been released.

Look out for the ultra-rare gold Woody of which only 25 were made. It was coated in 22ct gold leaf and accompanied with a certificate – watch out for fakes that have been sprayed gold.

A set of Wade National Westminster Bank ceramic piggy banks, comprising 'Sir Nathaniel Westminster' the father, 'Lady Hilary' the mother, 'Maxwell' the boy, 'Annabel' the girl and 'Woody' the baby.

The set aimed to encourage children to save – £3 was needed for Woody (who himself cost £1 of that sum), £25 for Annabel, £50 for Maxwell, £75 for Lady Hilary then £100 for Sir Nathaniel. In 1999, Natwest revisited the idea and released 'Cousin Wesley', also made by Wade. Although 5,000 were reputedly produced, few are known as a child had to invest £1,000 to get one!

1983-88

Tallest 7in (18cm) high

£150-200   **B&H**

A Wade Works Cat figure, produced at Burslem.

1994   3.25in (8.5cm) high

£40-50   **PSA**

A Wade 'Quack-Quacks' pattern nursery trio set, by Robert Barlow.

Plate 6.25in (16cm) diam

£15-20   **CHS**

A Wade's Orcadia ware vase, streaked in orange and green.

7in (18cm) high

£15-25   **CHEF**

COLLECTORS' NOTES

- Robert Methven Heron inherited his father's business, Fife Pottery in Kirkcaldy, Scotland in 1833. Together with Bohemian artist Karel Nekola, who had been hired by Heron Snr., they introduced Wemyss ware in 1882. The range included cat or pig-shaped items, jug-and-basin sets, doorstops, tablewares, candlesticks and inkstands, which were hand-painted with bright and bold designs including roses, fruit, birds and bees.

- By Nekola's death in 1915, the style of pottery was less popular with the public and the company was sold to the Devon-based Bovey Tracey Pottery in 1930, when pieces were marked "Plinchta" "Wemyss". Nekola's son Joseph worked there until his death in 1942.

A small Wemyss 'Jazzy' Lady Eva vase, painted in bright colours, brown painted mark "Wemyss 213".

6in (15cm) high

£120-180   **L&T**

An early 20thC Wemyss honey pot and cover, retailed by T. Goode & Co., painted with a hive in fenced landscape on the cylindrical sides and with large bees flying about, painted mark.

£250-350   **CHEF**

A Wemyss 'Cock and Hen' Low Kintore candlestick, painted with a frieze of a cockerel and three hens, impressed mark "Wemyss Ware".

4.5in (11cm) high

£350-450   **L&T**

A Wemyss 'Roses' pattern cylindrical jug, with applied handle, impressed and painted marks, "Wemyss".

7in (17.5cm) high

£220-280   **L&T**

A Wemyss ware tankard, decorated with thistles, with an applied handle.

5.5in (14cm) high

£280-320   **L&T**

A Wemyss 'Dog Roses' pattern teapot and cover, of ovoid form painted with sprigs of dog roses, unmarked.

5.5in (14cm) high

£180-220   **L&T**

A Wemyss 'Daffodils' pattern basket, with frilled rim and applied rope-twist handle, restored handle terminals, impressed "RH&S" mark, printed retailer's mark.

12in (30cm) wide

£550-650   **L&T**

A Plinchta figure of a cat, painted with cabbage roses, printed marks.

6in (15cm) high

£150-200   **L&T**

A Royal Worcester flatback jug, decorated with flowers on an ivory ground, puce mark.

1892   7in (17.5cm) high

£180-220   **WW**

A Royal Worcester leaf-moulded vase, shape No. 1947, with three leaf handles, decorated in green, orange and yellow.

c1900   6.25in (16cm) wide

£120-180   **WW**

A Royal Worcester squat vase, painted with blackberries by Micky Miller.

1953   3in (7.5cm) high

£150-200   **GORL**

A Royal Worcester flat back jug, signed "C. Baldwin".

1902   5.25in (13cm) high

£1,500-2,000   **AL**

A Royal Worcester flat back jug.

1901   5.5in (14cm) high

£200-300   **GCL**

A Royal Worcester flat back jug.

1901   5.25in (13.5cm) high

£200-300   **GCL**

A Royal Worcester yellow ground coffee set, each piece printed and painted with floral reserves, comprising six coffee cups and saucers, milk, sugar, coffee pot and cover, with date code.

1938

£80-120   **CHEF**

A Royal Worcester hand-painted demi-tasse cup and saucer.

c1925   3.75in (9.5cm) diam

£250-300   **GCL**

A Royal Worcester plate, painted by John Stinton Jnr after Corot, with a hillside view and two children, against primrose and deep blue borders elaborately gilded with acanthus scrolls and paterae, with date code.

1929   10.5in (26.5cm) diam

£250-350   **GORL**

A Royal Worcester nautilus shell vase, raised on a rocky base with tree stump and moulded with shells, printed mark.

1898   *7in (17.5cm) high*

£150-200   **WW**

A Royal Worcester 'January' figure, modelled by F.G. Doughty, as a little boy in the snow, base stamped "3452".

                    6.25in (16cm) high

£40-50   **BAD**

A Royal Worcester 'February' figure, base stamped "3453".

                    6.25in (16cm) high

£180-220   **GORL**

A Royal Worcester 'Grandmother's Dress' bone china figure, designed by Freda Doughty, with date code

1939   *6in (15cm) high*

£120-180   **GORL**

A Royal Worcester 'Cook' candle extinguisher, blue with white apron.

1912   *2.5in (6.5cm) high*

£180-220   **GCL**

A Royal Worcester 'Nun' candle extinguisher.

1903   *3.75in (9.5cm) high*

£200-250   **GCL**

A pair of Royal Worcester 'Miniature Cairo Water Carriers' models, painted with bronzed colours, green printed marks, one with date code, shape number "1250", man has restored rim to jar.

1901   *10in (25cm) high*

£550-650   **DN**

A pair of Royal Worcester 'Paul' and 'Virginia' lustreware figures, each standing on a rocky base and decorated with enamel details, impressed marks to Virginia.

c1865   *13in (33cm) high*

£550-650   **WW**

A Royal Worcester 'Yankee' figure.

c1890   *6.75in (17cm) high*

£300-400   **GHA**

CERAMICS

An Ault jardinière, designed by Christopher Dresser, with frilled rim moulded with dragons, applied and impressed factory marks.

£40-60   **L&T**

An Ault art pottery vase.

c1895   4.5in (11.5cm) high

£80-120   **TCS**

An Ault vase, attributed to Christopher Dresser, No. 467, with a moulded grotesque fish mask and brown ground.

Ault was founded by William Ault in 1887 in Staffordshire.

c1900   7.5in (19cm) high

£600-700   **TCS**

A small Ault vase, design attributed to Christopher Dresser, pattern No. 312A, olive running to yellow with moulded moth decoration.

This is a typical mark found on an Ault vase. Other marks include the name on a ribbon motif, the monogram 'AP' and 'ATLTD' and 'Aultcliff' after the merger with the Ashby Potters' Guild in 1923.

c1895

4in (10cm) high

£80-120   **TCS**

A William Adams tall blue and white vase.

This pattern was introduced by Adams in 1780 and is a copy of a Chinese pattern.

12.5in (31.5cm) high

£100-150   **BAD**

A Barum Ware cat figurine, in green, brown, and blue glossy glaze, restoration to ears and tail.

7in (18cm) high

£70-90   **DRA**

A Beswick 'Ballet' pattern cheese dish, from the Dancing Days series.

£15-25   **PSA**

An English blue and white transfer-printed plate.

c1815   10in (25.5cm) diam

£60-80   **GCL**

A pair of Boch vases, with tall necks and glaring frilled rims, printed and painted with panels of flowers on a floral ground, printed marks "Polychrome Boch, Belgium".

12.25in (30.5cm) high

£120-180   **L&T**

A rare Brannam fish-shaped jug, modelled by Thomas Liverton for the Hungarian Millennium exhibition, top fin on handle restored.

Charles Brannam joined the family pottery in 1879. He continued with traditional designs but also introduced more innovative lines.

1896   5.5in (14cm) high

£500-600   **TCS**

A pair of Brannam sgraffito vases, by John Dewdney.

John Dewdney, hired in 1882, was the first professional designer brought to the Brannam's Litchdon Street pottery.

1887   8in (20cm) high

£250-300   **TCS**

A C.H. Brannam, Barnstable vase.

c1890   7.75in (19.5cm) high

£140-160   **ADE**

A pair of Bretby jewelled vases.

The Bretby pottery was founded in 1883 by Henry Tooth and William Ault. The Bretby trademark was a sun rising over the word Bretby. After 1891 the word 'ENGLAND' was added and after 1921, 'MADE IN ENGLAND'.

c1920   7.5in (19cm) high

£300-400   **TCS**

A Bretby copperette four flower vase, pattern No. 1649, with jewelled cabochons, inscribed "9.1.6R10".

c1910   7.5in (19cm) high

£150-200   **TCS**

A Bretby two-handled bronzed vase, and another white.

A particular characteristic of Bretby is a ceramic designed to imitate metal, both in terms of form and colour.

10.5in (27cm) high

£40-60   **CHEF**

A Bretby flown glaze baluster vase, pattern No. 776, size C.

c1900   8.5in (21.5cm) high

£150-200   **TCS**

A Bretby bumpy four-flower vase, pattern No. 1716, in green, cream and brown flown glaze.

c1910   6.5in (16.5cm) high

£100-150   **TCS**

A Bretby Art Deco vase, of tapering square section, with ribbed diagonal panels picked out with shaded mauves and yellows against pale turquoise, with indented base forming bracket feet, factory marks on base.

6in (15.5cm) high

£150-200   **DN**

A Bristol 'Long Line' sugar jar, by Pountney & Co. Ltd, printed marks.

6.75in (17cm) high

£30-40   **CHS**

A Burleigh Ware ovoid vase, moulded with a frieze of owls, highlighted in gilt and covered in buff glazes, printed and painted marks.

7.25in (18cm) high

£80-120   **L&T**

An unusual Art Deco Burleigh Ware sandwich plate and five side plates, with hand-painted Art Deco fruit and geometric flowers and shape design.

c1930

Largest 11.5in (29cm) wide

£70-90   **BAD**

A 1930s Burleigh Ware 'Bullfinch' vase, the base stamped "BULLFINCH BAILEY SCOTT".

5in (13cm) high

£120-180   **BAD**

A Burmantofts turquoise art pottery spoon warmer, in the shape of a seated toad.

c1895

5in (13cm) high

£300-400   **TCS**

A Burmantofts turquoise art pottery vase, in the shape of a three-legged toad.

Burmantofts Pottery manufactured art pottery between 1881 and 1904. Although mainly known for strongly coloured glazes on Eastern inspired forms, after the 1890s it began to make a range of 'grotesques'. These appealed to a public desire for the unusual and have become immensely popular with collectors today. The three-legged toad is a Chinese symbol that is said to bring wealth.

c1895

6.75in (17cm) high

£300-400   **TCS**

A Bursley Ware ovoid vase, designed by Charlotte Rhead, shape No. 122, tube-lined and painted with stylized foliage, predominantly in orange lustre and pale brown, printed mark.

12.5in (31.5cm) high

£70-100   **GORL**

A 1930s Coronet Ware cake plate, on a chrome stand, with hand-painted and low relief image of a crinolined lady.

Plate 9in (23cm) diam

£40-60   **BAD**

A 1930s Fielding's Devon Ware Art Deco hand painted lily form vase.

6in (15cm) high

£50-70   **BAD**

A Crown Devon 'Mattita' hand-painted vase.

Crown Devon and Devon Pottery were names used by S. Fielding & Co, founded in 1870.

c1930   9.5in (24cm) high

£120-180   **BAD**

A CLOSER LOOK AT A CHARLOTTE RHEAD CHARGER

The designer Charlotte Rhead is considered one of the 'big three' ceramics designers of the early 20thC, also including Susie Cooper and Clarice Cliff.

'Byzantine' is considered one of Rhead's best and most complex designs for A.G. Richardson, for whom she worked for 11 years from 1931.

A Fielding's Crown Devon Castle lustre jug.

This style imitated both the lustre ware produced by Carltonware (known as 'Rouge Royale') and the more desirable and valuable 'Wedgwood Fairyland' 1920s designs by Daisy Makeig-Jones.

Her trademark was the tube lining technique, taught her by her father, the noted designer Frederick Rhead. 'Tube lining' is where a design is piped or 'drawn' onto a piece in liquid clay.

Visually highly impressive, the charger is large with a stylized design typical of the period. Despite her fame, her work is perhaps still undervalued compared to Cliff's and Cooper's.

A large 1930s Crown Ducal 'Byzantine' wall plate, by Charlotte Rhead, tube-lined and coloured with a broad band of stylized flowers and foliage, with chequered secondary border against a mottled pale brown ground, factory marks and tube-lined signature.

c1930   9.25in (23.5cm) high

17.25in (44cm) diam

£250-300   **BAD**

£450-550   **DN**

A 1930s Fielding's Crown Devon pumpkin lidded pot, with a witch sitting on top, with slightly lustred orange glaze, slight chips to peak of top hat.

4.75in (12cm) high

£80-120   **BAD**

A Crown Devon sugar sifter, with printed decorated of roses.

4.75in (12cm) high

£4-6   **MTS**

A Crown Ducal 'Manchu' vase, designed by Charlotte Rhead, the pale green slightly baluster ridged body decorated with a dragon and flaming pearl, printed marks, signed "C Rhead", impressed "No. 12".

8.5in (21.5cm) high

£180-220   **J&H**

A Crown Ducal vase, designed by Charlotte Rhead, tube-lined with stylized flowers and painted in bright enamels.

6.75in (17cm) high

£120-180   **GORL**

An Art Deco A. Dean hand-painted vase, decorated with ducks, with a pinched lip, signed "A. Dean".

7.5in (19cm) high

£25-35   **BAD**

A Ducal hand-painted dish, designed by Charlotte Rhead.

12in (30.5cm) long

£70-100   **BAD**

An Elton Ware vase with handle, the tall cylindrical shape moulded with flowers against the deep mottled green glaze, painted mark, restored.

14.25in (36cm) high

£150-200   **GORL**

An Editions Etling earthenware figure of a Gascony duck, modelled by Marcel Guillard, with crackled glaze impressed and incised marks "Hersent".

8.5in (21.5cm) high

£250-350   **L&T**

A pair of Fantoni Cubist-style Italian Renaissance figures of a man and woman, polychrome glazes, on wooden base, several small flakes and touch-ups, marked "Fantoni/Italy".

14.5in (37cm) wide

£350-450   **DRA**

A Fantoni charger, incised in sgraffito with figures exercising and stretching, some glaze losses in manufacture, signed "Fantoni/Italy".

14in (35.5cm) diam

£300-400   **DRA**

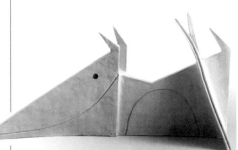

A Gambone ceramic dog sculpture, with carved details, covered in speckled ivory glaze, restoration to ears and muzzle, signed "Gambone/Italy".

33.5in (85cm) wide

£400-500   **DRA**

A pair of early 20thC Vereinigte Wiener & Gmunder Keramik pottery ducks, the two birds huddled on a green oval base, impressed marks.

3.75in (9.5cm) high

£100-150   **CHEF**

A Goebel bee-shaped honey pot, stamped on base "H6 1956".

4.25in (11cm) high

£100-150   **BAD**

A 1930s Goebel circular wall plaque, with a lady in a green dress dancing, incised marks.

Goebel is perhaps better known for producing a range of Art Deco figures and the ever-popular Hummel range of child figurines.

9.5in (24cm) diam

£200-300   **CHS**

A Goldscheider figure, by Linduer, moulded as a lady in a crinoline dress, chip to sleeve, printed marks.

8.75in (22cm) high

£100-150   **L&T**

A Gouda corseted vase, with geometric polychromatic design, several interior lines, marked "2073/Futurist/8/TNT/MH/Italiano".

6.75in (17cm) high

£120-180   **DRA**

An A. & E. Gray Pottery hand-painted charger, signed "A3829 AD".

Despite its appearance, this is not a Susie Cooper design, as she did not design any of Gray's patterns prefixed with an 'A'.

13.5in (34cm) diam

£300-400 BAD

An early 1930's Art Deco Grimwades 'Byzanta Ware' hand-painted lustre lidded urn.

Grimwades are best known for their transfer-decorated 'chintz' ware introduced in the mid-1920s.

8.75in (22.5cm) high

£180-220 BAD

A 1930s S. Hancock & Sons Rubens Ware hand-painted 'Pomegranate' bird, the base with holes for flowers.

7in (18cm) high

£80-120 BAD

A quirky 1930s Art Deco ceramic candlestick, in the form of a roaring lion, marked "Made in Japan".

3.25in (8.5cm) high

£50-70 BAD

A pair of 1930s Art Deco painted knife rests, in the form of pelicans, marked "Made in Japan".

4.25in (11cm) long

£45-55 BAD

A small 1930s Japanese lustre sitting dog egg cup.

2.75in (7cm) high

£30-40 BAD

A Johnson Bros. 'McDonalds Farm' pattern plate.

7in (18cm) diam

£12-18 CHS

A pair of early 20thC George Jones plates, encircled by gilt borders, signed "Birdbeck", factory marks.

8.5in (21.5cm) diam

£200-250 WW

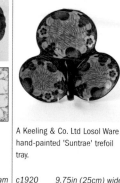

A Keeling & Co. Ltd Losol Ware hand-painted 'Suntrae' trefoil tray.

c1920 9.75in (25cm) wide

£60-80 BAD

A Keeling & Co. Ltd 'Losolware' hand-painted dish.

The purple background colour is highly unusual.

c1930 9.5in (24cm) diam

£180-220 BAD

A Liberty & Co. studio vase, of shouldered baluster form, painted with a frieze of fruited brambles, impressed marks.

9in (23cm) high

£35-45 | **L&T**

A 1930s Lingard 'An Old Woman Who Lived In A Shoe' teapot, milk jug and sugar bowl.

6.5in (16.5cm) wide

£60-80 | **BAD**

An unmarked Linthorpe slipper wall posy holder, with feather pattern, pattern No. 1768.

c1885   *7in (18cm) high*

£220-280 | **TCS**

A Linthorpe two-handled baluster vase, pattern No. 1308.

Linthorpe operated from 1879 to 1889 and produced some pieces by Christopher Dresser. The company was an inspiration to other designers in the late 19th and 20th centuries. At the closure of Linthorpe, many pottery companies benefited from the talents of their old work force.

c1884   *14in (35.5cm) high*

£250-300 | **TCS**

A Longwy Pottery footed dish, decorated with storks, stamped "Decore a la Main/Emaux de Longwy France", impressed "LONGWY".

The Longwy pottery was established in France in the late 1600s. From 1865 they made their characteristic earthenware decorated with 'cloisonné' style coloured enamels known as 'Emaux de Longwy'.

14.5in (37cm) diam

£250-350 | **SL**

A Longwy Pottery 'Primavera' large painted and glazed earthenware charger, stamped "PRIMAVERA LONGWY FRANCE", with damage.

14.75in (37.5cm) diam

£40-60 | **FRE**

A Longwy Pottery ceramic glazed earthenware bowl, stamped ink mark "LONGWY FRANCE".

2.5in (6.5cm) high

£150-200 | **FRE**

A Longwy Pottery ceramic glazed earthenware flower bowl, stamped ink mark "LONGWY FRANCE".

2.5in (6.5cm) high

£80-120 | **FRE**

A Longwy Pottery ceramic glazed earthenware trivet, stamped circular mark "EMAUX DE LONGWY" and "FRANCE".

£180-220 | **FRE**

A Longwy Pottery ceramic vase, two corners of foot chipped.

9.5in (24cm) high

£40-60 | **FRE**

A majolica pitcher, the aqua body with water lily motif.

7in (18cm) high

£100-150　　　　　　**DAW**

A majolica compote, the interior of bowl with four large leaves surrounded by a floral motif, losses.

10.25in (26cm) diam

£100-150　　　　　　**DAW**

A Portuguese majolica wallpocket, shaped as a bunch of radishes, with green and white glazes.

7in (18cm) high

£120-180　　　　　　**DRA**

An Etruscan majolica shell and seaweed teapot, impressed roundel, cover restored, some flakes.

Majolica is a corruption of 'maiolica', the term for Italian tin-glazed pottery and is characterised by brightly glazed earthenware.

c1875　　　　　　9.5in (24cm) long

£280-320　　　　　　**DRA**

A Geoffrey Maund hand-painted ceramic 'Gin Money' piggy bank.

The Geoffrey Maund Pottery was founded in 1950 and his work is growing in popularity.

6in (15cm) wide

£18-22　　　　　　**MTS**

An early 20thC German Art Nouveau pottery two-handled vase, painted with a bouquet of orchids on the green ground, flanked by foliate scroll handles, impressed mark for F.A. Mehlem and "2653".

12in (30.5cm) high

£120-180　　　　　　**S&K**

A Charles Meigh Bacchanalian Dance cup, relief-moulded in white parian, brown printed commemorative medallion mark.

c1850　　6.6in (16.5cm) high

£45-55　　　　　　**DN**

A Charles Meigh Bacchanalian Dance large jug, relief-moulded in buff stoneware, moulded mark incorporating registration diamond, metal lid missing.

1844　　11in (28.5cm) high

£50-60　　　　　　**DN**

A Charles Meigh Bacchanalian Dance jug, relief-moulded in white stoneware, moulded mark.

1844　　9in (23cm) high

£100-150　　　　　　**DN**

A 'Minster' jug, attributed to Charles Meigh, relief-moulded in white Parian with a blue ground, unmarked.

c1850　　10.5in (27cm) high

£50-70　　　　　　**DN**

CERAMICS

A late 19thC Minton bone china plate, titled 'Brantail', with reticulated border, the centre painted with a bird perched on a leafy branch, impressed marks.

9.5in (24cm) diam

£150-200   **WW**

A CLOSER LOOK AT A MYOTT VASE

The 'star' vase is one of Myott's best-known shapes and is typically Art Deco in form with its clean, angular lines and stepped form.

Little is known about Myott and its designs due to a fire that destroyed the factory in 1949. Many pieces are still affordable compared to other Art Deco ceramics.

The vase is hand-painted, in bright colours with stylised flowers typical of the Art Deco movement.

Look out for flaked paint, cracks and chips, as this devalues a piece.

A 1930s Myott ware star vase.

8.5in (21.5cm) high

£100-150   **RH**

A 1960s Lord Nelson Pottery "Caster Sugar" storage jar.

This design is a long way from the transfer-printed chintz patterns Lord Nelson Pottery made during the 1930s!

7.5in (19cm) high

£18-22   **MTS**

A Noritake Progression 'Blue Moon' pattern plate, printed marks.

8.25in (21cm) diam

£12-18   **CHS**

A Noritake Progression 'Up-Sa Daisy' pattern plate, printed marks.

8.5in (21.5cm) diam

£10-15   **CHS**

A Pearl Pottery of Hanley, England, hand-painted faceted Oriental inspired vase, the base also stamped "SANDON".

10.25in (26cm) high

£70-90   **BAD**

A Pilkingtons Royal Lancastrian large footed bowl, painted by Richard Joyce with an overall scale pattern in green brown on mottled orange ground, impressed mark, painted monogram.

Designer Richard Joyce worked at Pilkingtons from 1905 until he died in 1931. He is often credited with decorating more fine pieces than any other artist and favoured natural subjects. His work is sometimes signed with his initials in a square seal.

13.5in (34cm) diam

£80-120   **BONE**

A Pilkingtons Royal Lancastrian vase, painted by Richard Joyce, with stylized leaves and zigzag border in green and brown on grey ground, impressed mark, painted monogram.

9in (23cm) high

£60-80   **BONE**

A Pilkington Royal Lancastrian art pottery vase.

c1910   5in (13cm) high

£100-150   **TCS**

A Pilkington Lancastrian vase.

c1920   10in (25.5cm) high

£100-150   **TCS**

A Pilkington Lancastrian flown glazed vase.

The Pilkington Tile & Pottery Co was founded in 1891 and made art pottery between 1897 and 1937, as well as tiles and architectural pieces. The names 'Lancastrian' and 'Royal Lancastrian' were used from 1904 and 1913 consecutively. Pilkingtons' glazes are distinctive, from the glittering 'Sunstone' introduced in 1893, to lustre wares of 1906-1928, to sgraffito work.

c1915   11in (28cm) high

£120-180   **TCS**

An unusual Quenvit porcelain covered bowl, fashioned as a Negro minstrel, the domed cover being his cheerful smiling face, the base edged with a radiating turquoise-coloured ruff, impressed maker's mark on underside.

c1925   8.25in (21cm) diam

£180-220   **DN**

A Radford vase, matte painted with a tree and landscape in brown on mottled ochre ground, marked.

5in (12.5cm) high

£120-180   **DRA**

A pottery lamp base, attributed to Charlotte Rhead, typically slip-trailed with a band of palmettes on a net ground, numbered "5623".

8.25in (21cm) high

£80-120   **CHEF**

A Rosenthal young boy and bulldog figurine.

9.25in (23.5cm) high

£80-120   **BAD**

A Ruskin vase, covered in lustred pink and purple flambé glaze, marked.

The Ruskin Pottery, named after the great 19thC critic, operated in West Smethwick from 1901-35. The pottery is known for its glazes, a specialism of the founder William Howson Taylor. They are typically vibrantly or strongly coloured. Forms tend to be simple and Chinese in inspiration.

5.75in (14.5cm) high

£200-300   **DRA**

A Rosenthal porcelain coffee service, designed by Tapio Wirkkala, with three associated Rosenthal dishes, decorated with parquetry design, printed marks.

£120-180   **L&T**

CERAMICS

A Ruskin, West Smethwick jar, with short neck and foot, with overall sea green soufflé glaze, impressed marks.

1907   *6in (15cm) high*

£120-180   **CHEF**

A Ruskin bulbous vase, in celadon, amber, and indigo flambé crystalline glaze, stamped.

1931   *4.5in (11.5cm) high*

£250-350   **DRA**

A Ruskin stoneware crystalline glazed vase, impressed marks for 1931.

6.25in (16cm) high

£100-150   **WW**

A Ruskin bulbous vase, painted with green grapevines on a mottled lustred yellow ground, stamped, several hairlines.

7in (18cm) high

£60-80   **DRA**

A Ruskin high-fired bowl, the interior with a fawn glaze streaking to blue and orange towards the centre, impressed marks, dated 1930.

6in (15.5cm) diam

£60-80   **CHEF**

An Art Deco Shorter & Son Ltd Staffordshire hand-painted jug, decorated with pink daffodils.

9in (23cm) high

£100-150   **BAD**

An unusual Tuscan China figure 'Gypsy Girl', numbered "25" and inscribed "Potted by Plant".

The Plant family name has been associated with the Tuscan Works since the late 18thC.

6in (15cm) high

£180-220   **LFA**

A Vallauris lustre vase, by J. Gazietto, decorated with a wooded landscape scene, painted marks.

Vallauris is named after the region of South-eastern France in which it is made. A number of potteries are based there, most notably Massier and Foucard-Jourdan. The Madoura pottery made designs by Pablo Picasso who worked there briefly in 1946. Production today is dominated by cheerfully coloured tableware and vases.

11.5in (29cm) high

£350-450   **WW**

A pair of Vallauris pottery wall pockets, by Pierre Perret, each modelled as a pierrot, in colours, painted marks, damages.

8.5in (22cm) high

£100-150   **WW**

A Villeroy & Boch 'Acapulco' pattern tray, with printed marks.

£15-20   **CHS**

A Villeroy & Boch 'Izmir' pattern cup and saucer.

c1973   *6in (15cm) diam*

£25-30   **CHS**

A CLOSER LOOK AT A WEDGWOOD VASE

This vase was designed by Norman Wilson (1902-88), Wedgwood's production manager from 1927, as indicated by an 'NW' monogram on the base.

Wilson is closely connected to Keith Murray, one of Wedgwood's most famous 20thC designers. Wilson helped Murray with production processes and developing glazes in the 1930s and 1950s.

Although not matte like many of Murray's glazes, the design and glaze are typical of the period, being light in colour and with minimal decoration.

The form is also typical of the period and simple, recalling Murray's designs.

A Wedgwood vase, designed by Norman Wilson, covered in a pale blue glaze, impressed mark "NW".

6in (15cm) high

£200-250   **WW**

A Villeroy & Boch 'Glasgow' pattern teapot and sugar bowl, printed marks.

teapot 7in (18cm) high

£50-70 pair   **CHS**

A Villeroy & Boch cat cheese platter, printed marks.

10in (25.5cm) long

£50-70   **CHS**

A pair of Villeroy & Boch rabbit salt and pepper shakers, printed marks.

3.25in (8.5cm) high

£40-70   **CHS**

A Wedgwood 'Harvest Festival' pattern coffee pot, designed by Eric Ravillious.

£150-200   **GAZE**

A Wedgwood blue Jasperware cheese dish and cover, the knop as an acorn.

10.75in (27.5cm) diam

£150-200   **GAZE**

A Wedgwood hand-painted lidded box.

6in (15.5cm) wide

£70-100   **BAD**

A 1930s Woods ceramic square lidded 'beehive' box, with bee knop.

5.25in (13.5cm) wide

£60-70 BAD

A 20thC German porcelain swan bowl, with black and yellow feet and beak, the bowl within its wings.

6in (15cm) high

£20-30 CHEF

An Art Deco hand-painted figure of a budgie, by Weetman.

7.5in (19cm) high

£40-60 BAD

A Capo di Monte-style porcelain cat, seated on a cushion, playing with its tail.

4.5in (11.5cm) wide

£15-20 CHEF

A Haviland Limoges Art Deco style porcelain 'tête-à-tête', after Emile Sandoz, comprising a bird-form tea pot, a bird-form creamer, a duck-form covered sugar, a mushroom-form shaker, two teacups, two saucers and a tray, printed, impressed and incised marks, printed "hand painted from a design of E. Sandoz/edition limited/no 011/1000".

tray 15.75in (40cm) wide

£250-300 SL

Two horse-painted wares.

£20-30 CHEF

An English art pottery jug, in the style of Christopher Dresser, with angular handle.

c1890 *8in (20cm) high*

£70-100 TCS

A Czechoslovakian Bauhaus-inspired lidded jar, possibly 1930s, with hand-painted and gilt decoration and stepped form.

11.5in (29cm) high

£70-100 BAD

A 19thC English ceramic sardine lidded box, once used for storing sardines.

5.25in (13.5cm) wide

£30-40 BAD

A lithophane panel in holder, panel depicts young girl reading a scroll, wear to holder finish.

A lithophane is a moulded porcelain or ceramic object where a picture is created by the thickness of the material. Thick parts are darker in tone and show as shadows, whilst thin parts are lighter. They can be framed and hung in windows, but are also often found in the bottom of cups. They were developed by KPM Berlin in the 1820s.

16.25in (41.5cm) high

£350-450 JDJ

A 1950s Gund 'Popeye' vinyl and stuffed plush roly-poly toy, with bell inside, and original tag.

Popeye the Sailorman, the world's most famous spinach eater, first appeared in January 1929 in a comic strip drawn by Elzie Segar called 'Thimble Theater'. Originally about Olive Oyl (later to become Popeye's leading lady) and her family, Popeye soon took over and a whole new series of characters such as Swee'Pea the 'infink' and Brutus appeared. Over 600 cartoons were made by the Fleischer Studios, the first airing in 1933. Early memorabilia from the 1930s to the 1950s is usually highly sought after but condition is very important.

9in (23cm) high

£30-40   **WAC**

A Gund Mfg. Co. 'Popeye' hand puppet, with soft vinyl head.

9.5in (24cm) high

£30-40   **SOTT**

An 'Olive Oyl' push button puppet, by Kohner Bros. Hong Kong.

These puppets have become a collecting field in their own right.

4.25in (10.5cm) high

£20-30   **SOTT**

An early 'Popeye' cast and painted metal lamp.

This lamp would originally have come with a Popeye shade, but these were easily damaged and are hard to find.

11in (28cm) high

£100-150   **SOTT**

A 'Popeye' lithographed tinplate speedboat toy, possibly 1950s, with keywound mechanism, with box.

7in (18cm) long

£80-120   **CANT**

A 'Popeye' lithographed tin Dime Register Bank.

1929   2.5in (6.5cm) wide

£40-60   **DH**

An American 'Popeye' New York Evening Journal pin.

1in (3cm) wide

£30-40   **LDE**

A 1950s 'Popeye' wooden pipe, on original card.

9in (22.5cm) wide

£60-80   **SOTT**

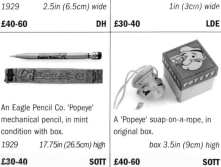

An Eagle Pencil Co. 'Popeye' mechanical pencil, in mint condition with box.

1929   17.75in (26.5cm) high

£30-40   **SOTT**

A 'Popeye' soap-on-a-rope, in original box.

box 3.5in (9cm) high

£40-60   **SOTT**

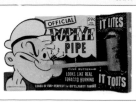

A 'Superman' plastic 'Spinball' pinball game, complete and with original coloured stickers.

A 'Superman' model SP-19 child's record player, by Dejay Corp, marked "©DC Comics 1978".

c1978   *11.75in (30cm) wide*

£150-200   **NOR**

Superman was originally devised in 1933 by high school students Joe Shuster and Jerry Siegel and first appeared in their fanzine 'Science Fiction' as a villain in 'The Reign of The Superman' series. By 1934, he had become a hero and began to be redesigned, but it was not until June 1938 and the publication of the first issue of 'Action Comics' that he appeared publicly in print and began his superhuman rise to prominence and worldwide fame. Today this comic could fetch as much as £250,000 in near mint condition! Interestingly, many claim that period styles for male bathing suits is the reason why the 'man of steel' wears his shorts as he does – many swimming trunks of the period were 'Speedo' like in shape and belted.

1967   *21.75in (55.5cm) long*

£100-150   **NOR**

A 'Superman' radio, lacks battery cover.

1973   *6in (15cm) wide*

£20-30   **NOR**

An American 'Superman-Tim Club' pin, reverse reading "MEMBER IN GOOD STANDING".

1in (2.5cm) wide

£15-25   **LDE**

A 'Superman' hairbrush, by Avon, in original box, both mint condition.

8.5in (21.5cm) high

£15-20   **NOR**

A 'Superman' soft vinyl and cloth handpuppet, by Ideal Toy Corp.

c1965   *11in (27.5cm) high*

£70-100   **NOR**

A 'Mighty Mouse' die-cut card figure.

'Mighty Mouse' first appeared in 1942 and was originally devised as a fly until one of the Terrytoons studio moguls came up with the idea of a mouse instead. The idea was to combine Superman-like powers with a small, insignificant animal. His initial name of 'Supermouse' was changed to Mighty Mouse in 1943 and from then he went on to star in comics from 1945 until the 1990s, and in numerous TV cartoon series in the 1970s and 1980s.

c1960   *11.5in (29cm) high*

£40-50   **SOTT**

A 1960s 'Supermen of America' pin, by National Periodical Publications Inc.

1961   *1in (3cm) wide*

£35-45   **LDE**

A Sesame Street 'Bert' soft vinyl money bank, marked on the back by "NEW YORK VINYL PROD CORP. 1971"

13.25in (33.5cm) high

£12-18   **WAC**

A late 1970s Muppets Inc. Sesame Street 'Bert' printed cloth pillow doll.

19.25in (49cm) high

£7-10   **AC**

An uncommon 'Cookie Monster' plush hand puppet, with pull-string and loop to operate mouth and spherical plastic eyes.

In better condition, he would fetch up to £25.

10.25in (26cm) high

£10-15   **WAC**

A licensed Sesame Street 'Oscar The Grouch' hand puppet, by Educational Toys Inc., with sunken plastic eyes and applied brown lashes, with cord to operate mouth.

10.25in (26cm) high

£10-15   **WAC**

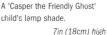

A 1960s 'Casper the Friendly Ghost' lithographed tin and celluloid musical pop-up box, by Mattel, with music arranged by Ted Duncan, marked "©1959 Mattel Inc.".

The celluloid head (with trembling eyes) of this toy is particularly thin and vulnerable to damage, so complete undamaged examples command a premium.

box 9.25in (14cm) high

A licensed Sesame Street 'Big Bird' plush speaking soft toy, with pull cord, with hole in back of head to move beak.

c1981   *21in (53cm) high*

£10-15   **WAC**

£40-60   **SOTT**

A 'Casper the Friendly Ghost' child's lamp shade.

7in (18cm) high

£30-40   **SOTT**

A 1960s 'Casper the Friendly Ghost' 'Spooky Slate', with wooden pencil.

Write on the slate with the pencil. Lifting up the top leaf causes the writing to mysteriously vanish!

11in (28cm) high

£20-30   **SOTT**

A Gund Gundikins 'Spooky' vinyl and plush doll, with card inserts in feet to allow him to stand.

9in (23cm) high

£60-80   **WAC**

A Gund 'Wendy The Good Little Witch' vinyl and stuffed plush doll, with original label and card inserts in feet to allow her to stand.

£60-80   **WAC**

A licensed Warner Bros Bugs Bunny hard plastic doll, by M&H Novelty Corp, with original clothes and tag, metal bars in his arms to pose, original baseball and hard foam white painted ball and felt carrot.

The fact that he is complete, clean and a very early example, makes this doll valuable.

A 1970s licensed Jim Henson's The Muppet Show 'Kermit The Frog' soft toy, by Fisher Price Toys, with Velcro pads on his hands and feet.

19.75in (50cm) high

A licensed Jim Henson's The Muppet Show 'Scooter' hugging doll, by Fisher Price Toys, with Velcro patches on his felt hands and hard plastic moulded feet.

c1975   16.25in (41.5cm) high

c1945

14.5in (37cm) high

£10-15 WAC | **£8-12** WAC | **£70-100** WAC

A 'Dopey' moulded and painted fabric-headed cloth-bodied doll, possibly by Ideal, in original felt clothes.

A Hanna Barbera's Yogi Bear 'Boo-Boo' vinyl and plush sitting toy, by Knickerbocker Toy Co., possibly 1960s, with original label.

A large 'Fred Flintstone' soft vinyl and fabric doll, by Knickerbocker Toy Co., with plush and felt clothing, card inserts in his feet to make him stand and original tag.

1938   11.5in (29cm) high

9in (23cm) high

c1961   17in (43cm) high

£70-100 WAC | **£30-40** WAC | **£40-60** WAC

A Warner Bros 'Tweety Pie' fabric and hard plastic headed finger puppet.

c1978   4in (10cm) high

A Bendy Toys 'Pink Panther' poseable toy.

The value of these toys is related to their condition as they can degrade very quickly, with the surface and eventually the material itself cracking and even fragmenting. This one has not yet degraded.

A Chipmunks 'Simon' soft vinyl musical doll, by Knickerbocker, with tag.

c1961   13in (33cm) high

A 1960s Ideal 'Mr Magoo' soft vinyl and stuffed fabric seated toy, with felt clothes, plush scarf and corduroy legs.

This toy was re-issued around 1988-89 and is usually worth under £12.

c1962   11.75in (30cm) seated

£7-10 WAC | **£30-40** WAC | **£40-60** WAC | **£60-80** WAC

COLLECTORS' NOTES

■ Although some sets can make several hundred pounds, the majority of cigarette cards are much more affordable, making them popular with collectors at all levels.

■ Card stiffeners were first added to paper cigarette packs by American tobacco manufacturers in 1879. These early cards were simply printed with text, but were replaced by pictorial cards from 1885.

■ W.D. & H.O. Wills were the first British tobacco company to include cigarette cards c1887. Production was aided by the use of colour lithography printing; which had been popularised in the 1860s.

■ As cards became commonplace, tobacco companies used them to retain customer loyalty, encouraging buyers to complete sets of cards. This was enforced

with a wide range of subjects ranging from flora and fauna, to cars, sports, and historical subjects.

■ Early cards from the 19thC are some of the most sought-after, particularly those from small, obscure companies such as Ainsworth of Harrogate, Alberge & Bromet of London, MacDonald of Glasgow and Taddy of London.

■ Cards that have never been glued into albums are preferable and collections should ideally be stored in sectioned plastic wallets. While individual cards from a particular set can have the same value, the first and last card in a series can often be damaged from sets bound with a rubber band.

■ Also desirable are non-standard shapes and sets that form a larger picture when placed together in order.

A series of 48 'Wild Animals' cigarette cards, issued by Gallaher Ltd.
1937   *2.75in (7cm) high*
£10-14   **CANT**

A series of 50 'Champions of 1936' cigarette cards, issued by Ogdens.
1936   *2.75in (7cm) high*
£50-70   **CANT**

A series of 25 'ABC of Sport' cigarette cards, issued by Ogdens of St. Julien Tobacco.
1927   *2.75in (7cm) high*
£45-55   **CANT**

A series of 50 'Celebrities of Sport' cigarette cards, issued by R. & J. Hill Ltd.
1939   *2.75in (7cm) high*
£60-80   **CANT**

A series of 25 'Feathered Friends' cigarette cards, issued by Abdulla & Co. Ltd.
1935   *2.5in (6.5 cm) high*
£15-25   **CANT**

A series of 48 'Aeroplanes' cigarette cards, issued by Gallaher Ltd.
1939   *2.75in (7cm) high*
£35-45   **CANT**

A series of 48 'Treasure Trove' cigarette cards, issued by W.A. & A.C. Churchman.
1939   *2.75in (7cm) high*
£8-12   **CANT**

A series of 48 'Holidays in Britain' cigarette cards, issued by W.A. & A.C. Churchman.
1938   *2.75in (7cm) wide*
£8-12   **CANT**

A series of 25 'British Butterflies' cigarette cards, issued by Godfrey Philips Ltd.
1927   *2.75in (7cm) high*

£15-20   **CANT**

A series of 36 'Ships That Have Made History' cigarette cards, issued by Godfrey Philips Ltd.
1938

2.5in (6.5 cm) wide

£30-40   **CANT**

A series of 30 'Our Dogs' cigarette cards, issued by Godfrey Philips Ltd.
1939   *2.75in (7cm) high*

£12-18   **CANT**

A series of 25 'British Live Stock' cigarette cards, issued by John Player & Sons.
1915   *2.75in (7cm) high*

£40-60   **CANT**

A series of 25 'Polar Exploration' cigarette cards, issued by John Player & Sons.
1915   *2.75in (7cm) high*

£40-50   **CANT**

A series of 50 'Game Birds & Wild Fowl' cigarette cards, issued by John Player & Sons.
1927   *2.75in (7cm) high*

£30-40   **CANT**

A series of 25 'Grandee Top Dogs Collection' cigarette cards, issued by John Player & Sons.
1979   *3.5in (7cm) wide*

£15-25   **CANT**

A series of 50 'Gardening Hints' cigarette cards, issued by W.D. & H.O. Wills.
1923   *2.75in (7cm) high*

£7-9   **CANT**

A series of 50 'Cricketers' cigarette cards, issued by W.D. & H.O. Wills.
1928   *2.75in (7cm) high*

£70-90   **CANT**

FIND OUT MORE...

'Card Time', *monthly magazine available by subscription from Magpie Publications, 70 Winifred Lane, Aughton, Ormskirk, Lancs. L39 5DL.*

'Murray's Cigarette Cards 2004', *published by Murray Cards (International) Ltd, 1993.*

COLLECTORS' NOTES

- Coin collecting is the oldest of the numismatic fields and the sheer range of types available can seem daunting to a new collector.

- It is generally advisable to concentrate on one area such as the ancient world, commemoratives, error coins, or simply examples from one specific period and place.

- When buying commemorative issues look at the edition number, those released in large numbers will appreciate less than more limited issues.

- Beware of facsimile collectors coins, which are common. Although not necessarily made to deceive, it can be hard to tell them from the genuine article.

- Coins should be handled as little as possible as condition is very important, invest in a good quality album and mounts to display and store your collection.

A silver facsimile Chinese coin with a military bust of Yuan Shih-Kai.

Original coins with this design can fetch £200, although the large number of facsimiles now in circulation has reduced the value of the originals.

1914   1.5in (4cm) diam

£2-3   **INT**

A Victorian crown, featuring the 'Old Head' portrait of Queen Victoria on the obverse and a representation of George slaying the dragon on the reverse, dated 1898.

1.5in (4cm) diam

£10-15   **INT**

A five pound coin, struck to commemorate Elizabeth II's Jubilee in 2002, featuring a portrait of the monarch on the obverse and an equestrian portrait of Elizabeth II on the reverse, surrounded by Latin script.

1.5in (4cm) diam

£5-6   **INT**

A 17thC coin, possibly from Flanders, found in the River Thames, very worn portrait and inscription on obverse, arms on reverse.

0.75in (2cm) wide

£6-8   **INT**

An Indian one rupee coin, struck with a portrait of Edward VII on obverse and Indian flora and script on reverse, dated 1909.

1.25in (3cm) diam

£5-7   **INT**

A Roman coin, featuring a portrait of the Emperor Gaius Caesar Augustus Germanicus on the obverse and three figures on the reverse, worn and discoloured.

cAD40   0.75in (2cm) diam

£10-15   **INT**

A J.R. Grundy trader's token, featuring a tobacco plant and inscribed "J.R. Grundy Merchant Ballarat 1861".

1861   1.5in (3.5cm) diam

£6-8   **INT**

A South African Commonwealth five shilling bullion coin, struck in 1952 to commemorate the tri-centennial of the establishment of the first Dutch settlement in South Africa, portrait of George VI on obverse and ship from Van Riebeeck's fleet on reverse.

1.5in (4cm) diam

£7-10   **INT**

FIND OUT MORE...

www.money.org – American Numismatic Association.

'Standard Catalog of World Coins', by Chester L. Krause & Clifford Mishler, published by Krause Publications.

COLLECTORS' NOTES

■ Although people tend to think of American Superheroes such as Superman and Spider-Man when talking about comics, interest in British comics is on the rise. This is possibly part of general wave of nostalgia and the increasing number of examples available on the Internet.

■ The earliest British comic was "Funny Folk" (1874-1894), the first to feature colour pages was Puck (1904-1940) and Mickey Mouse Monthly (1936-1955) was the first in full colour.

■ The 1930s is one of the key eras, and saw the launch of two of the most consistently popular titles, The Dandy (1937-) and The Beano (1938-). These two titles are very popular with collectors and very early examples can make hundreds of pounds although later issues can be under £1.

■ The equally popular Eagle (1950-1969) was founded by Reverend Marcus Morris and one of its most popular characters, Dan Dare, was the lead feature in the first issue. The popularity of the comic means that many issues were saved at the time, making them relatively easy to find and standard copies usually fetch under £10.

■ In general, girls' comics are less desirable although interest is growing and this could be a hot area for the future. Many girls' comics feature cut-out dolls or dolls' clothing, so look for complete examples.

■ As with any paper-based collectable, condition has a huge affect on value so look for complete examples without tears or graffiti and with clean, intact covers.

"Bunty", January 24th, 1959, published by D.C. Thomson & Co.

Bunty was among the vanguard of British comics for girls, it was very long lived, finally folding in 2001.

11.75in (29cm) high

£3-5 BPAL

"The Beano", August 1st, 1970, published by D.C. Thomson & Co.

11.75in (30cm) high

£6-8 VM

"The Beano", No. 1535, Dec 18th, 1971, published by D.C. Thomson & Co.

11.75in (30cm) high

£5-8 VM

"The Dandy", No. 293, May 26th, 1945, published by D.C. Thomson & Co.

11.5in (29cm) high

£20-25 BPAL

"The Dandy", No. 290, April 14th, 1945, published by D.C. Thomson & Co.

11.75in (29cm) high

£30-40 VM

"Classics Illustrated", No. 158A, featuring Ian Fleming's "Doctor No".

This is one of the rarest editions of the series and very sought-after.

c1950 *9.75in (25cm) high*

£250-350 BPAL

"Classics Illustrated", No. 100, featuring "Mutiny on the Bounty" by Nordoff & Hall.

9.75in (25cm) high

£5-10 BPAL

"The Dandy", No. 939, November 21st, 1959, published by D.C. Thomson & Co.

11.75in (29cm) high

£10-15 VM

"The Dandy", No. 1903, May 13th, 1978, published by D.C. Thomson & Co.

11.75in (29cm) high

£5-6 VM

"Eagle", No. 32, November 17th, 1950, published by Hulton Press.

Always look for examples in pristine condition. Due to the large print run these have the best chance of gaining in value.

13.75in (35cm) high

£20-25 VM

"Eagle", Vol. 3, No. 46, February 20th, 1953, published by Hulton Press.

13.5in (34cm) high

£4-6 BPAL

"Eagle", Vol. 8, No. 4, January 25th, 1957, published by Hulton Press.

13.5in (34cm) high

£10-15 VM

"Express Weekly", 31st March, 1956, published by Beaverbrook.

Express Weekly was larger than most comics of the time. As a result, if they were stacked amongst other comics they tended to get damaged around the edges, so fewer survive in top condition.

14in (35.5cm) high

£6-9 BPAL

"Rainbow", April 29th, 1944.

14.75in (37.5cm) high

£20-25 VM

"The Hotspur", No. 687, January 7th, 1950, published by D.C. Thomson.

First published in 1933, Hotspur was regarded as one of the 'Big Five' of early comics together with "Adventure", "Rover", "Skipper" and "Wizard".

11.75in (29cm) high

£6-8 BPAL

"Victor", No. 1099, March 13th, 1982, published by D.C. Thomson.

Victor first hit the streets in 1960, surviving until the early 1990s.

11.5in (29cm) high

£2-3 BPAL

"Wizard", No. 1821, January 7th, 1961, published by D.C. Thomson.

The original Wizard comic ran from 1922 to 1963.

11.5in (29cm) high

£5-6 BPAL

"Adventure Comics", No. 268, Jan. 1960, published by DC Comics.

£12-15   **MC**

"Adventure Comics", No. 294, Mar. 1962, published by DC Comics.

£6-8   **MC**

"Batman", No. 156, June 1963, published by DC Comics.

£10-15   **MC**

"Batman", No. 166, Sept. 1964, published by DC Comics.

£7-10   **MC**

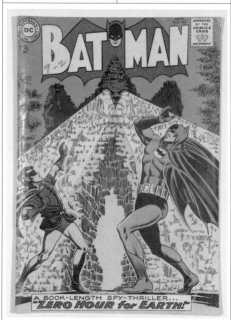

"Batman", No. 186, Nov. 1966, published by DC Comics.

£10-15   **MC**

"The Untold Legend of Batman", No. 3, Sept. 1980, published by DC Comics.

£2-3   **MC**

"Batman", No. 167, Nov. 1964, published by DC Comics.

£4-6   **MC**

"Detective Comics", No. 276, Feb. 1960, published by DC Comics.

£12-18   **MC**

"Green Lantern", No. 23, Nov. 1959, published by DC Comics.

£3-5   **MC**

"Justice League of America", No. 23, Nov. 1963, published by DC Comics.

£6-8   MC

"Superman", No. 150, Jan. 1962, published by DC Comics.

£4-6   MC

"Superman", No. 156, Oct. 1962, published by DC Comics.

£5-7   MC

"Action Comics", No. 286, Mar. 1962, published by DC Comics.

£1-2   MC

"Superman vs Kobra", No. 327, Sept. 1978, published by DC Comics.

£1-2   MC

"Giant Superman Annual" comic, No. 2, published by DC Comics.

£2-3   MC

"World's Finest ", No. 144, Sept. 1964, published by DC Comics.

£2-4   MC

"World's Finest", No. 137, Nov. 1963, published by DC Comics.

£3-5   MC

"Wonder Woman", No. 97, Apr. 1958, published by DC Comics.

£10-15   MC

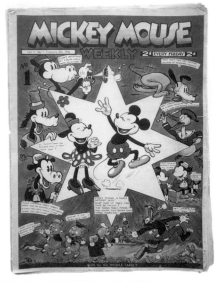

"Mickey Mouse Weekly", February 8th, 1936.

This was the first edition of this comic. The first issue of a title is usually one of the most desirable.

15in (38cm) high

£200-250   **BPAL**

"Walt Disney's Mickey Mouse and His Sky Adventure", No. 105, Feb. 1966, published by Gold Key.

£1-2   **MC**

"Tom and Jerry", No. 136, Nov. 1955, published by DC Comics.

£2-3   **MC**

"Walt Disney's Uncle Scrooge", No. 25, May 1959, published by Dell.

£7-10   **MC**

"Walt Disney's Comics and Stories", No. 2, Vol. 25, 1964, published by Gold Key.

£2-3   **MC**

"Woody Woodpecker", No. 59, Mar. 1960, published by Dell.

£1-2   **MC**

"Fightin' Army", No. 57, Mar. 1964, published by Charlton.

£1-2   **MC**

"Army War Heroes", No. 15, Aug. 1966, published by Charlton.

£1-2   **MC**

"Our Fighting Forces", No. 67, May 1963, publishes by Charlton.

£3-4   **MC**

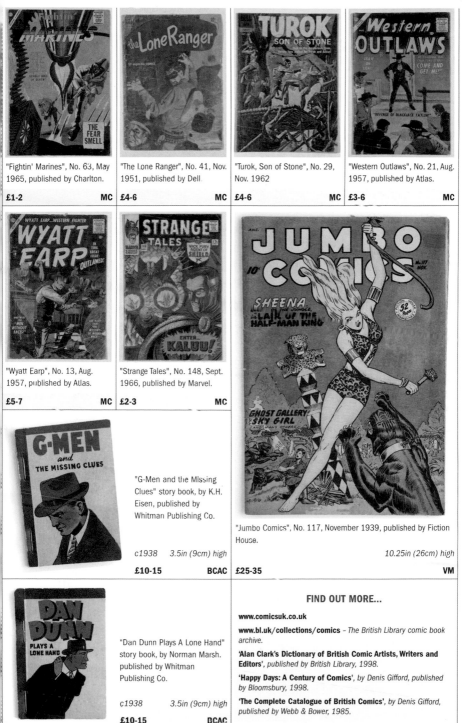

"Fightin' Marines", No. 63, May 1965, published by Charlton.

£1-2   **MC**

"The Lone Ranger", No. 41, Nov. 1951, published by Dell

£4-6   **MC**

"Turok, Son of Stone", No. 29, Nov. 1962

£4-6   **MC**

"Western Outlaws", No. 21, Aug. 1957, published by Atlas.

£3-6   **MC**

"Wyatt Earp", No. 13, Aug. 1957, published by Atlas.

£5-7   **MC**

"Strange Tales", No. 148, Sept. 1966, published by Marvel.

£2-3   **MC**

"G-Men and the Missing Clues" story book, by K.H. Eisen, published by Whitman Publishing Co.

c1938   *3.5in (9cm) high*

£10-15   **BCAC**

"Jumbo Comics", No. 117, November 1939, published by Fiction House.

10.25in (26cm) high

£25-35   **VM**

"Dan Dunn Plays A Lone Hand" story book, by Norman Marsh, published by Whitman Publishing Co.

c1938   *3.5in (9cm) high*

£10-15   **DCAC**

FIND OUT MORE...

www.comicsuk.co.uk

www.bl.uk/collections/comics - *The British Library comic book archive.*

'Alan Clark's Dictionary of British Comic Artists, Writers and Editors', *published by British Library, 1998.*

'Happy Days: A Century of Comics', *by Denis Gifford, published by Bloomsbury, 1998.*

'The Complete Catalogue of British Comics', *by Denis Gifford, published by Webb & Bower, 1985.*

COMMEMORATIVES

A bone china mug, in memoriam to William Gladstone, no maker's name.

c1898   *3.25in (8.5cm) high*

£80-110   **H&G**

A framed tile by Sherwin Cotton, in memoriam to William Gladstone, with a contemporary frame.

Although the frame can increase the desirability for Gladstone collectors, some collectors would look for an example without the frame. Always check that the frame has not caused any damage to the tile beneath.

c1898   *tile 8.5in (21.5cm) high*

£120-180   **H&G**

An earthenware plate, commemorating George Thomas, Speaker of the House of Commons, by Panorama Studios.

Panorama pieces are commonly decorated with a large amount of text.

1975   *10in (25.5cm) diam*

£60-80   **H&G**

An earthenware Edward Heath 'Ugly mug', produced for Private Eye, with illustration by Willie Rushton, printed with "Edward Heath's ugly mug".

c1974   *3.5in (9cm) diam*

£40-60   **H&G**

A Royal Worcester bone china plate, commemorating Margaret Thatcher's tenth year as Prime Minister.

c1989   *9in (23cm) diam*

£80-100   **H&G**

A 'Spitting Image' Margaret Thatcher egg cup.

A mug in the same design is also found, and can be worth up to 20% more than the egg cup.

c1983   *3.5in (9cm) high*

£50-60   **H&G**

A 'Women In Action' earthenware mug, commemorating the role of women in the miner's strike.

These, and other pieces commemorating the strike, were produced to raise money for the cause.

c1985 4.5in (11.5cm) high

£35-45   **H&G**

Three 'Spitting Image' mugs, with political subjects.

c1992   *3.5in (9cm) high*

£30-40 each   **H&G**

A bone china plate, by Crown Winsor, commemorating the abolition of the Greater London Council, from a limited edition of 500.

c1986   *11in (28cm) diam*

£50-70   **H&G**

A Royal Crown Derby bone china loving cup, commemorating John Major's election victory and the historic Conservative fourth term.

c1992   *3in (7.5cm) high*

£120-160   **H&G**

A bone china cup and saucer, by Chelsea China, commemorating victory in WWI.

1919   *5.5in (14cm) high*

£70-90   **H&G**

An earthenware mug by T.G. Green, commemorating the end of WWI.

T.G. Green of Derbyshire are more famous for their blue stripey 'Cornishware' domestic ceramics, produced from the 1920s.

1919   *3in (7.5cm) high*

£50-60   **H&G**

An earthenware jug, commemorating Prime Minister Lloyd George in WWI.

It is hard to find this type of jug in such good condition.

1914-16   6.25in (16cm) high

£70-90   **H&G**

A rare slipware pottery tankard, by Dickers of Sussex, commemorating the WWI battles of Louvain and Rheims, with "Never forget the Huns" around the base.

A technique dating back to the Romans, slipware designs are 'trailed' on using liquid clay before being glazed, typically in a lead based glaze giving the characteristic yellow colouring.

1914   6.75in (17cm) high

£280-380   **H&G**

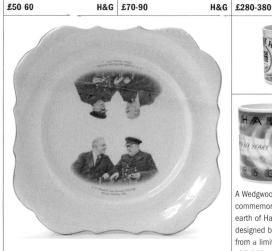

An earthenware mug, made to welcome home the Falkland Islands task force.

c1982   3.75in (9.5cm) high

£25-35   **H&G**

An earthenware plate, commemorating US President Roosevelt and Prime Minister Winston Churchill at the Atlantic meeting.

c1941   7.5in (19cm) diam

£100-150   **H&G**

A Wedgwood earthenware mug, commemorating the return to earth of Hayley's comet, designed by Richard Guyatt, from a limited edition of 2,000.

1986   4in (10cm) high

£70-90   **H&G**

A Wedgwood black basalt mug, commemorating the millennium, designed by Richard Guyatt.

Richard Guyatt started designing for Wedgwood in 1953 and his designs are avidly collected.

2000   4in (10cm) high

£120-180   **H&G**

COLLECTORS' NOTES

■ Clothes by globally renowned labels still tend to fetch the highest values when it comes to mid-late 20th century vintage clothes. Look for classic names such as Dior, Chanel, Pucci and Rhodes. Vivienne Westwood is currently a hot name, but pieces can be very hard to find. Some designer pieces that are only a few years old can be found at far less than their original retail price and may make a good investment if they are typical or from a noted collection.

■ Aim to buy pieces that represent the designer and their signature styles or that reflect the style of the period in terms of look, fit, colour and material. Examine designer labels to ensure that they haven't been added to a piece later on – the quality should speak for the name. It's not all about labels however – great pieces indicative of a look or period can be found by lesser names or bearing no name at all, but again look for quality in terms of material, design, fit and cut.

■ Along with the ever-popular 1960s names of Biba, Quant and Carnaby Street, 'street' fashion has long been sought after. Values for these clothes, from the more common vintage denims to unusual 'one-off' pieces that give the wearer individuality, have risen. Original vintage trainers have become hotly sought after, a trend led by the US and Japan, and have spurred a revival for yesterday's styles in 'new' ranges.

■ Fashions come and go, especially in vintage terms, but investing in high quality classics in any given notable 'look' is likely to be the best option. After the popularity of the '60s and '70s, the '80s is touted as the next target for revival. Always look for signs of damage such as excessive wear, tears (unless intended!), sweat marks and stains, as this reduces desirability and value – many pieces are still bought to be worn.

A 1970s Hardy Amies silk dress.

Sir Hardy Amies is known for his classically tailored suits and tweed and wool dresses. In 1955 he was appointed dressmaker to H.M. Queen Elizabeth II.

55in (139.5cm) long

£80-120 JV

A 1980s Amor ready-to-wear blue dress.

Born in 1949 in Tangiers, Faycal Amor made use of a new dying process and innovative structures. He created his own label, 'Plein Sud', in 1986.

44in (112cm) long

£180-220 RR

A 1960s Christian Dior military-style wool dress.

After Dior's death in 1957, Marc Bohan took over designing for the label. This dress echoes the feminine 'New Look' of the 1950s.

37.5in (95cm) long

£200-250 HP

A 1980s Christian Dior wool dress and jacket.

The striking colours and shoulder pads are typical of the 1980s 'power dressing' trend. The style was adopted by young and upwardly mobile professionals (yuppies) to whom labels, and moreover display of labels, became of immense importance to status.

Size 4

A Chanel sleeveless tunic dress, with square mother-of-pearl buttons.
2000   31in (118cm) long

£250-300 RR

A Robert Dorland lime green silk dress.

54in (137cm) long

£80-120 JV

A green evening dress and bolero, by Vernier Franka, London.

60in (152.5cm) long

£150-200 JV

£250-300 RR

A 1950s Hartnell dress.

40in (101.5cm) long

£100-150 RR

A 1970s Hartnell dress.

Size 16

£80-120 RR

A Guy Laroche black lace evening dress.

Laroche once said "It is my intention to try and adapt haute couture to modern requirements: to make dresses that are simple and chic". As well as re-introducing bright colours to collections, his evening dresses are known for a touch of the extravagant, including lace, beading and sequins.

35.5in (90cm) long

£200-250 HP

A Lilian eau de nil silk evening dress, with hand-beaded decoration.

55in (139.5cm) long

£100-140 JV

A 1980s Bruce Oldfield pink and green silk dress.

St Martin's School of Art graduate Oldfield launched his own label in 1978. He designed for Jerry Hall and Diana Ross and is famous for his evening wear. The puffed sleeves 'shout' 1980s.

55in (139.5cm) long

£180-220 RR

A CLOSER LOOK AT A ZANDRA RHODES GOWN

Rhodes is still a popular name and her designs are hotly collected - especially if vintage and typical. When worn, the collar, fitted waist and full, flowing silk skirt would create a look indicative of her style.

The neckline is hand-beaded, a motif repeated around the collar which has been cut to allow the printed design to form a garland pattern.

Rhodes' style is highly idiosyncratic and fanciful and often inspired by romantic themes – here the design harks back to Victorian and Edwardian styles.

Although the form is reminiscent of a bygone age, the bright colours and style of the printed pattern is highly evocative of the psychedelic 1960s and 1970s.

A 1970s Zandra Rhodes silk dress, with hand-beaded collar.

51in (129.5cm) long

£500-600 RR

A 1960s Oscar de la Renta dress.

Oscar de la Renta was born in 1932. He has become known for his opulent and romantic designs, often with ornate and extravagant patterning or detailing. Cinched waists are a particular hallmark of his designs.

38.5in (98cm) long

£150-200 RR

A Laura Phillips black hand-beaded dress.

50.5in (128.5cm) long

£80-120 JV

A 1980s Zandra Rhodes dress.

45in (114.5cm) long

£100-150 RR

A black polyester cocktail dress, by Rino Ross, with beaded bow detail.

£15-20 BR

A 1980s Salvatori silk dress.

38in (96.5cm) long

£150-200 RR

A 1980s Yves Saint Laurent printed cotton dress.

When buying famous names it pays to 'learn your labels'. A brand such as Yves Saint Laurent, as well as Versace and Ralph Lauren, will have many different ranges from the top-of-the-tree couture pieces down to the more commonly found high street ranges. Labels belonging to the different ranges will vary in wording, look and colour and often change over time.

57in (145cm) long

£150-200 RR

A 1970s Jean Varon dress.

54in (137cm) long

£80-120 JV

A 1960s Jean Varon printed dress.

Jean Varon was the label used by designer John Bates, who achieved popular success in the 1960s. Varon became costume designer for TV series 'The Avengers' in the 1960s, dressing popular characters such as Emma Peel (Diana Rigg) and Tara King (Linda Thorson). It is said that a design seen on screen one evening could be bought by 1960s fashionistas from his store the next day! Fabrics printed with strong graphics and dramatic designs were typical - look out for catsuits and black and white pieces like those worn by Mrs Peel.

56in (142cm) long

£100-140 JV

A chiffon dress, with matching cummerbund.

c1960 52in (132cm) long

£180-220 HP

A black polyester long dress, by Fashion III by Style Rite, with floral decoration.

£8-12 BR

A 1960s Miss Magninn printed silk dress.

56in (142cm) long

£70-100 JV

An unworn 1960s Italian dress.

50in (127cm) long

£70-100   **HP**

A 1960s chiffon dress, with sequin detail.

The contrast of the black top with its scarf-like neck and the psychedelically coloured, pleated and patterned skirt makes this piece not only extravagant, but also firmly rooted in the 1960s.

£220-280   **HP**

A violet crepe silk dress.

57in (145cm) long

£120-180   **JV**

A red and white shirt dress.

£40-50   **BR**

A copper knitted polyester long dress, by George's Factory, California.

£12-18   **BR**

A 1950s brown patterned day dress.

£45-55   **BR**

A black lace cocktail dress, with beaded detail.

£35-45   **BR**

A 1930s terracotta crepe silk dress.

£45-55   **BR**

A turquoise short dress, with a diamanté belt buckle.

£25-35   **BR**

A 1950s pink cocktail dress.

43.5in (110.5cm) long

£100-150   RR

A 1960s Saks Fifth Avenue silk dress.

Saks moved to its current home on New York's most prestigious shopping street in 1924. Saks' couture and high-end ready-to-wear department has stocked designs by Chanel, Madame Vionnet, Schiaparelli and, in the 1970s, Emilio Pucci. The couture department was closed during the 1970s.

40in (101.5cm) long

£100-150   RR

A 1950s Youth Guild of NY silk plaid dress.

Production from the late 1940s was dominated by clothes for teenagers, with a younger take on the influential 'New Look'. Much of the range was designed by Anne Fogarty who remained with the company until 1950. From 1960 to the mid-1970s, Liz Claiborne designed for the label.

42in (106.5cm) long

£70-100   RR

A Shearing Grecian-style dress.

c1960   52in (132cm) long

£100-170   HP

A copper sequinned short cocktail dress, with brown chiffon cape.

£25-35   BR

A 1950s London Town Model embroidered dress.

This dress is in the 'New Look' style, developed by Christian Dior in 1947, with its elegantly full skirt, cinched waist and fitted bodice. The dress is also valuable and desirable because of the level of hand-embroidered (still strikingly brightly coloured) decoration on the bodice and skirt.

45in (114.5cm) long

£280-320   HP

An orange and purple paisley dress and top, by Mister D, the top hand-beaded.

£30-40   BR

A cream long dress, with pink and gold bodice.

£15-20   BR

A silver and gold metallic quilted short dress.

£15-25   BR

A studded red leather short dress.

£20-30 BR

A yellow cotton sleeveless blouse, with lace trim and pin tuck front.

£12-18 CCL

A cream top, by Isla Engel, decorated with applied flowers and diamanté.

£22-28 CCL

A 1960s white ribbon Jackie O-style jacket.

£65-85 CCL

A 1950s paper nylon slip, with cream coloured ribbon.

£22-28 CCL

A red gingham full circle skirt, with lace trim.

£35-45 CCL

A hand-painted Mexican skirt, with Aztec motifs painted in gold-coloured paint, marked "S".

£65-85 CCL

A 1960s double-breasted horse hair coat, with a wide collar.

£180-220 BR

A striped fun fur coat, with leather trim.

£25-35 BR

A fur trimmed black coat, by Evans Furs exclusively at Crowleys.

£20-30 BR

COLLECTORS' NOTES

■ Over the past decade men have considered both grooming and fashionable clothing more closely, and as a result there has been a resurgence in interest in vintage styles. However, values for vintage men's clothing are often low compared to women's clothing. Consequently, famous name or well-made bargains still abound as the market has yet to reach its maturity. Many of the same rules apply here as to women's clothing.

A beige Western-style shirt, decorated with rural scenes, with brown cuffs and shoulders and black tassel trim.

£10-15   **BR**

An olive Western-style shirt, by Levi's, with hand-stitched mushroom decoration.

£15-25   **BR**

A brown satin Western-style shirt, with cream cuffs and shoulders, with hand-stitched decoration.

£20-30   **BR**

A blue printed Western-style shirt, from the Kenny Rogers Western Collection by Caravan, with navy piping.

£15-20   **BR**

A blue and silver Western-style shirt, by Caravan, with ruffle front.

£15-25   **BR**

A cream satin Western-style shirt, with hand-stitched floral decoration.

Look for western-style shirts produced in the 1940s and 1950s, the most popular decades for collectors and aficionados. Styles like this are still made today, so check the material and any decoration to date a shirt. Gabardine and heavier satins were frequently used for early shirts and the embroidery was hand-stitched, using a triple stitch, rather than machine-stitched. Embroidered pictures such as scenery or cowboy boots command a premium. Brands, such as 'H Bar C', are important and can also help to date examples.

1950s

£40-50   **BR**

A checked Western-style shirt, by Ron Rigo CA, with light blue cuffs and shoulders.

£10-15   **BR**

A cream Western-style shirt, by Mid Western Garment Co., with brown sleeves and collar.

£7-9   **BR**

A WWII embroidered black velvet souvenir jacket, decorated with a tiger and "Japan".

£80-120 BR

A Vietnam War embroidered nylon souvenir jacket, embroidered with Snoopy.

£100-150 BR

A WWII embroidered silk souvenir jacket, decorated with a dragon and "Shanghai China 1948".

Wartime souvenir jackets are still being made today, but it is the period pieces made up to the early 1950s that are sought after and valuable. It can be extremely hard to tell modern from vintage examples and the best way is to handle as many authentic pieces as possible. Areas to examine closely include the zip, which should be old, and any embroidery which must be hand executed, rather than machined. Older examples also often have the date embroidered on them, but period dates can appear on modern examples too. Older examples from the 1940s also tend to have satin/silk on both sides, with examples from the 1950s being made from satin/silk and velvet.

£400-500 BR

A US Navy woollen tunic, with white piping.

£55-65 BR

A 1960s Levi's 'Big E' denim jacket.

The 'e' in the Levi name on the red pocket tag is large, enabling it to be dated to a specific vintage period and making it very popular with collectors.

23in (58.5cm) long

£60-70 BR

A pair of 1960s Levi denim jeans, without a big 'E' on label.

By introducing the 'Engineered' and 'Anti-Fit' ranges, Levi has retained a top spot for jeans, despite seeing a slight low during the 1990s with their classic 501 brand. The most expensive vintage Levi's found to date are also the oldest known and are owned by Levi Strauss and Co., who bought them in an online auction on eBay. They date from 1880-1885, roughly a decade after denims were introduced by Levi Strauss in 1873 as the original hard wearing 'work wear' for manual workers. They were found in mud in a mining town in Nevada and fetched a staggering $46,532!

38in (96.5cm) long

£100-150 BR

A CLOSER LOOK AT A PUCCI TIE

Art Nouveau-style flowers updated with 1960s psychedelic colours – purples, blues, hot pinks and yellows – are typical of Pucci, as are geometrical designs.

Genuine Pucci products bear the name 'Emilio' as part of the printed design. Check carefully for original labels and silk linings woven with the 'Emilio' signature.

Pucci is usually associated with women's clothing, with men's ties still being affordable. Look out for Pucci menswear, such as shirts and suits, as it was purportedly only made for five years.

Now that Pucci has been re-launched (including a range of ties!), with the backing of luxury goods conglomerate LVMH, it is likely that original pieces will be even more sought- after.

A 1960s/70s Pucci black, blue and turquoise silk men's tie, with label marked "Italy" and "Emilio Pucci".

3.25in (8cm) widest

£35-45

NOR

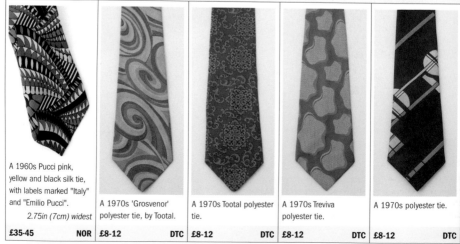

A 1960s Pucci pink, yellow and black silk tie, with labels marked "Italy" and "Emilio Pucci".

2.75in (7cm) widest

| £35-45 | **NOR** | £8-12 | **DTC** | £8-12 | **DTC** | £8-12 | **DTC** | £8-12 | **DTC** |

A 1970s 'Grosvenor' polyester tie, by Tootal.

A 1970s Tootal polyester tie.

A 1970s Treviva polyester tie.

A 1970s polyester tie.

A Govan Crusaders team jacket, red with cream trim.

£55-65 BR

A NBCHS Vikings team jacket, by Hunters Manf. Co., blue wool with cream shoulders and trim.

£20-30 BR

A Fort Edmonton yellow nylon college jacket, by Marv Holland.

£10-15 BR

A green nylon track top, by 'Boar', with white trim.

£10-15 BR

A St Anthony's college jacket, by Marv Holland, burgundy wool with cream shoulders and trim.

These jackets are still being made today, although modern examples usually have company brand names instead of college names. Look out for examples from the 1950s especially, but also up to the 1970s, as these tend to be the most popular. The years the original owner attended the particular college are often found on patches on authentic period examples.

£35-45 BR

A red and blue 'Sun & Surf' nylon jacket.

£7-10 BR

A Brooks ladies nylon jacket.

£10-15 BR

A 1980s nylon Patagonia jacket.

The Patagonia brand is particularly popular in Japan, perhaps due to the company's concern for the environment. Early examples from the 1980s have a larger label than those made throughout the 1990s.

£35-45 BR

A yellow ladies nylon short coat.

£7-10 BR

A red Patagonia children's waterproof jacket.

£7-10 B

A pale green Patagonia fleece jacket.

£75-85   BR

An Adidas navy sweat shirt, with light blue, green and white transfer decoration.

£15-25   BR

A Champion black sweat shirt.

£7-14   BR

A "Bears Cheerleader" navy sweat shirt, with orange transfer decoration.

£8-16   BR

A Nike green sweat shirt, with white and yellow transfer decoration.

Graphic design student Carolyn Davidson was originally paid just $35 for her now legendary 'Swoosh' design in 1971, at the birth of what was then a small company. Rough dates can be found by looking at the style and colour of the tick and the word 'Nike'. Look out for currently popular orange ticks where the word Nike is in blocky capital letters, indicating a date from 1978 to the mid-1980s.

£25-35   BR

An Adidas burgundy two-piece tracksuit.

Adidas, Champion and Nike are amongst the most popular names for vintage sportswear. It was not until the 1950s that most working men had enough spare time to play sports. During the 1980s, with the meteoric rise of celebrity sports stars, what was previously a form of 'workwear' became the height of fashion.

£35-45   BR

A pink towelling two-piece tracksuit, by Baycrest.

£10-15   BR

A black sweat shirt, with Mickey Mouse transfer decoration to front.

The mid-to late 1980s saw a fad for sweat shirts featuring popular cartoon characters. Look for authentic period examples which use a printed, rather than woven, label.

£15-25   BR

A knitted cotton one-piece playsuit, by Dominique.

£8-12   BR

A yellow bowling shirt, by Swingter, with brown trim, with "Victory Five" applied to the back.

£60-70 BR

A ladies teal blue bowling shirt, by Air Flow, with pin-shaped buttons, with "Barton Construction Bozeman" stitched on the back.

£45-55 BR

A pink bowling shirt, Hill & Dale Sports Ware, by Gilman, with black trim and marlin detail.

Look out for added details such as differently coloured trims, colourful embroidery, people's, teams or sponsor's names and pictorial logos, especially if related to bowling. Men's versions tend to be more popular than ladies' examples, but both are highly collectable - and wearable - particularly if from the most popular decades of the 1950s and 1960s.

£80-120 BR

A blue bowling shirt, by Master Bowler, with "Schrader Bros. Super Mkt." stitched on back.

£25-35 BR

A Dodgers red V-neck T-shirt, with navy and red trim and white transfer decoration.

£7-9 BR

A Nike navy vest, with light blue trim and yellow, white and navy transfer decoration.

£8-16 BR

A Ralph Lauren blue polo shirt.

Ralph Lauren once said "I'm not just selling clothes, I'm offering a world, a philosophy of life". This is certainly true of his ever-expanding empire, which includes homeware as well as ranges of mens and ladies clothing. His first designs were launched in 1967 (his first menswear in 1968) and were based around the polo player that later became his logo. The polo shirt is typical of his elitist, 'Ivy league' look as worn by East Coast 'W.A.S.Ps'. Vintage examples are often made in better quality cottons and are available in colours that are no longer produced today.

£5-6 BR

A pair of 1980s Adidas 'Montreal' white ladies trainers, with lavender trim.

£7-10   **BR**

A pair of Adidas 'Lady Boston' lavender ladies trainers.

£20-30   **BR**

A pair of Champion Air white and blue trainers.

£15-25   **BR**

A pair of Asics Tiger trainers.

The famous stripes on Onitsuka Tiger's Asics brand trainers were first seen on their 1966 'Mexico' training shoe, worn by the Japanese team in the 1968 Olympic Games.

£10-15   **BR**

A CLOSER LOOK AT A PAIR OF TRAINERS

John Boyd Dunlop developed the world's first commercial pneumatic tyre. He used his invention of bonding canvas to rubber to produce basic footwear in the 1830s.

Although it has remained constant for over 70 years with its Dunlopillo sole and distinctive styling, the design has changed slightly and no longer includes the curving 'S' flash.

A pair of Nike Air white and black trainers.

£12-18   **BR**

Green Flash sports shoes were introduced in 1933. They were worn by legendary tennis player Fred Perry when he won the 1934, 1935 and 1936 Wimbledon men's singles championships which stood as a record for 40 years.

A much-remembered favourite of grown-up schoolboys the world over, the Green Flash has recently enjoyed renewed popularity with the revival of vintage sneaker styles and continues to be a style icon.

A pair of original Dunlop 'Green Flash' 1555 tennis shoes.

£15-25   **BR**

A pair of Reebok white ladies trainers.

£7-10   **BR**

A pair of Nike Air Force Delta Hi-Top trainers.

Considered a classic, the Air Force was released in 1982 and was the first basketball shoe to have a full length 'air' sole. Look out for earlier examples of the many designs, especially in rare grey.

c1988   10.5in (27cm) long

£40-50   **BR**

A pair of black cowboy boots, with stitched decoration.

£30-40   **BR**

A pair of plain black cowboy boots, with simple stitched decoration.

£15-20   **BR**

A pair of grey leather cowboy boots, with snakeskin toes.

£25-35   **BR**

A pair of grey cowboy boots, with cream eagle head detail.

£20-30   **BR**

A pair black cowboy boots, with cream and turquoise details.

The condition, colour and quality of the detail, from patterning to accented decoration, are the usual indicators of value for cowboy boots.

£30-40   **BR**

A pair of light grey cowboy boots, with grey snakeskin detail.

£25-35   **BR**

A pair of terracotta cowboy boots, by Tony Lama.

£30-40   **BR**

A pair of three coloured ladies cowboy boots.

£15-20   **BR**

A pair of bronze coloured ladies cowboy boots, with cut-out detail.

£20-30   **BR**

COSTUME & ACCESSORIES

A pair of 1940s black leather utility wear peep-toe shoes, with 'diamond' pattern.

8.5in (22cm) long

£20-30 PC

A pair of 1940s black leather utility wear peep-toe shoes, with cross-over decoration.

9.5in (24cm) long

£20-30 PC

A pair of black vinyl and wood clogs.

c1960   9.5in (24cm) long

£5-8 AAC

A pair of 1920s men's speed skates by Canada Cycle and Motor.

11.5in (29cm) long

£35-45 TYA

A pair of 1940s grey suede utility wear shoes, by Oral, with bow decoration and in original box.

9in (23cm) long

£35-45 PC

A CLOSER LOOK AT A PAIR OF SHOES & HANDBAG

It is rare for such a set to retain the original box. The graphics on the box are brightly coloured, amusing and typical of the 1960s.

The silk is undamaged and still retains its bright, clashing colours that are typical of the modern look of the 1960s.

The bag is a substantial size and still retains its handle and lined interior.

The shoes and bag are in unworn and unused condition and remain together, which is rare.

A rare 1960s multi-coloured bag and matching shoes, by Hemphill Wells Geppetto, in Geppetto box.

bag 9in (23cm) wide

£40-60 NOR

COLLECTORS' NOTES

■ Beaded bags have been fashionable since the early 19thC, and are the most collectable form of vintage bag. They can also be the most valuable – a reflection of the hours of work that went into them, and their fragile nature.

■ The bright colours and intricate workmanship often mean they are more for display than use, but that does not diminish their appeal.

■ From 1910-1930 designs were inspired by flowers, chinoiserie, Eastern carpets and romantic medieval castles and Venetian scenes.

■ In the 1910s and 1920s, manufacturers used Venetian or Bohemian beads. Venetian beads are very small, slightly iridescent and with a pure colour that does not fade. Bohemian beads tend to be larger, coarser and fade over time.

■ High quality examples were made in France and Belgium during the late 1950s and early 1960s using fine beadwork, with attention to detail and elegant designs.

■ Clasps and handles are usually metal and often inset with glass or semi-precious stones. Bags were often lined with silk, which may have deteriorated far more than the exterior. A sympathetic replacement can enhance the value of a bag.

■ When buying beaded bags, consider whether the design suits the beads it is made from.

A CLOSER LOOK AT A BEADED BAG

The black fabric has been hand decorated with gold braid along the top.

The rear of the bag is made of a contrasting tapestry fabric.

A design of scattered leaves dominates the centre of the bag.

Sequins and gold and copper tone leaves have been used to embellish the surface.

A tapestry bag, by Caron of Texas, with applied leaves and sequins.

11.75in (30cm) wide

£50-70 FAN

A 1940s bag, by Caron of Texas, with hand-decorated front.

9in (23cm) wide

£40-60 FAN

A beaded bag, by Caron of Texas, hand-decorated with butterflies and jewels.

11.5in (29cm) high

£45-55 FAN

A 1950s hand-decorated bag, by Caron of Texas, with original sales tag.

11in (28cm) wide

£50-70 FAN

A 1950s hand-decorated bag, by Caron of Texas.

14.5in (37cm) wide

£30-50 FAN

A hand-decorated bag, by Caron of Texas, with butterflies and jewels.

11.5in (29cm) wide

£45-55 FAN

A 1950s plastic-coated linen bag, by Souré NY, with applied gold threading, studs and porcelain plaques featuring pastoral vignettes, leather interior.

11.75in (30cm) wide

£35-45 FAN

A 1950s black and pale green embroidered bag, probably by Souré NY, with applied beads, glass and leaves.

12.5in (32cm) wide

£70-100 FAN

A 1950s hand-decorated bag, by Souré NY, with a Bakelite handle.

13.75in (35cm) wide

£70-100 FAN

A 1950s black felt bag, by Souré NY, with applied paste.

11in (28cm) wide

£50-70 FAN

A 19thC scenic beaded bag, with metal frame.

7.25in (18.5cm) high

£150-200 GMC

A 1920s beaded bag, with bakelite frame decorated with leaves.

8in (20.5cm) high

£300-400 GMC

A 1920s beaded evening bag, with a floral beaded motif, the gold metal embossed frame decorated with red and green semi-precious stone inclusions and a pendant with a coloured rhinestone, a beaded fringe and chain handle.

9in (23cm) long

£250-350 AHL

A 1920s beaded bag.

6.75in (18.5cm)

£45-55 GMC

A 1930s white beadwork and woven gilt thread purse, with acorn-shaped ball clasps, with original hand mirror and pocket, with label reading "Bags by Josef HAND BEADED IN FRANCE".

9.75in (25cm) wide

£70-100 ROX

A 1920s silver sequin evening bag.

8.5in (21.5cm) wide

£50-60 GMC

A green glass beadwork purse, the cylindrical body with tucked 'loose' covering, lid with mirror to inside and lined throughout with brown silk lining.

c1920   *5in (12.5cm) high*

£120-180   **BY**

A 1930s French hand-beaded evening bag, with beaded and enamel frame and clasp marked "The French Bag Shop, 1116 Lincoln Road, Miami Beach, Florida."

9in (23cm) wide

£250-300   **RG**

A 1940s French gold and coloured bead clutch bag, with an enamelled clasp, decorated with micro-beading.

10in (25cm) wide

£400-500   **AHL**

A 1940s French hand-beaded evening purse, with tambour (tiny chain stitch) embroidery flowers, with gilt snake chain handles, black satin-lined with matching satin coin purse, marked "Made in France Pierre Marot Paris", unused.

10.25in (26cm) wide

£200-250   **RG**

A 1940s Dubinette gunmetal coloured glass bead box bag.

6in (15cm) wide

£70-90   **FAN**

A 1940s blue carnival bead bag.

7.75in (19.5cm) wide

£70-100   **FAN**

A 1950s mother-of-pearl sequin evening bag.

8in (20.5cm) wide

£35-45   **FAN**

A 1950s French hand-beaded evening purse, made for the American market, embroidered with hand-beaded frame set with two porcelain, Limoges plaques depicting on 18thC courting couple, cream satin lined with matching coin purse and snake chain handle, marked "Made in France by Hand, Walborg".

8in (20cm) wide

£200-250   **RG**

A 1950s French metal bead evening bag, the bag and handle in silver and gold beads, yellow satin lined, tagged "Hand Made in France", the clasp with rhinestones in an acorn shape.

9.5in (24cm) wide

£150-200   **RG**

A cream and white beadwork handbag, with circular catch lifting to open, interior lined with cream silk and with woven label reading "K&G Charlet Bag", with metal frame and gilt metal chain.

8.5in (21.5cm) wide

£120-180   **BY**

A 1950s Belgian white and gold-coloured glass beadwork purse, the ball catches inset with faceted rhinestones/glass jewels, lined with cream silk, with label reading "Jorelle Bags MADE IN BELGIUM".

9.75in (24.5cm) wide

£80-120   **ROX**

A rare flexible plastic and painted wood poodle handbag, possibly 1950s American, inlaid with gold thread and decorated with shell and bead, with wood support and gold-plated handle.

11.75in (30cm) wide

£250-300   **SM**

An early 1950s French black evening bag, decorated with rhinestone decoration, with a silver filigree frame, with a chain handle and cream satin lining.

8in (20cm) wide

£120-180   **AHL**

A 1950s three-way convertible bag, with a detachable reversible cover, cream and gold to one side and black to the other.

9in (23cm) wide

£30-40   **FAN**

A 1950s small evening bag, made in Hong Kong, decorated with faux pearl oval beads, small yellow and green glass beads, green bugle beads and rhinestones, with an embossed metal frame, chain strap and green satin lining.

6.75in (17cm) wide

£200-250   **AHL**

A black and gold beaded bag.

c1950   *9in (23cm) wide*

£40-60   **GMC**

An unmarked 1950s black beaded bag, with gold flowers.

8.5in (21.5cm) wide

£80-100   **FAN**

A large 1950s black fabric bag, with gold and black metal frame, a painted banjo motif and plastic gold flowers with gem insets and a leather handle.

14in (36cm) wide

£200-250   **AHL**

A 1950s hand-decorated bag, by Veldore of Texas.

9.25in (23.5cm) high

£40-60   **FAN**

A 1970s brocade bag, by La Jeunesse, studded with faux gems with gold metal surrounds, some with gold foil sparkles, the bead chain strap with multi-coloured diamantés interspersed.

8.75in (22cm) wide

£350-450   **AHL**

A floral tapestry purse, the gilt metal frame with applied enamelled metal Indian scrolling motifs and orange hardstone, the catch with hardstone cabochon, interior lined with cream silk, with suede-covered hand mirror.

c1910   *6.25in (16cm) wide*

£70-100   **ROX**

A 1920s woven tapestry purse, showing an 18thC Watteau-style pastoral scene, with gilt metal frame with applied semi-circles with pink painted dots, and padded tapestry strips, gilt metal chain, lined with cream silk.

9in (23cm) wide

£150-200   **ROX**

A 1930s pink woven wool tapestry purse, showing fish swimming over coral, with gilt metal frame inlaid with orange glass cabochons, lined with fawn silk.

9.25in (23.5cm) wide

£150-200   **ROX**

A 1960s tapestry gilt metal and vinyl bag, with brown vinyl handle, and metal button clasp, lined throughout with beige vinyl.

15in (38cm) long

£50-70   **ROX**

A 1950s white and brown woven and plush figural purse, showing a seated lute player with lady seated at a table, with gilt metal frame and button clasp in the form of an opening rose, lined with white silk and with gilt stamping to interior pocket reading 'Delill', pocket with original hand mirror in envelope, with chain handle and original shop gilt card tag reading 'A Delill Creation'.

12.25in (31cm) high

£50-70   **ROX**

A 1950s woven wool purse, with two donkeys eating daisies, with faux tortoiseshell plastic clasp and handle, with similar catch, lined with green fabric, with original purse in matching green fabric and hand mirror.

9.75in (25cm) wide

£150-200   **ROX**

A CLOSER LOOK AT A TELEPHONE BAG

This telephone bag was a cult object in the 1950s and 1960s. It was still being made in the 1970s.

The telephone could be plugged into a telephone socket so that calls could actually be made from them.

It was also made in white and red patent leather.

This example is in full working order.

A 1960s American 'Telephone' bag, in patent leather with an embossed design.

15in (38cm) wide

£450-550   **AHL**

A 1990s painted composition box bag, in the shape of a dalmatian's head, with black fabric interior, with label reading 'TIMMY WOODS Beverley Hills Collection Handmade in THE PHILIPPINES', with elasticated catch.

Former ballet dancer Timmy Woods started designing and manufacturing handbags in 1985. Her eye-catching designs were immediately snapped up by stores such as Bergdorf, Bendel's and Bloomingdales. She took a break from handbag design to work for Ken Done for the U. S. A. and B. J. Designs. Then, following serious injury in a car accident, Timmy's father, a real estate developer, suggested she join his lucrative business and include her design skills into real estate marketing. Although her new career proved lucrative it didn't hold the same appeal as the design world. In 1992, inspired by primitive carved wooden boxes she found at a market in the Philippines, Timmy launched Timmy Woods Beverly Hills. Timmy's bags are carried and collected by celebrities including Liz Taylor, Diana Ross, Jody Fisher, Melanie Griffith and Hillary Clinton.

4.5in (11.5cm) high

£100-150 | **ROX**

A 1950s Californian brown alligator bag, by 'Sydney' - stamped "Sydney California".

10.5in (27cm) wide

£150-200 | **RG**

A small, early 1950s red leather bucket bag, with two handles, polka dot lining, and a mirror on the inside of the lid.

8.75in (22cm) wide

£70-100 | **AHL**

A CLOSER LOOK AT A BELLESTONE BAG

Bellestone is one of the most popular names with collectors of vintage bags because the company used high quality skins which are flexible and durable and so have withstood the test of time.

The interiors of Bellestone bags usually feature pockets and are signed Bellestone. Condition affects value – especially interiors: linings can be suede and include change purses and mirrors.

The simple style of the bag is clean and classic.

This bag is in a roomy yet compact size making it a perfect everyday bag.

A 1950s American black alligator skin bag by Bellestone, un-used.

10in (25cm) wide

£200-250 | **RG**

A 1960s black crocodile skin bag, with black enamel frame, marked "Genuine Crocodile".

13in (33cm) wide

£200-250 | **RG**

A 1960s-70s Coronado leather bag, made in Spain, with stitched detailing, with a brass frame and feet.

15.75in (40cm) wide

£450-550 | **AHL**

A 1960s orange plastic clutch bag, with metal frame, lined with fawn fabric, with gilt metal clasp.

16.75in (42.5cm) wide

£25-35 | **ROX**

A 1970s Fendi brown leather purse with faux tortoiseshell closure, removable leather strap, and embossed central logo, with change purse.

Fendi was founded in Rome in 1925 by Edoardo and Adele Fendi and is famous for its luxury leather goods.

10.5in (26cm) wide

£120-180 | **TA**

A 1960s American pink faux snakeskin vinyl purse, with printed paisley fabric lining and clear polythene internal purse stamped 'Ethan Bags' on gilt metal chain, with silver finished plastic catch

14.25in (36.5cm) wide

£25-35 | **ROX**

A CLOSER LOOK AT A GUILD CREATIONS BAG

A mid-to late 1960s poodle sequin bag.

Sold as a craft kit, this type of bag would be hand-decorated by the purchaser. Although many designs were available, poodles are among the most popular and command higher prices.

10.5in (26.5cm) high

£80-120　　　　**FAN**

The bag is stamped on the inside with the company's logo.

The clasp is made from filigree metal decorated with rhinestones. This is a typical Guild Creations touch.

The felt is pleated at the top on both sides.

The bag is lined with satin and two small internal compartments.

A 1950s Guild Creations black felt bag with cathedral type frame, in used condition.

11in (28cm) wide

£70-90　　　　**FAN**

A 1950s classic black velvet bag, by Garay, with attached coin purse.

9.5in (24cm) high

£45-55　　　　**FAN**

A 1950s/60s leopard print felt Ingber bag.

12in (30.5cm) wide

£70-90　　　　**FAN**

A 1970s woven cotton psychedelic pattern tote bag.

13in (33cm) high

£20-30　　　　**MTS**

A 1920s fruits and greenery plastic bag frame.

Many collectors buy vintage bag frames and make new bags to fit them.

4.5in (11.5cm) wide

£100-150　　　　**GMC**

A 1950s Antler faux leopard skin vanity case.

11.5in (29.5cm) high

£50-70　　　　**MA**

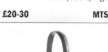

A 1970s velvet bucket bag, with a Lucite handle and brass button detail.

10.25in (26cm) wide

£120-180　　　　**AHL**

A 1940s amber bucket bag, with a bakelite lid, bronze beading to the body and handle, mirror fixed to the inside lid.

8in (20cm) wide

£180-220　　　　**AHL**

A 1950s translucent handbag, by JR USA, with gold vein decoration.

8.25in (21cm) high

£35-45 FAN

A 1950s resin-effect fitted bag.

6.5in (16.5cm) wide

£70-90 GMC

A CLOSER LOOK AT A LUCITE BAG

The clear Lucite handle is hinged.

The bag is fully lined in gold satin and has one interior pocket.

This cylindrical bag is made from Lucite and embossed, basketweave, gold-tone metal. The design was patented in 1945.

The bag has all four spherical brass feet.

A 1950s silver Lucite bag, by Dorset-Rex, 5th Avenue, with gold metal panel and gold effect ball feet, with a clear Lucite handle.

7in (18cm) wide

£200-250 AHL

A 1950s grey mottled Lucite box bag, with circular handle, the moiré silk lining with pockets.

9.5in (24cm) high

£200-300 ROX

A 1950s Lucite vanity handbag, with fitted interior.

6.5in (16.5cm) wide

£80-120 GMC

An American gold mesh bag.

Metal mesh bags were first made from precious metals in the 1820s, and by the end of the century mesh coin and finger purses, inspired by the trend for Medieval fashion, were in vogue. However, they were handmade and therefore expensive. In 1908 A.C. Pratt patented a mesh machine which meant affordable, mass produced bags could be made. In the 1920s designs started to be screen printed onto the mesh. The style was also a hit during the disco craze of the 1970s.

Mesh bags should be stored flat to prevent the mesh from buckling. Companies such as US firm Whiting and Davis – probably the biggest and most famous mesh bag maker - continue to make mesh bags today.

A marblized silver Lucite bag, with carved leaf design, double handles and scrolling initials "RJG" to the lid, and clear Lucite feet.

6.75in (17cm) wide

£200-250 AHL

A cut-steel beaded bag.

c1910 *9in (22.5cm) high*

£50-70 GMC

1920-25 *6.5in (16.5cm) high*

£70-100 GMC

An Art Deco bakelite compact, decorated with a lady's head.

c1930　　　*3.25in (8.5cm) d*

£100-150　　　**TDG**

An Art Deco compact, in green and silver, some damage to enamel on base.

c1930　　　*3in (7.5cm) diam*

£60-80　　　**TDG**

A powder compact by Coty, Paris, with printed powder puff decoration in peach and gold.

c1930　　　*2in (5cm) diam*

£40-50　　　**TDG**

A 1950s compact, with clear, purple and black paste decoration.

3in (7.5cm) diam

£70-90　　　**TDG**

A CLOSER LOOK AT A COMPACT

The bright orange colour and the design of the two stylized ladies is typically 1950s, with hairstyles that speak of the period and are derived from the 1930s.

American company Richard Hudnut is a known and collected name and produced a number of compacts and vanity cases.

Based in New York, they also owned the well-known DuBarry name.

The transfer of the ladies is unscratched and intact and the materials used are still in very good condition.

A 1940s/1950s 'Three Flowers' powder compact by Richard Hudnut, in paper.

2.75in (7cm) diam

£30-40　　　**TDG**

A Coty face powder compact, in original box, with orange and gilt decoration.

The noted maker, brightly coloured and complex design of the compact and the fact that it retains its original pictorial box make this a desirable example.

c1930

box 3.75in (9.5cm) wide

£120-180　　　**TDG**

A French Art Deco compact, with lovebirds.

c1925　　　*3in (7.5cm) wide*

£100-150　　　**TDG**

A rare 1920s/1930s Bourgois 'Evening in Paris' compact.

3.25in (8.5cm) wide

£80-120　　　**TDG**

A CLOSER LOOK AT A FAN

The scenes of courting lovers are delicately and skillfully hand-painted on silk – a more desirable and valuable feature than printed scenes on paper.

The leaf has much additional decoration. Panels have been cut out and lined with gauze, which is still intact. Gold-coloured threads have been woven into patterns incorporating sequins.

The overall condition is excellent, with bright colours and no tears, stains or losses to the silk leaf or sticks.

The sticks and guards are made from mother-of-pearl, a luxury material, and have been cut and painted with delicate, typically late-19thC designs.

A delicate French folding fan, with mother-of-pearl monture, the silk and mesh leaf with three cartouches boldly painted with couples, enclosed within ornate sequins.

c1880   *9.5in (24.5cm) long*

£1,000-1,500   **HD**

A 19thC fan, paper leaf painted in body colour with a lady and her suitor in a country setting, with ornately carved and pierced bone sticks and silver and gilt decoration, unusual guards with sea horse heads, some damage.

10.75 (27cm) high

£100-150   **BONM**

A mid-19thC Cantonese export fan, paper leaf painted with courtiers with applied ivory faces and silk robes, pierced and carved ivory sticks and fretwork guards, gilt metal rivets and silk tassels, some damage, in original lacquered box.

11in (28cm) long

£80-120   **BONM**

An 1880s sterling lipstick holder on chain, engraved with foliate designs.

2in (5cm) high

£8-12   **TAB**

A late 19thC to early 20thC fan, with a point de gaze leaf and mother-of-pearl sticks and guards, in a silk covered box.

11in (28cm) high

£350-450   **BONM**

An early 20thC point de gaze fan, with silk insertion, painted in body colour, simulated amber sticks, damage.

9.75in (25cm) high

£120-180   **BONM**

An Art Deco hatstand, possibly from Hamilton in Ontario.

c1930   *19in (48.5cm) high*

£40-60   **TYA**

A selection of Pochoir hand-stencilled prints, from 'Très Parisien'.

c1925   *11in (28cm) wide*

£55-65 each   **TDG**

COSTUME JEWELLERY

COLLECTORS' NOTES

■ Founded by 28-year old David McConnell from New York in 1886, Avon started life as the Californian Perfume Company. In 1929, the first products were offered under the Avon brand, a name supposedly inspired by William Shakespeare's birthplace, Stratford-upon-Avon. It was not until 1939 that the company itself became known as Avon.

■ In 1906, Avon printed its first colour brochure and began to run advertisements in Good Housekeeping magazine. By this time there were 10,000 sales representatives selling Avon products to women throughout America.

■ After expanding to Quebec, Canada, in 1914, the company continued to grow, and by 1928 the number of sales staff had more than doubled.

■ Avon successfully introduced a line of jewellery in the late 1920s. The reasonable prices and high quality of the pieces made the range immediately popular with American housewives. Today, the jewellery is not particularly valuable to costume jewellery collectors, but also appeals to collectors of Avon memorabilia.

■ Values are currently comparatively low, with many pieces being found for under £50, so a collection can be built on a budget. Look out for Christmas Tree pins produced by Avon as this is a popular and collectable type.

A pair of 1990s Avon Christmas present earrings, of goldwashed metal casting with clear rhinestone highlights.

0.5in (1.25cm) long

£15-20 **MILLB**

A pair of 1980s Avon Paisley motif earrings, of goldtone metal casting with three shades of pink enamelling.

1.5in (3.75cm) long

£12-14 **MILLB**

A pair of 1980s Avon earrings, with faux pearls, ruby rhinestones and green enamelling, on goldwashed metal castings.

The festive enamelled colours of these earrings show that these were made for sale around Christmas time.

1.5in (3.75cm) long

£20-30 **MILLB**

An unusual pair of late 1970s Avon knotted rope earrings, made from moulded faux ivory plastic.

1.25in (3cm) long

£12-14 **MILLB**

An Avon perfume owl pin, with hinged head, of goldwashed metal casting with emerald green rhinestone eyes.

c1980   2in (5cm) long

£25-30 **MILLB**

An Avon perfume basket pin, with hinged lid, of goldwashed metal casting with clear rhinestone highlights.

c1980   1.5in (3.75cm) long

£20-30 **MILLB**

A late 1970s Avon goldwashed metal necklace, with antiqued pendant with faux white and pink pearls and a pink plastic cabochon.

Necklace 24in (60cm) long

£20-30 **MILLB**

An Avon apple pendant necklace, of antiqued goldtone metal with semi-opaque clear plastic pendant.

c1970   Necklace 27in (68.5cm) long

£18-22 **MILLB**

A 1980s Avon silvertone white metal open bangle, of geometric form.

This item was originally promoted as part of a silver and gold 'pair'.

6.5in (16.5cm) long

£20-30 **MILLB**

A pair of late 1990s Dinny Hall pendant earrings, with gold fishhooks and pendant caps with semi-translucent white resin drops.

1.5in (4cm) long

£50-60 PC

A pair of Dinny Hall gold-plated silver earrings, in the form of elongated, stylized leaves.

c2001 1.5in (3.5cm) long

£80-100 PC

A pair of Dinny Hall large circular hoop silver earrings.

This piece was also produced in vermeil. This version can be worth 20 percent more.

c2001 1.5in (3.5cm) long

£60-70 PC

A pair of Dinny Hall earrings, with hand-crafted silver, Classical scrolling forms with with three icicle-form pendants of mauvish-blue resin.

c1992 2.5in (6.5cm) long

£60-80 PC

COLLECTORS' NOTES

■ Dinny Hall is considered one of Britain's leading jewellery designers and opened her first boutique in West London in 1992. In 1989 she was voted Accessory Designer of the Year by the British Fashion Council. In 1996 she was named 'Jewellery Designer of the year' following a vote by the readers of Marie Claire magazine. She counts Madonna, Liz Hurley and Uma Thurman amongst her clients.

■ Many of her designs are inspired by natural forms, such as leaves, icicles, droplets and starfish. Her style is understated and simple, with pared down settings, transcending passing fashions and fads.

■ Typical Dinny Hall pieces are simple and classic in style, showing a global influence and an attention to detail. Many pieces use high coloured resinous or precious or semi-precious stones against a simple setting and are created using traditional techniques. Hearts, crosses and floral designs are common features of her pieces. Each piece is handcrafted using fine quality materials, such as sterling silver and gold, and traditional jewellery making techniques.

A late 1990s Dinny Hall 'Diffusion Line' necklace and earrings, with silver chain, fishhooks and pendant caps and semi-translucent white resin drops.

Necklace 18in (46cm) long

£90-110 PC

A mid-1990s Dinny Hall 'Diffusion Line' necklace and earrings, with gold chain, fish hooks and scrolling hoops, with baroque pearl drops.

Necklace 15.5in (40cm) long

£90-110 PC

A Dinny Hall pendant necklace, with silver chain and pendant cap with semi-translucent violet resin drop.

c1992 Necklace 18in (46cm) l

£80-90 PC

A 1960s-1970s Accessocraft necklace, with beads of pearlized brown plastic and clear Lucite with white inclusions, and clear rhinestone roundels.

16in (40.5cm) long

£55-65   **ABIJ**

A 1960s ART snake bracelet, pin and earrings, gilt metal with turquoise-coloured stones.

Bracelet 7in (18cm) diam

£50-70   **JJ**

A 1940s Beaujewels floral pin and earrings, with fuchsia pink and pink aurora borealis rhinestones set in goldtone metal.

Pin 2in (5cm) long

£50-60   **JJ**

A 1950s-1960s Beaujewels floral wreath pin and earrings, with faux baroque pearls and aurora borealis rhinestones set in goldtone metal.

Pin 2.5in (6.25cm) diam

£50-60   **JJ**

A Bettina von Walhof floral pin, with hand-wired yellow, green and clear poured glass leaves and flowers, the latter with clear and jonquil crystal rhinestone centres, above a carved red and black medallion.

Flowers, leaves, fruit and animals are motifs commonly found in Von Walhof jewellery, which is all handmade, usually from vintage glass beads and 'poured glass' leaves and flowers.

c1980   *3.25in (8.5cm) high*

£450-550   **SUM**

A 1980s Butler and Wilson charm bracelet, of goldtone metal with pendant crowns and fleur-de-lis, and faux pearl drops.

7in (18cm) long

£40-50   **PC**

A 1970s-1980s Carolee bracelet, with round-cut clear crystal rhinestones set in white metal castings.

7in (18cm) long

£120-130   **JJ**

A 1980s Butler and Wilson three-strand, champagne-coloured faux pearl necklace, with gilt metal clasp.

16.25in (42cm) long

£30-40   **PC**

A 1950s Carolee star pin, of asymmetrical design in gold-plated base metal with embossed studs.

3in (8cm) wide

£55-75   **MILLB**

A 1980s-1990s Carolee necklace, with a chain of antiqued goldtone metal and a single strand of faux pearls.

16in (40.5cm) long

£20-30   **MILLB**

A late 1950s pair of Castlecliff floral motif earrings, set with bands and rings of ruby red crystal rhinestones.

£65-100 LB

A 1940s Danecraft bracelet, of sterling silver and vermeil sterling silver links and medallions, the latter with large, faceted purple pastes.

7in (18cm) long

£90-100 JJ

A late 1940s Castlecliff pendant necklace and earrings, with gold-plated Meso-american heads and motifs and semi-precious stone beads and drops.

Pendant 4.75in (12cm) long

£200-250 RTZ

A 1970s Givenchy necklace, with goldtone metal chain clasp and link, the latter threaded through a circular faux onyx ornament.

Necklace 17in (43cm) long

£25-35 MILLB

A 1930s German DRGM necklace, with rhodium-plated alloy chain and bib, the latter with clear crystal rhinestones and a cluster of rhinestones configured in a floral motif.

Necklace 14.5in (37cm) long

£250-300 LB

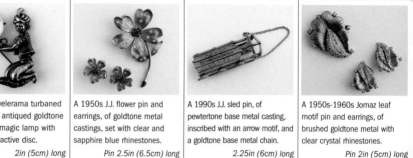

A 1960s Jewelerama turbaned genie pin, of antiqued goldtone casting and magic lamp with goldtone refractive disc.

2in (5cm) long

£20-25 JJ

A 1950s J.J. flower pin and earrings, of goldtone metal castings, set with clear and sapphire blue rhinestones.

Pin 2.5in (6.5cm) long

£40-45 MILLB

A 1990s J.J. sled pin, of pewtertone base metal casting, inscribed with an arrow motif, and a goldtone base metal chain.

2.25in (6cm) long

£12-15 MILLB

A 1950s-1960s Jomaz leaf motif pin and earrings, of brushed goldtone metal with clear crystal rhinestones.

Pin 2in (5cm) long

£50-60 ABIJ

A pair of 1970s Kenneth Jay Lane earrings, of gilt metal with prong-set faux jade and diamond cabochons, above rows of clear rhinestone baguettes.

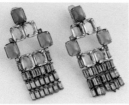

Lane's bright and bold designs designs are typified by creative reworkings of traditional styles, such as Egyptian designs, and unusual combinations of different materials.

2.5in (6.25cm) long

£55-80 ABIJ

A 1980s pair of Les Bernard interlaced scroll-form pendant earrings, of marcasite and clear and pale green rectangular and pear-cut rhinestones.

3.25in (8.5cm) long

£100-120 JJ

A pair of 1980s Moschino antiqued goldtone metal earrings, the clips with central faux pearl cabochons encircled by stamped "Moschino Bijoux" branding, and chained to peace symbol pendants.

3in (7.5cm) long

£20-22 MILLB

A pair of 1980s Richlieu earrings, of geometric form and highly polished, goldtone metal castings, the hinged pendants with three sections of pavé-set, round-cut, crystal clear rhinestones.

1.25in (3cm) long

£20-22 MILLB

A 1950s Robert figural pin, of an oriental man of gilt metal casting with bands of red and blue enamel.

Robert was founded in New York in 1942. Colours are usually strong, using rhinestones or enamelling. Pieces are marked 'Original by Robert'. The company closed in 1979.

2in (5cm) high

£165-175 JJ

A pair of 1950s Robert floral motif earrings, with gilt wired clusters of faux pearls and faceted clear crystal beads.

1.5in (3.75cm) long

£35-38 JJ

A pair of Sarah Coventry floral motif silvertone metal earrings, the latticework with faceted cabochon centres.

c1980   2.25in (5.75cm) diam

£20-28 MILLB

A late 1950s Trifari shoal-of-fishes pin, of gold-plated casting with small ruby red cabochons for the eyes.

Trifari was founded in New York in 1918, becoming immensely successful with its range of Art Deco jewellery in the 1930s. In 1952, President Eisenhower's wife commissioned a parure for the presidential inauguration ceremony, sealing the firm's enduring success and popularity.

2.25in (6.5cm) high

£75-85 ROX

A 1950s Trifari necklace.

Drop 3.5in (7cm) long

£40-45 TR

A pair of Trifari earrings, with original price tag.

1in (3cm) diam

£18-22 TR

A late 1970s Yves St Laurent bar pin, of gold tone metal set with square- and rectangular-cut fuchsia and pale amber glass stones.

2.5in (6.5cm) long

£50-55 MILLB

A pair of Yves St Laurent gold-plated earrings, of oval form with suspended lozenge-shaped centres set with faceted sapphire blue glass stones.

c1980   1.5in (4cm) long

£25-45 LB

COSTUME JEWELLERY

A rare, large, 1990s 'catwalk' butterfly pin of French jet, with pale blue glass beads and variegated agate stones, unsigned.

Jet is a black stone, mostly from Whitby, Yorkshire. It was popular during the late Victorian period, particularly for mourning jewellery. The unusual use of this material, the size, shape and level of carving make this a valuable piece. This piece would have been used as an accessory during a catwalk fashion show.

7.5in (19cm) wide

£250-300   **CRIS**

A 1980s Butler and Wilson dancing couple pin, with prong-set clear paste heads, the black-tie suit and dress of black and clear rhinestones.

This is typical of Butler & Wilson's production during the 1980s, which was very glitzy and studded with diamante. Look out for their lizard and spider-shaped pins which are considered classics.

4.75in (12cm) long

£40-50   **PC**

A 1950s Florenza floral bow pin, of antiqued silver tone metal, set with rows of small turquoise glass cabochons.

2.5in (6.5cm) long

£40-45   **ABIJ**

A Barry Parman '1920s Flapper' pin, in shades of grey, black and white resin with clear crystal rhinestone highlights.

c1975   *3.5in (9cm) high*

£100-150   **LB**

A 1960s Sarah Coventry leaves and berries medallion pin, of antiqued brushed goldtone metal with aurora borealis rhinestones.

2.5in (6.5cm) diam

£35-40   **ABIJ**

A 1970s-'80s Swoboda dragonfly pin, of gilt metal wire and casting with green and ruby glass stones, and channel-set coral and dark and pale brown glass stones.

Pins with coloured semi-precious or glass stones set in gold-plated settings typify Swoboda's production.

3in (7.5cm) long

£70-80   **JJ**

An unsigned 1920s-30s necklace, with gilt metal links and oval hoops of mottled amber-coloured glass.

15.25in (39cm) long

£40-70 ECLEC

An unsigned 1930s necklace, with silver links and hemispheres, roundels and baguettes of clear glass.

13.75in (35cm) long

£60-100 ECLEC

An unsigned 1950s triple-strand faux pearl necklace, with a pendant of gilt metal, clear crystal rhinestones and multiple faux pearl drops.

Necklace 14in (36cm) long

£140-160 CRIS

An unsigned 1950s necklace, with fruit and berry motifs, in yellow and green frosted glass interspersed with faux pearls and clear and aqua rhinestones.

22.5in (58cm) long

£80-100 CRIS

An unsigned 1950s-60s necklace, with green Murano glass leaves and yellow and orange-red Murano glass bead fruits.

16in (41cm) long

£75-120 LB

An unsigned 1960s necklace, with twin strands of faceted grey-blue glass beads and a floral motif of gilt metal with pink glass petals and faux pearls.

Necklace 17in (44cm) long

£170-200 CRIS

An unsigned 1960s necklace, with discs or rosettes in gilt metal with bead moulding encircling turquoise glass cabochons.

Necklace 18.25in (47cm) long

£65-75 CRIS

An unsigned 1940s floral motif necklace and earrings, of sterling silver vermeil set with faux pearls.

Necklace 14in (36cm) long

£60-75 RG

An unsigned mid-1950s necklace and bracelet, of gilt metal with peridot green rhinestones and glass cabochons and drops.

Necklace 14.75in (38cm) long

£90-100   **CRIS**

An unsigned 1930s bracelet, with rhodium-plated links and peridot green glass bead berry motifs.

6.75in (17cm) long

£150-175   **CRIS**

An unsigned 1950s bracelet, of gilt metal with 'butterfly wing' glass cabochons showing a tropical shoreline.

7in (18cm) long

£40-60   **ECLEC**

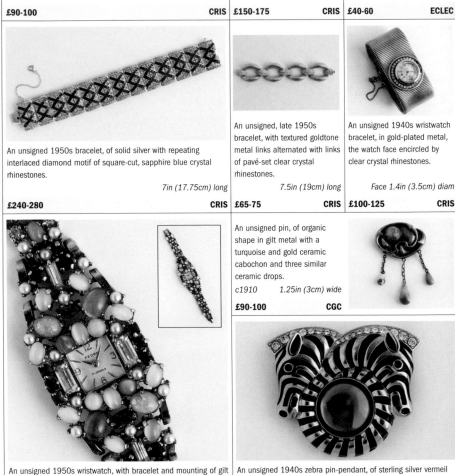

An unsigned 1950s bracelet, of solid silver with repeating interlaced diamond motif of square-cut, sapphire blue crystal rhinestones.

7in (17.75cm) long

£240-280   **CRIS**

An unsigned, late 1950s bracelet, with textured goldtone metal links alternated with links of pavé-set clear crystal rhinestones.

7.5in (19cm) long

£65-75   **CRIS**

An unsigned 1940s wristwatch bracelet, in gold-plated metal, the watch face encircled by clear crystal rhinestones.

Face 1.4in (3.5cm) diam

£100-125   **CRIS**

An unsigned pin, of organic shape in gilt metal with a turquoise and gold ceramic cabochon and three similar ceramic drops.

c1910   *1.25in (3cm) wide*

£90-100   **CGC**

An unsigned 1950s wristwatch, with bracelet and mounting of gilt metal set with polychrome glass beads, faux pearls and round- and baguette-cut rhinestones.

6.75in (17cm) long

£95-120   **CRIS**

An unsigned 1940s zebra pin-pendant, of sterling silver vermeil with black enamelling, clear crystal rhinestones and an emerald glass cabochon.

2in (5cm) long

£100-140   **ABIJ**

COSTUME JEWELLERY

An unsigned 1940s tropical fishes pin, possibly by Mazer Bros., of gilt metal casting with black and ivory enamelling, clear crystal rhinestones and 'metallic' faux pearls.

2.75in (7cm) wide

£140-160 CRIS

An unsigned 1940s triple flowerhead pin, of white metal casting set with clear crystal rhinestones.

2in (5cm) diam

£70-90 JJ

An unsigned 1950s floral pin, possibly by Schreiner, with clear, lime green and diamond-cut white crystal rhinestones, and a lime green glass cabochon.

3.25in (8.5cm) long

£120-145 CRIS

An unsigned 1950s floral pin, possibly by Schreiner, with prong-set ruby red and clear crystal rhinestones on a gilt metal back.

2in (5cm) diam

£100-120 CRIS

An unsigned 1950s butterfly pin, with gilt wire frame set with pink, mauve, ruby red and green rhinestones.

2.25in (5.75cm) wide

£75-85 CRIS

An unsigned 1950s floral motif pin and earrings, with aquamarine crystal rhinestones and dark blue glass cabochons prong-set in gilt wire backs.

Pin 2.75in (7cm) long

£75-85 CRIS

An unsigned 1940s pair of earrings, with prong-set aquamarine crystal rhinestones and prong-set amber and red glass cabochons.

1.25in (3.25cm) long

£80-100 PC

An unsigned 1950s pair of earrings, with gilt metal castings and prong-set orange-red glass cabochons and aurora borealis rhinestones.

1.5in (4cm) long

£35-45 CRIS

An unsigned 1930s pair of ruthenium-plated bow and pendant hoop earrings, with round and baguette-cut clear crystal rhinestones.

2.5in (6.5cm) long

£150-200 CRIS

An unsigned 1950s pair of earrings, with gilt wire frames, prong-set with topaz, olivine, and aurora borealis rhinestones.

1.5in (3.75cm) long

£30-35 CRIS

An unsigned 1950s pair of oval earrings, in textured goldtone metal with a trellis pattern with turquoise glass cabochon centres.

1in (2.5cm) long

£20-25 CRIS

An unsigned 1950s pair of floral motif earrings, with textured gilt metal castings, rings of faux pearls and larger faux pearl centres.

1in (2.5cm) diam

£30-35 CRIS

An unsigned 1960s pair of silvered metal casting earrings, with emerald green, turquoise and coral glass cabochons and faux baroque pearls.

1.25in (3.25cm) diam

£25-30 CRIS

An unsigned pair of Pop Art earrings comprising pendants of goldtone metal coins.

The form of these earrings hints at Antique Roman or Egyptian designs.

c1970   *4in (10cm) long*

£12-15 MILLB

FIND OUT MORE...

'Collector's Guide: Costume Jewellery' by Judith Miller, published by Dorling Kindersley, 2003.

www.dinnyhall.com

A 1980s Stanley Hagler Christmas tree pin, gold-plated metal filigree backing set with frosted white glass flowers, hand-wired red crystal rhinestones and red glass beads.

2.25in (6cm) high

£50-80　　　　**CRIS**

A CLOSER LOOK AT A CHRISTMAS PIN

Christmas Tree pins became popular in 1950, when American mothers and sweethearts wore and sent pins to their sons and lovers serving in the Korean War.

The three-dimensional design of this pin is typical of Hagler.

Hagler learnt to hand-wire beads while working for Miriam Haskell. It became a mainstay of his work.

The inclusion of a partridge is an unusual and festive addition.

A 1980s Stanley Hagler Christmas wreath pin, gold-plated metal filigree backing set with a central intaglio-carved panel of a partridge in a flowering wreath, mother-of-pearl, red and green glass flowers, frosted clear glass leaves, green bell flowers, red and green crystal rhinestones, hand-wired red glass beads, simulated pearl cabochons and rose montées.

Rose montées are flat-backed crystal rhinestones.

3.75in (9.5cm) high

£120-160　　　　**CRIS**

A 1980s Stanley Hagler Christmas tree pin, gold-plated metal filigree backing set with mother-of-pearl flowers, red and green glass beads and red crystal rhinestones.

2.75in (7cm) high

£60-100　　　　**CRIS**

A 1950s Art Christmas wreath pin, yellow-tone textured metal set with green and red enamel and multi-coloured crystal rhinestones.

1.75in (4.5cm) high

£35-45　　　　**CRIS**

A 1980s Stanley Hagler Christmas tree pin, gold-plated metal filigree backing set with moulded red glass flowers, opaque white glass and jadeite beads and red crystal rhinestones.

£60-100　　　　**CRIS**

A 1980s Bijoux Stern Christmas tree pin, textured gold-tone metal set with green and red enamel and multi-coloured crystal rhinestones.

2in (5cm) high

£20-35　　　　**CRIS**

A 1980s Stanley Hagler Christmas tree pin, gold-plated metal filigree backing set with blue and white moulded frosted glass flowers and leaves, blue glass beads with exposed silver foil cores and blue crystal rhinestones.

Most Christmas tree pins are green, red and gold, but wintry silver and blue examples such as this can also be found.

2.25in (6cm) high

£60-100　　　　**CRIS**

COLLECTORS' NOTES

- Bakelite jewellery saw its golden age from the 1920s-30s and provided an inexpensive splash of colour and style for ladies during the Great Depression and wartime. Pieces can attract prices usually paid for jewellery made with precious metals and stones.

- Look for bright, cheerful colours, such as cherry red. Combinations of colours also tend to be popular. Pieces showing intricate or deeply carved designs will usually attract higher prices, especially if they are large. Chips, cracks and burns reduce value.

- Although Bakelite was originally a trademark name, 'bakelite' has become a generic term for jewellery made from a range of plastics.

- Figurative, novelty-shaped and Art Deco styled pieces are often the most popular. Modern reproductions do exist, but these are usually lighter in weight, slightly shinier and have slightly different colours to period pieces – handle as many authentic pieces as possible to learn how to tell them apart.

An Art Deco chrome and bakelite Chinese design brooch.

c1930   2.25in (5.5cm) diam

£20-40   **GKA**

An Art Deco design bakelite brooch.

c1930   1.75in (4.5cm) diam

£30-40   **GKA**

A 1940s carved faux tortoiseshell circular bakelite brooch, carved with flowers.

2.25in (6cm) wide

£100-150   **BB**

A 1930s reverse carved brooch, the painted and filled ring of 'Apple Juice' bakelite.

2in (5cm) wide

£120-180   **BB**

A 1960s luminous pink and grey chequerboard brooch, possibly home-made.

2in (5cm) wide

£80-120   **BB**

A 1930s laminated cream and cherry red bakelite 'zig-zag' brooch.

2in (5cm) wide

£180-220   **PAC**

A rare 1930s laminated and hand-carved 'butterscotch' and 'creamed corn' bakelite triple-flower brooch.

3.25in (8.5cm) wide

£150-250   **PAC**

A 1930s multi-coloured bakelite fruit and leaf pendant brooch.

This example has many different types and colours of fruit making it desirable. Those with less fruit or less variety of colours are worth less.

3.25in (8cm) high

£550-650   **PAC**

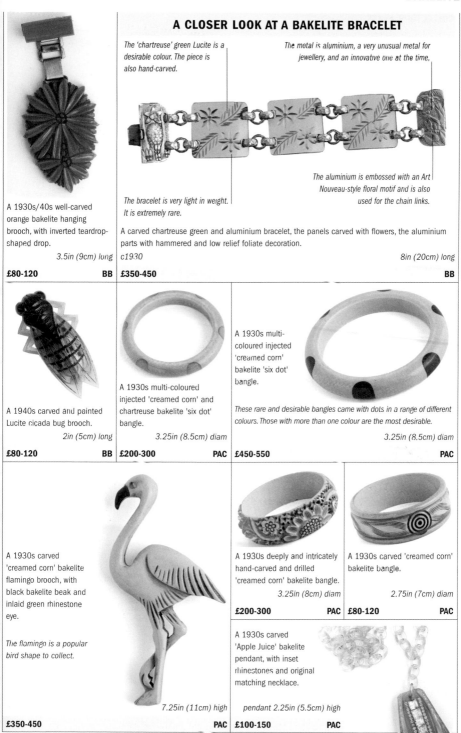

A 1930s/40s well-carved orange bakelite hanging brooch, with inverted teardrop-shaped drop.

3.5in (9cm) long

£80-120 BB

A CLOSER LOOK AT A BAKELITE BRACELET

The 'chartreuse' green Lucite is a desirable colour. The piece is also hand-carved.

The metal is aluminium, a very unusual metal for jewellery, and an innovative one at the time.

The aluminium is embossed with an Art Nouveau-style floral motif and is also used for the chain links.

The bracelet is very light in weight. It is extremely rare.

A carved chartreuse green and aluminium bracelet, the panels carved with flowers, the aluminium parts with hammered and low relief foliate decoration.

c1930   8in (20cm) long

£350-450 BB

A 1940s carved and painted Lucite cicada bug brooch.

2in (5cm) long

£80-120 BB

A 1930s multi-coloured injected 'creamed corn' and chartreuse bakelite 'six dot' bangle.

3.25in (8.5cm) diam

£200-300 PAC

A 1930s multi-coloured injected 'creamed corn' bakelite 'six dot' bangle.

These rare and desirable bangles came with dots in a range of different colours. Those with more than one colour are the most desirable.

3.25in (8.5cm) diam

£450-550 PAC

A 1930s carved 'creamed corn' bakelite flamingo brooch, with black bakelite beak and inlaid green rhinestone eye.

The flamingo is a popular bird shape to collect.

7.25in (11cm) high

£350-450 PAC

A 1930s deeply and intricately hand-carved and drilled 'creamed corn' bakelite bangle.

3.25in (8cm) diam

£200-300 PAC

A 1930s carved 'creamed corn' bakelite bangle.

2.75in (7cm) diam

£80-120 PAC

A 1930s carved 'Apple Juice' bakelite pendant, with inset rhinestones and original matching necklace.

pendant 2.25in (5.5cm) high

£100-150 PAC

COLLECTORS' NOTES

■ Dress clips were popular from the 1920s to the 1950s. They were worn at the neckline of a dress to highlight an outfit, particularly in the evening. They could also be used singly to grip or join the ends of scarves or fur stoles, or worn on hats or as collar or breast-pocket brooches.

■ Although examples in precious metals using diamonds and fine gems can be found, they are usually expensive. More affordable pieces from the 1920s and 1930s are made from rhinestones, glass, silver and plated base metals.

■ Look for the 'glitter' factor, and those with bright, well-cut 'stones'. Geometric Art Deco styles are particularly desirable and those produced in imitation of gems such as sapphires and rubies are popular. Look out for examples by known costume jewellery makers such as Trifari.

■ Bakelite examples are also highly collectable, with bright colours such as cherry red being the most desirable. Deep, intricate hand carving always adds value. Beware of chipped examples.

A 1930s lead and rhinestone dress clip.

2.5in (6.5cm) high

£50-80   **PAC**

A 1930s Trifari pink glass and rhinestone dress clip, the back stamped "KTF".

The mark indicates this was made after 1925, when Trifari, Krussman and Fishel was formed.

2in (5cm) high

£40-60   **PAC**

An Art Deco black Bakelite and red and clear rhinestone dress clip.

c1930   3in (7.5cm) high

£80-120   **PAC**

A large 1930s blue rhinestone dress clip, with pendant.

3.5in (9cm) high

£100-150   **PAC**

A 1930s rhinestone inlaid dress clip, with black glass cabochon.

2.5in (6.5cm) high

£40-60   **PAC**

A scarce mirrored and rhinestone inlaid dress clip.

Mirrored dress clips are scarce, especially those with bevelled edges.

1.5in (4cm) high

£40-60   **PAC**

A pair of 1930s Trifari coloured glass and rhinestone dress clips, with faceted clear glass bars, the backs marked "KTF".

1.5in (4cm) high

£60-80   **PAC**

A pair of red and rhinestone inlaid dress clips.

1.5in (3.5cm) high

£55-65   **PAC**

A pair of rare Art Deco 'Shooting Star' rhinestone dress clips.

1.5in (3.5cm) high

£70-100   **PAC**

A 1930s carved and polished wood and laminated Bakelite dress clip.

2.5in (6cm) high

£50-70 **PAC**

A CLOSER LOOK AT A DRESS CLIP

This plastic is a form of Lucite known as 'Apple Juice Bakelite' due to its colour.

Flowers are typical motifs and the colour is hand-applied.

The design is hand-carved onto the flat reverse side of the piece – look for intricate and detailed designs.

Look for large pieces such as bangles and brooches as this material and style is much sought after.

A reverse painted 'Apple Juice Bakelite' tear drop-shaped dress clip.

2.25in (5.5cm) high

£40-50 **PAC**

A 1930s red and yellow laminated and carved Bakelite curved dress clip.

2in (5cm) long

£30-50 **PAC**

A carved yellow Bakelite triangular dress clip, with inlaid mosaic of flowers made from glass tesserae.

2.5in (6cm) high

£20-30 **PAC**

A pair of laminated and carved red translucent Bakelite and wood dress clips.

2.5in (6cm) high

£40-50 **PAC**

A pair of 1930s deeply carved yellow Bakelite dress clips.

The intricate and deep hand carving makes this pair desirable.

2in (5cm) high

£40-50 **PAC**

A pair of 1930s carved green Catalin or cast-phenolic leaf-shaped dress clips.

1.5in (4cm) long

£20-25 **PAC**

A leaf-shaped green Bakelite dress clip, inlaid with diamanté.

2in (5cm) high

£20-25 **PAC**

A carved green Lucite dress clip.

3.25in (8cm) high

£25-35 **PAC**

COLLECTORS' NOTES

■ Walter Elias Disney (1901-66) started his own studio in Hollywood in 1923 with his partner and brother Roy, and developed the character of Mickey Mouse in 1928.

■ Disney was a pioneer in animation, constantly pushing his staff to new artistic heights and technological advances.

■ Licensing rights were first granted to George Borgfeldt of New York in 1930 and from 1932 'Kay' Kaymen also represented the characters, expanding the range of merchandise.

■ Collectors tend to prefer licensed pieces, however, very early unlicensed examples can be desirable – many were produced in Japan. Officially licensed items made in the US or Germany before 1938 should be marked with "Walt Disney Enterprises" or "Walter E. Disney". Those made in the UK should be marked

"Walt Disney Mickey Mouse Ltd". Post-1939 all items are marked "Walt Disney Productions".

■ The better known characters tend to be the most sought after, but are not necessarily the rarest. Date and condition are two of the most important indicators to value. The most popular period with collectors is the 1930s and includes soft toys, tinplate figures and games.

■ Mickey Mouse figures from this period can be identified by their rat-like bodies, a tail and "pie-cut" eyes. By the 1950s, the figures are plumper, often lacking a tail. Materials used and quality of production will also help in dating a piece.

■ As pieces from the 1930s become scarcer and more expensive, demand has grown for previously ignored pieces from the 1950s to the 1970s.

A Deans Rag Book Mickey Mouse crushed velvet soft toy, some repairs to feet, hands and shorts replaced.

Deans, together with Steiff, were awarded the first licenses to produced Disney soft toys in Europe.

c1930   12in (30cm) high

£100-150   **BONC**

A 1930s Deans Rag Book Mickey Mouse velveteen soft toy, with Deans Ragbook Co. button, missing one eye, tail and shorts, dirty and well played with.

9in (23cm) high

£50-70   **W&W**

A CLOSER LOOK AT A STEIFF MICKEY MOUSE DOLL

Steiff made Mickey Mouse dolls from 1931 to 1936.

Steiff soft toys are sought after in their own right making this toy doubly collectable.

The large size, together with original tags and stamping on the foot make this a desirable example.

This is example is wearing blue pants, the rarest colour variation.

A 1930s large Steiff Mickey Mouse soft toy, with applied felt 'pie-crust' eyes, original whiskers and tail, retains rubber stamping on foot, chest tag, ear tag and button, shows some very light darkening, excellent condition, front of pants somewhat faded, face shows some very light darkening.

18in (45.5cm) high

£9,000-10,000   **NB**

Five rare Britains Disney Characters, comprising a 16H Mickey Mouse, minor paint chips to face and body; a 18H Pluto, minor paint loss; a 19H Donald Duck, minor paint loss to beak, a 20H Clarabelle Cow; repaired arm, head support broken and a 21H Goofy, paint chips, small hole to back, all with detachable heads.

1939

£1,800-2,200 (set)   **VEC**

An unusual composition clockwork Pinocchio figure, with rocking action to feet and loose mounted head shakes, some cleaning required.

c1950 8in (20.5cm) high

£250-350 **W&W**

A limited edition Royal Doulton Disney Showcase 'Pinocchio' figure, style two designed by Shane Ridge, from an edition of 1,500, boxed with certificate.

1999 5.5in (14cm) high

£60-80 **PSA**

An American Ideal Pinocchio wood and composition figure.

As Pinocchio was less popular than other Disney characters at the time, fewer examples were produced, making this figure very collectable.

c1930 20in (51cm) high

£600-700 **BEJ**

A set of Chad Valley Seven Dwarfs, the cloth dolls with felt faces and painted features, paper labels, in original boxes.

'Snow White and the Seven Dwarfs' was the first feature length cartoon. It was considered madness at the time, but it proved a massive hit with the public and received a Special Academy Award (one full-sized Oscar and seven small ones) from the Motion Picture Academy in 1938.

1937 6in (15cm) high

£700-900 **BONC**

A Britains Snow White Series, comprising Snow White and the Seven Dwarfs, all very good condition.

£200-250 **VEC**

A 1970s Walt Disney Productions Donald Duck painted bisque figurine.

2.75in (7cm) high

£7-10 **TSIS**

A Cinderella painted china figurine, stamped "DISNEY JAPAN" on the base.

c1980 5.5in (14cm) high

£10-15 **TSIS**

A Royal Doulton 'Cruella De Vil' figure, DM1, designed by Martyn Alcock, from the Disney's 101 Dalmatians Collection.

1997-2001 6in (15cm) high

£40-60 **PSA**

A limited edition Royal Doulton Disney Showcase 'Thumper' figure, designed by Martyn Alcock, from an edition of 1,500, boxed with certificate.

1999 3.25in (8.5cm) high

£30-50 **PSA**

DISNEYANA

A 1930s Swiss Mickey Mouse lithographed biscuit tin, by Disch Ltd, marked "Par Aut. de Walt Disney Mickey-Mouse S.A. Concessionnaire Disch Othmarsingen".

8.5in (21.5cm) wide

£300-400   **DH**

A large 1930s Swiss Mickey Mouse lithographed biscuit tin, by Disch Ltd, marked "Par Aut. de Walt Disney Mickey-Mouse S.A. Concessionnaire Disch Othmarsingen".

10in (25.5cm) wide

£350-450   **DH**

A late 1930s English Mickey Mouse biscuit tin.

6in (15cm) high

£80-120   **DH**

A rare 1940s Australian Minnie Mouse triangular lithographed sweet tin, marked "W.D. Ent".

This tin was also made with an image of Mickey Mouse, Popeye and Donald Duck.

5.75in (14.5cm) wide

£100-150   **DH**

1939

£70-90

A Belgian 'Snow White' lithographed sweet tin, marked "Par Aut. Walt. Disney - Mickey Mouse S.A." and "Etabl. J. Schuybroek S.A. Hoboken-Anvers".

Another tin with a different scene from the film was also made and is worth a similar amount.

13in (33cm) wide

     DH

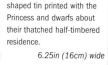

A mid-20thC Disney Snow White biscuit tin, the cottage-shaped tin printed with the Princess and dwarfs about their thatched half-timbered residence.

6.25in (16cm) wide

£60-80   **CHEF**

A 1930s Walt Disney Enterprises lithographed tin sand pail, with Minnie Mouse in a car, Mickey Mouse and Donald Duck.

8in (20cm) high

£100-150   **SOTT**

A Disney lithographed tin sand pail, by Happynak.

c1940   *6in (15cm) high*

£80-120   **DH**

A 1940s Disney lithographed tin sand pail, by Happynak, marked "by Permission Walt Disney Mickey Mouse".

5in (12.5cm) high

£70-90   **DH**

Christopher Finch, "The Art of Walt Disney, From Mickey Mouse To the Magic Kingdoms", published by Abrams.

"Walt Disney's Pinocchio", with illustrations from the film, very scarce.

1940

£70-90　　　　　　　**BIB**

"Walt Disney's Version of Pinocchio", with illustrations from the film, published by Collins, London.

1955

£40-50　　　　　　　**BIB**

1973

£40-50　　　　　　　**BIB**

An original pen, ink and dotted celluloid cartoon strip artwork, by Floyd Gottfredson, with Goofy, and Mickey, and signed 'Walt Disney', dated 8th August.

Gottfredson (1905-86) joined Disney as an apprentice animator in 1929. In 1930 he took over the production of the newly launched Mickey Mouse comic strip which he continued to run for 45 years until he retired in 1975. These strips originally appeared in daily newspapers and were later compiled into picture-books or comic books.

1962　　　　　　　*17.75in (45cm) wide*

£200-300　　　　　　　**MUW**

'Walt Disney's The Jungle Book', US title card.

This was issued for the 1980s re-release of the 1967 film.

14in (35.5cm) wide

£40-50　　　　　　　**ATM**

An original pen, ink and spotted celluloid cartoon strip artwork, by Floyd Gottfredson, showing Mickey and Minnie gardening, dated 8th September.

1962　　　　　　　*17.75in (45cm) long*

£200-300　　　　　　　**MUW**

An original pen and ink and blue wash cartoon strip artwork, by Floyd Gottfredson, showing Mickey Mouse and Mickey's son painting, signed "Walt Disney, 15th January".

1966　　　　　　　*18in (45.5cm) long*

£150-250　　　　　　　**MUW**

A 1940s Walt Disney Productions moulded card Multiplane Painting No. 13, 'Bambi Meets Little Flower, The Skunk', from Walt Disney's "Bambi", produced by Courvoisier, San Francisco.

1939-46　　　　　　　*8.75in (22cm) wide*

£70-100　　　　　　　**TM**

A 'Mickey Mouse Library of Games' card set, by Russell Mfg. Co, Leicester Mass.

c1946　　　　　　　*6in (15cm) long*

£40-60　　　　　　　**TM**

A Japanese Mickey Mouse Acrobat toy, celluloid figure on wire armature, cut-action.

Figure 6in (15cm) high

£180-220 **NB**

A clockwork Marx Donald Duck Duet, embossed lithographed tin, Goofy missing one ear.

10.5in (26.5cm) high

£250-350 **NB**

A 1930s Walt Disney Enterprises lithographed tin child's wash set toy, comprising washbasin, washboard, washing line and wooden pegs.

Bowl 9in (13.5cm) wide

£250-350 **SOTT**

Three 1980s Disney themed 'Viewmaster 3-D' reels, comprising "Peter Pan", "Cinderella" and "The Little Mermaid".

Cards 8.25in (21cm) high

£7-10 (each) **TSIS**

A Multiple Toymakers Walt Disney's Donald Duck Express, mint condition, in near mint condition window box.

1968

£200-250 **VEC**

A Multiple Toymakers Walt Disney's Donald Duck's Whirlybird, mint condition, in near mint condition box.

1968

£200-250 **VEC**

A Multiple Toymakers Walt Disney's Mickey Mouse's Tin Lizzy, mint condition, in excellent condition window box.

1967

£150-200 **VEC**

An unusual Happynak English tea set, each of the 15 pieces with printed Walt Disney character decorations, in original box.

Box 16in (40.5cm) wide

£250-350 **F**

A 1950s Walt Disney
Productions 'Minnie Mouse'
painted candle.

3.5in (9cm) high

£3-4   **TSIS**

A 1930s Mores Snow White
tooth brush holder.

6in (15cm) high

£100-150   **BEV**

A 1930s Mores Dopey tooth
brush holder.

3.75in (9.5cm) high

£100-150   **BEV**

A 1930s Mores Sleepy tooth
brush holder.

3.75in (9.5cm) high

£100-150   **BEV**

A pair of 1930s Japanese Mickey and Minnie Mouse painted bisque toothbrush holders,
with large heads and string tails, stamped "WALT DISNEY JAPAN", Minnie's head re-glued.

5in (12.5cm) high

£300-400   **SOTT**

A pair of 1980s Walt Disney 'Mickey
Mouse The Cook' salt and pepper shakers.

2.75in (7cm) high

£5-7   **TSIS**

A 1930s American Mickey Mouse pin, marked "Copyright Walt
Disney Enterprises".

1in (3cm) wide

£70-90   **LDE**

A Walt Disney Productions
'Mary Poppins' silver-plated
metal souvenir spoon, sealed in
polythene bag.

c1964   6in (15.5cm) long

£15-20   **TSIS**

A Walt Disney World blue and
clear iridescent glass souvenir
bell, by Crystal Arts, with
faceted glass clapper and acid-
etched Mickey Mouse motif,
dated 1986.

5.25in (13.5cm) high

£6-8   **TSIS**

A 'Ponytail' Barbie number 4 doll, by Mattel, in original black and white swimsuit.

Released in 1959, most collectors look for Barbies and outfits from before 1972 and date dolls by their face and hair.

c1960   11in (28cm) high

£150-250   **NOR**

A titian 'Bubble Cut' Barbie doll, by Mattel, in red swimsuit, with original box lacking ends.

Although the first 'Bubble Cut' Barbie was released in 1961, she originally wore a black and white striped swimsuit.

1962-67   11.5in (29cm) high

£120-180   **NOR**

A CLOSER LOOK AT A BARBIE DOLL

This outfit is No. 982 from the 'Fashion Set' series and is worn by a correct, period 'Bubble Cut' doll.

The outfit was sold from 1960-64, but re-released in 1989 on a porcelain doll and again in 1995.

She retains her floor-standing microphone, which was prone to breaking.

Her 'diva-like' outfit is nearly complete with pink scarf, black mules and long black gloves. She is only lacking her pearl necklace.

A brunette 'Bubble Cut' Barbie doll, by Mattel, in a 'Solo in Spotlight' outfit.

1962-3   11.75in (30cm) high

£150-200   **NOR**

A 'Ponytail' Barbie No. 4 doll, in 'Enchanted Evening' outfit.

This outfit is set No. 983 and dates from 1960-63. It is complete except for her pearl necklace and earrings. The name was re-used for a similar outfit in 1986. The exact gown was re-released in 1996 on a collector's edition doll.

1960-63   11.5in (29cm) high

£200-300   **NOR**

A 'Twist 'N' Turn' Barbie doll, by Mattel, in floral skirt and red top.

1969-70   11.5in (29cm) high

£70-100   **NOR**

A 'Twist 'N' Turn' 'Sweet Sixteen' Barbie doll, by Mattel, in short floral skirt, white sleeves.

'Twist 'N' Turn', often shortened to 'TNT', was a waist feature that was introduced in 1966.

c1973   11.5in (29cm) high

£70-100   **NOR**

A 'Twist 'N' Turn' 'Olympic Skater' Barbie doll, in red, white and blue outfit.

c1976-7   11.5in (29cm) high

£45-55   **NOR**

A limited edition 'Gay Parisienne Porcelain Treasures' porcelain Barbie doll, in correct outfit.

The original 1960s version of Barbie in this dress can fetch up to £350.

1991

£70-100   **NOR**

A Mattel 35th Anniversary Barbie doll, the replica doll with original 1959 shape, hair, clothes, box, complete with sunglasses, booklets, and box, all in mint condition.

1994   box 12.5in (32cm) high

£20-30   **MEM**

A flock-haired Ken No. 1 doll, by Mattel, in later football uniform.

This version was originally sold with a pair of red swimming trunks and red sandals.

c1961   12.25in (31cm) high

£70-100   **NOR**

An Allan doll, by Mattel, with bendable leg.

The straight leg version of Allan is less desirable and worth around £100.

c1965   12.5in (31.5cm) high

£100-150   **NOR**

A Skooter doll, by Mattel, in a yellow dress, bendable leg.

Skooter was first released in 1965 with a straight leg and is worth 50% of this later version.

1966   9in (23cm) high

£45-55   **NOR**

A blonde-haired Midge doll, by Mattel, with bendable legs and original and correct light and mid-blue two-piece swimming suit.

Midge was introduced in 1963. She has an identical body to Barbie, with a different head. She was only sold for a few years before vanishing (despite apparently being Barbie's best friend!) and returning in 1987 as 'California Midge'. Midge dolls with bendable legs or without freckles are usually worth more than straight leg versions. The clothing colours varied depending on hair colour.

1963-66   11.25in (28.5cm) high

£70-100   **NOR**

A CLOSER LOOK AT BARBIE'S FRIENDS

Ricky was Skipper's first male friend, later joined by Scott in 1979 and Kevin in 1990.

He is wearing his original outfit of blue shorts and a typically 1960s stripy beach jacket with terry collar, which are both in excellent condition.

He still retains his original tag, which is extremely rare as it was usually torn off or worn away with play.

He still has his original box and brochure and is in unworn and clean condition with no wear to his red-painted freckled face or hair.

A Ricky doll, by Mattel, in original box.

c1965   10in (25.5cm) high

£80-120   **NOR**

A 'Red Flare' Barbie outfit, by Mattel.

1962-65

£25-35   **DE**

A Mattel Barbie pink plastic handbag.

            2.25in (5.5cm) wide

£3-4   **DE**

A Mattel Ken vinyl doll case, dated 1961.

            12.75in (32.5cm) high

£35-45   **MA**

COLLECTORS' NOTES

■ Beatrice Alexander Behrman, later styling herself 'Madame Alexander,' was born in 1895 in New York. She opened her own business in 1923, making fabric dolls, which became very successful. Dolls were subsequently made in composition during the 1930s, plastic from 1948 and vinyl from the late 1950s. She died in 1990 at the age of 95, but the company continues today.

■ Madame Alexander dolls are noted and collected for their highly detailed and well-made costumes (rather than for the doll itself) which were made in over 6,500 variations. They were made to be displayed on a shelf rather than to be played with. Both the doll, and particularly the clothes, must be in clean, bright, mint and original condition complete with the original label and preferably with the box, to be of interest to most collectors. Values tumble if there are signs of wear or missing pieces.

■ The 'Storyland', 'Little Women' and 'International Series' are popular with collectors, the latter having been introduced in 1961 with each doll dressed in national costume from some 64 countries around the world. This series used the Wendy-kin/Alexander-kin 8in bent-knee walker doll until 1964. From then until 1972, a bent-knee, non-walking doll was used which was then replaced by the non-walking model still used today which had straight legs.

■ Each year the costumes of the International dolls were changed in some way, giving great scope to collectors who can collect either an entire year's variations across the countries, or one country across the years. Most collectors prefer the earlier (and usually more valuable) bent-knee versions, so examine a doll carefully before buying. Certain dolls made for short periods are rare - look out for the scarce Amish boy and Ecuador and Morocco dolls.

A Madame Alexander 'Brazil' doll, style 0773, with original tag, clothes and box, in mint condition.

9in (23cm) high

£50-70   MEM

A Madame Alexander 'China' doll, style 0772, from the 'International Dolls' series, with tag, original clothes, in mint condition with original box.

7.5in (19cm) high

£30-40   MEM

A Madame Alexander 'German' girl doll, style 563, with original tag, clothes and box, mint condition.

7.5in (19cm) high

£30-40   MEM

A Madame Alexander 'Indonesia' doll, from the 'International Dolls' series, with tag and original clothes, booklet and box.

8.25in (21cm) high

£35-45   MEM

A Madame Alexander 'Netherlands' girl doll, style 591, complete with original clothes and tag, in mint condition with original box.

7.75in (19.5cm) high

£30-40   MEM

A Madame Alexander 'Netherlands' boy doll, style 577, with original clothes and accessories, mint and boxed.

8in (20cm) high

£35-45   MEM

A Madame Alexander 'Turkey' doll, style 587, complete with original tag, clothes and box, in mint condition.

7.5in (19cm) high

£30-40   MEM

COLLECTORS' NOTES

■ When buying plastic dolls, consider condition as being of primary importance, as many dolls were mass-produced and played with. The plastic should be clean and blemish free. Any 'make-up' should not be rubbed off or worn and hair in particular should be in its original style and not cut, dyed or restyled. Costume is important, and clothes should be original, still brightly coloured and undamaged. Dolls made for display in particular should retain their boxes.

A Madame Alexander plastic 'Bride' doll, from the 'Storyland' series, in mint condition with tag, original clothes and in original card box.

The Storyland series represents different groups and cultures that make up the United States.

1972   doll 8.25in (21cm) high

£55-65   **MEM**

A Madame Alexander '8in Matthew' doll, style 26424, from the Storyland series, with original clothes and tag and box, in mint condition.

8.25in (21cm) high

£25-35   **MEM**

A later Madame Alexander 'Artists' Wendy doll, style 31250, with original clothes, tag and box, in mint condition, including brush and paints.

The paints and brushes were to be used by the child to paint their own picture.

8.25in (21cm) high

£45-55   **MEM**

A Vogue Ginny strung doll, with painted eyelashes, original outfit and box

The Ginny doll was released in composition in 1948 and made in hard plastic later that year. She was given sleeping eyes and painted lashes in 1950.

7.25in (18.5cm) high

£120-180   **SOTT**

A Ginny doll, by Vogue, with moulded marks to her back, in original clothes, with shoes, her head moves as she walks and her legs bend at the knee, ruffled hair.

1957-62   7.5in (19cm) high

£55-65   **MEM**

A Ginny 'Majorette' doll, by Vogue, with moulded marks to her head, head moves from side to side as her legs are moved, complete in original uniform.

9.5in (24.5cm) high

£70-100   **MEM**

A Madame Alexander 'Mary Cassatt Baby' doll, style 3360, with 'Mary Cassatt Baby' tag, original clothes and box, in mint condition.

Mary Cassatt (1844-1926) was an American painter who both supported the Impressionists and painted in their style. Her pictures are much loved and portray intimate domestic scenes, many featuring children or babies. This doll is based on one of her portrayals of a baby.

doll 14.25in (36cm) high

£100-150   **MEM**

A Steiff 'Ginny's Pup' soft toy dog, with ball and tag, marked "US ZONE GERMANY", no coat.

Steiff made this for the Ginny range but it was also released as a standard production line.

3.25in (8cm) high

£70-100   **SOTT**

A 1970s Ginny doll, by Vogue, with clothes, moulded marks to her back, mint condition, in original box.

box 9in (23cm) high

£15-25   **MEM**

An Ideal 'Shirley Temple' vinyl doll, with original tagged clothes and hair slide.

The Shirley Temple doll was designed by Bernard Lipfert and first made in the 1930s in composition. It helped propel Ideal to one of the highest positions in the doll industry. This large 15in (38cm) size is more unusual and valuable than the standard sizes.

1957   *15in (38cm) high*

£120-180   **MEM**

An Ideal 'Shirley Temple' doll, with original clothes, under clothes, socks, shoes, pearl necklace, hair slide and hat.

1957   *12in (30.5cm) high*

£120-180   **MEM**

An Ideal 'Shirley Temple' 'Stowaway' doll, with original clothes, mint condition, with bright clothes and box.

This character was taken from the 1936 film of the same name where Temple plays stowaway 'Ching-Ching' who ends up in America.

1983   *11.5in (29.5cm) high*

£20-30   **MEM**

An Ideal 'Shirley Temple' doll, with original clothes including under trousers, with curled hair, jewellery, shoes, box, mint with original net covering hair.

1982   *11.5in (29.5cm) high*

£35-45   **MEM**

An Ideal 'Saucy Walker' hard plastic doll, with original clothes and short hair, the back of the head moulded "IDEAL DOLL", plaits lost.

1951-55   *22in (56cm) high*

£60-80   **MEM**

An Ideal 'Saucy Walker' hard plastic doll, with original clothes and hair, with characteristic plaits.

1951-55   *22in (56cm) high*

£50-70   **MEM**

A rare Ideal 'Posie Walker' doll, with bent legs.

1954-56   *24.5in (62cm) high*

£80-120   **MEM**

An Ideal Revlon hard plastic bodied doll, with soft plastic head, original clothes, tights, shoes, underclothes and tag, hair with fragments of hair net and in very good condition.

1955-59   *18in (46cm) high*

£80-120   **MEM**

A CLOSER LOOK AT AN IDEAL DOLL

This Ideal doll is in mint condition, with a clean face with original make-up – her hair has also not been cut or restyled.

She retains her box, which has attractive and charming artwork in the style of the period.

Her clothes are still brightly coloured, original and complete with shoes and underclothes – she even retains her jewellery.

She retains her original booklet wrist tag.

A 1950s Ideal Revlon doll, with original clothes, underclothes, shoes, hair, jewellery, together with paperwork and booklet, in mint condition and boxed, box with sellotaped edges.

1955-59   *17.75in (45cm) high*

£450-550   **MEM**

A 1950s 'Tiny Terrilee' doll, with rare platinum hair, original clothes, socks and shoes, her head turns as she walks, with rouged cheeks and knees.

This doll has rare 'platinum' blonde coloured hair, echoing the hairstyles of famous models and personalities of the day such as Marilyn Monroe. It is the hardest colour to find and must not be confused with blonde, which is yellower in tone. Red is the next rarest colour. The value of this example is further heightened as the hair is in original condition with curls and ringlets.

10in (25.5cm) high

£100-150　　**MEM**

A 1950s Richmond 'Sandra Sue' hard plastic doll, with painted slippers, original clothes, hair and underwear.

7.75in (19.5cm) high

£70-100　　**MEM**

An 1950s unmarked hard plastic doll, with brunette hair, in original green taffeta dress.

18in (45.5cm) high

£100-150　　**SOTT**

A 1960s large Chiltern blown vinyl doll, with a blonde hair wig, in original box.

20in (51cm) high

£30-50　　**F**

A large Roddy blown vinyl doll, with a platinum hair wig, in original box.

20in (51cm) high

£30-40　　**F**

An Alice's Adventures In Wonderland doll, by Palitoy, with a battery operated walking mechanism and fitted miniature record player, with three double-sided discs playing the voice of Alice and songs from the Disney film, in original box.

23in (58cm) high

£100-150　　**CO**

An English Sasha 'Cora' plastic doll, No. 118, modelled as a black girl in a floral dress and original box.

£120-180　　**F**

A CLOSER LOOK AT A CRISSY DOLL

Her hair can be extended by pushing a button and pulling – then be wound back with a knob on her back. Hair on the earliest versions extended to her feet, but this was abandoned as it tangled easily.

Crissy was made between 1969 and 1975 and was mass-marketed and popular - later versions had moving hips and could 'talk'.

Her dress is in the style of the period, but her brown hair and dark eyes go against the blonde haired, blue eyed stereotype of the day.

A Crissy doll by Ideal, with 'hair that grows and grows and grows', original dress, shoes, 'Letter to Mother' care instructions and box with early wool handle.

In mint condition, she would command over £70.

1969

£45-55

18in (46cm) high

MEM

A Hasbro 'The World of Love' 'Flower' doll, that turns, twists and bends, in original box.

1971   *10.5in (26.5cm) high*

£50-70   **NOR**

A Hasbro 'The World of Love' 'Love' vinyl doll, in original box.

1970-71   *box 11in (28cm) h*

£30-50   **NOR**

A Topper 'Dawn' doll, with bendable legs and dressed in a yellow, gold and blue short-skirted dress.

'Dawn', the 6.5in (16.5cm) fashion doll, was released in 1970 as a smaller rival to Barbie. She clearly did not catch on as Barbie did and was withdrawn from production around 1973. She was produced in a number of ethnicities and variations, each now worth approximately the same. She also had a wardrobe of her own.

c1970   *6.5in (16.5cm) high*

£10-15   **NOR**

A Mego Corp 'Diana Ross' poseable doll, in original box, complete, in mint condition with clothing.

The price label on the box shows that a little girl could own Diana for "$12.39" (around £8).

1977   13in (33cm) high

£80-120   **MEM**

An Lyn 'Suntan Brooke Shields' poseable doll, with 'Year Round Funtan', original clothes and box.

This doll was released after Brooke Shields shot to fame as Emmele in the 1980 feature film 'The Blue Lagoon', in which two children were marooned and grew up on a desert island. The Brooke doll was available in many different costumes, or 'High Fashion Designs' as they were known.

c1982

£20-30   **MEM**

An American 'Cuddly Cathy' blown vinyl doll, in original box.

box 15.5in (39.5cm) high

£40-50   **F**

A Pedigree hard plastic bent leg black doll, in original box.

14in (35.5cm) high

£80-120   **F**

An early Palitoy painted celluloid doll, modelled as young black girl.

6in (15cm) high

£30-50   **F**

A late 1960s 'Heidi Pocketbook' doll, in a hard plastic carrying case, with clothes, missing one shoe, hair with damage.

If her hair was in perfect and original condition, the box was undamaged and her wardrobe was complete, the set would be worth around £40.

doll 5.5in (14cm) high

£15-25   **MEM**

A pair of Dean's Joan and Peter 'Dancing Dolls', in cloth with painted features, together with trade card, catalogue and instructions.

1928

£120-180   **BONC**

Two Dean's Rag Book 'The Lambeth Walk' cloth dolls, with moulded faces, together with sheet music and catalogue.

These dolls are based on the popular music hall star of the time, Lupino Lane, who popularised the song 'The Lambeth Walk' from the musical 'Me and My Girl'.

1939   *largest 11.75in (30cm) high*

£120-180   **BONC**

A 1930s Dean's Rag book doll, modelled as young girl, with moulded painted face and wearing a blue velvet winter suit with hand muff.

21in (53.5cm) high

£100-150   **F**

A Dean's Dutch Boy and Girl dolls, designed by Richard E. Ellett, with painted cloth heads, blonde hair on cloth bodies each wearing traditional Dutch costume, boy's right cheek dented and slight lose of paint.

1949   *33in (84cm) high*

£180-220   **BONC**

Seven Dean's 'Dolls of the World', designed by Richard E. Ellett, with hand-painted moulded rubber heads on cloth bodies, each wearing a traditional costume, Chinese boy, Irish boy, English girl, Dutch boy, Norwegian girl, Russian girl and Native American girl.

1949   *12.25in (31cm) high*

£180-220   **BONC**

Two Peggie and Teddie printed cotton cloth dolls.

1911   *15.75in (40cm) high*

£45-55   **BONC**

A Chad Valley cloth boy doll.

c1930   *24.75in (63cm) high*

£50-60   **HB**

An early 20thC Norah Wellings cloth doll, with moulded velvet upper body and felt lower body, modelled as an Native American Chief, in original box.

Norah Wellings dolls are hotly collected, particularly if in good condition with brightly coloured fabric and if an unusual or highly detailed character. Beware that there were many copies made at the same time and later and these look very much like Wellings dolls, particularly the sailors. Always look for the Norah Wellings label.

box 12in (30.5cm) high

£180-220   **F**

A Pedigree felt doll, designed by Nora P. Hill, with original label, in original box.

12in (30.5cm) high

£80-120   **F**

An early 20thC velvet doll, the moulded painted face with inset glass eyes, modelled as a South Seas maiden, dressed in a grass skirt, possibly Chad Valley.

12in (30.5cm) high

£40-60   **F**

A CLOSER LOOK AT RAGGEDY ANN & ANDY

The Volland company suggested illustrator and author John Gruelle made dolls to help sales of his stories. Early versions were made by Gruelle's family and are extremely rare, but from 1920 until 1934 the Volland company took over and these professionally produced dolls are valuable and sought-after.

Raggedy Andy was not developed until 1920. Gruelle chose another company, Beers, Keeler & Bowman, to make this character although Volland was responsible for sales – thus they were not produced as a matched pair.

Fabric does not generally wear well over time, but these dolls are in excellent condition – they have no tears or major stains and retain their clothes which still have their bright colours.

This is the smallest size made by Volland - a larger 29in (73cm) high version can fetch up to 50-70% more than this size if in similar condition.

An American cloth Volland 'Raggedy Ann' doll.

Raggedy Ann was a rag doll owned by the daughter of American illustrator John Gruelle who told his daughter stories of her 'adventures' when she was ill in 1915. She had been owned by Gruelle's mother and as her face had faded, he drew one on resulting in her rudimentary features. His daughter died in late 1915 and he wrote 'Raggedy Ann Stories' in 1918 in her memory.

An American cloth Volland 'Raggedy Andy' doll.

c1920-1934	*16.5in (42cm) high*	*c1930*	*15.75in (40cm) high*
£1,000-1,500	**HGS**	**£800-1,000**	**HGS**

An American 'Beloved Belindy' cloth doll, made by Georgene Novelties.

'Beloved Belindy' was another character from the hand of illustrator and author John Gruelle who also created the Raggedy Ann and Andy stories. The first cloth dolls were made by P.F. Volland from 1926, just before the book

was published. Georgene Novelties Co. took over production from 1938. This example dates from the first years of production – later versions from the 1940s onwards had forward, not sideways, facing feet. Georgene continued to produce 'Beloved Belindy' until the early 1960s and as well as being early, this doll is valuable as it is larger than the standard 15in (38cm) version.

1938   *18.5in (47cm) high*

£800-1,200   **HGS**

A Kathe Kruse doll, the painted moulded head modelled as a young child, on a fabric body, manufacturer's mark applied to the foot.

16in (41cm) high

£700-1,000   **F**

A cloth 'Brownie' doll, by an unknown maker, seated on a carved and painted toadstool.

A brownie is a mythical elf-like figure in Britain. It is said to help with domestic tasks, usually at night, in exchange for small gifts and food.

c1930   *33in (84cm) high*

£180-220   **BONC**

An Armand Marseille doll, bisque head with blue glass eyes, open mouth with row of teeth, brown wig, wooden body, restored, new dress.	An Armand Marseille doll, bisque head, blue sleeping eyes, open mouth with row of teeth, short-hair wig, wooden joint body, marked, restored.	An Ernst Heubach doll, bisque head, blue glass eyes, open mouth with teeth, wooden joint body, damaged, restored, new clothes, marked.	A Kestner bisque socket head doll, human hair wig, sleep eyes, remnants of plaster pate, jointed composition body, red stamp "Excelsior", impressed "Made in Germany 171".
c1905 24.75in (63cm) high	c1912 21in (53cm) high	c1915 23.5in (60cm) high	19in (48cm) high
£200-300 BMN	**£120-180** BMN	**£180-220** BMN	**£250-350** WHA

A CLOSER LOOK AT A BISQUE DOLL

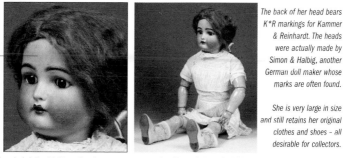

The bisque is undamaged, smooth and clean with no flaws and she has a desirable fully jointed body.

She has a row of teeth in her open mouth – Kammer & Reinhardt claimed to be the first company to introduce this feature on bisque-headed dolls.

The back of her head bears K*R markings for Kammer & Reinhardt. The heads were actually made by Simon & Halbig, another German doll maker whose marks are often found.

She is very large in size and still retains her original clothes and shoes – all desirable for collectors.

A Kammer & Reinhardt bisque headed doll, with blue sleeping eyes, open mouth with teeth, long dark blonde wig, jointed limbs on a composition body, original clothes with white leather shoes.

29.5in (75cm) high

£400-600   BMN

An early 20thC German bisque-headed doll, numbered "39", with auburn hair, lateral moving sleepy eyes, open mouth and jointed composition body.	A Gebrüder Heubach 'Piano Baby', in tinted bisque with moulded hair and intaglio eyes, impressed sunburst mark.	A German all-bisque doll, with articulated arms, in later knitted dress.	A glazed porcelain shoulder head black baby, with well matched five-piece body, dressed in Pierrot outfit, unmarked.
15.75in (40cm) high	15.75in (40cm) high	c1920 4.5in (11.5cm) high	c1930 19in (48.5cm) high
£200-300 CHEF	**£200-300** CHEF	**£150-200** BEJ	**£600-700** BEJ

A porcelain half doll, modelled as a lady wearing a wide-brimmed pink hat and pink dress, clasping a rose in her hands, incised marks.

Half dolls were popular from the late 19thC until the 1940s. Values depends on how well the doll is modelled and painted. Simple examples made from one mould are the least expensive, whilst those made from more than one mould with attached outstretched arms or extra details such as flowers or wide brimmed hats will be the most valuable. Other positive features to look for include fine painting, notable makers (such as Kestner, Goebel or Dressel & Kister) or popular fashions or styles of the day.

5in (12.5cm) high

£25-35   **F**

A porcelain half doll, modelled as a lady, her hands placed upon her head, wearing a flower decoration in her hair, incised marks "12756".

4.5in (11.5cm) high

£25-35   **F**

A porcelain half doll, modelled as a young lady with painted facial features, her hands placed upon her head, now dressed in a gold silk dress.

Many half dolls retain their original 'clothing' which was originally added to cover a cosmetic box, jewellery box, hairbrush or other object. Those in original period clothes in fine condition will command a premium, particularly if the doll itself is well-modelled and painted.

16.5in (42cm) high

£25-35   **F**

A porcelain half doll, modelled as a naked lady with her hands placed upon her chest.

4.5in (11.5cm) high

£25-35   **F**

An Art Deco painted wax half doll, modelled as a naked head and shoulder bust of an attractive young female, together with a pair of moulded bisque arms, in original box.

5.5in (14cm) high

£70-100   **F**

A bisque porcelain half doll, modelled as a pretty young lady with painted facial features, applied wig and jointed arms, now dressed in a black fabric dress.

20in (51cm) high

£35-45   **F**

A 'factory-made' tea cosy doll, with a bisque head and articulated arms, in Dutch costume.

c1920   11in (28cm) high

£200-250   **BEJ**

A Scottish novelty papier-mâché boy pin cushion, on a needle store base.

c1920   5in (12.5cm) high

£70-100   **BEJ**

A composition boy doll, with rigid limbs jointed at the shoulders and hips and with a moulded and painted head.

12.25in (31cm) high

£20-40   **HB**

A 1940s red and white unused doll's outfit, on original blue retail card, comprising underclothes, dress, hat and booties.

c1945

£100-150   **BEJ**

COLLECTORS' NOTES

- Many have cited early computers as being the 'next big thing' in collecting circles, with good reason as many are important examples of how technology has developed over the past two to three decades.

- It will be interesting to see if interest in this market actually does widen, as many models lack instant 'eye-appeal' and are bulky to store and largely unusable or 'useless' today.

- Look for complete examples in as close to mint condition as possible, as wear and missing parts reduce value considerably. Examples must also still work and preferably be useable for hobbies such as gaming.

- Try to buy the most important, landmark models from the mid-1970s through to the mid-1990s. Look for those that captured the public imagination and were popular, as nostalgia is also an important factor.

- Handhelds, calculators and personal organisers may offer a more attractive proposition due to their comparative size and near-usability. Look for names such as Amstrad, Apple and Sinclair: the latter is already highly collectable.

- Models that offered innovative systems, or the very first PDAs, may be the most likely to rise in popularity, but always consider condition as many were seriously worn when carried around.

A BBC Micro Computer with monitor and disk drive.

This reliable and expandable machine was promoted by the BBC as part of its Computer Literacy Project, and was the stalwart of most school computer rooms for many years. Acorn originally expected to produce about 12,000, but over a million were eventually sold throughout the 1980s.

c1982

£30-50 PC

An Acorn Atom home computer, the forerunner of the BBC microcomputer.

1980-83   15in (38cm) wide

£40-80 PC

An Amiga A600 home computer, by Commodore.

c1992   13.5in (34.5cm) wide

£20-30 PC

An Acorn Electron home computer, with Advanced Plus 1 expansion unit.

This was effectively a cut-down version of the BBC Acorn Micro and was released in 1983.

£30-40 PC

An Amstrad CPC 6128 home computer, with built-in three inch disc drive and with monitor and manual.

1985-90   20in (51cm) wide

£30-40 PC

A Dragon 32 home computer.

This was made in Port Talbot, South Wales.

1982

£30-40 PC

A Commodore C64 home computer, with Commodore tape drive, 'Terminator T2' games and user manual.

One of the most popular home computers from the company that later went on to produce the Amiga with sales in excess of £17 million! It had very good sound and graphics, as it was originally designed to work inside an arcade machine.

1982-93

£20-30 PC

An ORIC Atmos 48K home computer, with manual, 'Introduction To...' book and cover.

The 48K Atmos offered buyers more available, usable memory than equivalent competitors' products, even when programs and peripherals were running – quite a bonus at the time. A 16K version was also marketed, but it could not be upgraded and was thus not successful.

1984-86   11in (28cm) wide

£60-80   **PC**

A Sinclair QL home computer, with microdrive cartridges and manual.

Continuing Sinclair's reputation for innovation at affordable prices, the company released the 'Quantum Leap' in 1984 which was one of the first 32-bit home computers at under £400, placing it well ahead of its time. It also came with an innovative 'microdrive', but due to internal quality control and poor delivery, it was largely unsuccessful, making it comparatively hard to find today.

1984-86

£40-60   **PC**

A Jupiter ACE home computer, made by Jupiter Cantab.

Company owners Richard Altwasser and Steven Vickers previously worked for Sinclair on the Spectrum ZX81, which may explain the similarity this machine has to the Jupiter. This was the first and only computer made by the company and originally retailed for £89.95.

A Sinclair ZX Spectrum +2 home computer, with built-in tape drive.

This was actually made by Amstrad who had taken over Spectrum's computer arm in 1986 and is commonly found today due to its popularity at the time.

c1987   17in (43cm) wide

£15-20   **PC**

c1982   8.5in (21.5cm) wide

£70-100   **PC**

A Sinclair ZX81 home computer, with original packaging, game and power pack.

The third of Sinclair's home computers, it was the first that could be plugged in and used immediately. Despite offering just 1K of memory and having no sound or colour, over 1 million units were sold in the UK and US (via Timex) in the first two years.

c1981   13.5in (34.5cm) wide

£20-30   **PC**

A 'Mark-8' mini-computer, including six 'Mark 8' circuit boards, an Intel 8008 chip, two Signetics 8267 chips, two Signetics 8263 and eight National Semiconductor 1101 memory chips, and with a CD-ROM containing various magazine and newsletter pages regarding the computer.

Designed by Jon Titus, the Mark 8 was bought, assembled and housed by the purchaser. It was one of the very first home computers for computer 'hobbyists' offering an LED bulb-based display and 16 switches. It was marketed by 'Radio Electronics' magazine in July 1974.

c1974

£300-400   **ATK**

A Toshiba MSX HX-10 home computer, 64K.

c1983   14.5in (37cm) wide

£15-20   **PC**

An ORIC MCP-40 home computer, with ORIC colour printer, manual and games.

This has the same 6502 microprocessor as the BBC Micro and Acorn Electron.

1983

£25-35   **PC**

A TRS-80 model 100 portable home computer, by Tandy Radio Shack, with manual.

c1983   *11.5in (29cm) wide*

£30-40   **PC**

An Apple Newton MessagePad 100, with Stylus and soft vinyl pouch.

Despite being a market leader at the time, the MessagePad (Newton was actually the name of the Apple software), failed to be a hit. Marketing claims over handwriting recognition were arguably somewhat over-blown and it was large and expensive. The Palm system that replaced it was far more successful.

1993-98   *7.25in (18.5cm) high*

£15-20   **PC**

An Apple Macintosh Power Book 180.

The 180 was originally retailed for $4,110 and was the top of the range Powerbook of its time with a faster 33MHZ processor.

1992-94

            11.25in (28.5cm) wide

£20-30   **PC**

A Psion Series 3C organiser.

c1996

£10-15   **PC**

An HP 22 business calculator, by Hewlett Packard.

Originally sold for $165.

1975-78   *5in (12.5cm) high*

£20-30   **PC**

A Datamath TI-2500 II calculator, by Texas Instruments.

c1973   *5.5in (14cm) high*

£10-15   **PC**

A CLOSER LOOK AT A PDA

The five large keys are placed ergonomically reflecting the natural position of fingertips - this offered comfort and speed to the user and was first seen on the 1980 'Microwriter' writing machine that aimed to replace keyboards.

The innovative system of five buttons, which when pressed in certain sequences (chords) to match the rough shape of a letter, created that letter, was said to be faster than standard typing once learnt.

The main keyboard is arranged alphabetically and has very small buttons, encouraging use of the Microwriter keys. The four-line LCD screen is typically small.

The AgendA won a British Design Award in 1990. Unfortunately it did not cater for left-handed users!

An 'AgendA' Microwriter personal organiser, with 'microwriting' system originally developed by Cy Endfield and Chris Rainey in the 1970s.

c1989   *7in (18cm) wide*

£20-40   **PC**

An Amstrad Pen Pad PDA 600 personal organiser, with touch screen.

This was one of the first PDAs, running on three AA batteries and was offered by Amstrad as a less expensive competitor to the Apple Newton. Values vary depending on the condition of the screen.

c1993

£20-40   **PC**

A 1950s erotic ceramic mug, with moving, wired-on breasts and moulded wording reading "Let Them Swing", the base stamped "FOREIGN", and moulded "PATENT.T.T".

4.25in (10.5cm) high

£30-40 CVS

A 1950s ceramic erotic mug, with girl standing next to a tree trunk, with wired-on, moving ceramic bottom.

4.25in (11cm) high

£35-45 CVS

A 'South Carolina' erotic souvenir mug, with a cigarette girl, reading "If you don't see what you want, ask for it!"

The 1950s and 1960s saw a great many erotic novelty souvenir items, such as ashtrays and mugs, being sold in popular resorts such as Florida.

c1960 *4.75in (12cm) high*

£20-30 CVS

A 1950s erotic hand-painted ceramic small dish or ashtray.

Many of the erotic ceramics of the 1950s were made in Japan and can be identified by their lightweight material. Look for scratches and chips as this affects value.

4in (10cm) diam

£30-40 SM

Two English 1950s 'Glamour Girls' bone china gilt scalloped edge dishes, with transfer prints of semi-clad ladies in erotic poses.

4.75in (12cm) wide

£35-45 each CVS

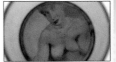

A 1950s Japanese erotic ceramic ashtray, with a semi-clad lady seated by a window and a motto reading "Lady Pull Down Your Shade, I Can't Go To Sleep", based stamped "JAPAN".

Although this was produced decades later, the form, bright colours and use of a motto on the base recalls German fairings – especially as they share the same 'naughty' seaside style humour.

4in (10cm) wide

£50-70 SM

A 1950s Japanese erotic ceramic ashtray, with a topless lady standing in front of a doctor and motto reading "But My Dear Young Lady, I'm A Foot Doctor", the back marked "JAPAN".

3.5in (9cm) high

£50-70 SM

A 1950s erotic Lucite shot glass, with photograph of topless busty seated lady in the base.

2.25in (6cm) high

£15-25 CVS

Charles Fay, "Pit of Shame", published by Emerald.

Often known as 'pulp' fiction, erotic paperbacks that peaked in popularity in the mid-1960s have become extremely collectable over the past decade. Condition is important to value as they were not made to last and often fall apart. The cover is one of the most important aspects, partly as the artwork is often so eye-catching, kitsch and typical of its period – when it would have been considered rather risqué!

1964   6.5in (16.5cm) high

£3-5   CVS

Kevin North, "The Golden Girls", published by Playtime Books.

1962   6.25in (16cm) high

£3-5   CVS

Clark Davis, "Knights of Lust", published by Spartan Line.

1967   6.5in (16.5cm) high

£3-5   CVS

A German tinted erotic photograph of a topless lady, in a towel and heels standing near a decorative log burner, together with two extravagantly designed brochures on the history of customs, one titled 'Forbidden Secret'.

c1960   photo 15in (38cm) high

£100-150   ATK

A 1950s American boxed set of plastic-coated erotic playing cards, made by "NOVELTIES MFG & SALES CORP", of St Louis MO, each card with a unique image of a posing naked lady protecting her modesty with a different object.

3.5in (9cm) high

£55-65   CVS

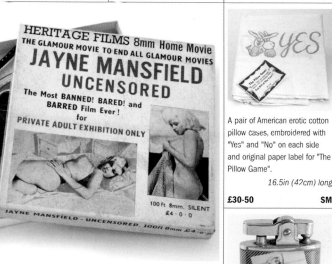

A very rare 1960s Heritage Films 8mm home movie of 'Jayne Mansfield Uncensored', boxed.

box 5.25in (13.5cm) wide

£120-180   CVS

A pair of American erotic cotton pillow cases, embroidered with "Yes" and "No" on each side and original paper label for "The Pillow Game".

16.5in (42cm) long

£30-50   SM

A 1950s erotic cotton bar towel.

30in (76cm) high

£20-30   SM

A 1950s PAC chrome-plated and plastic-sleeved erotic lighter, with photographic images of models posing on a beach.

2in (5cm) high

£40-50   CVS

"Playboy" from July 1977.

The label stuck to the cover indicates that pages 169-170 were removed from this issue for legal reasons, possibly due to pornography rules!

11in (28cm) high

£15-25 VM

"Playboy" from October 1978, with Dolly Parton cover.

11in (28cm) high

£20-30 VM

"Playboy" from January 1997, with commemorative Marilyn Monroe cover and containing new James Bond fiction.

11in (28cm) high

£40-50 VM

"Playboy" from May 1998, the cover with Geri Halliwell, 'Ginger Spice' of 'The Spice Girls', in her famous Union Jack dress.

11in (28cm) high

£20-30 VM

A Playboy bunny gold-plated necklace, the eye inset with a diamanté.

pendant 0.75in (2cm) high

£25-35 CVS

A 1960s Playboy bunny gold-plated bracelet, the eye inset with a red diamanté.

bunny 0.75in (2cm) high

£25-35 CVS

A pair of Playboy orange plastic sunglasses, with bunny decal on the arms near hinge and one arm stamped "PLAYBOY".

£70-100 VE

A Playboy Playmate 'Complete Playboy Centrefold' puzzle, complete and contained in a tin with paper label

c1965

5.75in (14.5cm) high

£50-80 P&I

A 1960s Playboy matchbook, from Phoenix.

The Playboy Club in Phoenix, Arizona opened on December 19th 1962.

2in (5cm) high

£3-4 DTC

COLLECTORS' NOTES

■ In recent years the interest in collecting eyewear has increased substantially. The four main indicators to value are: the style or look, the name of the maker or designer, the material and the condition. Look for styles or designs that sum up any period, the 1950s and 1960s are currently the most popular decades.

■ Values are not usually affected if lenses are missing unless they were unusual, such as having a graduated tone. Other lenses can be easily replaced.

■ The material counts – those made from real tortoiseshell or precious metals or those with large amounts of handcrafted work will usually be more valuable. Colour is also worth considering with the psychedelic colours of the 1960s much sought after.

■ Look out for famous fashion designers such as Christian Dior and Pierre Cardin, but also those more known for their eyewear designs such as Pierre Marly, Alain Mikli and Emmanuelle Khanh.

■ Frame condition is of vital importance as many collectors buy glasses to wear as well as to display. Splits and cracks reduce value considerably and examples with broken parts are rarely repairable.

A pair of 1960s French gold and black laminated plastic 'bug' sunglasses.

5.5in (14cm) wide

£200-250 VE

A pair of French laminated gold and clear plastic sunglasses, the arms with extra ovals, with paper label reading "Twist 1324".

1969-1970   5.25in (13.5cm) wide

£200-250 VE

A unique pair of French hand-cut faux tortoiseshell sunglasses, by Philippe Chevalier.

1954   5.75in (14.5cm) wide

£450-550 VE

A pair of French faux tortoiseshell plastic 'mask' sunglasses, by Paulette Gigner.

1958-1960   6in (15.5cm) wide

£350-450 VE

A pair of 1960s Pierre Cardin transparent brown plastic 'eyebrow' sunglasses, the arms stamped "Pierre CARDIN".

5.75in (14.5cm) wide

£200-250 VE

A pair of 1960s French laminated pearlised rust-coloured plastic bow tie-shaped sunglasses, the arm stamped "REGGAE" and with paper label reading "REGGAE".

5in (13cm) wide

£150-250 VE

A pair of 1950s French hand-cut, gold and white hand-painted black plastic frames, by Zyl, with inlaid rhinestones.

Zyl is also the trade name for the plastic zylonite, a form of cellulose acetate which originates from cotton and can be found in a wide range of colours.

8in (20.5cm) wide

£400-550 VE

A pair of 1950s French 'Fantasy' winged yellow snakeskin effect and clear laminated plastic 'wrap-around' sunglasses, the arms stamped "MADE IN FRANCE".

The laminated plastic has curved over the years making these fabulous sunglasses too small to wear now, although this may be reversed.

4.75in (12cm) wide

£150-200 VE

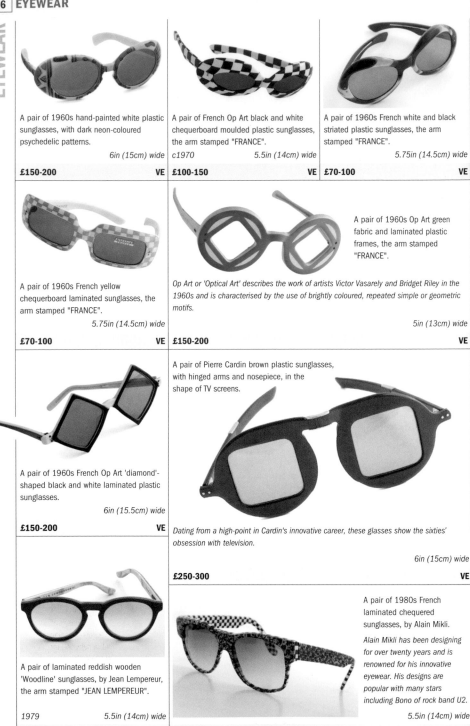

A pair of 1960s hand-painted white plastic sunglasses, with dark neon-coloured psychedelic patterns.

6in (15cm) wide

£150-200 VE

A pair of French Op Art black and white chequerboard moulded plastic sunglasses, the arm stamped "FRANCE".

c1970 *5.5in (14cm) wide*

£100-150 VE

A pair of 1960s French white and black striated plastic sunglasses, the arm stamped "FRANCE".

5.75in (14.5cm) wide

£70-100 VE

A pair of 1960s French yellow chequerboard laminated sunglasses, the arm stamped "FRANCE".

5.75in (14.5cm) wide

£70-100 VE

A pair of 1960s Op Art green fabric and laminated plastic frames, the arm stamped "FRANCE".

Op Art or 'Optical Art' describes the work of artists Victor Vasarely and Bridget Riley in the 1960s and is characterised by the use of brightly coloured, repeated simple or geometric motifs.

5in (13cm) wide

£150-200 VE

A pair of 1960s French Op Art 'diamond'-shaped black and white laminated plastic sunglasses.

6in (15.5cm) wide

£150-200 VE

A pair of Pierre Cardin brown plastic sunglasses, with hinged arms and nosepiece, in the shape of TV screens.

Dating from a high-point in Cardin's innovative career, these glasses show the sixties' obsession with television.

6in (15cm) wide

£250-300 VE

A pair of laminated reddish wooden 'Woodline' sunglasses, by Jean Lempereur, the arm stamped "JEAN LEMPEREUR".

1979 *5.5in (14cm) wide*

£150-200 VE

A pair of 1980s French laminated chequered sunglasses, by Alain Mikli.

Alain Mikli has been designing for over twenty years and is renowned for his innovative eyewear. His designs are popular with many stars including Bono of rock band U2.

5.5in (14cm) wide

£200-250 VE

A pair of 1960s laminated and tartan fabric clear plastic sunglasses, the arms stamped "Reminiscence MADE IN FRANCE".

5.75in (14.5cm) wide

£80-120 VE

A pair of Austrian painted black plastic and metal 'Playboy' sunglasses, with the bunny motif by the hinges.

1970 *5.5in (14cm) wide*

£80-120 VE

A pair of 1970s Italian Yves Saint Laurent laminated blue and white plastic squared 'Aviator' style sunglasses, arms stamped "YSL169 White/Blue/39 140 YVES SAINT LAURENT PARIS MADE IN ITALY".

These glasses benefit from a notable name, retain their original lenses and capture the look of the 1970s, making them highly desirable to collectors.

5.5in (14cm) wide

£250-300 VE

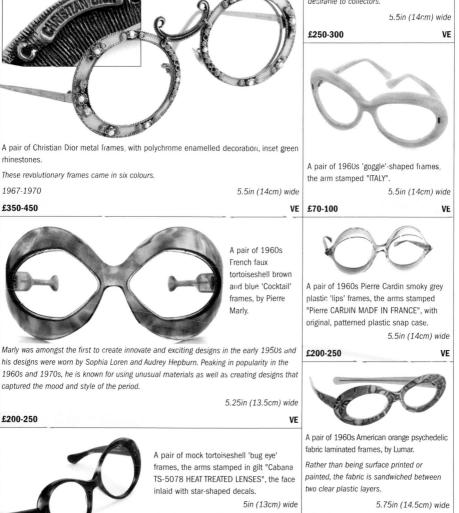

A pair of Christian Dior metal frames, with polychrome enamelled decoration, inset green rhinestones.

These revolutionary frames came in six colours.

1967-1970 *5.5in (14cm) wide*

£350-450 VE

A pair of 1960s 'goggle'-shaped frames, the arm stamped "ITALY".

5.5in (14cm) wide

£70-100 VE

A pair of 1960s French faux tortoiseshell brown and blue 'Cocktail' frames, by Pierre Marly.

Marly was amongst the first to create innovate and exciting designs in the early 1950s and his designs were worn by Sophia Loren and Audrey Hepburn. Peaking in popularity in the 1960s and 1970s, he is known for using unusual materials as well as creating designs that captured the mood and style of the period.

5.25in (13.5cm) wide

£200-250 VE

A pair of 1960s Pierre Cardin smoky grey plastic 'lips' frames, the arms stamped "Pierre CARDIN MADE IN FRANCE", with original, patterned plastic snap case.

5.5in (14cm) wide

£200-250 VE

A pair of mock tortoiseshell 'bug eye' frames, the arms stamped in gilt "Cabana TS-5078 HEAT TREATED LENSES", the face inlaid with star-shaped decals.

5in (13cm) wide

£25-35 BB

A pair of 1960s American orange psychedelic fabric laminated frames, by Lumar.

Rather than being surface printed or painted, the fabric is sandwiched between two clear plastic layers.

5.75in (14.5cm) wide

£150-250 VE

A pair of American laminated cream and black 'Eskimo' plastic frames, the arm marked "Victory Suntimer Bonetone ZYL".

1957   *6in (15cm) wide*

£200-250   **VE**

A pair of laminated pink and black frames.

5.75in (14.5cm) wide

£25-35   **BB**

A pair of white pearlised frames, the arms marked "BRO 5 1/4 U.S.A."

6in (15cm) wide

£20-30   **BB**

A pair of black and silver striated laminated plastic frames, the arm stamped "POP 360 5 3/4".

The winged area by the hinges is quintessentially 1950s and 1960s.

5.25in (13.5cm) wide

£25-35   **BB**

A pair of pink-tinted clear plastic frames, with glitter-like hexagonal silver metal fragments, with diamond-shaped decals.

5.5in (14cm) wide

£30-40   **BB**

A pair of 1950s clear plastic frames, with glitter-like hexagonal silver metal fragments and black thread laminated fabric.

5.5in (14cm) wide

£40-50   **BB**

A pair of subsurface metallic silver-finished, black and clear laminated plastic frames, with metal and rhinestone inserts, the arms stamped "U.S.A."

5.5in (14cm) wide

£30-40   **BB**

A pair of 1950s French brown plastic laminated frames, with curved, cut away 'eyebrow' rims above the eye, the arms marked "A Paris FRANCE".

Made from many layers of laminated plastic, the frames have been cut away to reveal the different colours.

6in (15cm) wide

£30-40   **BB**

A pair of pearlised gold plastic and carved black plastic laminated frames, the arms marked "A Paris Frame France".

5in (13cm) wide

£25-35   **BB**

A pair of laminated pink, grey and russet frames, with pearlised front face.

5.25in (13.5cm) wide

£20-25   **BB**

A pair of 1940s laminated clear plastic and psychedelic-chequered fabric frames, with metal flower-shaped decals.

5in (13cm) wide

£40-50 **BB**

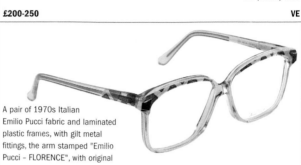

A pair of late 1970s American Emmanuelle Khanh plastic frames, covered with real ostrich skin.

Leather and animal skin-covered spectacles have seen a recent revival in popularity. Born in 1935, Khanh began at Cacharel in 1955 before becoming a model and setting up her own design label in the 1960s. She is often known as the 'French Mary Quant'. Her Paris shop has recently closed and there is now increased interest in her designs.

6in (15cm) wide

£200-250 **VE**

A pair of late 1970s American Emmanuelle Khanh clear plastic frames, covered with lace and lacquered.

6in (15cm) wide

£150-200 **VE**

A pair of 1950s reverse-carved Lucite frames, with painted and filled floral motifs.

These Lucite frames have been carved from the inside surface and then painted. This is a technique commonly found in clear and 'apple juice' coloured plastic jewellery from the 1930s onwards.

5.25in (13.5cm) wide

£30-50 **BB**

A pair of 1970s Italian Emilio Pucci fabric and laminated plastic frames, with gilt metal fittings, the arm stamped "Emilio Pucci – FLORENCE", with original shop display card.

Legendary Italian fashion designer Emilio Pucci is known for his wild psychedelic, geometric or swirling fabric patterns – original 1960s and 1970s pieces are hotly sought after, particularly as the label has been recently relaunched.

5.5in (14cm) wide

£200-250 **VE**

A pair of 1960s Italian laminated green and white plastic frames, stamped "MADE IN ITALY" on the arms.

5.25in (13.5cm) wide

£100-150 **VE**

A pair of Spanish laminated lime green-striped frames, the arms stamped "MAIORCA LOZZA R".

c1970 *5.5in (14cm) wide*

£150-200 **VE**

A pair of late 1970s French 'Woodline' wooden frames, by Jean Lempereur, with gilt metal decal reading "JEAN LEMPEREUR PARIS" to arm.

6in (15cm) wide

£150-200 **VE**

A pair of 1950s laminated clear and pearlised plastic round frames.

5.5in (14cm) wide

£20-30 **BB**

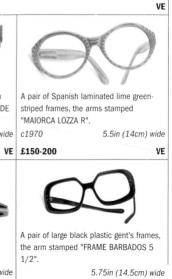

A pair of large black plastic gent's frames, the arm stamped "FRAME BARBADOS 5 1/2".

5.75in (14.5cm) wide

£20-30 **BB**

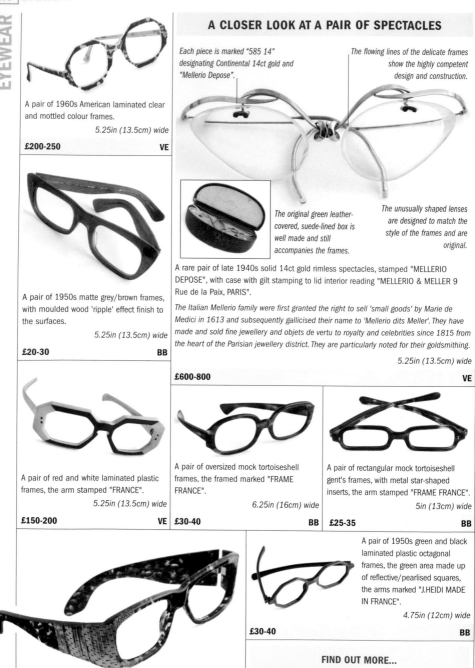

A pair of 1960s American laminated clear and mottled colour frames.

5.25in (13.5cm) wide

£200-250 VE

A pair of 1950s matte grey/brown frames, with moulded wood 'ripple' effect finish to the surfaces.

5.25in (13.5cm) wide

£20-30 BB

A pair of red and white laminated plastic frames, the arm stamped "FRANCE".

5.25in (13.5cm) wide

£150-200 VE

A CLOSER LOOK AT A PAIR OF SPECTACLES

Each piece is marked "585 14" designating Continental 14ct gold and "Mellerio Depose".

The flowing lines of the delicate frames show the highly competent design and construction.

The original green leather-covered, suede-lined box is well made and still accompanies the frames.

The unusually shaped lenses are designed to match the style of the frames and are original.

A rare pair of late 1940s solid 14ct gold rimless spectacles, stamped "MELLERIO DEPOSE", with case with gilt stamping to lid interior reading "MELLERIO & MELLER 9 Rue de la Paix, PARIS".

The Italian Mellerio family were first granted the right to sell 'small goods' by Marie de Medici in 1613 and subsequently gallicised their name to 'Mellerio dits Meller'. They have made and sold fine jewellery and objets de vertu to royalty and celebrities since 1815 from the heart of the Parisian jewellery district. They are particularly noted for their goldsmithing.

5.25in (13.5cm) wide

£600-800 VE

A pair of oversized mock tortoiseshell frames, the framed marked "FRAME FRANCE".

6.25in (16cm) wide

£30-40 BB

A pair of rectangular mock tortoiseshell gent's frames, with metal star-shaped inserts, the arm stamped "FRAME FRANCE".

5in (13cm) wide

£25-35 BB

A pair of 1950s green and black laminated plastic octagonal frames, the green area made up of reflective/pearlised squares, the arms marked "J.HEIDI MADE IN FRANCE".

4.75in (12cm) wide

£30-40 BB

A pair of American Emmanuelle Khanh faux tortoiseshell plastic frames, with hand-carved bamboo strips applied to the arms.

c1980 *5.75in (14.5cm) wide*

£200-250 VE

FIND OUT MORE...

'Specs Appeal – Extravagant 1950s & 1960s Eyewear', *by Leslie Pina and Donald-Brian Johnson, published by Schiffer Books, 2002.*

'Eyeglass Retrospective – Where Fashion & Science Meet', *by Nancy N. Schiffer, published by Schiffer Books, 2000.*

COLLECTORS' NOTES

■ The 1950s are often called 'the new 1930s' in terms of style and collectable potential. The decade certainly saw an optimistic 'New Look' at design as it emerged from the privations of war. This combined with today's vogue for 'retro' styling means that the market looks set to continue to grow.

■ Not all pieces produced during the 1950s meet with the exacting standards of today's collectors, and indeed interior decorators. Consider form and design, material, new technologies and surface decoration, as all should typify the period. Forms and shapes were often asymmetrically organic, but always clean-lined. They were quintessentially modern in a way linked to, but quite different from, the architectural Art Deco period - from kidney-shaped tables to tulip-like vases.

■ The 1950s saw a great number of new materials come to the fore. Plastic had been popularised in the 1920s and 1930s and development's from the 1950s had a great impact on design. Formica and laminated woods were increasingly used, along with other materials which allowed modern and fashionable forms to be produced efficiently and inexpensively.

■ Surface decoration is diverse, ranging from erotic or glamourous ladies to demure images of fashionable ladies with poodles - signs of a yearning for much desired luxury and prosperity. Polka dots, stars, playing card motifs, 'exotic' zebra prints and designs based around atomic designs were also common. Colours tend to be cheerfully bright, often taken from a pastel palette and are poles apart from the dominance of dull of the 1940s.

■ Condition is important, as many items were mass-produced. Damage or wear can reduce value dramatically unless the item is extremely rare or desirable. The work of leading designers should continue to be sought after. Do not ignore mass-produced items that cover as many of the above criteria as possible, as eye-appeal and adherence to the style of this key age usually counts for just as much to collectors and style gurus.

A Beswick 'Zebra Fur' vase, the shape designed by Albert Hallam in the late 1950s, marked "1351".

Jesse Tait's zebra-striped 'Zambesi' design, released in 1956, was so popular that it was widely copied. This example is by Jim Hayward for Beswick, who produced this pattern until 1963. The yellow interior is typical of the period.

9.5in (24cm) high

£70-90 L

A Sandland 'Zebrette' pattern vase.

6.5in (16.5cm) high

£15-20 GAZE

A Vulcanware vase, by Alban, England.

6.25in (16cm) high

£10-15 L

A Ridgways 'Barbecue' pattern bowl.

This pattern is much scarcer than the Homemaker pattern.

6.75in (17cm) diam

£20-30 GAZE

A 1950s Burleigh Ware white ground vase, with black and red leaf design.

11in (28cm) high

£15-20 GAZE

A 1950s ceramic vase, with hand-painted black glazed profile of a lady's head.

Both the 'organic' almost leaf like form and the black elegant lady are typical of the 1950s.

6.5in (16.5cm) high

£8-12 MA

A Ridgways Homemaker Cadenza coffee pot, with six black coffee cups and six saucers, two cups shown.

The ubiquitous and now legendary Homemaker pattern was designed by Enid Seeney in 1956-57 and was mass-produced, being sold through Woolworths in the UK until c1967. Although plates are common, coffee pots are not and are more valuable.

coffee pot 23.5in (60cm) high

£250-300 set GAZE

A set of four Old Foley 'Moonglow' pattern dishes, by James Kent, each with hand-painted decoration and gilt highlights.

largest 9.75in (25cm) wide

£8-12　　　　　**MA**

Five Ornamin plastic sandwich plates, and a bread plate.

largest 12.25in (31cm) long

£8-12　　　　　**GAZE**

A Japanese Shafford ceramic vitamin box, in the form of a lady's head, stamped on the base "C 1960 THE SHAFFORD CO. 5963Y", with silver label reading "AN ORIGINAL BY SHAFFORD JAPAN".

7.5in (10cm) high

£20-25　　　　　**DAC**

A 1950s ceramic dressing table set, with transfer of a lady's profile within a pink border.

7in (18cm) high

£50-60　　　　　**MA**

A Worcester Ware metal tea tray, with transfer decoration of ballerinas posing.

Very few trays have survived in this condition, as the pattern was easily scratched, and then went rusty.

c1957　　　　　*16.25in (41cm) wide*

£15-25　　　　　**MA**

A folding laminated wood cocktail tray, with four hand-painted cocktail pictures and four cocktail recipes with label reading "FOREIGN".

19in (48cm) long

£70-90　　　　　**CVS**

A rare, complete American plastic spice rack, with six 'black mamma' plastic spice jars, the lid coming off at the waist to reveal shaker.

c1955　　　　　*13.5in (34.5cm) long*

£250-350　　　　　**SOTT**

A set of ten 1950s Australian cast acrylic kitchen canisters, by Nylex, with gilt pictures and descriptions of contents.

largest 10in (25.5cm) high

£70-90　　　　　**MA**

A 1950s English plastic pineapple ice bucket.

Beware of later Japanese copies which can be identified by a deeper yellow plastic and a lightweight feel.

11in (28cm) high

£20-25　　　　　**DTC**

A 1950s acrylic Bovril advertising cup.

3.5in (9cm) high

50p-£1　　　　　**MA**

Two from a set of six plastic high ball tumblers, each encasing a lime green felt shark with gold studs and brown string fishing net.

1950s   *6in (15.5cm) high*

£60-80 set   **CVS**

Two from a set of eight American Federal frosted hi-ball glass tumblers, with transfer-printed lemons, ice cubes and cherries.

7in (17.5cm) h

£70-100 set   **CVS**

A 1950s black wire and wicker plant pot holder.

This is the middle height of three sizes of holder made.

7in (18cm) high

£12-18   **DTC**

A 1950s black wire and raffia paper rack.

9.5in (24cm) wide

£20-30   **DTC**

A 1950s black wire and wicker 'Miss Kitty' letter rack.

Letters can be stored in the ribs of her body, and a pen in her curling tail.

£20-30   **DTC**

A 1950s cream acrylic sailboat-shaped alarm clock, made in China.

6.75in (17cm) high

£60-80   **MA**

A 1950s black wire and raffia wine pourer.

An example of this wine pourer was included in the influential 'Austerity to Affluence - British Art & Design 1945-1962' exhibition held by the Fine Art Society, London in 1997 and can be seen in their catalogue.

£18-22   **DTC**

A CLOSER LOOK AT AN EAMES WALL HANGER

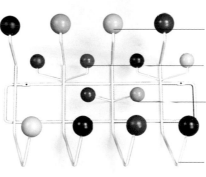

This was designed by designers and architects Charles & Ray Eames, who aimed to provide good modern design for all.

It was designed in 1952-53 and is still made today by Herman Miller Inc.

Scientific drawings or models of atoms inspired many designers of the period – just as the 'atomic age' was dawning.

It is produced in enamelled steel wire with painted maple wood balls in nine different colours.

An Eames 'Hang-It-All', produced by Herman Miller, recent manufacture, with 14-coloured wood balls on an enamelled metal rack, includes mounting hardware, as new.

£60-100   **FRE**

A Liberty of London alarm clock.

4in (10cm) wide

£20-30   **GAZE**

A 1950s boxed Taktelli metronome, in grey and red plastic.

6.25in (16cm) high

£12-18   **GAZE**

A 1950s wooden base and glass sphere money/piggy bank, with colour printed card pig on a rainy day, the back with a 'Money Meter' showing the values of different levels.

7in (18cm) high

£15-25   **TM**

A pair of 1950s chrome candlesticks, with prancing ladies with flowing hair, the bases stamped "REG 873891".

These candleholders and bases can be found on many other designs, which are usually worth much less if in wood - these Art Deco styled chrome ladies are much more desirable.

8.75in (22.5cm) high

£35-45   **MA**

An early 1950s guitar-shaped wall mirror, with hand-painted flower decoration.

Hard to find in such excellent condition, this type of mirror represents the beginning of the modern rock'n'roll movement in its shape, although amusingly not in the painted decoration!

17in (43cm) long

£45-55   **MA**

A CLOSER LOOK AT A TRETCHIKOFF PRINT

This is typical of the style of Russian-born, South African artist Vladimir Tretchikoff (b1913) in terms of its exotic subject, lighting, colour scheme and female subject gazing out at the viewer.

Look out for the scarcer and more desirable dancing girl pictures, such as 'Balinese Dancer'. Flowers are the least desirable of all subjects.

As well as being one of his most recognisable images, this print has its original, period frame, which is a desirable feature. It is also undamaged - many were stored away badly or thrown away when they fell out of fashion in the 1960s.

The kitsch style typifies the 1950s when many thousands of these highly fashionable, inexpensive reproductions were sold - they have now become highly fashionable again and have risen steeply in value.

A 1950s Tretchikoff 'Miss Wong' print, mounted on board and in period gilt frame, with addition retailer's label to rear for Bentalls Picture Department, Kingston.

27.5in (70cm) high

£50-70   **MTS**

A 1950s girls/ladies dressing table 'crinolined lady' lamp, painted plaster with pink net shade over a wired fabric base.

This form derives from the ceramic and wax half dolls popular during the early part of the 20thC. For more information, please see the 'Dolls' section.

c1952-53   15in (38cm) high

£15-25   **MA**

A 1950s Tretchikoff 'Chinese Girl' print, in period white-painted frame.

frame 25.25in (64cm) high

£40-60   **MTS**

A pair of American 1950s Japanese boy and girl figures, each carrying water buckets, with matte bodies and glazed faces, marked "Foreign".

8.5in (21.5cm) high

£30-40   **MA**

A 1950s long-necked cat ceramic vase, with lustre finish.

13.75in (35cm) high

£5-10   **MA**

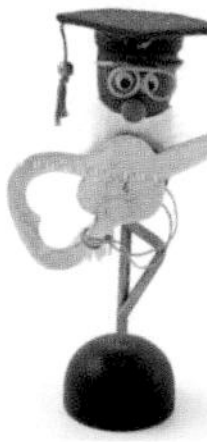

An unusual 'teacher' guitar playing bottle opener.

Found in a range of characters, including a Mexican, this version is rare. Presumably it would have been less popular than an exotic character at the time.

5.5in (14cm) high

£10-15   **MA**

A 1950s light blue Dansette Popular electric turntable, with built-in speaker.

12.5in (32cm) wide

£40-60   **MA**

A late 1940s Vogue "The House of Charm All-Girl Orchestral Choir" picture disc.

9.75in (25cm)diam

£40-50   **NOR**

A 1950s printed vinyl travelling bag.

13in (33cm) wide

£25-35   **NOR**

"Better Homes and Gardens Decorating Book", published by Meredith Publishing.

1956-61

10in (25.5cm) high

£70-80   **DTC**

A set of 1950s American iron-on 'Picture Patches', with portrait of 'Fabian'.

card 7.25in (18.5cm) high

£15-25   **MTS**

A Roland Rainer 'Town Hall' chair, produced by Pollak, Vienna, beech wood and layered wood painted in a greeny brown.

c1951

34.5in (88cm) high

£300-400   **QU**

COLLECTORS' NOTES

■ Many of the rules for 1950s memorabilia apply to 1960s and 1970s memorabilia as well. Look at styling in terms of form, decoration and material. Try to buy pieces that represent as many of these in the period as possible, preferably by notable makers.

■ Colour is an important aspect of this period, led primarily by the psychedelic 'flower power' movement. Bright, often acid colours dominated in an explosion of colour with clashing purples, oranges, lime greens and yellows. The use of plastics led to innovative designs in furniture and storage solutions.

■ Interest in all things futuristic, scientific and 'space-aged' continued, supported by movies and the 'space race'. UFO and space helmet shapes are common, formed in futuristic materials such as chrome and plastic. The world of flowers and sinuous plant stems was also popular, with Art Nouveau styling making a reappearance, but with a new make-over in the period palette.

■ Much of the market is governed by nostalgia and today's 'retro' fashion. Nostalgia becomes even more important with the 1970s, which is still a developing decade for collectors. Always look for brands, names or designs that people will remember, possibly as they owned them once or desired them at the time.

A 1960s J. and G. Meakin Studio 'Cornflower' pattern part coffee service, comprising coffee pot, sugar bowl and two cups and saucers.

The cylinder was a popular and fashionable shape for tableware and other objects during the 1960s, and shows any surface design off very well. The more notable factories of Midwinter and Portmeirion were at the forefront of this style, although Meakin currently offers a more affordable period alternative.

coffee pot 12in (30.5cm) high

£30-40   **DTC**

A 1960s Johnson Bros. coffee pot, in a variation of the 'Focus' pattern originally designed by textile designer Barbara Brown for Midwinter in 1964.

9in (23cm) high

£15-25   **MTS**

A Midwinter 'Tango' pattern coffee pot, designed by Eve Midwinter.

1969-76   *coffee pot 7.75in (19.5cm) high*

£12-18   **MTS**

A Midwinter 'Tango' pattern cup and saucer, designed by Eve Midwinter.

1969-76   *5.5in (14cm) diam*

£4-6   **MTS**

A 1960s Elizabethan English bone china 'Pop' pattern mug and saucer, shape designed by A. Kusmirek.

This came in a number of colours, all roughly of the same value.

saucer 5.75in (14.5cm) diam

£10-15   **MTS**

A 1960s Staffordshire Potteries storage jar, with psychedelic flower transfer decoration and plastic faux wooden lid.

4.25in (11cm) high

£15-20   **MTS**

A Lord Nelson Pottery 'Gaytime' flour sifter.

5in (12.5cm) high

£12-18   **MTS**

An English Ironstone Pottery Ltd 'Beefeater Steak and Grill Set' steak plate.

11in (28cm) wide

£8-12   **MTS**

A 1960s Burleigh 'Orbit' pattern dish, decorated with a psychedelic swirling 'Op Art' design.

7.75in (19.5cm) wide

£10-15   **MTS**

A 1970s Curran of Cardiff enamelled metal casserole dish and lid.

9.75in (25cm) wide

£18-22   **MTS**

A 1960s Finel enamelled metal saucepan and lid.

5in (13cm) high

£15-25   **MTS**

A set of three 1970s Pyrosil casserole dishes.

As they were inexpensive in their day and much used, it is rare to find a complete and undamaged set of three.

largest 11.75in (30cm) wide

£35-45   **MTS**

A 1960s enamelled metal kettle and matching lidded cooking pot, unused.

8.75in (22cm) high

£8-12   **GAZE**

A 1970s enamelled metal coffee pot, with remains of label to base.

7in (18cm) high

£12-18   **MTS**

A 1960s tomato red milk glass 'Whisky' decanter, with turned and painted wooden stopper.

9in (23cm) high

£22-28   **MA**

A set of six 'Babycham' glasses, in original box.

£30-45   **GAZE**

A 1960s lime green milk glass 'Gin' decanter, with turned and painted wooden stopper.

9in (23cm) high

£22-28   **MA**

A 1960s/70s German plastic and glass coffee set, comprising glass coffee jug with orange handle and lid, and six matching cups in orange, green and yellow.

coffee jug 6in (15.5cm) high

£22-28 **MA**

A 1970s Guzzini clear plastic ice bucket, with chrome-plated handle and plastic logo decal.

6.5in (16.5cm) high

£15-25 **DTC**

A 1960s American plastic fruit bowl condiment server, with pineapple salt shaker and grapefruit pepper shaker, the whole removing to allow access to the sugar bowl, the base moulded "STARKE DESIGN INC, BKLYN N.Y. MADE IN U.S.A.".

4.5in (11.5cm) wide

£20-30 **CVS**

A late 1970s Crayonne brown plastic ice bucket, retailed by Habitat.

6.75in (17cm) high

£12-18 **DTC**

A psychedelic lithographed string box.

4.75in (12cm) high

£10-15 **MTS**

A psychedelic lithographed biscuit tin, by Baret Ware, the lid with biscuit dryer.

7.75in (19.5cm) high

£18-22 **MTS**

A 1960s Worcester Ware lithographed tin 'flower power' waste paper bin.

7in (18cm) high

£10-15 **MTS**

A 1960s 'flower power' melamine bread board.

13.75in (35cm) long

£10-15 **MTS**

A pair of 1970s psychedelic elephant oven gloves.

6in (15.5cm) long

£7-10 **MTS**

A 1960s melamine four hook key rack.

11.75in (30cm) wide

£10-15 **MTS**

A set of 1960s psychedelic self-adhesive kitchen labels.

11.5in (29.5cm) high

£18-22   **MTS**

A 1970s West German vase, marked "549-21" and "W. German".

8.25in (21cm) high

£30-35   **DTC**

A 1970s West German Scheurich handled vase, marked "408-40".

A huge number of these moulded and glazed ceramic vases were produced during the 1960s and 1970s. Common colours are brown and orange and pieces bore a strong resemblance to Poole Pottery. Nearly all are marked on the base with numbers and a reference to Germany. Little more is known and this may turn out to be a developing market if more information is found. Eye appeal, size and condition are currently the major concerns for value, which rarely exceeds £80-100.

A 1970s West German vase, aqua glazed with abstract lava design, marked "285-18" and "W. German".

7in (18cm) high

£25-30   **DTC**

A 1960s Kilrush Ltd turquoise waisted vase, made in the Republic of Ireland.

7.5in (19cm) high

£12-18   **L**

15.75in (40cm) high

£50-60   **DTC**

A Shelley semi-matte turquoise glazed vase.

10in (25.5cm) high

£22-28   **L**

A 1970s Dialene red plastic party set, boxed.

This party set, often confused as a jewellery box, was made in a range of colours. The purple one is a rare colour.

10in (25.5cm) high

£15-25   **DTC**

A 1970s Carousel plastic lazy susan, in the form of a waterlily, with rare original box.

16in (40.5cm) diam

£22-28   **DTC**

An Italian 'Multiplor' red plastic storage box, designed by Rino Pirovano and produced by Rexite of Italy, with swing-out trays and marked "Art 900" and "R".

c1969   5.25in (13.5cm) high

£25-35   DTC

A 1970s green plastic desk tidy, probably Italian, with white plastic drawers.

4.5in (11.5cm) high

£10-12   DTC

A 'Dedalino' orange plastic pen holder, designed by Emma Gismondi-Schweinberger and made by Idarco.

These were designed in five different coloured plastics including a chrome-effect finish!

c1966   3.5in (9cm) high

£25-35   DTC

A red and white plastic vanity box.

4.75in (12cm) wide

£10-15   GAZE

A 1970s white desk lamp.

The 'space age' mushroom shaped lamp was a favourite for 1960s homes and was made by a number of companies. Value depends on the maker, designer, size and condition.

16in (41cm) high

£15-20   GAZE

A CLOSER LOOK AT A PAIR OF LAMPS

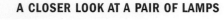

These lamps demonstrate the formal possibilities of plastic, being moulded from a single piece.

The form is also pure, clean lined and modern and almost resembles a space helmet.

They were produced in a range of colours, all bright and typical of the 1970s.

They were designed in 1969 by Italian architect Vico Magistretti (b1920), who began to design plastic furniture in the 1960s.

A pair of 1970s Italian Artemide 'Dalu' red plastic table lamps.

10.5in (26.5cm) high

£100-150   DTC

A Cosmo Designs chromed table lamp, with a four-piece revolving shade.

Different levels of coloured light could be created by turning successive leaves of the shade around. The idea is very similar to Danish designer Verner Panton's 'Moon Light' with is curving, revolving strips to alter the strength of the light.

13in (33cm) high

£20-40   GAZE

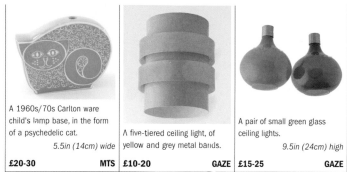

A 1960s/70s Carlton ware child's lamp base, in the form of a psychedelic cat.

5.5in (14cm) wide

£20-30   MTS

A five-tiered ceiling light, of yellow and grey metal bands.

£10-20   GAZE

A pair of small green glass ceiling lights.

9.5in (24cm) high

£15-25   GAZE

A Shattaline turquoise plastic resin lamp base, with a correct yellow spun fibreglass shade.

These mass-produced lamps were made from 1968 for sale in British Home Stores. They were made of cast resin and came in red, gold, orange, beige or turquoise. This is the middle of three sizes of lamp base.

c1968   *7in (18cm) high*

£35-45   DTC

A CLOSER LOOK AT A 1970S LAMP

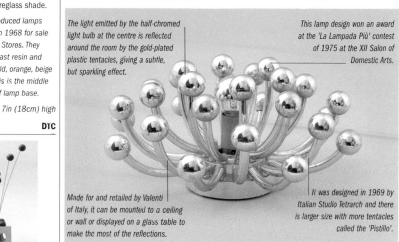

The light emitted by the half-chromed light bulb at the centre is reflected around the room by the gold-plated plastic tentacles, giving a subtle, but sparkling effect.

This lamp design won an award at the 'La Lampada Più' contest of 1975 at the XII Salon of Domestic Arts.

Made for and retailed by Valenti of Italy, it can be mounted to a ceiling or wall or displayed on a glass table to make the most of the reflections.

It was designed in 1969 by Italian Studio Tetrarch and there is larger size with more tentacles called the 'Pistillo'.

A 1970s Studio Tetrach 'Pistillino' gold-plated light, marked "Valenti eC Milano Mod. Pistillino Dep. Design Studio Tetrach".

12in (30.5cm) wide

£100-150   DTC

A 1970s wire and plastic sculpture.

13.5in (34.5cm) high

£25-35   DTC

An early 1970s 'bubble sculpture', with blue and green balls.

18in (45.5cm) high

£40-50   DTC

A Pifco table fan.

11in (28cm) high

£10-20   GAZE

A triangular display piece, with internal decoration, signed on the base "'71" and "J. Walter Thompson Co.".

1971   7.75in (19.5cm) high

£120-180   DTC

A 1970s stainless steel and chrome table lighter.
5.5in (14cm) high
£12-18 DTC

A 1970s Braun brushed steel table lighter.
3.5in (8.5cm) high
£15-25 DTC

A 1960s round wooden Ronson lighter.
4.25in (11cm) wide
£2-4 GAZE

A 1980s 4-D quartz clock, by Omni Clock Ltd.
5.5in (14cm) high
£30-40 DTC

A late 1970s Trebors Refreshers oversized advertising money box.
15.5in (39.5cm) long
£18-22 DTC

A 1970s Bossons 'Cheyenne' painted plaster wall plaque.
12.5in (32cm) high
£45-55 BAD

A BMF 'The Colani' yellow polyethylene chair, made by Top System, organic shape with writing surface.
c1972 26in (65cm) high
£500-600 QU

A Bossons 'Romany' hanging wall plaque, painted plaster.

Bossons was founded in 1946 by father and son W.H. and W. Ray Bossons, who released their first catalogue of hand-painted chalk wall plaques in 1948. Wall masks were added in 1959. The factory closed in 1996. Value is largely determined by condition, with mint examples being the most valuable. Those that have been repainted or varnished are worth the least.

9.5in (24cm) high
£45-55 BAD

A pair of Günter Beltzig 'Floris' fibreglass chairs, made by Beltzig Design, with artist's signature and number in felt-tip pen.

Designed in 1967, these chairs are from a limited edition of 100 produced in 1992. Made of moulded fibreglass resin, they fully explore the fluid nature of the material and have the appearance of an organic, natural form growing upwards from the floor. They were made in two parts and had to be handmade.

c1967 42.5in (106cm) high
£750-850 each QU

A pair of Alexander Begge 'Casalino' red plastic children's chairs, made by Casala Manufacture Lauenau, signed to underside.

c1970 20.75in (52cm) high
£120-180 QU

A 'Vicario' chair, with moulded ABS plastic body, designed by Vico Magistretti.

c1970

£100-150　　　　**BONBAY**

An American JVC Videosphere, made from 1969 to mid-1970s.

The design of this TV is clearly based on a spaceman's helmet and was influenced by the American lunar landing of 1969. They were made in white and orange in the UK and red, black and grey in the US. Red is the rarest colour. A chain allowed it to be hung from the ceiling. There is a later version with a radio and alarm clock in the base, which is usually more valuable.

13in (33cm) high

£250-350　　　　**DTC**

A 1960s Rexard Creation 'Gabrielle' display doll, designed by Odette Arden, in mint condition with original card tag and box.

12.25in (31cm) high

£15-25　　　　**MTS**

A 1960s Marx Toys of Swansea battery-operated 78rpm 'Kiddi-Tunes' record player, in original box.

box 13in (32.5cm) wide

£55-65　　　　**MA**

A CLOSER LOOK AT A TROLL

This troll was made by Thomas Dam of Denmark, the first and also considered the best and most collectable of toy troll makers, and is marked with his name.

This is one of the most common types of costume – look out for character costumes such as nurses and soldiers, which could also be bought separately.

He is in mint condition with clean plastic and original hair, and he retains his clothes and box.

Look out for black and animal trolls, which are rarer and more valuable, especially the legendary alligator troll.

A 1960s troll, by Thomas Dam, with green felt shorts and in original box.

Trolls were an immensely popular fad between the late 1960s and the early 1970s but were first created in the 1950s by Thomas Dam (pronounced Dom).

6in (15cm) high

£30-40　　　　**SOTT**

A 1970s "19" magazine clutch bag.

12in (30.5cm) wide

£30-40　　　　**DTC**

A 1970s 'Las Vegas' printed paper laminated and plastic magazine purse.

Made for carrying magazines and small items, these were mainly made in Italy and often contained fashion magazines.

11.75in (30cm) wide

£80-120　　　　**NOR**

A 1970s Panasonic "plunger" 8-track player, boxed.

The now obsolete 8-track format was developed in 1965 and was popular until the late 1970s. A great commercial success in its day, it lead to many developments in portable music and was best known for in-car entertainment being available in all Fords in 1966. Although successful, cheaper manufacturing led to use of plastic rollers which caused tape wear and jamming.

9in (23cm) high

£80-120　　　　**DTC**

FIFTIES, SIXTIES & SEVENTIES

A 'The Pussycats' vinyl lunch box and Thermos flask, by Aladdin Incorporated, the Thermos covered with a paper label.

c1966

£70-100   **NOR**

A 1960s 'Go Go' vinyl lunch box, lacks thermos, by Aladdin Incorporated.

These lunchboxes are very desirable for their funky period artwork that captures the fashions and evokes the music of the period. Splits in the vinyl will devalue them considerably.

c1966   *9in (22.5cm) high*

£70-100   **NOR**

A pair of 1960s Satellite jumping shoes (to give you a 'spring' in your step!), marked "Model 660", unused and in original box.

10.5in (26.5cm) high

£25-35   **NOR**

A 1970s Hai Karate aftershave and lotion gift set, distributed by Ross of Brighton Ltd.

5.75in (14.5cm) high

£10-15   **DTC**

A 1970s Hai Karate soap-on-a-rope, distributed by Ross of Brighton Ltd.

7.75in (19.5cm) high

£10-20   **DTC**

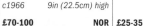

A 1970s Hai Karate body talc and aftershave gift set, distributed by Ross of Brighton Ltd.

7.25in (18.5cm) high

£15-25   **DTC**

A pair of yellow 'Smiley' printed canvas shoes, by the Newport Rubber Co.

The ubiquitous smiley face was invented by American artist and inventor Harvey Ball (1922-2001) in 1963 for an insurance company looking for a way to improve company morale. He was paid $45 for sole rights to his creation, which was used on badges. In 1970, two Philadelphia brothers Bernard and Murray Spain used the face on a massive range of items with peace themes and the ensuing fad reached its high point over the next two years. The computer smiley face was born later, however, being first used online in late 1982.

c1971   *10.25in (26cm) long*

£70-100   **NOR**

Left: A 1970s Hai Karate musk talc, distributed by Ross of Brighton Ltd.

5.5in (14cm) high

£6-7   **DTC**

Right: A 1970s Hai Karate advertising mug.

3.75in (9.5cm) high

£3-4   **DTC**

A 1977 Biba diary, unused.

8.25in (21cm) high

£35-45   **DTC**

COLLECTORS' NOTES

■ Born in 1937, Peter Max has grown to become one of America's foremost 'pop' culture artists. His childhood was filled with magic and mystery as he travelled with his family between Shanghai, China, Africa, India and Israel, where he first developed his love of planets and astronomy.

■ He also drew inspiration from comic books seen as a child and began studying art in Paris before emigrating to the US with his family in 1953. Here he furthered his studies in art and worked in photography. By the 1960s, his photographs gave way to a new quasi-psychedelic style, often called 'Cosmic 60s', for which he is best known. Bright, acid colours and bold, curvaceous forms often inspired by Art Nouveau and the popular cultural movements of the time dominate his work.

■ Look for pieces that typify this style, preferably from the 1960s and 1970s when Max began to shoot to fame. Posters and particularly original artworks fetch high sums but even items produced in great numbers, such as his tin trays, can fetch high prices. Many were disposed of, causing them to be rare today. Ceramics and glass, as well as paper pieces and books, are also popular. Condition is important with such items and scratches, tears and fading reduce the value.

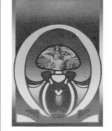

A Peter Max poster, printed by Security Printing, New York, with bright, psychedelic colours and swirling, free-flowing style.

1967   *36in (90cm) high*

£80-120   **SWA**

An 'Aries' printed card, designed by Peter Max, cut from a book.

£10-15   **NOR**

A Peter Max poster book, published by Crown Publishers Inc.

15.75in (40cm) high

£80-120   **NOR**

A Manhattan 'Yellow Pages' cover for 1970, designed by Peter Max.

This would be worth up to twice as much with the original book.

1970   *10.75in (27cm) high*

£80-120   **NOR**

A 'Do Not Disturb' hotel door sign, designed by Peter Max.

This was taken from a Manhattan hotel where much of the interior decoration and accessories were designed by Max.

£40-60   **NOR**

An Iroquois China 'Love' ashtray, designed by Peter Max.

5in (12.5cm) diam

£40-50   **NOR**

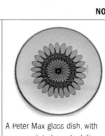

A Peter Max glass dish, with screen-printed psychedelic flower decoration.

8.25in (21cm) diam

£80-120   **NOR**

A Peter Max 'Happy' tin tray.

12.75in (32.5cm) diam

£30-40   **NOR**

FIND OUT MORE...

'The Art of Peter Max', *by Charles A. Riley II and Peter Max, published by Harry N. Abrams, 2002.*

COLLECTORS' NOTES

■ Film and TV props are the closest thing an enthusiast can get to being part of their favourite film or show. Collecting in this industry is continuing to grow.

■ Memorabilia connected to the golden age of Hollywood and its glamorous stars is the pinnacle of this collecting field. As props were not considered desirable at the time, many were discarded after filming, or altered and re-used on other productions.

■ Another popular area is cult science fiction and horror films and shows such as "Star Wars", "Star Trek", "Aliens" and "Dr Who", as well as the perennial spy film favourite "James Bond".

■ Today, major studios sell off props as soon as filming is complete. While this means you may not get a 'bargain', each piece should come with a letter of

authenticity from the studio guaranteeing that it is genuine. Provenance is vitally important, so always ask the seller for a history of the piece.

■ Props that appeared in key scenes or had a significant role in a film are usually the most desirable, but be aware that multiple copies will often be made in case of damage, or to display stages of usage. Examples that are used in the background will often be of poor quality or less detailed, but can be more affordable.

■ Promotional items and crew kit can also be an inexpensive way of entering the film and TV memorabilia market, as they are produced in relatively large amounts but would not have been available to the general market.

A prop 'Floats Like A Butterfly, Stings Like A Bee' badge from "Ali", made to the same design as the original with Will Smith's image replacing Cassius Clay.

The date "Oct. 30th '74" on the badge refers to the day Clay defeated George Foreman in Kinshasa, Zaire. It was the first heavyweight championship fight to be held in Africa.

2001   *2.75in (7cm) diam*

£35-45   **PSL**

AXL/2B.S.
VID-CON REET.I.
WARRANT OFFICER E. RIPLEY
USS NOSTROMO 1128 .9.A.
MISSION C.N8V.

A floppy disc from "Aliens", with label "AXCL/2B.S. VID-CON REET. I. WARRANT OFFICER E. RIPLEY USS NOSTROMO 1128.9.A. MISSION C.N8V".

Made for the inquest scene at the beginning of the film, when Ripley (Sigourney Weaver) is asked to give her account of events aboard the Nostromo. Despite being mentioned in the script, the disks were never used.

£150-200   **PSL**

An unworn grey promotional t-shirt for "American Beauty".

1999

£15-20   **PSL**

An unworn black promotional t-shirt for "Apollo 13".

£15-20   **PSL**

A replica alien head from "Alien Resurrection", the fibreglass head with clear dome, polyurethane neck and hand-painted details.

The fourth film from the Alien franchise, the screen play was written by Buffy creator Joss Whedon.

1997   *34in (87cm) wide*

£300-400   **PSL**

A visual effects Oscar nomination pack for "Armageddon", containing loose pages of information on the crew involved in the special effects.

This exclusive pack is only sent out to members of the Academy who can vote for the Oscar for best visual effects.

£40-50   **PSL**

A rubber stunt pistol from the Babylon 5 spin-off TV series "Crusade".

1999   *6in (15cm) wide*

£150-200   **PSL**

Two prop 'Joker' $50 bills from "Batman", mounted, framed and glazed.

Seen in the film when the Joker (Jack Nicholson) parades through the streets, throwing money to the crowds.

21in (53cm) wide

£100-150 PSL

A prop 'Oswald Means Order' metal button from "Batman Returns".

Seen in the film when The Penguin (Danny DeVito) runs for office.

1995 4in (10cm) wide

£70-100 PSL

A 'Diamond Exchange Security' sew-on patch from "Batman Forever", made for the film but never used.

Similar badges can be seen when Two Face (Tommy Lee Jones) and The Riddler (Jim Carrey) rob the diamond exchange.

1995 4in (10cm) high

£8-12 PSL

A pair of 'Gotham Observatory' metal security badges from "Batman & Robin", mounted, framed and glazed.

21in (54cm) wide

£400-500 PSL

A prop map from "The Beach", mounted, framed and glazed.

This is the map that Richard (Leonardo DiCaprio) draws on screen to show his new travelling friends the way to 'The Beach'. It is also seen as the other travellers arrive at the adjoining island, as seen through Richard's binoculars.

c2000

£800-900 PSL

A two-piece Colonial Warrior costume from "Battlestar Galactica", consisting of trousers and tunic made of heavy quilted cotton, the tunic shows signs of wear, with embroidered emblem on each arm featuring a series of triangles within a larger circle.

After successfully 're-imagining' the original series, Ronald Moore is producing 13 more episodes for the Sci-Fi Channel, due to air in 2005.

c1978

£400-500 PSL

A sheet of numbers from "A Beautiful Mind", mounted with four stills from the film, framed and glazed.

c2001 24in (60cm) high

£200-300 PSL

A 'Southern City Savings & Loans' blank cheque from "Big Fish", used by Edward Bloom (Ewan McGregor), mounted framed and glazed.

c2003 15in (38cm) wide

£70-100 PSL

A limited edition reproduction of the original artwork for the 'Machine Pistol' from "Blade 2", by R.T. Ruben, dated November 2000 and titled "Blade's Mach II – Blade Bloodhunt", from an edition of 50, mounted, framed and glazed.

£30-50 PSL

A CLOSER LOOK AT A BUFFY THE VAMPIRE SLAYER PROP

A 'Blair Witch Project Dossier', signed on the cover in silver pen by Daniel Myrick and Eduardo Sanchez, the film's writers and directors.

The Dossier represents a (fictionalised) in-depth investigation into the disappearance of the three students in the Black Hills of Maryland, and also an analysis of the Blair Witch legend itself.

1999

£80-120   **PSL**

This newspaper appeared in the famous season six 'musical' episode 'Once More With Feeling', where the characters uncontrollably burst into song throughout the episode, revealing their inner most fears. It was voted into the top 20 in Channel 4's 100 Greatest Musicals poll.

While not a key prop, the episode is a fan favourite, making it desirable.

When Buffy finished in 2003, many of the props were auctioned off for charity and on eBay.

Now that the "Buffy" spin-off show "Angel" has been cancelled, it is likely that interest in props from these two shows will rise.

A 'Sunnydale Press' prop newspaper from "Buffy The Vampire Slayer", the headline reading 'Mayhem Caused, Monsters Certainly Not Involved, Officials Say', the rest of the front page with unrelated articles copied from a real newspaper, mounted, framed and glazed.

2001

36in (92cm) high

£600-700   **PSL**

Three pieces of prop currency from "Buck Rogers In the 25th Century".
1979-81
   largest 2in (5cm) diam

£100-150   **PSL**

An official pictorial moviebook for "Catch Me If You Can", with detailed account of the making of the film, production photographs of locations, props, costumes and archive photographs from the real life Frank Abagnale's collection.

2003

£10-15   **PSL**

A prop newspaper from "Chicago", from the scene when Roxie (Renee Zellweger) first gets her story in the newspaper, mounted, framed and glazed.
2002   *33in (83cm) high*

£600-700   **PSL**

A prop shield from "Clash of the Titans", fibreglass with handpainted detailing.

These shields were used by Jappa's guards, when Perseus asks the Princess to tell her riddle. Also seen when the Princess is about to be sacrificed to the Krackon.

1981   *27.75in (70cm) d*

£400-500   **PSL**

A cream dress shirt from "The Curse Of The Jade Scorpion", worn by C.W. Briggs (Woody Allen), with labels "Anto, Beverly Hills" and 'W.A. Sept 2000".

Woody Allen wardrobe pieces are scarce.

2001

£200-250   **PSL**

A CLOSER LOOK AT A DOCTOR WHO COSTUME

A reproduction 'sonic screwdriver' from "Doctor Who", machined from high-grade aluminium and brass with a red anodised ring, with spring-loaded top section.

The screwdriver was carried by all the Doctors from Patrick Troughton to Peter Davison. This version is synonymous with the fourth Doctor, played by Tom Baker and, while it is a reproduction, it is well made and accurate.

9in (22cm) long

£150-200   **PSL**

This uniform appears in episode 10 of the Colin Baker story "Trial of a Time Lord – Terror of the Vervoids". The episode is part of a huge 14-story arc revolving around the Doctor's trial for interfering in the affairs of other planets.

This episode is set on board the starliner 'Hyperion III'. The 'Duty Officer' would have been a member of the liner's crew.

Although the fourth Doctor, Tom Baker, is generally considered one of the most popular incarnations of this character, the fifth Doctor Colin Baker and the sixth Peter Davison are gaining in popularity.

The new series of Doctor Who is due to air in 2005, staring Christopher Eccleston as the ninth Doctor. This is likely to increase interest in the franchise.

A 'Duty Officer' (Mike Mungarvan) costume from "Doctor Who", the cream-coloured trousers and tunic with a brown fleck pattern, padded shoulders, a zip-up back and silver coloured detailing around the neck and on the sleeves, label reading "Made in BBC Television Workroom" together with the actor's name added in pen.

1986

£500-600   **PSL**

A promotional cap for "E.T. the Extra-Terrestrial".

1982

£10-15   **PSL**

An unworn white crew t-shirt from "From Hell", size large.

2001

£35-45   **PSL**

A prop alien knife and sheath from "Galaxy Quest", made of resin in the shape of an alien animal bone, faux alien animal hide grip, the hard plastic scabbard covered with soft scales.

The knife can be seen throughout the film and in particular at the end, as General Sarris (Robert Sachs) attacks the crew as the ship plummets towards Earth.

1999   *17in (44cm) long*

£200-300   **PSL**

An original pencil and ink storyboard from "Ghostbusters", showing the 'Slimer' ghost scene in the dining room of the 'Sedgewick Hotel', dated 1983 and stamped "Copyright Columbia Pictures Inc", mounted, framed and glazed.

1984   *21in (53cm) wide*

£400-500   **PSL**

An unworn long-sleeved white and dark blue crew shirt from "Harry Potter - The Prisoner Of Azkaban", size XL.

2004

£65-75 PSL

A promotional Nike holdall from "I Know What You Did Last Summer", embroidered with "Production Crew 1997".

£25-35 PSL

A crew cap from "James Bond – The World Is Not Enough".

c1999

£25-35 PSL

A prop Russian-language document folder from "James Bond - The World Is Not Enough".

1999

£70-100 PSL

A crew cap from "Harry Potter: The Prisoner Of Azkaban".

2004

£25-35 PSL

A black cast and crew sweatshirt from "James Bond – Tomorrow Never Dies".

1997

£40-60 PSL

A replica 'Puzzle Cube' from the "Hellraiser" film series, hand-made from brass and mahogany.

£100-150 PSL

A prop book from "The Hours", the book with facsimile covers for 'The Goodness Of Time' by Richard Brown (Ed Harris).

2002

£60-80 PSL

A 'Graves Ice Palace Hotel' postcard from "James Bond – Die Another Day".

This postcard was used as set dressing in the hotel lobby.

2002 6in (15cm) wide

£25-35 PSL

A scarce, unworn black crew T-shirt from "Lord Of The Rings", size XL.

£150-200 PSL

A premier party menu for "The Lord Of The Rings: The Return Of The King", with 'London Premiere Party December 11 2003' printed at the bottom.

2003 8in (21cm) high

£15-20 PSL

A visual effects Oscar nomination pack for "Mars Attacks", the card wallet containing loose pages of information on the crew involved with the special effects and details of scenes where the effects came to the fore.

1996

£35-45 PSL

A sweatshirt from "M.A.S.H.", screen used and signed by 'Radar' (Gary Burghoff), with a couple of small holes.

1972-83

£220-280 PSL

A US press kit for "The Matrix Reloaded", containing a double CD and a 'digital press kit' with photos, trailers, Quick Time videos and other information, together with a 56-page colour book with dozens of stills and French language text.

2003

£70-100 PSL

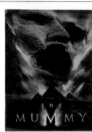

A press kit for "The Mummy", containing printed production information and a set of five black and white photographs of images from the film.

The kit would have been given to journalists reviewing the premiere or preview of the film.

1999

£15-20 PSL

A 'Coping with VD and Other Embarrassing Incidents' leaflet from "Red Dwarf", the folded paper leaflet with blurred print on the inside, the back page marked "JMC Medical Info".

c1999 7.5in (19cm) high

£60-80 PSL

A 'Leopard Lager' beer can from "Red Dwarf", with specially printed label with the fictional maker's name, purchased directly from Grant Naylor productions.

c1999 4.5in (11cm) high

£60-80 PSL

Two costume designs from "The Mighty Morphin Power Rangers", the two copied drawings show multi-coloured designs for three spacesuit-type outfits and a green suit with a cape that can be seen in the film.

1995 12in (30.5cm)

£25-35 PSL

Two original pencil storyboards for "Robin Hood Prince Of Thieves", featuring six frames, the second page titled 'scene 118. ext. Nottingham Castle Dungeon Gate. Day'.

1991

£80-120   **PSL**

A large prop book from "Scooby Doo", titled 'Thumbs Down', made from faux leather with a polystyrene core.

2002   *12in (30.5cm) high*

£150-200   **PSL**

An advertising flyer for 'The Company Of Players' from "Shakespeare In Love".

1998   *7.5in (19cm) high*

£60-80   **SL**

An oversized 'John Dorian' (Zach Braff) ID badge from "Scrubs".

8in (20cm) wide

£180-220   **PSL**

THE SHiNiNG

A limited edition reproduction photo of the last scene from "The Shining", taken from the original, from an edition of 50, mounted, framed.

16in (34cm) high

£80-120   **PSL**

A CLOSER LOOK AT STAR TREK PROPS

Made of soft rubber, this example would have been used in a fight or action scene where it could not cause any physical injury to the cast.

This larger more detailed prop phaser would have been used by a key cast member, or when it could be clearly seen on screen.

The plain, un-detailed version would be been used in the background.

Together with the iconic communicators, phasers are particularly sought after. Obviously more detailed examples are more popular and also more expensive, as fewer would have been made.

A Federation 'cobra-head' phaser from "Star Trek: The Next Generation", the soft rubber prop weapon with very little colour but detailed with various buttons and markings.

8.25in (21cm) long

£200-300   **PSL**

A large Federation 'cobra-head' phaser from "Star Trek: The Next Generation", painted silver with black detail, the underside tinted blue, the buttons on top numbered "U6" and "U7", used in the third season.

1989   *9in (23cm) long*

£800-1,200   **PSL**

An 'engineering PADD' from "Star Trek: The Next Generation", used by chief engineer 'Geordi LaForge' (Levar Burton), no longer functioning, with a row of buttons missing from the bottom leaving glue marks.

This distinctive red prop can be seen in more than one episode including 'The Masterpiece Society' and 'Realm Of Fear'.

1992   6in (15cm) high

£550-650   **PSL**

An 'isolinear chip' from "Star Trek: The Next Generation", with printed paper label and yellow printed circuit board effect on the main body.

                3in (8cm) high

£180-220   **PSL**

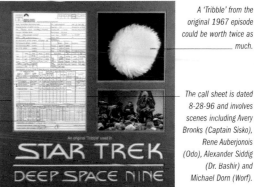

A plastic bottle from 'Quark's Bar' in "Star Trek: Deep Space Nine", the sports water bottle decorated with gold paint and coloured stickers.

This bottle was used in the bar at Quark's casino in the first series.

1993   10in (26cm) high

£80-120   **PSL**

A CLOSER LOOK AT A STAR TREK PROP

This prop was used in the 30th anniversary episode 'Trials & Tribble-ations', which re-used footage 'The Trouble with Tribbles' episode from the original series.

Call sheets are a vital part of the television-making process and inform members of the cast and crew where and when to be on set.

A 'Tribble' from the original 1967 episode could be worth twice as much.

The call sheet is dated 8-28-96 and involves scenes including Avery Brooks (Captain Sisko), Rene Auberjonois (Odo), Alexander Siddig (Dr. Bashir) and Michael Dorn (Worf).

A 'Tribble' and call sheet from "Star Trek - Deep Space 9", the Tribble made from faux white fur, mounted, framed and glazed.

1996   27in (68cm) wide

£600-700   **PSL**

A rare pre-release promotional sticker from "Star Wars", with 'Luke Over Yavin' logo and the title of the movie as "The Star Wars".

This sticker was never taken up by Fox after the 'The' was dropped from the title.

1975   3in (8cm) high

£15-20   **PSL**

A prop 'science award medal' from "Star Trek: Voyager", the gold coloured pendant engraved with characters, framed and glazed.

                pendant 2.5in (6cm) long

£450-550   **PSL**

A rare crew sew-on patch from "Star Wars".

This is the first version of the now iconic logo and was designed by Ralph McQuarrie.

c1975   3in (8cm) wide

£100-150   **PSL**

A rare press badge from "Star Wars".

This peel and stick press badge was given to the media for press conferences in 1977. Although very similar to the famous logo, the 'W' is slightly different, this version appears on the first advance posters in Christmas 1976, but was changed by George Lucas in 1977.

                4in (10cm) wide

£15-25   **PSL**

A rare 'Intergalactic Passport' given to cast, crew and special guests on the set "Star Wars - The Empire Strikes Back", the 18-page book with hard blue cover with unique ID number inside.

These individually stamped and numbered passports were given to visitors to the soundstages at Elstree Studios in England. The pass allowed guests to visit all areas of the production. There are also fun stamps in the book for 'Moss Eisley', 'Bespin' and 'Tatooine' as well as many others. There is an ID info page and foreign exchange facilities. Only 450 examples were produced and the vast majority are retained by George Lucas' Industrial Light & Magic archives.

c1980   *6in (15cm) high*

£300-400   **PSL**

A rare crew sew-on patch from "Star Wars - The Empire Strikes Back", unused.

Graphic artist Ralph McQuarrie initially worked at Boeing and later illustrated the Apollo lunar landings. This proved to be the perfect background when he was invited to provide some conceptual drawings for Star Wars. McQuarrie worked on designs for many characters and vehicles including Darth Vader, R2-D2 and the Death Star and went on to work on the rest of the original trilogy. His artwork has also been used in other cult sci-fi classics including "Battlestar Galactica", "Star Trek" and "E.T.".

c1980

£70-100   **PSL**

A rare promotional drink coaster from "Star Wars - The Empire Strikes Back", mint condition.

These were given out to crew members on the set. They are made from uncoated card and virtually all of them were destroyed after just one use.

c1980   *4in (10cm) wide*

£40-60   **PSL**

A rare original promotional shirt from "Star Wars - The Empire Strikes Back", with Ralph McQuarrie artwork, unworn.

c1980

£80-120   **PSL**

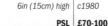

A blood analysis device from "Stargate SG-1", the hand-held fishing game sprayed silver, used in season 3 episode 'New Ground', with MGM certificate of authenticity.

1999   *6.5in (17cm) long*

£350-450   **PSL**

A rare pressbook for "THX 1138", together with an original lobby card.

"THX 1138" was George Lucas' first feature film.

1973   *14in (35cm) high*

£40-50   **PSL**

A bottle of Moët & Chandon champagne from "Titanic", the label and gold foil with White Star company name on them and a gold foil neck.

1997   *12in (30cm) high*

£180-220   **PSL**

A visual effects Oscar nomination pack for "Stuart Little", containing information on the crew involved with the special effects, and two glossy colour photos of some of the moments from the movie.

1999

£15-25   **PSL**

A pair of 'K White Star Line's' luggage labels from "Titanic", mounted, framed and glazed.

1997   *9.75in (25cm) wide*

£220-280   **PSL**

A prop cheque from "Trading Places", used by Lewis Winthorpe III (Dan Ackroyd), mounted, framed and glazed.

An earpiece worn by 'Lara Croft' (Angelina Jolie) in "Tomb Raider".

In much the same way that Nokia linked their 8146 mobile phone with "The Matrix", so Ericsson used 'product placement' to increase exposure on their Bluetooth earpiece.

2001   6in (15cm) long

£800-1,200   **PSL**

1983   14.5in (37cm) high

£250-300   **PSL**

A pair of sunglasses from "Waterworld", with pale green plastic lenses, a rough resin frame and wire arms, with a rubber cord at the back and rubber tubing on the bridge of the nose.

c1995

£60-80   **PSL**

A phone used as set dressing in "Wayne's World 2".

The Chicago Blackhawks phone can be seen in the Donut shop frequented by Wayne (Mike Myers) and Garth (Dana Carvey).

1993   8in (20cm) long

£100-170   **PSL**

A pair of glasses from "X-Men", worn by the main surgeon during the flashback scene where Wolverine (Hugh Jackman) has adamantium bonded to his skeleton, marked "Hero Doctor".

c2000

£150-250   **PSL**

COLLECTORS' NOTES

■ Increasing nostalgia for the 1970s and 1980s has had a dramatic effect on collecting cult film and TV memorabilia and toys.

■ Science fiction first zoomed across our screens in the 1930s and enjoyed a golden age in the 1950s, but the period gaining in popularity with collectors now is the 1980s. Many shows from that period are re-run on cable TV and also released on DVD and video.

■ British institution Doctor Who is a prime example of the burgeoning popularity of the 1980s. Later incarnations of the Doctor have traditionally been less popular, but interest in Peter Davidson (1981-84) and Colin Baker (1984-86) is growing steadily. With the ninth Doctor set to appear in 2005 in the form of Christopher Eccleston, this series looks set to continue as one of the most popular shows on TV.

■ Memorabilia made at the beginning of a show's run is often the hardest to find as smaller quantities were produced. Condition is very important, as is the original box and any instructions or certificates, particularly for more recent examples.

■ Items produced during an unpopular period can be bought at more reasonable prices and may well increase in value if the series gains a new generation of fans.

A handcrafted Doctor Who 'TARDIS' model, by Britannia Miniatures.

c1996   5.5in (14cm) high

£20-30   **TP**

A pewter Doctor Who 'Cyberman' bottle stopper, by Scifi Collector.

c2002   1.5in (4cm) high

£7-10   **TP**

A Denys Fisher Doctor Who 'Leela' figure, in original box.

1976   box 10in (25.5cm) high

£180-220   **F**

A set of pewter Doctor Who 'Dalek' salt and pepper shakers, by Asmortartz Productions.

2001   3in (7.5cm) high

£70-90   **TP**

A Doctor Who 'Cyberman Attacking' figure, by Media Collectables.

2002   figure 2in (5cm) high

£6-8   **TP**

A Doctor Who 'The Ice Warriors Collection' video box set, by the BBC.

1998   7.5in (19cm) high

£35-45   **TP**

A Doctor Who 'Out of the Darkness' audio CD, by the BBC.

1998   5.5in (14cm) wide

£20-25   **TP**

Two Doctor Who 'The Secrets of Doctor Who' audio cassettes, tapes one and three.

These cassettes were given away with the 1996 Doctor Who calendar.

1996   4.25in (11cm) high

£6-8 each   **TP**

A Doctor Who 'Theme from the BBC TV Series' LP, with hologram sleeve.

1986   *12in (30.5cm) wide*

£7-10   **TP**

A Doctor Who card, with 'Short Trips' audio CD, by the BBC.

1998   *7in (18cm) wide*

£15-25   **TP**

A signed Colin Baker Doctor Who publicity postcard, from 'The Two Doctors' episode.

*   6in (15cm) high*

£6-8   **LCA**

A Doctor Who 'The Legend' trading card, by Cornerstone, signed by Sophie Aldred, who played Ace.

1995   *3.5in (9cm) wide*

£7-10   **TP**

A Doctor Who 'The Web Planet' BT phone card, by Jonder International Promotions, with factsheet.

1994-97   *card 3.5in (9cm) w*

£10-15   **TP**

A Doctor Who 'Adventures' trading card, by Cornerstone, signed by Nicola Bryant (Peri).

1995   *3.5in (9cm) wide*

£7-10   **TP**

A Doctor Who 'The Aztecs' BT phone card, by Jonder International Promotions, with factsheet.

1994-97

card 3.5in (9cm) wide

£10-15   **TP**

A publicity pack for Tom Baker's autobiography 'Who on Earth is Tom Baker?'

1994

£20-25   **TP**

A 'Doctor Who and the Daleks' 2000 calendar, by Slow Dazzle Worldwide.

2000   *14in (35.5cm) high*

£6-8   **TP**

A Doctor Who calendar, from the Radio Times, in original packaging.

2001   *12in (30.5cm) wide*

£4-5   **TP**

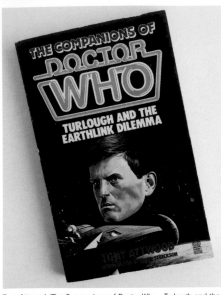

Tony Attwood, 'The Companions of Doctor Who – Turlough and the Earthlink Dilemma', published by Target.

1986 *7in (18cm) high*

£8-12 **TP**

Paul Cornell, 'Doctor Who The New Adventures – Love and War', published by Virgin Publishing.

Paul Cornell is one of the writers signed to work on the new Doctor Who series due in 2005.

1992

£8-10 **TP**

Terrance Dicks, Doctor Who 'Planet of Giants', published by Target.

1990 *7in (18cm) high*

£7-10 **TP**

Victor Pemberton, Doctor Who 'The Pescatons', published by Target.

1991 *7in (18cm) high*

£4-6 **TP**

Justin Richards, Doctor Who 'The Missing Adventures – System Shock', published by Virgin Publishing.

1995

£7-8 **TP**

Nigel Robinson, Doctor Who 'The Sensorites', published by Target.

1987 *7in (18cm) high*

£3-6 **TP**

Eric Saward, Doctor Who 'Attack of the Cybermen', published by Target.

1989 *7in (18cm) high*

£7-10 **TP**

Gary Russell, Doctor Who 'The Missing Adventures – Invasion of the Cat-People', published by Virgin Publishing.

1995

£8-10 **TP**

Victor Pemberton, Doctor Who 'Fury from the Deep', published by Target.

1986 *7in (18cm) high*

£15-20 **TP**

A 'The James Bond 007 Secret Service' board game, by Spears, in original box.

box 14.25in (36cm) wide

£25-35   **F**

A James Bond lunchbox with Thermos flask, by Aladdin Industries.

1966

£100-150   **TH**

An Airfix 'James Bond's Autogyro' kit, of 'Little Nellie' in 1:24 scale, featured in the film 'You Only Live Twice', with transfers, instructions and box.

Bond films are well-known for their cool gadgets and vehicles. 'Little Nellie' is a fan favourite and features in a key sequence in this Sean Connery film.

9in (23cm) wide

£80-120   **W&W**

A late 1960s base metal ring, with 'winking' image of James Bond's 'Little Nellie' from 'You Only Live Twice', and flying over an enemy helicopter.

0.75in (2cm) high

£7-10   **CVS**

A 1960s base metal ring, with 'winking' image of James Bond in a white dinner suit and in scuba gear.

0.75in (2cm) high

£8-12   **CVS**

A James Bond 'Moonraker' deluxe figure, by Mego Corp., with helmet and backpack.

A standard version without a helmet or backpack, was also released but is less desirable.

c1979

£200-250   **TH**

A James Bond 'Moonraker' Collegeville costume and mask, by EON Productions.

1970s

£40-50   **TH**

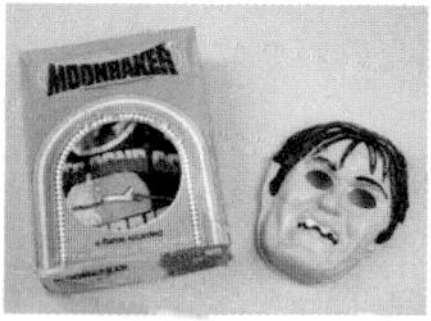

A James Bond 'Moonraker' Collegeville costume and mask of Jaws, by EON Productions.

1970s

£35-45   **TH**

A scarce Lone Star James Bond 'Moonraker' Space Gun, of diecast construction with plastic parts, finished in black and white, with original box, minor wear.

12in (30.5cm) long

£80-120   **W&W**

'Showtime', November 1964, with feature on Sean Connery as James Bond.

11in (28cm) high

£20-25   VM

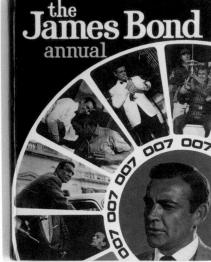

A James Bond annual, including pictures from 'Goldfinger' and 'You Only Live Twice'.

1968   *10.75in (27.5cm) high*

£50-60   VM

'Film Review', August 1977, featuring 'The Spy Who Loved Me'.

10.75in (27.5cm) high

£10-15   VM

A 1960s Arrows 'Goldfinger' jigsaw.

£80-120   VEC

A signed Roger Moore publicity postcard.

6in (15cm) high

£10-20   LCA

A signed Pierce Brosnan publicity photograph.

10in (25.5cm) high

£35-45   LCA

A 1960s Arrows 'Thunderball' jigsaw.

£80-120   VEC

A signed Ursula Andress 'Dr. No' publicity photograph.

The iconic white bikini Andress wears when she emerges from the sea sold at Christies for £60,000 in 2001.

10in (25.5cm) high

£40-50   LCA

A signed Honor Blackman 'Goldfinger' publicity photograph.

10in (25.5cm) high

£35-45   LCA

A signed Star Trek publicity photograph, signed by George Takei, James Doohan, Nichelle Nichols and Walter Koenig, mounted with another photograph titled 'Space, the final frontier...'.

£70-90   **GAZE**

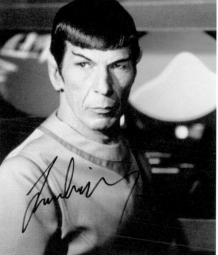

A signed Leonard Nimoy 'Star Trek: The Motion Picture' publicity photograph.

10in (25.5cm) high

£65-75   **LCA**

A Star Trek annual, authorised by the BBC.

1973   *10.5in (27cm) high*

£6-8   **MTS**

A signed George Takei Star Trek publicity photograph.

10in (25.5cm) high

£30-40   **LCA**

A Star Trek 'Champions' Spock pewter figure, by Racing Champions Inc., inspired by 'Star Trek: The Motion Picture', from a limited edition of 9,998.

1998   *box 9.25in (23.5cm) high*

£40-50   **TP**

A Star Trek 'Champions' Khan pewter figure, by Racing Champions Inc., inspired by 'Star Trek: The Wrath of Khan', from a limited edition of 9,998.

1998   *box 9.25in (23.5cm) high*

£40-50   **TP**

A Star Trek 'Champions' Kirk pewter figure, by Racing Champions Inc., inspired by 'Star Trek: The Motion Picture', from a limited edition of 9,998.

1998   *box 9.25in (23.5cm) high*

£40-50   **TP**

A signed Patrick Stewart 'Star Trek: The Next Generation' publicity photograph.

10in (25.5cm) high

£35-45   **LCA**

A signed Brent Spiner 'Star Trek: First Contact' publicity photograph.

10in (25.5cm) high

£30-40   **LCA**

'Astounding', July 1940, science fiction magazine.

9.25in (23.5cm) high

£10-15 VM

A signed Sarah Michelle Gellar 'Buffy the Vampire Slayer' publicity photograph.

10in (25.5cm) high

£35-45 LCA

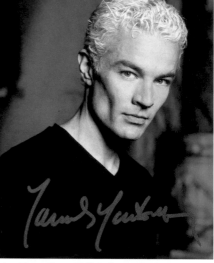

A signed James Masters 'Buffy the Vampire Slayer' publicity photograph.

10in (25.5cm) high

£40-50 LCA

A signed David Boreanaz 'Angel the Series' publicity photograph.

10in (25.5cm) high

£25-35 LCA

A 'Buffy the Vampire Slayer' action figure, by Moore Action Collectibles.

2001

£7-10 TP

A 'Buffy the Vampire Slayer' crucifix corkscrew.

2001

£10-20 TP

A limited edition 'Buffy the Vampire Slayer' figurine, by Steve Varner, from an edition of 4,500.

2000 9in (23cm) high

£60-70 TH

A limited edition 'Lorne the Host' bust from 'Angel the Series', sculpted by Jeremy Bush for Moore Creations, from an edition of 3,000.

2002 6in (15cm) high

£20-30 TP

A 'Countdown' annual, published by Purnell and Sons Ltd, featuring 'UFO', 'Doctor Who', 'Thunderbirds' and 'Captain Scarlet'.

1971   11in (28cm) high

£7-10   **MTS**

A 1980s 'Dukes of Hazzard' LCD quartz watch, by Unisonic, boxed.

A big-screen remake of this popular TV series is due in 2005.

10.25in (26cm) wide

£25-35   **DTC**

A 1980s 'Dukes of Hazzard' LCD quartz watch, by Unisonic, in bubble pack.

1981   9.5in (25cm) high

£20-30   **DTC**

A King Features number 990 'Flash Gordon' ray gun, on backing card.

1976

£40-60   **VEC**

A signed Daniel Radcliffe, Rupert Grint and Emma Watson 'Harry Potter' publicity photograph.

10in (25.5cm) high

£60-80   **LCA**

An 'Incredible Hulk' bubble bath bottle, by Cliro Perfumeries, with motto reading 'Combat The Evil of Grime With The Hulk's Power', boxed.

c1979   box 7in (18cm) high

£7-10   **MTS**

A 1970s Marx 'Lone Ranger' Butch Cavendish fully jointed action figure, in original box.

box 10in (25.5cm) high

£25-35   **F**

A signed Viggo Mortensen 'Lord of the Rings' publicity photograph.

10in (25.5cm) high

A signed Christopher Lee 'Lord of the Rings' publicity photograph.

10in (25.5cm) high

£25-35   **LCA**

£35-45   **LCA**

A signed Elijah Wood 'Lord of the Rings' publicity photograph.

10in (25.5cm) high

£35-45 | **LCA**

A signed Orlando Bloom 'Lord of the Rings' publicity photograph.

10in (25.5cm) high

£30-40 | **LCA**

A 'The Man From U.N.C.L.E.' annual, published by World Distributors.

1968 | *10.5in (27cm) high*

£7-11 | **MTS**

A 1960s base metal ring, with 'winking' image of Illya Kuryakin and Napoleon Solo from 'The Man From U.N.C.L.E.'.

0.75in (2cm) high

£8-12 | **CVS**

Nine rare Lone Star 'The Man From U.N.C.L.E.' triangular plastic badges, with the 'U.N.C.L.E.' logo and number 11 in gold with a black background, each with a safety clip fastener, mounted on an associated period backing.

10.5in (26.5cm) high

£180-220 | **W&W**

A 'Masters of the Universe' Modulok figure, by Mattel.

c1985

£15-20 | **TH**

A Bell Records 'The Partridge Family Shopping Bag' album, containing real shopping bag.

1972 | *12.25in (31cm) wide*

£8-12 | **MTS**

'Planet Stories', No. 9, published by Love Romances Publishing Co. Inc.

1953 | *10in (25.5cm) high*

£2-3 | **MTS**

Two 'Super Pops for the Stylophone' sheet music books, with Rolf Harris on the covers, published by EMI.

11in (28cm) high

£7-9 each | **DTC**

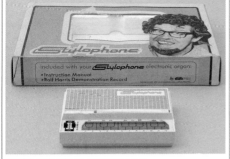

A Rolf Harris Stylophone, by Dübreq, boxed.

c1969-70   *box 13in (33cm) wide*

£55-65   **DTC**

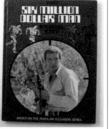

A 'The Six Million Dollar Man' annual, published by Stafford Pemberton.

1977   *10.5in (27cm) high*

£6-8   **MTS**

A miniature 'Smurf' novelty figure, modelled as a spaceman wearing a clear plastic bubble helmet.

2in (5cm) high

£8-12   **F**

A bottle of 'Monsieur le Stud' eau de toilette.

This aftershave was released as merchandising for the 1978 Joan Collins movie. It was advertised on the back of the movie's soundtrack album.

c1978   *6in (15cm) high*

£10-16   **DTC**

A 'Starsky and Hutch' annual'.

1979   *11in (27cm) high*

£7-9   **MTS**

A signed Gerry Anderson 'Stingray' publicity postcard.

6in (15cm) wide

£12-18   **LCA**

A 'Tarzan' holster, by Lone Star, on original backing.

c1966

£35-45   **TH**

A 'Terminator 2 Judgement Day' 'Cyberdyne T-800 Endo Skeleton' kit, by Tsukuda.

c1991

£20-25   **TH**

A 'TV21' annual, published by City Magazines, featuring 'Captain Scarlet', 'Fireball XL5', 'Thunderbirds', 'Stingray' and 'Zero X'.

1969   *12in (30.5cm) high*

£7-10   **MTS**

COLLECTORS' NOTES

■ Chance was established in West Smethwick, near Birmingham in the mid-19thC and initially focused on industrial and optical glass. It developed domestic glass from the 1920s, manufacturing both pressed and heat resistant glass.

■ In 1951 it launched its new Fiestaware range, manufactured in the same way as its short-lived 'Aqualux' range, but made of lighter and thinner glass and decorated with modern patterns. These were transfer-printed or screen-printed on to the piece. Dish or tray shapes are typically low and flat and often have wavy rims and gold rims.

■ During the 1950s and 1960s, designers such as Michael Harris and Margaret Casson created many patterns that are typical of the period in terms of both colour and design. These include 'Calypto', 'Night Sky' and brightly coloured flower patterns. Textured Fiesta glass dates from 1970 onwards.

■ One of its most recognisable designs is the 'handkerchief vase', produced from the 1950s until the late 1970s, and often found with bright, striped or chequered applied patterns. They were inspired by the similarly shaped vases, often known as 'fazzoletto', which were produced by prestigious Italian glass company Venini. The Chance factory closed in 1981.

■ When examining Chance, look at the condition of the pattern as scratches will devalue a piece considerably.

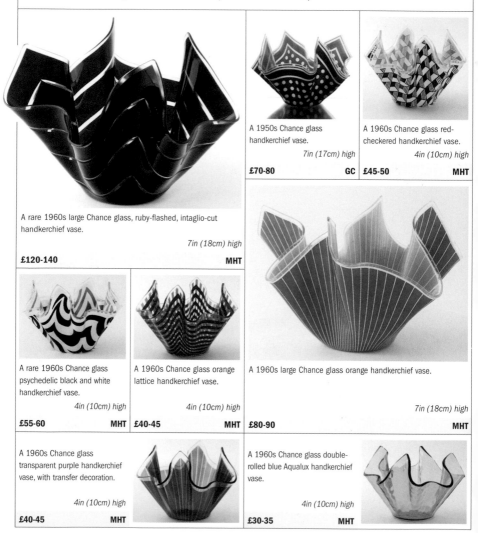

A 1950s Chance glass handkerchief vase.

7in (17cm) high

£70-80   GC

A 1960s Chance glass red-checkered handkerchief vase.

4in (10cm) high

£45-50   MHT

A rare 1960s large Chance glass, ruby-flashed, intaglio-cut handkerchief vase.

7in (18cm) high

£120-140   MHT

A rare 1960s Chance glass psychedelic black and white handkerchief vase.

4in (10cm) high

£55-60   MHT

A 1960s Chance glass orange lattice handkerchief vase.

4in (10cm) high

£40-45   MHT

A 1960s large Chance glass orange handkerchief vase.

7in (18cm) high

£80-90   MHT

A 1960s Chance glass transparent purple handkerchief vase, with transfer decoration.

4in (10cm) high

£40-45   MHT

A 1960s Chance glass double-rolled blue Aqualux handkerchief vase.

4in (10cm) high

£30-35   MHT

GLASS

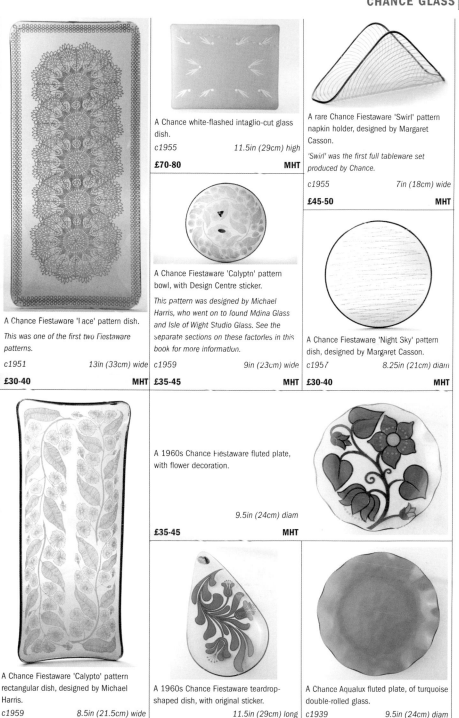

A Chance Fiestaware 'Lace' pattern dish.

This was one of the first two Fiestaware patterns.

c1951   13in (33cm) wide

£30-40   **MHT**

A Chance white-flashed intaglio-cut glass dish.

c1955   11.5in (29cm) high

£70-80   **MHT**

A Chance Fiestaware 'Calypto' pattern bowl, with Design Centre sticker.

This pattern was designed by Michael Harris, who went on to found Mdina Glass and Isle of Wight Studio Glass. See the separate sections on these factories in this book for more information.

c1959   9in (23cm) wide

£35-45   **MHT**

A rare Chance Fiestaware 'Swirl' pattern napkin holder, designed by Margaret Casson.

'Swirl' was the first full tableware set produced by Chance.

c1955   7in (18cm) wide

£45-50   **MHT**

A Chance Fiestaware 'Night Sky' pattern dish, designed by Margaret Casson.

c1957   8.25in (21cm) diam

£30-40   **MHT**

A Chance Fiestaware 'Calypto' pattern rectangular dish, designed by Michael Harris.

c1959   8.5in (21.5cm) wide

£20-30   **MHT**

A 1960s Chance Fiestaware fluted plate, with flower decoration.

9.5in (24cm) diam

£35-45   **MHT**

A 1960s Chance Fiestaware teardrop-shaped dish, with original sticker.

11.5in (29cm) long

£35-40   **MHT**

A Chance Aqualux fluted plate, of turquoise double-rolled glass.

c1939   9.5in (24cm) diam

£40-50   **MHT**

COLLECTORS' NOTES

■ During the 1920s and 1930s, traditional styles remained popular with both makers of cut glass and the public. However, some forward-thinking and highly skilled designers such as Ludwig Kny of Stuart & Sons and Keith Murray, working for Royal Brierley, were keen to experiment with new, modern Art Deco forms and styles seen in Scandinavian glass of the period, creating strongly modern designs.

■ The 1934 'Modern Art for The Table' exhibition held at Harrods showcased many new designs and was to become a major influence on designers such as W. Clyne Farquharson and William Wilson during the 1930s, but also during the 1950s. Here, the influences mentioned above, combined with a post-war optimistic move towards modernity, influenced designers such as John Luxton, Geoffrey Baxter and Irene Stevens. Nevertheless the movement was not widely popular and makers soon reverted to traditional styles.

■ This is still a new collecting area and is just beginning to receive the attention it deserves. Look for the 1930s-1950s work of key factories such as Stuart & Sons, Walsh Walsh and Webb Corbett. Also consider the design, which should be modern and strikingly cut. Circular 'lenses', clean, often deeply-cut, lines and stylized natural motifs are typical features. Condition is important and liming, chips and scratches devalue examples.

A late 1940s Edinburgh & Leith cut glass vase, with panels of mitre-cut stylized grasses, marked "E & L made in Scotland".

6.5in (16.5cm) high

£200-300   **JH**

A 1930s John Walsh Walsh cut glass bucket vase, with geometric patterns of ovals and flutes, marked "Walsh Birmingham".

This is one of a few of Walsh Walsh's Art Deco designs not by Clyne Farquarson.

6.5in (16.5cm) high

£240-280   **JH**

A Royal Brierley cut bowl, with mitre, lens and flute cutting, pattern number 68449 and 50.

c1937-38   *8.5in (22cm) high*

£300-400   **JH**

A 1960s Webb Corbett vase, with cut lenses, designed by David Queensbury, known as 'Queensway'.

4.25in (11cm) high

£200-300   **JH**

A Richardson conical footed vase, deeply cut with three jazzy zig-zagging panels between vertical flutes, marked "Richardson".

c1930-33   *8in (20cm) high*

£200-300   **JH**

A Webb Corbett footed vase, designed by Freda M Coleton, with a slice neck above panels of stylized leaves and flutes, pattern number 15344, marked "Webb Corbett".

c1938   *10in (26cm) high*

£300-400   **JH**

A Walsh Walsh clear cut glass biscuit jar, designed by Clyne Farquarson, with cut-leaf pattern, the base acid etched "WALSH ENGLAND" and signed "Clyne Farquarson NRD 39".

c1939   *7in (17.5cm) high*

£60-90   **GC**

A 1950s Thomas Webb & Sons engraved and cut glass footed vase, designed by David Hammond.

9.75in (25cm) high

£300-400   **JH**

COLLECTORS' NOTES

■ Dartington Glass was founded in 1966 in Torrington, Devon by the Dartington Hall Trust, in an attempt to bring work and prosperity to the area. The chief designer was Frank Thrower (1932-87), who had worked alongside Ronald Stennett-Willson (see King's Lynn & Wedgwood in this book) at British importers Wuidart from 1953 to 1960, where he had learnt about Scandinavian designs.

■ The factory initially employed Scandinavian blowers. Tableware dominated output and Thrower was responsible for over 500 designs. A smokey grey known as 'Midnight' was a key colour, with other brighter colours only used in the first few years. Pieces tend to have concave and convex moulded decoration.

■ Thrower's designs have not yet reached the levels of appreciation and value that Geoffrey Baxter's and Stennett-Willson's have, but this may change. Wedgwood acquired 50% of Dartington in 1982 and Thrower continued to design ranges for it until his death in 1987. The company returned to private hands in 1994, primarily producing crystal ware.

A Dartington Kingfisher blue vase, designed by Frank Thrower, shape no. FT88 'Hexagonal', with a moulded square and dot motif.

c1970   *3.25in (8cm) high*

£20-30   **GC**

A 1970s Dartington Kingfisher blue vase, designed by Frank Thrower, with textured square body and plain flared rim.

4in (10cm) high

£20-30   **GC**

A Dartington Kingfisher blue vase, designed by Frank Thrower, shape no. FT56, moulded with circular flowers, diamonds and squares and with a 'hammered finish' effect.

c1970   *5.25in (13.5cm) high*

£20-30   **GC**

A 1970s Dartington 'Hexagonal Nipple Vase', designed by Frank Thrower, shape no. FT95, with a moulded pattern of highly stylised flowers.

c1968   *6in (15cm) high*

£15-20   **GC**

A Dartington 'Greek Key' Midnight grey large vase, with square base, moulded and plain flared rim.

9.75in (24.5cm) high

£60-80   **GC**

A Dartington clear glass tankard, designed by Frank Thrower, shape no. FT1 commemorating the first English penny, with applied, moulded medallion reading "OFFA REX".

1971 4.75in (12cm) high

£20-25   **GC**

A 1970s Dartington Midnight grey medium 'Daisy Vase', designed by Frank Thrower, shape no. FT95.

6in (15cm) high

£25-35   **GC**

A Dartington 'Cylindrical Candleholder', designed by Frank Thrower, shape no. FT141.

This shape was available in different sizes, with larger examples being slightly more valuable.

6in (15cm) high

£8-12   **GC**

COLLECTOR'S NOTES

■ King's Lynn Glass was established in King's Lynn, Norfolk, by Ronald Stennett-Willson in 1967. It produced fine quality tableware and decorative glass along Scandinavian lines and styles. Stennett-Willson had previously gained much experience with Scandinavian factories when working for British importers Wuidart and others in the 1950s and 1960s.

■ The factory enjoyed great success as Scandinavian design was very much in vogue and in 1969 it was acquired by Wedgwood, who continued to use Stennett-Wilson's designs. Colours tend to be either coolly classical or strong. Lines are clean and modern. Candleholders are very popular with collectors and the range, size and colour affect value.

■ In 1982, Wedgwood acquired a controlling 50% stake in Dartington Glass and gained the design impetus of Frank Thrower, who had designed the majority of Dartington's pieces. Tablewares and vases still dominated production. Wedgwood was itself acquired by Caithness in 1988 and the King's Lynn factory closed in 1992. As colour and simple form are so important, the appearance is easily disrupted by chips, scratches and internal liming, so avoid buying these pieces. The market has expanded considerably over the past five years as interest has grown.

A rare 1970s Wedgwood 'Brancaster' light blue candlestick, designed by Ronald Stennett-Willson.

8in (20cm) high

£60-70   **MHT**

Two 1970s Wedgwood 'Sandringham' topaz candlesticks, designed by Ronald Stennett-Willson.

Left: 5in (12.5cm) high

£25-30   **MHT**

Right: 6.5in (16.5cm) high

£35-45   **MHT**

A 1970s Wedgwood 'Sheringham' candlestick, designed by Ronald Stennett-Willson, with nine disc-shaped knops and acid-etched "WEDGWOOD ENGLAND" mark to base.

The Sheringham candlestick was designed with one, two, three, five, seven and nine discs, each of increasingly taller size and greater value, and was produced in up to seven different colours. It was originally designed for King's Lynn Glass and featured in their first catalogue in 1967, also winning a Queen's Award for Industry.

12in (30.5cm) high

£250-300   **JH**

A Wedgwood 'Brancaster' purple candle holder, designed by Ronald Stennett-Willson, with acid etched "WEDGWOOD ENGLAND" mark to base.

c1970   *5.5in (14cm) high*

£25-30   **GC**

A Wedgwood 'Brancaster' dark blue candle holder, designed by Ronald Stennett-Willson, with acid-etched "Wedgwood" mark to base.

These were produced in three different sizes, the largest currently fetching around £70.

c1970   *5.5in (14cm) high*

£25-30   **GC**

A 1970s Wedgwood 'Sheringham' green candlestick, designed by Ronald Stennett-Willson, with two discs.

5in (12.5cm) high

£25-35   **GC**

A 1970s Wedgwood 'Sheringham' blue candlestick, designed by Ronald Stennett-Willson, with three discs.

6in (15.5cm) high

£30-50   **GC**

A 1970s Wedgwood 'Sandringham' pink candlestick, designed by Ronald Stennett-Willson.

7.25in (18.5cm) high

£45-55 **MHT**

A rare 1970s 'Sandringham' green candlestick, by Ronald Stennett-Willson, with bulbous stem, marked "Wedgwood" to base.

Although this piece has a candle holder in the form of an Sheringham candlestick, the bulbous knop is extremely unusual. Featured in the 1967 King's Lynn catalogue, it is pictured next to the Sandringham range and bears shape number 'RSW 152'.

4.5in (11.5cm) high

£50-60 **MHT**

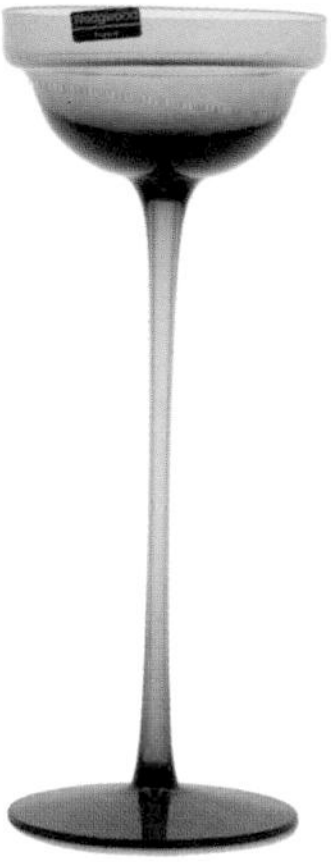

A 1970s Wedgwood 'Cromer' blue candlestick, with acid-etched mark.

8.75in (22cm) high

£40-60 **JH**

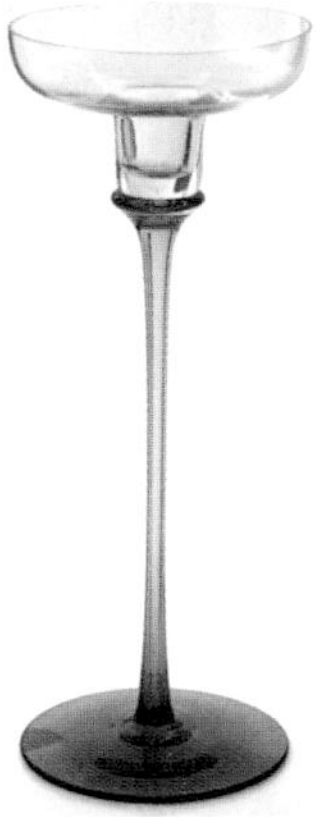

A Wedgwood Topaz and clear glass candlestick, designed by Ronald Stennett-Willson, with acid-etched mark reading "WEDGWOOD ENGLAND".

c1969 9.75in (25cm) high

£80-100 **GC**

A 1970s Wedgwood textured vase, designed by Ronald Stennett-Willson, marked "Wedgwood England" to base.

4.25in (11cm) high

£30-35 **MHT**

A King's Lynn 'Top Hat' vase, designed by Ronald Stennett-Willson.

c1967 8in (20.5cm) high

£70-90 **GC**

A 1970s Wedgwood 'Top Hat' white opal bowl, model number RSW21/1, designed by Ronald Stennett-Willson.

7in (18cm) wide

£65-75 **MHT**

A 1970s Wedgwood topaz and clear glass decanter, designed by Ronald Stennett-Willson.

12.25in (31cm) high

£55-65 **GC**

A rare set of six 'Harlequin' tumblers, designed by Ronald Stennett-Willson for Lemington Glassworks.

Lemington Glassworks was also known as G.E.C. Osram Glassworks and the technology used to produce these was the same used to produce Osram's famous lightbulbs. Stennett-Willson was still working with Wuidart when he designed these glasses.

c1959 3.5in (9cm) high

£100-150 **MHT**

A Wedgwood decanter, produced to commemorate Winston Churchill, with applied blue Jasperware plaque with profile of Winston Churchill, the base acid-etched "WEDGWOOD ENGLAND", designed by Ronald Stennett-Willson.

10.25in (26cm) high

£80-100 **GC**

Three Wedgwood 'Brutus' Midnight grey hexagonal vases, designed by Frank Thrower.
c1982   *tallest 10in (25.5cm) high*

£20-60 each   **GC**

A Wedgwood 'Brutus' Violet hexagonal candlestick, designed by Frank Thrower, with heavy foot.
c1982   8.25in (21cm) high

£15-20   **GC**

A Wedgwood short 'Brutus' Midnight grey vase, designed by Frank Thrower, with Wedgwood plastic factory label.
c1982   5.5in (14cm) high

£15-20   **GC**

A Wedgwood 'Brutus' Midnight grey hexagonal bowl, designed by Frank Thrower.

c1982   4in (10cm) high

£15-20   **GC**

A Wedgwood Midnight grey 'Devon Floral' vase, designed by Frank Thrower, shape no. WFT106, from the 'English County Crystal' series.

The English County Crystal series was designed by Frank Thrower, produced at the Dartington factory but sold under the Wedgwood name between 1984 and 1987. This particular shape was reputedly taken from an earlier design by Thrower for Dartington.

1984-87   8.25in (21cm) h

£25-30   **GC**

A Wedgwood Midnight grey 'Orson' vase, designed by Frank Thrower, from the 'English County Crystal' series.

1982-84   6in (15cm) high

£10-15   **GC**

A Wedgwood Midnight grey vase, designed by Frank Thrower, from the 'English County Crystal' series.

1982-84   3.5in (9cm) high

£10-15   **GC**

A Wedgwood Midnight grey 'Arthur' candle holder with shade, designed by Frank Thrower, from the 'English Country Crystal' series, and a similar taller candleholder without shade.

Note the similarity in form to Stennett-Willson's earlier 'Brancaster' candleholders.

Left: 7.75in (19.5cm) high

LEFT: £25-30 RIGHT: £35-45   **GC**

A Wedgwood Midnight grey 'Grace' candleholder, designed by Frank Thrower, from the 'Devon' range of 'English County Crystal' series, with flared rim.

This shape was only produced in Midnight grey.

9.5in (24cm) high

£15-20   **GC**

COLLECTORS' NOTES

■ Mdina was founded on Malta in 1969 by ex-Royal College of Art tutor Michael Harris. Here he took the new studio glass techniques to a commercial level until 1972 when he left the factory. Pieces tend to reflect the surrounding landscape, such as the blue-green of the sea and the golden tortoiseshell colours of sandy beaches. Most pieces, but not all, are signed 'Mdina'. Pieces signed by Michael Harris from this factory are extremely rare and desirable. As most pieces produced were small targetting the tourist market, large pieces also command a premium.

■ Isle of Wight Studio Glass was founded in 1973 and continues today, although Harris died in 1994. Signed pieces again command a premium due to their rarity. Also look for early ranges such as 'Seaward' and 'Blue Aurene', which are stamped with a stylized 'flame' prunt on the pontil on the base.

■ In 1979 they released their innovative 'Azurene' range developed by William Walker and Michael Harris. The exterior was decorated with gold and silver foil. The colour of the base glass, style of label and finish of the base will help to date a piece. Both factories are becoming considerably more collectable.

A Mdina cased blue and green oviform vase, with an iridescent streak, signed to the base "Mdina".

7.5in (19cm) high

£30-40   PSA

A Mdina glass cased 'axe-head' type vase, signed on the base "Mdina 1984".

This is one of the most typical forms designed by Michael Harris for the Mdina factory, and was produced until recently.

9.25in (23.5cm) high

£100-150   MHC

A rare and exceptionally large 1970s Mdina sand, aquamarine and white cased bulbous glass vase.

Mdina glass is primarily produced as souvenirs for tourists. Large pieces were heavy and difficult to pack into luggage, meaning few large pieces were produced, making this example rare.

7in (18cm) high

£120-180   MHC

A 1970s Mdina glass display goblet, with clear glass stem and foot and craggy knop, the base unsigned.

7.5in (19cm) high

£70-100   MHC

A Mdina blue and green swirled glass footed bowl, signed to the base.

4in (10cm) high

£20-30   GAZE

A rare, large Mdina glass 'knot' type sculpture, signed on the base "Michael Harris Mdina Glass Malta", the date obscured by scratches.

These abstract sculptures were more commonly produced as smaller paperweights, which are usually worth under £40. The rarity, size and fact that it is signed by Michael Harris make this example valuable.

c1970

£300-500

33cm (13in) high

PC

An early Isle of Wight studio glass vase, with an iridescent finish and early rectangular "Handmade Isle of Wight" paper label to base.

3.757in (9.5cm) high

£40-60   **MHC**

An Isle of Wight 'Tortoiseshell' bulbous glass vase, with Isle of Wight 'flame' mark to pontil and triangular Isle of Wight label.

1979   17cm (6.75in) high

£50-80   **TGM**

An early Isle of Wight 'Seaward' glass vase, signed on the base by Michael Harris and with unimpressed 'broken' pontil mark.

This dates from the period after Harris had set up his second factory in 1973, but before he had received his pontil stamp.

c1973   4.25in (11cm) high

£180-220   **TGM**

An Isle of Wight 'Tortoiseshell' glass bowl, with 'flame' pontil mark.

1973-79 5.25in (13.5cm) wide

£30-40   **TGM**

An Isle of Wight studio glass 'Black Azurene' spherical glass vase.

6in (15cm) tall

£50-80   **EAB**

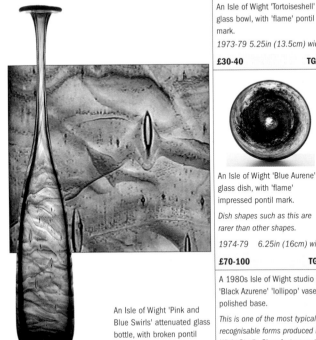

An Isle of Wight 'Blue Aurene' glass dish, with 'flame' impressed pontil mark.

Dish shapes such as this are rarer than other shapes.

1974-79   6.25in (16cm) wide

£70-100   **TGM**

A 1980s Isle of Wight 'Blue Azurene' 'lollipop' glass vase, with gold and silver foil decoration and polished base.

6.25in (15.5cm) high

£50-70   **TGM**

An Isle of Wight 'Pink and Blue Swirls' attenuated glass bottle, with broken pontil mark.

c1973-74   15.25in (39cm) high

£80-120   **PC**

A 1980s Isle of Wight studio glass 'Black Azurene' 'lollipop' vase and polished base.

This is one of the most typical and recognisable forms produced by Isle of Wight Studio Glass factory and is derived from Michael Harris' designs for Mdina.

8.25in (21cm) high

£60-90   **EAB**

COLLECTORS' NOTES

■ Monart was produced by the Moncrieff Glassworks of Perth, Scotland. Designs were produced from 1924 by Spanish glassmaker Salvador Ysart and his son Paul who had both joined the factory in 1921. They were shortly to be followed by Salvador's other sons Antoine, Augustine and Vincent. Over 300 free-blown shapes were inspired by Oriental forms including vases, bowls, lamps and perfume bottles.

■ Shapes were simple to show off the cloudy, mottled effects of the glass which were created by rolling the glass gather in enamel powder. The effect achieved was almost that of glazes on Chinese ceramics. Look out for 'Paisley Shawl' examples where the enamel colours were pulled into curling 'S' shapes. Production never exceeded 10% of the Moncrieff factory output and ended in 1961. Often covered with a paper label, pontil marks, and sometimes the rim of the foot, are polished flat on Monart, which distinguishes it from its later cousins, produced under the names 'Vasart' and 'Strathearn'.

A Monart baluster glass vase, the mottled yellow and orange body with green, amethyst and aventurine inclusions to the rim, bears paper label, "No.JJ.VI+".

10in (25cm) high 7.5in (19cm) high

£120-180 L&T

A Monart glass beaker vase, with red and orange mottled body.

5.25in (13cm) high

£40-60 L&T

A Monart glass vase, of bulbous tapering form with cylindrical neck, the mottled orange body with amethyst inclusions to the rim.

8.75in (22cm) high

£250-350 L&T

A Monart glass vase, with a straw or yellow swirled body and polychrome rim.

c1924-61   4in (10cm) high

£120-140 NBEN

A Monart glass vase, with yellow abstract design with polished pontil mark.

8.25in (21cm) high

£150-250 B&H

One of a pair of Monart ovoid glass vases, each having mottled green bodies with aventurine and amethyst inclusions to the rim, both baring paper labels "No. VII.A.162".

6.75in (17cm) high

£200-300 pair L&T

A Monart glass vase, of baluster form, with green mottled decoration, bearing original paper label and mark "SA. VI".

8in (20.5cm) high

£180-220 HAMG

A Vasart glass posy basket, mottled turquoise and green, with flared rim and handle formed by pulling the rim.

8.5in (21cm) high

£30-50 L&T

COLLECTORS' NOTES

■ Although associated with glassmaking since the 14th century, glass design on the island of Murano underwent a rebirth in the 1950s that took them far away from the intricate confections of previous years. Designs became more modern, with clean lines, bright colours and an exuberance quite unlike anything that had been seen before.

■ Key designers leading this movement included Paolo Venini, Fulvio Bianconi, Dino Martens, Gio Ponti and Carlo Scarpa. Their designs are much sought-after, and as such are often highly priced. The popularity of their pioneering work led to designs and styles being copied and imitated amongst the large number of factories on the island, mainly to fuel the burgeoning tourist market. Many of these generic pieces are eminently affordable today.

■ The 'sommerso' (submerged) technique was popular and large, coloured pieces with pulled rims can fetch high prices. Many are not signed, although identifying a known maker or designer will add value. Compare style, technique, form and colour to examples in reference books to help you identify makers or designers. Condition is important, especially for more common, mass-produced pieces, so avoid scratched or chipped glass.

A 1950s Murano glass dish, with colourful millefiori canes in yellow glass and original Seguso label.

4.5in (11.5cm) diam

£35-45 AG

A 1950s Italian glass tray, in cream glass set with murrines.

10in (25.5cm) wide

£20-30 BB

A 1950s Murano ruby glass dish, probably by A.V.E.M. from the 'Bizzantina' range, with silver, coloured and twisted cane inclusions.

6.25in (16cm) diam

£45-55 AG

A 1950s Murano emerald green glass bowl, possibly by A.V.E.M., with murrine and aventurine inclusions, two indents.

5.5in (14cm) diam

£25-35 AG

A 1950s Murano glass ashtray, in blue and gold bullicante.

This ashtray was from the Hotel Excelsior Palace, Venice.

4in (10cm) wide

£25-35 AG

A 1950s Murano glass ashtray, by Toso, in blue and clear glass.

4.25in (11cm) wide

£35-45 P&I

A 1950s Murano square glass ashtray, by Toso, in blue, green and clear glass.

4.25in (11cm) wide

£50-60 P&I

A 1950s Murano glass dish, by Cenedese, in red, orange and clear glass.

7in (18cm) wide

£60-80 P&I

A 1950s Murano glass ashtray, by Seguso, in yellow, green and turquoise.

6in (15cm) wide

£55-65 P&I

A pair of Murano glass ashtrays, pink with gold leaf inclusions, ribbing and folded rims.

4.5in (11.5cm) wide

£50-60 AG

A 1950s Murano glass clover leaf bowl, by Seguso.

10in (25.5cm) diam

£80-120 AG

A late 1960s/early 1970s Murano heavily cased 'Sommerso' glass ashtray.

5.75in (14.5cm) wide

£40-60 P&I

A 1960s Murano triple-cased 'Sommerso' glass ashtray with faceted sides

Such facet-sided vases and ashtrays were popular in the 1960s, and a large number were sold. Always examine the edges and corners for chips as this detracts from the optical, reflective effect created by the facets.

4in (10cm) high

£80-120 DTC

A 1960s Murano double-cased glass ashtray with faceted sides.

The shape of the aperture indicates that this ashtray would originally have held a lighter.

4in (10cm) high

£80-120 DTC

An early 1970s Murano heavily cased glass vase, grey and clear with textured sides.

The combination of the Sommerso and textured techniques used here recalls Scandinavian designs.

5in (12.5cm) high

£45-55 P&I

A late 1960s/early 1970s Murano heavily cased tall glass vase, amethyst and clear with textured sides.

7in (18cm) high

£60-80 P&I

A 1950s Murano 'Sommerso' glass vase, red and yellow cased in clear glass, with original label.

Although the strong colour and technique is typical of Murano, the organic bud-like form echoes the work of Holmegaard designer Per Lütken in the late 1950s and early 1960s.

4.5in (11.5cm) high

£55-65 AG

A Murano teal and red glass vase, with spherical base and collared neck, unmarked but with gilt label for Bucella Cristalli, Murano.

7in (17.5cm) high

£180-220   **TA**

A Murano glass circular pillow vase, with yellow, blue and clear glass in plaid pattern, unmarked but similar to designs by Ludovico Diaz de Santillana for Venini.

c1963   9.5in (24cm) high

£100-150   **TA**

A rare 'cherry' murrine vase, designed and made by Vittorio Ferro at the Fratelli Toso factory.

Showing the skill of Ferro as a glassmaster, these murrines are technically extremely competent and have not been repeated. These murrines can be found used in paperweights, but rarely vases, making this example one of a handful known to collectors.

1950-70   8in (20.5cm) high

£3,500-4,500   **PC**

A rare 'flower' murrine vase, designed and made by Vittorio Ferro at the Fratelli Toso factory.

Murrine decoration uses small coloured tiles or 'tesserae', made by cutting long glass rods, with internal decoration, into thin sections. These are then laid down in a pattern and 'picked up' by rolling a hot gather of molten glass over the mosaic. This vase uses five different types of murrine. Each acts differently when heated and cooling, contracting or expanding. As a result, distinct open gaps can be felt between the columns of murrines, and sometimes between the murrines themselves.

1950-70   6.25in (16cm) high

£1,200-1,800   **PC**

A Venini 'a canne' glass vase, with alternating broad red and blue vertical stripes with clear glass, unmarked.

9in (22.5cm) high

£220-280   **TA**

A Venini Verticali 'Tasce' carafe, designed by Gio Ponti, with an acid stamp for 'Venini Murano'.

1955   10in (25cm) high

£400-600   **AL**

A CLOSER LOOK AT A MURRINE VASE

The factory, style and design of the murrines reflect the rarity and value of a piece – this was made by Fratelli Toso, renowned for their historic murrine designs.

These murrines were designed for use on a small series of vases made to commemorate the life and work of designer and factory owner Ermanno Toso upon his death in 1973.

As well as being complex, these murrines are extremely rare. Very few vases were made incorporating them.

'San Nicolo' is the patron saint of glassmakers, hence the name of this vase.

An extremely rare Fratelli Toso 'San Nicolo' vase.

1973   7in (18cm) high

£4,000-6,000   **PC**

A CLOSER LOOK AT A MURANO VASE

This vase is typical of the exuberance of many 1950s Muranese glass designs, with bright clashing colours and irregular modern forms. _____

Dating from c1949, this vase can be considered a forerunner of the revolution in the 1950s which brought Murano worldwide fame in the mid- to late 20thC. _____

Dino Martens (1894-1970) is particularly renowned for his 'painterly' style. His innovative designs were considered shocking at the time. _____

This vase retains its original label from the Aurellano Toso factory. _____

A Murano glass vase, designed by Dino Martens, made by Aureliano Toso, with original label.

c1949   12.25in (30.5cm) high

£1,800-2,200   FIC

A 1950s Italian glass vase, of baluster form with frilled rim, opaque and blue spiral inclusions and etched marks.

10in (24cm) high

£70-100   L&T

A Murano opaque glass vase, of hour-glass form, maker's label attached.

12in (30.5cm) high

£40-60   GAZE

A Giulio Biancholli heavy clear glass triangular vase, with etched signature and date.

1999   10in (25cm) wide

£450-550   TA

A 1960s Murano 'pinnacolo' glass bud vase, designed by Luciano Gaspari for Saluti, in amethyst, turquoise and clear glass.

13.75in (35cm) high

£70-100   P&I

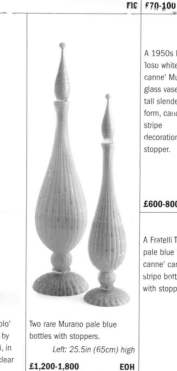

Two rare Murano pale blue bottles with stoppers.

Left: 25.5in (65cm) high

£1,200-1,800   EOH

Right: 20.5in (52cm) high

£800-1,200   EOH

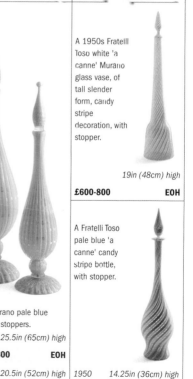

A 1950s Fratelli Toso white 'a canne' Murano glass vase, of tall slender form, candy stripe decoration, with stopper.

19in (48cm) high

£600-800   EOH

A Fratelli Toso pale blue 'a canne' candy stripe bottle, with stopper.

1950   14.25in (36cm) high

£500-600   EOH

A 1950s Barbini footed glass jar with lid, the orange glass with internal gold foil inclusions and trails of spots.

13.75in (35cm) high

£800-1,200 **EOH**

A selection of Italian cased wine glasses.

6.75in (17cm) high

£20-30 each **EOH**

Two Italian cased purple wine glasses.

Left: 9.5in (24cm) high

£30-40

Right: 8.25in (21cm) high

£20-30 **EOH**

One of six Italian caramel cased glasses, with pitcher.

pitcher 10.25in (26cm) high

£200-300 set **EOH**

A pair of 1950s Murano 'Sommerso' swans, in cobalt blue with air bubbles encased in clear glass.

Novelty designs such as these swans and the figures on this page have been produced in their millions by a number of factories on Murano, mostly to feed a growing tourist market. Value largely depends on the maker or designer (if known) and the quality of the design and workmanship.

7.5in (19cm) high

£80-120 **AG**

A 1950s Murano glass wild boar figure, by V. Nason and Co., in grey and clear glass, with sticker.

5.25in (13.5cm) wide

£30-40 **P&I**

An early 1960s Cesare Toso moulded mauve glass figure of a little girl, in the style of Mabel Lucy Attwell.

4in (10cm) high

£12-18 **AG**

An unusual Seguso free-form glass sculpture, of spiralling serpentine form, signed on edge "Seguso Arte" and "Seguso Murano" on base.

£400-500 **DN**

A pair of 1950s Venetian glass figures, in the form of a Regency couple, some restoration.

gent 11.5in (29.5cm) high

£100-170 **GMW**

A 1950s Murano glass fish figure, signed "Franco Bottaro, Murano" on the base.

5in (13cm) high

£30-40 **P&I**

FIND OUT MORE...

'DK Collectors Guide: 20th Century Glass', *by Judith Miller, published by Dorling Kindersley, 2004.*

'Murano Magic', *by Carl T. Gable, published by Schiffer Publishing, 2004.*

COLLECTORS' NOTES

■ Founded in 1825 on the Danish island of Zealand. Jacob Bang (1899-1965) was the first to bring modern designs to the company when he joined in 1927. He was succeeded by Per Lütken (1916-98) in 1941, whose cool-coloured, thick-walled and small vases in greys and blues are often signed on the base with the company name, his initials and a date. Forms tend to be organic with bud-like or teardrop shapes focusing on the plasticity of the material. Avoid scratched or chipped examples as these detract from the purity of colour and the form.

■ Lütken was also responsible for the 'Pop' inspired 'Carnaby' range of the 1960s and 1970s, which went to the other pole in terms of colours and form – being bright and largely geometric. The series was mould blown and opaque with a white interior layer and shares similarities with the 'Palet' range designed by Jacob Bang's son, Michael between 1968 and 1976. First admired by interior decorators, these pieces are now being collected. The Kastrup factory merged with Holmegaard in 1965 enabling production to be expanded to meet demand.

A pair of Danish Holmegaard red cased candlesticks/vases, from the 'Carnaby' range, designed by Per Lütken.

8in (20cm) high

£150-170   **RWA**

A pair of 1960s Danish Holmegaard candlesticks, from the 'Carnaby' range, designed by Per Lütken, one with original paper label.

6in (15.5cm) high

£150-200   **RWA**

A 1970s Danish Holmegaard red cased 'Gulvase', designed by Otto Brauer in 1962, based on a design by Per Lütken from 1958.

This is arguably the most popular colour for this shape, with the cased opaque version shown here being more valuable and desirable than the transparent coloured versions. Larger sizes command higher values, and were designed to sit on the floor rather than on a table or shelf.

17.75in (45cm) high

£550-650   **EOH**

A small Danish Holmegaard red cased vase, from the 'Carnaby' range.

6in (15cm) high

£180-220   **EOH**

A small Danish Kastrup & Holmegaard red cased vase, with straight sides, from the 'Palet' line by Michael Bang.

1968-76   *6.25in (16cm) high*

£180-220   **EOH**

A Danish Holmegaard blue cased 'Gulvase', designed Otto Brauer.

c1962   *14.5in (37cm) high*

£400-500   **EOH**

A Danish Holmegaard blue cased spherical vase, with short neck and collar, probably designed by Per Lütken, unmarked.

5in (13cm) high

£75-90   **RWA**

A Danish Holmegaard 'Gulvase' green cased vase, from the 'Palet' range, designed by Michael Bang, unmarked.

£150-200   **RWA**

A Danish Holmegaard yellow cased waisted vase, from the 'Carnaby' line.

8in (20cm) high

£100-150 EOH

A 1960s Danish Holmegaard clear cased white shaped vase, probably from the 'Palet' range, by Michael Bang.

8.75in (22cm) high

£120-180 RWA

A Danish Holmegaard clear Capri Blue pin-blown vase, designed by Per Lütken, with small opening.

6.25in (16cm) high

£180-220 EOH

A Danish Holmegaard clear Antique Green vase, designed by Per Lütken, with small lip.

8.75in (22cm) high

£400-500 EOH

A 1950s Danish Holmegaard clear Aqua pin-blown elliptical bowl, designed by Per Lütken.

4.75in (12cm) high

£200-250 EOH

A 1950s Danish Holmegaard clear Aqua heart-shaped vase, designed by Per Lütken.

7in (18cm) high

£250-350 EOH

A Kastrup opaline and cane pitcher and glasses, by Jacob E. Bang.

c1960 *pitcher 8.75in (22cm) high*

£280-320 EOH

A limited edition Danish Holmegaard 'Four Seasons' glass disk for 'Spring', designed by Per Lütken.

Released in 1976 to commemorate the 150th anniversary of the Holmegaard factory in an edition of 2,500.

£200-250 RWA

A 1960s Danish Holmegaard light blue suncatcher, with three moulded swirls.

7in (18cm) high

£12-18 RWA

A 1960s Finnish Riihimaën Lasi Oy cased red vase.

Founded in 1910 in Finland, the factory became known as Riihimaën Lasi Oy in 1937 and was known for producing domestic and industrial glass. During the late 1930s and 1940s talented new designers joined including Helena Tynell, Nanny Still, Aimo Okkolin and Tamara Aladin. Their designs of the 1950s and 1960s are typically strong in colour, cased and mould blown – often with strongly linear, geometric forms. Pieces appeal to the wide base of those interested in interior or Scandinavian design.

10in (25.5m) high

£30-50　　　　　　　　**JH**

A Finnish Riihimaën Lasi Oy tapering rocket-shaped cased red glass vase, designed by Aimo Okkolin.

c1970　9.25in (23.5cm) high

£35-40　　　　　　　**GC**

A Finnish Riihimaën Lasi Oy cased red glass vase, designed by Aimo Okkolin.

c1970　9.25in (23.5cm) high

£32-38　　　　　　　**GC**

A Finnish Riihimaën Lasi Oy cased green waisted glass vase, designed by Aimo Okkolin.

c1970　9.25in (23.5cm) high

£25-35　　　　　　　**GC**

A Finnish Riihimaën Lasi Oy blue mould-blown vase, designed by Nanny Still, unmarked.

£50-80　　　　　　　**RWA**

A Finnish Riihimaën Lasi Oy cased blue glass tapering vase, designed by Aimo Okkolin.

c1970　7.25in (18.5cm) high

£30-40　　　　　　　**GC**

A Finnish Riihimaën Lasi Oy pressed glass sunbottle, designed by Helena Tynell.

This design was produced in four different sizes and in six colours.

c1967-74　5in (13cm) high

£45-55　　　　　　　**RWA**

A Finnish Riihimaën Lasi Oy mould-blown green cased vase, designed by Tamara Aladin.

10.75in (27.5cm) high

£50-80　　　　　　　**RWA**

GLASS

A Flygfors 'Coquille' glass basket, in pink and white, signed to base.

6.25in (16cm) high

£35-45 **GAZE**

A Hyllinge glass vase, of ovoid form, designed by Bengt Orup, decorated with black specks, signed to base, with sticker on side.

£20-30 **GAZE**

A 1960s Boda bottle, designed by Eric Hogland, from the 'People' series, mould blown green glass, with cork stopper.

Hogland's designs for Boda are known for their 'primitive' feel and appearance and are typically produced in thickly rendered green, orange or red glass.

10.75in (25cm) high

£80-120 **JH**

A 1950s Ekenas green glass vase, designed by John Orwar Lake.

Little is known about the Ekenas factory and its chief designer and art director John Orwar Lake, but vases such as these with applied moulded bands or ribbons are typical.

5.5in (14cm) high

£40-60 **MHC**

A Humppila cased vase of attenuated waisted form, with spiral internal decoration, signed "Humppila" to the base.

c1958   12.5in (31.5cm) high

£160-180 **MHT**

A 1950s Iittala vase, designed by Tapio Wirkkala, with organic form, pulled rim and thickly rendered body, cut with lines.

4in (10cm) high

£100-120 **JH**

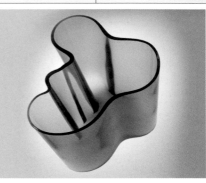

An Iittala 'Savoy' green glass vase, designed by Alvar Aalto, of waved organic cylindrical form, with etched marks.

This vase by world-renowned architect and designer Alvar Aalto (1898-1976) has been in continuous production since its introduction in 1937. It was designed for the Savoy Hotel in Helsinki, also designed by Aalto.

£300-400 **L&T**

A CLOSER LOOK AT A SCANDINAVIAN VASE

This vase was designed by Tapio Wirkkala, one of the leading exponents of Finnish glass design, and among the most influential of all 20thC designers.

It is signed on the base "TAPIO WIRKKALA 3729".

The form and texture shows Wirkkala's interest in the Scandinavian landscape that surrounded him – he was influenced by the textures and appearances of bark and ice.

It is in excellent condition with no damage, polished repairs and has a good variation of textures.

An Iittala textured glass 'Iceberg' vase, designed by Tapio Wirkkala and signed on the base.

6.5in (16.5cm) high

£75-85 **GC**

An Iittala 'Arkipelago' series glass vase, designed by Timo Sarpeneva.

c1978   *5in (13cm) high*

£25-40   **GAZE**

A large Kosta glass sculpture, signed "Goran Warff, Sweden".

£25-40   **GAZE**

A Kosta Boda cased glass vase, designed by Goran Warff, with blue and green interior layers, etched signature and number, and Kosta Boda label.

Warff first worked for Kosta between 1964 and 1975 and then from 1985 to the present. His wife, Ann, worked for Kosta between 1964 and 1978.

9.5in (24cm) high

£200-250   **TA**

A Kosta clear glass decanter, with suspended bubble decoration to base and stopper, marks to base.

15in (38cm) high

£20-30   **GAZE**

A Nuutajärvi Notsjö vase, designed by Kaj Franck, the body decorated with diagonal cut lines, dated.

1953   *3.25in (8cm) high*

£120-140   **JH**

A handmade Kosta Boda tall glass bottle, signed "K. Engmann".

15in (38cm) high

£60-90   **GAZE**

A Kosta cased glass vase, by Vicke Lindstrand, of swollen and waisted shape with inset canes, etched mark.

12.25in (31cm) high

£80-120   **GORL**

A 1960s Magnor clear and yellow cased bowl.

Magnor was founded in Norway in 1896 close to the Swedish border and continues to produce glass today.

15in (38cm) wide

£35-45   **MHT**

A 1960s Nuutajärvi Notsjö cased blue vase, designed by Kaj Franck, with small clear glass foot.

12in (30cm) high

£280-320   **JH**

A Strombergshyttan brown tinged glass vase, designed by Edvard Stromberg.

1930s-50s.   *8.25in (21cm) high*

£75-85   **GC**

A set of four Nuutajärvi Notsjö blue goblets, designed by Kaj Franck, with etched marks.

1962-64   *6.5in (16.5cm) wide*

£120-180   **DRA**

A Skruf hexagonal textured and polished vase, designed by Bengt Edenfalk, with abstract decoration and signed "Skruf Edenfalk".

c1974   *8.25in (21cm) high*

£90-100   **MHT**

An Orrefors heavy glass inkwell.

2.5in (6.5cm) high

£20-30   **AG**

A CLOSER LOOK AT A SWEDISH VASE

This vase was made at the Swedish Strombergshyttan, the company founded by Gerda and Edvard Stromberg after they left the Eda glassworks in 1933.

Stromberg designs are often confused with Orrefors, especially when they are engraved with patterns – however, the rims, heavy walls and bases are different.

A Stromberg elliptical vase.

£200-300

It has a typically thick body and a boldly square-cut and polished rim indicating it was designed by Gerda Stromberg.

The colour is austere and cool recalling ice, and was developed by the Strombergs' son Eric along with similar pale colours that typify the factory.

7in (18cm) high

EOH

A 'Bamboo' mould-blown blue cased white vase, from an unknown factory and designer.

8.5in (21.5cm) high

£35-45   **RWA**

Two Stromberg ice-buckets, with Danish sterling silver handles.

Left: 6in (15cm) high, Right: 4.75in (12cm) high

LEFT: £800-1,200 RIGHT: £700-900   **EOH**

A Stromberg thick walled tapering smokey glass vase, engraved with a fish swimming around pond weed.

6in (15cm) high

£30-50   **GC**

COLLECTORS' NOTES

■ Founded in the 17th century and known as James Powell & Sons from 1834 until 1962, Whitefriars became known for its appealing art glass from the early 20th century. Peaking in popularity around the 1910s-1930s and from the 1950s-1970s, the factory closed in 1980 due to the difficult economic climate.

■ In 1954 a talented young designer, Geoffrey Baxter, was employed and injected new impetus into the factory's designs. Key themes for forms and shapes were asymmetric organic shapes, often with pulled rims or knobbles, gently curved and cased designs and fashionable modern shapes with textured surface effects.

■ Colour varied from the fashionably psychedelic and bright, such as 'tangerine', to a number of subtle colours such as 'sea green'. It was either employed in pure, resonant and saturated tones in line with Scandinavian styles, often also being cased, or streaked through a piece.

■ Textured glass was popular during the 1960s and 1970s and Baxter was heavily inspired by natural forms and patterns, as seen in the cylindrical 'bark' effect vases as well as man-made forms, such as the 'drunken bricklayer' vases.

■ When buying textured glass, aim to buy pieces with excellent variation in texture. The texture on the iron moulds became worn after periods of use so pieces with varied texture were made early on and adhere to the intended design better.

■ Examine clear glass pieces for scratches that detract from the purity of the coloured glass and look at textured pieces for smoothed-off areas that may indicate polished out damage.

A Whitefriars green drape vase.

Although designed during the 1920s, this vase was produced from then until the 1970s.

c1920-70   12.25in (31cm) high

£60-80   **JH**

A large Whitefriars 'Antique' green and clear streaky vase.

c1954   9in (23cm) high

£100-150   **TCS**

A Whitefriars 'Antique' brick vase.

c1954   9in (23cm) high

£100-140   **TCS**

A Whitefriars emerald cased ovoid teardrop-shaped lamp, with original metal fitting.

c1960   11.5in (29cm) high

£50-70   **TCS**

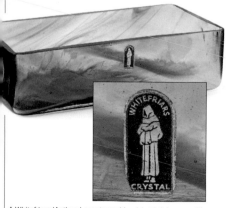

A Whitefriars 'Antique' sanctuary-blue lying brick vase, with Whitefriars label showing the factory logo.

c1954

9in (23cm) long

£150-200   **TCS**

A Whitefriars dark brown glass teardrop-shaped lamp.

This non-standard colour may have been specially made for Heals and was a revival of a colour used by Whitefriars (then known as James Powell & Sons) at the turn of the 20th century.

c1957   11.5in (29cm) high

£60-80   **TCS**

GLASS

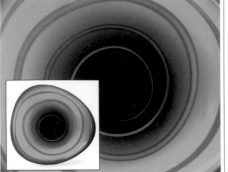

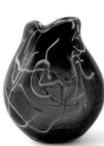

A Whitefriars blue triangular bowl, designed by Geoffrey Baxter, with white enamel snake decoration, pattern no. 9570.

The asymmetrical, organic form of this bowl is typically 1950s, whilst the 'vortex' pattern hints at the approaching psychedelia of the Sixties.

c1961   11.5in (29cm) diam

£280-320   TCS

A Whitefriars blue ovoid vase, designed by Geoffrey Baxter, with pinched lip and random white enamel lines, pattern no. 9577.

c1961   6in (15cm) high

£180-220   TCS

A Whitefriars shadow-green, concave-sided vase, designed by Geoffrey Baxter, mould blown, pattern no. 9638.

c1963   7.5in (19cm) high

£60-80   TCS

A Whitefriars midnight blue vase, designed by Geoffrey Baxter, mould blown, with white enamel decoration, pattern no. 9639.

c1963   7in (18cm) high

£120-180   TCS

A 1960s Whitefriars green optical ribbed bowl, designed by Geoffrey Baxter.

7.5in (19cm) high

£120-140   MHT

A Whitefriars cinnamon 'ham bone' vase, pattern no. 9656.

c1967   6in (15cm) high

£35-55   GAZE

A Whitefriars blue 'Knobbly Glass' vase.

9.5in (24cm) high

£30-45   GAZE

A Whitefriars 'Knobbly Glass' vase, with green streaked decoration.

5.5in (14cm) high

£35-55   GAZE

A Whitefriars 'Knobbly Glass' vase, with streaked decoration.

9.5in (24cm) high

£30-45   GAZE

A CLOSER LOOK AT A WHITEFRIARS GLASS VASE

Due to the complex manufacturing process, the Peacock range was expensive to make and was only made for a couple of years.

The hand applied strapping is random, making each piece unique.

The design was influenced by the growing studio glass movement.

Pieces from this range are usually signed 'Whitefriars' and dated on the base.

A Whitefriars 'Peacock' Studio range tall cylinder vase, designed by Peter Wheeler, with silver nitrate random strapwork on gold rim, signed and dated 1969, pattern no. S6.

1969   *9.5in (24cm) high*

£800-1,000   **TCS**

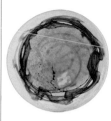

A Whitefriars 'Peacock' Studio range platter, designed by Peter Wheeler, with petrol green centre and random gold strapwork boarder, pattern no. S14.

c1969   *12in (30.5cm) diam*

£350-450   **TCS**

A Whitefriars Studio range orange twilight cased circular platter, with white enamel interior, surface bubbles, pattern no. S14.

c1969   *12in (30.5cm) diam*

£100-150   **TCS**

A large Whitefriars Studio range barrel vase, designed by Peter Wheeler, orange over white lining, pattern no. S6.

Peter Wheeler was a young art-school graduate who worked briefly at Whitefriars during 1969. Designing the 'Studio' range, his designs are typified by strong colours and overlays.

1969   *10in (25.5cm) high*

£300-400   **TCS**

A Whitefriars tangerine 'Drunken Bricklayer' vase, pattern number 9673.

c1969   *8.25in (21cm) high*

£60-100   **GAZE**

A medium-sized Whitefriars kingfisher blue bark log vase, designed by Geoffrey Baxter, pattern no. 9690.

c1969   *7.5in (19cm) high*

£20-30   **TCS**

A Whitefriars tangerine bark-textured cylindrical vase, pattern number 9690.

c1969   7.5in (19cm) high

£20-30   **GAZE**

A large Whitefriars meadow-green bark log vase, designed by Geoffrey Baxter, pattern no. 9691.

c1969   9in (23cm) high

£70-90   **TCS**

A large Whitefriars aubergine bark log vase, designed by Geoffrey Baxter, pattern no. 9691.

c1969   9in (23cm) high

£70-100   **TCS**

A Whitefriars sage textured cased 'Coffin' vase, designed by Geoffrey Baxter, pattern no. 9686.

c1969   6in (15cm) high

£40-60   **TCS**

A small Whitefriars pewter grey bark log vase, designed by Geoffrey Baxter, pattern no. 9689.

c1971   6in (15cm) high

£15-20   **TCS**

A rare Whitefriars 'Cirrus' asymmetric vase, designed by Geoffrey Baxter, pattern no. 9887.

This vase was made in the last year of production, and Baxter was particularly pleased that the neck of each of the vases was uniquely formed.

c1980   9.5in (24cm) high

£150-200   **TCS**

A Whitefriars arctic-blue penguin, designed and blown by Vicente Boffo.

Experienced Italian glass artist Vicente Boffo and his son Ettore helped Michael Harris found Mdina glass on Malta from 1967.

c1962   6.5in (16.5cm) high

£280-320   **TCS**

A low Whitefriars lilac textured candle holder, designed by Geoffrey Baxter, pattern no. 9733.

c1971   2in (5cm) high

£20-30   **TCS**

A Whitefriars cased lobed glass bud vase.

c1980   9.5in (24cm) high

£15-25   **GAZE**

COLLECTORS' NOTES

■ Born in 1907, Alexander Hardie Williamson studied textiles at the Royal College of Art in London. This training influenced his designs for surface patterns, for which he is particularly noted. During the 1930s he had designed press-moulded glass for Bagley of Knottingley but in 1944 he joined United Glass, where he remained as designer until his retirement in 1974. Hardie Williamson died in 1994.

■ Patterns are typically three dimensional, colourful and screen-printed with styles typical of the period. His designs were mass-produced on factory-made glassware and found their way into a huge number of fashionably 'modern' post war homes of the 1950s and 1960s. From 1956 he designed for Sherdley, which became known as Ravenhead in 1964. In total he was responsible for over 1,711 designs in styles to suit every taste and occasion – meaning there is great scope for the collector today.

■ 'Conical' is the most common glass shape. The barrel shaped 'Chubbie', and 'Chunkie' with its tapered base are both slightly rarer. The rarest form is 'Gaytime', with a gold rim. His designs were not considered collectable until the mid-1990s when both a Broadfield House exhibition and the 'Austerity To Affluence' exhibition at the Fine Arts Society in London featured his work. Now collectors are beginning to re-appraise his work and values are starting to rise. As his glasses were mass-produced, always aim to buy in the best condition possible.

A Sherdley 'Festival' pattern Conical tumbler, designed by Alexander Hardie Williamson.

This was produced in two colourways (red as shown here and blue) for the Festival of Britain in 1959.

1959   4.75in (12cm) high

£4-5   **EWC**

A Sherdley 'Festival' pattern Conical tumbler, designed by Alexander Hardie Williamson.

1959   4.75in (12cm) high

£4-5   **EWC**

A Sherdley 'Skylon' pattern Conical tumbler, designed by Alexander Hardie Williamson.

This was from a series produced to commemorate the Festival of Britain. It features the shape of the famed 'Skylon' monument in the pattern.

1959

£4-5   **EWC**

A Sherdley 'Lotus' pattern Conical tumbler, designed by Alexander Hardie Williamson.

1959   4.75in (12cm) high

£4-5   **EWC**

A Sherdley 'Clematis' pattern Conical glass, designed by Alexander Hardie Williamson.

1959   5in (12.5cm) high

£4-5   **EWC**

A Sherdley 'Cocktail Party' shot glass, designed by Alexander Hardie Williamson.

This was one of the very few Conical designs to be made in a smaller size.

3.25in (8.5cm) high

£7-8   **EWC**

A Sherdley 'Chubbie' tumbler, designed by Alexander Hardie Williamson, with blue leaf pattern.

4.5in (11.5cm) high

£8-10   **EWC**

A Sherdley 'Chinese Lantern' Slim Jim, designed by Alexander Hardie Williamson.

1964   5.75in (14.5cm) high

£5-7   **EWC**

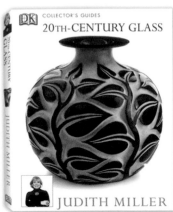

A Ravenhead 'Royalty' Slim Jim, designed by Alexander Hardie Williamson.

1964   5.75in (14.5cm) high

£5-7   EWC

A Ravenhead 'Bamboo' pattern Slim Jim, designed by Alexander Hardie Williamson.

1964   5.75in (14.5cm) high

£5-7   EWC

A 1960s Ravenhead 'Maple' pattern Chunkie tumbler, designed by Alexander Hardie Williamson.

4.5in (11.5cm) high

£8-10   EWC

A Ravenhead 'Gaytime' tumbler, designed by Alexander Hardie Williamson.

With its gold rim, this ultimate party glass is the hardest shape to find. Avoid buying examples with worn gold rims.

£8-10   EWC

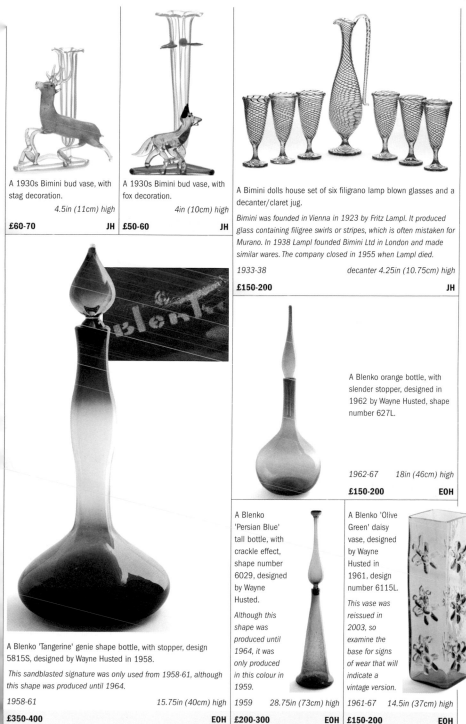

A 1930s Bimini bud vase, with stag decoration.

4.5in (11cm) high

£60-70 JH

A 1930s Bimini bud vase, with fox decoration.

4in (10cm) high

£50-60 JH

A Bimini dolls house set of six filigrano lamp blown glasses and a decanter/claret jug.

Bimini was founded in Vienna in 1923 by Fritz Lampl. It produced glass containing filigree swirls or stripes, which is often mistaken for Murano. In 1938 Lampl founded Bimini Ltd in London and made similar wares. The company closed in 1955 when Lampl died.

1933-38 *decanter 4.25in (10.75cm) high*

£150-200 JH

A Blenko orange bottle, with slender stopper, designed in 1962 by Wayne Husted, shape number 627L.

1962-67 *18in (46cm) high*

£150-200 EOH

A Blenko 'Tangerine' genie shape bottle, with stopper, design 5815S, designed by Wayne Husted in 1958.

This sandblasted signature was only used from 1958-61, although this shape was produced until 1964.

1958-61 *15.75in (40cm) high*

£350-400 EOH

A Blenko 'Persian Blue' tall bottle, with crackle effect, shape number 6029, designed by Wayne Husted.

Although this shape was produced until 1964, it was only produced in this colour in 1959.

1959 *28.75in (73cm) high*

£200-300 EOH

A Blenko 'Olive Green' daisy vase, designed by Wayne Husted in 1961, design number 6115L.

This vase was reissued in 2003, so examine the base for signs of wear that will indicate a vintage version.

1961-67 *14.5in (37cm) high*

£150-200 EOH

GLASS

A Royal Bohemia 'Matches' pattern clear glass ashtray.

1970-72   8in (20cm) long

£20-30   **GC**

A 1960s Royal Bohemia light blue glass vase, designed by Jiri Repasek, with heavy geometric press moulded design.

Royal Bohemia was founded in the 1960s with the merger of a number of Czechoslovakian glassworks. This design is typical of the moulded, textured pieces produced from then until the 1980s. Most examples have square-cut, raised bases and thick walls.

8in (20cm) high

£30-40   **MHC**

A Caithness Twilight Blue bowl, designed by Domhnall O'Broin.

As the glass becomes thinner towards the rim, the glass becomes less vividly blue.

c1965-67   4.25in (11cm) high

£20-25   **GC**

A large 1930s yellow carnival glass tazza table centrepiece, with repeated alternating grape on sycamore leaf and sycamore leaf design.

8.25in (21cm) high

£20-30   **MAC**

An orange carnival glass vase.

10.75in (27.5cm) high

£15-25   **BB**

A Davidson Cloudy amethyst glass candlestick.

c1920   4in (10cm) wide

£12-18   **GKA**

A marigold carnival glass 'Leaf Rays' pattern nappy.

6.75in (17cm) long

£25-35   **BA**

A Hartil glass ashtray or bowl, by Harrachov.

The Hartil art glass range was introduced by the Czechoslovakian Harrachov factory in 1955 and is recognised by its internal fine network of net-like lines. It was designed by Milan Metelak and Milos Pulpitel. Pieces are often mistaken for Murano glass due to their forms.

c1955   4.75in (12cm) wide

£40-60   **JH**

An Imperial purple carnival glass 'Diamond Lace' pattern water pitcher and six beakers.

Created by spraying inexpensively press-moulded glass with metal oxides to achieve the iridescent effect, carnival glass has become extremely popular. This pattern was first seen in The Imperial Glass Co.'s 1909 catalogue in crystal. This set is desirable due to its completeness and excellent level of iridescence. This pitcher is only known in this colour in this pattern.

c1930   pitcher 8.75in (22cm) high

£250-350   **MAC**

A Johann Lötz 'Chiné' footed vase, purple glass with scattered relief string decoration, three clear glass iridescent feet, slight damage.

c1896 7.5in (18.5cm) high

£70-100 FIS

A mid-1950s thick-walled Maastricht vase, with exaggerated freeblown form with vertical spines.

8.25in (21cm) high

£120-180 JH

A Nailsea glass pink and blue pulled trail flask, over an opaque white base.

The Nailsea Glassworks was founded in 1788 in Nailsea, near Bristol. Due to high taxes on flint glass, many factories such as Nailsea used plain bottle or window glass to make decorative objects and decorated them with speckled or trailed opaque white or coloured patterns. Flasks are a common form as are pipes and other functional objects made more decorative due to their rendering in glass. Not all Nailsea pieces were made at Nailsea and the term covers similar glass made around Bristol, the Midlands and Scotland.

c1880 8in (20cm) high

£150-250 AB

A Nailsea glass transparent pink and white flask.

c1880 8.25in (21cm) high

£100-150 AB

A Nailsea glass transparent ruby and clear rolling pin.

c1880 12.5in (31.5cm) l

£120-180 AB

A transparent pink and opaque white pulled trail 'whimsy' pipe.

Whimsical, decorative pieces such as this pipe were made by glassworkers during their breaks and in 'spare' time to display their virtuosity and skill. They come in a variety of shapes and sizes.

c1880 16.25in (41cm) long

£200-300 AB

A mid-19thC hand-finished Nailsea caviar barrel.

This colour is also typical of Nailsea glass, being derived from the colour of the bottle glass used to make it.

4in (10cm) high

£15-25 AG

A cased mottled greeny blue Nazeing glass vase with flared rim.

Founded in 1928 at Broxbourne, Hertfordshire, Nazeing originally produced light bulbs and hanging lamps. In 1935 it began to produce mottled 'Cloud' glass decorative ware, coloured by rolling the gather in powdered enamels. *Production ended in 1939 but was revived after the war until the mid-1950s, with pieces often having a clear, cased base and different colourways.*

4.75in (12cm) high

£25-35 GC

A graduated mottled green Nazeing vase with rounded base and flared rim.

4.75in (12cm) high

£25-35 GC

A 1950s Nazeing cased pink Cloud glass vase, with clear foot and broken pontil mark.

5in (13cm) high

£35-40   **GC**

A 1930s Nazeing speckled white and blue tinged waisted glass vase.

4.75in (12cm) high

£25-35   **GC**

A 1930s Nazeing Cloud pink spherical lampbase, with chrome-plated light fitting.

6.75in (17cm) high

£55-65   **GC**

A Nazeing deep mottled green ashtray, with shaped base.

3.25in (8.5cm) high

£20-25   **GC**

A Stevens and Williams 'Pompeiian Swirl' rose bowl, blue and brown swirls with a box pleated top and chartreuse interior colour.

6.25in (16cm) diam

£1,500-2,000   **JDJ**

A Stevens and Williams swirl vase, amber shading to pink with inverted ruffle top and light blue interior.

5.5in (14cm) wide

£550-650   **JDJ**

A nine-piece tea set, by Schott and Genossen of Jena, Germany, made of heat-resistant borosilicate glass.

By the start of WWII, the town of Jena had become world-renowned for producing extremely fine quality optical glass, particularly that made by lens maker Zeiss, and also laboratory glass. This design, extremely modern for its time, was by Heinz Loffelhardt, one of Germany's leading designers of the period. He was also a student of the notable designer Wilhelm Wagenfeld, a professor of design in Berlin and designer for WMF, who had designed a similar teapot before. The mark on the base shown in the inset thumbnail is shown on a black background for clarity.

c1957   *teapot 5.75in (14.5cm) high*

£100-200   **MHT**

A Stevens and Williams pull-up vase, small amber and white vase with clear amber applied base and decoration, minor chipping to applied amber decoration.

5in (12.5cm) high

£120-180   **JDJ**

A Stevens and Williams green glass vase, designed by Keith Murray, acid-etched mark and signature.

10.5in (26.5cm) high

£400-500   **WW**

A 1960s Strathearn speckled and lime green glass vase, with paper Strathearn sticker.

Strathearn was the final incarnation of the factory and designs that had begun with Monart and continued under Vasart. These almost acid colours are typical of the decade of psychedelia that it was produced in, but hark back to Monart's cloudy, mottled glass of the 1920s and 1930s.

3.75in (9.5cm) high

£20-30　　　　　　TGM

A Walsh Walsh 'Pompeiian' green baluster vase.

The Pompeiian range was introduced in 1929. Formed from glass with random internal bubbles, lower production costs kept the range reasonably priced. Blue, green and amber were the most popular colours, with amethyst, and particularly pink, being slightly rarer as fewer items were produced in these colours.

c1930

9.5in (24cm) high

£120-140　　　　　　GC

A Walsh Walsh 'Pompeiian' light green glass vase.

c1930　　10in (25.5cm) high

£100-150　　　GC

A Walsh Walsh 'Pompeiian' yellow glass spherical vase.

c1930　　5.75in (14.5cm) high

£80-120　　　GC

A Webb's 'Cameo Fleur' vase, of flared trumpet form, the clear body overlaid in transparent red glass with stylized lilies reserved on an acid-etched ground, acid-etched Webb mark to conical foot, small rim and foot-rim chips.

c1930　　　　10in (25cm) high

£300-400　　　　　　DN

A Laurence Whistler 'The Alternatives' stipple-engraved goblet, showing a male figure, signed "L.W." and dated 1979.

Sir Laurence Whistler CBE (1912-2000), was Britain's leading practitioner of hand-engraved glass during the 20thC. Using only a single vibrating steel point, he stipple-engraved images onto lead crystal bodies made to his design and specification.

1979　　9.5in (24cm) high

£600-700　　　DN

A 1930s WMF Ikora centre bowl, with folded lip and applied pedestal foot, with rust and maroon powdered trapped in the body and silvery white internal crackled pattern.

13.75in (35.5cm) diam

£120-180　　　AG

A 1970s German blue vase, designed by Atelier Schott-Zwiesel, made by Schott-Zwiesel Glassworks Germany.

10.25in (26cm) high

£120-180　　　JH

A 1950s/60s freeform studio art glass sculpture, by Ken Allen.

11.5in (29cm) high

£25-35　　　AG

A studio glass dish, signed by James Carcass.

9.75in (25cm) long

£10-15 **GAZE**

A 1980s Sam Herman brown and orange cased glass vase, from the Camberwell series, with stylised torso shape.

Sam Herman studied art at the University of Wisconsin, then came to London where he became head of the newly founded Royal College of Art's glass department in 1967 and helped found the influential 'Glasshouse' in 1969. The Victoria and Albert Museum held an exhibition of his work in 1971 and his pieces are in private and public collections the world over.

8.75in (22cm) high

£300-500 **JH**

A Jack-in-the-pulpit iridescent glass vase, by Siddy Langley.

Born in 1955 and studying and then working with Peter Layton at London Glass Blowing between 1979 and 1987, Siddy Langley has become one of Britain's leading studio glass artists. Often observing the natural world, this 'jack-in-the-pulpit' style vase is typical of her work in terms of form and colour – her work is becoming increasingly collectable on the secondary market.

£25-35 **GAZE**

A free blown cane glass ornament.

c1970   4.75in (12cm) high

£10-15 **AG**

A 'Super Nova' glass charger, by Louis Thompson, etched with stellar motifs and covered with an iridescent lustre wash, dated.

Thompson graduated from the North Staffordshire Polytechnic in 1988 and went on to study and then teach at the Pilchuck Glass School in Seattle. He also works at Peter Layton's London Glass Blowing.

1990   15in (38cm) high

£120-180 **L&T**

An extremely unusual lime green glass vase, of geometric form, painted with Egyptian motif bands, unmarked.

This rare and unusual painted vase has caused some controversy in the glass world recently. Although originally thought to be designed by Dr. Christopher Dresser, it is now believed to be the work of Moser of Karlsbad, dating from around 1895.

c1895   10.75in (27cm) high

£220-280 **WW**

An Italian art glass vase, pink and yellow shading with a large flared ruffled top.

9in (23cm) high

£40-60 **JDJ**

An Orrefors-type handkerchief-shaped vase, with cobalt blue shading to a pale blue colouring, signed on the base "OFGWX1460/4".

6in (15cm) high

£40-60   **JDJ**

An unusual German enamelled glass vase, of broad and flared cylindrical shape, painted in bright enamelled colours with a frieze of women engaged in various pursuits, against a pale mottled milky ground, signed "K.Roner" and dated.

1941   *11.75in (30cm) high*

£550-650   **DN**

A 1960s cylindrical glass vase, the clear glass overlaid in purple and cut to the angles.

10in (26cm) high

£50-70   **L&T**

A clear glass slab bud vase, with textured wave pattern design.

8in (20.5cm) high

£15-25   **GAZE**

A blue trailed art glass vase.

9.75in (24.5cm) high

£15-25   **GAZE**

A dimpled glass vase.

£10-15   **GAZE**

A moulded glass vase.

6.25in (16cm) high

£10-15   **GAZE**

A turquoise glass wine pitcher and four goblets, one shown.

pitcher 8in (20cm) high

£120-180 set   **EOH**

A Victorian turquoise blue freeblown glass eyebath, shaped bowl with nipped-in corners, pedestal-type with circular base and ground pontil.

3in (7.5cm) high

£250-350   **BBR**

COLLECTOR'S NOTES

■ The 19th century saw ladies' hats and hairstyles grow ever more extravagant and elaborate. In order to hold one successfully to the other, hatpins were developed as an alternative to ribbons. With hats freed of ribbons, they became a functional sign of equality with men, their styles, decoration and materials showing the wealth and status of the lady who wore them.

■ Hatpins saw the beginning of their heyday in 1832, with the invention of the pin-making machine which enabled pins to be produced in larger numbers and more economically than previous hand-crafting techniques. They proceeded to peak in popularity from the 1870s until the 1920s, when fashions changed again and women 'bobbed' their hair short, rendering the hatpin obsolete.

■ They were made in a wide variety of materials from silver and gold to enamelled and painted base metals. Styles varied with the fashions of the day, and Art Nouveau examples are particularly favoured today. Some had concealed functions such as compacts – these are rare and valuable. As well as precious materials, look for fine levels of well-executed detail, good representations of a particular style and notable makers.

■ Fakes or reproductions are often found – always look at the base of a hatpin 'head' when buying to check that the pin fits well into the head without damaging it. Examples with soldering, gluing or rough and damaged areas should be treated with caution as they may have been converted from earrings or other jewellery. The design should work well visually – think about how it would have been worn and displayed.

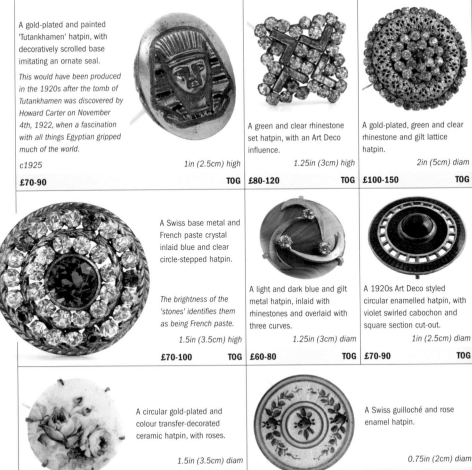

A gold-plated and painted 'Tutankhamen' hatpin, with decoratively scrolled base imitating an ornate seal.

This would have been produced in the 1920s after the tomb of Tutankhamen was discovered by Howard Carter on November 4th, 1922, when a fascination with all things Egyptian gripped much of the world.

c1925   1in (2.5cm) high

£70-90   **TOG**

A green and clear rhinestone set hatpin, with an Art Deco influence.

1.25in (3cm) high

£80-120   **TOG**

A gold-plated, green and clear rhinestone and gilt lattice hatpin.

2in (5cm) diam

£100-150   **TOG**

A Swiss base metal and French paste crystal inlaid blue and clear circle-stepped hatpin.

The brightness of the 'stones' identifies them as being French paste.

1.5in (3.5cm) high

£70-100   **TOG**

A light and dark blue and gilt metal hatpin, inlaid with rhinestones and overlaid with three curves.

1.25in (3cm) diam

£60-80   **TOG**

A 1920s Art Deco styled circular enamelled hatpin, with violet swirled cabochon and square section cut-out.

1in (2.5cm) diam

£70-90   **TOG**

A circular gold-plated and colour transfer-decorated ceramic hatpin, with roses.

1.5in (3.5cm) diam

£40-60   **TOG**

A Swiss guilloché and rose enamel hatpin.

0.75in (2cm) diam

£70-100   **TOG**

HATPINS

A silver-plated base metal hatpin, depicting a bird in flight.

2.25in (6cm) wide

£70-100 TOG

An English hollow silver hatpin, in the shape of a trumpeting elephant's head, with inlaid ruby-red rhinestone eyes and hallmarks for "A.J.S." of Chester.

1909 1.5in (4cm) long

£70-100 TOG

A CLOSER LOOK AT A HATPIN

The back is stamped with an interlaced "UB" mark, showing it was made by the notable Unger Bros of Newark NJ who flourished between 1895-1907.

Unger Bros were well known for their repoussé work in silver, particularly in the Art Nouveau style, as can be seen with this example.

The level of detail is excellent for such a small object - from the lion's mane to the bent blades of long grass in the background.

This well-composed design is very lifelike.

An American Unger Brothers sterling silver hatpin, moulded in the form of a lion's head, the back stamped with Unger Bros "UB" monogram and marked "Sterling".

1in (2.5cm) diam

£150-250 TOG

An English hollow-moulded silver teddy bear hatpin, on a swivelling joint, with inlaid red rhinestone eyes, with hallmarks for Birmingham.

1909 bear 1in (2.5cm) high

£180-220 TOG

A finely detailed hollow repoussé sterling silver 'Indian Chief' hatpin, stamped on the nape of the neck "Sterling".

This desirable hatpin is part of the 'Hiawatha' set which also comprises a similar silver 'Princess Laughing Water' hatpin and a nickel-plated holder decorated with the 'Song of Hiawatha' poem by Henry Wadsworth Longfellow. The 'Princess' is harder to find than the chieftain.

head 1.75in (4.5cm) high

£150-250 TOG

An American sterling silver Art Nouveau-styled hatpin, in the form of a lady's head, the back stamped "Sterling".

0.75in (2cm) diam

£40-50 TOG

A Scottish white metal 'Irish Harp' shaped hatpin, inset with green hardstone, with three-leaf clover motif and hand-engravings.

1.5in (3.5cm) high

£150-200 TOG

An American diamond-shaped hatpin, with polychrome enamelled thistle and leaves motif, stamped on the reverse "Sterling".

1in (2.5cm) long

£80-120 TOG

A transfer-printed and hand-painted ceramic oval hatpin, showing an elegant Georgian lady.

1.5in (3.5cm) high

£120-180　　　**TOG**

A Japanese white metal and hand-painted ceramic 'Geisha Girls' hatpin, with seven Geisha girls, the back stamped with an 'X' in a circle.

1.25in (3cm) diam

£200-300　　　**TOG**

An oval gilt metal and glass shaped tesserae mosaic hatpin, possibly Italian.

1in (2.5cm) long

£80-120　　　**TOG**

An English Art Nouveau-style hatpin, with lily and bow motif border and circular iridescent silver foil under glass cabochon, with hallmarks for "PPL" of Birmingham.

1909

£150-250　　　**TOG**

A gilt metal and ruby red rhinestone set floral bouquet-shaped hatpin.

1.25in (3cm) high

£80-120　　　**TOG**

A faux amethyst faceted glass hatpin, surmounted with a gilt-metal boss inlaid with rhinestones.

0.75in (2cm) wide

£60-80　　　**TOG**

An English silver and enamel Art Nouveau-style hollow hatpin, in the form of a flattened flower bud.

1895-1910　　　*1.5in (3.5cm) high*

£220-280　　　**TOG**

An American hardstone and faceted amber glass hatpin, the back stamped "Sterling Silver".

1.75in (4.5cm) long

£180-220　　　**TOG**

A black glass egg-shaped hatpin, with sterling silver filigree overlay.

c1900　　　*0.75in (2cm) high*

£80-120　　　**TOG**

A CLOSER LOOK AT A HATPIN

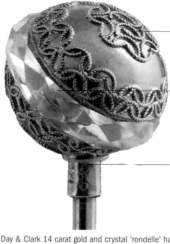

This hatpin is stamped "14K" showing it is made of 14ct gold.

The faceted crystal band is known as a 'rondelle', and imitates diamonds.

There is a small stamp, shaped like a miniature dumbell, on the finding. This shows that the hatpin was made by Day & Clark, who made pieces for jeweller and retailer Tiffany & Co.

The shaft of the pin is also marked, showing it has a solid gold sleeve - this part is often missing.

A Day & Clark two-colour gold bulbous hatpin, the top inset with a green jade cabochon, maker's mark to base of pin head, lacking gold sleeve on the shaft.

1in (2.5cm) high

£80-120   **TOG**

A Day & Clark 14 carat gold and crystal 'rondelle' hatpin, with faceted crystal band and 'chain link' wire overlay, stamped "14" and with maker's mark to the finding.

0.5in (1cm) high

£70-90   **TOG**

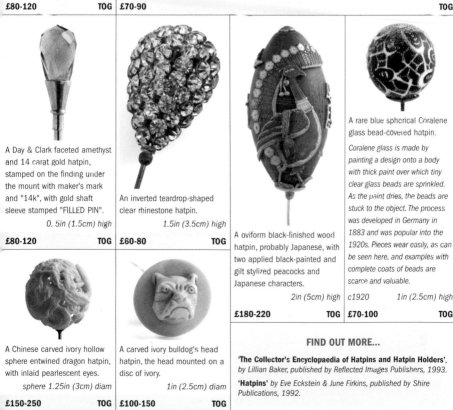

A Day & Clark faceted amethyst and 14 carat gold hatpin, stamped on the finding under the mount with maker's mark and "14k", with gold shaft and sleeve stamped "FILLED PIN".

0. 5in (1.5cm) high

£80-120   **TOG**

An inverted teardrop-shaped clear rhinestone hatpin.

1.5in (3.5cm) high

£60-80   **TOG**

A oviform black-finished wood hatpin, probably Japanese, with two applied black-painted and gilt stylized peacocks and Japanese characters.

2in (5cm) high

£180-220   **TOG**

A rare blue spherical Coralene glass bead-covered hatpin.

Coralene glass is made by painting a design onto a body with thick paint over which tiny clear glass beads are sprinkled. As the paint dries, the beads are stuck to the object. The process was developed in Germany in 1883 and was popular into the 1920s. Pieces wear easily, as can be seen here, and examples with complete coats of beads are scarce and valuable.

c1920   *1in (2.5cm) high*

£70-100   **TOG**

A Chinese carved ivory hollow sphere entwined dragon hatpin, with inlaid pearlescent eyes.

sphere 1.25in (3cm) diam

£150-250   **TOG**

A carved ivory bulldog's head hatpin, the head mounted on a disc of ivory.

1in (2.5cm) diam

£100-150   **TOG**

FIND OUT MORE...

'The Collector's Encyclopaedia of Hatpins and Hatpin Holders', by Lillian Baker, published by Reflected Images Publishers, 1993.

'Hatpins' by Eve Eckstein & June Firkins, published by Shire Publications, 1992.

COLLECTORS' NOTES

■ Holiday memorabilia is continuing to grow in popularity on both sides of the Atlantic and prices continue to rise. Early German examples from the first few decades of the 20th century are the most sought-after and expensive. Later pieces, generally in plastic, from America, are still very affordable.

■ Santa Claus is the most common figure for Christmas collectables, and has his roots in European folklore. The jolly, red-suited figure we know today became popular from the 1880s and other popular Christmas characters include snowmen and snowbabies, elves and reindeer.

■ Most Hallowe'en memorabilia is connected to confectionery, due to the popularity of the 'trick-or-treat' tradition, where children go from door to door asking for bribes of sweets and chocolate. Pumpkin 'jack-o-lanterns', witches and black cats are all typical.

■ Early examples are usually made from pulped card or papier-mâché, which is fragile, or from lithographed tin, which is easily scratched. By the 1960s these materials had been replaced by plastic. Condition affects value greatly and pieces should be as complete as possible with no repainting. Look out for rare colours or complex forms with moving parts.

A 1940s German composition Christmas candy container.

3.25in (8cm) wide

£150-200   **SOTT**

A 1950s American Christmas pressed card candy container, by The Pressed Pulp Company, in the form of Santa holding his sack.

10in (25.5cm) high

£70-100   **SOTT**

A 1930s German coated pressed card Christmas candy container, with "Venetian" glass decoration.

4in (10cm) high

£70-100   **SOTT**

A Christmas cake decoration, in the form of Santa's elf.

1in (2.5cm) high

£15-20   **LG**

A German Snowbaby, standing on a sledge.

c1900   *2in (5cm) high*

£80-100   **BEJ**

A seated Snowbaby, with black shoes.

1.5in (3.5cm) high

£20-30   **LG**

A rare kugel Christmas ornament, in blue with cream and gold decoration.

The term kugel (German for 'ball') is used to describe early decorative glass balls that were made in Germany from 1848. It became traditional to give kugels as gifts at Christmas and they can range in size from 1in (2.5cm) to 18in (47cm) in diameter. They arrived in the US in c1880. The larger versions would have been too heavy to hang from a tree so would be suspended from a ceiling.

4in (10.5cm) wide

£150-200   **CA**

A 1950s-60s Santa Claus plastic figure, with rabbit fur trim.

4.75in (12cm) high

£15-20   SOTT

A Santa Claus plastic electric light, to display in a window.

7in (18cm) high

£15-20   SOTT

A 1960s Santa Claus plastic rattle.

4.75in (12cm) high

£10-15   SOTT

A Santa Claus plastic lolly holder, with outstretched arms.

3.75in (9.5cm) long

£10-15   SOTT

A Santa Claus in a sled plastic candy container.

5in (12.5cm) long

£10-20   SOTT

A Santa Claus in a yellow sled candy container.

5in (13cm) long

£15-20   SOTT

A 1950s Santa Claus in a sled plastic lolly holder.

4.75in (12cm) long

£10-15   SOTT

A Santa Claus on a bike plastic lolly holder, with yellow wheels.

3.75in (9.5cm) long

£20-30   SOTT

A 1960s Santa Claus on green skis plastic lolly holder.

£8-12   SOTT

A Santa Claus on a green cart plastic figure, with red wheels.

4.5in (11.5cm) high

£25-35   SOTT

A CLOSER LOOK AT A HALLOWE'EN CANDY HOLDER

A 1950s press moulded card 'cat on a fence' Hallowe'en lantern, with original paper eye insert and wire handle.

To find the original eye insert is very rare.

7.5in (19cm) high

£120-180 **SOTT**

While snowmen are typically connected to Christmas, this one is the pumpkin orange colour more usually found on Hallowe'en merchandise. This makes the piece rare.

A snowman in a more traditional colour would be worth under £20.

The first few items to come out of the injection-moulding machine immediately after the coloured plastic was changed, would be in the colour of the previous batch. In this case, the snowman has been 'accidentally' made in the orange plastic used for Hallowe'en novelties.

This example retains its removeable pipe, making it more desirable.

A Hallowe'en plastic snowman candy holder, with removeable pipe.

These candy containers are used to hold 'bribes' for trick or treating children.

5in (13cm) high

£40-60 **SOTT**

A 1960s Hallowe'en plastic pumpkin lolly holder.

4.25in (10.5cm) wide

£20-30 **SOTT**

A 1940s tin Hallowe'en noisemaker, by Empress, with lithographed decoration of a black cat, wooden handle.

5in (12.5cm) long

£30-40 **SOTT**

A Hallowe'en printed tin noisemaker, with wooden handle and two wooden balls inside.

5.5in (14cm) high

£45-55 **DAC**

A Hallowe'en printed tin noisemaker, the handle as a kazoo, the pan with a printed paper face.

9in (23cm) high

£45-55 **DAC**

A 1930s German Hallowe'en card screech owl siren horn.

6.75in (17cm) high

£40-50 **SOTT**

A late 1940s Japanese Hallowe'en paper horn.

6.75in (17cm) long

£8-12 **SOTT**

A Hallowe'en orange and black plastic candy holder.

3.25in (8cm) wide

£15-20 **SOTT**

A 1930s Bonzo salt and pepper set, marked "Foreign".

3in (7.5cm) high

£40-60   **BEV**

A Victorian silver pepper caster, by George John Richards, London.

As well as the material, the attractive and intricate engraving makes this a desirable shaker.

1851   *4in (10cm) high*

£80-120   **CHEF**

A pair of 1970s Homepride Flour 'Fred' salt and pepper shakers, made by Spillers.

'Fred' was designed in 1964 and appeared on Homepride flour bags from 1965. He was so popular that a plastic flour shaker was introduced in 1969, with salt and pepper shakers coming shortly after.

4.25in (11cm) high

£8-12   **L**

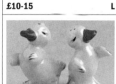

A pair of 1970s coated metal salt and pepper shakers, with incised decoration showing the underlying metal.

3.5in (9cm) high

£10-15   **L**

A pair of Japanese hand-painted duck-shaped salt and pepper shakers.

£20-30   **PC**

A rare 1930s Carltonware pepper shaker, in the form of a stylised blue and green toucan.

3in (7.5cm) long

£70-90   **AGO**

A 1930s pair of Kensington cottageware salt and pepper shakers.

2.75in (7cm) high

£18-22   **BAD**

A set of 1930s torpedo-shaped, fluted green and black Catalin salt and pepper shakers.

2.25in (6cm) high

£70-100   **BB**

A pair of Grimwade Royal Winton salt and pepper shakers.

c1940   *6in (15.5cm) high*

£80-120   **JF**

A 1950s Carltonware salt and pepper set, in the shape of fruits.

6.75in (17cm) wide

£30-40   **BAD**

A pair of 1960s Secla salt and pepper shakers on a tray, made in Portugal.

6.5in (16.5cm) wide

£10-15   **L**

A Susie Cooper bone china cruet set, with dot in a circle design on a green ground.

Mustard 3in (7.5cm) wide

£45-55   **BAD**

A 1930s Beswick cruet set, in the form of tomatoes on cabbage leaves.

tray 6in (15.5cm) long

£20-40   **BAD**

A Japanese ceramic pixie and mushroom cruet set, the mushroom top lifting off to reveal a pot, the pixies as salt and pepper shakers.

c1930   *5.5in (14cm) wide*

£50-70   **BAD**

A CLOSER LOOK AT A CRUET SET

The clean-lined form is quintessentially modern but also reminiscent of the Art Deco style.

It is made from solid silver by Gordon Hodgson with the silver contrasting strongly against the lids made of black wood and ivory.

The form is extremely unusual with the shakers fitting neatly around the mustard dish.

It is in excellent condition with no dents or splits which would detract from the form of the pieces by causing irregular reflections.

A silver cruet set, by Gordon Hodgson, comprising a mustard dish of cylindrical form with dished bowl, and a salt and pepper each of crescent form with unstained ivory and black hardwood removable lids with pouring apertures, each fitting around the mustard to form a cylinder, hallmarked London 1969-70.

2.5in (6.5cm) high

£650-750   **L&T**

A 1930s Carlton ware pink 'Lily' pattern cruet set.

This is a rare colourway and is complete, hence its high value. 1930s floral Carltonware is highly collectable.

5.5in (14cm) wide

£100-150   **BEV**

A 1930s 'cook and housekeeper' cruet set.

3in (7.5cm) high

£40-60   **BAD**

A 1930s German orange-glazed ceramic cruet set, in the form of three pumpkins, spoon missing.

3.75in (9.5cm) wide

£30-40   **BAD**

A 19thC copper ale muller, the conical shape with a tapering tubular iron handle to one side ending in a baluster wooden handle.

Ale mullers were conical in form and used to warm beer or wine over a fire in cold weather. They often come with handles or hooks to hang by a fireplace. Examples with splits, serious dents or handles that have been drilled to allow hanging are less desirable and valuable.

5.25in (13.5cm) diam

£70-100   **CHEF**

A late 19thC copper saucepan, with tinned interior, brazed seams and iron handle.

12.25in (31cm) diam

£70-100   **CHEF**

A late 19thC brass preserve pan, the tapering cylindrical sides below a fixed iron strap handle of round arch shape.

12.5in (31.5cm) diam

£45-55   **CHEF**

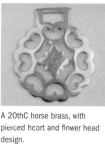

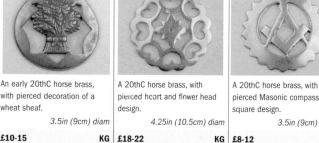

A graded set of three copper cider measures, each of the tapering cylindrical shapes with brass labels and iron handles, the interiors tinned, inscribed "Cider".

Damage to the interior lining and splits or serious dents reduce value. Those made of unlined, thin gauge copper are often modern reproductions, despite having signs of 'wear'.

largest 5.25in (13.5cm) diam

£100-150   **CHEF**

A late 19thC horse brass, of pierced anchor design.

3.75in (9.5cm) diam

£8-12   **KG**

A late Victorian horse brass, with pierced decoration of a crown.

4.25in (11cm) diam

£18-22   **KG**

An early 20thC horse brass, with pierced decoration of a wheat sheaf.

3.5in (9cm) diam

£10-15   **KG**

A 20thC horse brass, with pierced heart and flower head design.

4.25in (10.5cm) diam

£18-22   **KG**

A 20thC horse brass, with pierced Masonic compass and square design.

3.5in (9cm) diam

£8-12   **KG**

A mid- to late 19thC Cetem Ware ceramic jelly mould, with shell motif.

£40-60   **SSC**

A late 19thC large ceramic jelly mould, with lion motif.

9in (23cm) wide

£40-60   **SSC**

A pair of late 19th/early 20thC sycamore butter pats.

9in (22.5cm) long

£15-20   **SSC**

A hand-held butter table.

9in (23cm) diam

£15-25   **SSC**

A CLOSER LOOK AT A SPICE TOWER

These names are applied by transfer and although show signs of wear, they are still present and readable. This is unusual for an item which would have been handled a great many times.

This spice tower is large, well-made with a good level of patina to the wood and has no splits or chips.

Kitchenalia, treen (the name given to small, carved wooden utilitarian items), and transfer-decorated Mauchlineware are all highly collectable areas, meaning this item appeals to three types of collectors.

The spices shown are typical of the time and would have been popular and comparatively expensive.

A mid-19thC Mauchline-style spice tower, the four cylindrical sections screwing together and printed with "Mace", "Nutmegs", "Ginger" and "All Spice" on banners.

8.25in (21cm) high

£300-400   **CHEF**

A cast iron London Royal Mail horse-drawn carriage doorstop, with red, yellow and green enamel, minor losses.

12in (30.5cm) long

£50-80   **TA**

A Maypole Dairy Co. butter crock.

6in (15cm) high

£65-75   **SSC**

A 19thC European brass iron, with turned wooden handle, marked with "31 March 1754".

6.25in (16cm) long

£200-250   **ATI**

A GEC electric fan, designed in 1946.

7in (18cm) h

£45-55   **L**

A ceramic pink and green pie bird.

This pie funnel was given away as a promotion by Pillsbury.

5.25in (13.5cm) high

£30-40   **DAC**

A 1940s Bruton chrome-plated bar heater.

15in (38cm) high

£60-80   **L**

A Goebel ceramic egg timer, in the form of two red rabbits.

The German porcelain factory of Goebel is better known for its Art Deco figurines and ceramics and for Hummel figurines, which are covered in the 'Ceramics' section of this book.

c1950   *3.5in (9cm) high*

£70-100   **DAC**

A Homepride Flour 'Fred' parmesan cheese or herb shaker, by Spillers.

4.25in (11cm) high

£4-5   **L**

A ceramic blackbird pie funnel.

3.75in (9.5cm) high

£40-60   **DAC**

A 1960s painted ceramic egg timer, in the form of a mouse in a yellow dress and bonnet.

This timer bears similarities to the Beatrix Potter range of figurines by Beswick and she may have been made to copy the style. Egg-timers were not made in the Beswick range and here the colours are brighter.

3.5in (9cm) high

A 1950s painted ceramic egg timer, in the form of a small girl and dog.

Egg timers like this one are prone to damage, especially as the ceramic is comparatively delicate. This example is in excellent condition.

3.5in (9cm) high

A painted wooden egg timer, in the form of a cockerel.

c1945   *4.5in (11.5cm) high*

£15-20   **DAC**

£15-20   **DAC**

£70-100   **DAC**

COLLECTORS' NOTES

■ Lady head vases were originally sold inexpensively as gifts in florists' shops where they were filled with flowers. With styles dominated by fashionably or elegantly dressed ladies, production began in the late 1940s and peaked from the 1950s to the late 1960s. Cute children and teenagers can also be found. The majority were thrown away after the flowers had died.

■ Desirability and values are determined by the complexity of the moulding, level of detail and realistic painting, elegance of the form and particularly the 'attitude' or facial expression of the head. Many have been given names by collectors, some related to their theme and form.

■ Look out for good moulding, wide-brimmed hats, applied hands, jewellery, intricately curled hair and an elegant, well-painted portrayal of facial features.

Learn to recognise the faces of icons of the period – Marilyn Monroe and Jackie Onassis Kennedy vases are particularly sought-after and valuable.

■ Makers' names do not necessarily add value. Although some were made in the US, most were made in Japan for export and names include NAPCO (National Potteries Corporation) Enesco, INARCO (International Artware Corporation), Irice and Rubens.

■ Condition is vital – the ceramic is often thin and easily chipped or cracked. Mint condition examples will command a financial premium. Examine vases closely for cracks and chips and look at protruding parts such as fingers, curls, bows, and hat brims to ensure they have not been reglued, as this will lower the value.

A 1950s American lady head vase, by Relpo of Chicago, with gloved hand and faux pearl necklace and earrings, stamped on the base "K1633".

6.75in (17cm) high

£80-120   DAC

A small 1950s lady head vase, with moulded black eyelashes, base marked "D-3220".

5in (13cm) high

£80-120   DAC

A very rare lady head vase, with earrings and unusual large bow in her hair, with label for "CAFFCO JAPAN", the base marked "E3287".

5.5in (14cm) high

£80-120   KK

A rare INARCO lady head vase, the base marked "INARCO E5623".

The pleasing expression, jewellery and easily damaged curl on top of her head make this example rare and desirable.

6in (15cm) high

£80-120   KK

A Rubens Originals 'The Teenager' lady head vase, with label to base reading "Rubens Originals Los Angeles MADE IN JAPAN".

From a series of four, this example is distinguished by its realistic brown 'hair' eyelashes.

4.25in (10.5cm) high

£80-120   KK

A NAPCO 'The Engagement' lady head vase, with diamanté inlaid ring on her finger, marked on base "NAPCOWARE C5037".

This example still retains the original jewellery. These were often given, full of flowers, to recently engaged couples.

5.75in (14.5cm) high

£80-120   KK

A large cold-painted lady head vase, the base marked "T-1647".

This can be identified as cold-painted as the paint is matte and applied to the surface. If washed, the paint will rub off, so the dirty cheeks are acceptable and a sign that it is in original condition.

6.75in (17cm) high

£70-100   K

A Japanese contemporaneous copy of a Betty Lou Nichols lady head vase, with removable hat.

Copies of Betty Lou Nichols vases do exist, and are usually Japanese. Those made at the time are collectable, those made after the 1960s are not. This period copy has a removable hat – a desirable and rare feature.

5in (13cm) high

£100-150   **KK**

A rare Liftons yellowy green lady head vase, the base marked "MR-4556" and with label reading "Liftons JAPAN".

As well as her pleasing expression, her rare yellowy-green colourway is more desirable and rarer than the more common bluey-green colourway.

5.5in (14cm) high

£70-100   **KK**

A 'Praying Girl' lady head vase.

There is also a 'Praying Boy' version in blue with brown hair – the two clasped hands are a rare feature, and they are more commonly found with one or no hands. The cowl is easily damaged, but this example is in mint condition.

5.75in (14.5cm) high

£70-100   **KK**

An unmarked lady head vase, her unusual eyelashes with white undersides and grey tops.

4.75in (12cm) high

£70-100   **KK**

A NAPCO 'Southern Belle' lady head vase, with realistic eyelashes, the base marked "C3812B NAPCO 1959".

5.5in (14cm) high

£80-120   **KK**

A 1950s Japanese Rubens lady head vase, with lady in riding clothing and blue top hat, base with label reading "A Rubens Original" and stamped "R 531 JAPAN".

7.75in (19.5cm) high

£150-250   **DAC**

An INARCO lady head vase, with unusual feather form, the base marked "INARCO E-191/M/C".

c1961

5.5in (14cm) high

£80-120   **KK**

An Enesco 'The Secretary' lady head vase, with gilt and red foil Enesco label to base.

5.75in (14.5cm) high

£80-120   **KK**

A 1950s Japanese lady head vase, with gloss glaze, with moulded black eyelashes and applied pink rose on hat.

6.75in (17.5cm) high

£60-80   **DAC**

A pair of Louis Vuitton stacking automobile trunks, covered in brass-studded black cloth, brass mounts stamped "L.V.", each interior with a detachable tray, paper label.

33.5in (85cm) wide

£500-600 **CLV**

A Louis Vuitton trunk, with removable lid, originally made for the Encyclopedia Britannica, one removable divider missing, with stamped maker's marks to the leather, handle and metalwork, inscribed "Specially made for the Encyclopedia Britannica by Louis Vuitton, 149 New Bond St, London".

Vintage Louis Vuitton trunks are currently enjoying popularity as small pieces of furniture. Those made for specific purposes, such as this example, are also of interest to dedicated collectors of Louis Vuitton luggage.

35.5in (90cm) long

£700-800 **DN**

A large American trunk, for long ship passages, with applied stickers including "Norwegian American Line", inscribed with motto "P&S - Trunks That Wear - Everywhere".

38in (97cm) wide

£120-180 **ATK**

A brown leather suitcase, with two straps, reinforced corners and nickel-plated locks.

c1910   *28.75in (73cm) wide*

£100-150 **TDG**

A 1930s Gladstone-type gentleman's toilet case, by Clark of 33 New Bond Street in London, the divided hinged lid opening to reveal an interior fitted with compartments, silver hallmark for London.

1932   *15.5in (39cm) wide*

£350-450 **L&T**

A gentleman's travelling toilet set, including cut-glass vessels with hallmarked silver fittings and two ivory brushes, with green leather interior and felt protective cover.

Look closely at maker's marks on both the case and the lids of the contents. Good central London retailers or manufacturers such as Asprey, Leuchars or Mappin and Webb add interest and value, as does fine decoration in lacquer or enamel. A case must be complete with all its original, matching contents to fetch high values.

1935

£300-500 **TAG**

An Italian alligator briefcase, by Hamilton Hodge for de Vecchi, with fitted interior.

17.5in (44.5cm) wide

£550-650 **S&K**

A maid's travelling nécessaire, the rexine-covered case containing a portable iron and stand and a small plated kettle and stand, both with raffia handles, and a folding pair of wooden-handled curling tongs.

Case 8in (20.5cm) wide

£120-180 **DN**

A black leather briefcase, the flap with the royal cypher of George VI, in mint condition.

1936-52   *17in (43cm) wide*

£50-70 **MHC**

An Adco-Liberty 'The Lone Ranger' lunch box, and Thermos flask.

c1954   *8.75in (22cm) wide*

£400-500   **STC**

An Adco-Liberty Walt Disney's 'Mickey Mouse' and 'Donald Duck' lunch box.

The Thermos flask is extremely rare and can fetch up to five times the price of the lunch box on its own.

c1954   *9in (22.5cm) wide*

£150-250   **STC**

A CLOSER LOOK AT A LUNCH BOX

The earlier version has a shaped character decal, not a rectangular decal as this example dating from 1952 has.

Hoppalong Cassidy was the first 'character' to feature on a metal lunch box, in 1950.

Both versions were also available in blue, which carry a similar value.

Industrial designer Robert Burton was responsible for the artwork, and went on to produce most of Aladdin's lunch boxes designs during the 1950s.

A metal 'Hoppalong Cassidy' lunch box with Thermos flask, by Aladdin Industries of Nashville, Tennessee, near mint condition.

c1952   *8in (20.5cm) wide*

£350-450   **STC**

A 1950s 'Casey Jones' lunch box, with a few scratches and light dents.

8.75in (22.5cm) long

£150-250   **STC**

An Aladdin Industries 'Zorro' lunch box and Thermos bottle.

1958   *8in (20.5cm) wide*

£120-180   **STC**

A Thermos 'Central Station' and 'Firehouse' dometop lunch box and Thermos bottle.

Note the side view of the shaped lid, which is a characteristic of Thermos lunch boxes and does not appear with Aladdin dome topped lunch boxes. The bottom of this finely decorated box lists fire safety practices.

1959   *9in (22.5cm) wide*

£250-350   **STC**

An Aladdin 'Jetsons' dometop lunch box and Thermos bottle.

1963 9in (22.5cm) wide

£1,000-1,500 STC

A 1960s promotional 'Volkswagen Campervan' lunch box and Thermos bottle, manufactured by Omni-Graphics Inc, Yonkers N.Y., with styrofoam-lined plastic Thermos.

£700-900 STC

A Thermos Fireball XL5 lunch box and Thermos bottle.

The artwork for this box was created by Wally Wood, a top artist for EC Comics in the 1950s and beyond.

1964 8.75in (22cm) wide

£180-220 STC

An Aladdin Industries Inc 'Voyage To the Bottom Of The Sea' lunch box, with embossed relief details.

c1967 8in (20.5cm) wide

£600-800 STC

A Thermos 'MLB' baseball lunch box and Thermos bottle, with rare magnetic game counters still present, to play game on reverse.

c1968 8.75in (22cm) wide

£180-220 STC

A Thermos 'Beatles Yellow Submarine' metal lunch box and Thermos bottle.

1968 8.75in (22cm) wide

£700-1,000 STC

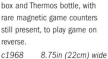

A Thermos 'Chitty Chitty Bang Bang' lunch box.

This example lacks its matching Thermos flask which affects that value detrimentally.

An Aladdin Industries 'Gentle Ben' lunch box and bottle, copyright Ivan Tors Films.

c1968

£100-150 TC

An Aladdin Industries 'Peter Pan' lunch box and Thermos flask.

1969 8.75in (22cm) wide

£100-150 STC

1969 8.75in (22cm) wide

£60-80 STC

A Thermos 'Snoopy' dometop metal lunch box and Thermos flask.

1970   *9in (22.5cm) wide*

£120-180   **STC**

An Aladdin Enterprises 'U.S. Mail' lunch box and Thermos bottle.

c1970   *9in (22.5cm) wide*

£80-120   **STC**

A Thermos 'Kiss' lunch box and Thermos bottle, near mint.

c1977   *8in (20cm) wide*

£150-250   **STC**

A Thermos 'Star Wars' lunch box and Thermos flask.

1978   *8.75in (22cm) wide*

£120-180   **STC**

An Aladdin Industries 'Charlie's Angels' lunch box and Thermos bottle.

c1978   *8in (20cm) wide*

£100-150   **STC**

An Aladdin Industries 'Popeye' lunch box, mint with plastic 'Pop-Top' Thermo flask, tag and instructions.

1980   *8in (20.5cm) wide*

£80-120   **STC**

A Thermos 'Rambo' lunch box, with plastic Thermos bottle.

'Rambo' was the last metal lunch box produced, which is ironic considering the issue during the 1970s concerning children using them as playground weapons!

c1985   *8.75in (22cm) wide*

£60-80   **STC**

A Thermos 'Star Wars - The Empire Strikes Back' lunch box and bottle.

1981   *8.75in (22cm) wide*

£70-100   **STC**

An Aladdin Industries 'E.T. The Extra-Terrestrial' lunch box and Thermos bottle.

1982   *8in (20.5cm) wide*

£40-50   **STC**

FIND OUT MORE...

'The Illustrated Encyclopaedia of Metal Lunch Boxes', *by Allen Woodall and Sean Brickell, published by Schiffer, 1999.*

'The Fifties and Sixties Lunch Box', *by Scott Bruce, published by Chronicle Books, 1998.*

COLLECTORS' NOTES

- The three main factors that determine a magazine's value are its cover, content and condition.

- Fashion magazines appeal to students and collectors of fashion and fashion history and are also collected for their decorative covers. Artwork should typify a period, such as the elongated, stylised faces of 1920s Art Deco, the austerity of post-war design or the bright day-glo colours of the 1960s and 70s.

- Covers featuring celebrities such as Princess Diana, famous models such as Twiggy or any of the 'Super Models' of the 1980s and 1990s also attract a premium, particularly if they are that model's first appearance.

Also look for artwork or photographs by famous names such as Cecil Beaton, Horst P. Horst or Mario Testino.

- News and current affairs magazines such as "Life" and "Picture Post" that cover major events such as royal events, celebrity weddings or the moon landings are sought-after. However, beware of special editions that were printed in large amounts and were often kept as a memento, making them common today.

- As with all paper-based collectables, condition is of upmost importance when it comes to value and desirability. This includes rips and tears as well as doodles, missing pages and cutout sections.

A CLOSER LOOK AT A VINTAGE MAGAZINE

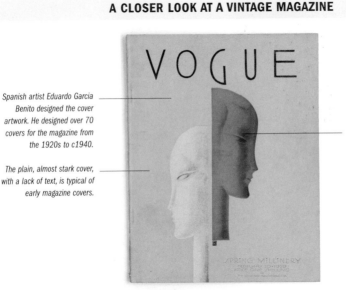

Spanish artist Eduardo Garcia Benito designed the cover artwork. He designed over 70 covers for the magazine from the 1920s to c1940.

The plain, almost stark cover, with a lack of text, is typical of early magazine covers.

The architectural style of this sans serif font is typical of the 1930s.

The elongated mask-like faces are reminiscent of Amadeo Modigliani's (1884-1920) paintings and sculptures, which were inspired by African masks and primitivism. This style epitomises the late 1920s/early 1930s.

"Vogue", February 20th, 1929, cover artwork by Eduardo Garcia Benito.

12.75in (32.5cm) high

£100-150   VM

"Vogue", September 1st, 1937, 21st birthday issue.

Unicorns were a popular motif for Vogue covers.

12.75in (32.5cm) high

£70-100   VM

"Vogue Beauty Book", February 22nd, 1939, with cover artwork by Eduardo Garcia Benito.

12.75in (32.5cm) high

£70-100   VM

"Vogue", September 1951.

11.5in (29cm) high

£30-50   VM

"Vogue", September 1954.

11.5in (29cm) high

£20-40 VM

"Vogue", April, 1964.

The amusing use of the "O" and "G" from Vogue over the model's eyes are in the style of the 'bug-eye' glasses that were highly fashionable in the 1960s.

11.5in (29cm) high

£25-35 VM

"Vogue", August 1966.

11.5in (29cm) high

£20-30 VM

"Vogue", December 1974, with Twiggy cover.

To many, Twiggy was the face of the 60s and appeared on the cover of Vogue four times.

12in (30.5cm) high

£20-40 VM

"Vogue", June 1976.

11.5in (29cm) high

£10-20 VM

"Vogue", January 1988, with Cindy Crawford on the cover.

11.5in (29cm) high

£10-20 VM

"Vogue", August 1981, the Royal Wedding issue.

11.75in (30cm) high

£15-25 VM

"Vogue", October 1989, with Claudia Schiffer cover.

11.5in (29cm) high

£10-15 VM

"Vogue", December 1991, with Mario Testino portrait of Diana, Princess of Wales on the cover.

11.75in (30cm) high

£20-25 VM

"Harper's Bazaar", August 1948.
11.5in (29cm) high

£50-70   **VM**

"Harper's Bazaar", August 1951.
11.5in (29cm) high

£30-50   **VM**

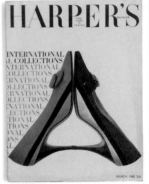

"Harper's Bazaar", March 1962.
12.5in (32cm) high

£20-30   **VM**

"The Queen", August 1949.
12.5in (32cm) high

£20-40   **VM**

"The Queen", January 4th, 1961.
12.5in (32cm) high

£20-30   **VM**

"The Queen", October 23rd, 1962, with Jane Fonda cover.
12.5in (32cm) high

£20-40   **VM**

"The Queen", December 10th/January 6th, 1970.
12in (30.5cm) high

£10-20   **VM**

"The Queen", July 1970.
15in (38cm) high

£15-25   **VM**

"Harper's Bazaar & Queen", July 1972.
12in (30.5cm) high

£7-10   **VM**

"My Home", November 1929.
11.75in (30cm) high

£20-30   VM

"Good Housekeeping", December 1937.
11.5in (29cm) high

£20-40   VM

"House Beautiful", July 1949.
12.75in (32.5cm) high

£15-25   VM

"House & Garden", January 1956.
11.5in (29cm) high

£20-30   VM

"Homes & Gardens", January 1972.
11.5in (29cm) high

£18-22   VM

A 1974 "Habitat" catalogue.
11.75in (30cm) high

£20-30   VM

"House & Garden", July/August 1976.
12in (30.5cm) high

£10-15   VM

A 1978/9 "Habitat" catalogue.
11.75in (30cm) high

£15-25   VM

A 1980/81 "Habitat" catalogue.
11.75in (30cm) high

£15-25   VM

"Life", July 25th, 1938, with Queen Elizabeth cover.

14in (35.5cm) high

£60-80 VM

"Life", December 6th, 1953, with John F. Kennedy funeral cover.

14in (35.5cm) high

£60-80 VM

"Life", October 23rd, 1961, International edition with Elizabeth Taylor as 'Cleopatra' cover.

14in (35.5cm) high

£60-80 VM

"Life", December 19th, 1969, rare edition with Charles Manson cover.

Charles Manson shocked the world when his 'Family' brutally slaughtered six people including Sharon Tate, the eight-month pregnant wife of film director Roman Polanski, in 1969. The horrific nature of these murders meant that few people kept anything featuring Manson, making this rare today.

14in (35.5cm) high

£150-200 VM

"Life", January 20th, 1969, with Earth seen from Apollo VIII cover.

The Apollo VIII lifted off on December 21st 1968 and returned six days later. It was the first manned lunar orbit mission.

14in (35.5cm) high

£40-60 VM

"Picture Post", December 4th, 1944.

13.25in (33.5cm) high

£15-25 VM

"Picture Post", January 16th, 1954, with Gregory Peck cover.

13in (33cm) high

£15-25 VM

"Picture Post", December 3rd, 1955, with Marlon Brando in "Guys & Dolls" cover.

13in (33cm) high

£30-50 VM

"Picture Post", August 4th, 1956, with James Mason cover.

13in (33cm) high

£15-25 VM

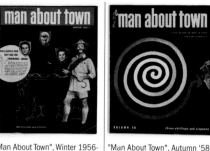

"Man About Town", Winter 1956-7, including a feature on Saville Row suits.

Man About Town was the UK's first glossy magazine for men, and from 1957 was published by Michael Heseltine, later Tory MP.

11in (28cm) high

£20-40　　　　　　　　**VM**

"Man About Town", Autumn '58

11in (28cm) high

£20-40　　　　　　　　**VM**

"Health & Efficiency", February 1941.

The world's longest running naturist magazine, Health & Efficiency has been published since 1900.

11in (28cm) high

£20-40　　　　　　　　**VM**

"Dude", May 1962.

11in (28cm) high

£10-15　　　　　　　　**VM**

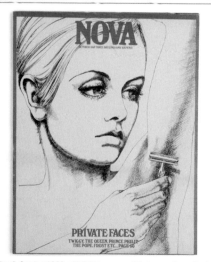

"Nova", October 1968, with Twiggy cover and feature on Henry Ford.

Nova was first published in 1965 and became the style bible for the 60s and 70s. As well as fashion, it covered heavy duty issues such as homosexual law reform when the issue was politically controversial. It closed in 1975 and was briefly relaunched in 2000 but closed again a year later.

13.5in (34.5cm) high

£25-35　　　　　　　　**VM**

"Penthouse", Vol.1 No. 9 1960s, with Nudest Miss World cover.

Published by Bob Guccione in the UK since 1965 and the US since 1969. Guccione resigned in 2003 after the magazines publisher filed for bankruptcy the same year.

11in (28cm) high

£10-20　　　　　　　　**VM**

"Nova", May/June 1969, with Oliver Reed feature.

13.5in (34.5cm) high

£25-35　　　　　　　　**VM**

"Dude", November 1971.

11in (28cm) high

£10-15　　　　　　　　**VM**

FIND OUT MORE...

'Collectible Magazines: Identification and Price Guide' *by David K. Henkel, published by HarperCollins 2000.*

COLLECTORS' NOTES

- Marbles are usually divided into three types – German 'handmade' made from c1860-c1920, American 'machine made' produced from c1905 and contemporary marbles, primarily American in origin.

- 'Handmade' marbles usually have one or two distinct pontil marks where they were broken off a rod of glass. Also look for symmetry and complex designs as well as large examples. Leading US companies include Akro Agate Company and the Peltier Glass Company. 'Eye appeal' is an important aspect – one that appeals to one collector may not to another.

- Condition is vital with 'machine-made' and contemporary marbles, but less so with 'handmade' examples. However, serious play-wear such as scratching and chipping (especially if it obscures or disturbs the design) will devalue any marble – sometimes by half or more.

A handmade German 'Solid Core Swirl' marble, with an outer swirl of latticinio (white glass) threads.

1860s-1920s   *0.75in (2cm)*

£20-40   **AB**

A German handmade English-style 'Latticinio Core Swirl' marble, with a core of orange 'latticinio' strands and an outer layer of coloured strands.

1860s-1920   *0.625in (1.5cm)*

£20-30   **AB**

A German English-style 'Joseph's Coat' marble, with blue, orange and white strands and two pontil marks.

1860s-1920   *0.625in (1.5cm)*

£50-70   **AB**

A German handmade English-style swirl marble, with predominately orange, but also white and black strands and a clear pontil mark.

Collectors call these 'English-style' as, until the fall of the Berlin Wall revealed an Eastern German factory that primarily exported to Britain, it was thought that they were made in the glass factories of Bristol, England.

1860s-1920   *0.625in (1.5cm)*

£80-120   **AB**

A handmade German 'Banded Lutz' marble, with yellow and white bordered Lutz swirls.

Lutz marbles have copper flakes suspended in glass which give the impression of gold.

1860s-1920s   *0.75in (2cm)*

£100-150   **AB**

A handmade German 'Indian' marble, with black base and white banded navy blue swirl and green and yellow strand swirl.

Indian marbles have a black base. The more colours seen in the swirls, the more valuable and desirable it is likely to be.

1860s-1920s   *0.75in (2cm)*

£80-120   **AB**

A handmade German 'Mica' glass marble, with single pontil mark.

Both the single pontil and the fact that the mica does not go all the way through the marble (see detail) show this came from the end of a rod, making this example rarer and more valuable than other mica marbles.

1860s-1920   *0.75in (2cm)*

£50-80   **AB**

MARBLES

A machine-made American Akro Agate Company swirl oxblood marble.

c1930-45   0.625in (1.5cm)

£12-18   **AB**

A machine-made American Akro Agate 'Corkscrew' marble.

This is the most commonly found Akro Agate marble. There are over 1,000 colour combinations enabling a diverse collection to be built!

c1930s   0.625in (1.5cm)

£10-20   **AB**

A Christensen Agate Company slag marble.

c1927-29   0.625in (1.5cm)

£40-60   **AB**

A contemporary glass marble, by Edward Seese, with a ribbon swirl and a green aventurine band, signed "FES".

2003   1.25in (3cm)

£20-30   **BGL**

A CLOSER LOOK AT A SULPHIDE MARBLE

Painted figures or those which feature named people are scarcer and fetch higher values, as do those with coloured glass.

The figure inside is made from a white, porcelain-like material. The technique is also found in paperweights.

They require great skill from the glass artist to make. The position of the figure as well as the air bubbles affect this marble's value.

A handmade German sulphide marble, with white standing lion.

1870s-1920s   1.5in (3.5cm)

£100-150   **AB**

A machine-made American 'Turkeyhead-Swirl' marble, by the Christensen Agate Company.

0.625in (1.5cm)

£120-180   **AB**

A selection of machine-made modern American marbles.

Although colourful, these were mass-produced after the 1960s and are of little interest to collectors.

Each 0.25in (0.5cm)

20p-30p each   **AB**

A contemporary glass marble, by William Murray, a solid core-banded Lutz, with a violet swirl, signed "WPM02".

2002   1.25in (3cm)

£30-50   **BGL**

FIND OUT MORE...

'Marbles – Identification & Price Guide', *by Robert Block, published by Schiffer Publishing, 2003.*

www.marblecollecting.com

A 1920s Mexican painted wood carnival or festivity mask.

11.75in (30cm) high

£70-100   **ANAA**

A 1930s Mexican red painted wood mustachioed Devil mask.

11.75in (30cm) high

£60-80   **ANAA**

A 1930s Dutch painted papier-mâché carnival mask, from Amsterdam.

12.5in (32cm) high

£70-100   **ANAA**

A 1930s painted fabric mule's head carnival mask.

10.5in (27cm) high

£12-18   **ANAA**

A Guatemalan carved wooden face tribal mask.

8.75in (22cm) high

£80-120   **ANAA**

A Mexican painted wooden festival mask, possibly related to the figure of Death, with label reading "MUERTO CUERTZAIA".

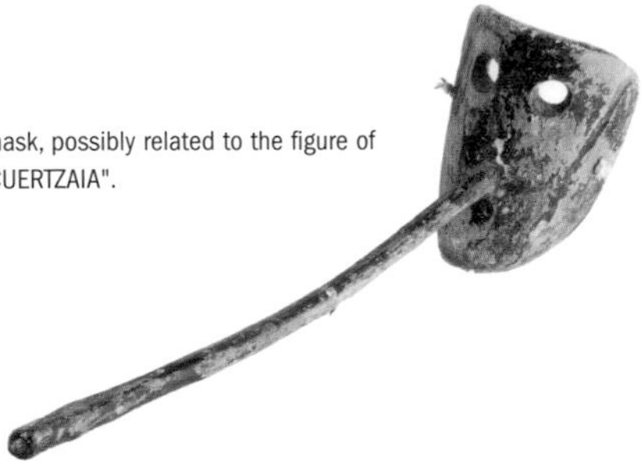

c1915   *24.5in (62cm) long*

£60-80   **ANAA**

An American painted metal gauze and black horsehair bearded man ceremonial mask, from an Odd Fellows' meeting hall.

The Odd Fellows, originally founded in England in the 18thC, staged their first US meetings in 1819. One of the largest fraternal societies in the US, its key tenets are friendship, love, truth and support for the needy.

c1910   *12.25in (31cm) high*

£40-60   **ANAA**

An American painted metal gauze and grey horsehair bearded man ceremonial mask, from an Odd Fellows meeting hall.

c1910   *15.25in (39cm) high*

£40-60   **ANAA**

A 1920s wood, composition and plaster painted mask of a demon's face.

1920s   *15in (38cm) high*

£200-300   **ANAA**

MECHANICAL MUSIC

COLLECTORS' NOTES

■ The gramophone was developed in 1887 by Emile Berliner and became popular around the turn of the century. It soon took over from other methods of reproducing sound, such as Thomas Edison's phonograph which used wax cylinders, and the 19th century metal cylinder and disc musical boxes.

■ Table-top examples are found with both integral and external horns. Those with original decorative external horns tend to be the most popular, although beware of modern reproductions of HMV examples, with bright yellow brass, dark, pixellated HMV transfers and use of dark, reddish tropical woods for the case.

■ Portable gramophones can make an affordable collection that is easy to display and store. Look out for well-known makers and unusual forms or shapes. Children's tinplate-cased examples can be very desirable and can fetch higher values than those made for the adult market.

A Madison table gramophone, with metal case, minor damage to reproducer.

c1930

£60-80 ATK

A Swiss Maestrophone portable gramophone, by Paillard, with mahogany case and original reproducer.

Paillard is also well known for its fine quality cylinder mechanical music boxes made in the 19thC.

c1930

£220-280 ATK

An English Cameraphone, small folding portable gramophone, with oak case, spherical imitation tortoiseshell 'Saturn' sound box replaced.

7in (17.5cm) long

£220-280 ATK

A Swiss portable Thorens folding gramophone, with metal case, complete with one record entitled "Karnevals-Shimmy".

£320-380 ATK

A portable Belgian Colibri gramophone, with original Swiss soundbox and spring motor.

c1930

£250-300 ATK

A Czechoslovakian portable Supralion gramophone.

c1930

£40-60 ATK

A Bing of Nuremburg toy gramophone, lithographed tin case, with one record entitled "Pigmynette", good working condition.

Bing is known for its tinplate toys, recognised by a "GBN" trademark.

£220-280 ATK

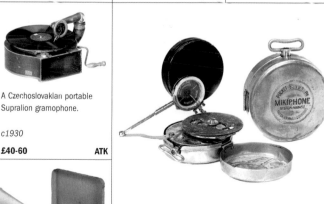

A Mikiphone pocket phonograph, clockwork mechanism, nickel case, good condition.

The entire mechanism folds down into the circular metal case which is slightly bigger than a large pocket watch.

4.5in (11.5cm) long

£400-500 ATK

A decorative horn gramophone, small oak case with Swedish dealer's label, coloured tin horn, 'Veni-Vidi-Vici' soundbox, needs restoration.

12.5in (32cm) long

£200-250   **ATK**

A 19thC Swiss cylinder musical box, playing 20-airs, faux rosewood and stencilled case.

24in (61cm) wide

£700-800   **LC**

A CLOSER LOOK AT A GRAMOPHONE

The Xb is the largest standard production gramophone ever made.

The case, mechanism and horn are all handmade and hand assembled.

The enormous horn is made from papier-mâché, and easily damaged. This example is in excellent condition.

Due to the quality of materials and sound, many claim this to be the finest acoustic gramophone ever made.

An English EMG gramophone, model 'Xb', with a large papier-mâché horn.
c1935

horn 33.5in (75cm) diam

£3,000-4,000   **ATK**

An HMV 'Model 460' gramophone, with special pleated diaphragm by Lumière, mahogany case, brass-plated fittings, automatic stop function.

Rather than using a horn to amplify the sound, a vibrating gilt-finished pleated paper diaphragm was used – values plummet if the paper is torn. This rare model was produced only for the English market between 1924 and 1925.

c1925   15.5in (39cm) wide

£1,800-2,200   **ATK**

An Edison 'Gem Model C' phonograph, two- and four-minute gearing, replaced brass horn, original wooden case, complete with three cylinders.

c1910

£700-800   **ATK**

A brass singing bird cage, with a mechanism of small bellows which operates a slide whistle and emits a warbling sound, complete but not working.

c1950

£200-250   **ATK**

A 'Sewing Lady' musical box, the plastic female figure with full-skirted dress and storage for eight cotton spools and a tape measure, hand-painted features and flowers.

c1958   7.5in (19.5cm) high

£80-120   **ATK**

A ceramic 'Phonograph' plate, by Creil & Montereau, with an illustration of a phonograph and French text.

8.25in (21cm) diam

£80-120   **ATK**

A Liberty and Co. Tudric pewter vase, the open-work tapering sides with three loop handles and embossed with a band of berries and leaves on a round base, with a green glass liner, stamped beneath "Tudric 0957".

8.75in (22cm) high

£300-400 **DN**

A Liberty and Co. Tudric pewter bowl, stamped "English Pewter, Made by Liberty and Co. 0277", some wear and pitting to inside.

5in (12.5cm) diam

£220-280 **DN**

A pair of Liberty and Co. Tudric pewter vases, each with S shaped handles, stamped beneath "English Pewter 030, Solkets".

7in (18cm) high

£400-500 **DN**

A pair of Liberty and Co. Tudric pewter candlesticks, each with circular base and cylindrical stem above open-work section, the tops of the stems moulded with stylized foliage, detachable sconces, stamped "TUDRIC 022".

5in (12.5cm) high

£350-450 **GORL**

A Liberty and Co. Tudric pewter twin-handled bowl, designed by Archibald Knox, of circular form with pierced sides cast with stylized leaves and tendrils, lacks liner, stamped marks "0320".

9in (23cm) wide

£120-180 **L&T**

A Liberty and Co. Tudric round caddy, designed by Archibald Knox, the cylindrical caddy decorated with stylized flowers, the cover with concave centre and horizontal flat handle, stamped beneath "T", "Tudric" and "0193".

4in (10cm) high

£450-550 **DN**

A CLOSER LOOK AT ART NOUVEAU METALWORK

One of a pair of Liberty and Co. Tudric pewter glass holders, designed by Archibald Knox, each of cylindrical form, the body diagonally pierced and cast with entwined foliage and leaves, stamped marks "0534".

3in (7.5cm) high

£60-100 pair **L&T**

The naturalistic, tapering and curving handles are typical of the Art Nouveau movement.

Stylized floral and foliate decoration was a popular theme of the movement.

The pierced areas draw attention to the shapes and forms and allow the glass inside to be seen, providing contrast.

The Württemberg Metalwork Factory (W.M.F.) became known for its elaborate Art Nouveau styled metalware and its success inspired the design of the Liberty and Co. 'Tudric' range.

A W.M.F. Art Nouveau pewter siphon stand, with two tendril handles, pierced and embossed with leaves, impressed marks.

8in (20cm) high

£150-200 **LFA**

METALWARE

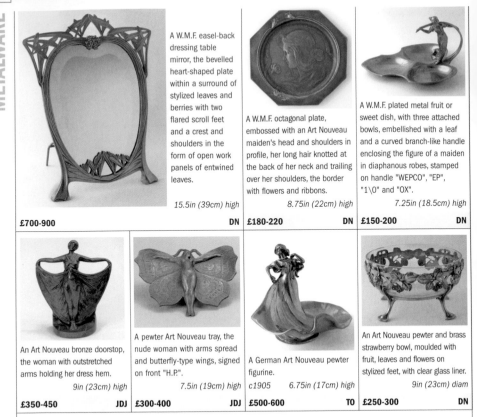

A W.M.F. easel-back dressing table mirror, the bevelled heart-shaped plate within a surround of stylized leaves and berries with two flared scroll feet and a crest and shoulders in the form of open work panels of entwined leaves.

15.5in (39cm) high

£700-900 DN

A W.M.F. octagonal plate, embossed with an Art Nouveau maiden's head and shoulders in profile, her long hair knotted at the back of her neck and trailing over her shoulders, the border with flowers and ribbons.

8.75in (22cm) high

£180-220 DN

A W.M.F. plated metal fruit or sweet dish, with three attached bowls, embellished with a leaf and a curved branch-like handle enclosing the figure of a maiden in diaphanous robes, stamped on handle "WEPCO", "EP", "1\0" and "OX".

7.25in (18.5cm) high

£150-200 DN

An Art Nouveau bronze doorstop, the woman with outstretched arms holding her dress hem.

9in (23cm) high

£350-450 JDJ

A pewter Art Nouveau tray, the nude woman with arms spread and butterfly-type wings, signed on front "H.P.".

7.5in (19cm) high

£300-400 JDJ

A German Art Nouveau pewter figurine.

c1905 6.75in (17cm) high

£500-600 TO

An Art Nouveau pewter and brass strawberry bowl, moulded with fruit, leaves and flowers on stylized feet, with clear glass liner.

9in (23cm) diam

£250-300 DN

[DK] The Complete Picture

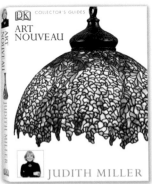

- Profiles of all the major designers and makers
- Over 1,000 full-colour photographs
- Up-to-date valuations
- Tips for collectors
- Analysis of iconic pieces
- Includes furniture, glass, ceramics, jewellery, metalware, sculpture, and posters

ART NOUVEAU

JUDITH MILLER

COLLECTORS' NOTES

- Badges and brooches form a popular collecting area that requires little space to store or display. Badges vary in type although may look similar, so examine the shape and format of a badge to find out where it was used. Changes in the Army occurred frequently, meaning insignia often changed. It can be interesting to track a regiment through its changing insignia.

- Before 1881 all regiments were known by number, but the Cardwell reforms of 1881 saw the loss of numbers and the adoption of names based on the county of location. Some regiments were also merged and many spent the next few decades trying to alter their names to correctly reflect their heritage.

- Cap badges were made from metal until 1945 when more inexpensive plastics took over allowing costs to be cut. Although these have been less popular with collectors than metal badges, rarities are being identified and their popularity is growing.

- Many of the cap badges and buttons available have been made recently, often from original dies. They are inexpensive and are often used by collectors to fill gaps in a collection but are also collectable in their own right.

- Beware of 'restrikes,' which have been artificially aged or worn to make them appear original. Handle and examine as many authentic examples as possible so that you can learn to recognise an authentic example.

A post 1902 silver-plated plaid brooch of The Highland Light Infantry, badge as for Glengarry with wreath bearing battle honours to South Africa on plain circle.

£180-220　　　　　　　　**W&W**

A piper's silver-plated plaid brooch of The Royal Scots, St Andrew and Cross, in Victorian crowned wreath on plain circle with title scroll below.

£60-80　　　　　　　　**W&W**

A Victorian officer's silver-plated pouch belt badge, Prince of Wales feathers on backing plate within crowned laurel wreath, probably Cheshire, two studs with original looped nuts and washers.

£250-300　　　　　　　　**W&W**

An officer's cast silver-plated plaid brooch of the 1st Volunteer Battalion The Seaforth Highlanders, engraved in script on the back "AFM".

£150-200　　　　　　　　**W&W**

An officer's gilt and silver slouch hat badge of the Northamptonshire Imperial Yeomanry, little gilt remaining.

£300-400　　　　　　　　**W&W**

An other ranks white metal Glengarry badge of the South Mayo Rifles.

£180-220　　　　　　　　**W&W**

A pair of Victorian brass bit bosses of The 5th (Princess Charlotte of Wales) Dragoon Guards, two copper studs each.

£120-180   **W&W**

An officer's cap badge of the Chota Nagpur Regiment, by J R Gaunt London, marked "S" on the back, blades missing.

£80-120   **W&W**

A Victorian other ranks helmet plate, of The Royal Marines Light Infantry, one lug missing, ray tips slightly bent.

£150-200   **W&W**

A Victorian officer's silver-plated helmet plate of the 2nd Volunteer Battalion The Cheshire Regiment.

Helmet plates made from white metals were issued to volunteers only. Brass plates were issued to regular soldiers.

£400-500   **W&W**

A scarce other ranks white metal Glengarry badge of the 4th-7th Battalion The Black Watch.

£120-180   **W&W**

An officer's silver-plated pouch badge of the Chester Volunteer Rifles, three studs.

£280-320   **W&W**

A standard Light Cavalry silver yeomans pouch, London hallmarks.

1842

£300-400   **CS**

A Georgian other ranks oval cast brass shoulder belt plate of the Strathspey Fencibles, bearing crown over thistle spray, with title around the top, hook and two stud fastening.

The regiment was raised in March 1793 under Sir James Grant, Bart.

£150-200   **W&W**

A silver-coloured cap badge of the 28th County of London Battalion (Artists Rifles), by Mappin & Webb, with slide, and a pair of matching collars marked "Mn & Wb Silver".

£100-150   **W&W**

A WWI Prussian officer's pickelhaube, white metal plate and mounts including tall spike with beaded base chinscale, state and national rosettes, silk lining, minor crazing to skull, lining slightly worn, one brass spike retaining rivet missing, in its lined and padded carrying case with leather strap and handle.

The instantly recognisable pickelhaube has remained a collectors' favourite due to its variety and wide price range, from a few hundred pounds to a couple of thousand pounds for a helmet from the Kaiser's Lifeguard.

£1,000-2,000   **W&W**

A WWI Prussian Reserve Artillery Officer's Kugelhelm, gilt brass plate with silver Landwehr cross, gilt brass mounts, chinscales, yellow skin lining, minor crazing to skull, some wear to gilt, star rivets replaced, rear peak stitching loose.

£550-650   **W&W**

A Prussian Infantry other ranks pickelhaube, black leather skull with brass fittings and gilt plate, leather chinstrap and nine segments lining, painted cockades, Berlin maker's stamp inside crown, and inside rear peak stamped "J R 152 1907 2B", brass peak trim missing, some wear overall and minor rust patches.

£280-320   **W&W**

A WWI Prussian other ranks pickelhaube and cover, grey-finished steel mounts and plate, maker's stamp and date inside skull, state and national rosettes, the rear peak stamped "R 39", some bubbling to peaks, rosettes repainted, chinstrap replaced, with its scarce khaki linen cover with felt number 39 to front.

1915

£300-350   **W&W**

An Imperial German military band NCOs pickelhaube, state rosette only, leather.

£400-500   **W&W**

A WWI German other ranks pickelhaube of the State of Reuss, gilt plate with superimposed white metal state arms, maker's stamp on inside of skull, rosettes repainted, chinstrap replaced.

Each German state had its own individual device, which adds another interesting dimension to collecting this type of helmet.

£900-1,200   **W&W**

A WWI Saxon other ranks pickelhaube, stamped "RA XII 16".

£350-450   **W&W**

A scarce officer's scarlet cloth peaked cap of the South Nottinghamshire Hussars, patent leather peak and chinstrap with plain buttons, silver badge with Birmingham hallmark and makers mark "F&S", patent leather congealed, minor marks and surface moth traces.

1904

£220-280   **W&W**

A well-made copy of a Russian Garde Hussar busby, possibly silver fox fur, with enamelled Garde star and brass honours scroll above.

£800-1,000   **W&W**

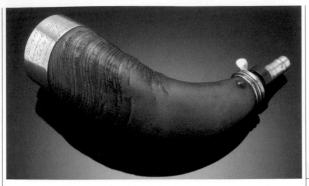

A rare early 18thC silver-mounted pocket ramshorn powder flask, with an engraved inscription on the base, with silver nozzle and turned mount decorated with incised line turning, secured by two screws, the base with screw top silver cap.

The early date, good level of work, materials and condition make this a valuable and desirable flask.

6in (15cm) long

£1,500-2,500   **L&T**

A late 18thC Spanish belt powder horn, sprung common top with vase-shaped brass nozzle, steel end plate, sprung steel belt hook with suspension ring, some small filled holes.

10in (25.5cm) long

£100-150   **W&W**

A German engraved horn powder flask, engraved with hunting scenes, nozzle inlaid with two eyes, wooden base plate.

10in (25.5cm) long

£100-200   **W&W**

A German silver cap dispenser, by Sykes.

£200-250   **W&W**

A small copper pistol flask, the tapered body stamped "Sykes", common brass top, fixed nozzles.

3.75in (9.5cm) long

£120-180   **W&W**

Three medals comprising The Royal Victorian Order, Lieutenant's breast badge; Edward VII Coronation 1902; George V Coronation 1911, mounted court-style; together with a miniature group of four: St Michael & St George breast badge, Coronation 1902, Coronation 1911, mounted as worn.

£250-300   **W&W**

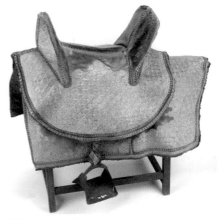

An officer's levée dress belt of The Scots Guards, gilt lace on red morocco, gilt and silver-plated waist belt clasp with green enamel backing to centre thistle.

£250-300   **W&W**

A 19thC Moroccan saddle, wooden tree covered with tooled leather and with further leather covers decorated with bullion embroidery in a repeated geometric design, tall pommel and cantle, iron stirrups mounted on a wooden display stand, some age wear overall.

£800-1,000   **W&W**

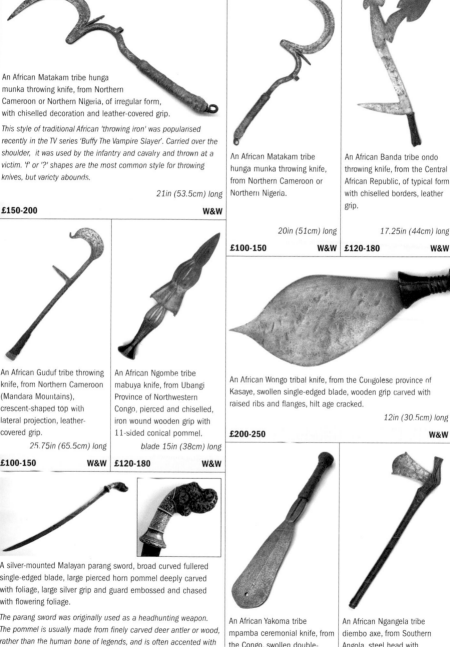

An African Matakam tribe hunga munka throwing knife, from Northern Cameroon or Northern Nigeria, of irregular form, with chiselled decoration and leather-covered grip.

This style of traditional African 'throwing iron' was popularised recently in the TV series 'Buffy The Vampire Slayer'. Carried over the shoulder, it was used by the infantry and cavalry and thrown at a victim. 'f' or '?' shapes are the most common style for throwing knives, but variety abounds.

21in (53.5cm) long

£150-200 W&W

An African Matakam tribe hunga munka throwing knife, from Northern Cameroon or Northern Nigeria.

20in (51cm) long

£100-150 W&W

An African Banda tribe ondo throwing knife, from the Central African Republic, of typical form with chiselled borders, leather grip.

17.25in (44cm) long

£120-180 W&W

An African Guduf tribe throwing knife, from Northern Cameroon (Mandara Mountains), crescent-shaped top with lateral projection, leather-covered grip.

25.75in (65.5cm) long

£100-150 W&W

An African Ngombe tribe mabuya knife, from Ubangi Province of Northwestern Congo, pierced and chiselled, iron wound wooden grip with 11-sided conical pommel.

blade 15in (38cm) long

£120-180 W&W

An African Wongo tribal knife, from the Congolese province of Kasaye, swollen single-edged blade, wooden grip carved with raised ribs and flanges, hilt age cracked.

12in (30.5cm) long

£200-250 W&W

A silver-mounted Malayan parang sword, broad curved fullered single-edged blade, large pierced horn pommel deeply carved with foliage, large silver grip and guard embossed and chased with flowering foliage.

The parang sword was originally used as a headhunting weapon. The pommel is usually made from finely carved deer antler or wood, rather than the human bone of legends, and is often accented with tufts of goat hair. The blade on earlier examples is usually decorated.

c1800

blade 28.5in (72.5cm) long

£280-320 W&W

An African Yakoma tribe mpamba ceremonial knife, from the Congo, swollen double-edged blade, iron wound wooden hilt.

blade 9in (23cm) long

£100-150 W&W

An African Ngangela tribe diembo axe, from Southern Angola, steel head with punched decoration, carved top to wooden haft.

21in (53.5cm) long

£50-70 W&W

A 19thC Malayan parang sword, watered swollen heavy single-edged blade, carved wooden hilt with foliate embossed silver ferrule, in ebony sheath with carved wooden top and two silver mounts, wood of fine grain, minor chips.

blade 14in (35.5cm) long

£250-300   **W&W**

A 19thC silver-mounted Malayan bade bade dagger, silver hilt embossed and chased with foliage, in wooden sheath, horn top carved in relief with foliage, silver mounts en-suite with narrow silver bands.

blade 8in (20cm) long

£180-220   **W&W**

A CLOSER LOOK AT AN EDGED WEAPON

All dhas have a single edge, but the tip may be squared off for domestic uses, or tapered.

The blade of higher quality examples can be damascened, or bear designs executed in silver wire.

Higher quality examples have silver covering on the hilt and scabbard, which can be decorated with engravings or chasing.

The quality of a dha and its decoration usually indicates its use from domestic and mundane to ceremonial.

A Burmese silver-mounted dha dagger, curved single-edged blade, ivory hilt with silver filigreed ferrule and sheath, green cotton belt cord, some patches of light rust.

A dha can come in a many different lengths and is the national edged weapon of Burma.

12.5in (31.5cm) long

£100-150   **W&W**

A silver mounted Burmese dha dagger, octagonal silver ferrule with silver wire filigree decoration, tapered octagonal ivory grip, in silver-covered sheath.

blade 9in (23cm) long

£100-150   **W&W**

A 19thC Indian dagger, recurved blade with thickened point etched with foliage, silver-plated hilt with lion's head pommel, ribbed grip, recurved quillons, in fabric-covered sheath with silver-plated pierced mounts, locket with birds at top, chape with stylized animal head finial, minor age wear.

blade 9in (23cm) long

£280-320   **W&W**

An 18thC Indian watered steel katar, blade of finely watered Oriental damascus steel, deep fullers and ribs, thickened steel armour piercing tip, hilt of conventional form with swollen faceted handlebars, good condition.

17.25in (18.5cm) long

£300-400   **W&W**

A scarce WWI French military dagger (Stephens No 95), diamond section blade stamped "Le Vengeur De 1870" and "76", steel crosspiece, shaped fruitwood grip, in steel sheath, minor rust marks to sheath.

blade 6in (15cm) long

£100-200   **W&W**

A scarce 19thC Swiss military saw-backed shortsword, broad single-edged blade, stamped "S J G HEJH (?) 17345-89" with Swiss cross, brass cruciform hilt of gladius type, in brass-mounted leather scabbard with frog stamped "Felix Widmer, Sattler, Granichen", with Swiss cross above "K".

blade 20.5in (52cm) long

£200-300   **W&W**

A well-made copy of an American Bowie knife, clipped back blade stamped "Rose New York", white metal crosspiece, two-piece ivory grips with white metal mounts, in white metal-mounted leather sheath, aged for effect.

blade 10in (25.5cm) long

£1,000-1,500   **W&W**

A first pattern field service military knife, by Wilkinson Sword Co Ltd, London, approx 1mm of tip broken off, chape rivet missing.

7in (18cm) long

£300-400   **W&W**

A well-made copy of an American Bowie knife, clipped back blade engraved "W & S Butcher Sheffield-For Graveley & Wreaks New York", white metal crosspiece with large leaf-shaped quillons, white metal gripstrap and mounts, two-piece mother-of-pearl grips, in white metal-mounted leather sheath, well aged for effect.

blade 10in (25.5cm) long

£500-600   **W&W**

A Scottish Skean dhu garter dagger, carved bog oak handle with white metal mounts, embossed pommel, in leather sheath, age worn, blade cleaned.

The name derives from the Gaelic 'sgian' for dagger and 'dubh' for black, as the handle was usually carved from black bog oak. The word black can also indicate 'secret' as it was usually concealed.

8in (20cm) long

£100-150   **W&W**

An unusual 19thC Continental carved casein ritual dagger, hilt and sheath carved with foliage surmounted by satanic, horned and bearded heads.

10in (25.5cm) long

£250-350   **W&W**

An Edwardian folding hunting knife, clipped back blade with white metal crosspiece and mounts, sprung thumb catch for release, two-piece natural staghorn grips with vacant shield-shaped escutcheon, in leather sheath, tip of blade re-shaped.

blade 7in (18cm) long

£35-45   **W&W**

A CLOSER LOOK AT A BAYONET

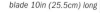

This bayonet was designed by Lord Elcho, the 9th Earl of Wemyss & March in 1870 and initial trials saw great success.

It has an integral saw for chopping trees or bushes on the top of the blade and was made to fit the Martini-Henry rifle in trial at the time.

It is well balanced allowing excellent performance in cutting and chopping as well as attack and defensive moves.

Genuine examples were made by Enfield and others - those marked 'AC' and bearing a motif of scales or marked with the name of the bayonet are likely to be fakes.

A rare 1871 Elcho sword bayonet, regulation saw-back blade with broad arrow, "WD" and two Enfield inspector's stamps, crosspiece stamped "8/84", steel pommel, sprung catch, two-piece chequered leather grips, age worn and cleaned overall, one grip well worn.

This bayonet was developed in 1870 and in 1871 modifications were made to produce a final design. Despite its initial success, it was costly to produce and met with some resistance, so the design was short-lived and other bayonets were adapted instead.

blade 20in (51cm) long

£500-600   **W&W**

An Ashmor porcelain figure of a Battle of Britain pilot, 'A Royal Air Force Fighter Pilot of Churchill's Few', from a limited edition of 250.

£200-300   **W&W**

An Ashmor porcelain figure, 'Field Marshal The Viscount Montgomery of Alamein, KGB, DSO', from a limited edition of 375.

£200-300   **W&W**

An Ashmor porcelain figure of a Gurkha soldier in the Falklands Campaign, 'A Soldier Representing the 1st Battalion 7th Regiment of The Duke of Edinburgh's Own Gurkha Rifles', from a limited edition of 250.

£180-220   **W&W**

An Ashmor porcelain figure, 'United States 8th Army Air Force Pilot, 1942-1945', from a limited edition of 250.

£180-220   **W&W**

An unframed watercolour '1st Royal Dragoons'.

10in (25.5cm) high

£200-300   **L&T**

A watercolour, signed "E Benassit", depicting a French Revolutionary period reconnaissance party seeking local knowledge from a peasant.

16in (40.5cm) wide

£500-600   **W&W**

A silver-coloured metal cup, engraved "Presented to Bertie Beresford Hart by his godfather Lord William Beresford 9th Lancers VC Calcutta 30".

8in (20cm) high

£250-300   **W&W**

A brass candlestick, made from the hilt of an Imperial German infantry officer's sword, regulation hilt with crowned eagle in guard, crowned WWII device to wire bound leather-covered grip, brass base and sconce mounted on section of blade.

11in (28cm) long

£50-70   **W&W**

A Scottish oval plated military shooting match trophy shield, on wooden back plate, decorated with an angel holding laurel wreaths above two soldiers with Martini falling block rifles and with St. Giles, Edinburgh Castle and the Scott Monument all framed by thistles.

Known as the Artisan Challenge Shield, it was started in 1891 and shot for until the outbreak of WWII in 1939, there is a gap in the list of named winners from 1913-28, in part due to WWI.

28in (71cm) high

£450-550   **L&T**

A scarce and interesting Georgian officer's campaign knife and fork, two-pronged steel fork, curved knife, the blade unclearly stamped "MIL/...PD", tapered hexagonal agate handles with scalloped edge bands, in velvet-lined, fitted leatherette case, some rust pitting, one band restored, few worn patches to case.

£250-300   **W&W**

COLLECTORS' NOTES

■ The speed at which the technology developed makes this a particularly interesting subject and early examples with their cumbersome and blocky designs are among the most sought-after.

■ Designs that have become iconic through media coverage are also desirable. When the Nokia 8110 had a pivotal role in the sci-fi blockbuster 'The Matrix' it instantly became the must-have handset of the moment. This marketing ploy proved so successful that Samsung specifically designed a handset for the first sequel.

■ Mobile phones are now seen as an indispensable part of everyday life and handsets are regularly upgraded as new designs and technology are released. Look for examples that are complete and in good condition.

■ The market is still in infancy with very little literature available to collectors other than the original catalogues, company literature or magazine reviews, and no standardised structure, so it will be interesting to see how the market develops.

An Alcatel HD1 mobile phone, with blue fascia.

6in (15cm) high

£20-30 GC

A British Telecom ebony TCR M0600 mobile phone, made by Matsushita, with extending aerial.

6.75in (17cm) high

£20-30 GC

An Ericsson GA628 GSM mobile phone, with green fascia.

c1997   6.5in (16.5cm) high

£15-25 GC

An Ericsson GA628 GSM mobile phone, with coloured fascia, and fixed aerial.

This model came in a variety of colour finishes.

c1997   6.5in (16.5cm) long

£20-35 GC

An Ericsson GH198 mobile phone, with flip aerial.

5.5in (14cm) high

£20-35 GC

A Maxon SL500 mobile phone, in the form of a walkie talkie.

8in (20cm) long

£50-60 GC

A black Motorola 6800X mobile phone and base battery unit, with cord and revolving aerial.

9.5in (24cm) long

£90-120 GC

A grey Motorola Star-TAC GSM mobile phone.

c1996   3.75in (9.5cm) long

£50-60 GC

A grey Motorola Independent mobile phone, the fixed aerial unscrews.

7.75in (19.5cm) long

£75-85   GC

A grey NEC Jade P3 ETACS mobile phone, lacks aerial.

c1992-3   6.5in (16.5cm) long

£15-20   GC

A black Nokia THX-6X mobile phone, with extending aerial, illuminating keys and three lines for speaker.

7.25in (18.5cm) long

£20-35   GC

A Nokia NHK-4RY mobile phone, with black keys and grey panels under screen.

6.75in (17cm) high

£20-35   GC

A Philips Fizz blue and black GSM mobile phone, with extending aerial.

c1997   7in (18cm) high

£20-30   GC

A silver Siemens J7 Digiphone mobile phone, with extending aerial.

6.75in (17cm) high

£20-30   GC

A white Storno 220 mobile phone.

9.75in (19.5cm) high

£85-95   GC

A Technophone PC2215T mobile phone, with extending aerial.

c1993   7.75in (19.5cm) long

£75-85   GC

A Sony CM-R111 ETACS mobile phone, with flip arm microphone.

c1993   4.25in (11cm) high

£80-100   G

A Faust magic lantern, by Gebrüder Bing, together with 12 3in slides, electrified.

Contained in a fitted box with small glass slides of children's stories, these lanterns were popular toys. Look for complete examples in excellent condition.

c1905   14.5in (37cm) high

£150-200   **ATK**

A 'Lampadophore' magic lantern, by Lapierre, Paris, in original wooden box, with 28 glass slides.

c1880

£650-750   **ATK**

A Lanterne Riche magic lantern, by Gebrüder Lapierre, Paris, for 2.5in slides, some patches of rust, lacks burner.

Lapierre are known for their brightly coloured, novelty-shaped tin lanterns – condition is important to value with splits, wear and rust devaluing examples considerably. Look for examples in the shapes of buildings, such as the Eiffel Tower, which are very valuable.

c1880

£320-380

12in (30.5cm) high

ATK

A mahogany mechanical, hand-painted magic lantern chromotrope slide.

c1890

£100-150   **ET**

A French mahogany stereoviewer, by Unis-France, together with a binocular type stereoviewer.

£350-400   **ATK**

A mahogany and brass 'Lothian' magic lantern by A.H. Baird of Edinburgh, with fabric bellows on a sliding focusing mechanism.

This magic lantern design was illustrated in the 1st November, 1892 edition of 'The Practical Photographer' and was said to be both of good value and excellent design. Baird was a photographic dealer based at 15 Lothian Street, Edinburgh.

18.5in (47cm) high

£300-500   **ET**

An unusual floor-standing Mutoscope, by the International Mutoscope Reel Co. Inc., New York, USA, with Mutoscope reel No. 7698, featuring a semi-naked maiden, holding a harp, dancing in the forest.

Mutoscopes held 'wheels' of single photographic images - turning a handle would rotate the wheel and show a sequence of images in quick succession, giving the impression of movement. Many were found at the seaside and other tourist attractions.

A walnut table-mounted stereoviewer, probably French, with 50 erotic stereocards.

17.75in (45cm) high

£450-550   **ATK**

An incomplete mahogany-cased Praxinoscope Theatre, by Emile Reynaud of Paris.

c1879   9.75in (25cm) wide

£350-400   **F**

c1900   56in (143cm) high

£1,500-2,000   **ATK**

COLLECTORS' NOTES

■ The 'classic' period of paperweight manufacture was between c1845 and c1860 and was centred in France around the glasshouses of Clichy, Baccarat and St Louis. Millefiori canes arranged in different patterns are the most common types, along with 'posy' weights of flowers. Look for complex and densely packed 'set-ups' and large 'magnum' or smaller 'miniature' sizes.

■ America and Scotland in particular led the revival of paperweight art during the 20th century, with names such as Paul Ysart, Charles Kaziun and later Paul Stankard and John Deacons. Natural designs still dominate as does the use of millefiori canes, but lamp or torch worked forms have also become important, further demonstrating the skill of the maker. Unlike 19th century examples, most are signed or contain canes with monograms making identification easy.

An 1850s Baccarat 'Anemone' paperweight.

2.25in (6cm) diam

£700-1,000 BGL

An 1850s/60s French Baccarat 'Primrose' paperweight, with star-cut base.

2.75in (7cm) diam

£750-850 BGL

An 1850s French Baccarat 'Anemone' paperweight, with red flower on a white latticework ground.

2.5in (6.5cm) diam

£700-800 BGL

An 1850s St Louis 'Double Clematis' paperweight, with amber ground and pink flower.

2.25in (5.5cm) diam

£750-850 BG

A 19thC St Louis 'Fruit Bouquet' paperweight.

2.75in (7cm) diam

£700-800 BGL

A rare Clichy paperweight, green and white carpet ground with millefiori canes, underneath a Clichy rose.

c1850 2.75in (7cm) diam

£700-900 FIS

A 19thC Bohemian-Czechoslovakian magnum paperweight, with a three-dimensional sulphide of a white rabbit.

4in (10cm) diam

£300-400 LHS

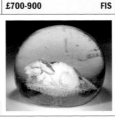

A mid-19thC Baccarat paperweight, two stone formations and moss glass imitations of green glass, concave base.

2.5in (6.5cm) diam

£250-350 WKA

A mid-to late 19thC Baccarat 'Sand Dune' paperweight.

These almost abstract patterns are made of unmelted sand and fragments of mica and green glass.

2.5in (6.5cm) diam

£70-100 AI

An unsigned Perthshire millefiori paperweight.

2.5in (6.5cm) diam

£50-70   **BGL**

A 20thC Perthshire paperweight, on a dark red glass cushion millefiori canes and white strings of glass, in the centre a flower, blossom and leaves, concave base.

Perthshire Glass was formed by Stuart Drysdale in 1968. He had worked with the Ysarts at Caithness and continued to make paperweights in that style.

3in (8cm) diam

£300-400   **WKA**

A 20thC Perthshire paperweight, with millefiori canes on a clear glass cushion, overlaid in red, cut through with circular panels and with star-cut base.

3.25in (8cm) diam

£250-350   **WKA**

A 1960s/70s Perthshire paperweight, with blue ground and millefiori rods arranged in a chain link star, with paper label to base for "Perthshire Paperweights Crieff Scotland".

2.25in (6cm) diam

£150-200   **BGL**

A 1970s Ysart paperweight, with bubbles emerging from a multicoloured ground, with blue PY sticker to base.

Paul Ysart is considered one of the fathers of 20thC paperweight design and began making paperweights in the 1930s for Monart at the Moncrieff glassworks and then Caithness Glass from 1963. He then set up his own company specialising in paperweight production in 1970 which ran until 1982.

2.25in (5.5cm) high

£150-250   **AB**

A William Manson 'Blue Dahlia' paperweight, signed to the base "William Manson SNR 2001".

2.5in (6.5cm) diam

£80-120   **BGL**

A late 1970s Charles Kaziun Pansy with Gold Bee' paperweight, the bee in gold foil resting on a milky pale yellow base, signed with a gold signature "K".

1.75in (4.5cm) diam

£800-1,200   **BGL**

A CLOSER LOOK AT A PAPERWEIGHT

Kaziun aimed to revive French paperweight manufacture techniques. Both the ground, known as 'muslin', made up of sections of canes, and the flower are typical of this.

The rose is 'lampworked' using a small gas blow torch to manipulate the glass before it is centred and cased in flawless clear glass – all typical features of many 20thC artist made paperweights.

Kaziun had admired and studied roses made by noted American paperweight and glass designer and maker Emil Larson (1879-unknown).

An American Charles Kaziun 'rose on muslin' paperweight, signed with "K" signature cane.

Kaziun is one of the 20thC's foremost and influential paperweight artists, beginning his work in 1939. He was self-taught and worked from his studio at his home, kick-starting a 'studio artist' movement in paperweight manufacture.

c1955

2.25in (5.5cm) diam

£800-1,200   **BGL**

A unique William Manson footed 'Strawberry Patch' paperweight, signed to the base "William Manson SNR 1/1 1999 Joyce Manson", with "William Manson Made in Scotland" paper label to base.

2.75in (7cm) diam

£100-150 **BGL**

A William Manson 'master sample' 'Almond Tree Flowers' type paperweight, with pink, blue and white cherry flowers on a green ground, signed inside with 'WM' cane, and to base "William Manson 2002 Master Sample".

William Manson founded his factory in Perth, Scotland in 1997 with his family. Each piece bears a signature cane in the design and an inscribed signature, number and date on the base. Many are released in limited editions, with unique examples such as this 'master sample' being highly sought after.

2002 *2.25in (6cm) diam*

£150-250 **BGL**

A John Deacons millefiori paperweight, with label to base, signed with "JD 2004" double hearts and thistle cane.

2004 *2.75in (7cm) diam*

£70-100 **BGL**

A Gordon Smith paperweight, with coral on a grey-blue ground and a red-black frog over a clear glass base, signed with a monogram cane and engraved with the year of production.

1944 *3in (7.5cm) diam*

£220-280 **WKA**

A John Deacons 'Pom Pom' paperweight, signed to the base with "JD 2002 cane".

2.75in (7cm) diam

£220-280 **BGL**

A Lewis and Jennifer Wilson faceted orange frog, snake and flowers paperweight, signed with blue 'CM' cane.

2.75in (7cm) diam

£180-220 **BGL**

A Daniel Salazar cherry blossom and dragonfly paperweight, signed to rim "Daniel Salazar Lundberg Studios 2003 06/927".

In 1974 Salazar and Steven Lundberg launched what has become known as the 'California' style, using complex, 3-D torchworked designs.

2.5in (6.5cm) high

£300-400 **BGL**

A large Steven Lundberg moon and cherry blossom paperweight, the moon made from gold foil, the base signed "Steven Lundberg Lundberg Studios 1995 051128".

3.5in (9cm) diam

£300-400 **BGL**

A Lindsay Art Glass 'New Zealand Coral Reef' dichroic paperweight, signed "Lindsay Art Glass 2002" on base.

3in (7.5cm) diam

£150-250 **BGL**

A crown paperweight, with radiating canes separated by twisted canes.

£70-100 **ROS**

A CLOSER LOOK AT A DUNHILL NAMIKI PEN

The box increases the desirability of this piece. Boxes are rare as they were often lost or damaged and thrown away.

This pen was made under a partnership between British luxury goods retailer Alfred Dunhill Ltd and the Japanese Namiki Mfg Co. Ltd, who were responsible for the lacquerwork decoration.

The decoration was painstakingly hand-painted by skilled artists over a period of weeks onto a black lacquered background using clear and coloured lacquer and gold and silver dust.

The decoration is artistically applied around the entire body of the pen, encouraging it to be turned around to view the entire design. A part of the design is shown however the pen is held.

A 1930s Dunhill Namiki three-quarter size lacquer fountain pen, showing a duck in flight on the barrel, with reeds on the barrel and cap, in original Dunhill Namiki box, artists signature on the barrel.

£1,500-2,000   **GORL**

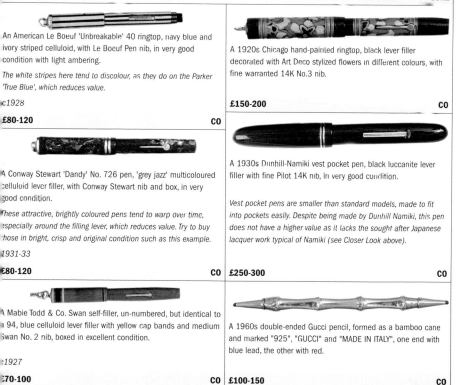

An American Le Boeuf 'Unbreakable' 40 ringtop, navy blue and ivory striped celluloid, with Le Boeuf Pen nib, in very good condition with light ambering.

The white stripes here tend to discolour, as they do on the Parker 'True Blue', which reduces value.

c1928

£80-120   **CO**

A Conway Stewart 'Dandy' No. 726 pen, 'grey jazz' multicoloured celluloid lever filler, with Conway Stewart nib and box, in very good condition.

These attractive, brightly coloured pens tend to warp over time, especially around the filling lever, which reduces value. Try to buy those in bright, crisp and original condition such as this example.

1931-33

£80-120   **CO**

A Mabie Todd & Co. Swan self-filler, un-numbered, but identical to a 94, blue celluloid lever filler with yellow cap bands and medium Swan No. 2 nib, boxed in excellent condition.

c1927

£70-100   **CO**

A 1920s Chicago hand-painted ringtop, black lever filler decorated with Art Deco stylized flowers in different colours, with fine warranted 14K No.3 nib.

£150-200   **CO**

A 1930s Dunhill-Namiki vest pocket pen, black luccanite lever filler with fine Pilot 14K nib, in very good condition.

Vest pocket pens are smaller than standard models, made to fit into pockets easily. Despite being made by Dunhill Namiki, this pen does not have a higher value as it lacks the sought after Japanese lacquer work typical of Namiki (see Closer Look above).

£250-300   **CO**

A 1960s double-ended Gucci pencil, formed as a bamboo cane and marked "925", "GUCCI" and "MADE IN ITALY", one end with blue lead, the other with red.

£100-150   **CO**

PENS & WRITING

A late 1920s Mabie Todd & Co. Swan 172-53, scarlet celluloid ringtop lever filler with black cap bands and fine Swan No.2 nib, in fair to good condition.

£50-70 CO

A late 1920s Mabie Todd & Co 54 ETN pen, pearl and black veined and marbled celluloid lever filling ringtop with fine Swan Eternal 4 nib, in very good condition with mild ambering.

£70-100 CO

A Mabie Todd & Co Swan Eternal E644B, mottled red and black hard rubber lever filling pen with medium Swan Eternal No.6 nib, in good but over-polished condition.

Large sized pens are desirable. The price would have increased by around 30% if it had not been overpolished.

c1920

£70-100 CO

A late 1930s Mabie Todd & Co 'Cygnet' stylo, un-numbered burgundy and black marbled celluloid lever filler with 'PATENT APPLIED FOR' barrel imprint and chrome trim.

Stylos or 'ink pencils' have thin, tubular nibs instead of a standard nib.

£60-80 CO

A late 1920s Mabie Todd & Co. self-filling pen, un-numbered jade green celluloid lever filler with fine Swan No.2 nib, in very good condition with a little brassing to the clip.

£50-80 CO

A 1980s Parker 75 Lacque pen and pencil set, 'thuya' lacquer cartridge/convertor filler with Parker 585 france nib and matching push cap ballpen, in near mint condition.

Although still deemed 'modern', the 75 has become a hot, niche collecting market. Pens must be in mint condition or have unusual finishes to be of interest to most collectors.

£50-80 CO

A Wahl Eversharp Skyline, sapphire blue pearl and black striped celluloid cap and barrel, with gold filled cap top and Eversharp nib, in excellent condition.

This is an unusual colour for a comparatively common pen.

c1943

£100-150 CO

A Montblanc 14k gold No. 744 pen and No. 772 pencil, stamped "585", fully working, no dents, engraved name.

This set is in excellent condition with crisp engine turned decoration and no dents or engraved names. Not all overlays on fountain pens were made or approved by the maker. Look carefully for authentic maker's marks. Many marks were added later by jewellers or added by unscrupulous collectors to raise the value of the pen.

c1955

£1,000-1,500 ATL

A 19thC brass rectangular inkstand, with leaf-chased handles, two cut-glass wells and a central recess, on round feet.

11.75in (30cm) wide

£300-400 DN

An unusual brass building-shape inkstand, with 'lift-up' roofs revealing inkwells, "Samuel Thompson & Sons/ Midland Maltings/ Smethwick Birmingham" in raised lettering to middle section with lift-off roof to take pens.

10.75in (27.5cm) long

£220-280 BBR

A German 'inky boy' bisque inkwell.

c1900 *5in (12.5cm) high*

£100-150 BEJ

A late 19thC brass novelty dog inkwell, after Landseer, in the form of a begging terrier, with glass eyes on circular beaded base.

The finely modelled and comparatively large form is much like the terrier seen in 'Macaw, Love Birds, Terrier, and Spaniel Puppies' painted by Sir Edwin Landseer in 1839. The painting is now owned by H.M. Queen Elizabeth II and is in the Buckingham Palace Collection, London.

7in (17.5cm) high

£400-500 GORL

A white metal stags head inkstand, the base engraved "Ryton Regatta 1894/ Steeplechase & Swimming/ J Geo Joicey", some damage to inkwells.

7in (18cm) wide

£40-60 BBR

A 19th/20thC Louis XV-style gilt-bronze and porcelain inkwell, the lobed porcelain bowl decorated in the Imari style, the dish base with scroll mounts, with scroll cast cover.

7in (17.5cm) high

£120-150 SL

A 1950s Parker green glass pen base, by Whitefriars, with internal bubble decoration, to hold a Parker 51 pen.

ball 2.75in (7cm) high

£30-40 GC

A Continental satinwood, ebony and brass standish, rectangular table-top form supported by turned standard resting on rectangular satinwood plinth with in-curved sides and single drawer.

13.75in (35cm) long

£300-400 SL

A Victorian electroplate inkstand, with pierced gallery and foliate moulded feet, mounted centrally with an underglaze blue painted ink reservoir in the Chinese taste, flanked by moulded pen trays.

c1870 *9.75in (25cm) wide*

£100-150 BONS

An English Victorian papier-mâché standish, rectangular box with single drawer having central carrying handle and pair of pen trays and pair of clear glass inkwells, decorated with floral mother-of-pearl inlaid design.

14in (35.5cm) long

£150-250 SL

A CLOSER LOOK AT A STAPLER

The chrome-plated body and the green Bakelite handle are colourful and typical of the Art Deco period.

The Catalin is still bright and undamaged and the chrome is clean and largely un-pitted.

This model is styled unlike any other stapler made by the ACE Fastner Corp. Their staplers were usually solidly made with large door-knob shaped striking heads and little attention to decorative styling.

The form is typical of the 1930s style, with the clean lines and futuristic streamlining seen in the plastic bar and curving bracket.

An American Ace Model 502 stapler, by Ace Fastner Corp. of Chicago, Illinois, with a chrome-plated body and green Catalin handle.

The Ace Fastner Corp made many staplers during the 1930s, with names such as 'Pilot', 'Scout' and 'Cadet'. Although they never recovered fully after being made to support the war effort during WWII, certain models such as the 'Pilot' are still available today.

c1938

£30-50 ATK

A Victorian silver bookmark, in the form of a trowel, with mother-of-pearl handle, Birmingham hallmark.

1894 2.75in (7cm) long

£40-50 AGO

A 1920s brass bookmark, in the form of a Lincoln pixie standing on one leg.

3in (7.5cm) long

£25-35 AGO

A late 19thC Persian hand-painted papier-mâché pen case, with painted flowers and delicate floral patterns in reds and earthy tones.

Condition is important on these, as is the level of decoration. Splits to the body or losses to the finish are highly detrimental to value.

9.5in (24cm) long

£180-220 EPO

A Victorian metal bookmark, possibly Scottish, in the form of a sickle, with striated agate handle.

c1880 3.5in (9cm) long

£30-40 AGO

A cast-iron stamper, with revolving holder for this and other stamps.

£100-150 ATK

An English letter scale, with weights, wooden base with brass weights and official weight divisions.

£250-300 ATK

COLLECTORS' NOTES

■ Perfume bottles fall into one of two categories: decorative bottles into which perfume is decanted, and commercial bottles that are designed for and sold with a specific perfume. It is the latter that are covered in this section.

■ Commercial perfume bottles came into their own when Rene Lalique began designing perfume bottles for his friend François Coty in 1907. As well as Coty, he went on to work with Guerlain, Caron, Worth and Lucien Lelong. Needless to say, his designs are highly sought-after, as are those by rival glass producer Baccarat.

■ The field expanded further in 1921 when Coco Chanel became the first couturier to release a perfume. She intended that women who could not afford her clothes, could buy her perfume. Since then virtually every fashion designer releases at least one perfume and continues the trend of employing popular artists and designers of the day to design the bottles.

■ The value of commercial perfume bottles can vary greatly, making them popular with collectors at many levels. Many collectors specialise in a particular designer such as Lalique or Dali, a company such as Guerlain or Schiaparelli or even individual fragrances such as 'An Evening in Paris' by Bourjois.

A set of three Elizabeth Arden miniature perfume bottles, comprising My Love (1948), Night & Day (1935) and On Dit (1944).

These bottles were probably part of a miniatures gift set.

2.75in (7cm) high

£15-20 each   **LB**

A Quadrille by Balenciaga, France perfume bottle, clear glass bottle with plastic lid and embossed leather slip case.

This is a classic 1950s perfume and this example has a leather slip case to protect the bottle while in the handbag.

1956   bottle 2in (5cm) high

£15-25   **LB**

A Jolie Madame by Balmain perfume bottle, introduced in 1957.

bottle 2.75in (7cm) high

£25-35   **LB**

A 1930s Evening in Paris by Bourjois of Paris, novelty perfume bottle, with tassle.

Introduced in 1928, Evening in Paris became one of the best known perfumes in the world. The Christmas novelty bottle, shaped as the Eiffel Tower, is very desirable and worth around £220. The 1930s version of this bottle with a Bakelite stopper is worth approximately £35.

3.25in (8.5cm) long

£70-90   **LB**

A Kobako by Bourjois of Paris perfume bottle, the bottle designed by Borsse and in Chinese red Bakelite box, introduced in 1936.

bottle 2.75in (7cm) high

£250-350   **LB**

A Le Narcisse Noir by Caron perfume bottle, with black glass flower stopper and box, introduced in 1911.

bottle 3in (7.5cm) diam

£60-80   **LB**

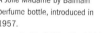

Two Voeu de Noel by Caron of Paris tester perfume bottles, one lacks label, etched "Caron", introduced in 1940.

2.5in (6.5cm) high

£15-25 each   **LB**

A CLOSER LOOK AT A CHANEL PERFUME BOTTLE

Legend has it that Coco Chanel's perfumier presented her with a selection of numbered samples. She chose "No. 5", and it went on to become her lucky number.

The simple, classic design of the bottle and packaging, which was in stark contrast to the elaborate bottles of the time, has changed little over the years. Values for even the earliest examples are relatively low.

A limited edition 'Three Gold Pearls' So Pretty by Cartier perfume bottle, the crystal bottle containing a pink, white and yellow gold 'pearl', in Harrods box, introduced in 1995.

bottle 5.75in (14.5cm) high

£200-300 LB

Chanel No. 5 is perhaps the most famous perfume in the world and was the first to carry the name of a fashion designer.

A Chanel No. 5 perfume bottle, with box, introduced in 1921.

£15-25 LB

Marilyn Monroe boosted sales when she claimed it was the only thing she wore to bed.

bottle 3.75in (9.5cm) high

LB

A L'Aiment by Coty perfume bottle, introduced in 1928.

Established in 1904, Coty was a pioneer in the industry and was considered the world's premier perfumier by 1910.

bottle 2.5in (6.5cm) high

£35-45 LB

A Dashing by Lily Daché perfume bottle, in a padded pink satin box topped with a fabric rose, also in pink, introduced in 1941.

bottle 5in (12.5cm) high

£250-350 LB

A set of two Celui by Jean Dessès perfume bottles, introduced in 1921.

5in (12.5cm) high

£150-200 LB

A 1920s Le Dandy by D'Orsay of Paris black geometric perfume bottle and stopper, introduced in 1926.

It is unusual to find these bottles with their original label.

2.5in (6.5cm) high

£70-100 LB

A Fabergé perfume bottle, the crystal bottle made exclusively by St Louis Cristalleries, France.

bottle 6in (15cm) high

£600-700 LB

A Fragile by Jean-Paul Gaultier perfume bottle introduced in 2001.

bottle 2.75in (7cm) high

£15-25 LB

A 1990s set of two Parfums Grès perfume bottles, comprising Cabochard and Cabotine.

The company was started in 1959 and Cabochard was launched the same year. Cabotine was launched in 1990.

bottles 2in (5cm) high

£15-25   **LB**

PIERRE-FRANÇOIS GUERLAIN

Pierre-François Guerlain founded Guerlain in Paris in 1828 after studying medicine and chemistry in England. His success was such that he was appointed perfumer to the French Imperial court in 1853. Pierre's sons Aimeé and Gabriel took over in 1890 and were responsible for one of the first uses of synthetic oils in 'Jicky'. Pierre's grandson Jacques was made creative director in the early 20thC and was responsible for some of the company's most popular perfumes such as 'L'Heure Bleu' and 'Shalimar'. The company has now produced over 200 different perfumes and until 1996 was still a family run business.

A No. 90 by Guerlain perfume bottle.

When a rival company launched a perfume using the name of an existing Guerlain perfume 'Shalimar', the company temporarily changed the name to it's stock number 'No. 90' while copyright issues were dealt with.

5.75in (14.5cm) high

£70-90   **LB**

A Chant de Arômes by Guerlain perfume bottle, the frosted and clear glass bottle with rosebud-shaped stopper, introduced in 1962.

bottle 4.5in (11.5cm) high

£50-70   **LB**

A Guerlinade by Guerlain perfume bottle, signed by Jean-Paul Guerlain, introduced in 1989.

This limited edition bottle was released in 1989 and commemorated the bicentenary of the company.

bottle 4.5in (11.5cm) high

£60-80   **LB**

A Jardins de Bagatelle by Guerlain perfume bottle, introduced in 1983.

13.75in (35cm) high

£500-600   **LB**

A L'Heure Bleue by Guerlain perfume bottle, introduced in 1912.

L'Heure Bleue was created by Jacques Guerlain, grandson of the company founder, Pierre.

12in (30.5cm) high

£60-80   **LB**

An early Liu by Guerlain perfume bottle, with clear glass bottle and stopper, paper label to base, introduced in 1926.

This perfume was named after the slave girl in Puccini's opera 'Turandot' and is now discontinued.

2.5in (6.5cm) high

£60-80   **LB**

A Mahora by Guerlain perfume bottle, with applied hammered gold-coloured disc, in original bag, introduced in the 1980s.

5in (12.5cm) high

£15-25   **LB**

A 1960s Vol de Nuit by Guerlain perfume bottle, with zebra-pattern printed box, glass bottle with plastic stopper, introduced in 1933.

3.5in (9cm) high

£80-120   **LB**

A large Mitsouko by Guerlain perfume bottle, introduced in 1919.

10in (25.5cm) high

£60-80   **LB**

A Parure by Guerlain perfume bottle, introduced in 1975.

4.5in (11.5cm) high

£30-50   **LB**

A Shalimar by Guerlain perfume bottle, introduced in 1919.

This perfume was named after the famous gardens commissioned by Shah Jahan for his wife in 1637 in Lahore, Pakistan. The bottle was originally designed by Baccarat.

6in (15cm) high

£70-100   **LB**

A Calèche by Hèrmes perfume bottle, the box with silk Hermes cushion, introduced in 1961.

bottle 3.75in (9.5cm) high

£70-90   **LB**

A DuBarry by Richard Hudnut gift set, comprising perfume bottle, compact and lipstick.

bottle 2.75in (7cm) high

£80-120   **LB**

A Magie Noire by Lancôme perfume bottle, introduced in 1978.

bottle 3in (7.5cm) high

£30-50   **LB**

A Trésor de Lancôme perfume bottle, with engraved glass stopper and box, introduced in 1952.

bottle 3in (7.5cm) high

£70-100   **LB**

A Magie de Lancôme special presentation perfume bottle, the icicle-shaped bottle with an engraved stopper and a ring for hanging it around the neck, introduced in 1949.

4.5in (11.5cm) long

£120-180   **LB**

A limited edition 'Pyramid and Crystal' Trésor by Lancôme perfume bottle, from a numbered edition of 10,000, introduced in the 1980s.

bottle 2.5in (6.5cm) high

£70-100   **LB**

An Arpège by Lanvin dummy perfume bottle, introduced in 1929.

Initially launched in 1929, this perfume was relaunched in 1994 in an updated version of the original round bottle.

9in (23cm) high

£500-600 LB

A My Sin Extrait by Lanvin perfume bottle.

bottle 2.5in (6.5cm) high

£25-35 LB

A Gardenia by Lucien Lelong perfume bottle.

5.5in (14cm) high

£70-100 LB

PERFUME
Indiscrete
LUCIEN LELONG
DISTRIBUTORS · NEW YORK · CHICAGO
CONTENTS 1 FLUID OUNCE
NO. 1000

An Indiscrete by Lucien Lelong of Paris, perfume bottle, with bow-shaped stopper, introduced in 1935.

Indiscrete was Lelong's best selling perfume.

3.75in (14.5cm) high

£80-120 LB

A rare and early Tweed by Lentheric of Paris perfume bottle, clear glass bottle and stopper, introduced in 1935.

3in (7.5cm) high

£80-120 LB

A Wind Song by Prince Matchabelli perfume bottle.

bottle 2.75in (7cm) high

£80-120 LB

A small Prince Matchabelli perfume bottle, the crown-shaped bottle decorated with gilt.

Prince Matchabelli was a Russian emigré who fled to New York. He began make perfume for his friends in the 1930s and based the bottle design on his family's crown. Most examples have lost their labels, making it difficult to tell which fragrance they contained.

c1925

2in (5cm) wide

£100-150 LB

A glass crown-shaped perfume bottle, with label for eau de cologne by Curtis.

6in (15cm) high

£60-80 LB

A Crêpe de Chine by F. Millot perfume bottle, introduced in 1929.

bottle 3.25in (8.5cm) high

£70-90 LB

A 1930 to 1940s Le Narcisse Bleu by Mury of Paris perfume bottle, clear glass with blue Bakelite top, the bottle with floral decoration.

4.25in (11cm) high

£50-70   **LB**

A Joy by Jean Patou perfume bottle, in box.

bottle 2in (5cm) wide

£25-35   **LB**

A Joy by Jean Patou perfume bottle, clear glass with gold label, introduced in 1993.

2in (5cm) high

£40-60   **LB**

A large Joy by Jean Patou display perfume bottle, black with red stopper, pictured with a smaller version to show scale.

7.25in (18.5cm) high

£70-100   **LB**

A small Joy by Jean Patou display perfume bottle, black with red stopper.

These bottles are influenced by Oriental fashions and are similar in shape to 19thC snuff bottles.

2.25in (5.5cm) high

£25-35   **LB**

A Moment Suprême by Jean Patou miniature perfume bottle, introduced 1929.

2.25in (5.5cm) high

£40-60   **LB**

A Replique by Raphael perfume bottle, designed by Lalique, in the form of a pine cone with orange ribbon, introduced in 1944.

2in (5cm) high

£150-200   **LB**

A Chichi by Renoir of Paris, perfume bottle, heart-shaped and in clear glass, made in France for the US market, introduced in 1942.

3in (7.5cm) high

£150-200   **LB**

A Coeur Joie by Nina Ricci perfume bottle, designed by Lalique, the clear glass bottle with three heart-shaped motifs and a gold-plated stopper, introduced in 1946.

3.25in (8.5cm) high

£80-130   **LB**

A Coeur Joie by Nina Ricci of Paris perfume bottle, designed by Lalique, introduced in 1946.

This was the first perfume released by Nina Ricci.

2.5in (6.5cm) high

£180-220 LB

A L'Air du Temps by Nina Ricci perfume bottle, in yellow satin-covered box.

bottle 4in (10cm) high

£80-120 LB

A Femme by Rochas perfume bottle.

bottle 3in (7.5cm) high

£25-35 LB

ELSA SCHIAPARELLI

■ Italian born fashion designer Elsa Schiaparelli (1890-1973) opened her first shop in Paris in 1929.

■ A passionate advocate of Surrealism, Schiaparelli collaborated with artists such as Salvador Dali and Jean Cocteau, and incorporated the elements of the school into her own designs.

■ Her first perfume, 'Salut' was launched in 1934, and her most famous 'Shocking' in 1937. The 'Shocking' bottle was in the shape of a lady's torso and is said to be based on the dressmaker's dummy sent to Schiaparelli by Mae West to use for fitting her clothes.

A Coeur Joie by Nina Ricci perfume bottle, designed by Lalique, lacks label.

4in (10cm) high

£70-100 LB

A set of three Deci Delà by Nina Ricci perfume bottles, each with heart-shaped stoppers, introduced in the 1980s.

bottles 2in (5cm) high

£25-35 LB

A limited edition L'Air du Temps by Nina Ricci 'The Winged Bottle' perfume bottle, designed by Lalique.

bottle 4.25in (11cm) high

£60-80 LB

A Violette by Rosine of Paris perfume bottle, in clear glass with gilt decoration and large key-shaped stopper, introduced in 1924.

Rosine was owned by couturier Paul Poiret and named after his daughter.

4in (10cm) high

£70-90 LB

A Shocking by Schiaparelli perfume bottle, shaped as a tailor's dummy, with frosted stopper.

15.5in (39.5cm) high

£800-1,000 LB

A Zut by Schiaparelli perfume bottle, formed as the lower half of a lady with her skirt around her ankles, decorated with gilt.

1948-49   *5.75in (14.5cm) high*

£350-450   **LB**

A CLOSER LOOK AT A PERFUME BOTTLE

Bottles with their hair and labels, like these, are more desirable.

These designs, which today are considered 'politically incorrect', are based on the character created by Florence K. Upton in 1895.

Vigny also produced a perfume pin in the form of a Golliwog head and a rare trio set of bottles called 'Jack-Junior-Jill'.

Golliwogs are collectable in their own right, which makes these perfume bottles very sought-after.

Two Le Golliwogg by Vigny of Paris perfume bottles, with seal fur hair, introduced in 1918.

largest 3.5in (9cm) high

LARGE: £250-350 SMALL: £220-280   **LB**

A miniature Schiaparelli sample perfume bottle, in the form a female torso.

2in (5cm) high

£100-150   **LB**

A Head Over Heels by Ultima II perfume bottle, the stopper in the form of a pair of lady's legs, boxed, introduced in the 1980s.

bottle 7in (18cm) high

£70-90   **LB**

A limited First by Van Cleef and Arpels perfume bottle, introduced in the 1990s.

bottle 4in (10cm) high

£70-100   **LB**

A Je Reviens by Worth of Paris, perfume bottle, designed by Lalique and decorated with stars, introduced in 1932.

bottle 4in (10cm) high

£50-70   **LB**

A Dans la Nuit by Worth of Paris perfume bottle, designed by Lalique, in round, blue glass.

This perfume and style of bottle was first introduced in the 1920s and relaunched in 1985.

c1985

£30-50   **LB**

bottle 3.5in (9cm) high

A Vers Le Jour by Worth of Paris perfume bottle, with square clear glass bottle, introduced in 1926.

2in (5cm) high

£15-25   **LB**

COLLECTORS' NOTES

- Photography has become an extremely popular and diverse sector of the collecting market in recent years. High prices are paid for early examples and masterpieces by noted, often surrealist, photographers. Away from this higher end, interesting collections can still be built for hundreds of pounds, or under.

- Always consider the type of photograph that you have, as this will help you identify the time period when it was taken. Also look at the clothes the sitter is wearing, as this will also give information about the date. If the sitter can be identified as a notable person, this can raise value – 'nobodies' are usually not of high value, unless there is another redeeming feature. A photograph of a 'nobody' with an early date, size or one depicting a quirky or unusual subject, such tools of a trade, are of interest.

- Not all images of famous people are rare and valuable, as some were printed in large quantities or are not sought after by collectors. The photographer also may have a bearing on value – look on the back and corners for a printed or stamped mark. Condition is important, with cut down images, tears, scuffs and fading all reducing value.

An American sixth-plate daguerreotype, anonymous, showing an elder in the 'Odd Fellows', his dark sash and gloves signify his rank, roses decorate his sash, and an arc laden with fruit is visible on his apron, resealed, one tiny spot on plate.

Although small, this image is crisp and clear and would be of interest to 'Odd Fellows' collectors as well as to collectors of photography. It will be rarer than other daguerreotypes showing unknown members of the public. For other items relating to and a brief explanation of the 'Odd Fellows', see the 'Masks' section of this book.

£400-500   **CHAA**

A sixth-plate hand-tinted daguerreotype of a young man, in complete leather case.

3.75in (9.5cm) high

£30-40   **ANAA**

A quarter-plate ambrotype of a baby girl, in a partial leather-covered case, the reverse with paper label reading "Edith Harper, Born in San Francisco, California".

4.75in (12cm) high

£40-50   **ANAA**

A sixth-plate daguerreotype of a husband and wife, in complete leather case.

3.5in (9cm) high

£40-50   **ANAA**

An ambrotype of a rather portly and frumpy seated lady, in a bonnet, in a complete leather-covered case.

The inset image shows the case closed. This is a typical case for many such early photographic images.

3.5in (9cm) high

£30-40   **ANAA**

A sixth-plate daguerreotype, of two men, one with arm on shoulder, case lacks lid.

The inset image shows the silvery reflective appearance of daguerreotypes, an effect not found on ambrotypes or tintypes.

3.75in (9.5cm) high

£30-40   **ANAA**

An American sixth-plate ruby ambrotype, anonymous, of a three-story clapboard building under construction, the scaffolding is visible at the right side of the building, in full pressed paper case.

£100-150   **CHAA**

An American Civil War albumen photograph, by the Brady Studio, titled "71st Regiment NY. Navy Yard, Washington, D.C." with an 1861 copyright line, mounted on board.

14.75in (37.5cm) wide

£250-350 **CHAA**

A photograph album with musical movement, black leather-bound album contains historical carte de visites and photographs and incorporates a key-wound music box with two tunes.

10.5in (27cm) high

£200-300 **ATK**

An American carte de visite of Edwin Booth, an actor, by Gurney & Son, New York.

Edwin Booth (1833-93) had noted acting skills, which were described at the time as 'a spell from which you can not escape'.

c1864

£200-250 **AAC**

A tortoiseshell photograph album, the cover with a central strapwork cartouche and a wide border in piqué and pose d'or, with purple moiré silk lining.

The condition and quality of materials and decoration affect the value of a Victorian photograph album such as this. Here the gilt tooling and use of tortoiseshell on the cover add to the value.

9.25in (23.5cm) long

£400-500 **HAMG**

A black and white photograph of Edward Prince of Wales (later King Edward VIII), signed and entitled "H.M.S. Renown Nov 1919", framed and glazed.

Between 1919 and 1925, Edward made four tours on the HMS Renown, then the newest and largest Royal Navy battleship, including voyages to Canada, the US, New Zealand and over 40 other countries. This image was taken upon his return journey from the US in November 1919.

8in (20cm) high

£150-200 **CLV**

A Japanese photograph of General Pershing and dignitaries, by R. Maruki of Tokyo, showing General Pershing, Ambassador of Knox and eight other dignitaries on front porch of house, mounted on board that exhibits some warping, surface soiling and corner bumps.

10.5in (26.5cm) wide

£100-200 **AAC**

A CLOSER LOOK AT A CARTE DE VISITE

Cartes de visites (or CdVs) were inexpensive photographs mounted on standard sized cards and given out as gifts and stored in albums - many millions were produced.

This CdV is by Edward Anthony of New York City, a prolific producer throughout the 1860s.

The photograph shows Edwin Perrin, a US expediter. He was sent to New Mexico in 1862 by the Secretary of War to help arm New Mexican troops for conflict in the Southwest. This CdV is more valuable as it shows a known person with a military connection.

It was taken in 1862, at the height of the CdV fashion, which lasted from around 1860 until 1866.

A rare American carte de visite, probably taken in Albuquerque, January 1862, showing Edwin Perrin, seated on a burro, wearing a fringed jacket, armed with a bowie knife, a sword and a carbine, with a tin cup and other utensils, Anthony backmark, lower corners clipped.

1862

£1,000-1,500 **CHAA**

COLLECTORS' NOTES

■ Bakelite was developed by Belgian chemist Dr Leo Baekeland in 1907 and was dubbed 'the material of 1,000 uses'. It is usually found in plain and mottled browns and black, with brighter colours such as blue and red being more desirable, and often more valuable.

■ Not all plastics are Bakelite, which can be recognised by rubbing a piece with a finger, which produces a strong carbolic smell. Other desirable plastics include cast phenolic, often known as Catalin. Many pieces were produced for the home, particularly the kitchen.

■ When buying plastics look for bright colour and good period styling – pieces showing the clean lines of the Art Deco style are often the most desirable. Damage such as chips, cracks and burn marks will always devalue a piece, but if a piece is extremely rare it may still be worth adding to your collection.

A black vulcanite circular box with lid, marked "Stipendum Reg. Greaseproof".

Vulcanite, also sometimes known as 'ebonite' is another name for 'hard rubber', which was patented by Charles Goodyear in 1844. It is recognisable by a strong sulphuric smell when rubbed.

c1910   3.25in (8cm) diam

£10-15   **JBC**

A 1920s green, maroon and black mottled Bakelite bowl.
5in (13cm) diam

£10-15   **JBC**

A 1940s multicoloured speckled urea-formaldehyde bowl.
4in (10cm) diam

£3-5   **MHC**

A 1920s dark green mottled Bakelite lidded pot.
4in (10.5cm) diam

£10-15   **JBC**

A 1930s lidded maroon mottled Bakelite pot.
3.5in (9cm) diam

£10-15   **JBC**

A brown mottled Bakelite tray, the base marked "Made in England MCC122", the centre with moulded profile of a stylish 1930s lady.

c1930   12in (30.5cm) diam

£30-40   **MHC**

Two 1920s English celluloid simulated tortoiseshell dressing table items.

£3-5 each   **JBC**

A pair of 1930s black Bakelite salt and pepper shakers, with very rare sterling "HJNS" tops.
2.25in (5.5cm) high

£40-60   **BB**

A rare 1930s Catalin salt and pepper shaker set, in the form of the Washington Monument.
4.25in (10.5cm) high

£80-120   **MHC**

A set of three small Art Deco sherry glasses and three wine glasses, made from orange Catalin-type plastic with chromed stems, moulded to base "NEWDAWN U.S.A. PAT. APPLD FOR".

£80-120   **BB**

PLASTICS

A 1930s fruit knife with a blue and white mottled urea formaldehyde handle, stainless Sheffield steel blade, leather holder.

4.5in (11.5cm) long

£5-10   **JBC**

A celluloid hand mirror, green with painted decoration of a lady and glitter.

c1930   *3.75in (9.5cm) l.*

£100-150   **TDG**

A General Electric alarm clock, with spherical face and ribbed orange Bakelite housing, marked on face and backplate.

4.5in (11.5cm) high

£180-220   **DRA**

A 1930s green and yellow Catalin mantel clock, by Viking.

Both the combination of colours and the shape make this clock desirable.

3.5in (9cm) high

£120-180   **CBU**

A 1930s tortoiseshell-effect cast phenolic-handled umbrella, the handle carved as a Scottie dog.

24.75in (63cm) long

£120-180   **ROX**

A Diehl 'Ribbonaire' Bakelite table fan, with two speeds and original grosgrain ribbons and wire, in working order.

9.75in (25cm) high

£200-250   **DRA**

A scarce 1940s Carvacraft green blotter, made by Dickinson Products.

The green is considerably scarcer than the amber or yellow.

6in (15.5cm) long

£70-100   **MHC**

A 1930s cherry red cast and carved Catalin magnifying glass, with folding handle.

4.25in (11cm) long

£30-50   **MHC**

A very rare Catalin scarab desk accessory.

Egyptian motifs were popular in the 1920s and 1930s following the discovery of Tutankhamun's tomb by Howard Carter in 1922.

c1930   *3.25in (8.5cm) wide*

£80-120   **MHC**

A 1930s French brown mottled Bakelite fountain pen.

4.75in (12cm) long

£20-30   **JBC**

COLLECTORS' NOTES

■ Picture postcards as we know them today were available from c1902 when the Post Office dropped its strict regulation that the message should be on one side of the card and the address on the other. They proved to be extremely popular and vast numbers were printed, mostly in Germany.

■ The most popular period for collecting is from the early 1900s to the start of WWI when materials were limited, German imports were banned and as a result their popularity waned. They became a common form of correspondence again after WWI until the 1950s. Later cards were mainly produced for the tourist market. These tend to lack variety and artistry and are not as sought-after.

■ Scenic postcards are common but the value ranges from under £1 to around £50. Of most interest are examples that show towns that have since been modernized, buildings which were demolished or destroyed during WWII and period scenes of everyday life that are of interest to local or social historians. Those showing one-off or unusual events such as natural disasters and local village or town gatherings are also popular.

■ Landscape and church scenes are less popular as the view is unlikely to have changed much over the years.

■ Postcards that have a crossover appeal, featuring railway stations and trains, cruise liners, military scenes with submarines or zeppelins and sporting events, will also fetch a premium.

■ Look for examples in good condition, creases and bends will detract from the value as will removed stamps. Unused, mint condition cards are the most desirable, but don't pass over used cards as the postmarks are useful for dating the card and the messages themselves can be interesting.

A postcard of a couple in a wicker buggy.

c1920   5.5in (14cm) wide

£7-10   **CANT**

A postcard of a man in a horse and carriage.

c1910   5.5in (14cm) wide

£10-15   **CANT**

A location postcard of 'Alveston Green, Empire Day', dated 31.MY.09.

5.5in (14cm) wide

£15-25   **CANT**

A 'Dymock Flower Show & Sports, August 25th, 1910. The "Grand Stand"' postcard.

5.5in (14cm) wide

£20-25   **CANT**

A 'Unionist Fete, 1913' postcard.

5.5in (14cm) wide

£15-20   **CANT**

A 'Bandstand and Pier, New Brighton' postcard, published by Valentine's.

5.5in (14cm) wide

£2-4   **CANT**

A location postcard of 'Stratford on Avon Mop I' fairground, published by Harvey Barton & Sons Ltd.

Fairgrounds are unusual and sought-after topics for postcards.

5.5in (14cm) wide

£20-30 CANT

A 'Royal Agricultural Show, Doncaster' postcard, featuring windmills, published by Regina Co.

5.5in (14cm) wide

£10-15 CANT

A location postcard of 'West Tytherley Post Office', published by A.E. Brundle, dated AU.6.12.

Postcards of Post Offices are rare and desirable.

5.5in (14cm) wide

£12-18 CANT

A '5440 Saltburn The Lift CN' postcard, published by the Photochrom Co. Ltd., dated SP.14.05.

5.5in (14cm) wide

£8-12 CANT

A location postcard of 'Flood at Minehead', dated 25th August 1938.

5.5in (14cm) wide

£8-12 CANT

A location postcard of 'German Raid, Dece 16th 1914, The Old Barracks, Castle Hill, Scarborough', published by J. Ashworth & Son, Scarborough.

5.5in (14cm) wide

£7-10 CANT

An 'Everton F.C. 1932-33, Winners of the First League' postcard, published by Carbonora Co.

The centre forward here is 'Dixie' Dean, who scored the most goals ever (60) in a professional season.

5.5in (14cm) wide

£50-70 CANT

A signed postcard of Al Harris, dated June 30 1936.

5.5in (14cm) wide

£8-12 CANT

A signed postcard of Alfred Holmes, indistinctly dated, probably 1920s.

5.5in (14cm) wide

£7-10 CANT

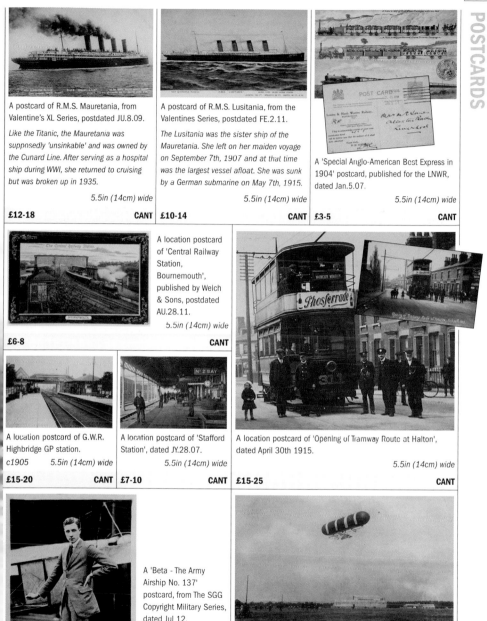

A postcard of R.M.S. Mauretania, from Valentine's XL Series, postdated JU.8.09.

Like the Titanic, the Mauretania was supposedly 'unsinkable' and was owned by the Cunard Line. After serving as a hospital ship during WWI, she returned to cruising but was broken up in 1935.

5.5in (14cm) wide

£12-18 CANT

A postcard of R.M.S. Lusitania, from Valentines Series, postdated FE.2.11.

The Lusitania was the sister ship of the Mauretania. She left on her maiden voyage on September 7th, 1907 and at that time was the largest vessel afloat. She was sunk by a German submarine on May 7th, 1915.

5.5in (14cm) wide

£10-14 CANT

A 'Special Anglo-American Best Express in 1904' postcard, published for the LNWR, dated Jan.5.07.

5.5in (14cm) wide

£3-5 CANT

A location postcard of 'Central Railway Station, Bournemouth', published by Welch & Sons, postdated AU.28.11.

5.5in (14cm) wide

£6-8 CANT

A location postcard of G.W.R. Highbridge GP station.

c1905   5.5in (14cm) wide

£15-20 CANT

A location postcard of 'Stafford Station', dated JY.28.07.

5.5in (14cm) wide

£7-10 CANT

A location postcard of 'Opening of Tramway Route at Halton', dated April 30th 1915.

5.5in (14cm) wide

£15-25 CANT

A 'Beta - The Army Airship No. 137' postcard, from The SGG Copyright Military Series, dated Jul 12.

5.5in (14cm) wide

£10-15 CANT

A 'Nulli Secundus - The Army Airship' postcard, published by Gale & Polden Ltd, postdated "MR 16 '10".

The Nulli Secundus was the first complete military airship in England and was built in 1907. She was rebuilt in 1908 as Nulli Secundus II.

5.5in (14cm) high

£8-12 CANT

A 'H.M.S. Centurian and Zeppelin L.3, Kiel, June 1914' postcard.

5.5in (14cm) wide

£6-8   **CANT**

A 'German Submarine UB131 Ashore Near Hastings' postcard, postdated JAN.9.21.

5.5in (14cm) wide

£8-16   **CANT**

A WWI 'H.M. Submarine "L.16"' postcard, published by Gieves Ltd.

5.5in (14cm) wide

£6-8   **CANT**

A 'Colonel C.M. Ryan D.S.O. Leaving Ludgershall March 20' postcard.

1915   *5.5in (14cm) wide*

£8-12   **CANT**

A WWI 'R.A.O.B. Second Motor Ambulance' postcard.

5.5in (14cm) wide

£20-25   **CANT**

A postcard with Insurance Acts political cartoon.

5.5in (13.5cm) wide

£3-4   **LG**

A "Free Trade" postcard, with "Vote for Herman-Hodge" message on reverse.

5.5in (13.5cm) wide

£2-3   **LG**

A patriotic postcard of Winston Churchill, in aid of The Daily Sketch War Relief Fund.

1939   *5.5in (13.5cm) high*

£6-8   **LG**

A postcard of Winston Churchill.

5.5in (13.5cm) high

£3-5   **LG**

FIND OUT MORE...

'Picture Postcards: Introduction to the Hobby', *by C W Hill, published by Shire, 1999*

'Collecting Picture Postcards', *by Geoffrey A Godden, published by Phillimore & Co., 1996*

www.postcard.co.uk

COLLECTORS' NOTES

■ As modes of travel expanded in scope and variety from the early to mid-20th century, and people became better able to afford holidays, travel posters increased in popularity. Ocean liner and railway company posters are amongst the earliest and most prolific designs. Today these categories remain the most popular with collectors.

■ A notable designer adds value, but it is the image that is often of primary importance – striking designs, bold use of colour and adherence to a popular styles, such as Art Deco or the 1950s 'modern' style, are important indicators of value.

■ Most posters were aimed at luring people away from the 'daily grind' and show seductive or exotic, brightly coloured landscapes. Evocative scenes, from the rolling hills of England to the sun soaked shores of Africa, tend to be the most popular.

■ Travel posters often have important socio-economic tales to tell. They document changing fashions and lifestyles, and highlight technological change. For example, they show how airlines began to compete commercially with cruise liners from the 1950s.

■ Condition is important – before posters became popular collectables, many were stored folded, so folds are acceptable and often easily removed. Tears that extend into the image, or more seriously, damage to the surface of the image, will reduce value considerably.

'St. Andrews, The Home of the Royal & Ancient Game', designed by H.G. Gawthorn, featuring figures in swimwear beside the course and clubhouse with monument and town beyond, lithographic print.

29.25in (74cm) wide

£550-650   **L&T**

'Canterbury By Southern Railway', ad no. 4525, designed by Shep (Charles Shepherd), published by SR, printed by Baynard, vertical folds.

1938   *50in (127cm) wide*

£400-500   **ON**

'York On The Track Of The Flying Scotsman', designed by Fred Taylor, published by LNER, mounted on linen.

50in (127cm) wide

£650-750   **ON**

'Aberdeen Brig O Balgownie', designed by Algernon Talmadge, published by LMS RA Series No. 5, printed by Thos. Forman, folds and small losses.

50in (127cm) wide

£280-320   **ON**

'The Treasurer's House York', designed by Fred Taylor, printed for the LNER by Dangerfield Printing Ltd, folds.

50in (127cm) wide

£450-550   **ON**

'The Palace of Holyrood Edinburgh', designed by Fred Taylor, printed for the LNER by John Waddington Ltd, folds.

Fred Taylor was a prolific poster designer from 1908-40. He worked for the Empire Marketing Board as well as the LNER and others. He also regularly exhibited paintings at the Royal Academy in London.

50in (127cm) wide

£800-1,000   **ON**

'Edinburgh (Trams)', signed with monogram, printed for LNER by John Waddington Ltd, folds.

50in (127cm) wide

£550-650   **ON**

'Llandudno for Sun Ray and Sea Spray, Travel in Comfort by LMS', designed by Warren Williams, printed by John Horn Ltd, mounted on linen.

This is typical of the type of railway poster that aimed to attract the public into taking affordable holidays at the many British seaside resorts that sprung up in the early 20thC. Along with the LMS, the notable LNER, the GWR and the SR were the leaders in graphic railway posters. LNWR had begun the trend by commissioning Norman Wilkinson as designer in 1905.

50in (127cm) wide

£800-1,000   **ON**

'Buxton The Mountain Spa', designed by S.J. Lamorna Birch, published by LMS, The Best Way Series No. 37, printed by Thos. Forman, folds with small losses.

Folds such as this are commonly found on railway posters, especially large ones, as they were often stored folded before posters became so sought after. Providing the surface is not damaged, they can usually be made to 'disappear' by a professional.

50in (127cm) wide

£400-600   **ON**

'Cornwall', designed by Ronald Lampitt, published by GWR, printed by J. Weiner, mounted on linen with minor repairs to bottom margin.

The evocative subject matter, the strong colours suggesting sunshine and the familiar holiday location, make this an extremely desirable poster. The unusual 'mosaic' style is a hallmark of Lampitt's work, used in posters from c1936.

50in (127cm) wide

£1,000-1,500   **ON**

'The Clyde Coast The Narrows, Kyles of Bute', designed by Alasdair Macfarlane, printed for BRSR by McCorquodale.

50in (127cm) wide

£400-600   **ON**

'Northern Ireland', designed by Hesketh Hubbard, published by LMS, printed by Jordison.

50in (127cm) wide

£500-600   **ON**

'The South Downs', ad no. 6657/A3, designed by Jack Merriott, printed for BRSR by Baynard, folds.

50in (127cm) wide

£400-600   **ON**

'Waterloo Station A Centenary of Uninterrupted Service During Peace and War 1848-1948', ad no. 5416 1946, designed by Helen McKie, published by SR, printed by Baynard, two folds and small tears to margin.

McKie's incredibly detailed and complex watercolour aimed to show how little service at Waterloo had varied in times of peace or war.

c1948   *50in (127cm) wide*

£2,500-3,000   **ON**

'Alnwick Castle Northumberland', designed by Fred Taylor, printed for the LNER by Dangerfield Printing Ltd, folds.

50in (127cm) wide

£600-800   **ON**

'Huntingdonshire Hemingford Grey', by Edward Wesson, published by BRER, printed by Waterlow.

50in (127cm) wide

£350-450   **ON**

'Callander The Trossachs Gateway', LMS Best Way Series No. 52, designed by Archibald Kay, printed by McCorquodale.

50in (127cm) wide

£180-220   **ON**

'Another Convoy Is Discharged The Lines Behind The Lines', No. 522, designed by Frank H. Mason, published by BR, printed by Haycock, vertical folds.

50in (127cm) wide

£800-1,200 ON

'Unceasing Service The Lines Behind The Lines', designed by Frank H. Mason, published by BR, printed by Haycock, folds.

c1945 50in (127cm) high

£1,200-1,800 ON

'On Early Shift, Greenwood Signal Box New Barnet', designed by Terence Cuneo, printed for the the Railway Executive by Waterlow ltd, mounted on linen.

50in (127cm) wide

£1,800-2,200 ON

'The Continent', designed by W. Smithson Broadhead, printed for GW, LMS, LNE & Southern Railways by the Haycock press.

W. Smithson Broadhead was also a well-known portrait and horse painter. This finely detailed and painted poster depicting café society was designed for a number of companies to promote travel to the Continent.

50in (127cm) wide

£4,500-5,500 ON

'Somerset', designed by Jack Merriott, published by REWR, printed by Jordison, small tears to bottom margin.

40.25in (102cm) high

£250-300 ON

'Suffolk Codenham', designed by Leonard Squirrell, printed for BRER by Waterlow, mounted on linen.

40.25in (102cm) high

£500-700 ON

'Worcestershire', designed by Frank Sherwin, published by BRWR, printed by Waterlow, mounted on linen.

40.25in (102cm) high

£280-320 ON

'The Dales Of Derbyshire Monsal Dale And The River Wye', designed by S.R. Badmin, published by BRLMR, printed by McCorquodale, small tear to bottom right corner.

40.25in (102cm) high

£450-550 ON

'Ullswater The Lake District for Holidays', designed by Clodagh Sparrow, printed for the LMS by Stafford Ltd, mounted on linen.

40.25in (102cm) high

£400-500 ON

'North Wales For Holidays Dolbarden Castle Llanberis', designed by John Mace, published by LMS, bottom margin slightly trimmed.

39.5in (100cm) high

£250-350 ON

'Guildford Picturesque And Historic', ad no. 1480, designed by Walter E. Spradbery, published by SR, printed by Waterlow.

Guildford's notable Tudor landmark, Abbott's Hospital, was founded in 1619 by Archbishop Abbot as an almshouse. This poster may have more local, rather than tourist, interest from collectors.

1931

£55-65 ON

'Shrewsbury Ireland's Mansion', designed by Claude Buckle, published by GWR No. 198, printed by Lowe and Brydone.

40.25in (102cm) high

£450-550 ON

'Tamworth Castle Staffordshire', designed by Ronald A. Maddox, published by BRLMR, printed by Jordison.

40.25in (102cm) high

£120-180 ON

'Chester The Gateway To North Wales', designed by S.R. Badmin, published by RELMR, printed by Jordison.

40.25in (102cm) high

£450-550 ON

'Skipton Castle', designed by Greene, published by BRLMR, printed by Waterlow, staining to top right corner.

40.25in (102cm) high

£60-80 ON

'Loch Derg Ireland for Holidays', designed by Paul Henry, printed for the LMS by Jordison Ltd.

1949   40.25in (102cm) high

£450-550 ON

'Isle of Man', designed by Clive Uptton, published by RELMR, printed by Waterlow.

40.25in (102cm) high

£80-120 ON

'Rothesay Isle of Bute', designed by Frank H. Mason, published by BRLMR, printed by McCorquodale.

40.25in (102cm) high

£120-180 ON

'Montrose', designed by Austin Cooper, published by LNER, printed by McCorquodale, folds.

40.25in (102cm) high

£30-40 ON

'Winter In Warmth at Bournemouth', ad no. 2500, colour photographic, printed for SR by Waterlow.

1933   40.25in (102cm) high

£250-300 ON

'Northern Ireland The Amphitheatre Giants Causeway', designed by Eric Lander, published by RELMR, printed by Waterlow.

1952   40.25in (102cm) high

£250-300   ON

'Dolgoch Station On The Talyllyn Railway', designed by Terence Cuneo, published by TR, printed by Waterlow.

40.25in (102cm) high

£120-180   ON

'Essex Coast Oysters', designed by Frank H. Mason, published by LNER, printed by Ben Johnson, mounted on linen.

39.75in (101cm) wide

£350-450   ON

'North East Coast Crabs', designed by Frank H. Mason, published by LNER, printed by Ben Johnson, mounted on linen.

40.25in (102cm) wide

£350-450   ON

'Warrenpoint Co. Down Ireland', designed by Odin Rosenvinge, The Best Way Series No. 32, published by LMS, printed by McCorquodale, folds.

Born in Newcastle-upon-Tyne of Danish descent, Rosenvinge (1880-1957) is known for his designs that incorporate a striking use of orange – he used such bright colours with great, eye-catching effect.

40.25in (102cm) high

£800-1,000   ON

'Greatstone By The Romney Hythe And Dymchurch Railway', designed by N. Cramer Roberts, printed by Vincent Brooks Day.

40.25in (102cm) wide

£200-250   ON

'East Coast Route To The Lake District', published by North Eastern Railway, printed by McCorquodale, mounted on linen.

40.25in (102cm) high

£300-350   ON

'Take The Family To The Lancashire Coast', designed by Septimus E. Scott, published by LMS, printed by Beck and Inchbold.

40.25in (102cm) high

£220-280   ON

'Butlins For Holidays', designed by Mervyn Scarfe, published REER, printed by Jarrold, mounted on linen.

Holiday camps were popular tourist destinations, and posters featuring them appeal as much to collectors of camp memorabilia as to railway collectors. They show the changing tastes of the British public.

40.25in (102cm) high

£400-500   ON

'Bath In 1828 By The New Steam Carriage Today By Western Region', designed by Eric Fraser, published by BRWR, printed by Waterlow.

40.25in (102cm) high

£120-180   ON

'Skegness Is So Bracing, The Jolly Fisherman celebrates his Golden Jubilee', designed by John Hassall, printed for BRER by Baynard Press.

This is the third version of this famous railway poster that first appeared in 1908. The main difference from the earlier LNER version is the addition of the pier, and it can also be found in a landscape format. Skegness was a popular holiday destination – in 1871 Skegness had a population of 500, but by 1907 it attracted some 300,000 tourists per year.

1958   40.25in (102cm) high

£1,800-2,200   ON

'Weston-Super-Mare', designed by Tom Purvis, published by the Railway Executive, printed by Jordison.

1949   40.25in (102cm) high

£800-1,000   ON

'Ireland The Land of Eternal Youth', designed by R. Breslin, printed for the Great Southern Railways by Alex Thom Ltd Dublin, mounted on linen with restoration.

39.75in (101cm) high

£180-220   ON

'The Peak District', designed by Ralph Mott, printed for LMS by S.C. Allen, mounted on linen.

40.25in (102cm) high

£600-700   ON

'Swanage', designed by Broomfield, published by BRSR, printed by Baynard, folds.

40.25in (102cm) high

£350-450   ON

'Colwyn Bay', designed by Bruce Angrave, published by BRLMR, printed by Baynard.

40.25in (102cm) high

£150-200   ON

'Lovely Llandudno Holds All The Aces!', designed by Amstutz, published by RELMR, printed by McCorquodale, small tear to bottom margin.

1952   40.25in (102cm) high

£150-200   ON

'Southern England', designed by Albert Brenet, printed for BRSR by Waterlow Ltd, mounted on linen.

40.25in (102cm) high

£250-350   ON

'The Lune Valley In England's Enchanting North West', designed by Bradshaw, published by BRLMR, printed by Wood, Rozelaar & Wilkes.

40.25in (102cm) high

£120-180   ON

'Metropolitan Railway, Look on the back of your ticket "It's a pity to puncture the picture"', designed by John Hassall, printed for R.H. Selbie General Manager by David Allen.

42.25in (107cm) high

£700-800 ON

'When In Doubt Take The Underground', designed by John Hassall, printed by the Hassall Designs Co., mounted on linen with restoration.

40.25in (102cm) high

£600-700 ON

'Edgware by Tram', designed by E.A. Cox, printed for Electric Railway House by Avenue Press, mounted on linen.

1916 30in (76cm) high

£280-320 ON

'Cunard LNER The United States & Canada link with the East Coast and the Continent', printed by Thos. Forman & Sons Ltd, mounted on linen.

The two powerful images of a cruise liner and a steaming train, combined with the Cunard name, make this an evocative and desirable poster depicting typical forms of travel of the era.

39.75in (101cm) high

£3,000-4,000 ON

A CLOSER LOOK AT A RAILWAY POSTER

Cassandre is the pseudonym used by Adolphe Mouron, one of the 20th century's most respected poster designers.

The poster sums up the 1930s perfectly – the style is the epitome of Art Deco, with its clean, angular lines.

The power and speed of the steam engine are emphasised in a graphic manner.

The angularity of the design, exaggerated perspective and use of muted colours are typical of Cassandre's designs.

'Nord Express', designed by A.M. Cassandre (Adolphe Mouron 1901-68), printed by Hachard & Cie Paris, mounted on Japanese paper, with repaired tear to top margin and slight fading.

1927 41.25in (105cm) high

£4,500-5,500 ON

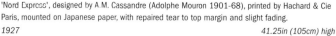

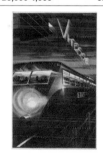

'Vitesse', designed by Hildenbrand.

1934 39.25in (98cm) high

£650-750 SWA

'Summer In Germany', designed by E. Frommbold, published by the German Railways.

39.75in (101cm) high

£150-200 ON

'Summer days on German Lakes', designed by Von Axster-Heudhab, published by the German Railways.

39.75in (101cm) high

£150-200 ON

'Lucerne Springtime A Delightful Season', designed by O. Landolt, printed for SFR by Fretz Bros Zurich, pin holes and small losses.

35.5in (90cm) high

£50-60 ON

'Bex Solbad Simplon-Linie Klimatischer Kurort-Golf', designed by Nico Heart, printed by Paul Attinger Neuchatel for SBB (Swiss Federal Railways), small losses and pin holes.

37.5in (95cm) high

£150-200 ON

'Giorgio Viola di C Trieste', printed by Modiano Trieste for ENIT and Italian Railways, small loss to top left corner.

40.25in (102cm) high

£70-100 ON

'L'Aquila Degli Abruzzi', designed by Umberto Noni, printed by Besozzi Milano for ENIT and Italian Railways, losses to bottom left margin.

1931   39.75in (101cm) high

£120-180 ON

A CLOSER LOOK AT A RAILWAY POSTER

Canadian designer, Peter Ewart is a noted artist who designed many posters for Canadian Pacific.

The snowy peaks of the Rockies highlighted by the sun and the shadowy forest are evocative of Canada's natural landscape.

The perspective, taken from close to the ground, and the dark, black train against the bright colours suggest the power and speed of the train.

The Canadian Pacific united Canada coast to coast and grew to be known as 'The World's Greatest Travel System'. By 1903 it sailed ships across the Pacific and Atlantic

'Travel Canadian Pacific Across Canada', designed by Peter Ewart.

c1950   35.75in (89cm) high

£1,400-1,800 SWA

'Norway 1931', designed by W. Midelfart, printed for Norwegian Railways by Hagen & Kornmann Oslo, pin holes.

39.75in (101cm) high

£80-120 ON

'Norway Summer Season June-September', designed by Ben Blessum, printed by A. Worner for Norwegian State Railway.

39.75in (101cm) high

£120-180 ON

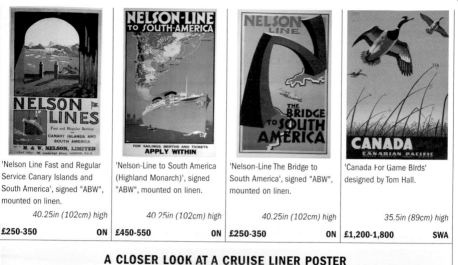

'Nelson Line Fast and Regular Service Canary Islands and South America', signed "ABW", mounted on linen.

40.25in (102cm) high

£250-350   **ON**

'Nelson-Line to South America (Highland Monarch)', signed "ABW", mounted on linen.

40.25in (102cm) high

£450-550   **ON**

'Nelson-Line The Bridge to South America', signed "ABW", mounted on linen.

40.25in (102cm) high

£250-350   **ON**

'Canada For Game Birds' designed by Tom Hall.

35.5in (89cm) high

£1,200-1,800   **SWA**

A CLOSER LOOK AT A CRUISE LINER POSTER

Although by an anonymous artist, this poster design is striking.

The use of the towering ship's bow motif is similar to the famous poster designed by Adolphe Mouron (Cassandre) for the 'Normandie' in 1935.

The simple lines, flat planes of colour and type of font are all in the desirable Art Deco style.

At around 1m (3ft 4in) in size, it is a popular size ideal for display in many homes.

'NSNC' (Nelson Steam Navigation Company), stock poster showing line up of ships, signed "AW", mounted on linen.

40.25in (102cm) high

£600-800   **SWA**

'Canada For Game Fish' designed by Peter Ewart, printed by Exhibits Branch, C.R.R. for Canadian Pacific, a trout fighting the line in its mouth, against a blue background.

35.75in (89cm) high

£1,400-1,800   **SWA**

'Cruise on the Great Lakes / Canadian Pacific' designed by Peter Ewart, a young woman against a blue background, lettering in khaki and blue.

35in (87.5cm) high

£650-750   **SWA**

'Blue Star Line, Mediterranean Cruises', designed by Maurice Randall, printed by Philip Read London, small losses and folds.

Similar to many railway posters, the colours used in cruise liner posters are often bright and saturated, giving the impression of bright sun. Exotic views of other peoples were a further draw for those stuck in the grey, humdrum life in a town or city.

40.25in (102cm) wide

£200-250   **ON**

'Welsh Norway Luxury Cruises by Blue Star Line', printed by Philip Reid London, small losses and folds.

40.25in (102cm) high

£220-280   **ON**

'Orient Pleasure Cruises by "Orontes" and "Ophir"', designed by John Hassall, mounted on linen.

40.25in (102cm) high

£250-350   **ON**

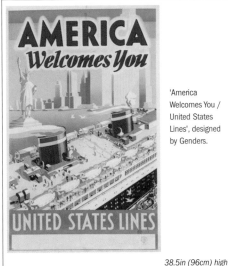

'America Welcomes You / United States Lines', designed by Genders.

38.5in (96cm) high

£750-850   **SWA**

'Mediterranean Cruises Hamburg–Amerika Linie', designed by Otto Anton, small tears to margins.

40.25in (102cm) high

£180-220   **ON**

'Cruises Around Africa, German African Lines', designed by Otto Anton, printed by Kunst I.M. Druck August 1936'.

39.75in (101cm) high

£200-250   **ON**

'Linea Rapida Para Habana Y Veracruz, Com Cie Gle Transatlantique (Liner Espagna)', printed by Champenois, mounted on linen.

40.25in (102cm) high

£220-280   **ON**

'Ellerman's City & Hall Lines to & from Egypt-India-Ceylon, (SS City of Benares)', designed by Frank H. Mason, printed by S. Straker and Sons London, small tears and folds.

40.25in (102cm) high

£350-450   **ON**

'Messageries Maritimes Mediterranean', loss to bottom margin.

The damage greatly reduces the value of this poster.

40.25in (102cm) high

£30-40   **ON**

'Orient-Royal Mail To Australia', designed by John Hassall, Managers F. Green & Co., mounted on linen.

40.25in (102cm) high

£350-450   **ON**

ONSLOWS
THE POSTER PEOPLE

19th & 20th Century Posters
For over 20 years Onslows have been developing the market in Posters which have seen remarkable growth in value.

Areas of particular interest include those published by the pre war railway companies LNER, LMSR, GWR and SR, London Transport, Imperial Airways, BOAC and BEA, Shipping Companies including Cunard White Star, Shell and BP, Motoring and Sporting including Racing, Skiing and the Olympics, The Empire Marketing Board, War Propaganda and Pop Art, European Posters, and any other vintage advertising.

Onslow's Collectors Auctions are held twice yearly. Colour illustrated catalogues are available by post or can be viewed free of charge on our website.

John Hassall Skegness Is So Bracing, printed for the LNER by Waterlow & Sons Ltd.- 102 x 127 cm. Estimate £2000 - 2500

Please contact **Patrick Bogue** for advice on selling and catalogues.
We have an extensive Picture Library of Poster Images available for Media and Publishing purposes.

ONSLOW AUCTIONS LTD. THE COACH HOUSE, STOURPAINE, DORSET. DT11 8TQ
TEL: 01258 488838   enquiries@onslows.co.uk   WWW.ONSLOWS.CO.UK

'Cunard U.S.A. / Etats Unis Et Canada' designer unknown, a French poster showing dramatically-angled view of three towering, red funnels, with colourful, stylized men and women waving farewell from the ships deck.

40.5in (101cm) high

£750-850   SWA

'West Indies and Spanish Main by French Line SS Colombie SS Cuba', designed by E.J. Kealey, printed by Hill Siffken London, small losses and tears to margin.

40.25in (102cm) high

£180-220   ON

'Scotland's Wonderland by Macbraynes Steamers', designed by E.C. Le Cadell, printed by McCorquodale, small losses, tears and pinholes to margin, fold.

40.25in (102cm) high

£300-400   ON

'Shaw Savill & Albion Line New Zealand Direct, Mt Egmont sighted by Captain Cook 1770', designed E. Walters.

40.25in (102cm) high

£200-250   ON

'Aberdeen and Commonwealth Line To Australia', designed by P. H. Yorke, printed by Howard Jones, mounted on linen.

40.25in (102cm) high

£220-280   ON

'British European Airways The Key to Europe', designed by Abram Games, printed by Broderna Lagerstrom.

1946   40in (101.5cm) h

£250-350   **ON**

'BOAC It's A Small World By Speedbird', designed by Tom Eckersley, small loss to top right corner.

1947   39in (99cm) high

£180-220   **ON**

'British European Airways The Key To Europe', designed by Lee-Elliott, printed by Curwen Press August 1946.

40.25in (102cm) h

£350-450   ON

'BOAC flies to all 6 continents', designed by Abram Games, printed by Baynard, mounted on linen.

1953   39.75in (101cm) high

£200-250   **ON**

'Dublin Fly There By Aer Lingus', P241, designed by Melai, printed by Hely's Ltd, mounted on linen.

40.25in (102cm) high

£300-400   **ON**

'Dublin fly Irish Air Lines Aer Lingus', designed by Beaumont, mounted on linen.

40.25in (102cm) high

£220-280   **ON**

'Air France, Riviera in five hours flight from London and Paris...', designed by Jean Miller, folds.

40.25in (102cm) wide

£220-280   ON

'Air France Flying Holidays This Year!', small tears and folds.

Air France is a popular airline amongst collectors and their posters are often cleverly designed, as with this example.

39.75in (101cm) high

£350-450   ON

'Imperial Airways Map of Empire & European Air Routes April 1936', printed by Curwen Press London, small tears to margins.

1939   40.25in (102cm) wide

£120-180   **ON**

'Bailie's B.B. Tours to Ulster, Seven Glorious Days', mounted on linen.

30in (76cm) high

£200-250 **ON**

'Northern Ireland', designed by Griffin, published by British Travel Association, printed by James Upton.

1955 *40.25in (102cm) high*

£50-60 **ON**

'Come to Ulster For A Happy Holiday', designed by Bernhard Higham, published by Ulster Tourist and Development Association, printed by S.C. Allen, mounted on linen.

40.25in (102cm) wide

£300-350 **ON**

'Ireland Invites You', designed by Melal, printed for the National Tourist Organisation by Browne & Nolan Ltd Dublin, mounted on linen.

40.25in (102cm) high

£280-320 **ON**

'Country Houses And Gardens In Britain', designed by Rowland Hilder, published by British Travel Association, printed by James Upton.

1954 *40.25in (102cm) high*

£80-120 **ON**

'London Piccadilly Circus', designed by Leonard Squirrell, published by the British Travel Association, printed by W. Cowell.

30in (76cm) high

£250-350 **ON**

'Bournemouth Britain's All Season Resort, A Place In The Sun', designed by Eustace Nash, published by the Town Council.

30in (76cm) high

£60-80 **ON**

'Farming', designed by James Arnold, published by the LT, printed by Curwen Press.

1950 *40.25in (102cm) high*

£200-300 **ON**

'Adelboden', designed by W.I., printed by Wolfsberg, Zürich, a partial view of a man mid-tennis game, against a blue and white mountainscape and a green and yellow pasture, text banner in red.

39.75in (99cm) high

£650-750 **SWA**

'National Parks Zetu Zinaleta – Donated by the Frankfurt Zoological Society', designed by Anon, printed by P.R. Wilk.

32.75in (83cm) high

£120-180   **ON**

'Hungary Hortobagy', designed by Fery Konecsni, printed by G. Klosz Budapest for Hungarian National Office for Tourism.

37in (94cm) high

£180-220   **ON**

'Jutland Denmark, The Bathing Beach of the Continent', designed by Henrik Hansen, printed by Chr. Olsen, small losses.

39in (99cm) high

£80-120   **ON**

'Sweden Värmland An Unspoiled Mekka for Tourists', designed by Beckman, printed by J Olsens Stockholm.

39.75in (101cm) high

£50-60   **ON**

'Davos Switzerland', designed by Otto Glaser, printed by Basler Druck Basel, small tears to margin.

40.5in (103cm) high

£60-70   **ON**

A CLOSER LOOK AT A TRAVEL POSTER

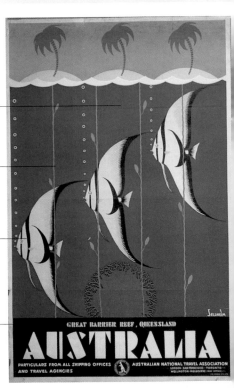

Gert Sellheim (1901-70) was one of the first designers commissioned by the Australian National Travel Association (est. 1929) to design posters to attract tourists to Australia.

Sellheim's most famous design is the leaping kangaroo logo for airline Qantas, designed in 1947.

The flat plane of perspective is typical of much of Sellheim's designs – also look out for his use of Aboriginal motifs in his other travel poster designs.

His hallmark brightly coloured and overtly modern designed posters were displayed in ANTA's London, Bombay and San Francisco travel offices.

'Camping', 1950s French sporting poster, artwork by Brocherun.

52in (132cm) high

£100-150   **CL**

'Australia Great Barrier Reef Queensland', designed by Sellheim, published by Australian National Travel Association, tear top margin.

40.25in (102cm) wid

£1,000-1,500   **O**

COLLECTORS' NOTES

■ Indicators to value for skiing posters are the destination, the artist and the design itself. Look for notable resorts and striking, powerful imagery.

■ These posters combine travel, sport and fashion – as well as modern design. Vibrantly coloured and romantic, they also combine many already collected forms of travel from railways to ships and planes.

■ Skiing has long been a fashionable pursuit, with great cachet. As it has become a more accessible pastime in recent decades, the audience has grown, leading to ever healthier prices, with many specialist poster sales devoted to them.

■ Skiing posters can be considered less common than others types, railway posters for example, and comparatively fewer were produced. Look out for Winter Olympic posters as this combines two popular collecting areas.

'Ski New York' designed by H.W., printed by Stecher-Traung, Rochester, a seldom seen image promoting skiing in the Empire State.

Here the typography is angled in opposition to the slope to create a dynamic graphic.

26in (65cm) high

£700-800   **SWA**

'Austria', designed by Prof. Kirnig (Atelier), printed by Christoph Reisser's Wein for the Austrian Railways, small tear to top margin.

37.5in (95cm) high

£500-600   **ON**

'New Hampshire' designed by Hechenberger, an orange haired woman holding a brown pair of skis on her shoulder, against a bright blue background.

36in (90cm) high

£1,000-1,500   **SWA**

'Sun Valley Idaho / Gretchen', colour photomontage of local hero Gretchen Fraser.

Gretchen Fraser won the 1948 St. Moritz Winter Olympics Women's Slalom.

1948   38in (95cm) high

£400-500   **SWA**

'Mürren Schweiz', colour photographic, designed by Helios, published by Amstutz & Herdeg, small tears to margins.

41in (104cm) wide

£350-450   **ON**

'Villars Chesières Switzerland', colour photographic, printed by Brugger SA Meiringen, small tears to margin.

40.25in (102cm) wide

£180-220   **ON**

'Alpes & Jura', designed by Eric De Coulon, printed by Le Novateur, Paris.

1933   39in (97.5cm) high

£500-600   **SWA**

'Ski-High Skiing / Lackawanna R. R.' designed by Beverly Towles.

28.5in (71cm) high

£400-600   **SWA**

'Winter In Italy', printed by Pizzi & Pizio Milano for ENIT and Italian Railways.

39.5in (100cm) wide

£300-400   **ON**

COLLECTORS' NOTES

■ Pictorial posters became a popular form of advertising during the early years of the 20th century. Posters from the 1950s are becoming increasingly valuable and collectable. The advent of television effectively saw the end of the golden age of the poster. Look out for oddities produced in small numbers, or those advertising brands that are already popular.

■ Certain long-lived brands are considered 'household names' and are already desirable and sought-after. They usually fetch high prices, particularly if they exemplify the Art Nouveau or Art Deco movements of the 1900s-30s. However, if the artwork is strong, evocative or by a noted designer, then look at lesser brands that currently may not be as sought-after.

■ Consider posters advertising what have grown to be modern-day classics, as many posters from the 1970s onwards are not as comparatively highly priced. These may be worth investing in, particularly if nostalgia for a certain product or brand grows in the future.

■ Always look for noted designers, iconic products and striking, colourful and attractive artwork that sums up a period or a style associated with it. Condition is important too, particularly with posters from the 1970s onwards, so always aim to buy those in as close to 'mint' condition as possible, avoiding those with tears and damage to the surface.

'Son & Co. BOS Blended Old Scotch Whisky', English advertising poster, artwork by Pease, printed by Walter Scott on three sheets, damp staining and losses to edges.

67in (170cm) high

£200-250　　　　　**ON**

'Stromness "OO" Old Orkney Whisky, You want a change My Boy I know Sample a bottle of Double "O"', English advertising poster, artwork by John Hassall.

25.25in (64cm) high

£30-50　　　　　**ON**

'John Kenyon Ltd Light Dinner Ales & Oatmeal Stout', English advertising poster, artwork by John Hassall, printed by Kingsway Press, repaired tear and small losses to margin.

30in (76cm) high

£100-150　　　　　**ON**

'Cognac Jacquet', 1920s French advertising poster, artwork by Camille Bouchet.

63in (160cm) high

£550-650　　　　　**CL**

'Cognac Otard', 1920s French advertising poster.

63in (160cm) high

£1,200-1,800　　　　　**CL**

'Toni-Kola', 1930s French advertising poster, artwork by Roby.

78in (198cm) high

£1,000-1,500　　　　　**CL**

'Aubel & Fils', 1930s French advertising poster.

47in (120cm) high

£800-1,000　　　　　**CL**

'Pastis Olive', 1930s French advertising poster, artwork by Marc.

78in (198cm) high

£500-600 CL

'Double Diamond, He's only here for the beer', English advertising poster, artwork by David Langdon.

39.75in (101cm) wide

£50-70 ON

'Double Diamond, I'm only here for the beer', English advertising poster, artwork by David Langdon.

39.75in (101cm) wide

£100-150 ON

'Absolut Les Bains', 1990s French advertising poster.

68in (172.5cm) high

£70-100 CL

'Absolut Queen', 1990s French advertising poster.

68in (172.5cm) high

£80-120 CL

'Absolut China Club', 1990s French advertising poster.

68in (172.5cm) high

£70-100 CL

'Absolut Vodka', 1990s American advertising poster, artwork by Ellen Steinfeld.

37in (94cm) high

£200-300 CL

A CLOSER LOOK AT AN ADVERTISING POSTER

This poster design was produced specially for an appearance in the popular TV series 'Sex and the City', where it was displayed in bus stops.

It was inspired by 1970s' campaigns featuring Burt Reynolds on a rug and Farah Fawcett in a swimsuit.

It was not released generally and features Smith Jared (actor Jason Lewis), a popular character from the hit TV show.

Very limited numbers of the official poster were produced, with the copyright wording showing it is not simply a reproduction of the photograph.

'Absolut Hunk', rare 2000s American faux advertising poster.

36in (91cm) high

£100-150 CL

'Bally', 1970s French advertising poster, artwork by Jacques Auriac.

22in (56cm) high

£100-150   CL

'Bally', 1970s French advertising poster, artwork by Jacques Auriac.

22in (56cm) high

£100-150   CL

A CLOSER LOOK AT AN ADVERTISING POSTER

The simple lines, minimal decoration and limited use of wording are striking and entirely modern.

The position of the legs and style hints strongly at desirable elegant and romantic night-time dalliances.

The use of flat planes of bright colour against a black background is eye-catching.

Bernard Villemot is a celebrated poster designer and was the first to use such designs for Bally.

'Bally', 1980s French advertising poster, artwork by Bernard Villemot.

c1981   *24in (61cm) high*

£70-100   CL

'Bally – La Chaussure Qui Habille', 1950s French advertising poster, artwork by Hervé Morvan.

63in (160cm) high

£400-500   CL

'Bally', 1980s French advertising poster, artwork by Bernard Villemot.

63in (160cm) high

£550-650   CL

'Bally', French advertising poster, artwork by Bernard Villemot.

The design, style and use of colour hark back to paintings by famous modern painter Matisse.

c1975   *68in (172.5cm) h*

£200-250   CL

'Bally', 1980s French advertising poster, artwork by Fix-Masseau.

66in (167.5cm) high

£300-400   CL

'Abercrombie & Fitch', 1990s American advertising poster, with photograph by Bruce Weber.

51in (125cm) wide

£80-120   CL

'Abercrombie & Fitch', 1990s American advertising poster.

Photographer Bruce Weber is known for his images that emphasise the male body, often in a voyeuristic way

.

56in (142cm) high

£100-150   CL

'United Colors of Benetton', 1980s Italian advertising poster.

31in (78.5cm) wide

£80-120 CL

'United Colors of Benetton', 1980s Italian advertising poster.

Italian fashion retailer Benetton have long delighted and shocked the world with their high profile, different stance to advertising. Social, political and economic statements often dominate their campaigns.

36in (91cm) wide

£80-120 CL

'Levi's', 1970s Belgian advertising poster.

37in (94cm) high

£150-200 CL

'Levi's', 1970s Belgian advertising poster.

37in (94cm) high

£150-200 CL

'Chanel No. 5', 1990s French advertising poster, featuring Carole Bouquet.

68in (172.5cm) high

£80-120 CL

'Chanel No. 5', 2000s French advertising poster, featuring Estella Warren.

68in (172.5cm) high

£80-120 CL

'Jean Paul Gaultier, Classique', 1990s French advertising poster.

The perfume bottle illustrated has become a collectable classic. It is said to have been modelled on Madonna and the classic 1930s 'Shocking' perfume bottle by Schiaparelli.

68in (172.5cm) high

£70-100 CLG

'Jean Paul Gaultier, Le Male', 1990s French advertising poster.

The striped 'matelot' (sailor) sweater has become a trademark for fashion designer Jean Paul Gaultier and is echoed by the models hat.

68in (172.5cm) high

£70-100 CLG

'Dior, Eau Sauvage', 1990s French advertising poster, artwork by René Gruau.

René Gruau was born in 1909 and began his career as a fashion designer, before turning exclusively to advertising from 1949. He worked for some of the greatest names in fashion, including many magazines such as Marie Claire. His work is characterised by economical use of line and bright colour.

63in (160cm) high

£70-100 CL

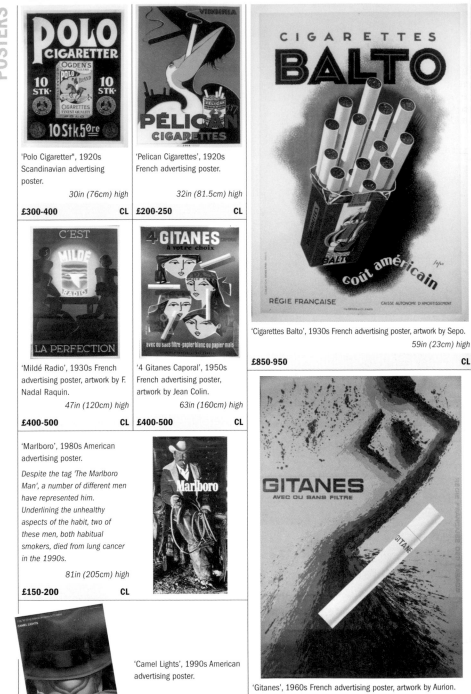

'Polo Cigaretter", 1920s
Scandinavian advertising
poster.

30in (76cm) high

£300-400   **CL**

'Pelican Cigarettes', 1920s
French advertising poster.

32in (81.5cm) high

£200-250   **CL**

'Mildé Radio', 1930s French
advertising poster, artwork by F.
Nadal Raquin.

47in (120cm) high

£400-500   **CL**

'4 Gitanes Caporal', 1950s
French advertising poster,
artwork by Jean Colin.

63in (160cm) high

£400-500   **CL**

'Cigarettes Balto', 1930s French advertising poster, artwork by Sepo.

59in (23cm) high

£850-950   **CL**

'Marlboro', 1980s American
advertising poster.

*Despite the tag 'The Marlboro
Man', a number of different men
have represented him.
Underlining the unhealthy
aspects of the habit, two of
these men, both habitual
smokers, died from lung cancer
in the 1990s.*

81in (205cm) high

£150-200   **CL**

'Camel Lights', 1990s American
advertising poster.

68in (172.5cm) high

£200-250   **CL**

'Gitanes', 1960s French advertising poster, artwork by Aurion.

58in (147.5cm) high

£400-500   **CL**

'Oxo For Cup And For Cooking', English advertising poster, published by Oxo Ltd Thames House London, folds.

60in (152cm) wide

£300-400 ON

'Oxo Health And Vigour Thanks To Oxo', English advertising poster, published by Oxo Ltd Thames House London, folds.

60.25in (153cm) wide

£300-400 ON

'Ovaltine', English advertising poster, the central part of a multiple sheet hoarding poster, small tears, together with three other sheets from the poster, folds and small tears.

c1930

£180-220 ON

'Ovaltine', incomplete English advertising sheets from multiple sheet hoarding poster, small tears and folds.

c1930 61in (155cm) high

£22-28 ON

'Perrier', 1960s French advertising poster, artwork by Bernard Villemot.

25in (60cm) high

£70-100 CL

'Orangina', 1980s French advertising poster, artwork by Bernard Villemot.

36in (91.5cm) high

£150-200 CL

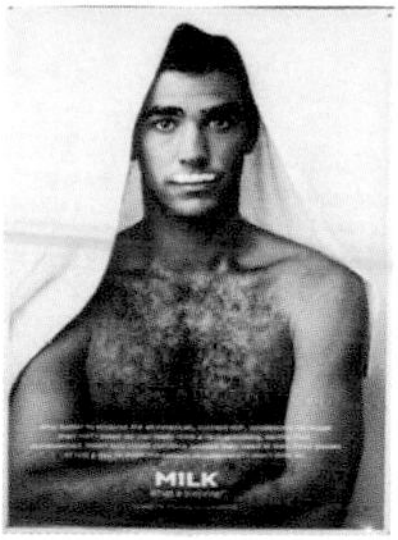

'Milk', 2000s American advertising poster, with Pete Sampras.

33in (80cm) high

£70-100 CL

'Olio Radino', 1940s Italian advertising poster, artwork by Boccasile.

55in (140cm) high

£450-550 CL

'Maison Bresilienne, Cafe Sao Paulo', 1900s French advertising poster, artwork by Villefroi.

37in (94cm) high

£600-800 CL

'Cigno', 1950s Italian advertising poster.

28in (71cm) high

£100-150 CL

'Philips, Prêt Pour Le 2eme Programme', 1960s French advertising poster, artwork by Saint-Genies.

63in (160cm) wide

£250-350 CL

'La Musique C'est Philips', 1960s French advertising poster.

63in (160cm) wide

£250-350 CL

'Electrophones Philips A Tête Diamant', 1950s French advertising poster, artwork by Eric.

63in (160cm) wide

£300-400 CL

'Lampes Philips', 1950S French advertising poster, artwork by Paul Igert.

63in (160cm) wide

£650-750 CL

'Disques Radio-Télé', 1950s French advertising poster, artwork by Eric.

63in (160cm) high

£550-650 CL

'Join the Olivetti Girls', 1990s Italian advertising poster.

26in (66cm) high

£70-100 CL

'Yum. Think Different', 1990s American advertising poster for Apple iMacs.

Ownership of home computers has increased dramatically since the 1980s and most homes now own one. Apple revolutionised typical designs with the release of the 'Bondi Blue' iMac in August 1998. It made the home computer fashionable, covetable and worthy of display. Unsurprisingly, it has gone on to become a design classic.

36in (91cm) high

£60-70 CL

'Radio la Voix de Son Maitre, Pathe Marconi', 1950s French advertising poster.

63in (160cm) wide

£350-450 CL

DER SCHWEDISCHE QUALITÄTSWAGEN

'British Vacuum Cleaner Model FF, A Perfect Electric Vacuum Cleaner', English advertising poster, artwork by John Hassall, printed by Hill Siffken, small tears and creases.

15.75in (40cm) wide

£500-600 ON

'"Dusmo" The Dustless Sweeping Powder, Cleans The Carpet And The Floor And By Jove It Kills The Germs Too!', English advertising poster, artwork by John Hassall, printed by John Hassall Designs Co, small tears.

30in (76cm) high

£200-250 ON

'Francisco Tamango Terrot Dijon Cycles Motocycles', French advertising poster, printed by Romanet, mounted on linen.

53.25in (135cm) high

£350-450 ON

'Volvo', 1950s Swiss advertising poster.

Here, the famed reliability and durability of Scandinavian-built Volvo cars is alluded to as they give you 'the key to the world'.

51in (125cm) high

£200-300 CL

'Cycles de Dion - Bouton', 1920s French advertising poster, artwork by Fournery.

47in (120cm) high

£700-1,000 CL

'Peugeot', 1930s French advertising poster, artwork by Faure.

47in (120cm) high

£500-600 CL

'Beeston Tyres Go By Themselves!', artwork by John Hassall, tears and losses.

1896

30in (76cm) wide

£120-180 ON

'Fiat Panda', 1970s Italian advertising poster.

The exploration of 'space', links the two disparate vehicles.

55in (140cm) high

£180-220 CL

'The Hartford Shock Absorbers "Make Every Road A Good Road" "Any Garage can fit Them"', English advertising poster, artwork by John Hassall, printed by John Waddington.

30in (76cm) high

£150-200 ON

POSTERS

'The Weekly Telegraph, On the Road', English advertising poster, artwork by John Hassall, printed by Sir W.C. Leng & Co., London.

25.25in (64cm) high

£120-180   **ON**

'The Printseller, A Monthly Journal Devoted to Prints & Pictures Ancient & Modern', English advertising poster, artwork by John Hassall.

26.5in (67cm) high

£80-120   **ON**

A CLOSER LOOK AT AN ADVERTISING POSTER

The design is typically Art Nouveau; a style in vogue at the time pictorial posters began to become popular forms of advertising.

Writing equipment is a popular subject with many collectors.

The wording is shown in an Art Nouveau font and fits seamlessly as part of the design.

The elegant pose and clothing, thoughtful gaze and flowing clouds and locks of hair exemplify the style.

'Encre L. Marquet', French advertising poster, artwork by Eugene Grasset, printed by Malherbe, mounted on old linen with restoration.

1892   *45.75in (116cm) high*

£700-900   **ON**

'Penthouse', 1980s American advertising poster, featuring Jessica Hahn.

Jessica Hahn shot to fame after her affair with religious televangelist Jim Bakker was revealed in 1987. After a brief career in soft pornography, during which she appeared on the front cover of Playboy and Penthouse, she married and now lives in California.

45in (114.5cm) high

£60-80   **CL**

'"Give 'em all Kodaks", Brownie's message from the Kodak girl', English advertising poster, artwork by John Hassall, small tears to margin.

Kodak is a popular brand to collect. This poster is also desirable because of the bright, colourful depiction of Santa Claus and the festive season.

30in (76cm) high

£450-550   **ON**

'Tudor by Rolex', 1960s Swiss advertising poster.

Tudor is a sub-brand of Rolex and their watches can generally be found for more affordable prices than similar Rolexes.

51in (125cm) high

£300-400   **CL**

'Zotos Prevents Sea-Sickness (SS Rol Polley), No. Tips!! "Zotos has done for me!!!"', English advertising poster, artwork by John Hassall.

30in (76cm) wide

£450-550   **ON**

'Cooper's Dip, The Happy Shepherd', English advertising poster, artwork by John Hassall, printed by William Cooper & Nephews, small tears.

35in (89cm) high

£220-280   **ON**

COLLECTORS' NOTES

■ The value or desirability of a poster depends on a number of factors. The popularity of a film and the actors in it make a poster sought-after. Posters for little-known films, unless they have a cult following, will be less desirable.

■ Posters are often re-issued if the film is re-released, or when the video or DVD is released. These are not as desirable and buyers should be careful they are not buying a poster for a re-release instead of an original.

■ Posters are produced for each country a film is released in and will tend to have different artwork. The poster from the film's country of origin is usually the most desirable, however posters from other countries such as Czechoslovakia and Poland are

known for their visually stunning artwork. US one sheets or British quads are the standard and most popular sizes.

■ Some collectors concentrate on posters by particular artists, such as Saul Bass, Robert Peak or Giuliano Nistri.

■ Early film posters were not made to last and were often thrown away after the film's release. Those that survived were often folded and damaged from being displayed – water stains, tears and fading will all affect the value of a poster. A professional restorer can repair many of these faults, and can also back a poster onto linen to make it more robust and easier to display.

"Alias the Champ", featuring Gorgeous George.

1949

£25-35   **GAZE**

"American Graffiti", UK quad poster.

1973   *40in (101.5cm) wide*

£350-450   **P**

"An American In Paris", US one sheet poster.

1951   *41in (104cm) high*

£1,000-1,500   **P**

"Annie Get Your Gun", US one sheet poster.

1950   *41in (104cm) high*

£250-350   **P**

"Bambi", by Walt Disney, Argentine Spanish language stone lithographed poster.

1942   *43in (109cm) high*

£800-1,200   **P**

"Blade Runner", US one sheet poster, with artwork by John Alvin.

1982   *41in (104cm) high*

£400-500   **P**

"For Your Eyes Only", UK quad poster.

1981   *40.25in (102cm) wide*

£30-40   **ON**

"From Russia With Love", Italian language locandino poster, mounted on linen.

1964   *26.75in (68cm) wide*

£200-250   **ON**

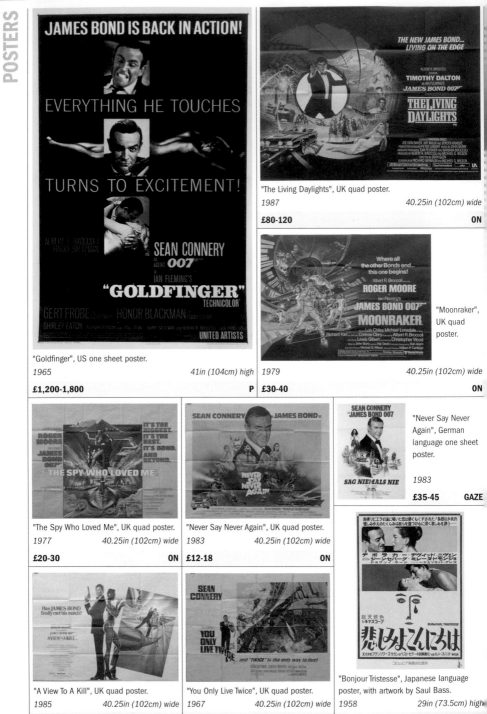

"The Living Daylights", UK quad poster.
1987   *40.25in (102cm) wide*
£80-120   **ON**

"Goldfinger", US one sheet poster.
1965   *41in (104cm) high*
£1,200-1,800   **P**

"Moonraker", UK quad poster.
1979   *40.25in (102cm) wide*
£30-40   **ON**

"The Spy Who Loved Me", UK quad poster.
1977   *40.25in (102cm) wide*
£20-30   **ON**

"Never Say Never Again", UK quad poster.
1983   *40.25in (102cm) wide*
£12-18   **ON**

"Never Say Never Again", German language one sheet poster.
1983
£35-45   **GAZE**

"A View To A Kill", UK quad poster.
1985   *40.25in (102cm) wide*
£180-220   **ON**

"You Only Live Twice", UK quad poster.
1967   *40.25in (102cm) wide*
£120-180   **ON**

"Bonjour Tristesse", Japanese language poster, with artwork by Saul Bass.
1958   *29in (73.5cm) high*
£450-550   **P**

"Breakfast At Tiffany's/Sabrina", re-release US one sheet double-bill poster.
1965   *41in (104cm) high*
£450-550   **P**

"Carry On England", poster.
£10-15   **GAZE**

"Carry On Round The Bend", poster.
£10-20   **GAZE**

"Casablanca", re-release Italian fotobusta poster.
1961   *27in (76cm) wide*
£400-500   **P**

"Casablanca", 1940s Austrian German language poster.
34in (86.5cm) high
£800-1,200   **P**

"Citizen Kane", 1960s re-release Italian locandino poster.
28in (71cm) high
£350-450   **P**

"Clockwork Orange", UK quad poster, folded.
1971
£200-300   **ON**

A CLOSER LOOK AT A HORROR FILM POSTER

"The Creature from the Black Lagoon" is one of the most popular monster movies of all time.

Horror movie posters are the most popular genre with collectors and usually make the most money.

Although this Argentine version is desirable, the US version can be worth around £12,000.

The stone lithography printing process produces a high quality image and can offer a wide range of tones and colours.

"Creature From The Black Lagoon", Argentine Spanish language stone lithographed poster.
1954   *43in (109cm) high*
£2,000-3,000   **P**

"Dangerous Years", US half-sheet poster.

This was one of Marilyn Monroe's first movies.

1947   28in (71cm) high

£120-180   **ATK**

"Death Wish II", poster.

1982

£10-20   **GAZE**

One of the most stunning and powerful films of all time.

"The Deer Hunter", UK quad poster.

1978   40.25in (102cm) wide

£35-45   **ON**

"Destination Gobi", poster.

1953

£25-35   **GAZE**

"Dirty Harry", Australian daybill poster.

1971   30in (76cm) high

£250-350   **P**

"Fantasia", Argentine Spanish language poster.

1940   43in (109cm) high

£800-1,200   **P**

"The Dirty Dozen", US one sheet poster.

1967   41in (104cm) high

£350-450   **P**

"A Fistful of Dollars", US one sheet poster.

1964   41in (104cm) high

£800-1,000   **P**

"Finder Keepers", UK quad poster.

1967

£40-50   **GAZE**

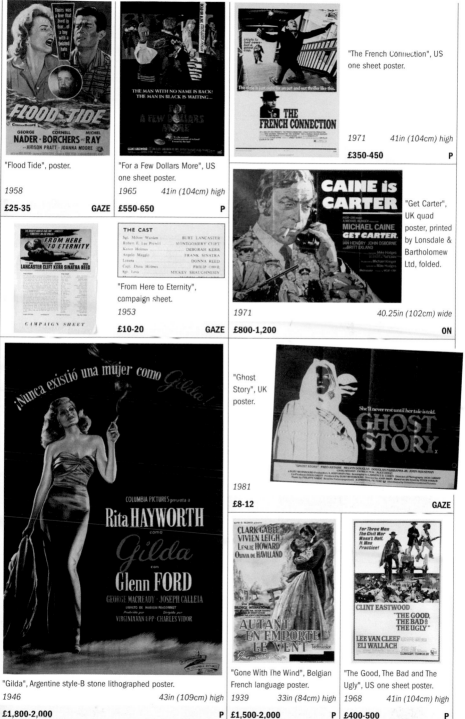

"Flood Tide", poster.

1958

£25-35   **GAZE**

"For a Few Dollars More", US one sheet poster.

1965   *41in (104cm) high*

£550-650   **P**

"The French Connection", US one sheet poster.

1971   *41in (104cm) high*

£350-450   **P**

"From Here to Eternity", campaign sheet.

1953

£10-20   **GAZE**

"Get Carter", UK quad poster, printed by Lonsdale & Bartholomew Ltd, folded.

1971   *40.25in (102cm) wide*

£800-1,200   **ON**

"Ghost Story", UK poster.

1981

£8-12   **GAZE**

"Gilda", Argentine style-B stone lithographed poster.

1946   *43in (109cm) high*

£1,800-2,000   **P**

"Gone With The Wind", Belgian French language poster.

1939   *33in (84cm) high*

£1,500-2,000   **P**

"The Good, The Bad and The Ugly", US one sheet poster.

1968   *41in (104cm) high*

£400-500   **P**

"The Guns of Navarone", UK quad poster.

1961   *40.25in (102cm) wide*

£50-60   **ON**

"Harry Potter and the Philosopher's Stone", UK quad advance poster, signed by Daniel Radcliffe, who played Harry Potter, together with a sheet of Daniel Radcliffe headed note paper.

This film was released as "Harry Potter and the Sorcerer's Stone" in the US.

23in (58.56cm) high

£120-180   **CO**

"Horror House", US poster.

1970

£10-20   **GAZE**

"Hot Spell", poster.

1958

£25-35   **GAZE**

"Hud", US one sheet poster.

1963   *41in (104cm) high*

£250-350   **P**

"In Prison - Behind Bars", 1950s German poster.

£60-70   **GAZE**

"If....", photo-montage UK quad poster, printed by W.E. Berry Ltd, folded.

1968   *40.25in (102cm) wide*

£250-350   **ON**

"A Jolly Bad Fellow", US one sheet poster.

1964

£10-20   **GAZE**

"Janis: A Film", US one sheet poster.

1974   *41in (102cm) high*

£70-100   **CO**

"La Dolce Vita", Japanese language poster.

1960   *29in (73.5cm) high*

£700-1,000   P

"Les Diaboliques", French language petite poster, with artwork by French artist Raymond Gid.

Raymond Gid (1905-2000) was a typographer who designed many film posters. He also worked for Club Méditerranée, Bally shoes, and Amnesty International.

1955   32in (81.5cm) high

£700-1,000   P

"Le Mans", US one sheet poster.

1971   41in (104cm) high

£400-500   P

"Love In The Afternoon", Japanese language poster.

1957   29in (73.5cm) high

£400-500   P

"A Man and a Woman", Japanese language poster.

1966   29in (73.5cm) high

£600-800   P

"The Manchurian Candidate", UK quad poster.

1962   40in (101.5cm) wide

£350-450   P

"Lawrence Of Arabia", 1970s re-release Italian fotobusta poster.

27in (76cm) wide

£250-350   P

"The Man With The Golden Arm", US one sheet poster, with artwork by Saul Bass.

Saul Bass (1920-96) became famous with his design concept for this film. After working with famous directors such as Alfred Hitchcock, he began making his own films in the 1960s. He returned to graphic design in the 1970s.

1954   41in (104cm) high

£1,200-1,800   P

"The Man Who Fell To Earth", UK quad poster, with artwork by Vic Fair.

Vic Fair also designed a rare "James Bond - A View to a Kill" poster, featuring Roger Moore in a white tuxedo.

1976   40in (101.5cm) wide

£400-500   P

POSTERS

"The Man Who Knew Too Much", US one sheet poster.

1956   *41in (104cm) high*

£550-650   **P**

"Mean Streets", Italian language fotobusta poster.

1975   *27in (76cm) wide*

£250-350   **P**

A CLOSER LOOK AT AN ALFRED HITCHCOCK FILM POSTER

This is the original first release, one sheet poster of this film, making it the most desirable example.

Posters from the film's country of origin, such as this one, are usually the most sought-after.

Hitchcock films and posters are very popular and are a collecting area in their own right.

Cary Grant and Ingrid Bergman were Hollywood legends and this film featured one of the most famous screen kisses in cinema history, which is hinted at in the poster image.

"Notorious", US one sheet poster.

1946   *41in (104cm) high*

£4,000-5,000   **P**

"The Outlaw Josey Wales", UK quad poster.

1976   *40.25in (102cm) wide*

£8-12   **ON**

"The Pink Panther Strikes Again", UK quad poster, folded and torn.

1976

£70-100   **ON**

"Walt Disney's One Hundred and One Dalmatians", US one sheet poster.

1961   *41in (104cm) high*

£350-450   **P**

"Psycho II", German language one sheet poster.

1983

£10-20   **GAZE**

"Renaldo and Clara", Spanish language one sheet poster.

1978   39in (99cm) high

£80-120   CO

"Repulsion", Japanese language poster.

1965   29in (73.5cm) high

£450-550   P

"Rock Show", US one-sheet poster.

1979   41in (104 cm) high

£50-70   CO

"Sidewalks Of New York", Australian one sheet stone lithographed poster.

1931   41in (104cm) high

£1,800-2,200   P

"The Rocky Horror Picture Show", one sheet poster.

1975

£80-120   GAZE

"Shaft", Italian language locandino poster, with artwork by Giuliano Nistri.

1971   28in (71cm) high

£200-300   P

"Singin' In The Rain", Argentine Spanish language stone lithographed poster.

1951   43in (109cm) high

£700-1,000   P

"Some Like It Hot", rare US soundtrack poster.

1959   25in (63.5cm) high

£350-450   P

"Spellbound", re-release US insert poster.

1949   36in (91.5cm) high

£350-450   P

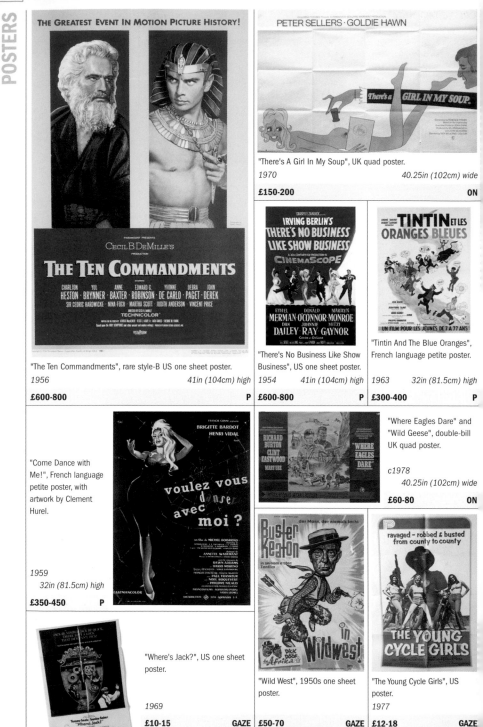

THE GREATEST EVENT IN MOTION PICTURE HISTORY!

PARAMOUNT PRESENTS
CECIL B DEMILLE'S
PRODUCTION
THE TEN COMMANDMENTS
CHARLTON   YUL   ANNE   EDWARD G.   YVONNE   DEBRA   JOHN
HESTON · BRYNNER · BAXTER · ROBINSON · DE CARLO · PAGET · DEREK
SIR CEDRIC HARDWICKE · NINA FOCH · MARTHA SCOTT · JUDITH ANDERSON · VINCENT PRICE
DIRECTED BY CECIL B. DEMILLE
TECHNICOLOR®

"The Ten Commandments", rare style-B US one sheet poster.
1956   *41in (104cm) high*
£600-800   **P**

PETER SELLERS · GOLDIE HAWN

There's a GIRL IN MY SOUP

"There's A Girl In My Soup", UK quad poster.
1970   *40.25in (102cm) wide*
£150-200   **ON**

DARRYL F. ZANUCK
IRVING BERLIN'S
THERE'S NO BUSINESS
LIKE SHOW BUSINESS
A 20th CENTURY-FOX PRODUCTION IN
CINEMASCOPE

ETHEL   DONALD   MARILYN
MERMAN·O'CONNOR·MONROE
DAN   JOHNNIE   MITZI
DAILEY·RAY·GAYNOR
COLOR BY DE LUXE

"There's No Business Like Show
Business", US one sheet poster.
1954   *41in (104cm) high*
£600-800   **P**

ANDRE BARROT   ROBERT LAMONT
TINTIN ET LES
ORANGES BLEUES

UN FILM POUR LES JEUNES DE 7 A 77 ANS

"Tintin And The Blue Oranges",
French language petite poster.
1963   *32in (81.5cm) high*
£300-400   **P**

FRANCIS COSNE
BRIGITTE BARDOT
HENRI VIDAL

voulez vous
danse
avec
moi ?

un film de MICHEL BOISROND
ANNETTE WADEMANT

EASTMANCOLOR
DISTRIBUTION LES ARTISANS S.A.

"Come Dance with
Me!", French language
petite poster, with
artwork by Clement
Hurel.

1959
       32in (81.5cm) high
£350-450   **P**

RICHARD
BURTON
CLINT
EASTWOOD
MARY URE

WHERE
EAGLES
DARE

"Where Eagles Dare" and
"Wild Geese", double-bill
UK quad poster.

c1978
       40.25in (102cm) wide
£60-80   **ON**

JACK BE NIMBLE, JACK BE QUICK,
THERE JUST A LOCK,
THAT JACKSON'S PICK

"Where's Jack?", US one sheet
poster.

1969
£10-15   **GAZE**

der Mann, der niemals lacht
Buster
Keaton
in seinem ersten
Tonfilm

DAWN ADDAMS
DARIO MORENO

PAUL FRANKEUR
NOEL ROQUEVERT
PHILIPPE NICAUD

in
Wildwest
DICK DOOR
in Afrika

"Wild West", 1950s one sheet
poster.

£50-70   **GAZE**

ravaged – robbed & busted
from county to county

THE YOUNG
CYCLE GIRLS

"The Young Cycle Girls", US
poster.
1977
£12-18   **GAZE**

COLLECTORS' NOTES

■ As part of an overall change in the direction of graphic design during the 1960s, commercial artists in San Francisco began to advertise concerts in a different way. They looked to previous styles such as Art Nouveau and presented it in a new way.

■ They were particularly inspired by poster artists Toulouse Lautrec and Alphonse Mucha. The text often dominates, forming part of the overall design. Colours are usually bright and reflective materials are common.

■ Collectors often concentrate on one artist, many of whom were performing artists themselves, such as Hapsash and the Coloured Coat or Rick Griffin.

A Berkeley Bonaparte 'Psychedelic Dream' poster, designed by Rick Griffin.

c1967   *35in (89cm) high*

£150-200   **CO**

A Pink Floyd and Jimi Hendrix silkscreen poster, for two concerts at The Saville Theatre, The Pink Floyd on 01.10.67 and The Jimi Hendrix Experience 08.10.67., designed by Hapshash and the Coloured Coat, published by Osiris Visions.

55in (140cm) high

£650-750   **CO**

A Pink Floyd 'Games For May' concert poster, at the Queen Elizabeth Hall, May 12th, designed by Barry Zaid, featuring three dancing silhouetted fairies, tears to bottom edge but otherwise complete.

1967   *30in (76cm) high*

£4,000-5,000   **CO**

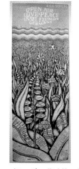

A rare alternative Jimi Hendrix "Open Air, Love & Peace Festival" poster, in Insel Fehmarn, Germany, 4-6 September 1970.

The festival was Jimi's last official performance, the bassist was sent home due to ill health and the remainder of the tour was cancelled. By September 18th Hendrix was dead.

43in (109cm) high

£120-180   **CO**

A Dr. Strangely Strange silkscreen poster, at Southampton University Students Union Entecom, Saturday 6th March, black on yellow ground, very good condition.

This poster was produced by Southampton Students Union and designed by the then Publicity Officer, John Liverton.

1971   *30in (76cm) high*

£20-30   **CO**

A Colosseum in concert with the New Jazz Orchestra poster, at the Guildhall, Portsmouth, Thursday 28th May at 7.45pm, silkscreened in cerise pink on blue ground, very good condition.

1970   *30in (76cm) high*

£120-180   **CO**

An Isle of Wight Festival 'Psychedelic Drummer' promotional poster, for August 26th-30th 1970, designed by David Roe.

c1970   *30in (76cm) high*

£180-220   **CO**

FIND OUT MORE...

'High Art: A History of The Psychedelic Poster', *by Ted Owen & Denise Dickson, published by Sanctuary Publishing Ltd, 2001.*

A Ferodo First Dutch Grand Prix poster, for Zandvoort 22nd June, 1975.

1975   *29.5in (75cm) high*

£60-80   ON

A Ferodo First Le Mans poster, by Dexter Brown.

1975   *29.5in (75cm) high*

£22-28   ON

A 1950s Crystal Palace Motor Racing poster, illustration by Raymond Groves, Whit Monday at 2 p.m., small tear to lower right corner.

                         30in (76cm) high

£300-400   SAS

A 1950s Goodwood Easter Monday International Programme poster, for 11th April 1.30 p.m.

30in (76.5cm) high

£280-320   SAS

A Brighton Speed Trials poster.

1996

£12-15   CARS

A Dieppe Retro poster.

1995

£25-30   CARS

A CLOSER LOOK AT A
MOTOR RACING POSTER

The bold red car is striking and is in a design of the period.

The Alps and forest add 'romance' and hint at the location of the race.

The 'streaking' implies speed as does the dizzying perspective.

Executed in a modern style, Hans Thoni also designed a version without the forest for the 1936 race.

IIME Grand Prix Automobile De Suisse' designed by Thoni.

1935   *38.25in (95.5cm) high*

£2,500-3,000   SWA

COLLECTORS' NOTES

- Both World Wars required participation from every citizen – a theme that can be seen in posters produced at the time, which ranged from call-up posters for the Army, Air Force or ancillary units to posters produced for the home front to encourage careful use of supplies or investing in savings schemes to fund the war effort.

- All types used encouraging imagery, bolstering the public's morale as much as encouraging them to fulfil the act required. Many designs were striking and employed bold colours – patriotic themes and images were widely used.

- Look out for modern designs by leading designers of the time such as Abram Games and Norman Wilkinson. Posters with a humorous element by artists such as Fougasse and H.M. Bateman are also popular.

"Bones help to fire the guns... save more ships", by Beverley Pick, printed for HMSO by Fosh & Cross Ltd, folds.

Pick was a member of the Society of Industrial Artists. She designed posters and displays at Charing Cross Underground station for the Ministry of Information during WWII. After the war she worked for airlines B.O.A.C. and B.E.A. Her style is indicative of the 'modern' designs produced by the leading poster artists of the day, but slightly less innovative.

30in (76cm) high

£35-45 ON

"Kitchen waste feeds pigs & poultry, kitchen scraps are wanted to produce bacon and eggs, don't waste kitchen scraps the Nation needs them now", by Beverley Pick, printed for HMSO by Fosh & Cross Ltd, folds.

30in (76cm) high

£80-120 ON

"Plan before you buy", by Beverley Pick, photo montage printed for HMSO by Fosh and Cross, folds.

30in (76cm) high

£55-65 ON

"Miles and miles of silk – a parachute for every airman, no silk for new frocks convert your old...", printed for HMSO by Multi Machine Plates Ltd.

30in (76cm) high

£35-45 ON

"The man who wasted power!", by H.M. Bateman, issued by the Ministry of Fuel and Power, printed for HMSO by Chromoworks, folds.

30in (76cm) high

£180-220 ON

"The worker who left the lights on! Don't be fuel-ish, wasted electricity means less fuel to make weapons we need for victory", by H.M. Bateman, issued by the Ministry of Fuel and Power, printed for HMSO by J. Weiner, fold.

Bateman had become famous for his cartoons showing the uproar caused by social gaffes - he was the caricaturist for 'The Tatler' and 'Punch' amongst others.

15in (38cm) wide

£35-45 ON

"The Hun and the home... back up the men who have saved you", by David Wilson, folds.

30in (76cm) high

£80-120 ON

"Electricity, 100 tons of coal to build a Spitfire, electric fires should be used only when absolutely necessary", printed for HMSO by Multi Machines Plates Ltd, folds.

29.5in (75cm) high

£180-220 ON

LEND TO DEFEND HIS RIGHT TO BE FREE
BUY NATIONAL SAVINGS CERTIFICATES

"Lend to defend his right to be free - Buy National Savings Certificates", by Tom Purvis, printed for H.M. Stationery Office by Fosh & Co. Ltd.

This popular and attractive poster appeals to collectors of Meccano as well as wartime poster collectors.

c1940   30in (76cm) high

£200-300   PC

CONVOY YOUR COUNTRY TO VICTORY
BUY NATIONAL SAVINGS CERTIFICATES

"Convoy your country to victory - Buy National Savings Certificates", designed by Rowland Hilder, printed for H.M. Stationery Office by J. Weiner Ltd.

c1940   30in (76cm) high

£100-150   PC

WAR SAVINGS ARE WARSHIPS

"War savings are warships", by Norman Wilkinson, published by National Savings, printed by J Weiner, folds.

30in (76cm) high

£120-180   ON

Keep mum – she's not so dumb!
CARELESS TALK COSTS LIVES

"Keep mum - she's not so dumb! Careless talk cost lives", by A. Forster, published by HMSO, printed by Lowe & Brydone, folds and small tears.

30in (76cm) high

£180-220   ON

"Careless talk costs lives" by Fougasse, four of eight posters including the 'Telephone Box'.

Fougasse's small "Careless talk costs lives" posters are perhaps the best known posters of their type - each scene contains a 'hidden' Hitler or Goering eavesdropping on a conversation in a public place.

12.5in (32cm) high

£500-600   ON

A CLOSER LOOK AT A WARTIME POSTER

The designer Abram Games is well known for his graphic design work across industrial, commercial and government sectors from the 1930s-1960s.

He also favoured simple graphics, obtaining 'maximum meaning' from 'minimum means' as seen in the patriotically coloured, heroic soldier's profile against a camouflage background.

He was designated official war artist in 1942 due to his experience and contacts made at Shell before the war.

Games wanted his wartime posters to be as seductive and striking as commercial art, combining eye catching imagery and typography.

SALUTE THE SOLDIER
SAVE MORE   LEND MORE

"Salute the soldier, save more, lend more", by Abram Games, issued by National Savings Committee London, printed by Alf Cooke Ltd.

1944   14.5in (37cm) high

£350-450   ON

"An appeal to you", published by PRC No. 88, printed by Roberts and Leete, folds.

40.25in (102cm) high

£150-200   **ON**

"Come and do your bit, join now", published by PRC No. 93, printed by David Allen, folds.

1915   *50in (127cm) wide*

£100-150   **ON**

"Everyone should do his bit, enlist now", by Baron Low, published by PRC No. 121, printed by Roberts and Leete.

1915   *30in (76cm) high*

£200-250   **ON**

"Fall in, answer now in your country's hour of need", by E. J. Kealey, published by PRC No. 12, printed by Hill Siffken.

1914   *30in (76cm) high*

£100-150   **ON**

"It's a real man's life, join the Regular Army", by E. Earnshaw, published by the War Office, printed by Stott Bros.

15in (38cm) high

£6-8   **ON**

"Take up the sword of Justice", by Bernard Partridge, published by PRC No. 105, printed by David Allen.

1915   *40.25in (102cm) high*

£180-220   **ON**

Lord Kitchener says enlist to-day", colour photographic poster published by PRC No. 117, printed David Allen, folds.

1915   *50in (127cm) wide*

£120-180   **ON**

"Join the Regular Army", published by the War Office.

30in (76cm) high

£7-10   **ON**

"Serve with the Coldstream Guards", by Charles Wood.

17.75in (45cm) high

£12-18 ON

"Boys come over here you're wanted", published by PRC No. 82, printed David Allen, folds.

1915 *50in (127cm) wide*

£100-150 ON

"A message.. to ambitious men.. join the Royal Signals", poster.

15in (38cm) high

£6-8 ON

"There are vacancies in the Intelligence Corps", mono-photographic poster, published by the War Office.

15in (38cm) high

£80-120 ON

"The De Havilland 'Mosquito' light bomber", colour cutaway with technical details, copyright of The Aeroplane, folds.

28.75in (73cm) wide

ON

"ATS at the wheel", by Beverley Pick, photo montage printed for HMSO by Field Sons & Co Ltd.

The ATS was the Army Transport Service.

29.5in (75cm) high

£350-450 ON

The British Handley Page "Halifax II", colour cutaway with technical details, copyright of The Aeroplane, folds.

28.75in (73cm) wide

£120-180 ON

"Aircraft Torpedo Sight, Air Diagram 2385, June 1943", prepared by Ministry of Aircraft Production, printed for HMSO by Alf Cooke Ltd London.

19.75in (50cm) wide

£25-35

FIND OUT MORE...

'Images of War: British Posters 1939-45', by J.D Cantwell 1989.

The Imperial War Museum, Lambeth Road, Kennington, London SE1 6HZ.

COLLECTORS' NOTES

- Pot lids are currently enjoying a particularly buoyant period, with collectors from the US and Australia in particular showing strong interest in English pot lids.

- Among the most popular pot lids are those made for bear's grease, which was used in large quantities by barbers for use as a gentlemen's hair styling product. These are followed by toothpaste pot lids with good, detailed pictures. 'Regional' lids are also sought after as they are rare – the majority were made for London-based companies.

- Condition of the face is important and any damage should not affect the image. The flange and rim underneath the face are often damaged, but this does not have a great impact on the value.

- There are a number of reproductions on the market at present so buyers should be wary, particularly of internet transactions. Original examples will have the glaze applied over the transfer decoration rather than vice versa, and will have a shiny appearance. Run your finger over the lid – if it is a reproduction you may be able to feel the texture of the transfer. Other copies have paper transfers stuck on plain pot lids, which are then lacquered – check that you can't feel the edge of the transfer with your nail.

- Collectors are not interested in the pot base, unless it is also decorated. Complete pots are popular with casual collectors, however, as they are often easier to display.

A 'Bears At School' Pratt pot lid, number 9, from the Pratt factory, in cream-coloured wooden frame.

4.75in (12cm) diam

£45-55   **BBR**

A 'Bear, Lion and Cock' Pratt pot lid, number 19, from the Pratt factory, clearly printed with colours

1854-55   *3.25in (8.5cm) diam*

£45-55   **BBR**

An 'Allied Generals' Pratt pot lid, number 168, from the Pratt factory, signed "J. Austin".

The numbers refer to Pratt pattern design numbers, as listed in 'Price Guide to Pot Lids' by A. Ball, published by the Antique Collectors' Club.

c1855

£100-150   **BBR**

An 'Eastern Repast' Pratt-type pot lid, number 98, from the Mayer Factory.

3in (7.5cm) diam

£25-35   **BBR**

An 'Eleanor Cross, London' Pratt-type pot lid, number 194, probably by Bates, Brown-Westhead, Moore and Co.

4in (10cm) diam

£60-80   **BBR**

A 'Volunteers' Pratt-type pot lid, number 214, probably by Bates, Brown-Westhead, Moore and Co., in strong colours.

c1860   *3in (7.5cm) diam*

£100-150   **BBR**

A 'Rifle Contest, Wimbledon 1865' Pratt-type pot lid, number 224, titled with blue marbled surround, some minor staining and chips to flange.

4.75in (12cm) diam

£280-320   **BBR**

POT LIDS

A "Dr Ziemer's Alexandra Tooth Paste" pot lid, with a portrait of Princess Alexandra to the centre with gold border, some outer edge restoration.

3.5in (9cm) diam

£45-55   **BBR**

A "Carbolic Tooth Paste" pot lid, with brown print, inner hairline crack to flange.

2.5in (6.5cm) wide

£70-100   **BBR**

An early "Hindoo Tooth Paste" pot lid, with slight body discolouration.

3in (7.5cm) diam

£120-180   **BBR**

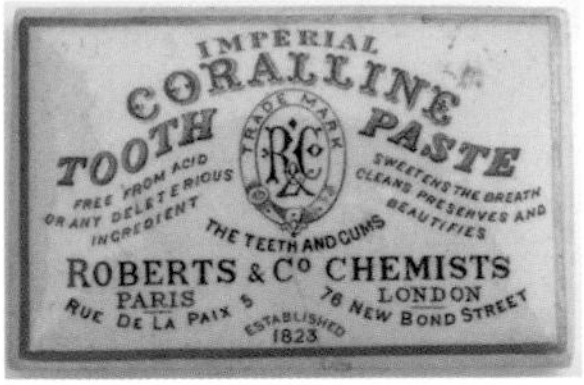

An "Imperial Coralline Tooth Paste" oblong pot lid, hairline crack at the bottom.

3.75in (9.5cm) wide

£40-50   **BBR**

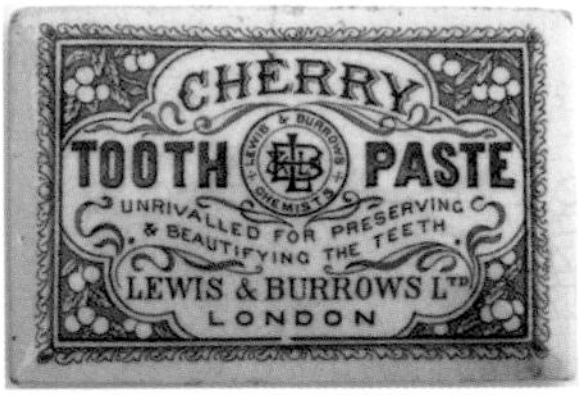

A Lewis and Burrows Ltd "Cherry Tooth Paste" oblong pot lid, hairline crack down top side.

3.75in (9.5cm) wide

£40-50   **BBR**

A Lorimer and Co. "Cherry Tooth Paste" pot lid, with a large bunch of cherries plus an arm holding a globe, flange hairline crack.

2.5in (6.5cm) diam

£70-100   **BBR**

A "Maw's Indian Betel Nut Or Areca Tooth Paste" pot lid.

2.5in (6.5cm) diam

£18-22   **BBR**

A "St. Paul's Cherry Tooth Paste" pot lid, with a pictorial trademark of St. Paul's.

2.75in (7cm) diam

£18-22   **BBR**

A May Roberts "Cherry Tooth Paste" pot lid, the detailed transfer depicting a young bonnetted girl, arms folded, leaning on wall, with trade mark below.

2.75in (7cm) diam

£180-220   **BB**

A "James Atkinson's Bears Grease" pot lid, with a fine and sharp black transfer of a chained and muzzled bear, restored chip to flange.

2.5in (6.5cm) diam

£50-70   BBR

A "Holloway's Ointment" pot lid, flange chips.

3.25in (8.5cm) diam

£20-30   BBR

A Knowle's "Esauline or Pomade D'Esau" pot lid, with a portrait of a gentleman with a long moustache, marked "I Used It", some crazing, clear dark transfer.

3in (7.5cm) diam

£220-280   BBR

A "Genuine Russian Bear's Grease" pot lid, with a pictorial transfer showing bear with trees in background, flange chips.

2.75in (7cm) diam

£120-180   BBR

A "Genuine Russian Bears Grease" pot lid, with a strong black pictorial transfer of two bears, flange chips and hairline crack.

3in (7.5cm) diam

£100-150   BBR

A "Savage's Celebrated Peruvian Balm" pot lid, with a large vase of flowers pictured to centre.

2.75in (7cm) diam

£80-120   BBR

A very rare "Spaks Wonderful" hair restorer pot lid, with St George slaying the dragon pictured to centre, small chip under top edge.

3.75in (9.5cm) diam

£320-380   BBR

A rare "The Children's Pomade" ceramic domed lidded pot, with a boy and girl pictured either side.

4.25in (11cm) high

£250-300   BBR

An early John Bell "Pure Cold Cream of Roses" pot lid, with a large and highly detailed chemists shop front pictured on the flat top.

3in (7.5cm) diam

£400-500 BBR

A "Sharp Brothers Cold Cream" pot lid, with a harp pictorial above banner and decorative outer border, minor crazing.

2.75in (7cm) diam

£180-220 BBR

A "Squire Cold Cream" pot lid, with gold border intact, overall crazing.

3.25in (8.5cm) diam

£45-55 BBR

A French "Icilma Crème" pot lid, with a sharp and stylish pictorial of a girl holding a pot, atop waterfall landscape, flange repair and some crazing.

3.75in (9.5cm) diam

£100-150 BBR

A Buisson Freres "Ambrosial Shaving Cream" pot lid.

3.25in (8.5cm) diam

£35-45 BBR

A "Roussel's Shaving Cream" pot lid, top edge chip repair and damage, repair underneath.

3.25in (8.5cm) diam

£35-45 BBR

A very rare "Isola Bishop's Balm" ointment pot, the black transfer with an image of a bishop with mitre in hand, with a swan and a church behind.

1.75in (4.5cm) high

£350-450 BBR

A "Blanchflower" pot lid, the farmyard scene showing a cow, bull, sheep, pigs and hens, two chips to underside flange.

3.75in (9.5cm) diam

£250-350 BBR

A "Bales Mushroom Savoury" pot lid, with brown transfer decoration of mushrooms.

3.5in (9cm) diam

£70-90 BBR

COLLECTORS' NOTES

■ The making of patchwork quilts probably dates from the early 1700s but because they are made from worn scraps of material, it may be that earlier examples have not survived.

■ This use of recycled fabric also meant that patchwork was often associated with the lower classes having to 'make do'. In Victorian times, when it became fashionable for women to do needlework as a hobby, this perception changed. However it was the Americans that turned the patchwork quilt into a work of art.

■ The value of a quilt tends to depend on the fabric used and the complexity and artistic quality of the design. As scraps of fabric were hoarded, it is not unusual to find pieces of 18th century fabric in a quilt assembled in the 19th century and these early additions can make a quilt more sought-after.

■ Although complete quilts are generally more desirable, unfinished examples are often more affordable (and can be fun to complete). These are of interest to students of quilting as they demonstrate techniques.

A late 19thC 'squares and triangles' pattern quilt, with turkey red, Oxford shirting and printed cottons, with 'strippy' back.

86in (218cm) long

£100-150 DN

A late 19thC piece of 'strippy' coverlet, applied with hexagons and inscribed "JJ(?) Smith, April 1886" verso.

87in (221cm) long

£180-220 DN

A late 19th/early 20thC patchwork quilt, of a design with hexagons set out in lines, with other printed cottons.

91in (231cm) long

£40-60 DN

An early 20thC double-sided patchwork quilt, with hexagons and stripes in plain and printed cottons.

91in (231cm) long

£22-28 DN

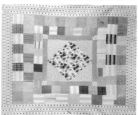

An 1860s/70s North Country frame patchwork quilt, with a central pattern of square on point, with printed cottons.

94in (239cm) long

£80-120 DN

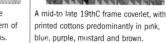

A mid-to late 19thC frame coverlet, with printed cottons predominantly in pink, blue, purple, mustard and brown.

91.25in (232cm) long

£200-250 DN

A late 19thC patchwork cot quilt, predominantly in white, with other printed cottons.

49in (125cm) long

£50-100 DN

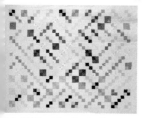

A late 19thC frame patchwork quilt, with a turkey-red and printed cottons, including cheater-cloths.

94in (239cm) long

£100-150 DN

A block pattern frame patchwork quilt, with printed cottons and other fabrics, predominantly late 19thC.

81.5in (207cm) long

£40-60 DN

A late 19thC double-sided tied patchwork coverlet, with a pattern of bordered squares of printed cottons.

77.5in (197cm) long

£60-80 DN

A late 19thC frame patchwork quilt, of a block design of printed cottons, with chevron quilting, with a cheater-cloth verso.

86in (218cm) long

£30-50 DN

A North Country frame patchwork quilt, with a central pattern of a turkey-red star and four baskets, with extensive use of Oxford shirting and other fabrics.

85in (216cm) lon

£45-55 DI

A late 19thC patchwork coverlet, of hexagon design, with printed cottons and turkey-red.

86.5in (220cm) long

£100-150 DN

An early 20thC patchwork top, of hexagon design, with printed cottons including turkey-red and portraits of a lady.

99in (251cm) lor

£100-150 D

A late 19thC pieced quilt top, with predominantly pink, blue and purple printed cotton hexagons including fabric samples.

94in (239cm)

£35-45 DN

An early 20thC honeycomb design piece quilt, hand stitched with printed cotton fabrics, the pierced area mounted with machine stitching on a white cotton pan

A 19thC patchwork quilt top of harlequin design, worked entirely in late 19thC and other silks.

86.5in (220cm) long

£180-220 DN

An early 20thC patchwork quilt, of hexagonal design, with printed cottons and turkey-red including Kate Greenaway design and 'that pink', with some fabrics dating from the early 19thC.

86.25in (219cm) long

£180-220 DN

Provenance: *Made by Mary Eleanor Bell, whose husband was a fabric salesman; th quilt was made from his fabric sample books.*

83in (211cm) lc

£80-120 DN

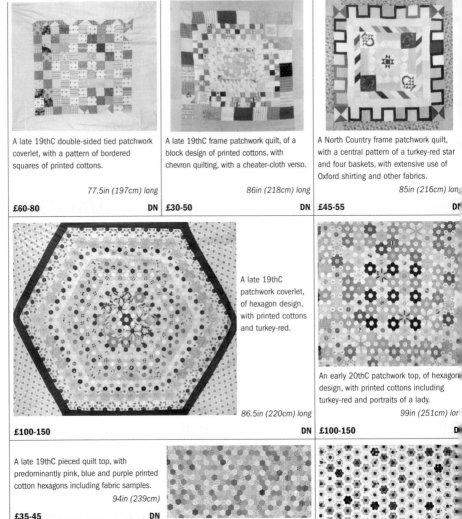
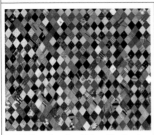

COLLECTORS' NOTES

■ With vintage radios, the case, rather than the quality of the electronics or sound, makes the most difference to value. During the 'golden age' of the radio between the 1920s and 1950s, many were produced in revolutionary 'Bakelite' cases. Although Bakelite was originally a trademark name, 'bakelite' has become a generic term for a range of plastics. When buying vintage radios, do discriminate – look for those in cases that either reflect the style of the period, such as Art Deco, or those in brightly coloured cases.

■ Condition is crucial. Bakelite, and its more colourful cousin 'Catalin', was prone to cracking, warping or chipping, all of which affect value. Feel the surface and edges of a radio to discover such faults. Look for classic forms and names such as Fada and Emerson. Many valve radios can be restored to working order, but always seek professional advice before plugging an example in. Many transistor radios from the 1960s and 70s exhibit the funky styling so beloved today.

A Philips 'Superinductance Type 830 A' radio, five valves, long and medium wave bands, needs new cloth.

Rather than Bakelite, this radio is Arbolite, a material specific to Philips, made from plastic laminated board.

c1932

£180-220 ATK

A German SABA Bakelite radio, with four valves and replaced speaker cloth.
1934
£150-250 ATK

A German Siemens '23 WL' radio, with bakelite case, original cloth, three valves and single circuit receiver.
1932
£200-300 ATK

A TFK '33 WL' radio, case in very good condition, cloth worn, missing lever on right side.
£100-150 ATK

A CLOSER LOOK AT A CATALIN RADIO

* retains both of its knobs, which is desirable. The knobs are smooth and rounded - correct for the period. After WWII ended, bbed knobs were used.

It is deemed a 'classic' radio and is in excellent condition with no cracks, chips or burn marks from the heat of the valves.

A Fada 5F60 butterscotch and blue grilled Catalin radio, with ribbed knobs.

This model was one of the first Catalins radio to be designed and produced by Fada. It was also made with a wooden body, which was much less expensive than its Catalin counterpart at the time.

1936   8in (20.5cm) wide
£2,500-3,000 CAT

is very rare 'All American' triotic colour combination was oduced just before the US tered WWII.

White Catalin oxidizes and changes colour to a butterscotch tone over time. Restoring the colour takes hours of skilled polishing.

n American Fada Streamliner Model 189 'Bullet' radio in white, ue and red Catalin, with smooth knobs.
941   10.25in (26cm) wide
2,000-2,500 CAT

A 'Telefunken 340W' radio, known as 'Katzenkopf', bakelite case, five valves, straight receiver. *1931*
£400-500 ATK

A Fada L-56 lapis lazuli blue and alabaster Catalin radio.
1939   9in (23cm) widest
£1,500-2,000 CAT

A Sentinel Model '284-NR' cherry or ox-blood red and yellow Catalin radio, with later grille cloth.

This radio was prone to cracking that was caused by the Catalin shrinking over the metal chassis, which did not shrink. It was also produced in a rare, but less unappealing, version without a grille.

1945   11in (28cm) wide

£800-1,200   **CAT**

A Bendix model '526 C' jade green, white marbled and black Catalin radio.

1946   11in (28cm) wide

£500-700   **CAT**

A Kadette Model 'L' Art Deco radio, in cream, with a yellow top and a marbled mustard coloured grille.

Along with many Catalin radios, this model came in a range of colours. The metal top and grille can also be found in different colours, including green.

         7.75in (20cm) high

£1,000-1,500   **CA**

A Emerson 'tombstone' Model 'BT245' butterscotch radio, with original turtle transfer to top and other transfers, cream grille and knobs, lacks two knobs.

1937   9.75in (25cm) high

£1,000-1,500   **CAT**

A Swedish radio, in the form of a miniature grand piano, with AGA radio and 78rpm record player, rare construction.

1948

£250-350   **ATK**

A Decca Transistor radio model 'TPW 70', in plastic, with dial and pointer volume controls.

This radio was produced to hang on a wall, resembling a clock. It originally cost £18, 7/6d.

1962

£60-70   **ROS**

A 1970s Weltron '2001' or 'Space Ball' radio cassette recorder, in an ivory plastic case, spherical form on a circular stand.

      11.75in (30cm) high

£120-180   **QU**

An early 1970s National Panasonic 'Pana Pet 70' radio, with original box and instructions.

Without the original box, this radio would be worth approximately £30.

      box 5.5in (14cm) high

£65-75   **DTC**

A yellow Panasonic 'Tootaloop' bangle transistor radio.

When closed, this radio could be worn around the wrist like a bangle. It was produced in a number of colours. Mauve, lilac and lime green are the rarest.

c1972   6in (15cm) dia

£55-65   **DT**

COLLECTORS' NOTES

■ Since Stephenson's 'Rocket' of 1814, we have had a fascination for steam travel. Unfortunately, memorabilia from these early days is extremely difficult to find today, and collectors focus on slightly more modern items.

■ The railway network grew rapidly and by the turn of the 20th century forty railway companies existed, which were amalgamated into just four in 1921. These four groups were the London, Midland & Scottish (LMS), London & North Eastern Railways (LNER), the Southern Railway (SR), and the Great Western Railway (GWR). Today, pieces from the 1920s are the earliest that are readily available to a collector and as a result the most sought-after. Collectors will often focus on one particular company, which can have a personal or geographical connection for them.

■ The next most popular period to collect is the 1950s. It is preceded by nationalisation in 1948 and closely followed by Dr. Beeching's rationalisation, which saw a number of lines closed.

■ Nameplates form the upper echelons of railwayana collecting with the current world record set at £54,000, paid at auction in 2002 for "Sir William A. Stanier FRS". The relative rarity of good quality name plates and a strong demand means that values are likely to remain high. Other railway signage can be much more affordable and may rise in value, with 'smokebox' and 'cab side' number plates in particular being popular with collectors.

A 'Clan Cameron' locomotive nameplate, a deflector mounted rectangular plate from the British Railways steam loco No. 72001, which entered service in December 1951, the second in a class of ten authorised in 1949.

6in (15cm) high

£30,000-40,000 **L&T**

A BR(E) 'Alford Town' totem station sign.

Ex-GNR station between Boston and Louth, closed October 1970.

£2,000-3,000 **GWRA**

A BR(M) 'Ambergate' totem station sign.

Ex-Midland Railway main line station between Derby and Chesterfield.

£900-1,200 **GWRA**

A BR(M) 'Besses o' th' Barn' totem station sign, wall-fitting variety with four integral fixing-holes.

Station signs, known as 'totems', are gaining in popularity. Each region has a different colour, for example the Eastern region totems are dark blue and North Eastern examples are orange.

£4,500-5,500 **GWRA**

BR(S) 'BUDE' dark green totem station sign, with all white flange, one small, easily repairable ding to the lower right edge.

Ex-LSWR station on the North Cornwall coast and Branch Line off the 'Withered Arm'.

£7,000-8,000 **GWRA**

BR(M) 'Kings Norton' totem station sign, with slight mottling.

Ex-Midland Railway station between Birmingham New Street and Bromsgrove.

£350-450 **GWRA**

A rare BR(M) 'Polesworth' totem station sign, some small repairs and slight mottling.

Ex-LNWR West Coast main line station between Nuneaton and Tamworth.

£550-650 **GWRA**

A BR(M) 'Witton' totem station sign, with slight mottling.

Ex-LNWR station a short way from Birmingham New Street, just beyond Aston. This sign would be of interest to football memorabilia collectors, as Witton is the stop for Aston Villa FCs ground at Villa Park.

£550-650 **GWRA**

EAST FINCHLEY

A London Transport 'East Finchley' enamel destination indicator, with brass ends.

£55-65 GWRA

LONDON BRIDGE

A London Transport 'London Bridge' enamel target station sign.

This is a desirable location because it is not only a Northern Line station, but also a British Railways station.

£220-280 GWRA

NEASDEN

A London Transport 'Neasden' enamel destination indicator, with brass ends.

£150-200 GWRA

87 E

A '87E' shed plate, oval alloy, face possibly restored, back predominantly clean, edge retains original green paint and there are plenty of traces of original paint over the rest of the plate.

£120-180 GWRA

PLATFORM 1

A rare BR(NE) 'Platform 1' enamel sign, with black-edged lettering, some chipping but good colour and shine.

24in (61cm) wide

£60-80 GWRA

FAVERSHAM

A scarce Southern Railway 'Faversham' enamel target sign.

Ex-SECR station between Sittingbourne and Canterbury.

£400-500 GWRA

LYDNEY G.F.

A British Railways 'LYDNEY G.F.' pressed alloy ground frame sign.

15in (38cm) long

£100-150 GWRA

41206

A '41206' smoke box number plate.

Ex-Ivatt 2-6-2T Class 2MT, built Crewe 1946.

£2,000-3,000 GWR

A 'Children' alloy road sign, bears the original maker's name "The Royal Label Factory".

CHILDREN

£150-200 GWRA

Claude Buckle, 'Canterbury Cathedral', carriage print from the Southern Railway Series (A), unmounted and unframed with slight damage to corners.

£70-100 GWRA

Claude Buckle, 'Exeter Cathedral', carriage print from the Southern Railway Series (A), unmounted and unframed with a couple of small tears and corner fold along base.

£150-200 GWRA

Hesketh Hubbard, 'Guernsey', carriage print from the Southern Railway Post - War Series, unframed and unmounted, some periphery damage.

£250-300 GWRA

Claude Buckle, 'Salisbury Cathedral', carriage print from the Southern Railway Series (A), unmounted and unframed, with some damage around periphery.

£120-180 GWRA

Hesketh Hubbard, 'Hockworthy Bridge, Dartmoor', carriage print from the Southern Railway Post - War Series, mounted but unframed, a few paint smudges bottom left.

£280-320 GWRA

Claude Buckle, 'Winchester Cathedral', carriage print from the Southern Railway Series (A), unmounted and unframed, with some damage around periphery.

£120-180 GWRA

Four GWR Photochrom carriage prints, all of Avon Gorge, three of which are different views of the Clifton Suspension Bridge.

£70-100 GWRA

Five GWR Photochrom carriage prints, all of Devon and including Lynton, Clovelly, Saltash Bridge, Dartmeet and Dartmouth, unframed.

£100-150 GWRA

An LNER and Cunard Line 'The Historic Side of Britain' brochure, 32-pages with an image of Lincoln Cathedral and Edinburgh Castle on the cover.

c1930

£40-50 GWRA

A very rare 1930s Great Eastern Railway wooden fixed distant signal arm and mono spectacle.

As these signs were exposed to the elements constantly, they are usually found with weather damage, meaning examples in good condition can fetch a premium.

c1930s   33in (85cm) long

£50-80   GWRA

An official British Railways working cut-away model of Walschaert's valve gear.

£350-450   GWRA

An LNWR Fletchers Block & Bell signal box instrument, from Lichfield No. 2 box, bearing three ivorine plates "No.1 Box", "Platform Lines" and "And Walsall Lines", rear stamped "LNWRy Tele Dept No. 3931".

£180-220   GWRA

A Tyers type-B token instrument, from an intermediate section.

£700-800   GWRA

A scarce Somerset & Dorset three-aspect hand lamp, embossed "LMS, Midland Pattern" and "S & D" properly stamped on the reducing cone, unrestored and complete with reservoir and unmarked burner.

Look for stamps by the railway company and ensure that all the internal pieces are present as this helps increase value.

£120-180   GWRA

A GWR brass-cased drum clock, by Kays of Paris, stamped on the case, back cover and movement "5092", with location pencilled on the inside cover "Chalford".

£300-350   GWRA

A GWR oak-cased fusee clock, bearing original ivorine plate "G.W.R 1560", restored and face bears the roundel style company initials.

face 12in (30.5cm) diam

£800-1,200   GWRA

A GWR locomotive/tail lamp, brass-plated on the chimney and stamped "Emergency Use Only - Return To Severn Tunnel East Signal Box".

£1,000-1,500   GWR.

FIND OUT MORE...

'British Locomotive Builders' Plates', by Keith Buckle and David Love, published by Midland Publishing Ltd, 1994.

'The Book of British Railway Station Totems', by Dave Brennand and Richard Furness, published by Sutton Publishing Ltd, 2002.

'A Collector's Guide to Railwayana', Handel Kardas (editor), published by Ian Allan Publishing Limited, 2001.

'Nameplates on Display', by Ian Wright, published by Pennine Publications, 1986.ß

www.railwayanapage.com

A scarce 1930s LMS peaked cap, the embroidered badge with laurel leaf either side.

£25-35   GWRA

COLLECTORS' NOTES

- As far as rock and pop memorabilia is concerned, Elvis Presley is still 'The King' and The Beatles still top the popularity charts. Due to the long careers of these acts and the high quantity of merchandise, memorabilia is available for all budgets. Other popular acts include The Rolling Stones, The Doors, Jimi Hendrix and The Who.

- Pieces personally owned or used by the artist are the most desirable, but are also the most expensive. Provenance is vital so always ask for a letter of authenticity or details of the item's history.

- Merchandise was produced in vast amounts, but much was damaged or destroyed over the years. Look for licensed examples in good condition, images of the star's faces on the original packaging are desirable.

- Posters, programmes and tickets are all popular collecting areas. Collectors often concentrate on concerts they attended in person or legendary or notable performances. Always look carefully at the condition of paper-based collectables as it has a huge effect on value.

- Anything signed by an artist is desirable, but beware that signatures obtained from fan clubs were often printed or signed by a secretary or assistant and that band members often signed for each other. Look for items with signatures from the whole band, preferably not crossing each other. Beatles signatures are among the most faked so make sure to have them authenticated by a recognised expert.

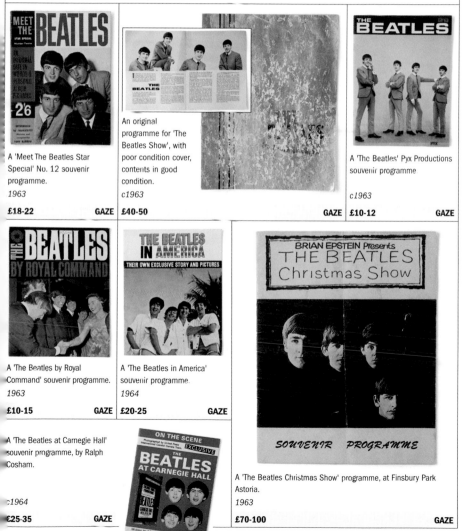

A 'Meet The Beatles Star Special' No. 12 souvenir programme.
1963
£18-22   GAZE

An original programme for 'The Beatles Show', with poor condition cover, contents in good condition.
c1963
£40-50   GAZE

A 'The Beatles' Pyx Productions souvenir programme.
c1963
£10-12   GAZE

A 'The Beatles by Royal Command' souvenir programme.
1963
£10-15   GAZE

A 'The Beatles in America' souvenir programme.
1964
£20-25   GAZE

A 'The Beatles Christmas Show' programme, at Finsbury Park Astoria.
1963
£70-100   GAZE

A 'The Beatles at Carnegie Hall' souvenir programme, by Ralph Cosham.
c1964
£25-35   GAZE

A rare Beatles Australian Tour concert programme, June 1964.

£150-200 GAZE

A programme for 'Another Beatles Christmas Show' 1964/65 at the Hammersmith Odeon, together with an original ticket stub for a second performance on Friday January 8th 1965.

£150-200 GAZE

A 1971 'FAB·208 annual', published by L.P.C. Magazines, featuring an interview with DJ Tony Blackburn at home, The Beatles and Steve McQueen.

1971 10.5in (27cm) high

£10-15 MTS

A 1970 'Teenbeat' annual, compiled by Albert Hand, featuring The Beatles, Status Quo, Jimi Hendrix, The Beach Boys, The Monkees and more.

1969 10in (25.5cm) high

£10-14 MTS

A 'Beatles on Broadway' souvenir booklet, by Sam Leach.

1964

£6-8 GAZE

A rare 'The Beatles' official magazine, No.1 Sept.-Nov. 1964, published by Dell.

First issues of a series are always desirable. This comprehensive magazine also shows the band in their prime.

10.25in (26cm) high

£250-350 NOR

'The Beatles Illustrated Lyrics', published by Gilvrie Misstear and David Hillman, edited by Alan Aldridge.

1969

£60-80 GAZE

A copy of The Daily Mirror, Wednesday December 10th 1980, "John Lennon Shot Dead" special issue.

£22-28 GAZE

A lilac-coloured ticket stub for The Beatles / Roy Orbison show at the Gaumont Theatre Ipswich, for the first performance on Wednesday 22nd May 1963.

£80-120 GAZE

A Nems Enterprises Beatles scrap book and contents.

£18-22   GAZE

A 'Yellow Submarine' set of eight re-issue lobby cards.

1999

£22-28   GAZE

A Beatles printed ring binder, by Nems Enterprises Limited.

11.5in (29.5cm) high

£200-300   NOR

A 1960s set of 20 Beatles 'Yellow Submarine' pop out art decorations.

15in (38cm) high

£55-65   NOR

A 'The Beatles Book' issue calendar for 1964, lacks June.

£35-45   GAZE

An American The Beatles 'Yellow Submarine' eight-track tape, released by Capitol.

c1967   *5in (13cm) high*

£12-18   NOR

An early American 'Introducing The Beatles England's No. 1 Vocal Group' stereophonic LP, on Vee-Jay label, No. SR1062.

£100-150   B&H

A Beatles biscuit plate, with transfer decoration.

£20-30   GAZE

A Parlaphone presentation gold disc for the soundtrack to The Beatles film 'A Hard Days Night', in recognition of sales exceeding 100,000 in the UK.

1964

£80-120   GAZE

An 'I Love Ringo' badge.

3.5in (9cm) diam

£10-15   **NOR**

A 1960s Beatles silver plastic button, showing two people dancing.

0.75in (2cm) diam

£3-5   **CVS**

A 'Help Stamp Out "Beetles"' badge.

"Beetles" is mis-spelt as this was not a licensed product. It could also be connected to when John Lennon made anti-Christian comments in 1966 in the San Francisco Chronicle.

3.5in (9cm) diam

£10-15   **NOR**

A rare Beatles signed photograph, featuring Stuart Sutcliffe, at their first ever foreign engagement at the Indra Club, Hamburg in 1960, signed by the original drummer Pete Best, with the group's name and date of the photograph.

£35-45   **GAZE**

A Beatles signed photograph, featuring the group onstage at The Cavern Club in 1961, signed by their original drummer Pete Best who has also added the groups name below his signature, mounted and framed with the heading "The Beatles" and photograph description.

£45-55   **GAZE**

A Beatles signed photograph, featuring the group wearing their first ever stage suits, and signed by their original drummer Pete Best, mounted with a description of the first time they wore the suits in 1962.

£40-50   **GAZE**

A white single cover sleeve, signed by Paul McCartney, John Lennon, Ringo Starr and George Harrison.

£250-350   **GAZE**

A handwritten letter from John Lennon's aunt, Mimi Smith, to a fan, dated 9th December 1963, plus a typed list of George Harrison's biography with facsimile signature.

John's aunt Mimi famously bought him his first guitar and is quoted as saying "The guitar's all right John, but you'll never make a living with it".

£70-100   **GAZE**

An American United Artists Corp press release, detailing the opening week's figures in Chicago for the second Beatles film "Help".

1965

£4-6   **GAZE**

A set of four Richard Avedon Beatles posters, German issue.

Commissioned by Nems, the Beatles' management company, these images were licensed to US magazine 'Look', UK newspaper 'The Daily Express' and German magazine 'Stern'.

1967

£300-400   **GAZE**

A early 1970's French Beatles "Oldies But Goldies" promo poster for the LP.

£12-18   **GAZE**

"Let It Be", German one sheet poster.

1971

£70-100   **GAZE**

A black and white Elvis Presley photograph.

£7-10   **GAZE**

A 1963 Star Pics Elvis Presley calendar, lacks 'September'.

£4-5   **GAZE**

"Love Me Tender", poster signed by Debra Paget (Cathy Reno) and James Drury (Ray Reno).

1956

£45-55   **GAZE**

A 1950s Elvis Presley necklace, the metal frame with a portrait of Elvis Presley.

pendant 0.75in (2cm) high

£40-50   **CVS**

A CLOSER LOOK AT A LOCK OF ELVIS PRESLEY'S HAIR

The hair and accompanying letter of authenticity are professionally mounted with a photograph of the famous haircut, making an attractive display.

Locks of Elvis' hair have come up for sale in the past and attract great interest, a clipping the size of a cricket ball sold for £70,000 in 2003.

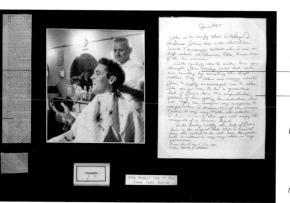

Letters of authenticity are vital when considering celebrity memorabilia - always ask the dealer or auction house how the item was obtained.

Elvis was drafted into the US Army on March 24th, 1958 and was posted to Fort Chaffee, Arkansas. He had his regulation haircut the next day at the local barber shop and his manager made sure no hair was stolen.

A lock of Elvis Presley's hair, mounted with a photograph of Elvis getting his Army hair cut, a letter of provenance from the winner of the lock in a competition and a related newspaper article.

24in (9.5cm) high

£1,000-1,500   **LCA**

An Elvis Presley 'The King of Rock & Roll 1935-77' commemorative badge, by Boxcar Enterprises.

c1977   3in (7.5cm) diam

£3-4   **NOR**

An Elvis Presley 'striking' match book.

2in (5cm) high

£1-2   **NOR**

A 1980s box of Elvis Cologne by Elvis Fragrances Inc, licensed by Elvis Presley Enterprises.

2.5in (6.5cm) high

£18-22   **CVS**

An Elvis Presley doll, by Eugene Doll Co. Inc., endorsed by Graceland Elvis Presley Enterprises, boxed.

c1984   14.75in (37.5cm) high

£80-120   **NOR**

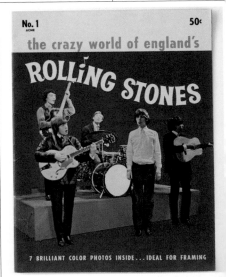

"The Rolling Stones Book", souvenir booklet of pictures and features.

c1964/65

£18-22   **GAZE**

An Elvis Presley radio, with dressed figure of Elvis.

c1978   9.75in (25cm) high

£40-50   **NOR**

An "On The Scene - The Rolling Stones" souvenir booklet, by June Knight.

1964

£28-32   **GAZE**

A Rolling Stones publicity photograph, issued by the BBC, in original envelope.

1964

£35-45   **GAZE**

An American "The Crazy World of England's Rolling Stones" souvenir programme, Summer 1964 Issue No 1.

£40-50   **GAZE**

A programme for the Rolling Stones concert at the London Palladium, with the original ticket stub for the second evening performance on Sunday 1st August.

£120-180   GAZE

An original programme for The Rolling Stones, at Romford ABC cinema, with two original ticket stubs for the second performance on Thursday 18th March, with Compliments of the Manager slip.
1965

£150-200   GAZE

A 1960s Rolling Stones transfer sheet, with line drawn busts and facsimile signatures.

£20-30   GAZE

An original show souvenir programme supplement for a tour featuring The Rolling Stones, Ike & Tina Turner, The Hollies, the Small Faces and others.

c1965

£50-60   GAZE

A Rolling Stones 66 souvenir brochure, featuring Ike and Tina Turner, The Yardbirds and others.

£60-70   GAZE

A "Stones In The Park - Full Story behind the TV show" magazine.

c1969

£50-60   GAZE

A Rolling Stones concert poster, from a 1973 concert in Frankfurt.

£80-120   GAZE

An Animals fan club badge.

3.25in (8.5cm) diam

£10-20   NOR

A very rare 1970s boxed bar of 'ABBA The Soap', by J. Grossmith, the bar in the form of a green audio tape.

£22-28   MTS

A 1960s card and plastic Bay City Roller lampshade.

8.25in (21cm) high

£22-28 **MTS**

A 1970s Bay City Rollers 'We Love You' purple fabric patch.

3.25in (8.5cm) wide

£5-7 **MTS**

A Bee Gees 'One Night Only' concert programme.

1998

£6-8 **GAZE**

A 1970s David Bowie Pick-A-Patch patch, with gold coloured details.

3.25in (8.5cm) high

£8-12 **MTS**

A David Bowie 'Serious Moonlight' tour concert programme.

1983

£15-20 **GAZE**

A guitar scratch plate signed by all four members of Bush, together with a 'Local Crew' access pass dated "Feb 22 2000".

£20-25 **GAZE**

An original programme for "The Dave Clark Five Show", with original ticket stub for a second performance on Thursday 9th April.

£40-60 **GAZE**

A guitar scratch plate signed by The Charlatans guitarist Mark Collins, together with two crew access passes, dated 24th 25th April 2000, framed.

£18-22 **GAZE**

A John Denver at the London Victoria Apollo concert programme, together with two ticket stubs.

1982

£6-8 **GAZE**

A concert programme for The Everly Brothers, with two ticket stubs.

1985

£7-10   **GAZE**

A Bob Dylan at the NEC concert programme, together with ticket stub.

1989

£10-15   **GAZE**

A Sophie Ellis-Bextor signed "Murder on the Dance Floor" CD single, annotated with "Don't steal the move!! Be good. Love Sophie", mounted with a photograph.

£20-30   **GAZE**

A pair of Mick Fleetwood signed wooden drum sticks.

£15-20   **GAZE**

An Emerson, Lake & Palmer concert poster, for Germany 28th November 1970 or 71, artwork by Gunter Kieser.

£70-100   **GAZE**

A Fleetwood Mac 'Tango in The Night' tour concert programme.

1987

£8-12   **GAZE**

A programme and ticket stub for Larry Parnes "Big Star Show", featuring Billy Fury, the ticket stub for the first performance on Sunday 13th October.

£40-50   **GAZE**

An original programme and ticket stub for "The Sunday Special" show, featuring Billy Fury at the Britannia Theatre, Great Yarmouth.

£30-40   **GAZE**

1960

£55-65   **GAZE**

An original programme for the Larry Parnes "Billy Fury Show - Meet The Beat", at the Britannia Theatre, Great Yarmouth.

Pop impresario Larry Parnes (1930-89) managed acts including Tommy Steele, Marty Wilde and Billy Fury. He turned down the opportunity to manage Cliff Richard and The Beatles on more than one occasion.

An original Arthur Howes and Brian Epstein programme, featuring Gerry and the Pacemakers, The Kinks, Gene Pitney and others, together with the ticket stub for Wednesday 25th November.

£35-45   **GAZE**

An original Arthur Howes programme, featuring Gerry and the Pacemakers, Del Shannon and others.

£18-22   **GAZE**

A 1970s plastic 'Pink Pop Bag' carrier bag, with facsimile signatures and portraits of Mark Bolan, Michael Jackson.

14.75in (37.5cm) high

£10-16   **MTS**

A KISS printed souvenir mirror.

5in (12.5cm) high

£8-12   **NOR**

A CLOSER LOOK AT A SET OF KISS DOLLS

These dolls were packed in card boxes with cellophane fronts, the backs were printed with cut-out instruments for the band.

These are very rare and sought-after today. A complete set is more desirable than individual dolls – single dolls are worth £70-100 each.

US toy manufacturer Mego Corp. made dolls and action figures from 1970 and held licenses for a large number of franchises. The high quality of their lavish figures makes them popular with collectors today.

Make sure the dolls retain all their original clothing and accessories and that their hair is in good condition.

A set of four KISS dolls, by Mego Corp.
c1977

13.25in (33.5cm) high

£550-650   **NOR**

"Kiss – A Marvel Comics Super Special", No. 1 Sept. 1977, published by Marvel Comics.

The comic was printed with ink containing the band's blood.

10.75in (27.5cm) high

£70-100   **NOR**

"TV Guide", Sept. 23-29 1967, 'The Day the Monkees Rebelled'.

1967   *7.25in (18.5cm) h*

£20-30   **NOR**

An 'Official Monkee Puzzle', by E.E. Fairchild, 340-pieces, complete.

c1967   *13in (33cm) wide*

£60-80   **NOR**

A Gary Moore signed scratch plate, framed with an 'all areas' access pass dated 28th March 2000.

£35-45   GAZE

A reproduction Roy Orbison concert poster.

Reproductions of early 'boxing' style posters such as this differ from the originals in that they contain the year of the event as well as the day and month. As the posters were destined for the rubbish bin as soon as the concert was over, the date was considered unnecessary and is missing from the vast majority of the original examples.

£10-15   GAZE

A scarce vinyl Jimmy Osmond pennant, with tassles.

15.75in (40cm) long

£15-20   MTS

An American Teen Pin-Ups magazine, June 1974, featuring the Osmonds, the Jackson Five and others.

This magazine originally retailed for 15p in England.

10.75in (27.5cm) high

£2-3   MTS

A 1970s Donny Osmond plastic face mask.

12in (30.5cm) long

£10-16   MTS

"Pink Floyd: Live at Pompeii", US one sheet poster.

1973

£180-220   GAZE

A The Osmonds' annual for 1976, by Osbro Productions.

10.5in (27cm) high

£6-8   MTS

A Pink Floyd World tour concert programme.

1987

£18-22   GAZE

A 'Paul Revere Interviews The Raiders' picture disc, 33.5rpm, with exclusive interview.

6in (15cm) diam

£25-35   NOR

A "Meet Cliff and The Shadows in Wonderful Life" Star Special magazine, together with a Cliff "Life With the Stars" magazine.

£15-20　　　　**GAZE**

A late 1950's Cliff Richard programme for "Oh Boy Its Cliff Richard" Cliff and the Dritlers, together with Pop Weekly No.1 with Cliff Richard front cover.

£12-18　　　　**GAZE**

A Roxy Music concert poster, from their 1973 tour of Europe, with artwork by Gunter Kieser.

£50-60　　　　**GAZE**

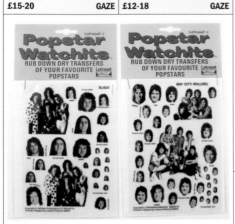

A 1960s set of Popstars Watchits Slade transfers, together with card of Bay City Rollers transfers.

10in (25.5cm) high

£10-16　　　　**MTS**

A 1970s Marc Bolan T-Rex fabric patch, with red flock lettering.

3in (7.5cm) diam

£10-15　　　　**MTS**

A Tina Turner 'Break Every Rule' tour concert programme.

1987-8

£8-12　　　　**GAZE**

A Bonnie Tyler 'Bitterblue' five track CD, framed with a signed photograph.

c1991

£7-10　　　　**GAZE**

A 1960s 'Yes' psychedelic reflective belt buckle.

3.25in (8.5cm) wide

£10-15　　　　**NOI**

A Wham 'Club Fantastic' tour concert programme.

1983

£5-7　　　　**GAZE**

COLLECTORS' NOTES

■ The development of transfer printing in the late 18th century allowed commemorative ceramics to became more widely available. As the technique spread and distribution methods grew during the 19th century, it became more popular.

■ As the variety of items available is so vast, many collectors choose to collect pieces related to a single monarch or member of the Royal family, or a single event in a monarch's life. Interest in the young Princes William and Harry is growing.

■ The quality of the piece is a key indicator to value, with those by well-known makers made from high quality materials and with fine decoration usually

being the most valuable. Condition is also vital as so many of each item were produced – always buy in the best condition you can, as this will help value remain constant or grow.

■ As well as ceramics, many other different items have been produced to celebrate events such as coronations and jubilees. Some, such as biscuit tins, were special versions of usual items, whilst some were specially produced for the event itself.

■ These 'ephemeral' items, including magazines and card and paper items, can be found regularly at affordable prices and can make a satisfying collection – again try to buy in the best condition you can.

A Tunnicliffe 'Queen's Diamond Jubilee' commemorative match holder and striker, printed mark, small bruise to top rim.

It is thought this match holder was given by William Tunnicliffe to Colonel Harry Johnson, chairman of the Johnson Pottery to celebrate the Jubilee.

c1897   3in (7.5cm) high

£45-55   **WW**

A Victorian découpage picture of the Royal family, including Queen Victoria and her children.

Découpage is a decorative technique involving cutting out paper designs. The inked inscription of the back adds desirability as it indicates that the picture was made by Lady Churchill, a Lady-in-waiting to Queen Victoria, on September 20th 1843, an excellent dated attribution close to the Queen.

1843   6.75in (17cm) high

£150-200   **GAZE**

A Queen Victoria Golden Jubilee plate.

1887   8.75in (22cm) diam

£40-60   **GAZE**

A reproduction Parian ware bust of Queen Victoria, in Coronation robes.

16in (40.5cm) high

£60-90   **GAZE**

A limited edition Royal Doulton 'Queen Victoria' large character jug, D6788, from an edition of 3,000.

This was specially commissioned in 1988 in a limited edition of 3,000 by The Guild of Specialist China & Glass retailers.

1988   7in (18cm) high

£60-80   **GAZE**

An edition of the London Illustrated News, commemorating the marriage of Princess Louise of Wales, containing silks.

1889   *16.5in (42cm) high*

£22-28   **GAZE**

A handkerchief commemorating Queen Victoria's Diamond Jubilee, inscribed "Souvenir of Her Majesty's Reign, The Longest on Record 1837-1897", framed and glazed.

c1897   *19.5in (49.5cm)*

£30-40   **GAZE**

A horse brass, commemorating Queen Victoria's Diamond Jubilee.

1897   *3.5in (9cm) diam*

£6-9   **GAZE**

An Edward VII and Alexandra monochrome milk jug, dated June 26th 1902.

4.75in (12cm)

£30-40   **GAZE**

A copy of the Daily Mirror, the lead story being the funeral of King Edward VII.

1910   *15in (38cm) high*

£70-100   **GAZE**

A small Edward VII Coronation milk jug, inscribed with the date, "26th June 1902".

The June date shown was the proposed date of the Coronation, but the event did not actually take place until August 9th as the uncrowned King developed appendicitis. Look out for commemorative pieces with both dates or only the August date shown as these are usually more sought after.

1902   *3.75in (9.5cm) high*

£15-20   **GAZE**

An official paper programme and souvenir of King Edward VII and Queen Alexandra's Royal visit to the City and South London, on Saturday October 25th, frayed, torn and faded.

1902

£18-22   **GAZ**

A George V Silver Jubilee commemorative beaker.

1935   *4.25in (11cm) high*

£4-6   **GAZE**

A pair of Royal Doulton George V & Queen Mary commemorative beakers, inscribed "The Silver Jubilee 1910-1935"

c1935   *3.25in (8.5cm) high*

£20-25   **GAZE**

A matching pair of George V Silver Jubilee cups and saucers.

1935   *Saucer 5.75in (14.5cm) diam*

£15-25   **GAZE**

A Doulton plate, commemorating the coronation of George V and Queen Mary.

8in (20.5cm) diam

£30-50   **GAZE**

A signed Royal presentation photograph of Queen Mary, gilt-tooled and embossed crown decoration, signed "Mary R".

1936   *Photograph 8in (20.5cm) high*

£180-220   **GAZE**

A copy of "King Emperor's Jubilee", published by Daily Express Publications commemorating 25 years of rule by King George V, with extensive illustrations.

12in (30.5cm) high

£4-6   **GAZE**

A trio set, commemorating the proposed Coronation of Edward VIII.

1936-37

Plate 6in (15cm) diam

£15-25   **GAZE**

A Shelley mug, commemorating the proposed Coronation of Edward VIII.

1936-37   *3in (7.5cm) high*

£18-22   **GAZE**

An unusual Bretby 'Edward VIII' commemorative musical character jug, covered in a matt white glaze, impressed mark, lacks movement.

8in (20cm) high

£100-150   **WW**

A Poole Pottery 'Edward VIII' plaque, designed by Harold Brownsword, impressed "Poole England", facsimile signature "Harold Brownsword Sc", repaired damage.

11.25in (28.5cm) high

£80-120   **WW**

A metal badge of Edward VIII, with Union Jack.

1.25in (3cm) diam

£6-8   **LG**

A Tuscan china mug, commemorating the Coronation of George VI and Elizabeth.

1937   2.75in (7cm) high

£30-40   **GAZE**

A George VI Coronation trio set.

1937   7in (18cm) diam

£12-18   **GAZE**

A souvenir songbook for the Coronation of George VI and Elizabeth entitled "National Airs of the Empire".

1937   11.75in (30cm) high

£8-12   **GAZE**

A 1937 edition of the Radio Times, the cover illustrating the Coronation of King George VI.

1937   *11.5in (29cm) high*

£5-8   **GAZE**

A commemorative mug, made for the Coronation of George VI and Queen Elizabeth

1937   *3.5in (9cm) high*

£40-60   **GAZE**

A Coronation arrangement pamphlet, with map, for the Coronation of George VI and Elizabeth.

1937   *6in (15cm) wide*

£4-6   **DH**

A commemorative fold-out booklet, produced by Ogden's Tobacco, complete with a full collection of George VI's Coronation procession cigarette cards.

1937   *42.5in (108cm) long*

£5-8   **GAZ**

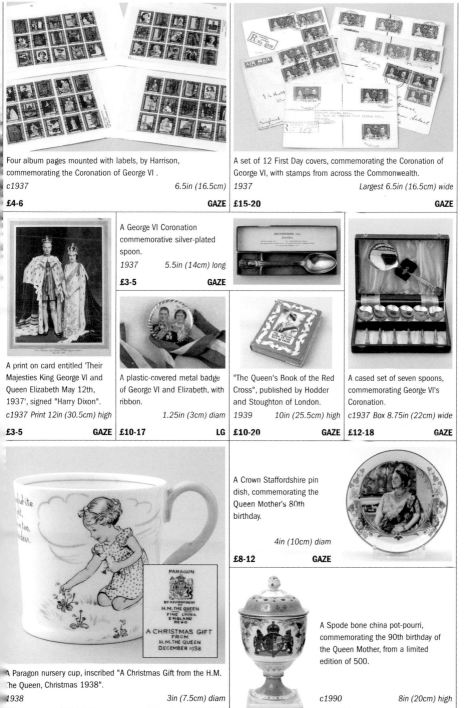

Four album pages mounted with labels, by Harrison, commemorating the Coronation of George VI .

c1937   *6.5in (16.5cm)*

£4-6   **GAZE**

A set of 12 First Day covers, commemorating the Coronation of George VI, with stamps from across the Commonwealth.

1937   *Largest 6.5in (16.5cm) wide*

£15-20   **GAZE**

A George VI Coronation commemorative silver-plated spoon.

1937   *5.5in (14cm) long*

£3-5   **GAZE**

A print on card entitled 'Their Majesties King George VI and Queen Elizabeth May 12th, 1937', signed "Harry Dixon".

c1937 Print 12in (30.5cm) high

£3-5   **GAZE**

A plastic-covered metal badge of George VI and Elizabeth, with ribbon.

1.25in (3cm) diam

£10-17   **LG**

"The Queen's Book of the Red Cross", published by Hodder and Stoughton of London.

1939   *10in (25.5cm) high*

£10-20   **GAZE**

A cased set of seven spoons, commemorating George VI's Coronation.

c1937 Box 8.75in (22cm) wide

£12-18   **GAZE**

A Crown Staffordshire pin dish, commemorating the Queen Mother's 80th birthday.

4in (10cm) diam

£8-12   **GAZE**

A Paragon nursery cup, inscribed "A Christmas Gift from the H.M. The Queen, Christmas 1938".

1938   *3in (7.5cm) diam*

£120-180   **GAZE**

A Spode bone china pot-pourri, commemorating the 90th birthday of the Queen Mother, from a limited edition of 500.

c1990   *8in (20cm) high*

£190-240   **H&G**

A Wedgwood Queen Elizabeth II Coronation mug, designed by Richard Guyatt, of cylindrical form with applied handle, in pink and brown colourway with gilt decoration, printed marks.

c1953   *4.75in (12cm) high*

£35-45   **L&T**

A Wedgwood commemorative mug, designed by Eric Ravilious, commemorating the Coronation of Queen Elizabeth II.

1953   *4.25in (11cm) high*

£200-400   **REN**

A Honiton Pottery earthenware mug, commemorating the Coronation of Queen Elizabeth II.

c1953   *4in (10cm) high*

£50-60   **H&G**

A Royal Albert Queen Elizabeth II loving cup, damaged.

If in perfect condition, these loving cups can fetch £200 or more.

7.5in (19cm) wide

£100-150   **GAZE**

A Thornton Crown ware trio set, to commemorate the Coronation of Queen Elizabeth II.

1953   *6in (15cm) wide*

£10-15   **GAZE**

A Royal Worcester bone china mask-head jug, commemorating the Coronation of Queen Elizabeth II.

c1953   *5.75in (14.5cm) high*

£70-90   **H&G**

A Minton bone china loving cup and cover, commemorating the Coronation of Queen Elizabeth II, designed by John Wadsworth.

Without the cover, the value of this piece falls to £160-190.

c1953   *5.75in (14.5cm)*

£340-390   **H&G**

A Burleigh hand-painted earthenware jug, commemorating the Coronation of Queen Elizabeth II.

c1953   *8.25in (21cm) high*

£150-200   **H&G**

Two Wade commemorative pin dishes, commemorating the Coronation of Queen Elizabeth II.

c1953   *4.75in (12cm) diar*

£10-20   **GAZ**

A CLOSER LOOK AT A COMMEMORATIVE ORB

A costume jewellery brooch, commemorating the Coronation of Queen Elizabeth II, in the form of her crown.

American costume jewellery company Trifari are perhaps the best known maker of crown-shaped pins, made from the 1930s to the late 1950s. In 1953, they released their popular 'Coronation gems' range. Look out for 1940s designs by Alfred Philippe for Trifari in vermeil which can fetch around £100-200 - these are more sought after than the re-issues of the 1980s.

c1953   1.5in (4cm) wide

£35-45   **GAZE**

The maker is well known, and only produced 600 examples of the design.

It is in mint condition with no wear to the gilding or any other damage.

It is made from bone china and the gilt decoration is finely applied.

Look out for coloured versions, each colour was made in a limited edition of only 60, and they can fetch up to £2,000 each.

A Minton bone china cup and cover, in the shape of an orb, commemorating the Coronation of Queen Elizabeth II, a limited edition of 600.

c1953   6in (15cm) high

£450-550   **H&G**

A scarf commemorating the Coronation of Queen Elizabeth II.

1953   28in (71cm) wide

£18-22   **GAZE**

A plastic-covered metal badge, commemorating the Coronation of Queen Elizabeth II.

1953   1in (2.5cm) diam

£10-15   **LG**

A Union Jack card shield, commemorating the Coronation of Queen Elizabeth II.

1953

£25-30   **DH**

A limited edition Paragon two-handled loving cup, from an edition of 750, commemorating the silver wedding anniversary of Queen Elizabeth II and Prince Phillip, complete with certificate.

1972   8.75in (22cm) wide

£70-100   **GAZE**

A limited edition Crown Staffordshire mug, commemorating the silver wedding anniversary of Queen Elizabeth and Prince Phillip.

1972   4.25in (11cm) high

£8-12   **GAZE**

A limited edition silver presentation plate, designed by Pietro Annigoni, commemorating the silver wedding anniversary of Queen Elizabeth II and Prince Philip.

1972   *Plate 9in (23cm) diam*

£20-30   **GAZE**

An earthenware mug, commemorating the Silver Jubilee of Queen Elizabeth II, the back decorated with other 20thC monarchs.

1977   *3.5in (9cm) high*

£10-15   **H&G**

A Kaleidoscope for Liberty & Co. earthenware mug, commemorating the Silver Jubilee of Queen Elizabeth II.

c1977   *3.25in (8.5cm) high*

£25-30   **H&G**

A Sheridan china bowl, commemorating the Silver Jubilee of Queen Elizabeth II.

1977   *6.25in (16cm) diam*

£8-10   **GAZE**

A Wedgwood lidded dish, commemorating the Silver Jubilee of Queen Elizabeth II.

1977   *4.5in (11.5cm) diam*

£10-15   **GAZE**

Two glass goblets, commemorating the Silver Jubilee of Queen Elizabeth II, boxed.

1977   *5in (12.5cm) high*

£8-12   **GAZE**

An earthenware teapot, by Chiswick Ceramics Community, commemorating the Silver Jubilee of Queen Elizabeth II, from a limited edition of 100.

c1977   *8in (20cm) high*

£180-220   **H&G**

A white metal presentation tray, commemorating the Silver Jubilee of Queen Elizabeth II.

1977   *12.5in (31.5cm) diam*

£18-22   **GAZE**

A pair of chromium-plated teaspoons, commemorating the Silver Jubilee of Queen Elizabeth II.

1977   4.75in (12cm) long

£8-12   **GAZE**

A Colman's Mustard commemorative pot, commemorating the Silver Jubilee of Queen Elizabeth II, in original presentation box.

1977

£7-10   **GAZE**

An oak footstool, with home-made commemorative Silver Jubilee tapestry cover.

1977   13.25in (33.5cm) wide

£10-20   **GAZE**

A Queen Elizabeth II Silver Jubilee commemorative stamp album, containing a complete set of stamps.

1977   8.25in (21cm) high

£5-8   **GAZE**

A Royal Crown Derby five-petal dish, commemorating the inauguration of Carsington Water by Her Majesty The Queen.

c1992   4.5in (11.5cm) wide

£40-50   **H&G**

A Rye Pottery child's mug, commemorating the Golden Jubilee of Queen Elizabeth II.

c2002   3in (6.5cm) high

£15-25   **H&G**

A Royal Doulton figure 'Her Majesty Queen Elizabeth', HN2878.

This design by E.J. Griffiths was released on the 30th anniversary of Her Majesty's reign in a limited edition of 2,500. Royal Doulton have modelled three other figurines of our current Queen, each taken from a different part of her reign.

1983   10.75in (27cm) high

£100-150   **L&T**

A bone china teapot, by The Royal Collection, commemorating the Golden Jubilee of Queen Elizabeth II, from a limited edition of 750.

c2002   11in (28cm) wide

£180-220   **H&G**

A Wood & Sons plate, for the wedding of Prince Charles and Lady Diana Spencer.

1981   Plate 10in (25.5cm) diam

GAZE

An enamel beaker, by Halcyon Days, commemorating the wedding of Prince Charles and Lady Diana Spencer.

1981   *3.5in (9cm)*

£80-120   **H&G**

A Wood & Sons tankard, commemorating the wedding of Prince Charles and Lady Diana Spencer.

1981   *5in (12.5cm) high*

£12-18   **GAZE**

1981

£10-20   **GAZE**

A pair of Wedgwood plates, commemorating the wedding of Prince Charles and Lady Diana Spencer.

1981   *4in (10cm) diam*

£8-12   **GAZE**

A pair of Carltonware 'walking' mugs, commemorating the wedding of Prince Charles and Lady Diana Spencer, the handles overlapping to form a heart shape.

1981   *5.25in (13.5cm) high*

£100-150   **H&G**

A Wedgwood lidded box, commemorating the wedding of Prince Charles and Lady Diana Spencer.

1981   *3in (7.5cm) wide*

£10-15   **GAZE**

A Royal Wedding commemorative mustard pot, for the wedding of Prince Charles and Lady Diana Spencer, boxed.

1981

£15-20   **GAZE**

A bottle of Adnams commemorative 'Prince's Ale', commemorating the wedding of Prince Charles and Lady Diana Spencer.

1981   *9.25in (23.5cm) high*

£2-3   **GAZE**

A silver-plated cake slice, commemorating the wedding of Prince Charles to Lady Diana Spencer.

1981   *9.5in (24cm) long*

£15-20   **GAZE**

A bone china mug, by Chown, commemorating the divorce of Prince Charles and Diana, Princess of Wales.

c1996   *3.75in (9.5cm) high*

£55-65   **H&G**

A rare Wedgwood basalt mug commemorating the investiture of Prince Charles as the Prince of Wales, designed by Richard Guyatt, a limited edition of 200.

c1969   *4in (10cm) high*

£250-300   **H&G**

A bone china plate, by Caverswall, commemorating the 30th birthday of H.R.H. The Princess of Wales.

c1991   *10.25in (26cm) wide*

£100-150   **H&G**

A Crown Staffordshire pin dish, commemorating the birth of Prince William.

1982   *4in (10cm) diam*

£8-12   **GAZE**

A Spitting Image Prince Charles mug, commemorating the marriage of Charles and Diana.

This mug is scarce as very few were made because they were so vulnerable to breakage.

c1981   *7.5in (19cm) high*

£180-220   **H&G**

A bone china mug, by Aynsley, commemorating the 18th birthday of Prince Harry, from a limited edition of 5,000.

c2002   3.75in (9.5cm) h.

£45-55   **H&G**

A Bells scotch whisky decanter, by Wade, commemorating the birth of Prince William.

Had this piece retained its rectangular card box, it's value could have been around 50% more.

1982   *8in (20.5cm) high*

£30-40   **GAZE**

A bone china mug, by The Royal Collection, commemorating the 21st birthday of Prince William.

c2003   *6in (15cm) high*

£20-25   **H&G**

A bottle of Adnams 'Wedding Ale', commemorating the wedding of Prince Andrew to Sarah Ferguson.

1986   9.25in (23.5cm) high

£2-3   **GAZE**

A Bells 'Old Scotch Whisky' decanter, by Wade, commemorating the birth of Princess Eugenie, unopened and boxed.

1990

Bottle 7.75in (19.5cm) high

£30-50   **GAZE**

A commemorative china mug depicting Prince Andrew and Sarah Ferguson, probably commemorating their wedding.

c1986   3.5in (9cm) high

£3-5   **GAZE**

A Crown Ducal bone china mug, featuring the young Princess Margaret, commemorating the Coronation of her parents.

A similar mug was made depicting Princess Elizabeth. Commemorative ware depicting the Royal children is particularly popular.

c1937   3in (7.5cm) high

£120-180   **H&G**

A late 1980s Duke and Duchess of York commemorative dish, with certificate, boxed.

4.25in (11cm) diam

£7-10   **GAZE**

A bone china lion-head beaker, by Sutherland Pottery, commemorating the 60th birthday of Princess Margaret, from a limited edition of 750.

c1990   4.5in (11.5cm) high

£50-70   **H&G**

A bone china mug, by Chown, commemorating Princess Alice, Duchess of Gloucester, the longest lived Royal, from a limited edition of 35.

The previous longest lived Royal was Queen Elizabeth, The Queen Mother.

c2003   3.75in (9.5cm) high

£30-40   **H&G**

A saucer in memoriam to Princess Charlotte, with pink lustre decoration.

The pink lustre makes this saucer appealing to collectors of lustreware as well as of commemorative ware. Princess Charlotte died in child birth at the age of 21.

c1817   5.5in (14cm) diam

£80-120   **H&G**

A Parian bust of Princess Mary, by Robinson and Leadbeater, made at the time of her wedding to the Duke of York.

A matching bust of the Duke of York was also produced.

c1893   8.5in (21.5cm) high

£280-320   **H&G**

A microscope by W. Watson & Sons of London, with original wooden box.

c1890   13.5in (34cm) high

£350-450   **ATK**

A microscope by E. Leitz of Wetzlar, with original wooden box.

c1890   14in (36cm) high

£500-600   **ATK**

A Culpeper-type brass microscope, with shuttered objective lens over four-division calibrated focus and circular stage supported within two tiers of S-scroll supports with mirror mounted below, on circular moulded mahogany base, in pyramid-shaped mahogany case with drawer containing accessories to interior and brass loop handle to top.

This type was first made from card and wood in the 1720s, and then in brass until the mid-19thC. Many are unsigned, but look for names such as Adams. Beware of reproductions and examine cases, which are being reproduced today.

c1800   13.75in (35cm) high

£1,000-1,500   **BAR**

A Burkhardt Arithometer, in oak case, damage to 'tens' transfer.

The Arithometer was invented by Charles Xavier Thomas de Colmar c1820 and was used up until the first decades of the 20thC. It could calculate all four arithmetic functions (addition, multiplication, subtraction and division). The Burkhardt was the first German calculating machine of this type.

1878

£850-950   **ATK**

A Curta 'Type 1' miniature calculation device, with original plastic box, shipping carton and two manuals.

£500-600   **ATK**

An early hour-glass in a tin frame, marked with four symbols including "CB" monogram.

c1850   5in (12.5cm) high

£250-300   **ATK**

An American WWII compass.

                    2in (5cm) diam

                    £35-45   **COB**

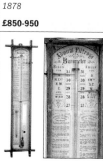

A 19thC 'Admiral Fitzroy's Barometer', with thermometer.

Named after Admiral Robert Fitzroy who re-organised the Meteorological Office from 1854, the more complex and decorative the example, the more valuable it is likely to be. Damage to the printed card backing reduces value dramatically.

c1870   41in (104cm) high

£100-150   **ATK**

A German orbit tellurium, by Columbus of Berlin, made for the Scandinavian market, electrified later.

Telluriums show the daily and annual movements of the Earth around the sun, with a candle/lightbulb and curved mirror acting as the sun.

c1920   20in (50cm) long

£550-650   **ATK**

SEWING

COLLECTORS' NOTES

■ Most surviving sewing tools found today date from the late 18th century and the 19th century, when sewing was a fashionable and virtuous hobby for a lady. Many were made to fill comprehensive work or sewing boxes, which have since been broken up. Whilst many were manufactured, some charming items were made at home, often with parts bought from a shop and assembled at home.

■ Materials vary, and value largely depends on this, as well as age and the quality of design and decoration. Wood, metals such as pressed brass, bone and ivory are common. 19th century and earlier silver and gold tools are usually much sought after and valuable, particularly if finely crafted. The quality of any carving is also worth considering.

■ Many items were sold as souvenirs, the most frequently found being Tunbridgeware from Kent, Mauchlineware from Scotland and carved wooden items from Switzerland. During the early decades of the 20th century, sewing machines became inexpensive, better quality factory needlework developed and sewing became less necessary and fell from fashion, resulting in a steady decline in the production of sewing tools.

■ Thimbles began to be machine-made from the mid-18th century, with Germany and England being notable producers. Early silver thimbles are often not marked as they were too small to be covered by the hallmarking laws. Look for intricately decorated thimbles, those in precious metals, or those by notable makers such as Charles Horner or Iles.

A French abalone shell-covered souvenir pin-case, with red silk interiors and loops to hold a stiletto.

c1890　　　　*2.25in (5.5cm) high*

£70-90　　　　　　　　　　**JSC**

A French carved ivory pin-case, covers with carved foliate design, with silk and material interior.

　　　　　　　　　2.5in (6.5cm) high

£120-160　　　　　　　　　**JSC**

A Tunbridgeware needle-case, the cover with stickwork and central mahogany panel, the paper-lined interior with materia pages.

Tunbridgeware is made from tiny, thin tiles o 'tesserae' of differently coloured woods glued to the surface.

　　　　　　　　　2.25in (5.5cm) hig

£80-120　　　　　　　　　　**JS**

An amboyna wood needle-case, lined with ebony and with ivory bands.

c1820　　　　　　　*3in (8cm) long*

£140-160　　　　　　　　　**JSC**

A glass needle-case and packet holder, showing Old Court, St Peter's College, Cambridge, with silver and gilt highlights and mirror as back cover.

Made from glass and painted with a scene from the reverse, these can be found with a series of notable buildings such as Osborne House.

　　　　　　　　　3.5in (8.5cm) high

£180-220　　　　　　　　**JSC**

An early 19thC beadwork needle-case, over a bone body.

　　　　　　　　　3.5in (9cm) long

£120-160　　　　　　　　**JSC**

A rare Tunbridgeware stickwork parasol-shaped needle-case, with turned mahogany handle pulling off to reveal storage in interior.

Both the form and the use of the woods in this manner are rare for Tunbridgeware.

c1840　　　　　　　*4in (10cm) lor*

£150-200　　　　　　　　　**JS**

A straw work needle-case, with fine mosaic-like pattern.

Straw work is made from flattened coloured strands of straw and is often associated with objects handmade by French prisoners of war during the Napoleonic wars of the early 19thC.

c1850   4.25in (11.cm) long

£70-90   **JSC**

A mid-19thC English milk glass needle-case, with painted flowers, gilt bands and paper lined interior.

3.75in (9.5cm) long

£150-200   **JSC**

A Tartanware needle-case, with label reading "Prince Charlie".

3.5in (8.5cm) long

£80-100   **JSC**

A Transferware torpedo-shaped needle-case, with colour transfer reading "A Happy Christmas" amidst holly.

3.75in (9.5cm) long

£60-90   **JSC**

A late 19thC black lacquerware needle-case, with transfer of flowers a dove and an envelope.

3.25in (8cm) long

£70-90   **JSC**

An early 19thC French ivory needle-case, in the form of a pea pod.

Both the material and the realistic carving of this piece makes it valuable and desirable.

4in (10cm) long

£180-200   **JSC**

An English vegetable ivory needle-case, with pineapple-shaped ends.

Vegetable ivory is not derived from animals as with other ivory, but is rather made from the 'coroso' or 'tagua' nut, the fruit of a tropical palm. When fresh it is a creamy white, but it yellows over time. Large pieces such as this are made from more than one nut.

c1860   3in (7.5cm) long

£70-90   **JSC**

A pressed brass 'Britannia Needle case', by W. Avery & Son, Redditch, with repoussé dolphin to centre, knob on reverse pushing to reveal 6/7 or 8/9 needles.

2.25in (5.5cm) high

£100-150   **CBE**

A 'Beatrice Case' accordion-style needle packet case, with different leaves unfolding, each holding a needle packet, with fitted case.

Patented on 3rd April 1867 by Lewis & Archibald, this case was made to commemorate the birthday of Princess Beatrice.

2in (5cm) high

£250-350   **JSC**

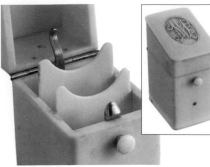

A leather pocket for needle packets, contained in a card case, the front with chromolithographic portrait of Jenny Lind, 'The Swedish Songbird'.

c1870   *3.5in (9cm) high*

£70-90   **JSC**

A 19thC ivory needle packet holder, with deeply engraved initials to top of hinged lid, with ivory dividers to interior.

2.75in (7cm) high

£250-300   **CBE**

A colour printed and embossed card needle packet holder box, interior with concertina holding different needle packets, the lid with inset mirror.

box 2.25in (6cm) wide

£30-40   **CBE**

A late 19thC English velvet-covered and colour lithographed card needle packet holder box, the interior with concertina of panels holding different needle packets.

box 2.75in (7cm) long

£45-55   **CBE**

A late 19thC card needle-box, with Baxter colour lithograph print of Prince Frederick of Prussia, from the 'Queen Mary' set.

2.25in (6cm) high

£30-40   **CBE**

A late 19thC card needle-box, with Baxter colour lithograph print of The Princess Royal, Princess F.W. of Prussia, from the 'Queen Mary' set.

2.25in (6cm) high

£30-40   **CBE**

A card 'Synoptical Needle case', patented on 14th November 1867, with applied embossed chromolithographic panel.

c1867 3.75in (9.5cm) high

£60-80   **JSC**

A German metal needle-holder, with blue fabric ribbon to hold needles, the finials as winders.

c1890   *4in (10cm) long*

£30-40   **JS**

A French silver thimble, commemorating WW1, stamped "PAX" and "LABOR" and marked "F.P. Lasserie".

These commemorative thimbles were sold as souvenirs to people who visited battlefields in France and are of interest to collectors. The use of silver and the sympathetic, comparatively intricate, low relief design also make this example desirable.

c1919

£250-350   CBE

A French silver commemorative thimble, for the "Exposition 1889", with French control marks.

£100-150   CBE

A cupro-nickel thimble, commemorating Queen Victoria's Golden Jubilee.

This thimble was also made in silver and brass.

c1887

£50-70   CBE

An early 20thC French silver thimble, with an applied band of leaves and flowers and punched dot design.

£40-60   CBE

An early 20thC German silver thimble, with applied scrolling band inset with coral cabochons, stamped "800".

0.75in (2cm) high

£60-80   CBE

A silver Queen Elizabeth II Coronation thimble, by James Swann & Son, with low relief scene of coronation carriage, Westminster Abbey etc, Birmingham hallmark.

The same scenes are found on the George and Mary commemorative thimble.

1953

£100-150   CBE

A sterling Irish-themed thimble, by James Fenton, with a band of clovers and a harp, Rd No. 202536 for 1892.

James Fenton of Birmingham was a very prolific thimble maker c1850-c1900, the last use of his mark was 1923. Many of his thimbles are highly desirable today.

£80-120   CBE

An early 20thC Continental brass thimble, with repeated 'star' design and milled band.

0.75in (2cm) high

£15-20   CBE

An American 'Patriotic' brass thimble, with an applied painted plaque of the 'Stars & Stripes'.

Probably produced to commemorate the American participation in WWI.

c1917   0.75in (2cm) high

£25-35   CBE

SEWING

A Tartanware barrel-shaped thimble-case, containing a silver thimble.

Tartanware thimble-cases are hard to find.

3in (4.5cm) high

£100-150 | **JSC**

A French sewing set, comprising a pair of scissors and thimble in a plush-lined fitted case marked "Languedoc Rue du Septembre 18", the scissors with applied miniature gold coronet and cross motifs.

Avoid buying sets where one or more pieces are missing as it can be extremely difficult to find an exact replacement.

c1870

£100-120 | **JSC**

An Edwardian silver novelty pin cushion, by Levi & Salaman, Birmingham, in the form of an old boot, with Reg No.

1907 | *2in (5cm) long*

£100-150 | **WW**

A handmade card, silk and beadwork pin holder.

c1800 | *1.5in (4cm) diam*

£30-40 | **JSC**

A scarce green plush-covered Iles thimble shop counter display case, with bevelled glass lid.

c1895

£50-60 | **CB**

Two white metal knitting needle-end covers, in the form of riding boots, stamped 'Rd No.491556' for 1906.

0.75in (2cm) high

£25-35 | **CBE**

An early 20thC chromolithographed card knitting needle case, with motto.

6.75in (17cm) lon

£15-20 | **CB**

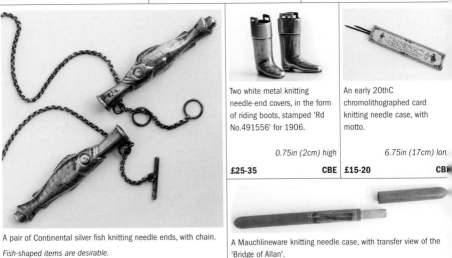

A pair of Continental silver fish knitting needle ends, with chain.

Fish-shaped items are desirable.

fish 2.25in (6cm) long

£120-180 | **CBE**

A Mauchlineware knitting needle case, with transfer view of the 'Bridge of Allan'.

9.75in (25cm) lon

£40-50 | **CB**

COLLECTORS' NOTES

- Although patents exist from the turn of the 19th century, the first functional sewing machine was developed by French tailor Barthelemy Thimonnier in 1830. Sewing machines did not go into commercial production until the 1850s when Isaac Singer and Elias Howe founded their companies.

- Although an interesting collection can be built comparatively inexpensively, collectors tend to seek out early or scarce machines from the 1850s-1870s, often from companies that were short-lived.

- Commonly found names include Willcox & Gibbs and Singer. Most Singer machines fetch under £30 unless early or scarce. Condition is important, look for machines which are complete and retain their bright, gilt transfers and, if applicable, their cases.

A Canadian domestic sewing machine, made by Wanzer, retailed in London.

Manufacturer R.M. Wanzer of Buffalo, NY ran the first Canadian sewing machine factory in Hamilton, Ontario between 1860 and 1886. In 1878, they bought the Canada Sewing Machine Company and also distributed their machines in London.

c1885

£150-200 ATK

A German 'Saxonia' lock-stitch sewing machine, probably made by Gustav Winselmann GMBH.

c1895

£80-120 ATK

A domestic sewing machine, probably German, retailed in London by 'American Sewing Machine Co.'

c1900

£100-150 ATK

An English sewing machine, by Jones, inscribed "As supplied to HRH the Princess of Wales".

c1890

£200-250 ATK

An American sewing machine, by Willcox & Gibbs, popular early version with wooden base and glass tension bar, inscribed with patent date "22nd March 1864".

c1870

£200-250 ATK

An extremely rare German 'Mignon' sewing machine, made by Schröder of Darmstadt, complete with original wooden box.

Only a very few examples of this comparatively early machine are known to exist, with this example retaining many of its bright, gilt transfers.

c1865

£2,000-3,000 ATK

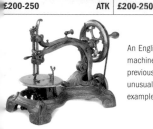

An English domestic sewing machine, by Taylor, previously bronzed, an unusual and desirable early example.

During the 1870s, this attractive 'Art Nouveau' styled machine was offered by S. Smith & Sons of Soho Bazaar, London for £4 4s.

1870

£300-350 ATK

A rare miniature 'Moldacot' lock-stitch sewing machine, with handcrank and shuttle.

The pocket-sized Moldacot was patented by S.A. Rosenthal of Berlin in 1885 and was made in both England and Germany from the late 1880s.

c1890

£300-400 ATK

FIND OUT MORE...

'Antique Needlework Tools and Embroideries', by Nerylla Taunton, published by Antique Collectors Club, 1997.

The Textile Museum, Vadienstrasse 2, 9000 St Gallen, Switzerland, www.textilemuseum.ch

COLLECTORS' NOTES

- Sheet music is collected as much for its decorative cover as for its musical content and is popular due to the quantities available and affordable prices.

- Demand for sheet music grew during the 19thC and, as colour printing became cheaper, so the designs became more detailed.

- Hand-illustrated covers reached their peak during the late 19thC but had been replaced by pictures or photographs of the performers by the 1930s and 1940s as their public images eclipsed that of the composers.

- Due to the vast quantities produced, very few examples of sheet music are rare. However, the quality of the paper was often poor so condition is still important. Look for complete copies with crisp colours and no tears or rips.

A Grieg's "Holberg-Suite" sheet music book.

12in (30.5cm) wide

£1-2   **CANT**

A "Sunset Trail" sheet music book.

1936   *12.25in (31cm) wide*

£1-3   **CANT**

An "Oh, What a Beautiful Mornin'" sheet music book, from "Oklahoma".

1943   *11in (28cm) wide*

£2-3   **CANT**

An "I Got The Sun in the Morning" sheet music book, from "Annie Get Your Gun".

1946   *11in (28cm) wide*

£2-3   **CANT**

An "Easter Parade" sheet music book.

1947   *11in (28cm) wide*

£3-4   **CANT**

A Mario Lanza "Because You're Mine" sheet music book.

1952   *11in (28cm) wide*

£3-4   **CANT**

A Frank Sinatra "I'm Walking Behind You" sheet music book.

1953   *11in (28cm) wide*

£4-5   **CANT**

A "(How Much Is) That Doggie In The Window?" sheet music book.

1953   *11in (28cm) wide*

£1-3   **CANT**

A Johnny Mathis "Misty" sheet music book.
1954 11in (28cm) wide
£1-3 **CANT**

A "My Fair Lady" sheet music book.
1956 11in (28cm) wide
£2-4 **CANT**

A "The Sound of Music" sheet music book.
1959 11in (28cm) wide
£4-6 **CANT**

A Carpenters "(They Long to be) Close to You" sheet music book.
1963 11in (28cm) wide
£4-5 **CANT**

An "If I Were a Rich Man" sheet music book, from "Fiddler on the Roof".
1964 11in (28cm) wide
£2-4 **CANT**

A Tom Jones "The Green Green Grass of Home" sheet music book.
1965 11in (28cm) wide
£2-3 **CANT**

A "Day by Day" sheet music book, from "Godspell".
1971 11in (28cm) wide
£1-3 **CANT**

A Roberta Flack "Killing Me Softly With His Song" sheet music book.
1972 11in (28cm) wide
£3-4 **CANT**

A Brotherhood of Man "Save Your Kisses for Me" sheet music book.
This song won the Eurovision Song Contest for England in 1976.
1976 11in (28cm) wide
£2-4 **CANT**

SMOKING ACCESSORIES

COLLECTORS' NOTES

■ Unlike other smoking-related collectables, many non-smokers collect ashtrays. Ashtrays became a popular collectable at the beginning of the 20thC when tyre manufacturers in the US started to produce them as advertising gimmicks. These form the base of many collections today.

■ Production of promotional ashtrays stopped during WWII but began again in earnest in the 1950s. Those made prior to WWII are highly sought-after, particularly ceramic ashtrays from the 1930s.

■ As well as advertising products, many examples are connected to travel and come from hotels, airlines and cruise liners. Look for designs that are typical of the period, and those made by companies that no longer exist such as BOAC and TWA.

■ Many ashtrays cross over to other collectable areas and this can help to push the price up. Examples that belonged to or are associated with famous smokers, such as Orson Welles, are also desirable.

■ Ashtrays are generally mass-produced and in everyday use, so condition is vital. Check carefully for chips and cracks.

A 1930s S.S. Santa Paula cast bronze ashtray, in the shape of a seahorse.

5.5in (14cm) long

£150-200   **CW**

A French ceramic ashtray, in the form of a ship's funnel.

3.25in (8cm) high

£80-120   **CW**

A 1930s Linea C ship's funnel ashtray.

3.5in (9cm) high

£35-45   **CW**

A T.G. Green Gresley ware Orient Line ceramic ashtray.

7.25in (18.5cm) wide

£60-80   **CW**

A 1930s French 'jadeite' glass French Line ashtray.

3.25in (8cm) wide

£60-80   **CW**

A Swedish-American Line ceramic ashtray, by Lagun of Gustavsberg, with ship-shaped silver inlay.

6in (15.5cm) wide

£100-150   **CW**

£180-220   **CW**

A pair of Royal Worcester presentation ashtrays, showing the 'Orestes' and 'Agamemnon' for the Blue Funnel Line Ltd, in original gift box.

Box 8.5in (21.5cm) wide

CW

A 1930s Art Deco Mobil Oil cast bronze ashtray, with Pegasus model.

5.75in (14.5cm) high

£180-220 **CW**

A 1950s German ceramic "Gebr. Vermeulen" advertising ashtray.

4.25in (11cm) wide

£30-50 **CW**

A 1940s Rookwood Pottery ashtray, showing a Woodburn 7895, the book stamped "Walter E. Schott Willy's Distributor Cash for Cars. 2320 Gilbert Ave. Cincinnati Ohio".

6.75in (17cm) wide

£300-400 **CW**

A 1950s square glass Vespa ashtray.

3.5in (9cm) wide

£70-100 **CW**

A 1960s glass Travette camper coach advertising ashtray.

6.75in (17.5cm) wide

£70-100 **CW**

A 1960s ceramic "Pontiac Fine Car" ashtray, the base stamped "Pontiac Fleet Sales".

6in (15cm) high

£70-100 **CW**

A 1960s Rose Cutri Pontiac enamelled tin advertising ashtray.

6in (15cm) wide

£70-100 **CW**

A 1970s Canadian Georgian China Ferrari 410 ceramic ashtray.

8.75in (22cm) wide

£60-80 **CW**

A "Try The Thunderbird" metal ashtray.

Despite this being an American car, the steering wheel is shown here on the right-hand side.

c1990 5.5in (14cm) wide

£7-10 **CW**

A brass "MCMXX ANVERS" Olympics commemorative ashtray.

The 1920 Olympics were held in Antwerp, Belgium. It was the first time that the Olympic oath was recited and also the first time the Olympic flag, with its famous five coloured rings, was flown.

1920   4in (10cm) high

£150-200   **CW**

A 1924 Paris Olympics commemorative pressed brass ashtray.

1924   5in (13cm) wide

£100-150   **CW**

A 1924 Paris Olympics metal ashtray, showing a boxer.

1924   5.5in (14cm) long

£150-200   **CW**

A 1936 Berlin Olympics commemorative clear glass ashtray.

1936   4.5in (11.5cm) wide

£180-220   **CW**

A rare 1950s Cleveland Indians milk glass ashtray, one of only 100 made.

7.25in (18.5cm) long

£150-200   **CW**

A German ceramic football stadium-shaped advertising ashtray.

Bild am Sonntag is a popular German Sunday paper. This ashtray advertises their coverage of the previous day's football.

7.5in (19.5cm) long

£40-60   **CW**

A rare Washington Pottery Football Association "World Cup Willie 1966" ashtray.

1966   4.75in (12cm) wide

£300-400   **CW**

A "Mexico 70" plastic football ashtray.

1970   4.25in (11cm) wide

£60-80   **CW**

A Faenza "Italia 90" ceramic ashtray.

1990   4.75in (12cm) wid

£40-60   **CW**

A 1920s Players advertising ashtray.

5in (12.5cm) wide

£70-90   BS

A 1920s Gilbeys advertising ashtray.

5in (12.5cm) wide

£25-35   BS

A 1920s Johnnie Walker advertising copper ashtray.

5in (12.5cm) wide

£60-80   BS

A 1920s Chester Northgate Ales brass ashtray.

4.5in (11.5cm) diam

£7-10   DH

A 1950s "Players Finest Virginia Weights" ceramic ashtray.

4.75in (12cm) diam

£6-8   DH

A 1950s ceramic Electrolux advertising ashtray, made by Sculptural Promotions Inc. of New York.

6.5in (16.5cm) wide

£40-50   BB

A 1930s Michelin Bakelite advertising ashtray.

5in (12.5cm) high

£80-120   DH

A 1950s "Black & White Scotch Whisky" ceramic advertising ashtray, by James Green & Nephew Ltd.

5.25in (13.5cm) wide

£60-80   CW

A 1950s German Ornamin Presswerk melamine advertising ashtray for Pepsi Cola.

4.25in (11cm) wide

£70-100   CW

A 1950s Bass ceramic ashtray.

5.25in (13cm) wide

£5-7   DH

COLLECTORS' NOTES

- Smoking accessories are hotly sought after, even though smoking is becoming rapidly more and more unfashionable. Lighters are perhaps the largest and most popular area and are divided into pocket and table lighters. Although many have already reached high values, they may yet have some way to go, particularly good quality table and integral compact case lighters. Other items, such as cases, tobacco jars and cigar cutters are also collectable. Look for quality in terms of material and form, and notable makers.

- Dunhill lighters are the most desirable, due to the high quality of their manufacture and materials, and the range available. Collectors tend to prefer the 'petrol' filled lighters of the 1920s-50s, but certain later examples in fine quality materials or with hidden features such as watches are also popular. Also look for Zippo lighters which are generally more affordable.

A Zippo 'Bahamas' souvenir pocket lighter.

c1972   2.25in (5.5cm) high

£20-30   **ML**

A Dunhill 'Tinder Pistol' table lighter, with wood handle and petrol fuelled mechanism, marked beneath "Prov.Pat 19273/34, Regd. No.794093".

There is also a 1960s gas filled version which is rare.

c1938

£150-200   **DN**

A Dunhill 'Aquarium' table lighter, the perspex body of shaped-oblong outline and decorated in reverse with fish amidst aquatic foliage and enclosing the petrol fuelled plated-brass mechanism, the hinged wick cover signed "Dunhill".

The quasi-kitsch 'Aquarium' lighter has become an immensely collectable model in recent years, partly due to the large number of variations available in terms of size and type of wildlife. Fish are the most common, but rarer birds and even an ultra-rare racehorse have been depicted in the reverse carved and painted perspex panels.

c1953   4in (10cm) long

£1,000-1,500   **DN**

A 1960s Swank table lighter, in the form of a television.

4in (10cm) wide

£15-25   **GAZE**

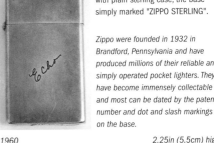

A small Swedish silver cigar or cigarette box, with heavily ribbed sides and plain lid, with mahogany lining,

c1920   4.25in (11cm) wide

£50-70   **GS**

A half-size or small Zippo lighter, with plain sterling case, the base simply marked "ZIPPO STERLING".

Zippo were founded in 1932 in Brandford, Pennsylvania and have produced millions of their reliable and simply operated pocket lighters. They have become immensely collectable and most can be dated by the patent number and dot and slash markings on the base.

1960   2.25in (5.5cm) high

£80-120   **ML**

An Arts & Crafts style copper cigarette box, with rivet decoration to the fish tail hinges and bracket feet.

7.5in (19cm) wide

£40-60   **CLV**

A Dunhill 'Bumper' or tankard table lighter, with engraved initials, with a thumb-piece activating petrol mechanism, marked "Reg. Des. Appl. No. 861972".

c1950   3.5in (9cm) high

£50-80   **DN**

A CLOSER LOOK AT A TOBACCO JAR

The lid is held on with a sprung arm mechanism that seals the jar making it airtight to preserve the tobacco - as such many can still be used today.

This jar was made by Royal Winton, a notable British factory well known for their transfer-decorated chintzwares and quality ceramics.

It was made for high quality historic pipe maker and retailer Comoy's of London, founded in 1879 by Henry Comoy.

The scene is delicately and realistically hand-painted onto the body rather than being applied by transfer. These sorts of 'sporting' themes are popular.

A Royal Winton hand-painted tobacco jar, for Comoy's of London, decorated with a scene of woodcocks in a field.

1920-1930   *5in (13cm) high*

£180-220   **BAD**

A Continental majolica match holder, in the form of a recumbent goat with panniers on its back, raised on a rockwork base.

4.75in (12cm) long

£60-80   **ROS**

An American Unger Bros. sterling fob cigar cutter, with grotesque mask.

For more information about Unger Brothers, see the first page of the 'Hatpins' section in this book.

1.75in (4.5cm) long

£100-150   **CAC**

An elegant porcelain smoke dispeller, in the form of a kneeling female figure.

After being plugged into an electric supply, an element inside the dish heated perfumed liquid and dispersed pleasantly smelling vapours around the room. The unusual form of a semi-clad 1920s flapper girl is well modelled, well painted and would have appealed greatly to gentleman smokers of the day.

1950   *8.5in (22cm) high*

£60-80   **ATK**

A meerschaum type pipe, carved with a dog chasing a monkey, in fitted case, with retailer name "Ludwig Hartmann Wien", losses.

£120-180   **ROS**

A Japanese Bonzo dog pottery matchbox holder, the blue and milky white glazed cartoon character seated beside a floral moulded rectangular trough.

4in (10cm) wide

£80-120   **CHEF**

A 14ct gold cigar cutter, with inset cabochons.

1.5in (3.5cm) long

£120-180   **CAC**

Three packets of 1960s airline branded Marlboro cigarettes.

3.5in (9cm) high

£10-15 each   **DH**

COLLECTORS' NOTES

- Snowdomes have been made since the late 19thC, although specific dates and manufacturers are unknown. Examples from this period can be identified by their materials, such as glass, ceramic and marble and, as a consequence, their heavy weight.

- Production grew during the 1920s, with religious themes becoming the most common. The explosion of cheap plastic production methods after this time led to a wider range of designs and themes.

- Snowdome collecting became popular in the late 1940s, and as workers became used to paid vacations and cheaper travel costs, the demand for holiday souvenirs grew.

- Europe and the US were the main manufacturers until the 1970s, when a number of Asian countries started to produce snowdomes. These often copy existing designs with small changes to details to avoid copyright laws, and in the main are of a lesser quality.

- Collecting became popular again in the 1980s, and in response manufacturers began making high quality pieces in traditional materials such as glass and wood, as well as novelty items like snowdome watches and T-shirts.

- Look for early pieces in good condition and unusual shapes from any period, especially those with a surround or moving parts inside. Advertising snowdomes are always popular as they often have a crossover appeal.

Three 1970s Mr Men snowdomes.

2.25in (5.5cm) high

£12-20 (each)　　　　　　　　**NWC**

A late 1990s South Park advertising snowdome, for the Comedy Channel.

This snowdome was made exclusively for executives at the Comedy Channel and was not available for retail.

5in (12.5cm) high

£25-50　　　　　　　　**NWC**

A 1990s Nickelodeon advertising snowdome.

3in (7.5cm) high

£15-25　　　　　**NWC**

A "Die Hard 2" advertising snowdome.

c1990　　2.25in (5.5cm) high

£20-30　　　　**NWC**

A late 1970s/early 1980s Jerry glass snowdome, by Rosarium.

4in (10cm) high

£15-20　　　　　　　**NWC**

A Media Markt advertising snowdome, made in Germany.

2.5in (6.5cm) high

£18-28　　　　　**NWC**

An HBO Couch Potatoes advertising snowdome.

3in (7.5cm) high

£15-25　　　　**NWC**

A 1960s Welsh souvenir snowdome.

6in (15cm) high

£10-20   **NWC**

A 1970s/80s London Bridge souvenir calendar snowdome.

4in (10cm) high

£12-20   **NWC**

A 1980s souvenir World Trade Centre, New York City snowdome.

3.25in (8.5cm) high

£10-20   **NWC**

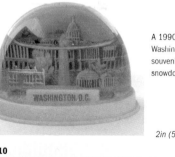

An early 1990s Lyon souvenir snowdome, with 'Lyon' upside down.

2in (5cm) high

£15-25   **NWC**

A 1990s Salzburg souvenir snowdome, made in Germany.

Snowdomes made in Germany can be identified by their fine snow flakes.

2in (5cm) high

£5-10   **NWC**

A 1990s Washington DC souvenir snowdome.

2in (5cm) high

£5-10   **NWC**

A 1990s London Bridge souvenir snowdome, produced missing the bridge.

These 'rejects' can make an amusing collecting area of their own.

2.25in (5.5cm) high

£15-25   **NWC**

A 1990s Taronga Zoo, New South Wales souvenir snowdome.

2in (5cm) high

£8-15   **NWC**

A 1990s Brussels souvenir snowdome.

3in (7.5cm) high

£4-10   **NWC**

FIND OUT MORE...

'Collector's Guide to Snowdomes: Identification & Values', *Helene Guarnaccia, Collector Books 1993.*

'Collectible Snowdomes', *Lélie Carnot, Flammarion, 2002.*

COLLECTORS' NOTES

■ Unlike other collecting areas, modern sporting memorabilia, and in particular football memorabilia, is as desirable as more vintage examples.

■ With soccer stars like David Beckham and Michael Owen holding pop star-like celebrity status, any items connected to these players are desirable.

■ Medals tend to fetch the best prices, and the higher the competition the better. Uniforms come a close second with items worn during a match, particularly a key game, being the most popular.

■ Despite record-breaking prices, memorabilia is available for all pockets, examples of programmes, as well as tickets, badges and collecting cards, can all be purchased for reasonable sums.

A set of Arsenal F.C. players autographs, the A4 size page depicting head and shoulder cut-outs of players with caricature bodies in pencil, each player signed in ink including Leslie Compton, Joe Mercer, Wally Barnes, Laurie Scott and George Swindon, dated August 26th 1949 in pencil.

These players were part of the club's League Championship team 1947-8.

1949

£80-120 **MM**

A signed Graham Le Saux publicity photograph, in Chelsea Football Club strip.

10in (25.5cm) high

£15-25 **LCA**

A signed David Beckham publicity photograph, from the England v Greece World Cup 2002 qualifying match.

10in (25.5cm) high

£65-75 **LCA**

A signed David Beckham 'Police' sunglasses advertising photograph.

10in (25.5cm) high

£65-75 **LCA**

A Sir Geoff Hurst signature, mounted together with the famous quote "They think it's all over...It is now!" and a photograph from the 1966 World Cup final.

£50-60 **GAZE**

A signed George Best publicity photograph, in Manchester United Football Club strip.

10in (25.5cm) high

£100-150 **LCA**

A CLOSER LOOK AT FOOTBALL SIGNATURES

Manchester United are arguably the most famous football club in the world, with a truly global following, unlike many other clubs.

Sir Matt Busby's 'Busby Babes', are considered one of the best teams to ever play together. 'Busby Babes' Memorabilia is very collectable.

In 1958, as they returned from a European Cup match, their aircraft crashed during take off killing eight members of the team as well as 15 other people. Items that feature the team members that died in the Munich air disaster are particularly sought-after.

A signed magazine centre spread of the 'Busby Babes', titled "The Team of the Century", depicting 19 players with Matt Busby and officials, autographed in ink by 15, including Duncan Edwards, Tommy Taylor, David Pegg, Eddie Coleman, Colin Webster, Liam Whelan, Dennis Violett, Jackie Blanchflower, Matt Busby, Jimmy Greaves and Fred Goodwin, framed and glazed.

15in (38cm) wide

£800-1,000 **MM**

A scarce set of album pages, signed by the 1948 Manchester United F.A. Cup Winners team, depicting cut-out head and shoulder pictures of all 11 players who played in the final, each signed below.

£350-450   **MM**

A World Cup collage depicting Hurst scoring the final goal and listing both teams plus all 3 World Cup 1966 stamps, signed in ink by Alf Ramsey.

£80-120   **MM**

A signed Jamie Redknap publicity photograph, in Tottenham Football Club strip.

10in (25.5cm) high

£30-40   **LCA**

25th ANNIVERSARY – ENGLAND WINNERS

July 30th, 1966, Wembley Stadium. "The crowd think it's all over... it is now" – the epic television commentary that rang out across the nation as Geoff Hurst rifled his third and decisive goal into the roof of the West German net. England had won 4-2, and the Cup had at last come to the country where football began.

A special World Cup stamp, which was approved by both the British Post Office and the Football Association, was banned by the Foreign Office. It showed the flags of the 16 participating nations which included North Korea, a country the British government did not recognise, resulting in the banning of the issue.

This special commemorative issue was quickly changed and a set of three stamps was issued. Following England's success, one value was overprinted with the words 'ENGLAND WINNERS' (above). Interestingly, not only was this the first British stamp to feature sportsmen, but it was also the first and indeed only stamp to be dealt on the London Stock Exchange. Because of its limited availability, dealers brought frantically and the price rocketed to many times its face value.

1966-1991

With the likes of Jimmy Greaves, Bobby Charlton and Roger Hunt all vying for a place in the team, Geoff Hurst was grateful to have been picked to play at all 25 years on, he is still the only player ever to have scored a hat-trick in the final.

England boss, Sir Alf Ramsey, described Martin Peters as 'ten years ahead of his time'. His vital goal, scored in the 78th minute, ensured England went on to play that decisive period of extra time following the German's last minute equaliser.

Bobby Moore, England's triumphant captain holds aloft the Jules Rimet Trophy amid the deafening cheers of Wembley's 87,000 strong crowd. As well as leading his side to victory, Bobby Moore was also named as player of the tournament.

A World Cup 25th Anniversary collage, depicting the famous after match image of Moore with the cup held aloft by the team, signed in ink by Bobby Moore, Geoff Hurst and Martin Peters.

£450-550   **MM**

A Birmingham City Football Club black blazer, with embroidered club crest and initials "B.C.F.C", made by G. & A. Smith Tipton.

This blazer was the property of John Vincent who played for the club between 1964 and 1970, making 168 appearances and scoring 41 goals.

£150-200   **MM**

A signed Michael Owen publicity photograph.

10in (25.5cm) high

£35-45   **LCA**

A signed Teddy Sheringham publicity photograph, in Tottenham Football Club strip.

10in (25.5cm) high

£20-30   **LCA**

A Leeds United F.A. Cup Final long-sleeved green shirt, by Umbro, embroidered "LUFC F.A. Cup Final 1973" to front with blue No. 1 to rear.

This shirt was worn by David Harvey during the Cup Final against Sunderland. This was Harvey's third Cup Final appearance in four years. He made 329 appearances during his 18 year career and won 16 caps for Scotland.

1973

£350-450   **MM**

A Leeds United long-sleeved green goalkeepers replica shirt, by Umbro, embroidered "LUFC FA Cup Final 1973", with "No.1" to rear.

This, and the shirt to its right, were specially commissioned as a prize for a national newspaper competition run prior to the Final. They were made to the same specification as the match shirts, but are in children's sizes.

£50-60　　　　**MM**

A Leeds United long-sleeved white replica shirt, by Umbro, embroidered "LUFC FA Cup Final 1973", "No. 8" to rear.

£45-55　　　　**MM**

A purple and cream eight-panelled England trial cap, with embroidered initials "FA" to front and "1919-20" to peak.

£350-450　　　　**MM**

A CLOSER LOOK AT A FOOTBALL CAP

Strips and uniforms comprise the top end of the football memorabilia market, particularly items from International games.

From the beginning of the 19thC, caps were awarded to players who were selected for a match. At that time, they were an important part of the strip.

This cap was awarded to Charles Murray Buchan (1891-1960) who played for Leyton Orient, Sunderland United and Arsenal, as well as for England.

This was Buchan's second cap for England; the match was against Wales at Highbury on March 15th 1920. Wales won 2-1 with Buchan scoring for England.

A red eight-panelled England International cap, with embroidered rose and "1920" to peak.

£850-950　　　　**MM**

An England Inter-League match white shield-shaped shirt badge, embroidered in blue and yellow with the wording "FL Irish Match 1912-13".

£100-150　　　　**MM**

A red eight-panelled England International cap, with embroidered rose and "1921" to peak.

This was Buchan's third Cap for England. The match was against Wales at Ninian Park, Cardiff, on March 14th 1921. The score was a 0-0 draw.

£850-950　　　　**MM**

A 1924 F.A. Cup Final ticket, Newcastle United v Aston Villa, some creasing.

£700-900　　　　**MM**

A 1962 World Cup Quarter Final ticket, Brazil v England, played at the Sausalito Stadium on the 10th June, central fold and stained but complete.

Brazil won this game 3-1.

£180-220　　　　**MM**

An early Bovril shop sign, depicting the Wolverhampton and West Bromwich Albion teams and fixtures for the 1911-12 season, clipped to the left-hand side affecting the Albion team picture and fixtures.

£45-55   MM

Three 1978 World Cup tickets, Brazil v Poland, W. Germany v Mexico and W. Germany v Columbia.

£100-150   MM

Ten 1982 World Cup tickets, for matches played in Barcelona and Madrid including England v West Germany, Argentina v N. Ireland and the Semi Final Italy v Poland match.

£200-300   MM

A 1950's 'Piktee' League Championship football game, appears complete with all cards and instructions, mint, in box.

£100-150   MM

A Minerva Supreme Sunderland F.C. autographed football, signed in ink by 11 players.

Sunderland were promoted to the 1st Division in the 1963-64 season.

1964

€80-120   MM

A Pelé signed football, signed in his official capacity as spokesperson for Mastercard International during the 1998 FIFA World Cup, with authenticity certificate.

£150-200   GAZE

A Sir Geoff Hurst signed limited edition football, signed in March 2002 to celebrate Hyundai's sponsorship of the 2002 FIFA World Cup, with authenticity certificate.

£70-100   GAZE

A Birmingham Challenge/Senior Cup enamelled medal, in the shape of an eight-pointed star, engraved to rear "Presented to W. Hewitt one of the 12 winners of the Birmingham Challenge Cup Feby. 10th 1877", the obverse reads "The Unity Foot Ball Club" with a segmented ball to centre.

This medal was awarded to Hewitt, the goalkeeper of Wednesbury, who defeated Stafford Rangers in the final, in which 12 players took part for each side. Although the medal states "The (Aston) Unity Foot Ball Club", records show they were defeated earlier in the competition by Salway but were awarded the medals as the winners.

1877

300-400   MM

A Football Association Charity Shield silver hallmarked plaque, mounted on an octagonal black Bakelite back plate, engraved "Chelsea F.C. v Newcastle United F.C. Wednesday, 14th September 1955".

This plaque was awarded to the Referee J. Kelly.

£550-650   MM

COLLECTORS' NOTES

- Golf originated in Scotland and developed slowly between the 15th and 17th centuries. By the late 19th century, it had become very popular.

- Pieces prior to this period are rarely found and most equipment dates from the late 19th century onwards.

- Golf clubs and balls tend to form the upper end of the market, but a wide range of merchandise and memorabilia with a golfing theme is available, including ceramics, prints and paintings, books and photographs.

- Collectors tend to focus on the historical aspect of the game, looking for pieces that depict old equipment, courses or clothing as well as famous players.

A long nose putter, indistinctly stamped, some later whipping and later grip, re-shafted.

£350-450   L&T

A centre shafted putter, possibly with later head.

£120-180   L&T

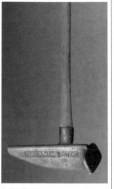

A Hardinghams patent putter, the face scored with 20 vertical lines, "C - V" markings to the back of the plate, later shaft, grip lacking, some damage.

£4,000-5,000   L&T

An early and rare sand iron, with large concave face, hosel with deep nicking.

c1825-35

£4,500-5,500   L&T

An 18thC iron, blacksmith-forged, nicked face, with replacement grip.

c1750

£8,000-12,000   L&T

A Spalding Gold Medal No. 4 Jigger, with hammer stamp and "Patented Jan 1914" and "Patented Aug 29, 1916", with perforated 'Lard' shaft and hand-punched dot face.

c1918

£1,500-2,000   L&T

A Banner spade mashie, with 'brick pattern face'.

£150-200   L&T

A rut niblick, stamped "Harrod. Ltd., London", with good original leather grip and under listing.

£60-80   M

John Vassos, 'Tee Shot', enamel on aluminium, signed lower right.

1971 *28in (71cm) high*

£450-550 FRE

George Houghton, 'The Green at the Treacherous 13th hole, at Muirfield,' signed and inscribed, pen and ink and watercolour.

15in (39cm) high

£800-1,200 FRE

Nash, Frederick, 'Bruntisfield Links, Edinburgh', signed with initials, dated.

1830 *11.25in (28.5cm) high*

£1,800-2,200 L&T

A signed Nick Faldo publicity photograph.

10in (25.5cm) high

£40-50 LCA

A mahogany ballot box, inscribed "AYE" and "NO", with circular opening and central division above a baize-lined draw.

£600-700 L&T

Tufts, Richard S., "The Scottish Invasion", first edition, published by Pinehurst Publishers.

1962

£60-70 MM

A Royal Doulton Golfing Seriesware 'Every Dog Has His Day And Every Man His Hour' plate.

8in (20cm) wide

£100-150 PSA

mahogany ballot box, with ory "YES" and "NO" inserts, two cking drawers with turned ood knob handles to the base.

16.75in (42.5cm) high

700-800 L&T

Hutchinson, Horace G., 'Golf (Badminton library)', second edition, published by Longmans, with publisher's half blue morocco, cloth boards, with fore-edge painting under the gilt depicting the author in plus fours with a club under one arm, together with a fore-edge painting display stand.

1890

£800-1,200 L&T

A Mohammad Ali photograph.

£12-18   **GAZE**

A signed Frank Bruno HP Sauce publicity postcard.

6in (15cm) wide

£10-15   **LCA**

A World Heavyweight Championship Joe Frazier v Muhammad Ali souvenir edition programme, 8th March 1971, together with a scarce large lapel badge for the fight.

£70-100   **MM**

A Muhammad Ali v Joe Bugner ticket, 14th February 1973, for a $100 ringside seat.

£150-200   **MM**

A World Heavyweight Championship Joe Frazier v Muhammad Ali programme, 8th March 1971.

£220-280   **MM**

A 'Bang – Boxing's Weekly Wallop' magazine, with Joe Louis on the cover, for week ending January 23rd 1937.

9in (23cm) high

£30-40   **VSC**

A signed Stirling Moss publicity postcard.

6in (15cm) high

£10-15   **LC**

A signed Damon Hill publicity photograph, in Arrows-Yamaha Formula 1 racing car.

10in (25.5cm) wide

£45-55   **LCA**

A signed Jonah Lomu publicity photograph, in New Zealand All Blacks strip.

10in (25.5cm) high

£35-45   **L**

COLLECTORS' NOTES

- The use of stamps as advance payment for postage was started in Britain in 1840 and had spread worldwide by 1860. There are now 350 stamp issuing authorities across the world.

- Due to this enormous variety, collectors tend to specialise in one particular area and British Commonwealth stamps are popular in the UK.

- The first UK stamp was the Penny Black and, although famous, is not rare – tens of millions were produced and used examples can be easily found.

- As a general rule, the higher the face value, the more desirable, as less of these would have been produced. Unusual cancellation marks, perforations and misprints will all add to a stamp's value.

- As the number of philatelists increases, supplies of classic stamps fall and so collectors are looking at more modern varieties. The Royal Mail will occasionally produce something out of the ordinary and those with a shrewd eye will spot this variation and buy before supplies run out.

A used 'penny black' stamp, with two clear margins and check letters "C" and "E" in bottom left and right corners respectively, in good condition.

Unused examples of the 'penny black' are rare and worth approximately £1,000.

1840   1in (2.5cm) high
£30-60   SD

A used 'two-penny blue' stamp, with magenta cancellation, lacking clear margins and with check letters "N" and "L" in bottom left and right corners respectively.

1840   1in (2.5cm) high
£30-50   SD

A used Victoria unified series 9d stamp.

This stamp is from the first set ever issued for both postage and revenue purposes, commonly known as the 'lilac and greens'. This 9d example is the most valuable.

1883   1in (2.5cm) wide
£60-90   SD

A used Victorian 2/6 stamp, lilac on white paper.

Versions of this stamp printed on blue paper are scarce, and examples in good condition can be worth up to £180-220.

1883   1.5in (3.5cm) high
£20-30   SD

A used Victoria 2d Jubilee series stamp.

The 'Jubilee' series replaced the 'lilac and greens' in 1887, to commemorate 50 years of Victoria's rule. This 2d stamp is among the most valuable from the series.

c1890   1in (2.5cm) high
£25-50   SD

A used George V 2/6 stamp.

The design on this series of stamps, commonly called 'Seahorses', is considered by many to be among the finest stamp designs of all time. The almost identical 1934 re-issue can be distinguished from this example by the cross-hatching behind the King's head.

c1913   1.75in (4.5cm) wide
£60-90   SD

unused sheet of ten Christmas 'Smilers' stamps, complete with labels and Christmas cracker design surround.

2000   11.5in (29.5cm) wide
80-120   SD

An unused sheet of ten 'Smilers' stamps, with personalised labels printed at The Stamp Show 2000' in Earl's Court.

2000   11.5in (29.5cm) high
£40-50   SD

FIND OUT MORE...

www.stanleygibbons.com - *comprehensive catalogues and other information and services from their website.*

Gibbons Stamp Monthly, *a magazine published by Stanley Gibbons with news and features about philately.*

National Philatelic Society Library, *British Philatelic Centre, 107 Charterhouse Street, London, EC1M 6PT, Tel 020 7336 0882.*

COLLECTORS' NOTES

■ Teddy bears have grown to be as important to the collecting world as they were to the children who owned them. Steiff are still the most recognised and valuable maker, but others such as the German firm Bing, British makers Farnell and Merrythought and American maker Ideal can fetch similarly large sums. Try to buy examples in good condition, or those by noted makers, but also look for those with 'eye-appeal'.

■ As pre-war teddies become increasingly scarce and valuable, fine quality postwar bears and modern limited edition bears by makers such as Steiff have begun to interest collectors, although the market for modern bears has perhaps yet to reach its peak.

■ To help identify bears, study images and books, but preferably the bears themselves as the shape of the head, limbs, wear and type of materials used will help you work out who made your bear and when. As with all high value markets, reproductions and fakes do exist, so learn to spot signs of intended wear. Always smell a bear as the smell of years of love cannot yet be faked!

A Bing tumbler bear, with stitched woollen nose and claws, boot button eyes.

German maker Bing were very well known for their mechanical bears, which are rare today. Their tumbler bears have typically extra long arms to allow them to tumble. Some did not have paw pads, others were dressed following a typical Bing fashion, but intact clothes are rarely found today.

1909-10   *11.5in (29cm) high*

£2,000-2,500   **HGS**

A Wendy Boston brown woollen teddy bear, with white woollen snout and pads.

Although this appears like many modern unjointed bears, Wendy Boston was a pioneering maker founded in Wales and active between 1954 and 1976. The majority of their bears were machine-washable and used synthetic fabrics.

15in (38cm) high

£15-25   **F**

MERRY THOUGHT
IRONBRIDGE SHROPS.
MADE IN ENGLAND
REGD DESIGN

A Merrythought 'Cheeky' bear, the ears fitted with bells, amber eyes and vertical stitched pointed Draylon snout, stitched white felt pads and makers label.

Merrythought's 'Cheeky' bear was introduced in 1957 and is still made today. He always has bells in his ears.

11in (28cm) high

£350-450   **F**

A 1950s Chad Valley teddy bear, with wide pricked ears, amber eyes, stitched snout and brown velvet pads.

19in (48.5cm) high

£120-180

A Chad Valley golden plush teddy bear, with wide pricked ears, amber eyes, stitched snout and brown velvet pads.

14in (35.5cm) high

£120-180   **F**

A Merrythought beige art silk 'Cheeky' bear, with fitted bells to the ears, amber eyes and stitched velvet snout.

10.5in (27cm) high

£100-150   **F**

A 1930s Chad Valley golden plush teddy bear, the bear with wide pricked ears, amber eyes and vertical stitched snout, jointed limbs and leatherette pads.

14.5in (37cm) high

£280-320

An unidentified American brown mohair bear, with boot button eyes, black wool stitched nose and fabric pads.

Although it is hard to specify a maker, he may be by Ideal due to his long and slender body, widely spaced ears and arms placed lower down on the body.

1906-08   12.5in (32cm) high

£700-900   HGS

A Tara Toys gold plush teddy bear, with wide pricked ears, amber eyes and stitched pointed snout.

This bear was made in Elly Bay, County Mayo, Ireland after 1953 when the name Erris Toys changed to Tara Toys. This form is also typical of post war bears from the 1950s and 1960s.

23in (58.5cm) high

80-120   F

A Steiff 'Amelia' collector's edition teddy bear, the dusty pink bear with recorded voice and ruffled red/white collar.

The form of this bear is based on the 'Teddy Clown' produced in a limited number of 9,000 between 1926 and 1928, but without the clown's hat.

1993   12.5in (32cm) high

150-200   RP

A 1950s Steiff small blonde bear, with original peach ribbon, paper chest tag and ear stud with raised "Steiff" logo.

7.5in (19cm) high

£500-700   HGS

A limited edition Steiff brown mohair muzzled bear.

13.5in (35.5cm) high

£80-120   F

An early Steiff miniature bear, with boot bead eyes and stitched woollen nose, metal ear stud with "Steiff" logo.

c1909   *3.5in (9cm) high*

£600-800   HGS

A 1950s English golden plush bear, with rexine pads, the head detached.

£50-70   ROS

A CLOSER LOOK AT A TEDDY BEAR

Long, thin limbs, a firm body and ears set widely apart are typical features of early American bears produced around 1910 after the re-election of Teddy Roosevelt in 1906.

The triangular shape of his head and pointy feet suggest the most popular American maker Ideal although his down turned paws also hint at Bruin. He is probably by an unknown maker who produced bears at this time when they were highly popular with the public.

At over two feet high, he is a very large size and has early 'boot button' eyes and a woven cotton nose.

He is still well proportioned and his mohair is in superbly furry condition with his feet and paws retaining their original felt pads, woven claws and card inserts.

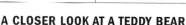

A scarce and early American golden mohair teddy bear, with black boot button eyes, woven nose and claws.

c1905   *24.5in (62cm) high*

£1,800-2,200   SOTT

A CLOSER LOOK AT A STEIFF SNAIL

Nelly the snail is typical of Steiff's creation of unusual, not normally cuddly, animals and is rare and sought after today.

She has a vinyl and velvet body and should not be confused with the furry plush version known as 'Cosili', which is still available today.

Of typically fine Steiff quality, she was made in two colourways for a comparatively short period of time between 1961 and 1963.

She is in excellent, bright condition and complete with her tentacles, shell fabric and paper tags, all in excellent condition.

A Steiff 'Nelly' snail vinyl and cotton soft toy, with original paper chest tag, ear stud with raised "Steiff" logo, and yellow "Made in Germany" tag.

1961-63

6in (15cm) long

£300-400 TCT

A 1930s Steiff finch soft toy, with wire feet and plastic beak, boot bead eyes, ear stud with raised "Steiff" logo and yellow label.

This example is larger than the less valuable miniature 'Pom-Pom' toys made from the 1930s until the 1950s. Pre-war examples have a wire internal body and feet, whilst post war examples have plastic feet.

5in (12.5cm) high

£120-180 TCT

A Steiff giraffe soft toy, with dappled body markings, date unknown.

9.25in (23.5cm) high

£20-30 RP

A Steiff kangaroo soft toy, with original tag.

2.25in (6cm) high

£15-25 RP

A 1950s Steiff Airedale terrier, in brown and black.

Famous German teddy bear maker Steiff, founded in 1877, are also well known for their stuffed or soft animals. Indeed, founder Margerete Steiff made these (initially as gifts) before introducing teddy bears. Pre-war animals can be expensive, but some of the more unusual post war examples can fetch higher prices. As with all stuffed toys, try to buy in as clean and undamaged condition as possible, preferably with labels. However also always consider the personal 'Aaah' factor which makes so many of them instantly appealing.

8in (20cm) long

£50-70 R

A 1960s Steiff cocker spaniel soft toy, in sitting position, with glass eyes.

10.25in (26cm) high

£55-65 RP

A miniature Steiff chimpanzee soft toy, with silver button and yellow label to ear.

4.5in (11.5cm) high

£25-35 F

A Steiff koala bear, with pad feet and nose, glass eyes, paper chest tag and ear stud with raised "Steiff" logo.

5in (12.5cm) high

£200-250

A Merrythought chimpanzee soft toy, in seated pose.

13in (33cm) high

£20-30   F

A Merrythought buffalo brown plush soft toy.

This label was used by Merrythought from 1957 until 1991.

20in (51cm) wide

£20-30   F

A 1950s American Agnes Brush Heffalump soft toy.

The 'never seen' Heffalump in A.A. Milne's short stories is as rare in reality as in the books, as indicated by its high value! This is possibly as it was less popular than the main characters, such as Winnie the Pooh, at the time.

13.75in (35cm) high

£700-900   HGS

Four Dean's printed cloth sitting cat soft toys.

c1906   8.25in (21cm) high

£80-120   BONC

A Chad Valley dog soft toy, with two-tone fur.

11.5in (29cm) high

£15-25   F

An amusing Merrythought camel soft toy.

14.5in (39cm) high

£20-30   F

A Schuco blond mohair cat, with faceted green glass eyes and pink stitched woollen nose and mouth, head movement controlled by tail.

German maker Schreyer & Co, known as Schuco, are renowned for their moving and miniature toys, but these are usually monkeys or teddy bears, with cats being less common. Postwar examples tend to have shorter, plumper limbs and fatter, more rounded bodies.

c1930   8.5in (21.5cm) high

£300-400   TCT

A Deans Childs Play chimpanzee fabric glove puppet, with tag and label.

10in (25.5cm) high

£15-25   F

A 1950s Chiltern 'Twurly Toys' cat plush soft toy, with poseable limbs, tag and label.

11in (28cm) high

£60-80   DE

1930s Farnell nightdress case, modelled as a monkey in recumbent pose.

British company J.K. Farnell are better known for their high quality 'Alpha' range of teddy bears which can fetch high prices today. This embroidered label was used on toys made from 1925 until c1945.

23in (58.5cm) long

£35-45   F

COLLECTORS' NOTES

■ Welsh toy company Mettoy, founded in the 1930s, released Corgi toys in 1956 as a competitor to Dinky's highly successful range of model vehicles. As well as having realistically glazed windows (leading to the slogan 'The Ones With The Windows'), from 1959 they often had extra features such as opening doors and bonnets, suspension and 'jewelled' headlights – exciting features for young boys!

■ Corgi are very well known for their large range of models produced during the 1960s and 1970s to tie-in with popular TV shows and films. These models were highly popular at the time and stole the lead from Dinky. They continue to be popular with fans of the series or film as well as with Corgi collectors today, which can leads to higher values due to increased competition, especially for some of the Bond cars.

■ As with other die-cast models, condition and unusual variations are key indicators to value. Collectors grade examples from 'poor' through 'good' and 'very good'

to 'excellent' and 'mint', with the top prices being paid for mint condition examples. Original boxes add a substantial amount to the value and the condition of the box is also important.

■ Unusual variations produced in small numbers or for short periods of time can also fetch high values and can add excitement to collecting and diversity to a collection. Look out for non-standard colours, different wheels, transfers or decoration that are unusual and consult a reference book to learn how to spot them.

■ Look out for models produced with 'Whizzwheels' as many are still comparatively affordable – but always buy in the best condition possible with boxes. Many tip these to be a good investment for the future. Some 1970s bubble-packed and carded examples from the 'Rockets' and 'Juniors' range are also worth looking out for and may even still be found in independent local toyshops.

A Corgi No. 408 "AA Road Service" Bedford Van, yellow, black, spun hubs, near mint condition, apart from very minor marks, in a good condition blue and yellow carded box.

1959-63

£120-180　　　　　　　**VEC**

A Corgi No. 403 "Daily Express" Bedford Van, blue, flat spun hubs, near mint condition, in a fair condition all-carded blue box.

1956-60

£55-65　　　　　　　**VEC**

A Corgi No. 421 "Evening Standard" Bedford Van, black, silver, flat spun hubs, excellent condition, in good condition blue and yellow carded box.

The variation with an 'AVRO BODE' logo in place of the Evening Standard logo and with a blue body can fetch up to twice the value of this variation.

1960-63

£100-150　　　　　　　**VE**

A Corgi No. 354 Commer Military Ambulance, green, dark tinted glass and roof light, near mint condition, very slight discolouration marks, in good condition blue and yellow carded box.

1964-66

£60-70　　　　　　　**VEC**

A Corgi No. 483 Dodge Kew Fargo Tipper, white, blue, graphite grey chassis, cast wheels, excellent condition, in good condition blue and yellow window box.

1968-72

£40-60　　　　　　　**VEC**

A Corgi No. 441 VW "Toblerone" Van, blue, lemon interior, spun hubs, mint condition, in slightly crushed, blue and yellow carded good condition box.

1963-67

£100-150　　　　　　　**VEC**

A Corgi No. 454 Commer Platform Lorry, lemon, silver, flat spun hubs and a No. 101 Platform Trailer, yellow, silver, flat spun hubs, in incorrect No. 100, box, both in good to excellent condition, in good condition blue and yellow carded boxes.

The trailer is worth under a quarter of the value of the lorry.

1957-63

£100-150　　　　　　　**V**

A Corgi No. 246 Chrysler Imperial, red, pale blue interior, cast wheels, excellent condition, in a fair condition, blue and yellow carded box.

The version of this model in metallic kingfisher blue is the most sought after and can fetch more than twice the value of this colour variation.

1965-68

£50-70 VEC

A Corgi No. 313 "Graham Hill" Ford Cortina GXL, metallic bronze, black roof, white interior, Whizzwheels, mint condition, in a good condition although crushed orange and yellow window box, complete with figure.

A variation with a tan body, black roof and number plate reading 'CORTINA' was released as a promotional model and can fetch up to double the value of this version.

1970-73

£80-120 VEC

A Corgi No. 238 Jaguar Mark 10, mid-blue, lemon interior, spun hubs, slightly superdetailed, excellent condition, in a good condition carded box.

1962-67

60-80 VEC

A Corgi No. 307 Jaguar E-type, graphite grey, red hood, spun hubs, mint condition, in a good condition blue and yellow plain carded box.

1962-64

£150-200 VEC

A Corgi No. 318 "I've Got a Tiger in My Tank" Lotus Elan, blue, black interior, spun hubs, figure, with small racing No. 20 decals, excellent condition, in a good condition blue and yellow carded box.

1965-67

£45-55 VEC

A Corgi No. 388 Mercedes C111, orange, black, Whizzwheels, near mint condition, orange and yellow window box.

1970-74

£18-22 VEC

A Corgi No. 230 Mercedes Benz SE Coupe, cream, red interior, spun hubs, excellent condition, in a good condition blue and yellow carded box.

1962-64

£70-100 VEC

A Corgi No. 330 Porsche Carrera 6, white, red, blue, cast wheels, racing number "60", excellent condition, slight surface corrosion to rear wheels, in a good condition blue and yellow carded box.

1967-69

22-28 VEC

A Corgi No. 485 "Surfing" Mini Countryman, turquoise, figure, two surf boards, excellent condition, in a good condition blue and yellow picture box.

It is essential that the surfer and boards are present with the box and model for examples to fetch this value.

1965-69

£150-200 VEC

A Corgi No. 389 Reliant Bond BUG, lime green, Whizzwheels, mint condition, in an excellent condition window box.

1971-74

£55-65 VEC

A Corgi Juniors No. E2529 "James Bond - The Spy Who Loved Me" twin-pack, comprising Lotus and Helicopter, mint condition, in an excellent condition film-strip picture card.

1977

£150-200 VEC

A Corgi Juniors No. E3019 "James Bond - Octopussy" gift set, comprising Land Rover, Trailer and small Jet Aircraft, mint condition, on a good condition blister card.

1983

£100-150 VEC

A Corgi No. 267 "Batman" Batmobile, black, clear screens, instruction pack containing folded leaflet and some missiles still attached to sprue, mint condition, in a good condition striped window box.

1967-72

£100-150 VEC

A Corgi Juniors No. 2601 "Batman" three-piece gift set, comprising Batmobile, Batboat on Trailer and Batcopter, mint condition, on an excellent condition bliste card.

1975-91

£180-220 VE

A Corgi No. 497 "The Man From U.N.C.L.E." Thrushbuster, blue, plastic lamps, cast wheels, Waverley ring, near mint condition, in a good condition inner pictorial stand an outer blue and yellow picture box.

1966

£150-200 V

A Corgi No. 290 "Kojak" Buick, gold, two figures and red roof light, near mint condition, in an excellent condition inner pictorial stand and a good condition outer window box, slight tear to front and grubby around corners, missing badge.

1976-77

£120-180 VEC

A Corgi No. 808 "Basil Brush car, yellow, red including plastic hubs, missing sound box, otherwise mint condition in a good condition box.

1971-73

£55-65 V

A Corgi No. 2 gift set, comprising Land Rover, beige, cream complete with trailer of same colour but with silver base, excellent condition, in a fair condition blue and yellow picture box.

1958-68

£150-200 VEC

A Corgi No. 7 "Daktari" Land Rover gift set, with figures and animals, good condition, box damaged.

1968-76

£45-55 CHEF

A Corgi No. 14 Hydraulic Tower Wagon gift set, with lamp standard, fair to good condition, box damaged.

1961-64

£20-25 CHEF

A Corgi No. 11 London Transport gift set, comprising Austin Taxi, Routemaster Bus and Mini Minor, all mint condition, including inner polystyrene packing and Policeman on dome, in a good condition outer with striped window.

The later No. 11 London Transport gift set, produced between 1980-82, does not include a Mini and is usually worth under a quarter of the value of this set.

1971-72

£100-150 VEC

A Corgi No. 13 Tour de France gift set, comprising Renault 16 "Paramount" Car, white, black, cast wheels, near mint condition, apart from slightly worn decal to front bonnet, excellent condition inner polystyrene tray, good condition outer blue and yellow window box.

1968-72

£120-180 VEC

A Corgi No. 31 Buick Riviera Gift Set, with No.245 Buick, red trailer, and Dolphin Cabin Cruiser towing lady water skier, fair to good condition, box rather misshapen and lacking two flaps.

1964-68

£80-120 CHEF

A Corgi No. 36 "Tarzan" gift set, in excellent condition window box, although grubby around corners.

1976-78

£200-250 VEC

A Corgi No. 14 "Daktari" gift set, comprising Bedford Giraffe Transporter, beige, brown; Land Rover, green, black; and Cattle Truck, blue, brown, plus various figures, near mint to mint condition, mint condition inner polystyrene packing, good condition outer blue and yellow picture box, excellent condition picture header card.

As well as being complete with all its packaging and models, the superb condition of the packaging, including the picture card, helped this example reach this value.

1969-73

£400-500 VEC

A Corgi No. 8101 Wings Flying School gift set comprising Land Rover, Trailer with Plane and Helicopter, all finished in silver, mint condition, excellent condition outer blue window box.

This gift set was produced by Corgi exclusively for Marks & Spencer.

1978

£150-200 VEC

A Corgi No. 503 "Chipperfields Circus" Bedford Giraffe Transporter, red, blue, spun hubs, mint condition including inner carded packing, excellent condition outer blue and yellow box, apart from slight tear to end flap.

1964-70

£120-180 VEC

A Corgi No. 23 "Chipperfields Circus" gift set, comprising Land Rover, six-wheeled Crane, Bedford Giraffe Transporter, Elephant Cage on Trailer and two Animal Cages, excellent to near mint condition, in a good condition inner polystyrene tray and fair condition but complete outer picture box.

This set was released in two variations. On the earlier, and usually more valuable, set produced between 1962-66, the giraffe transporter was replaced with a booking office.

1964

£300-400 VEC

A Corgi No. 1121 "Chipperfields Circus", red, yellow, blue, silver jib and hook, excellent condition, in a good condition blue and yellow picture box.

1963-69

£120-180 VEC

A Corgi No. 1139 "Chipperfields Circus" Scammell with Menagerie Trailer, red, blue, three animal cages, good condition, in a good condition, although grubby blue and yellow window box.

1968-72

£150-200 VEC

A Corgi No. 1123 "Chipperfields Circus" Animal Cage, red, blue, yellow, spun hubs, excellent condition, in a good condition all-carded blue and yellow picture box.

1963-68

£80-120 VEC

A Corgi No. 1111 Massey Ferguson 780 Combine Harvester, red including front and rear plastic hubs, yellow plastic tines, excellent condition, apart from a couple of very minor marks, in a good condition box.

1961-64

£150-200 VE

A Corgi No. 66 Massey Ferguson 165 Tractor, red, grey, white, mint condition, in an excellent condition blue and yellow carded box, apart from one side where price label has been removed.

1966-72

£150-200 VEC

A Corgi No. 412 Bedford "Ambulance", cream, flat spun hubs, excellent condition, in a goo condition all-carded blue box.

A very small number of this model were produced with labels reading 'HOME SERVICES', these are extremely scarce with none having been found recently, making values difficult to predict.

1957-60

£120-180 VE

Front: A Corgi No. 437 Cadillac Superior Ambulance, good condition, surface corrosion in places, in a good condition but grubby blue and yellow carded box.
1962-65

£30-40   **VEC**

A Corgi No. 448 BMC Mini "Police", one rear door hinge broken, in a good condition inner pictorial stand, Including tracker dog and policeman.
1964-69

£70-100   **VEC**

A Corgi No. 468 "Natural Corgi Toys" London Transport Routemaster Bus, with Corgi Classics side decals, red, spun hubs, excellent condition, in a good condition although grubby blue and yellow carded box.

Of the first casting series, the rarest of the Routemaster buses is the green, cream and brown example produced for the Australian market with a transfer reading 'NEW SOUTH WALES'.

1964-66

£70-100   **VEC**

A Corgi No. 1120 "Midland Red Birmingham to London" Motorway Express Coach, red, flat spun hubs, excellent condition, in a good condition box.

£100-150   **VEC**

Two Corgi Rockets, a No. 902 Jaguar XJ6, metallic green, near mint condition, and a No. 907 Cadillac Eldorado, gold, cream interior, mint condition, both on good condition blister cards.

The 'Rocket' series was produced to compete with Mattel's 'Hotwheels' series and was advertised as being stronger than other die-cast series. In general they are hard to find carded and in mint condition, which explains their comparatively high values for such modern die-cast toys.

1970-72

£50-80   **VEC**

A Corgi No. 486 Chevrolet Impala Kennel Club Van, white over red, cast wheels, mint condition, very minor marks, in an excellent condition carded box.
1967-69

£120-180   **VEC**

A Corgi No. 436 "Wildlife Preservation" Citroen Safari, missing rear window otherwise good condition, in a good condition blue and yellow carded box.
1963-65

£45-55   **VEC**

A Corgi No. 653 "Air Canada" Concorde, white, red, blue, near mint condition, in an excellent condition correct issue blue and yellow carded box.

Although not uncommon, interest in these models has increased due to Concorde being 'retired' by British Airways and Air France in 2003. The Japan Airlines and Air Canada versions are usually the most valuable.

1973-81

£250-300   **VEC**

A Corgi No. 438 Land Rover, metallic green, dark green plastic canopy, cast wheels, near mint condition, apart from slight marks to roof, in a good condition blue and yellow window box.

£40-60   **VEC**

A Corgi No. 1106 Decca Mobile Airfield Radar, beige, five orange stripes, flat spun hubs, good condition although one side showing slight discolouration in colour, in a good condition box.
1959-61

£70-100   **VEC**

FIND OUT MORE...

'Ramsay's British Die-cast Model Toys Catalogue', by John Ramsay, 9th edition, published Swapmeet Publications, 2001.

'The Great Book of Corgi Toys', by Marcel van Cleemput, published by New Cavendish Books, 2001.

COLLECTORS' NOTES

■ Dinky toys were first launched in 1931 as 'Meccano's Model Miniatures' – a range of accessories to Hornby train sets in die-cast and tinplate materials. Known under the 'Dinky' brand a year later, cars were first introduced in 1934.

■ The 1930s were one of Dinky's most successful decades with over 200 models to choose from by 1935. These pre-war toys are usually the most desirable and valuable.

■ 'Supertoys' were introduced in 1947 and 'Speedwheels' in the 1970s, to compete against the growing strength of competitors. Dinky's English factory closed in 1979 and since 2001, the name has been dormant.

■ Condition and variations in colour are two key indicators to value. Collectors prefer to buy examples in the best condition possible, using terms such as poor, fair, good, very good and mint to describe the models.

■ An original box can add 40% or more to the value, and the condition of the box is important too. Models without their boxes offer a more affordable option, but always try to buy in the best condition.

■ Variations in colour or detailing (such as an unusual transfer advertising a certain product) can have a major impact on value. National variations such as models made in France or models made for specific foreign markets such as South Africa are particularly noteworthy. Examine paintwork closely to ensure that the model has not been repainted.

■ In this section, where prices for variations of a particular model are given in the footnotes - they are for pieces in a similar condition to the piece shown.

A Dinky No. 342 Austin Mini Moke, light metallic green, greyish brown hood, spun hubs, near mint condition, in good condition box, slight repair to one end.
1966-72

£120-180   **VEC**

A Dinky No. 282 Austin 1800 Taxi, blue, white bonnet and boot, red interior, roof box, spun hubs, excellent condition, in good condition box.
1967-69

£50-80   **VEC**

A Dinky No. 152 Austin A40 Devon, deep yellow lower body, mid-blue upper and ridged wheels, excellent condition, in fair condition box, some sellotape repairs.

The rarest and most valuable colour variation of this model has an all-over tan body and green hubs and can fetch over three times the value of this variation.
1956-59

£180-220   **VEC**

Two Dinky No. 155 Ford Anglias, one pale green, red interior, spun hubs, excellent condition, in good condition box, slight tear to end flap, and one turquoise blue, good condition, in good condition box.

In 1966 only, Dinky released a cream version and a light blue version for the South African market. These are much rarer and can fetch over three times the value of the versions shown here.
1961-66

£150-200   **VEC**

A Dinky No. 154 Hillman Minx, lime green lower body, cream upper body and ridged wheels, near mint condition, small chip marks to rear of roof, in excellent condition box, small amount of graffiti to side.
1955

£250-300   **VEC**

A Dinky No. 38f Jaguar SS100, mid-blue, grey interior, black ridged wheels, treaded tyres, good condition.
1947-50

£60-90   **VEC**

A Dinky No. 157 Jaguar XK120, in original box.

1954-57

£80-120 F

A Dinky No. 172 Studebaker Land Cruiser, mid-blue, fawn ridged hubs, in good condition box, tear to end flap.

Look out for two-tone examples with a cream lower body as these can fetch up to 25% more.

1954-56

£70-100 VEC

A French Dinky No. 559 Ford Taunus 17M, light metallic gold, red interior, dished hubs, white tyres, good condition, including box, tear mark to one end.

£60-90 VEC

A French Dinky No. 542 Simca Arianne Taxi, black, red roof, metre and roof light, chromed hubs, white tyres, good condition, slight corrosion to hubs, in good condition box.

£80-120 VEC

A Dinky No. 108 MG Competition Midget, red, light tan interior, driver, racing number "24", red ridged wheels, good condition, including box.

The version produced for the US market is numbered '129' rather than '108'.

1955-59

£70-100 VEC

A French Dinky No. 1409 Chrysler 180, metallic sea-green, black roof, light beige interior, excellent condition, in good condition box.

£100-150 VEC

A French Dinky No. 531 Fiat Grande Vue, metallic bronze, off-white roof, chromed hubs, replacement front tyres, good condition, including box.

£60-90 VEC

A rare South African issue French Dinky No. 552 Chevrolet Corvair, pale blue, cream interior, concave chromed hubs, white tyres, excellent condition, in excellent condition dual language box, small tear mark to one end flap.

Production of Dinky toys in France began in 1934, at the Paris Meccano factory. Many were English models assembled in France but finished in different colours. Production recommenced after ceasing during the war, with a series of typical French family cars such as the Peugeot 203. During the 1950s a new series of cars and lorries was produced. In 1970 the factory moved to Calais but by 1971 increased competition led to a downturn in production and 1971 saw the last French catalogue.

£650-750 VEC

A South African issue French Dinky No. 555 Ford Thunderbird, metallic blue, red interior, driver, white tyres, slight corrosion to hubs and damage to windscreen, good condition, including box, slight marks to end flap.

1962-65

£300-400 VEC

A Dinky No. 501 Foden Diesel 8-wheel Wagon, first type cab, light grey, black chassis, red side flash and ridged wheels, herringbone tyres, no hook, good condition, in good condition box, space to side and split to one end.

The variation produced for only the US market is much sought after and can be identified by its red cab, back and hubs, black chassis, silver cab flash and no hook. It can fetch three to five times as much as some other variations.

1947-48

£200-250 VEC

A Dinky No. 501 Foden Diesel 8-wheel Wagon, first type cab, dark blue, black chassis, silver flash, dark blue ridged hubs, no hook, fair condition including box.

1947-48

£80-120 VEC

A Dinky No. 501 Foden 8-wheeled Wagon, first type cab, light grey cab and back, black chassis and wings, red side flash, red ridged wheels, herringbone tyres, no hook, good condition, some minor detailing to rear, in good condition buff box.

1947-48

£250-300 VEC

A scarce Dinky No. 935 Leyland Octopus Flat Truck with chains, dark blue cab and chassis, pale grey back, yellow band around cab, pale grey plastic hubs, rivetted back, fair condition, in poor condition box.

Although scarce, the rarest variation of this model has a blue cab and chassis, a yellow flash on the cab and a light grey flatbed and can fetch up to three times more than this version.

1964-66

£550-650 VEC

A Dinky No. 503 Foden Flat Truck with tailboard, first type cab, violet blue cab and chassis, burnt orange back and side flash, mid-blue ridged hubs, excellent condition, minor chip to right-hand side screen post and a few minor chips to edge of tailboard, in good condition box.

1948-52

£400-500 VEC

A Dinky No. 902 Foden Flat Truck, second type cab, orange cab and chassis, mid-green back and Supertoy wheels, excellent condition, some minor retouching to mudguards and cab roof, in good condition box.

1954-57

£150-200 VEC

A Dinky No. 438 Ford D800 Tipper Truck, metallic red cab, white interior, silver chassis, yellow back, yellow plastic hubs, near mint condition, in good condition box, dymo tape stuck over end flaps.

1970-77

£50-80 VEC

A Dinky No. 433 Guy Flat Truck with tailboard, first type cab, dark green cab and chassis, mid-green back and Supertoy wheels, good condition, in good condition yellow lift-off lid box, incorrect colour spot.

1956-57

£80-120 VEC

A Dinky No. 410 Bedford End Tipper, red cab and chassis, cream back, glazing to cab, red ridged hubs, excellent condition, small chip to roof, in good condition box, label applied to one end flap and puncture hole to one side.

Look closely at the hubs of this model. Die-cast hubs are earlier dating from 1954-61. Models with die-cast hubs are usually worth around 20-25% less than examples like this with plastic hubs.

1962-63

£150-200 VEC

A Dinky No. 25b Covered Wagon, type two, light green chassis, orange body, cream tin tilt, black smooth hubs, good condition, damage to rear hook and slight damage to chassis.

1936-40

£180-220   VEC

A Dinky No. 30v Job's Dairy Electric Milk Float, cream, red, red ridged wheels, excellent condition, unboxed.

1949-54

£100-150   VEC

A Dinky No. 436 Atlas Copco Compressor Lorry, very good condition, boxed.

1963-69

£40-60   CHEF

A Dinky No. 981 British Railways Horsebox, maroon, red Supertoy wheels, excellent condition, in good condition box.

A Dinky No. 29b Streamlined Bus, two-tone green, black ridged wheels, good condition.

If the rear window of the bus is open rather than filled in, the bus dates to between 1936-46, although values remain similar.

1954-60

£120-180   VEC

1947-50

£60-90   VEC

A Dinky No. 949 Wayne School Bus, deep yellow, red interior, red side flash and red plastic hubs, excellent condition, minor chips to protruding edges, in good condition box.

1961-66

£250-300   VEC

A Dinky No. 952 Vega Major Luxury Coach, pale grey, metallic maroon side flash, cream interior, silver cast hubs, flashing indicators, good condition, in good condition box.

1964-71

£40-60   VEC

A Dinky No. 886 Richier Road Grader, yellow, driver, red hubs, excellent condition, including box complete with inner packing.

1961-66

£100-150   VEC

A Dinky No. 60y Shell Aviation Service Thompson Pressure Refueller, red, white solid rubber wheels, black base, good condition, no visible signs of fatigue.

1938-40

£220-280   VEC

A Dinky No. 60r Caledonia Empire Flying Boat, silver, orange, plastic roller, red propellers, G-A DHM, gliding hook, fair condition, no visible signs of fatigue.

1937-40

£70-100   **VEC**

A Dinky No. 62y Giant Highspeed Monoplane, grey, dark green wing edges, red propellers, G-A TBK, good condition.

The post-war version, produced between 1945-49, has wing lettering reading 'G-ZBK'.

1939-40

£70-100   **VEC**

A Dinky No. 60w Clipper III Flying Boat, silver, red propellers, red plastic roller, USA NC16736, gliding pin and hole, nose of aircraft and engine cowls fatigued, repaired damage to one wing, good condition, in good condition box, slightly sunfaded.

The similarly valued US issue of this model is identical except for missing out the letters 'USA' on the left wing, retaining only the numbers.

1938-40

£70-100   **VEC**

A Dinky No. 62d Blenheim Bomber, camouflage, with two roundels to wings, black and white to underneath, red propellers, excellent condition, no signs of fatigue.

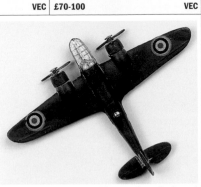

Many early and pre-war die-cast toys used a metal compound known as 'mazac' or 'zamac' comprising aluminium and zinc. If the metals were poorly combined, the cast metal began to 'fatigue' over time, crumbling and warping. This reduces value considerably and is often found on airplane wings and fittings. Handle models showing fatigue as little as possible and keep them at room temperature to stave off further damage.

1940-41

£180-220   **VEC**

A Dinky No. 62w Imperial Airways Liner, Frobisher class, Falcon, silver, red propellers, gliding pin and hole, G-A FDJ, good condition, slight distortion to one wing, in good condition but sunfaded box.

1939-41

£150-200   **VEC**

A Dinky No. 998 Bristol Britannia Canadian Pacific Airliner, white, silver, blue, red propellers, excellent condition, in good condition blue and white striped box, split to one corner, complete with inner packing.

1959-64

£250-300   **VEC**

A Dinky No. 700 Spitfire Mark II Diamond Jubilee of the Royal Air Force, chrome-plated, on marble effect plinth, near mint condition, in excellent condition box.

This model, which could be mounted on a plinth, was released to celebrate the Diamond Jubilee of the Royal Air Force and was sold in a special presentation box.

1979

£120-180   **VEC**

A Dinky No. 998 Bristol Britannia 'Canadian Pacific' Airliner, silver-grey, white, red, red propellers, CF-CZA, excellent condition, in yellow picture lift-off lid box.

1964-65

£180-220   **VEC**

A French Dinky No. 804 Noratlas, silver-grey, silver propellers, French rosettes to wings, near mint condition, in good condition box, puncture hole to one side, complete with inner packing.

£250-300   **VEC**

A Dinky No. 353 Shado 2 Mobile, in original box.

1971-79

£60-90   F

A Dinky No. 353 UFO Shado 2 Mobile, blue, black base, rollers and tracks, white interior, near mint condition, with mint condition inner polystyrene packing, in good condition outer window box.

The version with the blue finish is usually more desirable and more valuable than the version with the green finish, also shown on this page. However green-finished examples with a smooth, flat roof can fetch similar values to the blue variation.

1971-79

£300-400   VEC

A Dinky No. 351 UFO Shado Interceptor, green, red legs, blue tinted glass, excellent condition, in good condition inner pictorial stand and outer picture box.

1971-79

£220-280   VEC

A Dinky No. 101 Thunderbirds 2 and 4, metallic bluish-green, yellow legs, red thrusters, good condition, in mint condition bubble pack.

1973

£200-250   VEC

A Dinky No. 100 Thunderbirds Lady Penelope's FAB 1, pink, clear roof slides, cast wheels, excellent condition, base badly pitted and screen discoloured in places, in excellent condition bubble pack.

1970-75

£80-120   VEC

A Dinky No. 477 The Adventures of Parsley, Parsley's Car, with un-cut inner card in original box, excellent condition, in good condition box.

1970-72

£70-100   SAS

A Dinky No. 360 Space 1999, Eagle Freighter, white, blue, unapplied decal sheet, near mint condition including inner polystyrene moon display.

1975-79

£150-200   VEC

A Dinky No. 358, Star Trek U.S.S. Enterprise, in original box.

1976-80

£60-80   F

A Dinky No. 108 Joe 90 Sam's Car, chrome finish, lemon interior, red engine cover, cast wheels, near mint condition, excellent condition inner and outer picture box.

1969-71

£100-150   VEC

FIND OUT MORE...

'Ramsay's British Die-cast Model Toys Catalogue', *by John Ramsay, 9th edition, published by Swapmeet Publications, 2001.*

'The Great Book of Dinky Toys', *by Mike & Sue Richardson, published by New Cavendish Books, 2000.*

COLLECTORS' NOTES

■ Tri-ang launched the 'Spot-On' range in 1959 in direct competition with rivals Dinky Toys and the newly established Corgi Toys.

■ To differentiate their toys from other companies, Tri-ang modelled all the vehicles to an exact 1:42 scale – slightly larger than the competition and making them closer to models than toys.

■ Over 100 different models were produced at a new factory in Belfast. The range was expanded to include building and road signs, all to 1:42 scale.

■ Production ceased when Tri-ang bought Dinky in 1967, however some variations continued to be made in New Zealand for a couple of years

■ Each model came in a variety of rich colours and all variations are collectable today, particularly commercial vehicles and sets. Boxes are particularly fragile and boxed examples will fetch a premium.

A Tri-ang Spot-On No. 100 Ford Zodiac, lilac, cream interior, excellent condition, in fair condition box complete with leaflet.
1959

£120-180 VEC

A Tri-ang Spot-On No. 115 Bristol 406, metallic blue, cream interior, excellent condition, including box.
1960

£150-200 VEC

A Tri-ang Spot-On No. 101 Armstrong-Siddeley Sapphire, light green, black roof, cream interior, good condition, in fair condition box.

This is one of the most valuable colourways for this model.

1959

£100-150 VEC

A Tri-ang Spot-On No. 118 BMW Isetta, pale turquoise-green, cream interior, excellent condition, in good condition box with sellotape repair to end and slightly crushed.

1960

£100-150 VEC

A Tri-ang Spot-On No. 157SL Rover 3 litre, with lights, slightly darker shade of grey, light beige interior, slight chrome loss to plastic parts, good condition, in fair condition box.

This model was also released without lights and is worth approximately the same.

1963

£80-120 VEC

A Tri-ang Spot-On No. 119 Meadows Frisky, pale grey, black roof, blue interior, excellent condition, in excellent condition box with light tear mark.
1960

£70-100 VEC

A Tri-ang Spot-On No. 120 Fiat Multipla, very pale blue, cream interior, good condition, in poor condition box.
1960

£55-65 VEC

A Tri-ang Spot-On No. 154 Austin A40, red, cream interior, excellent condition, in good condition box.

1961

£80-120 VEC

A Tri-ang Spot-On No. 131 Goggomobile, pale yellow, black roof, cream interior, good condition, in good condition box, some sellotape repairs.
1960

£70-100 VEC

A Tri-ang Spot-On No. 165 Vauxhall Cresta, light beige, white interior, good condition, front suspension has dropped, in poor condition box.

The version of this car with a roof rack is worth approximately the same amount.

1961

£60-90 VEC

A Tri-ang Spot-On No. 166 Renault Floride, metallic green, cream interior, excellent condition, in fair condition box.

1962

£80-120 VEC

A Tri-ang Spot-On No. 184 Austin A60 Cambridge, with skis, bright pale blue, white interior, roof rack, skis and pole, near mint condition, in good condition box with slight tear mark to one side.

1963

£100-150 VEC

A Tri-ang Spot-On No. 193 NSU Prinz 4, red, cream interior, driver, excellent condition, in good condition box.

1963

£70-100 VEC

A Tri-ang Spot-On No. 185 Fiat 500, pale blue, cream interior, good condition, in excellent condition box.

The yellow and dark blue versions of this car are worth about 30% more than other colours.

1963

£70-100 VEC

A Tri-ang Spot-On No. 191/1 Sunbeam Alpine, with hard top, lilac, black roof, cream interior, excellent condition, in good condition box.

This and the yellow version are the most desirable for this model.

1963

£100-150 VEC

A Tri-ang Spot-On No. 215 Daimler SP250, light beige, cream interior, good condition, in poor condition box complete with leaflet.

1961

£60-90 VEC

A Tri-ang Spot-On No. 213 Ford Anglia, red, cream interior, near mint condition, in fair condition box.

1963

£180-220 VEC

A Tri-ang Spot-On No. 215 Daimler SP250, light beige, cream interior, good condition, in poor condition box complete with leaflet.

A Tri-ang Spot-On No. 217 Jaguar E-type, beige, white interior, excellent condition, in fair condition box.

1963

£100-150 VEC

A Chad Valley RMS Queen Mary, excellent condition, in good condition box.

£20-30 VEC

A CIJ Douglas "UAT", silver, yellow, blue, white, F-B GTX, excellent condition, some discolouration, in excellent condition box.

£150-200 VEC

A CIJ Boeing 707, white, red, blue, excellent condition including box.

£60-90 VEC

A J.R.D. articulated Berliet lorry No. 120, in red and white Kronenburg livery, complete and boxed, some wear, minor chips.

£120-180 W&W

A Lone Star Viscount "Aer Lingus", silver, green, white, four propellers, excellent condition, in fair condition box, complete with leaflet and a Bristol Britannia "British and Commonwealth", silver, blue, four propellers, good condition.

£150-200 VEC

A Mercury Models No. 416 Convair, silver, silver propellers, US decals to one wing and fuselage, good condition.

£100-150 VEC

A Mercury No. 402 Fiat G212, silver, Italian rosette decals to wings and fuselage, three propellers, good condition, in excellent condition box.

£50-80 VEC

A rare Matchbox series MB17 Bedford removals van, with "Matchbox Removals Service" with silver trim and metal wheels, minor rusting to axles.

£45-65 W&W

A scarce Mettoy Metair Hangar, finished in powder blue and red tinplate hangar with airsock and retractable doors, complete with two Vickers Viscounts and DeHavilland Comet plastic friction-drive aircraft and one Tudor Rose plastic aircraft, excellent condition, in good condition box.

£350-450 VEC

A Mettoy Luxury Motor Coach, blue, grey, clear roof, tinplate base, missing figures and luggage, good condition, in fair condition box.

£40-60 VEC

An Indian Milton Models, Double-Decker Bus, light blue lower body, white upper, white interior, excellent condition, in good condition box, some sellotape repairs.

£50-80 VEC

A Morestone No. 4 Express Delivery wagon, yellow cab and chassis, grey back, yellow wheels, near mint condition, in excellent condition box.

1955-57

£100-150 VEC

A Morestone No. 1 Foden Petrol Tanker "ESSO", red, red wheels, excellent condition, slight nick marks to decals to sides, in good condition box.

1955-57

£250-350 VEC

A Nickytoys, Calcutta, No. 999 DeHavilland Comet, silver, blue, white, good condition, in fair condition box.

£100-150 VEC

A Tekno No. 419 Ford Taunus Van "Solgryn", red, white, excellent condition, in good condition box, labels stuck to one end.

£220-280 VEC

A Tekno No. 787 Super Sabre, silver, FW-761, US decals to front nosecone and wing, near mint condition, in good condition box.

£120-180 VEC

A Tekno No. 834r Mustang Rally Car, white, dark blue, black roof, red interior, racing number "169", excellent condition, box in excellent condition, label on one end flap.

£60-90 VEC

A Tri-ang Minic No. 2 clockwork Jeep, khaki, complete with key and petrol can, good condition, including box.

£100-150 VEC

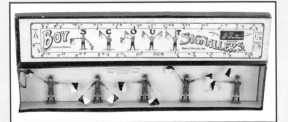

A CLOSER LOOK AT A LOCOMOTIVE

This is a rare shape for a model train and is based on the real-life 'Schienenzeppelin' that set a railway speed record on June 21st 1931 - this toy was released shortly after this event.

It is made of tinplate and is hand-painted, showing the quality of Märklin's toys - early versions of this model have a two, rather than four-bladed propeller.

A 1920s Hornby 0-gauge 4-4-0 and six-wheel tender LMA No. 2711, a clockwork locomotive, finished in black with gold, red lining to splashers and LMS shadow lettering, crest to cab sides and "RN" to tender, minor damage and wear.

15.25in (38.5cm) long

£220-280 **W&W**

This is the electric version, as indicated by the red flash on the nose, electric pick-up bar and two screw marks on the side - a clockwork version (No SZ970) with a keyhole was also available.

It is in very good condition with its original light gold finish and no serious dents or splits, but it would have sold for more if areas of the finish were not worn and it retained its window transfers.

A Märklin 0-gauge 'Schienenzeppelin' (track zeppelin) SZ 12970 locomotive, in working order.

This and the real-life Schienenzeppelin are based on the form of a Zeppelin airship, a popular and novel form of transport in the 1930s. The actual locomotive was designed by Franz Kruckenberg and only one example was ever made.

c1932-34

£500-600 **LAN**

A Märklin 1-gauge train set 'R 981/72/3', with a B-movement locomotive 981, a tender, two carriages 1872, eight curved and ten straight tracks, chromolithographed in green, sheet metal wheels, original box with old cover painting.

8in (20cm) wide

£800-1,000 **LAN**

A Märklin 0-gauge steam locomotive, two parts, with tender, hand-painted in black, movement in working order, some wear.

£550-650 **LAN**

A Hornby 0-gauge 4-4-2 tank locomotive, a clockwork No. 2 special tank locomotive finished in Southern 2091 green and black, paint chips, some sympathetic restoration.

£180-220 **W&W**

A Hornby 0-gauge 0-4-0 locomotive and tender, a well restored clockwork No. 1 special finished in Southern B343 black livery, coal load missing.

£100-150 **W&W**

A GCR 0-8-4 kit built 0-gauge electric tank locomotive, finely detailed with black livery and red line details.

12.25in (31cm) long

£180-220 **ROS**

A Mamod live steam model SC1 steam locomotive, with railway carriage, open wagon and track.

8in (20cm) wide

£150-200 **F**

A fine scale 0-gauge electric motored 2-6-2 tank locomotive, finished in LMS maroon, lettering to tank sided and RN2 to bunker and smoke box door, brass and diecast construction sprung buffers, with a fully detailed cab and fireman figure.

11in (28cm) long

£180-220 **W&W**

COLLECTORS' NOTES

■ Since their introduction as toys in the mid-19th century, trains have generally become more finely modelled, more realistic and smaller in size. The widths between the wheels, known as a 'gauge' (such as 'I', 'II', and 'III'), were standardised in 1891. The 'OO' gauge was introduced by Märklin and Bing in 1935 and by Hornby as 'Dublo' in 1938. Märklin introduced the 'HO' gauge in 1948. Plastic was introduced in the mid-1950s and became prevalent in the 1960s.

■ Collectors look for the most popular names in the industry and also often ones remembered nostalgically from childhood. Hornby, Märklin, Wrenn and Bassett-Lowke are popular, especially if early, large or of high quality. Condition is important unless the train is extremely rare. Wear through play, missing pieces or broken mechanisms reduce value dramatically, particularly for later sets from the 1950s onwards. Look out for boxes where possible, which should also be in good condition.

An Issmayer scenery train station, chromolithographed tinplate, marquee missing, wear.

7.25in (18cm) wide

£250-350   **LAN**

A Hornby 00-gauge Class A4 4-6-2 Mallard locomotive, in original box.

box 13in (33cm) long

£45-55   **F**

A Wren 00-gauge 4-6-2 Class A4 Mallard, in LNER blue, with original box, "RN 4468" to cab sides, "LNER" lettering to tender, minor wear.

11in (28cm) long

£120-180   **W&W**

A Wren 00-gauge 2-6-0 and tender 'Windsor Castle', in original box, finished in BR blue, splasher name plate RN 4082 to cab sides, BR symbol to tender, with paperwork, minor wear.

10.5in (26.5cm) long

£100-200   **W&W**

A Lima 00-gauge 'Vale of York' electric locomotive, in original box.

box 14in (35.5cm) wide

£40-50   **F**

A Märklin signal hut with signal, backrest of chair broken off, base with some colour damage.

4in (10cm) wide

£180-220   **LAN**

A lithographed tinplate train station, including a waiting hall and little shop, imitation of clock and telegraph, electrified.

20in (50cm) wide

£100-200   **LAN**

A Märklin 0-gauge locomotive TWE 12930, hand-painted in red and cream, two electrified headlights, roof restored, some wear.

13.25in (33cm) wide

£250-350   **LAN**

A CLOSER LOOK AT A TCO HIGHWAY COURIER

This car is marked "TCO" showing it was made by the notable maker Tipp and Co. of Nuremburg in Germany, founded in 1912.

At 14in (35cm) in length, this is a comparatively large example of a tinplate car.

This is a very rare pre-war model and is styled extremely attractively. It is also typical of the 1930s when Tipp and Co. made some of their best cars.

Although this model has signs of rust that devalue it, it is in relatively good condition for such a rare piece. It still works and has no serious damage to the bodywork or transfers.

A TCO chromolithographed tinplate highway courier, in light green and brown, with driver, movement in working order, slightly rusty.

14in (35cm) long

£4,500-5,500   **LAN**

A Märklin hand-painted tinplate torpedo boat 'Granatiere', no engine, partly overpainted.
In this condition this model is ideal for restoration, which would increase its value.

22.5in (56cm) long

£1,000-1,500   **LAN**

A Fleischmann single-funnelled tinplate clockwork model ocean liner, with cream and blue hull, brown decking and detailed superstructure.

20.5in (52cm) long

£600-800   **F**

A Lehmann chromolithographed tinplate taxi 755, with driver and taximeter, movement in working order, some wear.

7.25in (18cm) wide

£800-1,000   **LAN**

A Japanese T.N. trademark tinplate model Benz, battery-powered, boxed, in good condition.

11in (28cm) wide

£120-180   **CHEF**

A painted tinplate and wooden model veteran car, scratch-built, with four-seater open body.

13.75in (35cm) long

£10-15   **CHEF**

A Märklin green painted sheet metal steam boat, lacks burner, old finish, shows some wear.

15.25in (38cm) wide

£350-450   **LAN**

A Köhler polychrome chromolithographed turkey, movement in good order, slight wear.

4in (10cm) high

£60-80 LAN

An EBO 'Trili' chromolithographed tinplate jumping bird, with original box, slightly damaged.

7.25in (18cm) long

£350-450 LAN

A CLOSER LOOK AT A TINPLATE CAT

The whimsical form may suggest this is by a Japanese maker of the 1950s or 1960s. It is in fact made by well-known German maker Günthermann, operational from 1877 to 1965.

This simple and 'naïve' toy is made purely of tinplate. An examination of the finish reveals that it is hand-painted which means that it is an early tinplate toy dating from around the turn of the century.

Günthermann are well known for their humour and vitality of design as seen in this and the other examples on this page.

This figure is in good condition, with bright colours and a working moving and musical mechanism - if the base had not been restored it would have been worth £600-700.

A Günthermann hand-painted tinplate figure of a cat, with double bass, base restored.

c1908 *9.5in (24cm) high*

£450-550 LAN

A Günthermann hand-painted tinplate moving figure of a man on a bicycle, with hat and drum, movement in working order.

3.5in (9cm) w

£300-400 LAN

A Günthermann tinplate man riding on a pig toy, movement in working order, slight wear.

5.25in (13cm) long

£200-300 LAN

A Japanese Yonezawa tinplate battery-operated 'Sleeping Baby Bear' novelty toy, in part original box.

9.75in (25cm) wide

£70-100 F

A 'Funny Tiger' lithographed tinplate wind-up toy, by Marx Toys.

6.5in (16.5cm) high

£70-100 NOR

A 19thC painted tinplate toy engine, tender, and passenger coach, painted red, green, orange and black, paint loss, some breaks to wheel spokes.

9in (22.5cm) long

£100-150 FRE

A Japanese T.P.S. tinplate clockwork 'Clown on Roller Skates' novelty toy, in original box.

box 6.5in (16.5cm) wide

£200-300 F

COLLECTORS' NOTES

- Japan is considered the most important producer of toy robots, and the 1950s and 1960s are deemed the 'golden age'. Robots and space toys fascinated the public at this time when the 'space race' and Cold War dominated news, and cinemas showed endless science fiction movies.

- Forms vary and are rarely based on real spacecraft, instead focusing on fantasy and fiction. The majority in this period were made of tinplate decorated with brightly coloured transfers. Plastic began to dominate more and more from the 1960s onwards, eventually taking over completely as it was less expensive to produce. Pieces made before the mid-1950s are usually marked 'Made in Occupied Japan', changing to 'Made in Japan' after this period.

- Identifying the maker can be difficult as not all have their full names printed on them. Popular makers include Alps, who usually print their full name, Yonezawa, identified by a mark of a 'Y' in a flower and Masudaya, identified by the letters 'TM'. As there were so many makers of robots, many have fallen into obscurity and are simply known by their letters, such as 'SY'.

- Condition is an important indicator to value, with scratches to the lithographic transfers and dents or splits to the metal reducing value, especially if rust has taken hold. Rare, large and early robots and those that have complex functions, as well as those made by the major manufacturers, will usually hold the most appeal to robot collectors. The addition of an original box will also add to desirability and value - many of them have amusing and appealing graphics.

MECHANICAL WIND-UP
ATOMIC ROBOT

* WALKING FORWARD
* TURNING HEAD AND HANDS
* WITH NOISE

A 1960s Japanese Atomic Robot tinplate and plastic wind-up toy, with original printed card box.

robot 6in (15cm) high

£400-500   **RSJ**

A 1970s Japanese Rotate-O-Matic Super Astronaut robot, by SJM, in tinplate and plastic, with battery powered automatic 'stop 'n' go' action, blinking and shooting guns, firing noise and rotating body, in original box.

12in (30.5cm) high

£80-120   **W&W**

A Japanese Taiyo Blink-A-Gear tinplate and plastic toy robot, with walking action, panel to chest containing multi-coloured plastic gears, eyes with lights, swinging arms, damage to foot.

14in (35.5cm) high

£180-220   **W&W**

A late 1960s Japanese Laser 008 tinplate toy robot, by Daiya, with plastic arms, clockwork mechanism.

This style of arms, body and legs can also be found on Daiya's X20 Astronaut, which has a different head but similarly bright paintwork.

6.5in (16.5cm) high

£350-450   **RSJ**

A 1950s Japanese Revolving Flashing Robot remote control toy, by Alps, in original box.

The exact design and transfers of this robot is unique. It has a door that allows a view of part of the mechanism. The head is like the famous Robby the Robot, even though it has no precise face. Two pins in the feet allow it to waddle along. The rubber hands are prone to perishing, but are in good condition here. The excellent condition, original box and noted maker help account for the high value.

10in (25.5cm) high

£1,500-2,500   **RSJ**

A Super Space Explorer plastic battery operated toy robot, by HK, Hong Kong, with automatic 'stop 'n' go' action, rotating antenna and a large screen depicting the Apollo spacecraft, in original multi-coloured box.

11in (28cm) high

£100-150   **W&W**

A Japanese Engine Robot battery operated toy, by JH, with clear plastic box containing gear mechanism, blinking lights and swinging arms.

9in (23cm) high

£250-350   **RSJ**

A CLOSER LOOK AT A ROBOT

His head can be inverted to make a watering can, with the handle modelled as an ear. His body can be converted into a sand pail, which can be used with the spade that forms the carrying handle.

The lid of the pail can be used as a sieve and the legs make excellent sand moulds.

This rather unusual, comparatively simple looking robot has no mechanised parts but comes apart to make further toys to be played with.

Sand or earth would have scratched the lithographs and water rusted the tin plated material, but as he is in incredible condition with no dents, he must have rarely or never been played with!

An American Wolverine tinplate 'Mr Sandman Robot', with wooden arms and fragment of original box with instructions on his use.

c1956   *11in (28cm) high*

£400-500   **RSJ**

A 1960s Japanese 'Super Robot' mechanical wind-up toy, by Noguchi, with flashing lights and rotating arms, marked "N", complete with original box.

This unusual robot is wound by turning the yellow plastic arms. Once in motion, his arms hit the floor and move him in other directions.

5.5in (14cm) high

£150-250   **RSJ**

A Japanese Naito Shoten Deep Sea Robot, the tinplate wind-up toy marked "AN JAPAN", on the back.

Modern reproductions of this robot are known - they are taller than this authentic example and have plain, undecorated backpacks. They are also typically marked with a ToM logo.

7.75in (19.5cm) high

£550-650   **RSJ**

A Japanese mechanical toy spaceman, by SY, with spinning antenna and flapping feet, with 'NASA' insignia on shoulder, complete with original box.

6.5in (16.5cm) high

£280-320   **RSJ**

A Japanese tinplate clockwork toy robot, modelled as a spaceman.

5.5in (14cm) high

£40-60   **F**

A Japanese Yoshiya 'Mr Chief' smoking toy robot, by KO.

This is the hardest to find of the Yoshiya 'skirt' bodied robots, hence his high value. A small tube projecting from his domed head emits smoke which is puffed out by small bellows in the mechanism, hence his rather odd name. On the box he is called 'Chief Smokey', but the chest is marked 'Mr Chief'.

c1965   *11.75in (30cm) high*

£700-900   **RSJ**

A Japanese 'Moon Creature' mechanical toy, made by Louis Marx, box bears legend "Moves forward with mouth movement and sound".

A variation with the uniform depicted on the box is also known.

c1968   *6in (15cm) high*

£80-120   **RSJ**

A 1960s Japanese Space Radar Pilot battery powered tinplate and plastic toy, made by Asakusa Toy Co., for Asahi Trading Co., with handlebar controls, automatic stop action and mystery movement, with three discs that eject from launch point to the front of the craft, the plastic pilot with moveable arms, with original box.

8.25in (21cm) wide

£100-150 W&W

A Japanese Masudaya tinplate and plastic Space Capsule 3481, with battery powered mystery action, flashing lights and sound, two astronauts in nose cone, a landing ring for the floating astronaut, marked "TM, Japan", in original picture box and packing.

10in (25.5cm) wide

£120-180 W&W

A 1950s 'Friendship No. 7' battery operated tinplate spaceship, with spaceman dangling from rotating arm and driver with moving hands, complete with original box.

7.5in (19cm) wide

£250-350 RSJ

A Japanese tinplate wind-up robotic dog, with flapping ears and opening mouth.

7.25in (18.5cm) wide

£100-150 RSJ

A scarce Planet Explorer tinplate toy vehicle, by Alps of Japan, in silver litho blue tinplate, with mystery action, printed tracks, light to turret and moving twin guns, battery powered, on four small rubber wheels, with original box.

11.25in (28.5cm) wide

£120-180 W&W

A scarce Eagle Comic Dan Dare pocket watch, by Ingersoll, the face with a compass in unusual hand position rotates with movement, an engraved Eagle Comic logo on the reverse.

c1963 *2.75in (7cm) diam*

£150-200 W&W

A 1960s Japanese Nomura tinplate and plastic Lunar Bulldozer, battery operated mystery movement, with orange tinplate body, rotating action, with flashing lights, blue plastic half tracks and rear wheels, side handle for yellow dozer blade, "NASA" symbol to body, marked "TN, Japan", in original box.

10in (25.5cm) wide

£120-180 W&W

A Japanese SH model of an American space capsule, battery powered, in tinplate and plastic, a blue lithographed finish to the capsule body, the cockpit window showing an astronaut figure, a rotating beacon and two spring aerials, "United States NASA" to sides, some damage to canopy.

10.75in (27.5cm) wide

£70-100 W&W

A Japanese Masudaya X07 Space Surveillant tinplate and plastic toy craft, with battery powered mechanism, marked "TM, Japan", in original box.

c1963 *9in (23cm) wide*

£150-250 W&W

A scarce Dan Dare space control station, by Merit, comprising multi-colour plastic radio station, two remote handsets, an operating morse code key for hand set and a flashlight, with log book pad and instruction booklet, in original box.

box 13.75in (35cm) wide

£200-300 W&W

COLLECTORS' NOTES

- Lead figures and in particular soldiers, have been collected since the 19th century. William Britain, established in 1845, revolutionised the industry in 1893 when he developed a hollow-cast process using less materials, thus enabling him to undercut his competitors. To this day, Britains are one of the most sought-after manufacturers primarily due to their quality and accuracy and many collectors focus on this maker.

- Other makers of note include Mignot (1825-), Charbens (1920-55), John Hill (1898-1960) and Pixyland (c1920-33). Manufacturers often marked their names on the bases, so look here if you are unsure.

- After WWI, the popularity of soldiers waned and domestic themes such as farming, gardening and zoo became more popular. Interest grew at the time of Queen Elizabeth's Coronation and figures based on characters from the new children's television programmes helped maintain this for a short while, but by the beginning of the 1960s, lead had been replaced by cheaper plastic figures.

- Collectors look for good quality figures with fine detailing that retain their original paintwork as well as unusual characters or variations. Repainted and replaced or missing parts will detract from the value, so examine pieces closely. Boxes add value, particularly if in good condition or from a smaller manufacturer.

A 1960s scarce Britains set of 10 Hommes De Corvee (fatigue party), by C.B.G. Mignot, comprising 10 figures each with a wheelbarrow, broom, pick, shovel, bucket, two water cans, sack, billie can, set of four billie cans or a wood bale, all dressed in gloss white fatigue smock, red trousers and black cap.

2.75in (7cm) high

£250-300   **W&W**

A Britains British Infantry active service dress with helmets and gas masks set 258, comprising eight figures matching at the trail, in original Whisstock box. *c1927*

2.25in (5.5cm) high

£70-90   **W&W**

A 1930s Britains Royal Engineers General Service wagon set 1331, comprising of a two horse limbered wagon, in peaked cap service dress at the gallop.

8.25in (21cm) long

£220-280   **W&W**

A Britains Belgian Infantry set 1389, comprising eight Ors marching rifles at the slope, in khaki service dress greatcoats with packs and steel helmets, in original box. *1935*

2.75in (7cm) high

£150-200   **W&W**

A Britains set No.1611 gas mask men, comprising of seven men with rifles and fixed bayonets and an officer with a sword and pistol to hand, in original box.

3in (7.5cm) high

£80-120   **W&W**

A Britains RA regiment Gunners with shells set 1730, comprising four kneeling and three standing figures, all in khaki paint with moving arms, shells and steel helmets, all banded to original box, with Whisstock label.

c1939   *tallest 2.25in (5.5cm) high*

£80-120   **W&W**

A scarce Britains Danish Guard Hussar regiment set 2018, comprising of six men with swords and an officer, all on brown horses, and a trumpeter on a grey horse, in original box.

3.25in (8.5cm) high

£350-400   **W&W**

A rare Britains King George VI figure, in the uniform of Colonel-in-Chief of the Welsh Guards, produced to commemorate the Royal visit to South Africa, with unusual flat base.

c1947

3in (7.5cm) high

£600-800   **W&W**

A Britains Farm Series 5F Farm Wagon, dark green wagon, red wheels, non-matching brown horses, wagon floor has paint loss, carter with whip, very good condition, contained in a poor faded box, old tears, marks and repairs.

£70-100　　　　　　　　　　**VEC**

A Britains Set 161 Boy Scouts 1925 version, comprising scout master together with eight various scouts marching, two missing arms, with poles, very good condition, contained in a good condition box with illustrated label, lid paper lifting.

£180-220　　　　　　　　　　**VEC**

A Britains Hunt Series Set 1447 Full Cry, comprising galloping huntsman and huntswoman, side saddle, a fox and seven hounds, all very good condition.

£100-150　　　　　　　　　　**VEC**

A Britains Knight of Agincourt No. 1662 Mounted Knight with standard, excellent condition, in very good condition 'stone' type box, no insert.

£100-150　　　　　　　　　　**VEC**

A Britains Set 1664, Knights of Agincourt, five Foot Knights in various poses, excellent condition, in good condition box with Historical Series Label, small lid edge missing, no insert.

£120-180　　　　　　　　　　**VEC**

A Britains The Aga Khan Racing Colours, excellent condition, in very good condition box name label missing.

£220-280　　　　　　　　　　**VEC**

Seven Britains Cowboys on foot, various poses, excellent condition, in very good condition box with illustrated label, end label missing, lid edge has two tears.

£180-220　　　　　　　　　　**VEC**

A Britains 'Sunderland' Famous Football Teams Series, comprising ten footballers, goalkeeper and referee, goalpost, three corner flags, one base missing, excellent condition, with only minor chipping and paint loss unstrung and contained in a very good condition green box with illustrated label, three lid corners torn, one box base side partially crushed.

£1,000-1,500　　　　　　　　　　**VEC**

A Britains Circus Series Roundabout, six children on horses, cardboard ring and canopy with original hollowcast central organ.

This rare toy, first issued in 1936, is of an unusual subject and is in good condition, making it desirable.

£3,000-4,000　　　　　　　　　　**VEC**

A Charbens Costermonger's Cart, with man, donkey and two baskets of produce, good condition.

£35-45   **CHEF**

A Charbens, No.817 Tip Cart, yellow cart, red wheels and shafts, brown horse, excellent condition, in very good condition box.

£70-100   **VEC**

A Charbens Horse-Drawn Baker's Delivery Van, with horse and baker carrying basket, damage to van shaft, fair condition, in fair condition box.

£180-220   **CHEF**

A Charbens The Farm Wagon, green cart, red wheels, shafts and racks, brown horse, carter in yellow smock, very good condition, in good illustrated box.

£80-120   **VEC**

A Charbens Horse Drawn Tar Boiler from the Roadmenders set, together with watchman's hut, brazier, 'No Road' sign, two hurdles, also workmen with pickaxe, pneumatic drill, standing with shovel, digging with shovel, broken end.

£280-320   **VEC**

A Charbens Horse Roller from the Roadmenders set, together with a nightwatchman, watchman's hut and brazier, 'No Road' sign, three barrier supports, and two poles, all very good condition.

£120-180   **VEC**

Twenty Charbens Animals, including a crocodile, three monkeys, two lion cubs, pelican, tiger cub, polar bear, two moose, two walrus, a rhinoceros, bison, ostrich, goat and zebra.

£100-150   **VEC**

A Charbens No.500 Gypsy Caravan, comprising a blue caravan, tan wheels and shafts, brown horse, gypsy wife with baby, stool and washing line, mainly good condition, caravan roof has paint loss, contained in a fair/good condition box, end of lid and label missing.

£300-350   **VEC**

A Charbens Circus Figures set, comprising ringmaster, clown with hands in pockets, strongman with barbells, unicyclist, clown on stilts, clown with hoop and dog, acrobat on chair and policeman with truncheon.

£300-350   **VEC**

A John Hill Wedding Party, comprisᵒing two brides in white, one with hand broken, one bride in blue, no painted detail, hand broken, and one bridesmaid in green, good condition.

£50-70   VEC

A John Hill Tennis Players, two male players with rackets across their body, one male with overhead racket, also female player with racket to side, all good/very good condition.

£100-150   VEC

A John Hill Millers Series, corn bin, miller, man carrying sack, four various sacks, sack barrow, rare rat, pigsty, all very good condition.

£120-180   VEC

A John Hill Pirates Series, Captain Hook, pirate with eye patch, cutlass and pistol, Long John Silver with bottle, with hook hand and sitting on a barrel with accordion, all good/very good condition, except Captain Hook which is fair, hole to back and paint loss.

£180-220   VEC

A John Hill Police Issues series, motorcycle with sidecar, rider and cast in observer, together with a patrolman on motorcycle, both excellent condition.

£180-220   VEC

A John Hill Street Gas Lamp Set, comprising lamp, ladder and lighter, all very good condition, in very good condition box with illustrated label.

£150-200 VEC

A John Hill Blacksmith's Set, comprising a forge, blacksmith, anvil, horse, latter with broken hoof.

£70-100   VEC

A John Hill Stage Coach, brown coach, red wheels, pair of brown horses, driver and guard, all excellent condition, in very good condition box with illustrated label.

£150-200   VEC

A John Hill Stage Coach display set, comprising a standard stage coach, two horse team, driver and guard together with small scale figures, three standing cowboys firing rifles, two kneeling firing pistols, three Indians standing firing, two kneeling with bows and arrows, with box and illustrated label, end missing, lid end missing, old marks.

£200-250   VEC

A Pixyland Kew Father Christmas, together with a rare Town Crier, both in very good condition.

£60-80 each   VEC

A Pixyland Kew Lyons 'Nippy' Waitress, a rare promotional item, very good condition.

£100-150   VEC

A rare 1930s Kew Chicks on a Log, very good condition, together with a Gardener bending over to flower, fair/good condition.

£60-70   VEC

A Pixyland Kew Farmer with pitchfork, together with a scarecrow, tramp, landgirl with bucket and a dog, all good/very good condition.

£70-90   VEC

A rare Pixyland Kew figure of Monk, together with two girls in red coats, a small scale postman with sack, man carrying can, chimney sweep and a painted figure of man with cudgel.

£90-120   VEC

A large scale Pixyland Kew Man with hands in his pockets, together with a postman with sack, hand broken, postman with moveable arm, butcher with side of beef, another with knife, repainted man in trilby hat and a Huntswoman, side-saddle.

£80-120   VE

Ten Pixyland Kew Animals, comprising a camel, zebra, two hippopotami, a tiger, gorilla, ibis, mule, two peacocks, one with open plumage.

£100-150   VEC

Twenty six Pixyland Kew Farm Animals, including three cows, three bulls, swan, large cockerel, sheep dog, three ducks, begging dog, spitting cat, goose, rabbit and ten further animals and birds.

£50-70   VE

A Crescent Bullfighter, in full Spanish ceremonial dress including red cape, together with a charging bull, one bull's horn broken.

£55-65 VEC

A Crescent Highwayman on horse and foot, together with a civilian stretcher party with stretcher and patient, and a Dan Dare figure marching in green uniform, all good/very good condition.

£80-120 VEC

An Elastolin Wild West Covered Wagon, brown tin wagon, blue tin wheels, cotton tilt, driver with whip, two horses on wooden bases which also have four tin wheels, wagon driver, good, horses poor to fair condition.

£35-45 VEC

A rare Elastolin 2-D Wild West covered wagon, appearing flat to one side, broken shaft, very good condition, together with an Indian totem pole, man tied to tree, tomahawk missing, Indian tepee, camp fire with hanging meat and rock formation, all very good condition, minor damages.

£45-55 VEC

A F.G. Taylor Blacksmith set, comprising forge, horse, blacksmith, anvil, horseshoe, all very good condition, in fair/good condition illustrated box.

£100-150 VEC

A Taylor and Barrett Elephant Ride, elephant, keeper, keeper with fish, plastic elephant keeper and two children, all very good condition.

£80-120 VEC

A Timpo Station Passengers, porter carrying luggage, signalman with flag and whistle, railwayman with lamps, Mr. Brown, Mr. & Mrs Smith and soldier with kitbag, mainly very good condition.

£80-120 VEC

Timpo Arctic Series Sledge with Dog Team, together with an Eskimo with whip, shooting rifle and walking, polar bear, two penguins, all very good condition.

£55-65 VEC

A rare and unusual 18 piece set comprising mounted and foot Cowboys and Indians, by an unknown maker, depicting models by Timpo, Benbros etc, all very good condition and contained in a fair condition plain cardboard box, insert dirty and a little creased.

£200-250 VEC

COLLECTORS' NOTES

■ Action Man was released in 1966 by British maker Palitoy, and soon beat off his rival 'Tommy Gunn' produced by Pedigree. The basic jointed figure, based initially on the American 'G.I. Joe,' underwent a number of changes. Knowledge of these changes allows the collector to match the correct period figure to the relevant uniform.

■ The earliest figures had moulded and painted hair, used until 1969. 'Realistic' flock hair was used from 1970-76, gripping hands were introduced in 1973, and 'eagle eyes' used from 1977. In 1978, Action Man was remodelled and gained moulded blue pants. This model lasted until 1984, when the figure was discontinued due to the growing popularity of smaller action figures, particularly from the Star Wars range.

■ Despite being re-launched in 1993, collectors prefer examples from the late 1960s/70s, which is considered by many the gold age of Action Man. The uniforms of this time were incredibly complex and well made, with the most sought after being the ceremonial uniforms.

■ Always try to buy examples in the best possible condition, as so many were produced and played with, only the best will appeal to collectors unless extremely rare.

A 'Parachute Regiment' Action Man figure, by Palitoy.

The cloth beret was from the first issue of this uniform and is rare. Like many small items that were lost, it can be valuable today.

c1970   *11.5in (29cm) high*

£60-80   **NBC**

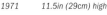

A 1970s 'Royal Marine Commando' Action Man figure, by Palitoy.

11.5in (29cm) high

£60-80   **NBC**

A 1960s 'British WWII Infantryman' Action Man figure, by Palitoy.

11.5in (29cm) high

£60-80   **NBC**

A 'British Sailor' Action Man figure, by Palitoy.

1971   *11.5in (29cm) high*

£50-70   **NBC**

A 1960s 'Navy Dress Parade Sailor' Action Man figure, by Palitoy.

11.5in (29cm) high

£70-100   **NBC**

A 1960s 'German Stormtrooper' Action Man figure, by Palitoy.

This uniform is the first from the 'Soldiers of The Century' series introduced in 1967. The helmet, first version of the belt and undamaged gun are the most collectable items.

11.5in (29cm) high

£70-100   **NBC**

A 1970s 'British Army Officer' Action Man figure, by Palitoy.

This uniform, released in 1972, features a shirt and elasticated tie, and shoes and socks, rather than just boots. This example, like many, lacks the rare baton.

11.5in (29cm) high

£70-100   **NBC**

A 1970s 'British Military Police' Action Man figure, by Palitoy.

A less expensive 'carded' version of this uniform was released in the 1980s, known as 'Front Liners'. It lacked the weapon, shirt and tie.

11.5in (29cm) high

£60-80   **NB**

A CLOSER LOOK AT AN ACTION MAN UNIFORM

This uniform is from the 'Ceremonials' range from the 'Famous British Uniforms' series introduced in 1970. It is renowned for its accuracy and detail due to design assistance from the regiment itself.

It is complete and undamaged - the helmet is particular is easily damaged - and was meant more for display than play.

It was first released in 1971 as 'The Royal Horseguards' (The Blues), but as the regiment had merged with the 'Royal Dragoons' (The Royals) in 1969, the name was soon changed.

It is similar to the Life Guards outfit, which has a red coat and a white plume - the cuirass (breast plate) did not come with the uniform and had to be purchased separately to complete it.

A 'Blues & Royals' Action Man figure, by Palitoy.
1971   *11.5in (29cm) high*
£150-200   **NBC**

A 'Red Devil Parachutist' Action Man figure, by Palitoy.

This uniform included a parachute that worked, enabling the hero to actually parachute into any dangerous situation.
1968   *11.5in (29cm) high*
£55-65   **NBC**

A 1980s 'Battle of Britain Pilot' Action Man figure, by Palitoy.

This uniform was launched in 1980 to commemorate the 40th anniversary of The Battle of Britain and is sought after by Action Man collectors and militaria collectors due to its incredible accuracy.
                              11.5in (29cm) high
£70-100   **NBC**

A 1970s 'Polar Explorer' Action Man figure, by Palitoy
11.5in (29cm) high
£70-90   **NBC**

A 1970s 'Crash Crew' Action Man figure, by Palitoy.
11.5in (29cm) high
£50-70   **NBC**

A 1970s 'Mountain Rescue' Action Man figure, by Palitoy.
11.5in (29cm) high
50-70   **NBC**

A 1960s 'Jungle Explorer' Action Man figure, by Palitoy.
11.5in (29cm) high
£50-70   **NBC**

A 1960s 'French Resistance Fighter' Action Man figure, by Palitoy.

The shoulder holster and machine gun with an elastic strap are the most sought after items from this uniform.
11.5in (29cm) high
£60-80   **NBC**

COLLECTORS' NOTES

■ The market for Star Wars toys is as strong as ever, as a pensioner in Flintshire discovered in 2003. In the late 1970s, this lady bought two sets of 20 action figures, one set for her grandson to play with and one to put in storage to replace any lost figures.

■ When put up for auction 20 years later, the Palitoy figures which remained in mint condition on their backing cards, made over £10,000. The top sellers were 'Luke Skywalker' and 'Chewbacca' who each made £1,000. In contrast, a standard loose Skywalker action figure would only be worth about £20.

■ The figures were originally issued in a set of 12 in 1978. The card backing featured a picture of all the characters and these, known as '12-backs', are the most desirable. The range was soon expanded to sets of 20 and to sets of 21 with 'Boba Fett'. These '20/21-backs' are also highly sought-after, particularly Boba sets.

■ Eventually, around 100 different figures were released, with a number of variations of each the figure.

■ In 1995, after a gap of nearly a decade, Kenner started making Star Wars toys again. These were called "The Power of the Force", reusing the name from the rare 1985 line. The action figure market had changed in those 10 years so the figures were re-modelled to be more muscular. At first these models were poorly received but interest from collectors grows slowly and the market continues to expand. Look for characters with lightsabers that have the re-issued short weapon in the original long tray in the packaging – it can be a valuable variation.

■ Condition and packaging also affect value when considering other toys such as vehicles or playsets. Look for complete examples and rare variations; invest in a specialist price guide, which lists the variations and their comparative values.

A Star Wars 'Luke Skywalker' large action figure, by Kenner, complete with lightsaber, grappling hook, boots and utility belt.

Kenner made 12 different large size figures between 1979 and 1980. The last was 'IG-88', issued in an 'Empire Strikes Back' box, and is the hardest to find.

1979-80   *12in (30.5cm) high*

£45-55   **W&W**

A Star Wars 'Princess Leia Organa' large action figure, by Kenner, lacks shoes, comb, brush and booklet.

1979-80

12in (30.5cm) high

£30-40   **W&W**

A Star Wars 'Darth Vader' large action figure, by General Mills Fun Group, lacks lightsaber.

1979-80

15in (38cm) high

£25-35   **W&W**

A Star Wars 'C-3PO' large size action figure, by General Mills Fun Group.

c1978

12.5in (31.5cm) high

£20-30   **W&W**

A Star Wars 'R2-D2' large size action figure, by General Mills Fun Group, plastic yellowed.

c1979

7.5in (19cm) high

£15-20   **W&W**

A Star Wars 'Boba Fett' large action figure, by Kenner, lacks equipment.

1979-80

13in (33cm) high

£15-20   **W&W**

A Star Wars 'Stormtrooper' large action figure, by General Mills Fun Group, with laser rifle, some age mottling to plastic.

1979-80

12in (30.5cm) high

£20-40   **W&W**

A Star Wars 'Death Star Droid' action figure.

c1979 *3.75in (9.5cm) high*

£10-15 KF

A Star Wars 'Hammerhead' action figure.

c1979 *4in (10cm) high*

£6-8 KF

A Star Wars 'Power Droid' action figure.

c1979 *2.5in (6.5cm) high*

£10-15 KF

A Star Wars 'R5-D4' action figure.

c1979 *2.5in (6.5cm) high*

£10-15 KF

A Star Wars 'Snaggletooth' action figure.

c1979 *3in (7.5cm) high*

£8-12 KF

A Star Wars - The Empire Strikes Back 'Lobot' action figure.

c1981 *3.75in (9.5cm) high*

£4-6 KF

A Star Wars - The Empire Strikes Back 'Bossk (Bounty Hunter)' action figure.

1980 *3.75in (9.5cm) high*

6-8 KF

A Star Wars - Return of the Jedi 'Bib Fortuna' action figure.

c1983 *4in (10cm) high*

£5-7 KF

A Star Wars - Return of the Jedi 'Han Solo in Carbonite Chamber' action figure with chamber.

c1985 *4.75in (12cm) high*

£40-60 KF

A Star Wars 'Patrol Dewback' figure, by Kenner, from the re-issued Collector Series, complete with saddle and reins, boxed.

The original version from 1979, identical except for the red 'sunburst' decal in the corner of the box is worth half as much again as this re-issue.

c1983   Box 11in (28cm) wide

£20-40   **W&W**

A Star Wars - Return of the Jedi tri-logo 'Sy Snootles and the Rebo Band' figures multi-pack, boxed.

c1984   Box 9.25in (23.5cm) wide

£20-30   **W&W**

A Star Wars - Power of the Force (II) 'Luke Skywalker and Tauntaun' figures, by Kenner, in green box.

c1998   Box 11in (28cm) wide

£8-12   **W&W**

A Star Wars - Power of the Force (II) 'Wampa with Luke Skywalker' figures, by Kenner, in green box.

c1998   Box 11in (28cm) wide

£10-15   **W&W**

A Star Wars 'Jawa' action figure, by Meccano, with cloth cape, on 20-back card.

Originally issued with a vinyl cape, it was quickly replaced with a cloth version as it was deemed 'cheap' looking. Vinyl examples are considerably more valuable, but fakes with other capes exist.

c1978

£40-60   **W&W**

c1980

£40-60

A Star Wars - The Empire Strikes Back 'Han Solo (Hoth Outfit)' action figure, by Palitoy, on 30-back card.

9in (22.5cm) high

W&W

A Star Wars - Return of the Jedi 'Ree-Yees' action figure, by Kenner, on 65-back card.

c1983   9in (22.5cm) high

£10-15   **W&W**

A Star Wars - The Empire Strikes Back 'Luke Skywalker (Hoth Battle Gear)' action figure, by Palitoy, in opened bubble pack.

c1982   9in (22.5cm) high

£30-40   **W&W**

A Star Wars - Return of the Jedi 'General Madine' action figure, by Kenner.

c1983   9in (22.5cm) high

£8-12   **W&W**

A Star Wars - Return of the Jedi tri-logo 'Death Star Droid' action figure, by Palitoy, bubble pack opened.

This multi-lingual packaging was intended to save money on a range losing public interest. These figures often have variations not found on standard US or UK figures.

1984-86 9in (22.5cm) high
£30-40 W&W

A Star Wars - Return of the Jedi tri-logo 'Luke Skywalker (in Battle Poncho)' action figure, by Palitoy.

1984-86 9in (22.5cm) high
£50-60 W&W

A Star Wars - Return of the Jedi 'Weequay' action figure, by Kenner, on 70-back card.

1984-86 9in (22.5cm) high
£12-18 W&W

A Star Wars - Return of the Jedi tri-logo 'Weequay' action figure, by Kenner, on 70-back card.
9in (22.5cm) high
W&W

A Star Wars - The Power of the Force 'Barada' action figure, by Kenner, on 92-back card, with special collectors coin.

Two years after 'Return of the Jedi' had been released, Kenner reissued 22 existing and 15 new figures in new packaging with a collectors coin. The ploy failed and few were bought. Today they are some of the rarest figures, particularly those only released outside the US.

A Star Wars - Shadows of the Empire 'Chewbacca' action figure, by Kenner, in 'Bounty Hunter Disguise', on multi-language red header card.

The Shadows of the Empire range of figures are based on the book and computer game of the same name that takes place between 'The Empire Strikes Back' and 'Return of the Jedi'.

c1996 9in (22.5cm) high
£3-4 W&W

c1985 9in (22.5cm) high
£60-80 W&W

An Italian Star Wars - Shadows of the Empire 'Luke Skywalker' action figure, by GIG under license to Kenner, in 'Imperial Guard Disguise', on red header card.

c1996 9in (22.5cm) high
£5-8 W&W

A Star Wars - The Power of the Force (II) 'Han Solo in Hoth Gear' action figure, by Kenner, on multi-language red header card.

c1996 9in (22.5cm) high
£5-8 W&W

A Star Wars - The Power of the Force (II) 'Luke Skywalker Jedi Knight' Theatre Edition action figure, by Kenner, on green header card, with Special Edition trilogy logo.

c1997 9in (22.5cm) high
£5-8 W&W

A Star Wars - The Power of the Force (II) 'Princess Leia' action figure, by Kenner, from Collection 1, on green Freeze Frame header card.

c1997 9in (22.5cm) high
£3-4 W&W

A Star Wars 'Landspeeder' vehicle, by Palitoy, mint condition in slightly worn box.

c1978

£60-80 W&W

A Star Wars - Return of the Jedi 'Scout Walker' vehicle, by Kenner.

c1982 *Box 11.5in high*

£12-18 W&W

A Star Wars - The Empire Strikes Back 'Millenium Falcon Spaceship' vehicle, by Palitoy, lacks lightsaber and radar screen, labels used, boxed.

c1977

£70-90 W&W

A Star Wars - Return of the Jedi 'Imperial Shuttle' vehicle, by Palitoy, boxed.

c1983 *18in (45.5cm) high*

£220-280 W&W

A Star Wars - Return of the Jedi 'Millennium Falcon' vehicle, by Palitoy, lacks ramp, boxed.

c1983

£50-80 W&W

A French Star Wars - Return of the Jedi 'Rebel Armoured Snowspeeder' vehicle, by Meccano.

c1983 *12.5in (32cm) wide*

£12-18 W&W

A Star Wars - The Power of the Force (II) 'TIE Fighter', by Kenner, with ejecting solar panel wings, in red box.

c1995 Box 11.5in (29cm) wide

£5-10 W&W

A Star Wars - The Power of the Force (II) 'Cruisemissile Trooper' vehicle, by Kenner, in green box.

c1997 Box 10.5in (26.5cm) wide

£4-8 W&W

A Star Wars -The Power of the Force (II) 'Darth Vader's TIE Fighter' vehicle, by Kenner, with multi-language green box.

c1997 Box 12in (30.5cm) wide

£10-15 W&W

A Star Wars - The Empire Strikes Back 'Radar Laser Cannon' accessory, by Kenner, boxed.

c1983

£7-9   **W&W**

A Star Wars - Return of the Jedi 'Vehicle Maintenance Energizer' accessory, by Kenner, sealed in box.

c1983   Box 6in (15cm) high

£7-10   **W&W**

A Star Wars - Return of the Jedi 'Ewok Assault Catapult', by Kenner, complete in box.

c1984   Box 6in (15cm) high

£7-10   **W&W**

A Star Wars - Return of the Jedi 'Ewok Combat Glider' accessory, by Kenner.

c1984   Box 6in (15cm) high

£7-10   **W&W**

A Star Wars - Return of the Jedi 'ISP-6 (Imperial Shuttle Pod)' mini-rig, by Kenner.

c1983   Box 6in (15cm) high

£6-8   **W&W**

A Star Wars - Return of the Jedi tri-logo 'Endor Forest Ranger' mini rig, by Palitoy, boxed.

c1984   Box 9in (23cm) wide

£10-15   **W&W**

A Star Wars 'Cantina' playset, by Palitoy, complete and boxed.

c1979   18in (45.5cm) wide

£100-150   **W&W**

A Star Wars - Return of the Jedi 'Jabba The Hut Dungeon' action playset, by Kenner, version two, complete and including 'EV-9D9', 'Amanaman' and 'Barada' action figures, in red box with instructions.

Version two was exclusive to Sears department store. Version one included with 'Klaatu', 'Nikto' and '8D8' is worth less than half of this version.

c1984   13.25in (33.5cm) wide

£80-120   **W&W**

A Star Wars - Return of the Jedi tri-logo 'One-Man Sail Skiff' mini-rig.

Also seen as 'Desert Sail Skiff' on standard boxes.

c1984   Box 5.5in (14cm) high

£6-8   **W&W**

A Star Wars 'Escape from the Death Star' board game, by Kenner.

c1979   *Box 18.25in (46.5cm) wide*

£6-8   **W&W**

A Star Wars 'Adventures of R2-D2' board game, by Parker.

c1977   *Box 17in (43cm) wide*

£6-9   **W&W**

A Star Wars 140-piece jigsaw puzzle, by Kenner, with a picture of Luke and Han in the Death Star trash compacter.

This puzzle is worth slightly more with a blue box.

1977-79

£3-4   **W&W**

A Star Wars 'Authentic R2-D2 (Artoo Detoo)' model kit, by Denys Fisher, complete and unmade.

c1977   *10in (25.5cm) high*

£8-12   **W&W**

A Star Wars - The Empire Strikes Back 'Slave I' model kit, by Airfix, complete and unmade.

c1980   *Box 14in (35.5cm) wide*

£10-15   **W&W**

A Star Wars 'Authentic C-3PO (See-Threepio)' model kit, by Denys Fisher, complete and unmade.

c1977   *10in (25.5cm) high*

£8-12   **W&W**

A Star Wars electronic 'Talking R2-D2', by Micro Games of America, carded.

c1995   *11in (28cm) high*

£4-5   **W&W**

A Star Wars 'Chewbacca' stuffed plush toy, by Kenner, with utility belt and original card tag, in mint condition.

c1977   *20.5in (52cm) high*

£70-90   **KNK**

A scarce Star Wars - The Empire Strikes Back 'Yoda' Magic 8-Ball fortune teller figure, by Kenner, the base with transparent plastic window revealing the liquid-filled body, with a white plastic dodecagonal dice with Yoda-style phrases such as 'Ready are you, no' and 'Certain I cannot be'.

c1981   *5.25in (13.5cm) hig*

£20-25   **KN**

A set of Star Wars - Return of The Jedi bubble gum cards, by Topps, unopened.

c1983   *3.5in (9cm) high*

£2-3   **KNK**

A Star Wars 'Darth Vader' plastic lunch box, by King Seeley Thermos.

c1978   *10in (25.5cm) wide*

£3-4   **W&W**

A Star Wars - The Empire Strikes Back 'Yoda' thermos flask, by King Seeley-Thermos.

c1980   *6.5in (16.5cm) high*

£2-4   **W&W**

An unused Star Wars 'C-3PO' bath-size soap bar.

c1978   *5.5in (14cm) high*

£1-2   **KNK**

A Star Wars 'Darth Vader' Pez dispenser, and a 'Stormtrooper' Pez dispenser, both carded.

c1997   *8.5in (21.5cm) high*

£1-2 each   **W&W**

Two Star Wars - Return of the Jedi toothbrushes, by Oral-B, comprising 'Darth Vader' and 'C-3PO and R2-D2', together with an Oral-B Dental Health Adventure Book.

c1983   *Book 6.75in (17cm) high*

£7-10   **W&W**

Seven Star Wars badges, including Darth Vader, R2-D2, C-3PO, Return of the Jedi, and others.

Pins are popular with collectors, but are easy to make and largely unlicensed. Most are worth between 50p-£1, the licensed ones being more desirable.

Largest 2in (5cm) diam

50p-£1 each   **W&W**

A Star Wars - Return of the Jedi 'Imperial Storm Trooper' costume and mask, by Acamus Toys.

c1982

£15-20   **W&W**

A rare Star Wars outfit pattern sheet, by McCall's, for 'Chewbacca', 'Leia', 'Yoda', a 'Jawa' and 'Darth Vader', in medium size, with instructions, contained in original envelope.

c1981   *8in (20cm) wide*

£10-15   **KNK**

FIND OUT MORE...

'Tomart's Price Guide to Worldwide "Star Wars" Collectibles', *by Stephen J. Sansweet, published by Tomart Publications, 1997.*

www.starwars.com - *official company website.*

www.toysrgus.com - *database of merchandise.*

A scarce Victory Models remote control battery operated Coles Ranger truck-mounted crane, finished in mustard-yellow, black, fair condition, missing some parts for jib attachment and other pieces, in fair condition box.

£300-400 VEC

A Mamod live steam model SR1A Road Roller, in original box.

box 11.25in (28.5cm) wide

£40-60 F

A Tri-ang Minic clockwork Series II Nuffield tractor, key missing, boxed.

£50-70 CHEF

An early Lesney large scale Massey Harris 745D tractor, the red body with gold detailing, yellow wheel hubs and front steerable axle with black rubber tyres, exhaust pipe detached but present.

£100-150 W&W

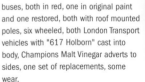

A pair of 1930s T&B cast lead trolley buses, both in red, one in original paint and one restored, both with roof mounted poles, six wheeled, both London Transport vehicles with "617 Holborn" cast into body, Champions Malt Vinegar adverts to sides, one set of replacements, some wear.

£80-120 W&W

A Märklin Metall box set 101/2, black and red, mostly complete.

Märklin changed the colour of their boxes relatively frequently, at certain points choosing red to match Meccano's of the time.

£400-500 LAN

A rare Victory Models battery powered Rapier mobile crane, orange, grey, black, excellent condition, slight marks to front wings, complete with leaflets, in good condition box, some sellotape marks to sides.

£700-800 VEC

A Märklin Metall polychrome box set 105/2, two layers, including sprockets, brass cogwheels and axle gears, mostly complete, in original box.

German Märklin Metall sets were direct competitors to the British Meccano sets. Märklin had a relationship with Meccano as German distributor from 1912, but upon the outbreak of war in 1914, Märklin took over all Meccano's rights and sold their own sets. The company came into its own when it stopped supporting the war effort in 1919. The 1930s were the golden age for Märklin, and the number of parts in the sets increased - there were over 700 parts in the biggest set in 1930. After 1947 fewer components were less tightly packed in larger boxes. The trademark of the company was a boy proudly standing next to a crane. Märklin Metall ceased production in 2000.

c1954

£650-850 LAN

A Victory Models conveyancer fork truck, finished in red and black, complete with three pallets, forks, instruction leaflets and original receipt, excellent condition including box.

£250-300 VE

A CLOSER LOOK AT A NOAH'S ARK

The figures and ark are made from 'Elastolin' the trade name for composition products made by German maker Hausser.

The ark pieces are made of a china clay powder mixed with sawdust and glue, which was heated and moulded around a wire frame.

A Märklin Metall box set 4, black, two layers, including propellers and chains, original box partly damaged.

£120-180 LAN

A Tri-ang plastic clockwork Indian elephant, the grey plastic elephant with walking action, upon his back a Howdah with Indian figures.

6.5in (16.5cm) high

£70-100 F

Elastolin was made from around 1910 and was first used for animal figures. This set dates from shortly after 1910.

The Noah's Ark is a traditional toy, popular in the 18th and 19thC as both an educational and moral plaything. Always try to buy examples in as complete condition as possible, although with more modern, mass produced sets such as these, replacement animals can sometimes be found.

A plush-covered clockwork novelty toy, modelled as a monkey wearing a pointed felt hat and playing a drum.

8.5in (21.5cm) high

An Elastolin Noah's Ark, the ark modelled as a log construction, with removable roof, opening door, working rudder and wheeled hull, with a good selection of figures.

ark 22.5in (57cm) wide

£650-850 F

£15-25 F

A cast iron 'walking' elephant, with 1878 patent mark.

An early 20thC American cast iron model of a French bulldog.

11in (28cm) high

3.5in (9cm) wide

A late 19th/early 20thC toy theatre, with printed decoration around the frame of the stage.

12in (30cm) high

180-220 ROS £50-70 ROS £150-250 GORL

TOYS & GAMES

An unusual 1950s German plastic clockwork novelty toy, modelled as two dancing figures on a mirror topped base, marked "Magneto, West German".

4.5in (11.5cm) wide

£12-18   **F**

A large German miniature theatre, by Jos Scholz of Mainz, complete with multiple backgrounds, seven scripts and approximately 150 actor figures.

c1920

£750-850   **ATK**

A 1960s slinky, by James Industries Inc, with box.

box 3.25in (8cm) wide

£10-15   **SOTT**

A Beeju Muffin the Mule toy TV set, by EVB Plastics, dated.

1948   *9.5in (24cm) wide*

£100-150   **DH**

A rare 1950s slinky, by James Industries Inc, with maroon box.

The Slinky was developed in 1945 by naval engineer Richard James, who was experimenting with tension springs to keep ship instruments steady. After dropping it and finding it 'walked', he and his wife decided to make it into an amusing toy. It saw its debut in the Gimbell's department store in Philadelphia in 1946. Since then, over a quarter of a billion Slinkys have been sold. This example is an early one, dating from the early 1950s and retains its rare box and excellent condition - note the difference in the design of the box to the later example above.

box 3.25in (8cm) wide

£15-20   **SOTT**

A large early wooden Pelham puppet, modelled as a skeleton, in original box.

18.5in (47cm) high

£80-120   **F**

A child's miniature white glazed ceramic tea set, with floral transfer decoration, in original box.

8.5in (21.5cm) wide

£12-18   **F**

An unusual 1970s official Batman plastic battery powered Zoomcycle, Batman with a cloak, seated on streamlined blue plastic and chromed motorcycle, separate battery pack which plugs into exhaust pipes to power rear wheel, made in Hong Kong and in original two part window lid box, internal packing, and outer plain card sleeve, almost mint, minor marking to battery box and cape.

£80-120   **W&**

A 1970s Hot Track No. 2 battery-operated model race set, in original box.

box 20in (51cm) wi

£10-20

A 1980s pack of 54 vinyl Nintendo 'Tactics' playing cards, crosshatch design on reverse with large 'T'.

3.75in (9.5cm) high

£15-20 INT

An incomplete set of 1870s De La Rue playing cards, with square corners, no indices, double figures, marked with numbers, reverse design of gold and green flora, eight cards missing.

The lack of indices suggests that these cards predate the 20thC, the double figures (two-headed picture cards) indicate that they are from the latter part of the 18thC as earlier cards had single figures.

3.75in (9.5cm) high

£3-5 INT

A set of 54 vinyl playing cards to commemorate the tri-centenary of Bevis Marks Synagoguc, ace of spades with of Yasha Beresiner, Master of the Worshipful Company of Makers of Playing Cards, reverse with arms of the Company.

A set of cards is commissioned every year for the annual dinner of the Worshipful Company of Makers of Playing Cards and distributed to the Livery only. A mint double pack from 1888 recently sold for £1,600.

2001 *3.25in (8.5cm) long*

£30-40 INT

A set of 50 tarot cards, made by Ferdinand Piatnik & Son, of Vienna.

1908-1928 *4.5in (11.5cm) long*

£35-45 INT

A set of 55 playing cards issued by the US military, to be distributed among Coalition forces in the aftermath of the 2003 war with Iraq, the cards bear portraits of the 52 most wanted members of the Ba'athist regime, the jokers have explanations of Iraqi military ranks and Arab titles, reverse pattern of army camouflage, in original plastic case.

2003 *3.25in (8.5cm) high*

£3-5 INT

A 1930s pack of 52 'Kargo' golf playing cards, made by Castell Brothers of London, complete with instruction booklet in original case.

3.5in (9cm) long

£25-35 INT

1930s pack of Walt Disney 'Silly Symphony' snap cards, by Chad Valley.

Box 4in (10cm) high

£40-60 DG

A Mickey and the Beanstalk card game, by Pepys, taken from Walt Disney's "Fun and Fancy Free".

c1945 *Box 3.5in (9cm) high*

£30-40 DG

A 1950s Famous Five card game.

Box 3.5in (9cm) high

£35-45 DG

A 'L'Attaque - The Game of Military Strategy' board game, by H.P. Gibson & Sons Ltd.

This is a very early version of the game and may well be from the first edition.

c1900   *box 12.5in (31.5cm) wide*

£80-120   **DG**

A 1930s 'Hokus-Pokus' magic set, boxed.

box 15.5in (39.5cm) wide

£80-120   **DG**

A 1940s 'Escalado' horse racing game, by Chad Valley.

box 11in (28cm) wide

£60-80   **D**

A 'Chasing Charlie' game, by Spears.

c1930   12.5in (31.5cm) wide

£60-80   **D**

A 1930s 'Peter Rabbit's Race Game'.

box 21in (53.5cm) high

£80-120   **DG**

A 'Journey by Air' board game, by Spears Games.

c1935   10in (25.5cm) wide

£35-45   **DH**

A 'Table Quoits' game, by Royal Letters Patent, with bone rings.

box 7in (9.5cm) wide

£20-30   **DG**

A 1930s 'Bob's Bridge Game'.

box 15.5in (39.5cm) wide

£55-65   **D**

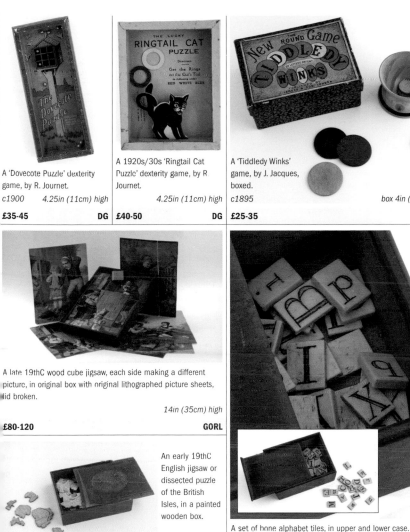

A 'Dovecote Puzzle' dexterity game, by R. Journet.

c1900   *4.25in (11cm) high*

£35-45   **DG**

A 1920s/30s 'Ringtail Cat Puzzle' dexterity game, by R Journet.

4.25in (11cm) high

£40-50   **DG**

A 'Tiddledy Winks' game, by J. Jacques, boxed.

c1895   *box 4in (10cm) wide*

£25-35   **DG**

A late 19thC wood cube jigsaw, each side making a different picture, in original box with original lithographed picture sheets, lid broken.

14in (35cm) high

£80-120   **GORL**

An early 19thC English jigsaw or dissected puzzle of the British Isles, in a painted wooden box.

7in (17.5cm) wide

£100-150   **PC**

A set of bone alphabet tiles, in upper and lower case.

c1900   *box 4in (10cm) wide*

£100-150   **DG**

An octagonal carved bone teetotum, for use with board games.

2.25in (5.5cm) high

45-55   **DG**

A carved ivory spinning top.

c1910   *1in (2.5cm) high*

£20-25   **DG**

A carved ivory spinning top.

c1910   *1in (2.5cm) high*

£20-25   **DG**

COLLECTORS' NOTES

■ Computer games irrevocably redefined children's play during the 1980s and 1990s. They have a growing base of collectors keen to build representative collections and nostalgically revisit the toys of their youth. 'Shoot 'em up' and 'Beat 'em up' games are popular with names such as Nintendo (particularly the Game & Watch series), TOMY and early names such as CGL being sought after.

■ Condition is extremely important and games should be undamaged and complete with their battery covers and preferably boxes and instructions. Games must work and always examine the battery cases for signs of damage from battery leakages.

A Bandai 'Missile Invader' hand-held game.

c1978 3.5in (9cm) wide

£20-30 HLJ

An Entex 'Raise the Devil' hand-held game.

c1980 5in (13cm) wide

£30-40 HLJ

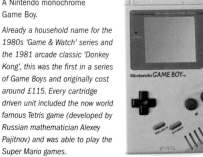

A Nintendo 'Spitball Sparky BU-201' Supercolor game and watch.

This unusual vertically-oriented game used coloured screen overlays to give the impression of colour - an innovative feature.

c1984 5.25in (4.5cm) wide

£100-150 HLJ

An Atari 'Asteroids' record and story book.

c1982

£15-20 HLJ

A Texas Instruments 'Speak & Spell' electronic game.

c1978 15.5in (39.5cm) high

£25-35 DTC

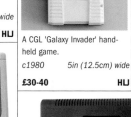

A CGL 'Galaxy Invader' hand-held game.

c1980 5in (12.5cm) wide

£30-40 HLJ

An MB Electronics 'Pocket Simon' game.

Milton Bradey's 'Simon' game debuted at the legendary nightclub 'Studio 54' in 1978 and went on to be a classic 1980s hit.

c1980 7in (18cm) high

£15-20 DT'

A Nintendo monochrome Game Boy.

Already a household name for the 1980s 'Game & Watch' series and the 1981 arcade classic 'Donkey Kong', this was the first in a series of Game Boys and originally cost around £115. Every cartridge driven unit included the now world famous Tetris game (developed by Russian mathematician Alexey Pajitnov) and was able to play the Super Mario games.

c1989 6in (15cm) high

£15-20 PC

An Atari 7800 ProSystem game console, with two games and a controller.

c1984 11.25in (29cm) wid

£15-25 P

COLLECTORS' NOTES

■ From the 1970s onwards, wristwatches with traditional mechanisms had to compete against those with newer, electronic technologies. A range of quartz and tuning fork movements, manual and electronic wind timepieces were all vying for market attention.

■ Case designs from this period are typically large and chunky, and were available in many non-traditional shapes. Bezels are often correspondingly heavy and bold.

■ Space travel was a particularly popular theme, inspiring both the design and names of watches. Andre Le Marquand's 'Spaceman Audacieuse', for example, is a much-valued classic of the period.

■ The design of a watch is often as important as its mechanism, those that sum up the style ethics of the period are often the most popular with collectors.

■ While collectors often concentrate on a particular designer or company, the quality of the mechanism and the iconography of the design, are also important factors to consider.

■ Many watches from this period can be found for sale in their original state, sold as 'old new stock'. They are, however, often purchased to be worn and so the amount of 'old new stock' available is diminishing all the time.

■ There is a growing market for all kinds of accessories from this period, fuelled in part by today's post-modern tendency to make sly references to yesterday's styles.

A 1970s Amida wristwatch, faux marble plastic bezel, cream dial, brown plastic strap.

Face 2in (5cm) wide

£25-35 **SEVW**

A Pierre Balmain manual wristwatch, wedge-shaped brushed steel bezel, signed silver dial, wine red numerals, on original wine red strap signed "PB" on the buckle.

Face 1.75in (4.5cm) wide

£100-150 **SEVW**

A Pierre Balmain manual wristwatch, wedge-shaped brushed chrome bezel, signed blue/black dial, on original black leather strap, signed "PB" on the buckle.

Pierre Balmain was a French fashion designer well known for dressing the aristocracy of Europe. Between 1971 and 1973 he designed about 30 watches.

Face 1.5in (4cm) wide

£100-150 **SEVW**

A 1970s Buler Super-Nova wristwatch, brushed chrome bezel, black dial, on black leather strap.

Face 1.75in (4.5cm) wide

£150-200 **SEVW**

A late 1960s Buler manual wristwatch, blue plastic bezel, white dial, blue Arabic numerals, original red plastic strap.

This watch was sold together with an interchangeable blue strap to change the style.

Face 2in (5cm) wide

£30-50 **SEVW**

A 1970s Buler Super-Nova wristwatch, brushed chrome bezel, black dial, on black leather strap.

Face 1.75in (4.5cm) wide

£150-200 **SEVW**

A rare mid-1960s Bulova Accutron Spaceview wristwatch, with tuning fork movement, stainless steel bezel, on black leather strap.

Face 1.5in (3.5cm) wide

£280-320 **SEVW**

WRISTWATCHES

A 1960s Clarina Incabloc ladies' manual wristwatch, shaped oval brushed and textured chrome bezel, scarlet dial, on original scarlet strap.

Face 2.25in (5.5cm) wide

£70-100　　　　**SEVW**

A 1970s Elka automatic wristwatch, steel bezel, deep bronze sunburst dial, date function, black strap.

Face 1.5in (4cm) wide

£70-100　　　　**SEVW**

A 1970s Eza automatic wristwatch, brushed steel bezel, blue dial, sweeping second hand, original strap.

Face 1.5in (3.5cm) wide

£60-90　　　　**SEVW**

A 1970s Josmar wristwatch, brushed steel bezel, red and light gold striped dial, red strap.

Face 1.5in (4cm) wide

£80-120　　　　**SEVW**

A 1980s Lip Datolip electronic wristwatch, gold bezel, 'lightning bolt' seconds hand, date function, on original, pierced strap.

This was the first electronic watch to have a date function.

Face 1.5in (4cm) wide

£150-200　　　　**SEVW**

A Lip wristwatch, with dark brown anodized metal body, brown dial, white Arabic numerals and brown leather strap.

This is one of a series of watches designed by French architect Isabelle Hebey for Lip.

1973　　　　*Face 1.25in (3cm) wide*

£220-280　　　　**SEVW**

A 1970s Lip hexagonal ladies manual wristwatch, steel bezel, silver herringbone dial, extended lugs, on original strap.

Face 1.5in (3.5cm) wide

£70-100　　　　**SEVW**

A 1970s Lordex manual wristwatch, brushed steel bezel, blue dial, on brushed steel bracelet.

Face 1.5in (4cm) wide

£70-90　　　　**SEVW**

A 1970s Lucerne Direct Time wristwatch, heavy chrome bezel, blue dial, on a new oiled black leather strap.

Face 1.75in (4.5cm) wide

£60-80　　　　**SEVW**

A 1970s Lucerne manual wristwatch, brushed steel bezel, blue dial, on steel bracelet.

Face 1.5in (4cm) wide

£70-100   **SFVW**

A 1970s Lucerne digital wristwatch, brushed steel bezel, blue dial, on pierced ridged steel bracelet.

Face 1.5in (4cm) wide

£120-180   **SEVW**

A 1970s Nelco manual wristwatch, with black, white and red dial and yellow second hand, brushed chrome bezel, original strap.

Face 1.5in (4cm) wide

£50-70   **SEVW**

A 1970s Sicura ladies' wristwatch, 17-jewel movement gold bezel, manual wind, bronze sunburst dial, on a thin black strap.

Face 1.5in (4cm) wide

£70-90   **SEVW**

An unusual mid-1970s Parger manual wristwatch, stainless steel hezel, black dial, on steel bracelet.

Face 1.5in (3.5cm) wide

£80-120   **SEVW**

A 1970s Daniel Perret ladies' manual wristwatch, gold-filled bezel, brushed at the front and polished at the sides, gold dial, on tan leather strap.

Face 1in (2.5cm) wide

£80-120   **SEVW**

A Pronto Automatic wristwatch, with silver and white dial, blue seconds hand and date function, black strap.

Face 1.5in (3.5cm) wide

£70-100   **SEVW**

A 1970s Ruhla manual wristwatch, green-striped white plastic bezel, white dial, green Arabic numerals, on original plastic strap.

Face 2in (5cm) wide

£40-60   **SEVW**

A very rare Sicura manual wristwatch, brushed steel bezel, champagne dial, on replaced metal bracelet.

Face 1.5in (4cm) wide

£150-200   **SEVW**

A 1970s Sorna bullhead Chrono World Time wristwatch, black world time bezel, black dial, stopwatch function with two subsidiary dials, on black leather strap.

Face 1.75in (4.5cm) wide

£200-250   **SEVW**

A 1970s Sorna Direct Time manual wristwatch, 17-jewel movement, brushed chrome bezel, two-tone blue dial, on original wet-look blue plastic strap.

Face 1.5in (3.5cm) wide

£100-150   **SEVW**

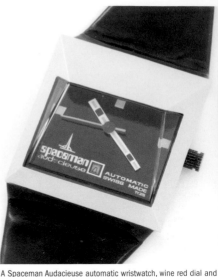

A Spaceman Audacieuse automatic wristwatch, wine red dial and original strap, with original promotional bauble.

Designed by André Le Marquand in 1972, for the Catena watch company and later manufactured by OMAX and Zeno. When they were released at the Basel Watch show in 1973 nobody thought they would sell, but eventually 150,000 were sold worldwide .

Face 1.5in (4cm) wide

£280-320   **SEVW**

An early 1970s Sorna Chrono World Time wristwatch, blue outer bezel and stainless steel inner bezel, blue dial, two subsidiary dials, date function, on black leather strap.

Face 2in (5cm) wide

£150-200   **SEVW**

A Spaceman Oval automatic wristwatch, brushed chrome bezel, blue dial with day-glo orange hands and date function, on original blue foam and plastic strap.

This is the other famous watch designed by André le Marquand in the late 1960s. Other colours made include red, white, brown and green, all worth approximately the same amount.

c1970   Face 2in (5cm) wide

£120-160   **SEVW**

A Vulcain Direct Time automatic wristwatch, steel surround, with all-in-one strap.

Face 1.5in (3.5cm) wide

£150-200   **SEVW**

A 1970s Vulcain ladies manual wristwatch, hexagonal gold-plated bezel, brown dial, on ridged gold-plated bracelet, with original tag.

Face 0.75in (2cm) wide

£60-80   **SEVW**

A Spaceman Audacieuse automatic wristwatch, by O.M.A.X., wedge-shaped steel bezel, black dial, date function, on metal bracelet.

Face 1.5in (4cm) wide

£280-320   **SEVW**

Collectors' Notes

- The first digital watch was designed by Hamilton in 1970. The earliest examples had light emitting diode (LED) displays that consumed a lot of power, and so the screens only lit up at the push of a button. It wasn't until the introduction of the liquid crystal display (LCD) that the numbers were permanently visible.

- The earliest Pulsar watches were very expensive when they were first sold. Various models were produced, some of them in solid gold. In Europe, the technology was repackaged by Omega in cases of their own design.

- Most digital watches keep time by sending an electric current through quartz crystals. Japanese-made quartz watches are both inexpensive and accurate, and have dominated the market for years.

- From the late 1970s, digital timepieces were sometimes combined with other features, such as calculators. These multi-function watches are particularly evocative of the period and eagerly collected by many.

- Condition is vital: ideally, a watch from this period should still have its original packaging. Many examples are marketed as 'new old stock', having never been worn. Replaced components and other signs of wear will have a detrimental effect on the value of a watch.

- It can be hard to locate original batteries to fit vintage digital watches today, although modern equivalents are usually available.

A Bulova Computron gold-plated LED watch, with Drivers-style shaped case and with hours, minutes, seconds and day and date displays on the side window.

c1975   *Face 1.5in (4cm) wide*

£200-250   **PC**

A 1970s Bulova LCD wristwatch, stainless steel bezel, on matching steel bracelet.

Face 1.25in (3cm) wide

£70-100   **SEVW**

A 1970s Bulova Accuquartz LCD wristwatch, textured gold-filled bezel, on matching bracelet.

Face 1.5in (4cm) wide

£200-250   **SEVW**

A 1980s Casio CA-505 LCD calculator/wristwatch, calculator, alarm, dual time, stopwatch, lap counter, time and date functions, on original metal bracelet.

Face 1.5in (3.5cm) wide

£40-60   **SEVW**

A rare early 1980s Casio 52 LCD wristwatch, time, day/date, stopwatch and chronograph function, on steel bracelet.

Face 1.5in (4cm) wide

£40-60   **SEVW**

A Commodore Time Master stainless steel bracelet LED watch, by Commodore Computers, with time and date functions.

c1979   *Face 1.5in (4cm) wide*

£150-200   **PC**

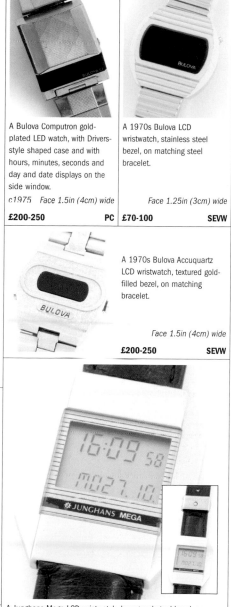

A Junghans Mega LCD wristwatch, hexagonal steel bezel, on original black leather strap.

This is the British version of the first watch to have the time radio-controlled by the Atomic Clock - it was designed by Frog Designs and synchronises itself at 2pm every day.

1991   *Face 1.75in (4.5cm) wide*

£180-220   **SEVW**

A Nivada CompuChron stainless steel bracelet LED watch, with time and date functions.

c1977   *Face 1.75in (4.5cm) wide*

£100-150   **PC**

A 1970s Novus LED wristwatch, gold-plated bezel, on gold-plated bracelet.

Face 1.5in (4cm) wide

£150-200   **SEVW**

A 1970s Novus LCD wristwatch, gold-plated bezel, on gold-plated bracelet.

Novus is the brand name for watches made by National Semiconductors, who made many of the early LCD watch modules.

Face 1.5in (4cm) wide

£150-200   **SEVW**

An Omega Time Computer stainless steel integral bracelet LED watch, with time and date functions.

c1974   *Face 1.5in (4cm) wide*

£200-250   **PC**

A 1980s Phasar LCD chronograph, made for retail by Sears, on metal bracelet.

Face 1.5in (4cm) wide

£40-60   **SEVW**

A Pulsar Calculator stainless steel integral bracelet LED watch, with time, date and calculator functions.

c1976   *Face 1.5in (4cm) wide*

£250-350   **PC**

A scarce 1980s Pulsar Sport Timer LCD wristwatch, on original black plastic strap.

This watch is unusual as it can time four people at once due to four combined stopwatch settings.

Face 1.5in (4cm) wide

£50-80   **SEVW**

A CLOSER LOOK AT A DIGITAL WATCH

Its calendar is programmed until 2100, hence its name.

The gold and black ceramic-coated versions are rare and can be worth in excess of £2,000.

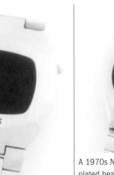

The two solar panels on top of the watch power it for up to a year when charged.

The unusual side mounting of the display made it ideal for drivers.

A Synchronar 2100 solar-powered watch with LED readout, with stainless steel bracelet.

This watch was designed by Roger Riehl, a pioneer of LED wristwatches development.

1973   *Face 1.5in (4cm) wide*

£800-1,200   **SEVW**

FIND OUT MORE...

'History of the Modern Wristwatch', *by Pieter Doensens, published by Snoeck-Ducaju & Zoon 1994.*

WINE & DRINKING

COLLECTORS' NOTES

■ One of the most collectable objects in this sector of the market is the corkscrew. There are 'straight pull' or 'mechanical' examples, where either the strength of the user or the ingenuity of the invented mechanism takes the strain. The 19th century is the most prolific period of production with many variations due to the large number of patents issued during the period. However many innovative and eminently more affordable examples can be found from the early decades of the 20th century.

■ Look for early examples, fine materials and good levels of decoration, particularly with straight pull examples. Consider the shape, material and decoration as these often hold clues to when the piece was made. The value of complex, innovative mechanisms such as the Thomason type is also enhanced by these factors. Notable names can make a considerable difference to value, so examine pieces closely for maker's marks.

■ As with corkscrews, many wine and drinking accessories can still be used, and thus a sense of fun is important with whimsical items often fetching comparatively high values due to their appeal – providing they are in appealing condition. Popularity of pieces from the 1930s and 1950s in particular continues to grow, with amusing or novelty designs more important than quality.

A German nickel silver base pocket-sized corkscrew, in the form of ladies' legs, with mother-of-pearl thighs and striped stockings, stamped "Germany".

A large number of variations of these screws, based on the 'CanCan' Girls of the Moulin Rouge and similar establishments, were produced in Germany during the 1890s. The use of mother-of-pearl is relatively unusual – others have stripy celluloid stockings and some have two-colour celluloid stocking panels. As well as acting as a pulling handle, the 'legs' fold down to protect the worm.

c1900	*2.5in (6.5cm) long*
£100-150	**CSA**

An English silver corkscrew, by Joseph Taylor of Birmingham, with a green stained two-fingered ivory grip and engraved stem.

This is the standard for many 18thC and early 19thC silver corkscrews, which are often Dutch in origin and include pipe tampers or nutmeg graters. The use of ivory for the handle of this example, particularly stained bright green, is unusual.

c1790	*3in (8cm) long*
£220-280	**CSA**

An English boar's tusk corkscrew, with steel stem and bladed worm.

c1890	*6.25in (16cm) long*
£30-40	**CSA**

An English turned corkscrew, with turned bone handle and dusting brush, fine baluster stem, fluted button cork-stopper, plain helical worm.

c1840	*5.5in (14cm) l*
£70-90	**CSA**

An English straight-pull corkscrew, with turned bone handle and dusting brush, tapered stem, helical worm.

c1850	*5.5in (14cm) long*
£40-60	**CSA**

A 1920s steel corkscrew, with bottle opener.

	4.5in (11.5cm) long
£30-50	**BS**

A late 19thC Corozo nut corkscrew, with carved grotesque face, droopy moustache and glass eyes.

This amusing corkscrew was carved from a Corozo or tagua nut, the fruit of a tropical palm and popular during the late 19thC. It is very dense and hard, making it ideal for carving and as it ages, it takes on an yellowy-amber colour. Here the darker outer layer has been used to represent hair and a beard.

	3.5in (9cm) wide
£70-100	**CSA**

An English silver-plated four-pillar rack-and-pinion 'King's Screw' corkscrew, with turned bone handle, dusting brush and side wind handle.

The 'King's' type can be recognised by the side handle. This operates a rack and pinion mechanism to draw the cork upwards. It came in both 'open' styles as here, and 'closed' styles, where a cylinder covered the mechanism.

c1820   7.75in (20cm) long

£450-550   **CSA**

A CLOSER LOOK AT A BOW CORKSCREW

This piece is marked with a maker's name, which is a rare feature. Without this it would be worth around £100.

As well as a corkscrew, this piece also includes a gimlet, buttonhook and screw. Each tool folds out and the protecting bow can be used as a grip.

The maker, Holtzapffel & Co., were founded in 1792 in London. They were renowned for their lathes and important, complex tool benches and sets which fetch very high values.

The more tools included and the larger the piece the higher the value will usually be.

A rare English steel 11-tool folding bow, stamped with maker's name "Holtzapffel & Co. 53 Haymarket".

c1840   3.25in (8.5cm) long

£600-700   **CSA**

A 19thC Thomason-type corkscrew, with bone handle and side brush above a rack and brass drum applied with a gilt Royal Coat of Arms.

A 'Thomason' type uses a special mechanism, patented in 1802 by Sir Edward Thomason. It enables the worm to be forced into the cork and the cork extracted by constant turning of the handle. Look out for decorated barrels, such as those moulded with gothic windows. These tend to be more valuable than this more common banded version with a coat of arms.

7.25in (18cm) long

£220-280   **GORL**

An English silver-plated pocket roundlet folding corkscrew, inscribed "Drew & Sons, Piccadilly Circus, London".

'Roundlet' corkscrews typically contain other tools in the tapering cylindrical sheath. Drew & Sons were a notable central London retailer of accessories, including picnic sets and gentlemen's and ladies' luggage and prerequisites.

c1880   3.25in (8.5cm) long

£22-30   **CSA**

An unusual left-handed screwed steel pocket corkscrew, with cyphered (or sharpened) worm.

Few of these screws have survived complete, as the cross bar is removable and was often lost.

c1850   4.5in (11.5cm) long

£70-90   **CSA**

An English faceted bow pocket corkscrew, in cut steel with a button hook for perforating perfume and ink bottles.

c1800   1.5in (3.5cm) long

£30-40   **CSA**

A 1920s cast brass corkscrew, in the form of a kilted Scotsman holding a bottle of Scotch and leaning on a walking stick, with registration number.

4.5in (11.5cm) high

£10-15   **CSA**

A Heeley 'King's Screw' mechanical corkscrew, with turned bone handle and brush, steel side handle, the brass barrel with applied Royal Coat of Arms, signed "Heeley".

8in (20cm) long

£300-400   **GOR**

A silver hipflask, with engine-turned decoration and an engraved crest, Birmingham hallmarks.

1873

£100-150   **CSA**

A clear glass hipflask, covered with silver and crocodile skin, with armorial motif, motto and initials, hallmark for JD&S, Sheffield.

1907   *5.5in (14cm) high*

£220-280   **GS**

A cocktail shaker, in the form of a dumb-bell.

11in (28cm) wide

£180-220   **DETC**

A 1930s silver and leather hip flask, makers mark for "J.D. & Sons", London hallmarks.

50-60   **CSA**

A 1930s silver fully overlaid clear glass hipflask, with plain finish, hallmarks rubbed.

5.25in (13.5cm) high

£60-70   **GS**

An 'Abyssinian' champagne tap, with original box.

c1880   *5.75in (14.5cm) long*

£35-40   **CSA**

A slim silver hipflask, with fine barley decoration, hallmark for JD&S, Sheffield.

1936   *5.5in (14cm) h*

£400-500   **GS**

An English silver-plate champagne tap, with Prince of Wales feather design and inscription "Maw & Son".

c1890   *4in (10cm) long*

£40-50   **CSA**

An English steel champagne wire clipper, handle for opening wooden crates with dusting brush.

c1880   *7in (18cm) long*

£30-40   **CSA**

An early 20thC faceted clear glass hip flask, with silver sleeve, hallmarks indistinct.

5.25in (13.5cm) high

£200-300   **GS**

A slim silver hipflask, with fine barley decoration, hallmark for JD&S, Sheffield.

1936   *5.5in (14cm) h*

£400-500   **GS**

A Stelton Cylinda-Line stainless steel cocktail shaker, designed by Arne Jacobsen, with original box.

Famed Danish architect and designer Arne Jacobsen is well known for his 'Ant' chair designs. The idea for his starkly modernist, functional cylinder shape 'Cylinda-Line' range of accessories, was reputedly first sketched on a napkin! The range was produced by the company of his foster son, Peter Holmblad.

c1968   *9in (23cm) high*

£60-80   **L**

A cocktail shaker in the form of a man, wearing a medal inscribed "Gin" hanging from his waistcoat and a female figure on his forehead, the stopper in the form of a top hat, paper label "Japan", original sticker "Yona original by Shafford Japan", inscribed "8001-Y".

We wonder what this 'gentleman' is preoccupied with!

£80-120   **DETC**

A pair of decanters within a case, in the form of an armoured torso, marked "Scotch" and "Bourbon", with helmet stoppers, together with six shot glasses.

12.5in (32cm) wide

£180-220   **DETC**

An unusual faceted soda siphon, with bird's head spout, mid-blue glass, faceted body, good condition.

12in (30.5cm) high

£12-18   **BBR**

An acid-etched glass cocktail shaker, with two of seven matching stem glasses.

10.5in (26.5cm) high

£80-120 set   **DETC**

A CLOSER LOOK AT A BAR SET

The 1950s saw a return to glamour and fun after WWII and a large number of whimsical, novelty bar designs were produced – look for those that are in great condition, are complete and have an appealing sense of fun with a period feel.

The plastic stirrers are shaped like gentleman's walking canes, continuing the theme of the upper class lounge lizard or 'boulevardier'.

Transfer-decorated glassware was popular during the 1950s – here the top hat motif is followed through in the design of the lid of the cocktail shaker.

The tray is designed to resemble a city park, complete with street lamps and handles modelled as benches.

A bar set, comprising a shaker and six glasses with cane-shaped stirrers, depicting gentlemen wearing top hats.

c1955   *16in (40.5cm) wide*

£300-400   **DET**

A Robj pottery spirit flask, in the form of a stylized image of Napoleon Bonaparte wearing a grey greatcoat with black buttons and a medal, his distinctive black hat for a stopper, signed "Robj Paris" and "Made in France".

10in (25.5cm) high

£150-250   **DN**

An English silver-plate wine bottle-holder, with shepherd's crook grip, the base with gadroon border and adjustable stem.

c1860   *12in (30cm) high*

£80-120   **CSA**

COLLECTORS' NOTES

■ The manufacture of contemporary glass spheres is one of the most dynamic and rapidly developing areas of the American contemporary studio glass movement. Many glassmakers have worked extensively in the field and have experience in related areas such as marbles or paperweights.

■ Available at a wide range of prices and easy to display due to their size, look out for key names and complex designs displaying the glassmaker's art. It is anticipated that they will increase in value as the field becomes more popular.

An American 'Joe Cool' contemporary glass sphere, by Harry Besett of the Vermont Glass Workshop, painted by artist Ken Leslie.

2001 2in (5cm) d

£350-450   **BGL**

An American 'Temari' contemporary glass sphere, by Dinah Hulet Tulet, inscribed very faintly with "Hulet 2002".

Hulet has worked with glass for over 30 years and is probably the best known studio glass artist producing spheres. She is a board member of the Glass Art Society and on the board of directors of the American Crafts Council.

2002   *1.5in (4cm) diam*

£200-300   **BGL**

A CLOSER LOOK AT A CONTEMPORARY SPHERE

The sphere is composed of four layers of coloured glass representing the sea, landmasses and clouds, plus clear layers.

The landmasses are marked out in 'dichroic' glass, a speciality of Beetem's. They change colour as the sphere is moved.

The cloud forms correctly represent the gulf/jet streams and peak at the pole.

The size of the sphere, and the fact that the design covers it entirely, creates a tactile effect.

An American 'World Marble' contemporary glass sphere, by Geoffrey Beetem, signed and numbered "GD Beetem 2003 C 1618".

Beetem studied glassmaking at Ohio State University and at the Pilchuk School. He worked with Lino Tagliapietra, before establishing his own shop in 1987.

2003   *3.5in (9cm) diam*

£600-800   **BGL**

An American 'School of Fish' contemporary glass sphere, by Cathy Richardson, with three layers of glass and signed "C Richardson 03".

Richardson is also known for her paperweights.

2003   *2in (5cm) diam*

100-150   **BGL**

An American contemporary glass sphere, by Douglas Sweet, with densely packed millefiori, signed "Sweet".

Sweet is a prolific and well-known American contemporary studio glass maker and is also known for his paperweights.

2003   *2in (5cm) diam*

£100-150   **BGL**

An American 'Hummingbird with flowers' contemporary glass sphere, by Jesse Taj, signed "Taj 03".

2003   *1.25in (3cm) diam*

£100-150   **BGL**

An American 'Cat In The Hat' contemporary glass sphere, by Jesse Taj, made from murrine canes worked with a hot torch, signed "Taj 03".

2003   *1.5in (4cm) diam*

£150-200   **BGL**

COLLECTORS' NOTES

■ Modern crafts, particularly in the medium of ceramics and glass, have become increasingly rated as works of art over the past few decades. This is partly due to the influence and growing importance of the studio movement of the mid-20th century. Although glass is still a little behind ceramics in the UK and parts of Europe, interest is growing (as it has already in the US) and the works of many designers seem set to become the collectables of the future.

■ Always look for fine workmanship and an understanding of design, often twinned with ancient techniques, as very little in this aspect of glass is new. Long-standing masters and innovators of new

movements are likely to remain popular. Spotting talented new artists early can be exciting and rewarding, but developing an eye for quality and design is important.

■ As each work is unique, they are usually one-offs, but some are released in limited editions. Unique pieces are more valuable and may remain so in the future, but do not underestimate limited editions. They appeal to a wider number of collectors, particularly if they embody the artist's typical style.

■ Only a single price is given as this reflects the retail price of that individual piece.

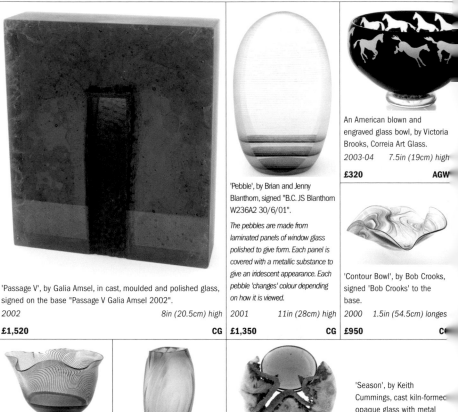

An American blown and engraved glass bowl, by Victoria Brooks, Correia Art Glass.

2003-04   *7.5in (19cm) high*

£320   **AGW**

'Pebble', by Brian and Jenny Blanthorn, signed "B.C. JS Blanthorn W236A2 30/6/01".

The pebbles are made from laminated panels of window glass polished to give form. Each panel is covered with a metallic substance to give an iridescent appearance. Each pebble 'changes' colour depending on how it is viewed.

2001   *11in (28cm) high*

£1,350   **CG**

'Contour Bowl', by Bob Crooks, signed 'Bob Crooks' to the base.

2000   *1.5in (54.5cm) longes*

£950   **C**

'Passage V', by Galia Amsel, in cast, moulded and polished glass, signed on the base "Passage V Galia Amsel 2002".

2002   *8in (20.5cm) high*

£1,520   **CG**

'Longitudinal Bowl', by Bob Crooks, blown and worked blue glass with solid blue base.

Crooks works in a flamboyant manner which matches and echoes his extravagantly shaped pieces.

2003   *8.5in (21.5cm) highest*

£390   **CG**

'Chisel Cut Vase', by Catherine Hough, in 'steel blue' glass, with matte finish.

2002   *13in (33cm) high*

£380   **CG**

'Season', by Keith Cummings, cast kiln-formed opaque glass with metal additions, with cast and polished glass additions.

Cummings' kiln-formed glass appears almost like ceramic or rock, due to the level of opaque enamels used. The technique of kiln-forming has been used since the Roman period.

2003   *5in (13cm) wid*

£1,100   **C**

'Windfall', by Keith Cummings, kiln formed opaque glass with metal and applied coloured glass 'cabochons'.

2000   *8.25in (21cm) long*

£900   **CG**

An American blown glass mantle vase, by Paul Cunningham.

2003-04   *4in (10cm) high*

£350   **AGW**

An iridescent blue and orange 'rose' murrine vase, designed and made by Vittorio Ferro, signed to the base "VITTORIO FERRO".

2000   *7.5in (19cm) high*

£850   **VET**

An American blown glass mantle vase by Paul Cunningham.

Cunningham has worked alongside legendary studio glass artists such as Dale Chihuly, Richard Marquis and Lino Tagliapietra. He has exhibited in Italy and across the US, including at the American Craft Museum, New York.

2003-04   *11.5in (29cm) high*

£1,900   **AGW**

A yellow and red murrine vase, designed and made by Vittorio Ferro from the 'Autumn Impression' series, with iridescent areas between the murrines, signed to the base 'VITTORIO FERRO'.

2002   *8in (20cm) high*

€650   **VET**

A grey and orange 'rose' murrine vase, designed and made by Vittorio Ferro, signed to the base "Vittorio Ferro V&A Murano 2000".

2000   *8in (20cm) high*

£800   **VET**

A green and red murrine cased vase, designed and made by Vittorio Ferro at Fratelli Pagnin, Murano, with iridescent areas around the murrines and a black foot, signed to the base "VITTORIO FERRO".

2004   *9.5in (24cm) high*

£900   **VET**

A glass chicken, by Vittorio Ferro.

One of Murano's leading glass artists, Ferro worked at Fratelli Toso and De Majo. His passion is for murrine work, and he has won many prestigious prizes in Italy.

2004   *9in (22.5cm) high*

£1,700   **VET**

An American yellow and purple clear glass plate stand, by David Garcia, Yacult, Washington.

2003-04 10.5in (26.5cm) high

£280 AGW

'Floral with vines' American perfume bottle, by Richard Gillian, iridescent finish to sides, front and back facets, using flamework painting, signed "R. Gillian 2002".

5in (12.5cm) high

£200 BGL

'Aesculus', by Kate Jones and Stephen Gillies, in cased coloured glass, signed on the base "Gillies Jones Aesculus 2004/01 Rosedale".

Designer and glass artist Kate Jones works with Stephen Gillies, her husband, who is the glass blower.

2004 *10in (25.5cm) diam*

£1,840 CG

An American hand-blown glass mantle vase, by Dale Heffernan, San Raphael, California.

2003-04 23in (57.5cm) high

£170 AGW

An Aerial 'stone form' cased vase, by Peter Layton.

Layton (b.1937) is one of Britain's most prominent glass artists and co-founded the 'Glasshouse' in London in 1969. This piece shows his current interest in the optical effects of casing – the clear outer layer reflects the design of the coloured core.

2004 *8in (20.5cm) high*

£1,500 PL

An Aurora cased 'stone form' vase, by Peter Layton.

2004 *9.25in (23.5cm) high*

£500 PL

A large Mirage bowl, by Peter Layton.

2004 *13.5in (34cm) wide*

£1,200 PL

A unique Skyline 'pebble form', by Peter Layton.

This piece is from a new and experimental range. Its delicate yet varied and vibrant colouration is highly appealing.

2004 *11.5in (29cm) wide*

£1,500 PL

A tall vase, by Annette Meech, from the 'Les Fauves' series, signed "Annette Meech Glasshouse de Savignon".

2002 *19in (48cm) high*

£136 C

A tall vase, by Annette Meech, from the 'Les Fauves' series, orange blown glass vase with red zig-zagging red trails, signed "Annette Meech Glasshouse de Savignon".

2002 16.25in (41cm) high

£136 CG

A Simon Moore blue jug, with fins along the back.

1986 13.5in (34cm) high

£700 JH

'Face Two Face' bowl, by Stephen Newell, blown and cased, with silver leaf inside, signed "Newell".

American born and trained Newell often tells stories or portrays emotions though his complex works. Examples can be found in public collections in Japan, Britain and the US.

2003 6in (15cm) high

£2,400 CG

An American glass perfume bottle, by Michael Nourot.

2003-04 6in (15cm) high

£120 AGW

An American glass perfume bottle, by Michael Nourot.

Michael Nourot (b.1949) has studied with glassblowers on the island of Murano, Italy and also with studio glass artist Marvin Lipofsky. He works with his wife, also a glass artist, in the US.

2003-04 6in (15cm) high

£120 AGW

'Por do Sol em Bozios' sommerso glass block, signed and dated by Bruno Pedrosa and bearing his cruciform monogram.

Multi-talented Brazilian artist Bruno Pedrosa (b.1950) began working in glass in 1995. He designs his pieces and then guides the glass master's hand, using it as a brush, to execute his designs. His work can be found in Museum of Modern Art, Rio de Janeiro and the Corning Museum of Glass, New York.

2003 11.25in (28.5cm) high

£1,900 VET

An American hand-blown glass jug, by Janusz Poznia, with cast clear glass handle.

2003-04 12in (30.5cm) high

£550 AGW

'Greek Head VIII', by David Reekie, kiln formed opaque glass, signed "Greek Head VIII David Reekie Norwich July94".

David Reekie (b.1947) trained at the Stourbridge College of Art. He is known for his often humorous and surreal depiction of the human form and its many feelings and attitudes. In this series, Reekie aimed to add more life and excitement to Ancient Greek head designs.

1994 16.75in (42.5cm) high

£3,600 CG

'Drifter Bowl', by Karlin Rushbrooke, orange glass with internal opaque white rounded rectangles, signed "Karlin Rushbrooke" on the base.

Well known for bottle forms, his glass has a fluid, flowing property as he works with very hot glass. He was one of the first people to have a hot glass studio of his own in the UK.

2003   12.75in (32.5cm) widest

£80   **CG**

An American 'Angelfish' perfume bottle, by David Salazar, ground glass aquarium scene, with clear stopper signed "D P Salazar 5/02".

Salazar is a leading practitioner of 'painting with glass' technique where the artist heats the glass rod and 'draws' a design onto hot glass, using the cane as coloured pencil.

2002   4in (10cm) high

£300   **BGL**

'Marine Light III', by Pauline Solven, blown and cased coloured glass, signed 'Pauline Solven 2003'.

The abstract patterns are created with powdered coloured enamels and inspired by marine light, as the title suggests.

2003   6in (15cm) high

£690   **CG**

'Paintwork XIV', by Pauline Solven, signed on the base "Pauline Solven 2004".

This is part of a series of 15 'vessels' inspired by the distressed state of painted boats in a dry dock.

2004   6.5in (16.5cm) high

£690   **CG**

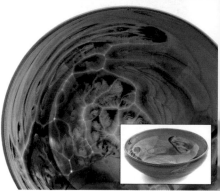

An American 'New Mexico Blue Bowl with Red Lip', by Josh Simpson, signed "Simpson 8-4-01".

Known for his 'planet' spheres, Simpson was inspired by the colour of the night sky in Summer to create this colour and range of bowls. Each is unique and uses metallic silver on cobalt blue glass. Each one is created in controlled conditions to create the right colour and pattern.

2001

£200   **BGL**

'Emerging Sun', by Pauline Solven, constructed from blown and cased elements, with sandblasted finish giving a matte texture, the individual segments adhered with ultraviolet bonding.

Solven is unusual in that she works alone in her studio, without assistants. She trained at the Royal College of Art in London, and worked at the Glasshouse with Sam Herman, before co-founding Cowdy Glass. Her finely coloured, painterly work is often inspired by nature and light.

2000   14in (35.5cm) high

£1,800   **CG**

A 'Mirrored Vase', signed and made by Anthony Stern, made using blown mirrored glass

2004   19.75in (50cm) high

£250   **ASG**

A large blown 'Seascape' bowl, by Anthony Stern.

Stern's expressive 'Seascape' pieces work with light to bring the design, which incorporates impressions of sea, sky and landscape, alive.

2003   8.75in (22cm) hig

£1,500   **AS**

A 'Rolling Stone Vase', by Anthony Stern, using images from original photographs taken by Stern when he was a photographer during the 1960s.

The photographic images of the 'Rolling Stones' seen here were captured by Stern in one of his early roles as a photographer during the 1960s. Using an innovative process, they are suspended between two clear layers of glass, over a core of opaque white glass.

2004   8.5in (21.5cm) high

£900   **ASG**

An American blown glass bowl, by Valerie Surjan, decorated with leaf and cherry motifs.

Surjan's highly detailed sand-blasted cameo work on hand-blown vessels is influenced by the world of nature, with exotic animals, fruits, vines and leaves being typical subjects. She has studied in Italy and has won a number of awards for her designs, many of which can be found in limited editions.

2003-04   5in (13cm) high

£650   **AGW**

A River Trout shaped stem goblet, by Milon Townsend, with lampwork fish stem and blown foot and bowl, signed "C Milon Townsend".

2000   8in (20cm) high

£180   **BGL**

'Quilt Platter 7', by David Traub, cased coloured glass dish comprising layers of coloured glass strips and clear glass.

American born and trained Traub now lives and works in Wanganui, New Zealand. His works, such as this, focus on pure form and resonant, vibrant colour.

2003   17.25in (44cm) square

£2,200   **CG**

'Waterfall Bowl', by Fleur Tookey, blown bowl with blue striations created by applying powdered colour to the glass gather, signed on the base "Fleur Tookey".

2003   7.25in (18.5cm) wide

£150   **CG**

An American blown glass mantle vase, by Lucy Vergamini.

2003-04   12in (30.5cm) high

£480   **AGW**

An American moulded and blown glass sculpture by Nikolas Weinstein.

2003-04   14.5in (37cm) high

£300   **AGW**

'String Ball', by Christopher Williams, free engraved with a fine wheel, signed on the base, "Christopher Williams Savignon".

2002   14.25in (36.5cm) high

£975   **CG**

An American moulded and blown glass sculpture, by Nikolas Weinstein.

2003-04   6in (15cm) high

£200   **AGW**

FIND OUT MORE...

'DK Collectors Guide: 20th Century Glass', *by Judith Miller, published by Dorling Kindersley, 2004.*

'Glass Art', *by Peter Layton, published by A & C Black Ltd, 1996.*

GLOSSARY

A

Acid etching A technique using acid to decorate glass to produce a matt or frosted appearance.

Albumen print Photographic paper is treated with egg white (albumen) to enable it to hold more light-sensitive chemicals. After being exposed to a negative, the resulting image is richer with more tonal variation.

Applied Refers to a separate part that has been attached to an object, such as a handle.

B

Baluster A curved form with a bulbous base and a slender neck.

Base metal A term describing common metals such as copper, tin and lead, or metal alloys, that were usually plated in gold or silver to imitate more expensive and luxurious metals. In the US, the term 'pot metal' is more commonly used.

Bisque A type of unglazed porcelain used for making dolls from c1860 to c1925.

Boards The hard covers of a book.

Brassing On plated items, where the plating has worn off to reveal the underlying base metal.

C

Cabochon A large, protruding, polished, but not faceted, stone.

Cameo Hardstone, coral or shell that has been carved in relief to show a design in a contrasting colour.

Cameo glass Decorative glass made from two or more layers of differently coloured glass, which are then carved or etched to reveal the colour beneath.

Cartouche A framed panel, often in the shape of a shield or paper scroll, which can be inscribed.

Cased Where a piece of glass is covered with a further layer of glass, sometimes of a contrasting colour, or clear and colourless. In

some cases the casing will be further worked with cutting or etching to reveal the layer beneath.

Charger A large plate or platter, often for display, but also for serving.

Chromolithography A later development of 'lithography', where a number of printing stones are used in succession, each with a different colour, to build up a multi-coloured image.

Composition A mixture including wood pulp, plaster and glue used as a cheap alternative to bisque in the production of dolls' heads and bodies.

Compote A dish, usually on a stem or foot, to hold fruit for the dessert course.

Craze/Crazed/Crazing A network of fine cracks in the glaze caused by uneven shrinking during firing. It also describes plastic that is slowly degrading and has the same surface patterning.

Cuenca A technique used for decorating tiles where moulded ridges separate the coloured glazes, like the 'cloisonne' enamelling technique.

Cultured pearl A pearl formed when an irritant is artificially introduced to the mollusc.

D

Damascened Metal ornamented with inlaid gold or silver, often in wavy lines. Commonly found on weapons or armour.

Dichroic Glass treated with chemicals or metals that cause it to appear differently coloured depending on how it is viewed in the light.

Diecast Objects made by pouring molten metal into a closed metal die or mould.

Ding A very small dent in metal.

E

Earthenware A type of porous pottery that requires a glaze to make it waterproof.

Ebonized Wood that has been blackened with dye to resemble ebony.

E.P.N.S. Found on metal objects and standing for 'electroplated nickel silver', meaning the object is made from nickel which is then electroplated with silver.

F

Faience Earthenware that is treated with an impervious tin glaze. Popular in France from the 16th century and reaching its peak during the 18th century.

Faceted A form of decoration where a number of flat surfaces are cut into the surface of an object such as a gem or glass.

Faux A French word for 'false'. The intention is not to deceive fraudulently but to imitate a more costly material.

Finial A decorative knob at the end of a terminal, or on a lid.

Foliate Leaf and vine motifs.

G

Guilloché An engraved pattern of interlaced lines or other decorative motifs, sometimes enamelled over with translucent enamels.

H

Hallmark The series of small stamps found on gold or silver that can identify the maker, the standard of the metal and the city and year of manufacture. Hallmark differ for each country and can consist only of a maker's or a city mark. All English silver made after 1544 was required to be fully marked.

IJKL

Incised Applied to surface decoration or a maker's mark that has been scratched into the surface of an object with a sharp instrument.

Inclusions Used to describe all types of small particles of decorative materials embedded in glass.

Iridescent A lustrous finish that subtly changes colour depending on how light hits it. Often used to describe the finish on ceramics and glass.

Lithography A printing technique developed in 1798 and employing the use of a stone upon which a pattern or picture has been drawn with a grease crayon. The ink adheres to the grease and is transferred to the paper when pressed against it.

MNO

Millefiori An Italian term meaning 'thousand flowers' and used to describe cut, multi-coloured glass canes which are arranged and cased in clear glass. When arranged with the cut side facing the exterior, each circular disc (or short cane) resembles a small flower.

Mint A term used to describe an object in unused condition with no signs of wear and derived from coinage. Truly 'mint' objects will command a premium.

Mount A metal part applied to an object made of ceramic, glass or another material, with a decorative or functional use.

Nappy A shallow dish or bowl with a handle used for drinking.

Opalescent An opal-like, milky glass with subtle gradations of colour between thinner more translucent areas and thicker, more opaque areas.

P

Paisley A stylized design based on pinecones and foliage, often with added intricate decoration. It originated in India and is most often found on fabrics, such as shawls.

Paste (jewellery) A hard, bright glass cut the same way as a diamond and made and set to resemble them.

Patera An oval or circular decorative motif often with a fluted or floral centre. The plural is 'paterae'.

Piqué A decorative technique where small strips or studs of gold are inlaid onto ivory or tortoiseshell on a pattern and secured in place by heating.

Pontil A metal rod to which a glass vessel is attached when it is being worked. When it is removed it leaves a raised disc-shaped 'pontil mark'.

Pot metal Please see 'Base metal'.

Pounce pot A small pot made of wood (treen), silver or ceramic. Found on inkwells or designed to stand alone, it held a gum dust that was sprinkled over parchment to prevent ink from spreading. Used until the late 18th century.

Pressed (Press moulded) Ceramics formed by pressing clay into a mould. Pressed glass is made by pouring molten glass into a mould and pressing it with a plunger.

R

Reeded A type of decoration with thin raised, convex vertical lines. Derived from the decoration of classical columns.

Relief A form of moulded, pressed or carved decoration that protrudes above the surface of an object. Usually in the form of figures of foliate and foliage designs, it ranges in height from 'low' to 'high'.

Repoussé A French term for the raised, 'embossed' decoration on metals such as silver. The metal is forced into a form from one side causing it to bulge.

S

Sgraffito An Italian word for 'little scratch' and used to describe a decorative technique where the outer surface of an object, usually in glazed or coloured ceramic, is scratched away in a pattern to reveal the contrasting coloured underlying surface.

Sommerso Technique developed in Murano in the 1930s. Translates as 'submerged' and involves casing one or more layers of transparent coloured glass within a layer of thick, clear, colourless glass.

Stoneware A type of ceramic similar to earthenware and made of high-fired clay mixed with stone, such as feldspar, which makes it non-porous.

T

Tazza A shallow cup with a wide bowl, which is raised up on a single pedestal foot.

Tooled Collective description for a number of decorative techniques applied to a surface. Includes engraving, stamping, punching and incising.

V

Vermeil Gold-plated silver.

Vesta case A small case or box, usually made from silver, for carrying matches.

W

White metal Precious metal that is possibly silver, but not officially marked as such.

Y

Yellow metal Precious metal that is possibly gold, but not officially marked as such.

INDEX TO ADVERTISERS

CLIENT	PAGE NO.	CLIENT	PAGE NO.
Dorling Kindersley	236	Dorling Kindersley	370
The Propstore of London	295	Onslows	405
Dorling Kindersley	332	Wallis & Wallis	526

KEY TO ILLUSTRATIONS

Every collectable illustrated in DK Collectables Price Guide 2005 by Judith Miller has a letter code that identifies the dealer or auction house that sold it. The list below is a key to these codes. In the list, auction houses are shown by the letter A and dealers by the letter D. Some items may have come from a private collection, in which case the code in the list is accompanied by the letter P. Inclusion in this book in no way constitutes or implies a contract or a binding offer on the part of any of our contributors to supply or sell the goods illustrated, or similar items, at the prices stated.

AAC (A)
Alderfer Auction Company
501 Fairgrounds Road, Hatfield,
PA 19440, USA
Tel: 001 215 393 3000
Fax: 001 215 368 9055
info@alderferauction.com
www.alderferauction.com

AAG (D)
Animation Art Gallery
13-14 Great Castle St,
London W1W 8LS
Tel: 020 7255 1456
Fax: 020 7436 1256
gallery@animaart.com
www.animaart.com

AB (A) (D)
Auction Blocks
P.O. Box 2321, Shelton, CT
06484 USA
Tel: 001 203 924 2802
auctionblocks@aol.com
www.auctionblocks.com

ABIJ (D)
Aurora Bijoux
Tel: 001 215 855 1921
aurora@aurorabijoux.com
www.aurorabijoux.com

ADE (D)
Art Deco Etc
73 Upper Gloucester Road,
Brighton, Sussex BN1 3LQ
Tel: 01273 329 268
johnclark@artdecoetc.co.uk

AG (D)
**Antique Glass at Frank Dux
Antiques**
33 Belvedere, Bath BA1 5HR
Tel: 01225 312 367
Fax: 01225 312 367
m.hopkins@antique-glass.co.uk
www.antique-glass.co.uk

AGO (D)
Anona Gabriel
Otford Antiques Centre, 26-28
High St, Otford, Kent TN15 9DF
Tel: 01959 522 025
info@otfordantiques.com
www.otfordantiques.co.uk

AGW (D)
American Art Glass Works Inc
41 Wooster St, 1st floor, New
York, NY 10013 USA
Tel: 001 212 625 0783
www.americanartglassgallery.com

AHL (D)
Andrea Hall Levy
P.O. Box 1243, Riverdale, NY
10471 USA
Tel: 001 718 601 4239
Mob: 646 441 1726
barangrill@aol.com

AL (D)
Andrew Lineham Fine Glass
The Mall Antiques Arcade,
359 Upper St, London N1
Tel: 020 7704 0195
Fax: 01243 576 241
Mob: 07767 702 722
andrew@andrewlineham.co.uk
www.antiquecolouredglass.co.uk

ANAA (D)
Anastacia's Antiques
617 Bainbridge St,
Philadelphia,
PA 19147 USA
Tel: 001 215 928 9111

ASG (D)
Anthony Stern Glass
Unit 205, Avro House,
Havelock Terrace,
London SW8 4AL
Tel: 0207 622 9463
Fax: 0207 738 8100
anthony@anthonysternglass.com
www.anthonysternglass.com

ATA (D)
Atomic Age
318 East Virginia Road,
Fullerton, CA 92831 USA
Tel: 001 714 446 0736
Fax: 001 714 446 0436
atomage100@aol.com

ATK (A)
Auction Team Köln
Postfach 50 11 19,
Bonner Str. 528-530,
D-50971 Köln, Germany
Tel: 00 49 (0) 221 38 70 49
Fax: 00 49 (0) 221 37 48 78
auction@breker.com
www.breker.com

ATM (D)
At the Movies
17 Fouberts Place,
London W1F 7QD
Tel: 020 7439 6336
Fax: 020 7439 6355
info@atthemovies.co.uk
www.atthemovies.co.uk

B&H (A)
Burstow & Hewett
Lower Lake, Battle, East Sussex
TN33 0AT
Tel: 01424 772 374
Fax: 01424 772 302
auctions@burstowandhewett.co.uk
www.burstowandhewett.co.uk

BA (D)
Branksome Antiques
370 Poole Road,
Branksome, Poole,
Dorset BH12 1AW
Tel: 01202 763 324 / 679 932
Fax: 01202 763 643

BAD (D)
Beth Adams
Unit GO43/4, Alfies Antique
Market, 13 Church St,
Marylebone, London NW8 8DT
Tel: 020 7723 5613
Fax: 020 7262 1576
badams@alfies.clara.net

BAR (D)
Dreweatt Neate (Bristol)
St John's Place, Apsley Road,
Clifton, Bristol BS8 2ST
Tel: 0117 973 7201
Fax: 0117 973 5671
bristol@dnfa.com
www.dnfa.com

BB (D)
Barbara Blau
South Street Antiques Center, 615
South 6th St, Philadelphia, PA
19147-2128 USA
Tel: 001 215 592 0256

BBR (A)
BBR Auctions
Elsecar Heritage Centre, Nr
Barnsley, South Yorks S74 8AA
Tel: 01226 745156
Fax: 01226 361 561
www.bbrauctions.co.uk

BCAC (D)
Bucks County Antique Center
Route 202, Lahaska,
PA 18931 USA
Tel: 001 215 794 9180

BEJ (D)
Bébés & Jouets
c/o Post Office, 165 Restalrig
Road, Edinburgh EH7 6HW
Tel: 0131 332 5650
bebesetjouets@u.genie.co.uk

BEV (D)
Beverley
30 Church St, London NW8
8EP
Tel: 020 7262 1576

BG (A)
**Bob Gowland International
Golf Auctions**
The Stables, Claim Farm,
Manley Road, Frodsham,
Cheshire WA6 6HT
Tel: 01928 740 668
bob@internationalgolfauctions.com
www.internationalgolfauctions.com

BGL (D)
Block Glass Ltd.
60 Ridgeview Avenue, Trumbull,
CT 06611 USA
Tel: 001 203 556 0905
blockglass@aol.com
www.blockglass.com

BIB (D)
Biblion
1/7 Davies Mews,
London W1K 5AB
Tel: 020 7629 1374
Fax: 020 7493 7158
info@biblion.com
www.biblion.com

BMN (A)
Auktionhaus Bergmann
Möhrendorfestraße 4, D-91056
Erlangen Germany
Tel: 00 49 (0) 9131 45 06 66
Fax: 00 49 (0) 9131 45 02 04
kontact@auction-bergmann.de
www.auction-bergmann.de

BONE (A)
Bonhams, Edinburgh
65 George St,
Edinburgh EH2 2JL
Tel: 0131 225 2266
Fax: 0131 220 2547
info@bonhams.com
www.bonhams.com

BONM (A)
Bonhams, Knowle
The Old House, Station Road,
Knowle, Solihull,
West Midlands B93 0HT
Tel: 01564 776 151
Fax: 01564 778 069
info@bonhams.com
www.bonhams.com

BONS, BONBAY, BONC (A)
Bonhams, Bond St
101 New Bond St,
London W1S 1SR
Tel: 01732 740 310
Fax: 01732 741 842
info@bonhams.com
www.bonhams.com

BPAL (D)
The Book Palace
Bedwardine Road, Crystal
Palace, London SE19 3AP
Tel: 020 8768 0022
Fax: 020 8768 0563
www.bookpalace.com

BR (D)
Beyond Retro
110-112 Cheshire St,
London E2 6EJ
Tel: 020 7613 3636
Fax: 020 7613 3636
sales@beyondretro.com
www.beyondretro.com

BS (D)
Below Stairs of Hungerford
103 High St, Hungerford,
Berkshire RG17 0NB
Tel: 01488 682 317
Fax: 01488 684 294
hofgartner@belowstairs.co.uk
www.belowstairs.co.uk

BY (D)
Bonny Yankauer
Tel: 001 201 825 7697
bonnyy@aol.com

CAA (D)
Contemporary Applied Arts
2 Percy St, London W1T 1DD
Tel: 020 7436 2344
Fax: 020 7436 2446
www.caa.org.uk

CAC (D)
Charles A. Cohn
P.O. Box 8835, Elkins Park, PA
19027 USA
Tel: 001 215 840 6112
cacint@comcast.net

CANT (D)
Carlton Antiques
43 Worcester Road, Malvern,
Worcestershire WR14 4RB
Tel: 01684 573 092
dave@carlton-antiques.com
www.carlton-antiques.com

CARS (D)
**Classic Automobilia & Regalia
Specialists**
4-4a Chapel Terrace Mews,
Kemp Town,
Brighton BN2 1HU
Tel: 01273 601 960
Fax: 01273 623 846

CAT (D)
Catalin Radios
5443 Schultz Drive, Sylvania,
OH 43560 USA
Tel: 001 419 824 2469
Mob: 001 419 283 8203
steve@catalinradio.com
www.catalinradio.com

CBE (P)
Christina Bertrand
neke@rcn.com

CBU (D)
Chéz Burnette
South St Antiques Center, 615
South 6th St, Philadelphia, PA
19147-2128 USA
Tel: 001 215 592 0256

CCL (D)
Cloud Cuckoo Land
6 Charlton Place, Camden
Passage, London N1 8EA
Tel: 020 7354 3141

CG (D)
Cowdy Gallery
31 Culver St, Newent,
Gloucestershire GL18 1DB
Tel: 01531 821 173
info@cowdygallery.co.uk
www.cowdygallery.co.uk

CGC (P)
Cheryl Grandfield Collection

CHAA (A)
**Cowan's Historic Americana
Auctions**
673 Wilmer Avenue, Cincinnati,
OH 45226 USA
Tel: 001 513 871 1670
Fax: 001 513 871 8670
info@historicamericana.com
www.historicamericana.com

CHEF (A)
Cheffins
The Cambridge Salerooms,
1&2 Clifton Road,
Cambridge CB1 7EA
Tel: 01223 213 343
fine.art@chcffins.co.uk
www.cheffins.co.uk

CHS (D)
China Search
P.O. Box 1202, Kenilworth,
Warwickshire CV8 2WW
Tel: 01926 512 402
Fax: 01926 859 311
helen@chinasearch.uk.com
www.chinasearch.uk.com

CL (D)
Chisholm Larsson
145 8th Avenue, New York,
NY 10011 USA
Tel: 001 212 741 1703
Fax: 001 212 645 6691
www.chisholm-poster.com

CLV (A)
Clevedon Salerooms
The Auction Centre, Kenn Road,
Clevedon, Bristol BS21 6TT
Tel: 01934 830 111
Fax: 01934 832 538
Info@clevedonsalerooms.co.uk
www.clevedon-salerooms.com

CO (A)
Cooper Owen
10 Denmark St,
London WC2H 8LS
Tel: 020 7240 4132
info@cooperowen.com
www.cooperowen.com

COB (D)
Cobwebs
78 Old Northam Road,
Southampton SO14 0PB
Tel: 02380 227 458
Fax: 02380 227 458
www.cobwebs.uk.com

CR (A)
Craftsman Auctions
333 North Main St,
Lambertville, NJ 08530 USA
Tel: 001 609 397 9374
Fax: 001 609 397 9377
info@ragoarts.com
www.ragoarts.com

CRIS (D)
Cristobal
26 Church St, Marylebone,
London NW8 8EP
Tel: 020 7724 7230
steven@cristobal.co.uk
www.cristobal.co.uk

CS (D)
Christopher Seidler
Stand G13, Grays Mews
Antique Market, 1-7 Davies
Mews, London W1K 5AB
Tel: 020 7629 2851
tomus@tinyworld.co.uk

CSA (D)
Christopher Sykes Antiques
The Old Parsonage, Woburn,
Milton Keynes MK17 9QL
Tel: 01525 290 259/ 290 467
Fax: 01525 290 061
sykes.corkscrews@sykes-
corkscrews.co.uk
www.sykes-corkscrews.co.uk

CVS (D)
**Cad Van Swankster at The Girl
Can't Help It**
G115, Alfies Antique Market, 13
Church St, Marylebone,
London NW8 8DT
Tel: 020 7724 8984
Fax: 020 8809 3923

CW (P)
Christine Wildman Collection
wild123@allstream.net

DAC (D)
**Dynamite Antiques &
Collectibles**
Tel: 001 301 652 1140
bercovici@erols.com

DAW (A)
**Dawson's Auctioneers &
Appraisers
now trading as Dawson & Nye**
128 American Road, Morris
Plains, NJ 07950 USA
Tel: 001 973 984 6900
Fax: 001 973 984 6956
info@dawsonandnye.com
www.dawsonandnye.com

DE (D)
The Doll Express
Ceased trading.

DETC (D)
Deco Etc
122 West 25th St,
New York, NY 10001 USA
Tel: 001 212 675 3326
deco_etc@msn.com
www.decoetc.net

DG (D)
Donay Games
34 Gower Road, Haywards
Heath, West Sussex RH16 4PN
Tel: 01444 416 412
donaygames@btconnect.com
www.donaygames.com

DH (D)
Huxtins
11 & 12 The Lipka Arcade,
288 Westbourne Grove,
London W11
Mob: 07710 132 200
david@huxtins.com
www.huxtins.com

DN (A)
Dreweatt Neate
Donnington Priory Salerooms,
Donnington, Newbury,
Berkshire RG14 2JE
Tel: 01635 553 553
Fax: 01635 553 599
auctions@dnfa.com
www.dnfa.com

DRA (A)
Rago Modern Auctions
333 North Main St,
Lambertville, NJ 08530 USA
Tel: 001 609 397 9374
Fax: 001 609 397 9377
info@ragoarts.com
www.ragoarts.com

DTC (D)
Design20c
Tel: 0794 609 2138
/ 0776 013 5203
sales@design20c.com
www.design20c.com

EAB (D)
Anne Barrett
Otford Antiques Centre,
26-28 High St, Otford,
Kent TN15 9DF
Tel: 01959 522 025
Fax: 01959 525 858
info@otfordantiques.co.uk
www.otfordantiques.co.uk

ECLEC (D)
Eclectica
2 Charlton Place, Islington,
London N1
Tel: 020 7226 5625
eclecticaliz@yahoo.co.uk

EOH (D)
The End of History
548 1/2 Hudson St, New York,
NY 10014 USA
Tel: 001 212 647 7598
Fax: 001 212 647 7634

EPO (D)
Elaine Perkins
Otford Antiques Centre,
26-28 High St, Otford,
Kent TN15 9DF
Tel: 01959 522 025
Fax: 01959 525 858
info@otfordantiques.co.uk
www.otfordantiques.co.uk

ET (D)
Early Technology
Monkton House,
Old Craighall,
Musselburgh,
Midlothian,
Scotland EH21 8SF
Tel: 0131 665 5753
michael.bennett-levy@virgin.net
www.earlytech.com

EWC (P)
Emma Wilson Collection
Tel: 07989 493 831

F (A)
Fellows & Sons
Augusta House, 19 Augusta St,
Hockley, Birmingham B18 6JA
Tel: 0121 212 2131
Fax: 0121 212 1249
info@fellows.co.uk
www.fellows.co.uk

FAN (D)
Fantiques
30 Hastings Road, Ealing,
London W13 8QH
Tel: 020 8840 4761
paulajraven@aol.com

FFM (D)
Festival
136 South Ealing Rd,
London W5 4QJ
Tel: 020 8840 9333
info@festival1951.co.uk

FIS (A)
Auktionhaus Dr Fischer
Trappensee-Schößchen, D-
74074 Heilbronn Germany
Tel: 00 49 (0)71 31 15 55 70
Fax: 00 49 (0)71 31 15 55 720
kunstauktionendr.fischer@t-online.de
www.auctions-fischer.de

FM (D)
Francesca Martire
F131-137, Alfies Antique
Market, 13 Church St,
Marylebone, London NW8 8DT
Tel: 020 7724 4802
martire@alfies.clara.net

FRE (A)
Freeman's
1808 Chestnut St,
Philadelphia, PA 19103 USA
Tel: 001 215 563 9275
Fax: 001 215 563 8236
info@freemansauction.com
www.freemansauction.com

G (A)
Guernsey's Auctions
108 East 73rd St, New York,
NY 10021 USA
Tel: 001 212 794 2280
guernsey@guernseys.com
www.guernseys.com

GAZE (A)
Thos. Wm. Gaze & Son
Diss Auction Rooms, Roydon
Rd, Diss, Norfolk IP22 4LN
Tel: 01379 650 306
sales@dissauctionrooms.co.uk
www.twgaze.com

GC (P)
Graham Cooley Collection
Mob: 07968 722 269
graham.cooley@metalysis.com

GCA (D)
Griffin & Cooper Antiques
South St Antiques Center, 615
South 6th St, Philadelphia,
PA 19147-2128 USA
Tel: 001 215 582 0418

GCL (D)
Claude Lee
The Ginnel Antiques Centre,
Harrogate, North Yorks HG1 2RB
Tel: 01423 508 857
info@theginnel.com
www.redhouseyork.co.uk

GEW (D)
Eileen Wilson
The Ginnel Antiques Centre,
Harrogate, North Yorks HG1 2RB
Tel: 01423 508 857
info@theginnel.com
www.redhouseyork.co.uk

GGRT (D)
Gary Grant
18 Arlington Way,
London EC1R 1UY
Tel: 020 7713 1122

GHA (D)
Hawkswood Antiques
The Ginnel Antiques Centre,
Harrogate, North Yorks HG1 2RB
Tel: 01423 508 857
info@theginnel.com
www.redhouseyork.co.uk

GKA (D)
Kismet Antiques
The Ginnel Antiques Centre,
Harrogate, North Yorks HG1 2RB
Tel: 01423 508 857
info@theginnel.com
www.redhouseyork.co.uk

GMC (D)
Mary Cooper
The Ginnel Antiques Centre,
Harrogate, North Yorks HG1 2RB
Tel: 01423 508 857
info@theginnel.com
www.redhouseyork.co.uk

GMW (D)
Geoffrey and Millicent Woolworth
Otford Antiques Centre, 26-28
High St, Otford, Kent TN15 9DF
Tel: 01959 522 025
Fax: 01959 525 858
info@otfordantiques.co.uk
www.otfordantiques.co.uk

GORL (A)
Gorringes, Lewes
15 North St, Lewes, East
Sussex BN7 2PD
Tel: 01273 472 503
clientservices@gorringes.co.uk
www.gorringes.co.uk

GROB (D)
Geoffrey Robinson
Stand GO77-78 & GO91-92,
Alfies Antiques Market, 13-25
Church St, London NW8 8DT
Tel: 020 7723 0449

GWRA (A)
**Gloucestershire Worcestershire
Railwayana Auctions**
Tel: 01684 773 487
/ 01386 760 109
www.gwra.co.uk

H&G (D)
Hope and Glory
131A Kensington Church St,
London W8 7LP
Tel: 020 7727 8424

HAMG (A)
Hamptons
Baverstock House,
93 High St, Godalming,
Surrey GU7 1AL
Tel: 01483 423 567
fineart@hamptons-int.com
www.hamptons.co.uk

HB (D)
Victoriana Dolls
101 Portobello Rd,
London W11 2BQ
Tel: 01737 249 525
Fax: 01737 226 254
heather.bond@totalserve.co.uk

HD (D)
Halcyon Days
14 Brook St, London W1S 1BD
Tel: 020 7629 8811
Fax: 020 7409 7901
info@halcyondays.co.uk
www.halcyondays.co.uk

HGS (D)
Harper's General Store
10482 Jonestown Rd, Annville,
PA 17003 USA
Tel: 001 717 865 3456
Fax: 001 717 865 3813
lauver5@comcast.com
www.harpergeneralstore.com

HLJ (D)
Hugo Lee-Jones
Tel: 01227 375 375
electroniccollectables@hotmail.com

HP (D)
Hilary Proctor
Vintage Modes, Grays Antiques
Market, 1-7 Davies Mews,
London W1Y 2PL
Tel: 020 7409 0400
Mob: 07956 876 428
hproctor@antiquehandbags.fsne
t.co.uk
www.vintagemodes.co.uk

INT (D)
Intercol
43 Templar's Crescent, Finchley,
London N3 3QR
Tel: 020 8349 2207
Fax: 020 8349 9539
yasha@intercol.co.uk
www.intercol.co.uk

J&H (A)
Jacobs and Hunt Auctioneers
26 Lavant St, Petersfield,
Hampshire GU32 3EF
Tel: 01730 233 933
Fax: 01730 262 323
auctions@jacobsandhunt.co.uk
www.jacobsandhunt.co.uk

JBC (D)
James Bridges Collection
james@jbridges.fsnet.co.uk

JDJ (A)
James D Julia Inc
P.O. Box 830, Fairfield,
Maine 04937 USA
Tel: 001 207 453 7125
Fax: 001 207 453 2502
lampnglass@juliaauctions.com
www.juliaauctions.com

JF (D)
Jill Fenichell
305 East 61st St, New York, NY
10021 USA
Tel: 001 212 980 9346
jfenichell@yahoo.com

JH (D)
Jeanette Hayhurst Fine Glass
32A Kensington Church St,
London W8 4HA
Tel: 020 7938 1539

JJ (D)
Junkyard Jeweler
937 West Beech St,
Suite 49, Long Beach,
NY 11561, USA
spignerc@aol.com
www.junkyardjeweler.com

JL (D)
Eastgate Antiques
SOO7/009, Alfies Antique
Market, 13 Church St,
Marylebone, London NW8 8DT
Tel: 0207 258 0312
Fax: 020 7724 0999

JSC (P)
Jean Scott Collection
jean@stanhopes.info
www.stanhopes.info

JV (D)
June Victor
Vintage Modes, Grays Antiques
Market, 1-7 Davies Mews,
London W1Y 2PL
Tel: 020 7409 0400
info@vintagemodes.co.uk
www.vintagemodes.co.uk

KF (D)
Karl Flaherty Collectables
Tel: 02476 445 627
kfckarl@aol.com
www.kfcollectables.co.uk

KG (D)
Ken Grant
F109-F111, Alfies Antique
Market, 13 Church St,
Marylebone, London NW8 8DT
Tel: 020 7723 1370
Fax: 020 7721 0999
k-grant@alfies.clara.net

KK (D)
Kathy's Korner
Tel: 001 516 624 9494

KNK (D)
Kitsch-N-Kaboodle
South St Antiques Center,
615 South 6th St,
Philadelphia,
PA 19147-2128 USA
Tel: 001 215 382 1354
kitschnkaboodle@yahoo.com

L (D)
Luna
23 George St,
Nottingham NG1 3BH
Tel: 0115 924 3267
info@luna-online.com
www.luna-online.com

L&T (A)
Lyon and Turnbull Ltd.
3 Broughton Place,
Edinburgh EH1 3RR
Tel: 0131 557 8844
Fax: 0131 557 8668
info@lyonandturnbull.com
www.lyonandturnbull.com

LAN (A)
Lankes Auktionhaus
Triftfeldstrasse 1,
95182 Döhlau
Germany
Tel: 0049 (0) 928 69 50 50
Fax: 0049 (0) 928 69 50 540
www.lankes-auktionen.de

LB (D)
Linda Bee
Stand L18-21, Grays Mews
Antique Market, 58 Davies St,
London W1Y 2LP
Tel: 020 7629 5921
Fax: 020 7629 5921
Mob: 07956 276384
www.graysantiques.com

LC (A)
Lawrence's Fine Art Auctioneers
The Linen Yard, South St,
Crewkerne, Somerset TA18 8AB
Tel: 01460 73041
Fax: 01460 74627
enquiries@lawrences.co.uk
www.lawrences.co.uk

LCA (D)
Lights, Camera, Action
6 Western Gardens, Western
Boulevard, Aspley,
Nottingham HG8 5GP
Tel: 0115 913 1116
nickstraw@ntlbusiness.com
www.lca-autographs.co.uk

LFA (A)
Law Fine Art Ltd.
The Long Gallery,
Littlecote House,
Hungerford,
Berkshire RG17 0SS
Tel: 01635 860 033
Fax: 01635 860 033
info@lawfineart.co.uk
www.lawfineart.co.uk

LG (D)
Legacy
G50/51, Alfies Antique Market,
13 Church St, Marylebone,
London NW8 8DT
Tel: 020 7723 0449
Fax: 020 7724 0999
legacy@alfies.clara.net

LHS (A) (D)
L.H. Selman Ltd.
123 Locust St, Santa Cruz, CA
950600 USA
www.selman.com

LOB (D)
Louis O'Brien
Tel: 01276 32907

LW (D)
Linda Warren
Otford Antiques Centre, 26-28
High St, Otford, Kent TN15 9DF
Tel: 01959 522 025
Fax: 01959 525 858
info@otfordantiques.co.uk
www.otfordantiques.co.uk

MA (D)
Manic Attic
Stand S011, Alfies Antiques
Market, 13 Church St,
London NW8 8DT
Tel: 020 7723 6105
Fax: 020 7724 0999
manicattic@alfies.clara.net

MAC (D)
Mary Ann's Collectibles
South St Antiques Center,
615 South 6th St,
Philadelphia,
PA 19147-2128 USA
Tel: 001 215 923 3247

MC (D)
Metropolis Collectibles, Inc.
873 Broadway, Suite 201,
New York, NY 10003 USA
Tel: 001 212 260 4147
Fax: 001 212 260 4304
orders@metropoliscomics.com
www.metropoliscomics.com

MCOL (P)
Mick Collins Collection
admin@sylvacclub.com

MEM (D)
Memory Lane
45-40 Bell Blvd,
Suite 109, Bayside,
NY 11361 USA
Tel: 001 718 428 8181
memlnny@aol.com
www.tias.com/store/memlnny

MHC (P)
Mark Hill Collection
Mob: 07798 915 474
stylophile@btopenworld.com

MHT (D)
Mum Had That
Tel: 01442 412 360
info@mumhadthat.com
www.mumhadthat.com

MILLB (D)
Million Dollar Babies
47 Hyde Boulevard, Ballston
Spa, NY 12020 USA
Tel: 001 518 885 7397

ML (D)
Mark Laino
South St Antiques Center,
615 South 6th St,
Philadelphia,
PA 19147-2128 USA

MM (A)
Mullock Madeley
The Old Shippon,
Wall-under-Heywood,
Church Stretton,
Shropshire SY6 7DS
Tel: 01694 771 771
Fax: 01694 771 772
info@mullockmadeley.co.uk
www.mullock-madeley.co.uk

MTS (D)
The Multicoloured Time Slip
Unit S002, Alfies Antiques
Market, 13-25 Church St,
London NW8 8DT
Mob: 07971 410 563
d_a_cameron@hotmail.com

MUW (D)
MuseumWorks
525 East Cooper Avenue,
Aspen CO 81611 USA
www.mwhgalleries.com

NB (A)
Noel Barrett Antiques &
Auctions Ltd
P.O. Box 300, Carversville,
PA 18913 USA
Tel: 001 215 297 5109
toys@noelbarrett.com
www.noelbarrett.com

NBC (P)
Nick Batt Collection
Tel: 020 8455 0719

NBEN (D)
Nigel Benson –
20th Century Glass
58-60 Kensington Church St,
London W8 4DB
Tel: 020 7938 1137
Fax: 020 7729 9875
nigelbenson@20thcentury-
glass.com
www.20thcentury-glass.com

NBS (P)
New Baxter Society
c/o Reading Museum and Art
Gallery, Blagrave St,
Reading RG1 1QH
baxter@rpsfamily.demon.co.uk
www.rpsfamily.demon,co,uk

NOR (D)
Neet-O-Rama
93 West Main St, Somerville,
NJ 08876 USA
Tel: 001 908 722 4800
www.neetstuff.com

NWC (P)
Nigel Wright Collection
xab@dircon.co.uk

ON (A)
Onslows
The Coach House,
Manor Rd, Stourpaine,
Dorset DT11 8TQ
Tel: 01258 488 838
Fax: 01258 488 838
enquiries@onslows.co.uk
www.onslows.co.uk

P (D)
Posteritati
239 Centre St, New York,
NY 10013 USA
Tel: 001 212 226 2207
Fax: 001 212 226 2102
mail@posteritati.com
www.posteritati.com

P&I (D)
Paola & Iaia
Unit S057-58, Alfies Antiques
Market, 13-25 Church St,
London NW8 8DT
Tel: 07751 084 135
paolaeiaialondon@hotmail.com

PAC (D)
Port Antiques Center
289 Main St, Port Washington,
NY 11050 USA
Tel: 001 516 767 3313
visualedge2@aol.com

PC (P)
Private Collection

PL (D)
London Glass Blowing
7, The Leather Market,
Weston St, London SE1 3ER
Tel: 0207 403 2800
Fax: 0207 403 7750
inf@londonglassblowing.co.uk
www.londonglassblowing.co.uk

PSA (A)
Potteries Specialist Auctions
271 Waterloo Rd, Cobridge,
Stoke-on-Trent ST6 3HR
Tel: 01782 286 622
Fax: 01782 213 777
enquiries@potteriesauctions.com
www.potteriesauctions.com

PSL (D)
The Prop Store London
Great House Farm, Chenies,
Rickmansworth,
Herts WD3 6EP
Tel: 01494 766 485
Fax: 01494 766 487
steve.lane@propstore.co.uk
www.propstore.co.uk

QU (A)
Quittenbaum
Hohenstaufenstraße 1, D-
80801, München Germany
Tel: 0049 859 33 00 75 6
Fax: 0049 089 33 00 75 77
dialog@quittenbaum.de
www.quittenbaum.de

REN (D)
Rennies
13 Rugby St, London WC1 3QT
Tel: 020 7405 0220
info@rennart.co.uk
www.rennart.co.uk

RG (D)
Richard Gibbon
34/34a Islington Green,
London N1 8DU
Tel: 020 7354 2852
neljeweluk@aol.com

RH (D)
Rick Hubbard Art Deco
3 Tee Court, Bell St, Romsey,
Hampshire SO51 8GY
Tel: 01794 513 133
www.rickhubbard-artdeco.co.uk

ROS (A)
Roseberry's
74-76 Knight's Hill,
West Norwood,
London SE27 0JD
Tel: 020 8761 2522
Fax: 020 8761 2524
enquiries@roseberys.co.uk
www.roseberys.co.uk

ROX (D)
Roxanne Stuart
Tel: 001 888 750 8869 / 001
215 750 8868
gemfairy@aol.com

RP (D)
Rosie Palmer
Otford Antiques Centre, 26-28
High St, Otford, Kent TN15 9DF
Tel: 01959 522 025
Fax: 01959 525 858
info@otfordantiques.co.uk
www.otfordantiques.co.uk

RR (D)
Red Roses
Vintage Modes, Grays Antiques
Market, 1-7 Davies Mews,
London W1Y 2PL
Tel: 020 7409 0400
sallie_ead@lycos.com
www.vintagemodes.co.uk

RSJ (D)
Roger & Susan Johnson
1701 Venture Farms Rd, Pilot
Point, TX 76258 USA
Tel: 001 940 365 9149
Fax: 001 940 365 4401
czarmann@aol.com

RTZ (D)
Ritzy
7 The Mall Antiques Arcade,
359 Upper St, London N1 0PD
Tel: 020 7351 5353
Fax: 020 7351 5350

RWA (D)
Richard Wallis Antiks
Tel: 020 8529 1749
Fax: 0870 051 5740
Mob: 07721 583306
info@richardwallisantiks.co.uk
www.richardwallisantiks.com

S&K (A)
Sloans & Kenyon
4605 Bradley Boulevard,
Bethesda, MD 20815 USA
Tel: 001 301 634 2330
Fax: 001 301 656 7074
info@sloansandkenyon.com
www.sloansandkenyon.com

SAS (A)
Special Auction Services
Kennetholme, Midgham,
Nr. Reading, Berkshire RG7 5UX
Tel: 0118 971 2949
Fax: 0118 971 2420
commemorative@aol.com
www.invaluable.com/sas

SCG (D)
Gallery 1930 Susie Cooper
18 Church Street,
Marylebone,
London NW8 8EP
Tel: 020 7723 1555
Fax: 020 7735 8309
gallery1930@aol.com
www.susiecooperceramics.com

SD (P)
Simon Dunlavey Collection
pennyblack@despammed.com

SEG (D)
Galerie Segas
34, Passage Jouffroy,
75009 Paris France
Tel: 00 33 (0) 1 47 70 89 65

SEVW (D)
70s Watches
graham@gettya.freeserve.co.uk
www.70s-watches.com

SL (A)
Sloans
Ceased trading.

SM (D)
Sparkle Moore at The Girl
Can't Help It
G100 & G116, Alfies Antique
Market, 13 Church Street,
Marylebone, London NW8 8DT
Tel: 020 7724 8984
sparkle.moore@virgin.net
www.sparklemoore.com

SOTT (D)
Sign of the Tymes
Mill Antiques Center,
12 Morris Farm Road,
Lafayette, NJ 07848 USA
Tel: 001 973 383 6028
jhap@nac.net
www.millantiques.com

SSC (P)
Sue Scrivens Collection

STC (D)
Seaside Toy Center
Joseph Soucy
179 Main St, Westerly,
RI 02891 USA
Tel: 001 401 596 0962

SUM (D)
Sue Mautner
Stand A18-19, Antiquarius, 135
King's Rd, London SW3 4PW
Tel: 020 7376 4419
Fax: 020 7531 5350

SWA (A)
Swann Galleries Image Library
104 East 25th St, New York,
NY 10010 USA
Tel: 001 212 254 4710
Fax: 001 212 979 1017
www.swanngalleries.com

TA (A)
333 Auctions LLC
333 North Main St,
Lambertville, NJ 08530 USA
Tel: 001 609 397 9374
Fax: 001 609 397 9377
www.333auctions.com

TAB (D)
Take-A-Boo Emporium
1927 Avenue Rd, Toronto,
Ontario M5M 4A2 Canada
Tel: 001 416 785 4555
Fax: 001 416 785 4594
swinton@takeaboo.com
www.takeaboo.com

TAG (D)
Tagore Ltd
302, Grays Antique Market, 58
Davies St, London W1Y 2LP
Tel: 020 7499 0158
Fax: 020 7499 0158
tagore@grays.clara.net

TCS (D)
The Country Seat
Huntercombe Manor Barn,
nr Henley on Thames,
Oxon RG9 5RY
Tel: 01491 641 349
Fax: 01491 641 533
info@whitefriarsglass.com
www.whitefriarsglass.com

TCT (D)
The Calico Teddy
Tel: 001 410 433 9202
Fax: 001 410 433 9203
calicteddy@aol.com
www.calicoteddy.com

TDG (D)
The Design Gallery
5, The Green,
Westerham,
Kent TN16 1AS
Tel: 01959 561 234
sales@thedesigngallery.uk.com
www.thedesigngallery.uk.com

TEN (A)
Tennants
The Auction Centre,
Leyburn,
North Yorkshire DL8 5SG
Tel: 01969 623 780
Fax: 01969 624 281
enquiry@tennants-ltd.co.uk
www.tennants.co.uk

TGM (D)
The Glass Merchant
Tel: 07775 683 961
as@titan98.freeserve.co.uk

TH (D)
Toy Heroes
42 Westway, Caterham-on-the-
Hill, Surrey CR3 5TP
Tel: 0188 334 8001
andydroon@aol.com
www.toyheroes.co.uk

TM (D)
Tony Moran
South St Antiques Center, 615
South 6th St, Philadelphia, PA
19147-2128 USA
Tel: 001 215 592 0256

TO (D)
Titus Omega
Tel: 020 7688 1295
www.titusomega.com

TOG (D)
A Touch of Glass
Tel: 001 973 857 2617
deold@antiqueconnection.com
www.antiqueconnection.com

TP (D)
Tenth Planet
Vicarage Field Shopping
Centre, Barking, IG11 8DQ
Tel: 020 8591 5357
Fax: 020 8591 3035
sales@tenthplanet.co.uk
www.tenthplanet.co.uk

TR (D)
Terry Rodgers & Melody LLC
30 Manhattan Art and Antique
Center, 1050 2nd Avenue,
New York, NY 10022 USA
Tel: 001 212 758 3164
Fax: 001 212 935 6365
melodyjewelnyc@aol.com

TSIS (D)
Three Sisters
South St Antiques Center, 615
South 6th St, Philadelphia, PA
19147-2128 USA

TWC (A)
T.W. Conroy
36 Oswego St,
Baldwinsville, NY 13027 USA
Tel: 001 315 638 6434
Fax: 001 315 638 7039
www.twconroy.com

VE (D)
Vintage Eyeware of New York
Tel: 001 646 319 9222
www.vintage-eyeware.com

VEC (A)
Vectis Auctions Limited
Fleck Way, Thornaby,
Stockton on Tees TS17 9JZ
Tel: 01642 750 616
Fax: 01642 769 478
enquiries@vectis.co.uk
www.vectis.co.uk

VET (D)
Vetri & Arte Gallery in Venice
Calle del Cappeler 3212,
Dorsoduro, 30123 Venice Italy
Tel: 0039 041 522 8525
contact@venicewebgallery.com
www.venicewebgallery.com

VM (D)
VinMagCo
39/43 Brewer St,
London W1R 9UD
Tel: 020 7439 8525
Fax: 020 7439 8527
sales@vinmag.com
www.vinmag.com

VV (D)
Vintage to Vogue
28 Milsom St,
Bath BA1 1DG
Tel: 01225 337 323
www.vintagetovoguebath.com

W&W (A)
Wallis & Wallis
West St Auction Galleries,
Lewes, East Sussex BN7 2NJ
Tel: 01273 480 208
Fax: 01273 476 562
auctions@wallisandwallis.co.uk
www.wallisandwallis.co.uk

WAC (D)
What A Character!
hughk@aol.com /
bazuin32@aol.com
www.whatacharacter.com

WHA (A)
Willis Henry Auctions Inc
22 Main St, Marshfield, MA
02050 USA
Tel: 001 781 834 7774
Fax: 001 781 826 3520
wha@willishenry.com
www.willishenry.com

WKA (A)
Wiener Kunst Auktionen -
Palais Kinsky
Freyung 4, A-1010 Wien
Tel: 00 43 15 32 42 00
Fax: 00 43 15 32 42 009
office@palais-kinsky.com
www.palais-kinsky.com

WW (A)
Woolley & Wallis
51-61 Castle St, Salisbury,
Wiltshire SP1 3SU
Tel: 01722 424 500
Fax: 01722 424 508
enquiries@woolleyandwallis.co.uk
www.woolleyandwallis.co.uk

DIRECTORY OF SPECIALISTS

If you wish to have any item valued, it is advisable to contact the dealer or specialist in advance to check that they will carry out this service and whether there is a charge. While most dealers will be happy to help you with an enquiry, do remember that they are busy people. Telephone valuations are not possible. Please mention the DK Collectables Price Guide 2005 by Judith Miller when making an enquiry.

ADVERTISING

Huxtins
11 & 12 The Lipka Arcade, 288 Westbourne Grove, London W11
Mob: 07710 132 200
david@huxtins.com
www.huxtins.com

ANIMATION ART

Animation Art Gallery
13-14 Great Castle St
London W1W 8LS
Tel: 020 7255 1456
Fax: 020 7436 1256
gallery@animaart.com
www.animaart.com

AUTOGRAPHS

Lights, Camera Action
6 Western Gardens, Western Boulevard, Aspley,
Nottingham NG8 5GP
Tel: 0115 913 1116
nickstraw@ntlbusiness.com
www.lca-autographs.co.uk

AUTOMOBILIA

Classic Automobilia & Regalia Specialists
4-4a Chapel Terrace Mews,
Kemp Town, Brighton NBN 1HU
Tel: 01273 601 960
Fax: 01273 623 846

BOOKS

Biblion
Gray's Mews Antiques Market,
1-7 Davies Mews,
London W1K 5AB
Tel: 020 7629 1374
Fax: 020 7493 7158
www.biblion.com

BONDS & SHARES

Intercol
43 Templar's Crescent, Finchley,
London N3 3QR
Tel: 020 8349 2207
Fax: 020 8349 9539
sales@intercol.co.uk
www.intercol.co.uk

CANES

Michael German Antiques
38b Kensington Church St,
London W8
Tel: 020 7937 2771

CERAMICS

Beth Adams
Alfies Antiques Market, Stand
G43/44, 13-25 Church St,
London NW8
Tel: 020 7723 5613
Fax: 020 7262 1576

Beverley
30 Church St
London NW8
Tel: 020 7262 1576

China Search
P.O. Box 1202, Kenilworth
Warwickshire CV8 2WW
Tel: 01926 512 402
Fax: 01926 859 311
helen@chinasearch.uk.com
www.chinasearch.uk.com

Eastgate Antiques
S007/009, Alfies Antique
Market, 13 Church St,
Marylebone, London NW8 8DT
Tel: 0207 258 0312
Fax: 020 7724 0999

Feljoy Antiques
Shop 3, Angel Arcade, Camden
Passage, London N1 8EA
Tel: 020 7354 5336
Fax: 020 7831 3485
joy@feljoy-antiques.demon.co.uk
www.chintznet.com/feljoy

Festival
136 South Ealing Rd,
London W5 4QJ
Tel: 020 8840 9333
sj@festival1951.demon.co.uk

Susie Cooper Gallery
18 Church St,
London NW8 8FP
Tel: 020 7723 1555
Fax: 020 7735 8309

Gary Grant Choice Pieces
18 Arlington Way,
London EC1R 1UY
Tel: 020 7713 1122

Gillian Neale Antiques
P.O. Box 247,
Aylesbury HP20 1JZ
Tel: 01296 423754
Fax: 01296 334601
gillianneale@aol.com
www.gilliannealeantiques.co.uk

Louis O'Brien
Tel: 01276 32907

Mad Hatter
Admiral Vernon Antiques
Market, Unit 83, 141-149
Portobello Rd, London W11
Tel: 020 7262 0487
madhatter.portobello@virgin.net

Rick Hubbard Art Deco
3 Tee Court, Bell St, Romsey,
Hampshire SO51 8GY
Tel: 01794 513133
www.rickhubbard-artdeco.co.uk

Geoffrey Robinson
Stand G077-78 & G091-92
Alfies Antiques Market, 13-25
Church St, London NW8 8DT
Tel: 020 7723 0449

Rogers de Rin
76 Royal Hospital Rd,
Paradise Walk,
London SW3 4HN
Tel: 020 7352 9007
rogersderin@rogersderin.co.uk
www.rogersderin.co.uk

Sue Norman
Antiquarius, Stand L4, 135
King's Rd, London SW3 4PW
Tel: 020 7352 7217
Fax: 020 8870 4677
sue@sue-norman.demon.co.uk
www.sue-norman.demon.co.uk

CIGARETTE CARDS

Carlton Antiques
43 Worcester Road, Malvern,
Worcestershire WR14 4RB
Tel: 01684 573 092
dave@carlton-antiques.com
www.carlton-antiques.com

COINS

Intercol
43 Templar's Crescent, Finchley,
London N3 3QR
Tel: 020 8349 2207
Fax: 020 8349 9539
sales@intercol.co.uk
www.intercol.co.uk

COMICS

Book & Comic Exchange
14 Pembridge Rd, London W11
Tel: 020 7229 8420

The Book Palace
Bedwardine Road, Crystal
Palace, London SE19
Tel: 020 8768 0022
Fax: 020 8768 0563
www.bookpalace.com

COMMEMORATIVE WARE

Hope & Glory
131a Kensington Church St,
London W8 7LP
Tel: 020 7727 8424

Recollections
5 Royal Arcade, Boscombe,
Bournemouth, Dorset BH1 4BT
Tel: 01202 304 441

Susan Rees
Tel: 01582 715 555
Fax: 01582 715 555

COSTUME & ACCESSORIES

Beyond Retro
110-112 Cheshire St,
London E2 6EJ
Tel: 020 7613 3636
sales@beyondretro.com
www.beyondretro.com

Cad van Swankster at The Girl Can't Help It
Alfies Antiques Market, Shop
G100 & G115, 13-25 Church
St, London NW8 8DT
Tel: 020 7724 8984
Fax: 020 8809 3923

Cloud Cuckoo Land
6 Charlton Place, London, N1
Tel: 020 7354 3141

Decades
20 Lord St West, Blackburn
BB2 1JX
Tel: 01254 693320

Fantiques
30 Hastings Rd, Ealing,
London W13 8QH
Tel: 020 8840 4761
paulajraven@aol.com

Linda Bee
Gray's Mews Antiques Market,
1-7 Davies Mews,
London W1Y 2LP
Tel/Fax: 020 7629 5921

Old Hat
66 Fulham High St,
London SW6 3LQ
Tel: 020 7610 6558

Sparkle Moore at The Girl Can't Help It
Alfie's Antiques Market, Shop
G100 & G116, 13-25 Church
St, London NW8 8DT
Tel: 020 7724 8984
Fax: 020 8809 3923
sparkle.moore@virgin.net
www.sparklemoore.com

Vintage Modes
Grays Antiques Market, 1-7
Davies Mews, London W1Y2PL
Tel: 020 7409 0400
info@vintagemodes.co.uk
www.vintagemodes.co.uk

Vintage to Vogue
228 Milsom St, Bath,
Avon BA1 1DG
Tel: 01225 337323

COSTUME JEWELLERY

Cristobal
26 Church St, London NW8 8EP
Tel: 020 7724 7230
steven@cristobal.co.uk
www.cristobal.co.uk

Eclectica
2 Charlton Place, London N1
Tel: 0207226 5625
eclecticaliz@yahoo.com

Richard Gibbon
34/34a Islington Green,
London N1 8DU
Tel: 020 7354 2852
neljeweluk@aol.com

Ritzy
7, The Mall Antiques Arcade,
359 Upper St, London N1 0PD
Tel: 020 7351 5353

William Wain
Antiquarius, 131-141 King's
Rd, London SW3 4PW
Tel: 020 7351 5353

DOLLS

Bébés & Jouets
c/o Post Office,
165 Restalrig Rd,
Edinburgh EH7 6HW
Tel: 0131 332 5650

Sandra Fellner
Gray's Antiques Market, 58
Davies St, London W1
Tel: 020 8946 5613

Victoriana Dolls
101 Portobello Rd,
London W11 2BQ
Tel: 01737 249 525
Fax: 01737 226 254
heather.bond@totalserve.co.uk

Yesterday Child
1 Angel Arcade,
118 Islington High St
London N1 8EG
Tel: 020 7354 1601

EPHEMERA

Legacy
G50/51 Alfie's Antiques
Market, 13-25 Church St,
London NW8 8DT
Tel: 020 7723 0449

FIFTIES, SIXTIES & SEVENTIES

Design 20c
Tel: 07946 092 138
/ 07760 135 203
sales@design20c.com
www.design20c.com

Luna
323 George St,
Nottingham NG1 3BH
Tel: 0115 924 3267
info@luna-online.co.uk
www.luna-online.co.uk

Manic Attic
Alfie's Antiques Market, Stand
S011, 13-25 Church St,
London NW8 8DT
Tel: 020 7723 6105
Fax: 020 7724 0999
manicattic@alfies.clara.net

The Multicoloured Timeslip
Unit S002, Alfies Antiques
Market, 13-2 Church Street,
London NW8 8DT
d_a_cameron@hotmail.com

FILM & TV

The Prop Store of London
Great House Farm,
Chenies, Rickmansworth,
Herts WD3 6EP
Tel: 01494 766 485
Fax: 01494 766 487
steve.lane@propstore.co.uk
www.propstore.co.uk

GENERAL

Alfie's Antiques Market
13-25 Church St,
London NW8 8DT
Tel: 020 7723 6066
info@alfiesantiques.com
www.alfiesantiques.com

Bartlett St Antiques Centre
5-10 Bartlett St, Bath BA1 2QZ
Tel: 01225 466689

Bermondsey Market
Crossing of Long Lane &
Bermondsey St,
London SE1
Tel: 020 7351 5353
Every Friday morning from 5am

Brackley Antique Cellar
Drayman's Walk, Brackley,
Northamptonshire
Tel: 01280 841 841
Fax: 01280 841 851

Camden Passage Market
Camden Passage,
Islington, London N1
Every Wednesday morning

The Ginnel Antiques Centre
Off Parliment St,
Harrogate,
North Yorkshire HG1 2RB
Tel: 01423 508 857
info@theginnel.com
www.redhouseyork.co.uk

Great Grooms at Hungerford
Riverside House,
Charnham St,
Hungerford,
Berkshire RG17 0EP
Tel: 01488 682 314
Fax: 01488 686 677
antiques@great-grooms.co.uk
www.great-grooms.co.uk

Heanor Antiques Centre
11-3 Ilkeston Rd,
Heanor, Derbyshire
Tel: 01773 531 181
Fax: 01773 762 759
sales@heanorantiquescentre.co.uk
www.heanorantiquescentre.co.uk

Heskin Hall Antiques
Heskin Hall,
Wood Lane, Heskin,
Chorley,
Lancashire PR7 5PA
Tel/Fax: 01257 452 044
heskinhallantiques@att.global.net

**Otford Antiques and
Collectors Centre**
26-28 High St, Otford,
Kent TN15 9DF
Tel: 01959 522 025
Fax: 01959 525 858
www.otfordantiques.co.uk

Portobello Rd Market
Portobello Rd, London W11
Every Saturday from 6am

Potteries Antique Centre
271 Waterloo Rd, Cobridge,
Stoke-on-Trent ST6 3HR
Tel: 01782 201518
Fax: 01782 201 518
www.potteriesantiquescentre.com

The Swan Antiques Centre
Tetsworth, nr Thame,
Oxfordshire OX9 7AB
Tel: 01844 281777
Fax: 01844 281770
antiques@theswan.co.uk
www.theswan.co.uk

**Woburn Abbey Antiques
Centre**
Woburn Abbey, Woburn,
Bedfordshire MK17 9WA
Tel: 01525 290 350
Fax: 01525 292 102

GLASS

Andrew Lineham Fine Glass
The Mall, Camden Passage,
London N1 8ED
Tel/Fax: 01243 576 241
www.andrewlineham.co.uk

**Antique Glass at Frank Dux
Antiques**
33 Belvedere, Bath BA1 5HR
Tel/Fax: 01225 312 367
www.antique-glass.co.uk

Francesca Martire
Stand F131-137, First Floor,
13-25 Alfies Antiques Market,
13 Church St,
London NW8 0RH
Tel: 020 7723 1370
www.francescamartire.com

Jeanette Hayhurst Fine Glass
32a Kensington Church St,
London W8 4HA
Tel: 020 7938 1539

Mum Had That
Tel: 01442 412 360
info@mumhadthat.com
www.mumhadthat.com

**Nigel Benson 20th Century
Glass**
58-60 Kensington Church St,
London W8 4DB
Tel: 020 7938 1137
Fax: 020 7729 9875

KITCHENALIA

Appleby Antiques
Geoffrey Van Arcade, Stand 18,
107 Portobello Rd,
London W11
Tel: 01453 753 126
applebyantiques@aol.com
www.applebyantiques.com

Below Stairs of Hungerford
103 High St, Hungerford,
Berkshire RG17 0NB
Tel: 01488 682 317
Fax: 01488 684 294
www.belowstairs.co.uk

Ken Grant
F109-111 Alfies Antiques
Market, 13-25 Church Street,
Marylebone, London NW8 8D
Tel: 020 7723 1370
Fax: 020 7721 0999
k-grant@alfies.clara.net

Ann Lingard
18-22 Rope Walk, Rye,
Sussex TN31 7NA
Tel: 01797 233 486
Fax: 01797 224 700

MECHANICAL MUSIC

Terry & Daphne France
Tel: 01243 265 946
Fax: 01243 779 582

The Talking Machine
30 Watford Way, London
NW4 3AL
Tel: 020 8202 3473
talkingmachine@gramophones.n
direct.co.uk
www.gramophones.ndirect.co.uk

MILITARIA

Boscombe Militaria
86 Palmerston Rd, Boscombe,
Bournemouth, Dorset BH1 4HU
Tel: 01202 733 696

Christopher Seidler
Gray's Mews Antiques Market,
South Molton Lane,
London W1K 5AB
Tel: 020 7629 2851

Q&C Militaria
22 Suffolk Rd, Cheltenham,
Gloucestershire GL50 2AQ
Tel: 01242 519 815
john@qcmilitaria.freeserve.
co.uk
www.qcmilitaria.com

PAPERWEIGHTS

Sweetbriar Gallery Ltd
Sweetbriar House, Robin Hood
Lane, Helsby,
Cheshire WA6 9NH
Tel: 01928 723 851
Fax: 01928 724 153
www.sweetbriar.co.uk

PLASTICS

Paola & Iaia
Alfie's Antiques Market, Stand
S050/051, 13-25 Church St,
London NW8 8DT
Tel: 07751 084 135

POSTCARDS

Carlton Antiques
43 Worcester Road,
Malvern,
Worcestershire WR14 4RB
Tel: 01684 573 092
dave@carlton-antiques.com
www.carlton-antiques.com

POSTERS

At The Movies
17 Fouberts Place, London
W1F 7QD
Tel/Fax: 020 7439 6355
info@atthemovies.co.uk
www.atthemovies.co.uk

Barclay Samson
65 Finlay St, London SW6 6HF
Tel: 020 7731 8013
richard@barclaysamson.com

DODO
Alfies Antiques Market, Shop
F071, 13-25 Church St,
London NW8 8DT
Tel: 020 7706 1545

The Reelposter Gallery
72 Westbourne Grove,
London W2 5SH
Tel: 020 7727 4488
Fax: 020 7727 4499
info@reelposter.com
www.reelposter.com

Rennies
13 Rugby St,
London WC1 3QT
Tel: 020 7405 0220
info@rennart.co.uk
www.rennart.co.uk

PENS & WRITING

Battersea Pen Home
PO Box 6128,
Epping CM16 4CG
Tel: 0870 900 1888
Fax: 0970 909 9888
info@penhome.com
www.penhome.com

Henry The Pen Man
Admiral Vernon Antiques
Market, Portobello Rd,
London W11
Tel: 020 8530 3277

RADIOS

On the Air Ltd
The Vintage Technology Centre,
The Highway,
Hawarden CH5 3DN
Tel: 01244 530 300
www.vintageradio.co.uk

ROCK & POP

Beatcity
PO Box 229, Chatham,
Kent ME5 8WA
Tel: 01634 200 444
www.beatcity.co.uk

More Than Music
PO Box 2809,
Eastbourne,
Sussex BN21 2EA
Tel: 01323 649 778
Fax: 01323 649 779
www.mtmglobal.com

Tracks
PO Box 117,
Chorley,
Lancashire PR6 0UU
Tel: 01257 269 726
Fax: 01257 231 340
sales@tracks.co.uk
www.tracks.co.uk

SCIENTIFIC & TECHNICAL, INCLUDING OFFICE, MEDICAL, OPTICAL

Arthur Middleton
12 New Row,
Covent Garden,
London WC2N 4LF
Tel: 020 7836 7042
Fax: 020 7497 2486

Branksome Antiques
370 Poole Rd,
Branksome,
Dorset BH12 1AW
Tel: 01202 763 324
Fax: 01202 769 932

Cobwebs
78 Old Northam Rd,
Southampton SO14 0PB
Tel: 02380 227 458
Fax: 02380 227 458
ww.cobwebs.uk.com

Early Technology
Monkton House,
Old Craighall Musselburgh,
Midlothian,
Scotland EH21 8SF
Tel: 0131 665 5753
michael.bennett-levy@virgin.net
www.earlytech.com

Stuart Talbot
PO Box 31525,
London W11 2XY
Tel: 020 8969 7011
talbot.stuart@talk21.com

SEWING & NEEDLEWORK

Thomas & Pamela Hudson
9 Watermore Rd,
Cirencester GL7 1JW
Tel: 01285 652 972
www.pwhudson.demon.co.uk

SMOKING

Richard Ball
richard@lighter.co.uk
www.lighter.co.uk

Tagore
Gray's Antiques Market,
Stand 302, 58 Davies St,
London W1Y 2LB
Tel: 020 7499 0158

Tom Clarke
Admiral Vernon Antiques
Centre, Unit 36,
Portobello Rd, London W11
Tel/Fax: 020 8802 8936

SPORTING MEMORABILIA

Fiona Taylor
Jubilee Hall Antiques Centre,
Oak St,
Lechlade GL7 3AE
Tel: 01367 253 777

Manfred Schotten
109 High St,
Burford,
Oxfordshire OX18 4RH
Tel: 01993 822 302
enquiries@schotten.com
www.schotten.com

Old Troon Sporting Antiques
49 Ayr St,
Troon KA10 6EB
Tel: 01292 311 822
Fax: 01292 313 111

Sean Arnold
1 Pembridge Villas,
London W2 4XE
Tel: 020 7221 2267
Fax: 020 7221 5464

Simon Brett
Creswyke House,
Moreton-in-Marsh GL56 0LH
Tel: 01608 650 751

Warboys Antiques
Old Church School, High St,
Warboys PE28 2SX
Tel: 01487 823 686
john.lambden@sportingantiques
co.uk
www.sportingantiques.co.uk

TOYS & GAMES

Automatomania
Gray's Antiques Market, Shop
124, 58 Davies St,
London W1K 5LP
Tel: 020 7495 5259
www.automatomania.com

**Collectors Old Toy Shop
& Antiques**
89 Northgate, Halifax,
North Yorkshire HX1 1XF
Tel: 01422 360 434

Colin Baddiel
Gray's Antique Market, Stand
B25, South Molton Lane,
London W1Y 2LP
Tel: 020 7629 7352
Fax: 020 7493 9344

Donay Games
34 Gower Rd,
Haywards Heath,
West Sussex RH16 4PN
Tel: 01444 416 412
donaygames@btconnect.com
www.donaygames.com

Garrick Coleman
75 Portobello Rd,
London W11
Tel: 020 7937 5524
coleman-antiques-antiques-
london@compuserve.com
www.antiquechess.co.uk

Hugo Lee-Jones
Tel: 01227 375 375
Mob: 07941 187 2027
electroniccollectables@hotmail.com

Intercol
43 Templar's Crescent,
Finchley,
London N3 3QR
Tel: 020 8349 2207
Fax: 020 8349 9539
sales@intercol.co.uk
www.intercol.co.uk

Karl Flaherty Collectables
Tel: 02476 445 627
kfcollectables@aol.com
www.kfcollectables.com

**Sue Pearson Dolls & Teddy
Bears**
18 Brighton Square,
Brighton,
East Sussex BN1 1HD
Tel: 01273 329 247
www.sue-pearson.co.uk

The Vintage Toy & Train Shop
Sidmouth Antiques &
Collectors' Centre,
All Saints' Rd,
Sidmouth EX10 8ES
Tel: 01395 512 588

Tim Armitage
99 Welsh Row,
Nantwich CW5 5ET
Tel: 01270 626 608

Wheels of Steel (Trains)
Gray's Mews Antiques Market,
Stand 349, 58 Davies St,
London W1Y 2LP
Tel: 020 7629 2813

Becca Gauldie Antiques
Scottish Antiques & Arts Centre
Abernyte,
Scotland PH14 9SJ
Tel: 01828 686 401

Pauline Parkes
Durham House Antiques Centre,
Sheep St,
Stow-on-the-Wold,
Gloucestershire GL54 1AA
Tel: 01451 870 404

Polly de Courcy-Ireland
PO Box 29,
Alresford,
Hampshire SO24 9WP
Tel: 01962 733 131

Susan Shaw Period Pieces
Solihull, West Midlands
Tel/Fax: 0121 709 1205

Peter Gibbons
Jubilee Hall Antiques Centre,
Oak St,
Lechlade GL7 3AY
Tel: 01367 253777

WATCHES

Kleanthous Antiques
144 Portobello Rd,
London W11 2DZ
Tel: 020 7727 3649
antiques@kleanthous.com
www.kleanthous.com

The Watch Gallery
129 Fulham Rd,
London SW3 6RT
Tel: 020 7581 3239
Fax: 020 7584 6497

WINE & DRINKING

Bacchus
Lombard St,
Petworth GU28 0AG
Tel: 01798 342844
Fax: 01798 342634

Christopher Sykes Antiques
The Old Parsonage,
Woburn,
Milton Keynes MK17 5AB
Tel: 01525 290 259
Fax: 01525 290061
sykes.corkscrews@sykes-
corkscrews.co.uk
www.sykes-corkscrews.co.uk

Tagore Ltd
Gray's Antiques Market, Stand
302, 58 Davies St,
London W1Y 2LB
Tel: 020 7499 0158

DIRECTORY OF AUCTIONEERS

This is a list of auctioneers that conduct regular sales. Auctioneers who wish to be listed in this directory for our next edition, space permitting, are requested to email info@thepriceguidecompany.com by 1st February 2005.

LONDON

Bloomsbury Auctions
24 Maddox St,
London W1S 1PP
Tel: 020 7495 9494
Fax: 020 7495 9499
www.bloomsburyauctions.com

Bonhams
101 New Bond St,
London W1S 1SR
Tel: 020 7629 6602
Fax: 020 7629 8876
www.bonhams.com

Christies (South Kensington)
85 Old Brompton Rd,
London SW7 3LD
Tel: 020 7581 7611
Fax: 020 7321 3311
www.christies.com
info@christies.com

Sotheby's (Olympia)
Hammersmith Rd,
London W14 8UX
Tel: 020 7293 5555
Fax: 020 7293 6939
www.sothebys.com

Rosebery's
74-76 Knights Hill, West
Norwood, London SE27 0JD
Tel: 020 8761 2522
Fax: 020 8761 2524

BEDFORDSHIRE

W. & H. Peacock
The Auction Centre,
26 Newnham St,
Bedford MK40 3JR
Tel: 01234 266366
Fax: 01234 269082
www.peacockauction.co.uk
info@peacockauction.co.uk

BERKSHIRE

Dreweatt Neate
Donnington Priory,
Donnington, Nr. Newbury,
Berkshire RG14 2JE
Tel: 01635 553553
Fax: 01635 553599
auctions@dnfa.com
www.dnfa.com

Law Fine Art Ltd
Firs Cottage, Church Lane,
Brimpton,
Berkshire RG7 4TJ
Tel: 0118 971 0353
Fax: 0118 971 3741
info@lawfineart.co.uk
www.lawfineart.co.uk

Special Auction Services
The Coach House,
Midgham Park,
Reading,
Berkshire RG7 5UG
Tel: 01189 712 949
Fax: 01189 712 420
commemorative@aol.com

BUCKINGHAMSHIRE

Amersham Auction Rooms
125 Station Rd, Amersham,
Buckinghamshire HP7 0AH
Tel: 01494 729292
Fax: 01494 722337
info@amershamauctionrooms.co.uk
www.amershamauctionrooms.co.uk

CAMBRIDGESHIRE

Cheffins
The Cambridge Saleroom,
2 Clifton Rd,
Cambridge CB1 4BW
Tel: 01223 213343
Fax: 01223 413396
fine.art@cheffins.co.uk
www.cheffins.co.uk

CHANNEL ISLANDS

Martel Maides
40 Cornet St,
St Peters Port, Guernsey,
Channel Islands GY1 1LF
Tel: 01481 722700
Fax: 01481 723306
auctions@martelmaides.co.uk
www.martelmaides.co.uk

CHESHIRE

Bonhams (Chester)
New House,
150 Christleton Rd, Chester,
Cheshire CH3 5TD
Tel: 01244 313 936
Fax: 01244 340 028
info@bonhams.com
www.bonhams.com

Halls Fine Art (Chester)
Booth Mansion,
30 Watergate St, Chester,
Cheshire CH1 2LA
Tel: 01244 312300
Fax: 01244 312112
general@halls-auctioneers.ltd.uk
www.halls-auctioneers.ltd.uk

**Bob Gowland International
Golf Auctions**
The Stables, Claim Farm,
Manley Rd Frodsham,
Cheshire WA6 6HT
Tel/Fax: 01928 740668
bob@internationalgolfauctions.com
www.internationalgolfauctions.com

CLEVELAND

Vectis Auctioneers
Fleck Way Thornaby, Stockton-
on-Tees, Cleveland TS17 9JZ
Tel: 01642 750616
Fax: 01642 769478
www.vectis.co.uk

CORNWALL

W.H. Lane & Son
Jubilee House, Queen St,
Penzance, Cornwall TR18 4DF
graham.bazley@excite.com

David Lay
The Penzance Auction House,
Alverton, Penzance,
Cornwall TR18 4RE
Tel: 01736 361414
Fax: 01736 360035
dlay@pzsw.fsnet.co.uk

CUMBRIA

Mitchells Auction Co.
Furniture Hall, 47 Station Rd,
Cockermouth,
Cumbria CA13 9PZ
Tel: 01900 828557
Fax: 01900 828073
MFineart@aol.com

Penrith Farmers' & Kidds
Skirsgill Saleroom, Skirsgill,
Penrith, Cumbria CA11 0DN
Tel: 01768 890781
Fax: 01768 895058
penrith.farmers@virgin.net

DERBYSHIRE

Noel Wheatcroft & Son
The Old Picture Palace,
Dale Rd, Matlock,
Derbyshire DE4 3LU
Tel: 01629 57460
Fax: 01629 57956
www.wheatcroft-noel.co.uk

DEVON

Bearne's
St Edmund's Court,
Okehampton St, Exeter,
Devon EX4 1LX
Tel: 01392 207000
Fax: 01392 207007
enquiries@bearnes.co.uk
www.bearnes.co.uk

Bonhams
Dowell St, Honiton, Devon
EX14 1LX
Tel: 01404 41872
Fax: 01404 43137
honiton@bonhams.com
www.bonhams.com

Charterhouse
Back Lane, Sherborne, Dorset
DT9 3JE
Tel: 01935 812277
Fax: 01935 389387
enquiry@charterhouse-
auctions.co.uk
www.charterhouse-auctions.co.uk

HY Duke & Sons
Weymouth Avenue, Dorchester,
Dorset DT1 1QS
Tel: 01305 265080
Fax: 01305 260101
enquiries@dukes-auctions.co.uk
www.thesaurus.co.uk/hyduke&son

Onslows
The Coach House, Manor Rd,
Stourpaine, Dorset DT11 8TQ
Tel: 01258 488838
Fax: 01258 488838
www.onslows.co.uk

Semley Auctioneers
Station Rd, Semley, Nr
Shaftesbury, Dorset SP7 9AN
Tel: 01747 855122
Fax: 01747 855222
semley.auctioneers@btinternet.com
www.semleyauctioneers.com

ESSEX

Ambrose
Ambrose House, Old Station
Rd, Loughton, Essex IG10 4PE
Tel: 020 8502 3951
Fax: 020 8532 0833
info@ambroseauction.co.uk
www.ambroseauction.co.uk

G.E. Sworder & Sons
14 Cambridge Rd, Stansted
Mountfitchet, Essex CM24 8BD
Tel: 01279 817778
Fax: 01279 817779
auctions@sworder.co.uk
www.sworder.co.uk

GLOUCESTERSHIRE

BK
The Tithe Barn, Southam,
Cheltenham,
Gloucestershire GL52 3NY
Tel: 01242 573904
Fax: 01242 224463
www.bkonline.co.uk

Dreweatt Neate (Bristol)
St John's Place, Apsley Rd,
Clifton, Bristol BS8 2ST
Tel: 0117 973 7201
Fax: 0117 953 5671
bristol@dnfa.com
www.dnfa.com

Cotswold Auction Co.
Chapel Walk Saleroom,
Chapel Walk, Cheltenham,
Gloucestershire GL50 3DS
Tel: 01242 256363
Fax: 01242 571734
info@cotswoldauction.co.uk
www.cotswoldauction.co.uk

Mallams (Cheltenham)
26 Grosvenor St, Cheltenham,
Gloucestershire GL52 2SG
Tel: 01242 235712
Fax: 01242 241943
cheltenham@mallams.co.uk
www.mallams.co.uk

HAMPSHIRE

Andrew Smith & Sons
Hankin's Garage, 47 West St,
Alresford, Hampshire
Tel: 01962 842841
Fax: 01962 863274
chrisjarrey@andrewsmithandson
.fsbusiness.co.uk

Jacobs and Hunt
Fine Art Auctioneers, 26 Lavant
St, Petersfield, Hampshire
GU32 3EF
Tel: 01730 233 933
Fax: 01730 262 323

HEREFORDSHIRE

Brightwells
The Fine Art Saleroom,
Ryelands Rd,
Leominster,
Herefordshire HR6 8NZ
Tel: 01568 611122
Fax: 01568 610519
www.brightwells.com

HERTFORDSHIRE

**Brown & Merry –
Tring Market Auctions**
Brook St, Tring,
Hertfordshire HP23 5EF
Tel: 01442 826 446
Fax: 01442 890 927

ISLE OF WIGHT

Ways, The Auction House,
Garfield Rd, Ryde,
Isle of Wight PO33 2PT
Tel: 01983 562255
Fax: 01983 565108
www.waysauctionrooms.
fsbusiness.co.uk

KENT

**Dreweatt Neate (Tunbridge
Wells)**
The Auction Halls, Linden Park
Rd, Pantiles, Tunbridge Wells,
Kent TN2 5QL
Tel: 01892 544500
Fax: 01892 515191
tunbridgewells@dnfa.com
www.dnfa.com

Gorringes
15 The Pantiles,
Tunbridge Wells,
Kent TN2 5TD
Tel: 01892 619670

LANCASHIRE

Capes Dunn & Co.
The Auction Galleries, 38
Charles St, Manchester,
M1 7DB
Tel: 0161 273 1911
Fax: 0161 273 3474

LEICESTERSHIRE

Gilding's
Roman Way Market,
Harborough, LE16 7PQ
Tel: 01858 410414
Fax: 01858 432956
sales@gildings.co.uk
www.gildings.co.uk

Heathcote Ball & Co.
Castle Auction Rooms,
78 St Nicholas Circle,
Leicester LE1 5NW
Tel: 0116 2536789
Fax: 0116 2538517
heathcoteball@clara.net

LINCOLNSHIRE

Golding Young & Co.
Old Wharf Rd, Grantham,
Lincolnshire NG31 7AA
Tel: 01476 565118
Fax: 01476 561475
enquiries@goldingyoung.com
www.goldingyoung.com

MERSEYSIDE

Cato, Crane & Co
6 Stanhope St,
Liverpool L8 5RE
Tel: 0151 709 5559
Fax: 0151 707 2454
www.cato-crane.co.uk

NORFOLK

T.W. Gaze
49 Diss Auction Rooms,
Roydon Rd, Diss IP22 4LN
Tel: 01379 650306
Fax: 01379 644313
sales@dissauctionrooms.co.uk
www.twgaze.com

Keys
8 Market Place, Aylsham,
Norfolk NR11 6EH
Tel: 01263 733195
Fax: 01263 732140
mail@aylshamsalerooms.co.uk
www.aylshamsalerooms.co.uk

Knights Sporting Auctions
The Thatched Gallery,
The Green, Aldborough,
Norwich, Norfolk NR11 7AA
Tel: 01263 768488
Fax: 01263 768788
www.knights.co.uk

NORTHAMPTONSHIRE

Heathcote Ball & Co.
Albion Auction Rooms,
Commercial St,
Northampton NN1 1PJ
Tel: 01604 622735

NOTTINGHAMSHIRE

Mellors & Kirk Auctioneers
Gregory St,
Nottingham NG7 2NL
Tel: 0115 9790000
melkirk@dircon.co.uk
www.mellors-kirk.co.uk

Neales
192 194 Mansfield Rd,
Nottingham NG1 3HU
Tel: 0115 9624141
Fax: 0115 9856890
fineart@neales.co.uk
www.neales.co.uk

T. Vennett-Smith
11 Nottingham Rd, Gotham,
Nottingham NG11 0HE
Tel: 0115 9830541
Fax: 0115 9830114
info@vennett-smith.co.uk
www.vennett-smith.co.uk

OXFORDSHIRE

Mallams
Pevensey House, 27 Sheep St,
Bicester, Oxfordshire OX6 7JF
Tel: 01869 252901
Fax: 01869 320283
bicester@mallams.co.uk

Mallams (Oxford)
Bocardo House, St Michaels St,
Oxford, OX1 2EB
Tel: 01865 241358
Fax: 01865 725483
oxford@mallams.co.uk
www.mallams.co.uk

SOAMES COUNTRY AUCTIONS

Soames Country Auctions
Pinnocks Farm Estate,
Witney,
Oxfordshire OX8 1AY
Tel: 01865 300626
soames@email.msn.com
www.soamesauctioneers.co.uk

SHROPSHIRE

Halls Fine Art (Shrewsbury)
Welsh Bridge Salerooms,
Shrewsbury,
Shropshire SY3 8LA
Tel: 01743 231212
Fax: 01743 246191
fineart@halls-auctioneers.ltd.uk
www.halls-auctioneers.ltd.uk

Walker Barnett & Hill
Cosford Auction Rooms,
Long Lane, Cosford,
Shropshire TF11 8PJ
Tel: 01902 375555
Fax: 01902375556
www.walker-barnett-hill.co.uk

Mullock Madeley
The Old Shippon,
Wall-under-Heywood,
Nr Church Stretton,
Shropshire SY6 7DS
Tel: 01694 771771
Fax: 01694 771772
info@mullockmadeley.co.uk
www.mullock-madeley.co.uk

SOMERSET

Clevedon Salerooms
Herbert Rd, Clevedon, Bristol,
Somerset BS21 7ND
Tel: 01275 876699
Fax: 01275 343765
clevedon.salerooms@cableinet.co.uk

Gardiner Houlgate
The Bath Auction Rooms,
9 Leafield Way,
Corsham, Bath,
Somerset SN13 9SW
Tel: 01225 812912
Fax: 01225 811777
auctions@gardiner houlgate. co.uk
www.invaluable.com/gardiner-
houlgate

**Lawrence's Fine Art
Auctioneers Ltd**
South St, Crewkerne,
Somerset TA18 8AB
Tel: 01460 73041
Fax: 01460 74627
enquiries@lawrences.co.uk
www.lawrences.co.uk

STAFFORDSHIRE

Potteries Specialist Auctions
271 Waterloo Rd, Cobridge,
Stoke-on-Trent,
Staffordshire ST6 3HR
Tel: 01782 286622
Fax: 01782 213777
www.potteriesauctions.com

Richard Winterton
School House Auction Rooms,
Hawkins Lane, Burton-on-Trent,
Staffordshire DE14 1PT
Tel: 01283 511224
Fax: 01283 568650
adrianrathbone@btconnect.com

Wintertons
Lichfield Auction Centre
Fradley,
Lichfield, WS13 8NF
Tel: 01543 263256
Fax: 01543 415348
enquiries@wintertons.co.uk
www.wintertons.co.uk

SUFFOLK

Diamond Mills
117 Hamilton Rd,
Felixstowe,
Suffolk IP11 7BL
Tel: 01394 282281
Fax: 01394 671791
diamondmills@easynet.co.uk

Neal Sons & Fletcher
26 Church St,
Woodbridge,
Suffolk IP12 1DP
Tel: 01394 382263
Fax: 01394 383030
enquiries@nsf.co.uk
www.nsf.co.uk

SURREY

Barbers
The Mayford Centre,
Smarts Heath Rd,
Woking, Surrey GU22 0PP
Tel: 01483 728939
Fax: 01483 762552
www.thesaurus.co.uk/barbers

Clark Gammon
Guildford Auction Rooms,
Bedford Rd,
Guildford, GU1 4SJ
Tel: 01483 880915
Fax: 01483 880918

Ewbank Auctioneers
The Burnt Common Auction
Rooms, London Rd,
Send, Woking,
Surrey GU23 7LN
Tel: 01483 223101
Fax: 01483 222171
antiques@ewbankauctions.co.uk
www.ewbankauctions.co.uk

Hamptons Auctioneers
93 High St,
Godalming,
Surrey GU7 1AL
Tel: 01483 423567
Fax: 01483 426392
fineart@hamptons-int.com
www.hamptons.co.uk

EAST SUSSEX

Burstow & Hewett
Lower Lake, Battle,
East Sussex TN33 0AT
Tel: 01424 772 374
Fax: 01424 772 302
auctions@burstowandhewett.co.uk
www.burstowandhewett.co.uk

Dreweatt Neate (Eastbourne)
46-50 South St,
Eastbourne,
East Sussex BN214QJ,
Tel: 01323 410419
Fax: 01323 416540
eastbourne@dnfa.com
www.dnfa.com

Gorringes
Terminus Rd,
Bexhill-on-Sea,
East Sussex TN39 3LR
Tel: 01424 212994
Fax: 01424 224035
bexhill@gorringes.co.uk
www.gorringes.co.uk

Gorringes
15 North St, Lewes,
East Sussex BN7 2PD
Tel: 01273 472503
Fax: 01273 479559
auctions@gorringes.co.uk
www.gorringes.co.uk

Raymond P. Inman
The Auction Galleries,
35 & 40 Temple St, Brighton,
East Sussex BN1 3BH
Tel: 01273 774777
Fax: 01273 735660
r.p.inman@talk21.com

Wallis & Wallis
West St Auction Galleries,
Lewes, East Sussex BN7 2NJ
Tel: 01273 480208
Fax: 01273 476562
grb@wallisandwallis.co.uk
www.wallisandwallis.co.uk

TYNE & WEAR

Anderson & Garland
Marlborough House,
Marlborough Crescent,
Newcastle Upon Tyne,
Tyne and Wear NE1 4EE
Tel: 01912 326278
Fax: 01912 618665
agarland@compuserve.com

Corbitts
5 Mosley St, Newcastle-upon-
Tyne, Tyne and Wear NE1 1YE
Tel: 0191 232 7268
Fax: 0191 261 4130
collectors@corbitts.com
www.corbitts.com

WARWICKSHIRE

Locke & England
18 Guy St, Leamington Spa,
Warwickshire CV32 4RT
Tel: 01926 889100
Fax: 01926 470608
info@leauction.co.uk
www.leauction.co.uk

WEST MIDLANDS

Bonhams, Knowle
The Old House,
Station Rd, Knowle,
Solihull, B93 0HT
Tel: 01564 776151
Fax: 01564 778069
knowle@bonhams.com
www.bonhams.com

Fellows & Sons
Augusta House,
19 Augusta St, Hockley,
Birmingham,
West Midlands B18 6JA
Tel: 0121 212 2131
Fax: 0121 212 1249
info@fellows.co.uk
www.fellows.co.uk

Walker, Barnett & Hill
Waterloo Rd, Salerooms,
Clarence St,
Wolverhampton,
West Midlands WV1 4JE
Tel: 01902 773531

WEST SUSSEX

John Bellman
New Pound Wisborough Green,
Billingshurst,
West Sussex RH14 0AZ
Tel: 01403 700858
Fax: 01403 700059
enquiries@bellmans.comuk
www.bellmans.co.uk

Denhams
The Auction Galleries,
Warnham, Nr Horsham,
West Sussex RH12 3RZ
Tel: 01403 255699
Fax: 01403 253837
denhams@lineone.net

Rupert Toovey
Star Rd, Partridge Green,
Horsham,
West Sussex RH13 8RA
Tel: 01403 411744
Fax: 01403 711919
auctions@rupert-toovey.com
www.rupert-toovey.com

WILTSHIRE

Finan & Co
The Square, Mere,
Wiltshire BA12 6DJ
Tel: 01747 861411
Fax: 01747 861944
post@finanandco.co.uk
www.finanandco.co.uk

Henry Aldridge & Sons
The Devizes Auctioneers,
Unit 1, Bath Rd Business
Centre, Devizes,
Wiltshire SN10 1XA
Tel: 01380 729199
Fax: 01380 730073
www.henry-aldridge.co.uk

Hamptons
20 High St, Marlborough,
Wiltshire SN8 1AA
Tel: 01672 516161
Fax: 01672 515882
saleroom@hamptons-int.com
www.hamptons.co.uk

Woolley & Wallis
51-61 Castle St,
Salisbury,
Wiltshire SP1 3SU
Tel: 01722 424500
Fax: 01722 424508
enquiries@woolleyandwallis.co.uk
www.woolleyandwallis.co.uk

WORCESTERSHIRE

Andrew Grant
St Mark's House,
St Mark's Close,
Cherry Orchard,
Worcester WR5 3DJ
Tel: 01905 357547
Fax: 01905 763942
fine.art@andrew-grant.co.uk
www.andrew-grant.co.uk

**Gloucestershire Worcestershire
Railwayana Auctions**
'The Willows',
Badsey Rd, Evesham,
Worcestershire WR11 7PA
Tel: 01386 760109
admin@gwra.co.uk
www.gwra.co.uk

Phillip Serrell
The Malvern Saleroom,
Barnards Green Rd, Malvern,
Worcestershire WR14 3LW
Tel: 01684 892314
Fax: 01684 569832
www.serrell.com

EAST YORKSHIRE

Dee, Atkinson & Harrison
The Exchange Saleroom,
Driffield,
East Yorkshire YO25 7LJ
Tel: 01377 253151
Fax: 01377 241041
exchange@dee-atkinson-
harrison.co.uk
www.dee-atkinson-harrison.co.uk

NORTH YORKSHIRE

David Duggleby
The Vine St Salerooms,
Scarborough,
North Yorkshire YO11 1XN
Tel: 01723 507111
Fax: 01723 507222
www.davidduggleby.com

Tennants
The Auction Centre, Leyburn,
North Yorkshire DL8 5SG
Tel: 01969 623780
Fax: 01969 624281
enquiry@tennants-ltd.co.uk
www.tennants.co.uk

SOUTH YORKSHIRE

A. E. Dowse & Sons
Cornwall Galleries, Scotland St,
Sheffield, S37 7DE
Tel: 0114 272 5858
Fax: 0114 249 0550
aedowse@talk21.com

BBR Auctions
Elsecar Heritage Centre,
5 Ironworks Row, Wath Rd,
Elsecar, Barnsley,
South Yorkshire S74 8HJ
Tel: 01226 745156
Fax: 01226 361561
sales@bbrauctions.co.uk
www.bbrauctions.co.uk

Sheffield Railwayana
43 Little Norton Lane,
Sheffield, S8 8GA
Tel: 0114 274 5085
Fax: 0114 274 5085
ian@sheffrail.freeserve.co.uk
www.sheffieldrailwayana.co.uk

WEST YORKSHIRE

Andrew Hartley Fine Arts
Victoria Hall Salerooms,
Little Lane, Ilkle,
West Yorkshire LS29 8EA
Tel: 01943 816363
info@andrewhuntleyfinearts.co.uk
www.andrewhuntleyfinearts.co.uk

SCOTLAND

Bonhams Edinburgh
65 George St,
Edinburgh EH2 2JL
Tel: 0131 225 2266
Fax: 0131 220 2547
edinburgh@bonhams.com
www.bonhams.com

Loves Auction Rooms
52-54 Canal St, Perth,
Perthshire, PH2 8LF
Tel: 01738 633337
Fax: 01738 629830

Lyon & Turnbull
33 Broughton Place,
Edinburgh EH1 3RR
Tel: 0131 557 8844
Fax: 0131 557 8668
info@lyonandturnbull.com
www.lyonandturnbull.com

Lyon & Turnbull
4 Woodside Place,
Glasgow G3 7QF
Tel: 0141 353 5070
Fax: 0141 332 2928
info@lyonandturnbull.com
www.lyonandturnbull.com

Thomson, Roddick & Medcalf Ltd
42 Moray Place,
Edinburgh EH3 6BT
Tel: 0131 220 6680
Fax: 0131 441 7455
mark.medcalf@virgin.net
www.thomsonroddick.com/trm/
.index.html

WALES

Bonhams Cardiff
7-8 Park Place, Cardiff,
Glamorgan CF10 3DP
Tel: 02920 727 980
Fax: 02920 727 989
cardiff@bonhams.com
www.bonhams.com

Peter Francis
Curiosity Salerooms, 19 King
St, Carmarthen, South Wales
Tel: 01267 233456
Fax: 01267 233458
www.peterfrancis.co.uk

Welsh Country Auctions
2 Carmarthen Rd, Cross Hands,
Llanelli, Dyfed SA14 6SP
Tel/Fax: 01269 844428

IRELAND

HOK Fine Art
4 Main St, Blackrock, Co
Dublin, Ireland
Tel: 00 353 1 2881000
fineart@hok.ie

Mealy's
The Square, Castlecomer,
County Kilkenny, Ireland
Tel: 00 353 56 41229
/41413
Fax: 00 353 56 41627
info@mealys.com
www.mealys.com

CLUBS, SOCIETIES & ORGANISATIONS

ADVERTISING

Antique Advertising Signs
The Street Jewellery Society, 11
Bowcdon Ter, South Gosford,
Newcastle-Upon-Tyne NE3 1RX

AUTOGRAPHS

Autograph Club of GB
47 Webb Cresent, Dawley,
Telford, Shropshire TF4 3DS
autographs@acogb.freeserve.co.uk
www.acogb.co.uk

BAXTER PRINTS

The New Baxter Society
c/o Reading Museum & Art
Gallery, Blagrave St, Reading,
Berkshire RG1 1QH
baxter@rpsfamily.demon.co.uk
www.rpsfamily.demon.co.uk

BANK NOTES

International Bank Note Society
43 Templars Crescent, London,
N3 3QR

BOOKS

The Enid Blyton Society
93 Milford Hill, Salisbury,
Wiltshire SP1 2QL
tony@blysoc.fsnet.co.uk

The Followers of Rupert
31 Whiteley, Windsor,
Berkshire SL4 5PJ

BOTTLES

Old Bottle Club of Great Britain
2 Strafford Avenue,
Elsecar, Nr Barnsley,
South Yorkshire S74 18AA
Tel: 01226 745 156

CERAMICS

Carlton Ware Collectors' International
The Carlton Factory Shop,
Copeland St, Stoke-upon-Trent,
Staffordshire ST4 1PU
Tel: 01782 410 504
Fax: 01782 412202
www.carltonwarecollectorsintern
ational.com

Chintz World International
Tel: 01525 220272
Fax: 01525 222442
www.chintzworld-intl.com

Clarice Cliff Collectors' Club
Fantasque House, Tennis Drive,
The Park, Nottingham NG7 1AE
www.claricecliff.com

Goss Collectors' Club
ilsa@schofieldhouse.fsnet.co.uk
www.gosschina.com

Hornsea Pottery Collectors' & Research Society
28 Devonshire St, Keighley,
West Yorkshire BD21 2QJ
ornsea@pdtennant.fsnet.co.uk
www.honseacollector.co.uk

M.I. Hummel Club (Goebel)
Porzellanfabrik, GmbH & Co. KG,
Coburger Str.7, D-96472
Rodental, Germany
Tel: +49 (0) 95 63 72 18 03
Fax: +49 (0) 95 63 9 25 92

Keith Murray Collectors' Club
Fantasque House, Tennis Drive,
The Park, Nottingham NG7 1AE
www.keithmurray.com

Lorna Bailey Collectors' Club
Newcastle Street,
Dalehall, Burslem,
Stoke-on-Trent ST6 3QF
Tel: 01782 837 341

Mabel Lucie Attwell
Abbey Antiques,
63 Great Whyte, Ramsey,
Huntingdon PE26 1HL
Tel: 01487 814753

Moorcroft Collectors' Club
Sandbach Rd, Burslem,
Stoke-on-Trent,
Staffordshire ST6 2DQ
Tel: 01782 820500
Fax: 01782 820501
cclub@moorcroft.com
www.moorcroft.com

Pendelfin Family Circle
Cameron Mill,
Howsin St, Burnley,
Lancashire BB10 1PP
Tel: 01282 432 301
www.pendelfin.co.uk

Poole Pottery Collectors' Club
The Quay, Poole,
Dorset BH15 1RF
Tel: 01202 666200
Fax: 01202 682894
www.poolepottery.co.uk

Potteries of Rye Collectors' Society
22 Redyear Cottages,
Kennington Rd, Ashford,
Kent TN24 0TF
barry.buckton@tesco.net
www.potteries-of-rye-society.co.uk

Royal Doulton International Collectors' Club
Minton House,
London Rd,
Stoke-on-Trent,
Staffordshire ST47QD
Tel: 01782 292292
Fax: 01782 292099
enquiries@royal-doulton.com
www.royal-doulton.com/collectables

Royal Winton International Collectors' Club
Dancers End, Northall,
Bedfordshire LU6 2EU
Tel: 01525 220 272
Fax: 01525 222 442

The Shelley Group
38 Bowman Road,
Norfolk,
Norwich NR4 6LS
shelley.group@shelley.co.uk
www.shelley.co.uk

Susie Cooper Collectors' Group
Panorama House,
18 Oaklea Mews,
Aycliffe Village,
County Durham DL5 6IP
www.susiecooper.co.uk

The Sylvac Collectors' Circle
174 Portsmouth Rd, Horndean,
Waterlooville, Hampshire
admin@sylvacclub.com
www.sylvacclub.com

Novelty Teapot Collectors' Club
Tel: 01257 450 366
vince@totallyteapots.com
www.totallyteapots.com

Official International Wade Collectors' Club
Royal Works, Westport Rd,
Stoke-on-Trent, Staffs ST6 4AP
Tel: 01782 255255
Fax: 01782 575195
club@wade.co.uk
www.wade.co.uk

Royal Worcester Collectors' Society
Severn Street,
Worcester, WR1 2NE
Tel: 01905 746 000
sinden@royal-worcester.co.uk
www.royal-worcester.co.uk

CIGARETTE CARDS

Cartopulic Society of GB
7 Alderham Avenue, Radlett,
Herts WD7 8HL

COINS

British Numismatic Society
c/o The Warburg Institute,
Woburn Square,
London WC1H 0AB
www.britnumsoc.org

Royal Numismatic Society
c/o The British Museum,
Dept of Coins and Medals,
Great Russell Street,
London WC1B 3DG
Tel: 020 7636 1555
RNS@dircon.co.uk
www.users.dircon.co.uk/~rns

COMMEMORATIVE WARE

Commemorative Collectors' Society
The Gardens,
Gainsborough Rd, Winthorpe,
nr Newark NG24 2NR
Tel: 01636 671377
chris@royalcoll.fsnet.co.uk

COMICS

Association of Comic Enthusiasts
L'Hopiteau, St Martin du
Fouilloux 79420, France
Tel: 00 33 549 702 114

Comic Enthusiasts Society
80 Silverdale, Sydenham,
London SE26 4SJ

COSTUME & ACCESSORIES

British Compact Collectors' Club
PO Box 131, Woking,
Surrey GU24 9YR

Costume Society
St. Paul's House, Warwick Lane,
London EC4P 4BN
www.costumesociety.org.uk

Hat Pin Society of GB
PO Box 74, Bozeat,
Northamptonshire NN29 7UD

DISNEYANA

Walt Disney Collectors' Society
c/o Enesco, Brunthill Road,
Kingstown Industrial Estate,
Carlisle CA3 0EN
Tel: 01228 404 062
www.wdccduckman.com

DOLLS

Barbie Collectors' Club of GB
117 Rosemount Avenue, Acton,
London W3 9LU
wdl@nipcus.co.uk'

British Doll Collectors Club
'The Anchorage', Wrotham Rd,
Culverstone Green, Meopham,
Kent DA13 0QW
www.britishdollcollectors.com

Doll Club of Great Britain
PO Box 154, Cobham, Surrey
KT11 2YE

The Fashion Doll Collectors' Club of GB
PO Box 133, Lowestoft,
Suffolk NR32 1WA
Tel: 07940 248127
voden@supanet.com

FILM & TV

James Bond 007 Fan Club &Archive
PO Box 007,
Surrey KT15 IDY
Tel: 01483 756007

Fanderson - The Official Gerry Anderson Appreciation Society
2 Romney Road,
Willesborough, Ashford,
Kent TN24 0RW

GLASS

The Carnival Glass Society
P.O. Box 14, Hayes,
Middlesex UB3 5NU
www.carnivalglasssociety.co.uk

The Glass Association
1, White Knobs Way
Caterham, Surrey CR3 6RH
geoffctim@btinternet.com
www.glassassociation.org.uk

Isle of Wight Studio Glass
Old Park, St Lawrence, Isle of
Wight, PO38 1XR
www.isleofwightstudioglass.co.uk

Pressed Glass Collectors' Club
4 Bowshot Close, Castle
Bromwich B36 9UH
Tel: 0121 681 4872
www.webspawner.com/users/
pressedglass

KITCHENALIA

National Horse Brass Society
2 Blue Barn Cottage,
Blue Barn Lane,
Weybridge,
Surrey KT13 0NH
Tel: 01932 354 193

The British Novelty Salt &
Pepper Collectors Club
Coleshill,
Clayton Road, Mold,
Flintshire CH7 15X

MARBLES

Marble Collectors Unlimited
P.O. Box 206
Northborough,
MA 01532-0206 USA
marblesbev@aol.com

MECHANICAL MUSIC

Musical Box Society of
Great Britain
PO Box 299,
Waterbeach,
Cambridge CB4 4PJ

The City of London
Phonograph and Gramophone
Society
2 Kirklands Park,
Fyfe KY15 4EP
Tel: 01334 654 390

METALWARE

Antique Metalware Society
PO Box 63, Honiton,
Devon EX14 1HP
amsmemsec@yahoo.co.uk

MILITARIA

Military – Crown Imperial
37 Wolsey Close, Southall,
Middlesex UB2 4NQ

Military Historical Society
National Army Museum,
Royal Hospital Rd,
London SW3 4HT

Orders & Medals Research
Society
123 Turnpike Link,
Croydon CR0 5NU

PAPERWEIGHTS

Paperweight Collectors Circle
P.O. Box 941,
Comberton,
Cambridgeshire CB3 7GQ
Tel: 02476 386 172

PENS & WRITING

The Writing Equipment Society
wes.membershipsec@virgin.net
www.wesoc.co.uk

PERFUME BOTTLES

International Perfume Bottle
Association
396 Croton Road, Wayne,
PA 19087 USA
www.ipba-uk.co.uk

PLASTICS

Plastics Historical Society
31a Maylands Drive,
Sidcup, Kent DA14 4SB
mail@plastiquarian.com
www.plastiquarian.com

POSTCARDS

The Postcard Club of Great
Britain
34 Harper House,
St. James' Crescent,
London SW9 7LW

POTLIDS

The Pot Lid Circle
Keith Mortimer
Tel: 01295 722 032

QUILTS

The Quilters' Guild of the
British Isles
Room 190,
Dean Clough, Halifax,
West Yorks 3HX 5AX
Tel: 01422 347 669
Fax: 01422 345 017
info@quiltersguild.org.uk
www.quiltersguild.org.uk

RADIOS

The British Vintage
Wireless Society
59 Dunsford Close,
Swindon,
Wiltshire SN1 4PW
Tel: 01793 541 634
www.bvws.org.uk

RAILWAYANA

Railwayana Collectors Journal
7 Ascot Rd, Moseley,
Birmingham B13 9EN

SCIENTIFIC, TECHNICAL & MEDICAL INSTRUMENTS

Scientific Instrument Society
31 High St,
Stanford in the Vale,
Farringdon SN7 8LH
www.sis.org.uk

SEWING

International Sewing Machine
Collectors' Society
www.ismacs.net

The Thimble Society
1107 Portobello Rd,
London W11 2QB
antiques@thimblesociety.co.uk
www.thimblesociety.co.uk

SMOKING

Lighter Club of Great Britain
Richard Ball
richard@lighter.co.uk
www.lighter.co.uk

SPORTING

International Football Hall of
Fame
info@ifhof.com
www.ifhof.com

British Golf Collectors Society
anthonythorpe@ntlworld.com
www.britgolfcollectors.wyenet.co.uk

STAMPS

Postal History Society
60 Tachbrook Street,
London SW1V 2NA
Tel: 020 7545 7773
john.scott@db.com

Royal Mail Collectors' Club
Freepost, NEA1431,
Sunderland, SR9 9XN

STANHOPES

The Stanhope Collectors' Club
jean@stanhopes.info
www.stanhopes.info

TEDDY BEARS & SOFT TOYS

British Teddy Bear Association
PO Box 290
Brighton, Sussex
Tel: 01273 697 974

Merrythought International
Collectors' Club
Ironbridge, Telford,
Shropshire TF8 7NJ
Tel: 01952 433 116

Steiff Club Office
Margaret Steiff GmbH,
Alleen Strasse 2, D-89537
Giengen/Brenz, Germany

TOYS

Action Man Club
PO Box 142,
Horsham, RH13 5FJ

The British Model Soldier Society
44 Danemead, Hoddesdon,
Hertfordshire EN119LU
www.model.soldiers.btinternet.co.uk

Corgi Collectors' Club
PO Box 323, Swansea, Wales
SA1 1BJ

Hornby Collectors Club
PO Box 35, Royston,
Hertfordshire SG8 5XR
Tel/Fax: 01223 208 308
hsclubs.demon.co.uk
www.hornby.co.uk

The Matchbox Toys
International Collectors'
Association
P.O. Box 120, Deeside,
Flintshire CH5 3HE
kevin@matchboxclub.com
www.matchboxclub.com

Historical Model Railway
Society
59 Woodberry Way,
London E4 7DY

The English Playing Card
Society
11 Pierrepont St, Bath,
Somerset BA1 1LA
Tel: 01225 465 218

Train Collectors' Society
P.O. Box 20340,
London NW11 6ZE
Tel: 020 8209 1589
tcsinformation@btinternet.com
www.traincollectors.org.uk

William Britain
Collectors Club
P.O. Box 32,
Wokingham RG40 4XZ
Tel: 01189 737080
Fax: 01189 733947
ales@wbritaincollectorsclub.com
www.britaincollectorsclub.com

WATCHES

British Watch & Clock
Collectors' Association
5 Cathedral Lane, Truro,
Cornwall TR1 2QS
Tel 01872 264010
Fax 01872 241953
tonybwcca@cs.com
www.timecap.com

COLLECTING ON THE INTERNET

■ The internet has revolutionised the trading of collectables. Compared to a piece of furniture, most collectables are easily defined, described and photographed. Shipping is also comparatively easy, due to average size and weight. Prices are also generally more affordable and accessible than for antiques and the Internet has provided a cost effective way of buying and selling, away from the overheads of shops and auction rooms. Many millions of collectables are offered for sale and traded daily, with sites varying from global online marketplaces, such as eBay, to specialist dealers' websites.

■ When searching online, remember that some people may not know how to accurately describe their item. General category searches, even though more time consuming, and even purposefully misspelling a name, can yield results. Also, if something looks too good to be true, it probably is. Using this book to get to know your market visually, so that you can tell the difference between a real bargain and something that sounds like one, is a good start.

■ As you will understand from buying this book, colour photography is vital – look for online listings that include as many images as possible and check them carefully. Beware that colours can appear differently, even between computer screens.

■ Always ask the vendor questions about the object, particularly regarding condition. If there is no image, or you want to see another aspect of the object – ask. Most sellers (private or trade) will want to realise the best price for their items so will be more than happy to help – if approached politely and sensibly.

■ As well as the 'e-hammer' price, you will probably have to pay additional transactional fees such as packing, shipping and possibly regional or national taxes. It is always best to ask for an estimate for these additional costs before leaving a bid. This will also help you tailor your bid as you will have an idea of the maximum price the item will cost if you are successful.

■ In addition to well-known online auction sites, such as eBay, there are a host of other online resources for buying and selling, such as fair and auction date listings.

INTERNET RESOURCES

Live Auctioneers
www.liveauctioneers.com
info@liveauctioneers.com
A free service which allows users to search catalogues from selected auction houses in Europe, the USA and the United Kingdom. Through its connection with eBay, users can bid live via the Internet into salerooms as auctions happen. Registered users can also search through an archive of past catalogues and receive a free newsletter by email.

Invaluable.com
www.invaluable.com
sales@invaluable.com
A subscription service which allows users to search selected auction house catalogues from the United Kingdom and Europe. Also offers an extensive archive for appraisal uses.

The Antiques Trade Gazette
www.atg-online.com
The online version of the UK trade newspaper, comprising British auction and fair listings, news and events.

Maine Antiques Digest
www.maineantiquesdigest.com
The online version of America's trade newspaper including news, articles, fair and auction listings and more.

La Gazette du Drouot
www.drouot.com
The online home of the magazine listing all auctions to be held in France at the Hotel de Drouot in Paris and beyond. An online subscription enables you to download the magazine online.

Auctionnet.com
www.auctionnet.com
Simple online resource listing over 500 websites related to auctions online.

AuctionBytes
www.auctionbytes.com
Auction resource with community forum, news, events, tips and a weekly newsletter.

Auctiontalk
www.auctiontalk.com
Auction news, online and offline auction search engines and live chat forums.

Go Antiques/Antiqnet
www.goantiques.com
www.antiqnet.com
An online global aggregator for art, antiques and collectables dealers who showcase their stock online, allowing users to browse and buy.

eBay
www.ebay.com
Undoubtedly the largest and most diverse of the online auction sites, allowing users to buy and sell in an online marketplace with over 52 million registered users. Collectors should also view eBay Live Auctions (www.ebayliveauctions.com) where traditional auctions are combined with realtime, online bidding allowing users to interact with the saleroom as the auction takes place.

Nielsen, Niels 67
nightdress cases 509
Nike 212-14
Nintendo 553, 556
Nistri, Giuliano 437
Nivada 562
Nixon, Harry 94
Noah's Arks 551
Noguchi 532
noisemakers 346
Noke, Charles 70, 92, 94, 96-7
Nokia 380
Nomura 533
Noni, Umberto 412
Noon, Jeff 40
Noritake 85, 182
North, Kevin 263
Norwegian
 ceramics 144
 glass 325
 posters 412
Nourot, Michael 571
Novus 562
Nuutajarvi Notsjo 325-6
Nyland, Gunnar 143, 144
Nylex 272
Nymølle 140, 143, 145
Nyquist, Kari 144

O
O'Broin, Domhnall 334
Ogdens 191
oil bottles, ceramic 143
Okkolin, Aimo 323
Old Foley 272
Oldfield, Bruce 203
Omega 561, 562
Omni-Graphics Inc. 356
Op Art sunglasses 266
optical instruments 381
oral 126
Ordnance Survey 48
ORIC 260
ornaments, Christmas 344
Ornamin Presswerk 472, 493
Orrefors 326, 339
Orup, Bengt 324
Ovaltine 425
oven mitts 278
Oxo 425

P
Pagnin, Fratelli 569
Paillard 367
pails, tin 244
paintings
 militaria 378
 sporting 503
Paintoy 253, 254, 540-1, 544-7
Palshus 144
Pan, masonic 283, 452
panels, lithophane 186
Panton, Verner 280
paper racks 273

paperweights
 ceramic 91, 139
 glass 382-4
papier-mâché
 masks 366
 pen cases 388
 pin cushions 258
 standishes 387
Paragon 85-6, 473, 475
Paramount 18
Parfums Grés 391
Parger 559
Parian ware 469, 480
Parker (board games) 548
Parker pens 386, 387
Parlophone 459
Parman, Barry 232
Parsons, Pauline 96, 97
Partridge, Bernard 443
Pascoe, Marilyn 163, 167
Patagonia 211, 212
patchwork quilts 449-50
Patou, Jean 394
Pavely, Ruth 126, 128
Pearl Pottery 182
Pedigree 254, 256
Pedley, Nada 94, 97
Pedrosa, Bruno 571
Pelham puppets 552
Pemberton, Gill 87, 88
Pemberton, Victor 298
pen cases 388
pen holders 280
pencils 11, 187, 385, 386
pendants, Bakelite 239
Pendelfin 125
penknives 14
penny farthing bicycles 34
pens and writing 385-8, 400
pepper shakers see salt and pepper shakers
Pepsi-Cola 11, 493
perfume bottles 389-96, 570-2
Perret, Daniel 559
Perret, Pierre 184
Perthshire glass 383
pewter 369
Peynet, Raymond 15
Pez dispensers 549
Phasar 562
Philips 380, 451
Philips, Godfrey 192
Phillips, Laura 203
Phoenix 86
phone cards 297
phones, mobile 379-80
phonographs 368
Photochrom Co. 402
photographs 397-8
 autographs 20-3
 erotica 263
 film and TV 300-4
 rock and pop 460, 462
 royal commemoratives 470
 sporting 498-9, 503, 504

see also postcards
'Piano Babies' 257
Piatnik, Ferdinand & Son 553
Picasso, Pablo 184
Pick, Beverley 441, 444
"Picture Post" 362
pictures
 découpage 469
 see also paintings; prints
pie birds 351
Pifco 281
piggy banks 170, 181
Pilkington Tile & Pottery Co. 182-3
pillow cases 263
pin-cases 482
pin cushions 258, 486
pin dishes 473, 474, 479
pinball game 188
Pinocchio 243, 245
pins
 advertising 11
 character collectables 187, 188
 Christmas tree 237
 costume jewellery 227, 229-32, 234, 235, 237-9
 Disneyana 247
pipes
 character collectables 187
 glass 335
 meerschaum 495
Pirovano, Rino 280
pitchers
 glass 320, 322, 334, 339
 majolica 181
Pixyland Kew 538, 539
planes, toy 515, 520, 524
Plant family 184
plant pot holders 273
planters
 Clarice Cliff 77
 Royal Doulton 90
 studio pottery 151
plaques
 Clarice Cliff 80
 commemorative ware 472
 Goebel 178
 Lorna Bailey 57
 Scandinavian ceramics 141, 145
 Sixties and Seventies 282
 sporting 501
 Troika 167
plastics 399-400
 ashtrays 492
 dolls 250-4
 Sixties and Seventies 278-80
plates
 Burleighware 176
 Clarice Cliff 77-9
 commemorative ware 200, 201, 469, 471, 478
 Coronet Ware 176
 Crown Ducal 177
 Denby 87, 88

Fifties 272
Fornasetti 102
George Jones 179
 glass 307, 570
Johnson Bros 179
Midwinter 109-14
Minton 182
Moorcroft 116
Noritake 182
pewter 370
Poole Pottery 127, 128, 130
Royal Crown Derby 139
Royal Doulton 99, 100
Royal Worcester 172
Scandinavian ceramics 145
 silver 476
Sixties and Seventies 277
Susie Cooper 81, 82
Troika 168
platters
 ceramic 185
 glass 329
Playboy 264
Player, John & Sons 14, 192, 493
playing cards 10, 263, 553
Pleydell-Bouverie, Katherine 150
Pochoir 226
pocket watches 29, 533
poison bottles 51
political
 commemoratives 200
 postcards 404
Pollak 275
polo shirts 213
Ponti, Gio 102, 318
Poole Pottery 126-30, 472
'Popeye' 187
porcelain see ceramics
De Porceleyne Fles 158
Porcelle 103
Portmeirion Pottery 131-2, 276
Portuguese
 ceramics 181
 salt and pepper shakers 348
postage stamps 473, 477, 505
postcards 401-4
 autographed 20, 21, 23
 ceramic 140
 domestic 401-2
 film and TV 297, 300, 305
 military 403-4
 political 404
 sporting 504
 transport 402-3
posters 405-44
 advertising 420-8
 automobilia 29
 film 429-38
 motor racing 440
 psychedelic 439
 rock and pop 461,

463, 465, 467, 468
Sixties and Seventies 285
 travel 405-19
 wartime 441-4
posy holders 153, 180
pot lids 445-8
pot-pourris 473
pots
 Crown Devon 177
 plastic 399
 Royal Copenhagen 135
Potter, Beatrix 44, 62-5, 351
pottery see ceramics
Pottinger, Sue 130
Pountney & Co. 176
powder compacts 225
powder flasks 374
Powell, James & Sons 327
Pozniak, Janusz 571
Pratchett, Terry 40
Pratt pot lids 445
preserve jars 78, 80, 98
preserve pans 349
Presley, Elvis 461-2
The Pressed Pulp Company 344
Price Bros. 83
Price's Candles 51
prints
 Baxter 32-3
 Fifties 274
 railwayana 455
programmes
 commemorative 470
 rock and pop 457-8, 462-8
 sporting 504
Pronto 559
props, film 286-95
Prussian militaria 373
Psion 261
psychedelic posters 439
Pucci, Emilio 210, 269
Pullman, Philip 39
Pulpitel, Milos 334
Pulsar 561, 562
punch pots 148
puppets 187-90, 552
Purvis, Tom 410, 442
puzzles, jigsaw 300, 466, 555
Pyrosil 277

Q
Queensbury, David 308
Quenvit 183
quilts 449-50

R
R.A.C. 24
Racing Champions Inc. 301
Rackham, Arthur 44
Radford 183
radios 188, 451-2, 462